GUIDE T
LITERARY AG

2019

Includes a one-year online subscription to **Guide to Literary Agents** on

THE ULTIMATE MARKET RESEARCH TOOL FOR WRITERS

To register your *Guide to Literary Agents 2019* and **start your one-year online subscription**, scratch off the block below to reveal your activation code*, then go to WritersMarket.com. Find the box that says "Purchased a Deluxe Edition?" then click on "Activate Your Account" and enter the activation code. It's that easy!

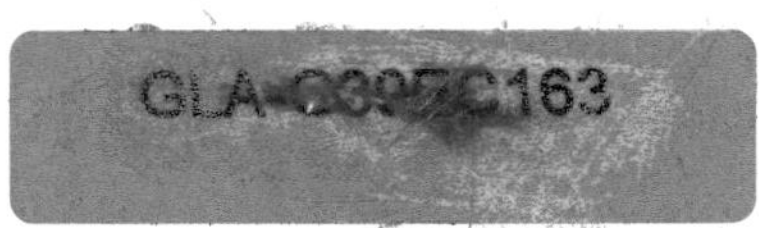

UPDATED MARKET LISTINGS

EASY-TO-USE, SEARCHABLE DATABASE • RECORD-KEEPING TOOLS

PROFESSIONAL TIPS & ADVICE • INDUSTRY NEWS

Your purchase of *Guide to Literary Agents* gives you access to updated listings related to literary agents (valid through 12/31/19). For just $9.99, you can upgrade your subscription and get access to listings from all of our best-selling Market Books. Visit **WritersMarket.com** for more information.

◂ 28TH ANNUAL EDITION ▸

GUIDE TO LITERARY AGENTS

2019

Robert Lee Brewer, Editor

WRITER'S DIGEST
BOOKS
WritersDigest.*com*
Cincinnati, Ohio

Writer's Market website: www.writersmarket.com
Writer's Digest website: www.writersdigest.com

Distributed in the U.K. and Europe by F&W Media International
Pynes Hill Court, Pynes Hill, Rydon Lane
Exeter, EX2 5AZ, United Kingdom
Tel: (+44) 1392-797680, Fax: (+44) 1626-323319
E-mail: postmaster@davidandcharles.co.uk

ISSN: 1078-6945
ISBN-13: 978-1-4403-5438-0
ISBN-10: 1-4403-5438-3

Attention Booksellers: This is an annual directory of F + W Media, Inc.
Return deadline for this edition is December 31, 2019.

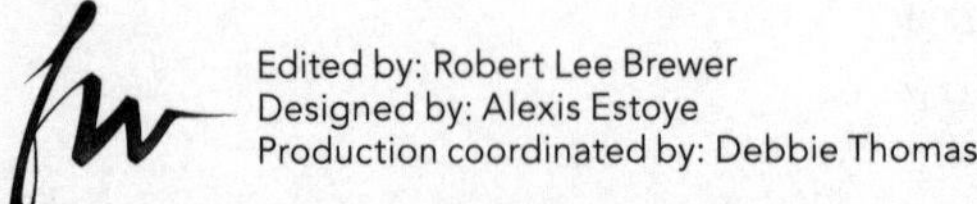

Edited by: Robert Lee Brewer
Designed by: Alexis Estoye
Production coordinated by: Debbie Thomas

CONTENTS

MARKETS

RESOURCES

INDEXES

FROM THE EDITOR

Unlike other Market Books, I've always thought of *Guide to Literary Agents* as more than a directory of agents and conferences. As the title implies, it's a guide to the world of literary agents who are the gatekeepers of the publishing industry.

As such, this edition of *Guide to Literary Agents* is filled with helpful information on how to find, contact, secure, and work with literary agents. The agent-writer relationship generally starts with a query or pitch, but it can grow into something much more significant with many writers and agents spending their careers together.

Of course, this year's *Guide to Literary Agents* is once again loaded with listings for literary agents and writers conferences, but there are also articles on crafting queries, debut authors, and writing the perfect synopsis.

Also, be sure to take advantage of the exclusive webinar for *Guide to Literary Agents* readers. Learn more at www.writersmarket.com/2019-gla-webinar.

Until next we meet, keep writing and marketing what you write.

Robert Lee Brewer
Senior Content Editor
Guide to Literary Agents
http://writersdigest.com/editor-blogs/poetic-asides
http://blog.writersmarket.com
http://twitter.com/robertleebrewer

HOW TO USE GUIDE TO LITERARY AGENTS

Searching for a literary agent can be overwhelming, whether you've just finished your first book or you have several publishing credits on your résumé. More than likely, you're eager to start pursuing agents and anxious to see your name on the spine of a book. But before you go directly to the listings in this book, take time to familiarize yourself with the way agents work and how you should approach them. By doing so, you will be more prepared for your search and ultimately save yourself effort and unnecessary angst.

READ THE ARTICLES

This book begins with feature articles organized into three sections: **Getting Started**, **Contacting Agents**, and **The Writer's Toolbox**. These articles explain how to prepare for representation, offer strategies for contacting agents, and arm you with vital tools in your journey. You may want to start by reading through each one and then refer back to relevant articles during each stage of your search.

Because there are many ways to make that initial contact with an agent, we've also provided an article called "Debut Authors Tell All." These personal accounts from just-published authors offer information and inspiration for any writer hoping to find representation.

DECIDE WHAT YOU'RE LOOKING FOR

A literary agent will present your work directly to editors or producers. It's the agent's job to get her client's work published or sold, and to negotiate a fair contract. In the **Literary Agents** listings section, we list each agent's contact information and explain both what type of work the agency represents and how to submit your work for consideration.

For face-to-face contact, many writers prefer to meet agents at conferences. By doing so, writers can assess an agent's personality, attend workshops, and have the chance to get more feedback on their work than they get by mailing or e-mailing submissions and waiting for a response. The **Conferences** section lists conferences agents and/or editors attend. In many cases, private consultations are available, and agents attend with the hope of finding new clients to represent.

UTILIZE THE EXTRAS

Aside from the articles and listings, this book offers a section of **Resources**. If you come across a term with which you aren't familiar, check out the Resources section for a quick explanation. Also, note the gray tabs along the edge of each page. The tabs identify each section so they are easier to flip to as you conduct your search.

Finally—and perhaps most importantly—there are the **Indexes** in the back of the book. These can serve as an incredibly helpful way to start your search because they categorize the listings according to different criteria. For example, you can look for literary agents according to their specialties (fiction/nonfiction genres).

LISTING POLICY AND COMPLAINT PROCEDURE

Listings in *Guide to Literary Agents* were originally compiled from detailed questionnaires and information provided by agents. However, the publishing industry is constantly in flux, and agencies change frequently. We rely on our readers for information about their dealings with agents, as well as changes in policies or fees that differ from what has been reported to the editor of this book. Write to the editor (*Guide to Literary Agents*, F+W, 10151 Carver Road, Suite 300, Cincinnati, OH 45242) or e-mail (robert.brewer@fwmedia.com) if you have new information, questions, or problems dealing with the agencies listed.

Listings are published free of charge and are not advertisements. Although the information is as accurate as possible, the listings are not endorsements or guarantees by the editor or publisher of *Guide to Literary Agents*. If you feel you have not been treated fairly by an agent or representative listed in *Guide to Literary Agents*, we advise you to take the following steps:

- First try to contact the agency. Sometimes one letter or e-mail can clear up the matter. Politely relate your concern.
- Document all your correspondence with the agency. When you write to us with a complaint, provide the name of your manuscript, the date of your first contact with the agency, and the nature of your subsequent correspondence.

- We will keep your letter on file and attempt to contact the agency. The number, frequency, and severity of complaints will be considered when we decide whether or not to delete an agency's listing from the next edition.

NOTE: *Guide to Literary Agents* reserves the right to exclude any agency for any reason.

FREQUENTLY ASKED QUESTIONS

1. **Why do you include agents who are not seeking new clients?** Some agents ask that their listings indicate they are currently closed to new clients. We include them so writers know the agents exist and know not to contact them at this time.
2. **Why are some agents not listed?** Some agents may not have responded to our requests for information. We have taken others out of the book after we received complaints about them.
3. **Do I need more than one agent if I write in different genres?** It depends. If you have written in one genre and want to switch to a new style of writing, ask your agent if she is willing to represent you in your new endeavor. Occasionally an agent may feel she has no knowledge of a certain genre and will recommend an appropriate agent to her client. Regardless, you should always talk to your agent about any potential career move.
4. **Why don't you list more foreign agents?** Most American agents have relationships with foreign co-agents in other countries. It is more common for an American agent to work with a co-agent to sell a client's book abroad than for a writer to work directly with a foreign agent. If you decide to query foreign agents, make sure they represent American writers (if you're American). Some may request to receive submissions only from Canadians, for example, or from United Kingdom residents.
5. **Do agents ever contact a self-published writer?** If a self-published author attracts the attention of the media, or if his book sells extremely well, an agent might approach the author in the hope of representing him.
6. **Why won't the agent I queried return my material?** An agent may not answer your query or return your manuscript for several reasons. Perhaps you did not include a self-addressed, stamped envelope (SASE). Many agents will discard a submission without a SASE. Or the agent may have moved. To avoid using expired addresses, use the most current edition of *Guide to Literary Agents* or access the information online at www.writersmarket.com. Another possibility is that the agent is swamped with submissions. An agent can be overwhelmed with queries, especially if the agent recently has spoken at a conference or has been featured in an article or book. Also, some agents specify in their listings that they never return materials of any kind.

WHAT AN AGENT DOES

A writer's job is to write. A literary agent's job is to find publishers for her clients' books. Because publishing houses receive more and more unsolicited manuscripts each year, or do not accept unsolicited manuscripts, securing an agent is becoming increasingly necessary. But finding an eager and reputable agent can be a difficult task. Even the most patient writer can become frustrated or disappointed. As a writer seeking representation, you should prepare yourself before starting your search. Learn when to approach agents, as well as what to expect from an author/agent relationship. Beyond selling manuscripts, an agent must keep track of the ever-changing industry, writers' royalty statements, fluctuating market trends—the list goes on.

So you face the question: Do I need an agent? The answer, more often than not, is a resounding yes.

WHAT CAN AN AGENT DO FOR YOU?

For starters, today's competitive marketplace can be difficult to break into, especially for unpublished writers. Many larger publishing houses will only look at manuscripts from agents—and rightfully so, as they would be inundated with unsatisfactory writing if they did not. In fact, approximately 80 percent of books published by the five major houses are acquired through agents.

But an agent's job isn't just getting your book through a publisher's door. The following describes the various jobs agents do for their clients, many of which would be difficult for a writer to do without outside help.

BEFORE YOU SUBMIT YOUR NOVEL

- Finish your novel manuscript or short story collection. An agent can do nothing for fiction without a finished product. Never query with an incomplete novel.

- Revise your manuscript. Seek critiques from other writers or an independent editor to ensure your work is as polished as possible.
- Proofread. Don't ruin a potential relationship with an agent by submitting work that contains typos or poor grammar.
- Publish short stories or novel excerpts in literary journals, which will prove to prospective agents that editors see quality in your writing.
- Research to find the agents of writers whose works you admire or are similar to yours.
- Use the Internet and resources like *Guide to Literary Agents* to construct a list of agents who are open to new writers and looking for your category of fiction. (Jump to the listings sections of this book to start now.)
- Rank your list according to the agents most suitable for you and your work.
- Write your novel synopsis.
- Write your query letter. As an agent's first impression of you, this brief letter should be polished and to the point.
- Educate yourself about the business of agents so you will be prepared to act on any offer. This guide is a great place to start.

Agents Know Editors' Tastes and Needs

An agent possesses information on a complex web of publishing houses and a multitude of editors to ensure her clients' manuscripts are placed in the right hands. This knowledge is gathered through relationships she cultivates with acquisitions editors—the people who decide which books to present to their publisher for possible publication. Through her industry connections, an agent becomes aware of the specializations of publishing houses and their imprints, knowing that one publisher wants only contemporary romances while another is interested solely in nonfiction books about the military. By networking with editors, an agent also learns more specialized information—which editor is looking for a crafty, Agatha Christie–style mystery for his fall catalog, for example.

Agents Track Changes in Publishing

Being attentive to constant market changes and shifting trends is another major requirement of an agent. An agent understands what it may mean for clients when publisher A merges with publisher B and when an editor from house C moves to house D. Or what it means when readers—and therefore editors—are no longer interested in Westerns while thrillers are flying off the shelves.

Agents Get Your Work Read Faster

Although it may seem like an extra step to send your work to an agent instead of directly to a publishing house, the truth is that an agent can prevent you from wasting months sending manuscripts that end up in the wrong in-box or buried in an editor's slush pile. Editors rely on agents to save them time as well. With little time to sift through the hundreds of unsolicited submissions arriving weekly in the mail, an editor naturally prefers work that has already been approved by a qualified reader (i.e., the agent) who knows the editor's preferences. For this reason, many of the larger publishers accept agented submissions only.

Agents Understand Contracts

When publishers write contracts, they are primarily interested in their own bottom line, not the best interests of the author. Writers unfamiliar with contractual language may find themselves bound to a publisher with whom they no longer want to work. Or they may find themselves tied to a publisher who prevents them from getting royalties on their first book until subsequent books are written. Agents use their experiences and knowledge to negotiate a contract that benefits the writer while still respecting the publisher's needs. After all, more money for the author will almost always mean more money for the agent—another reason they're on your side.

Agents Negotiate—and Exploit—Subsidiary Rights

Beyond publication, a savvy agent keeps other opportunities for your manuscript in mind. If your agent believes your book also will be successful as an audio book, a Book-of-the-Month-Club selection, or even a blockbuster movie, she will take these options into consideration when shopping your manuscript. These additional opportunities for writers are called subsidiary rights. Part of an agent's job is to keep track of the strengths and weaknesses of different publishers' subsidiary rights offices to determine the deposition of these rights regarding your work. After contracts are negotiated, agents will seek additional moneymaking opportunities for the rights they kept for their clients.

Agents Get Escalators

An escalator is a bonus an agent can negotiate as part of the book contract. It is commonly given when a book appears on a best-seller list or if a client appears on a popular television show. For example, a publisher might give a writer a $30,000 bonus if he is picked for a book club. Both the agent and the editor know such media attention will sell more books, and the agent negotiates an escalator to ensure the writer benefits from this increase in sales.

Agents Track Payments

Because an agent receives payment only when the publisher pays the writer, it's in the agent's best interest to make sure the writer is paid on schedule. Some publishing houses are notorious for late payments. Having an agent distances you from any conflict regarding payment and allows you to spend time writing instead of making phone calls.

Agents Are Advocates

Besides standing up for your right to be paid on time, agents can ensure your book gets a better cover design, more attention from the publisher's marketing department, or other benefits you may not know to ask for during the publishing process. An agent can provide advice each step of the way, as well as guide you in your long-term writing career.

ARE YOU READY FOR AN AGENT?

Now that you know what an agent is capable of, ask yourself if you and your work are at a stage where you need an agent. Look at the "Before You Submit" lists for fiction and nonfiction writers in this article and judge how prepared you are for contacting an agent. Have you spent enough time researching or polishing your manuscript? Does your nonfiction book proposal include everything it should? Is your novel completely finished? Sending an agent an incomplete project not only wastes your time but also may turn off the agent in the process. Is the work thoroughly revised? If you've finished your project, set it aside for a few weeks, then examine it again with fresh eyes. Give your novel or proposal to critique group partners (or beta readers) for feedback.

Moreover, your work may not be appropriate for an agent. Most agents do not represent poetry, magazine articles, short stories, or material suitable for academic or small presses; the agent's commission does not justify spending time submitting these types of works. Those agents who do take on such material generally represent authors on larger projects first and then adopt the smaller items as a favor to the client.

If you believe your work is ready to be placed with an agent, make sure you're personally ready to be represented. In other words, consider the direction in which your writing career is headed. Besides skillful writers, agencies want clients with the ability to produce more than one book. Most agents say they're looking to represent careers, not books.

WHEN DON'T YOU NEED AN AGENT?

Although there are many reasons to work with an agent, some authors can benefit from submitting their own work directly to book publishers. For example, if your project focuses on a very specific topic, you may want to work with a small or specialized press. These houses usually are open to receiving material directly from writers. Small presses often can give more attention to writers than large houses can, providing editorial help, marketing expertise, and other advice. Academic books or specialized nonfiction books (such as a book about the history of Rhode Island) are good bets for unagented writers.

Beware, though, as you will now be responsible for reviewing and negotiating all parts of your contract and payment. If you choose this path, it's wise to use a lawyer or entertainment attorney to review all contracts. Lawyers who specialize in intellectual property can help writers with contract negotiations. Instead of earning a commission on resulting book sales, lawyers are paid only for their time.

And, of course, some people prefer working independently instead of relying on others. If you're one of these people, it's probably better to submit your own work instead of potentially butting heads with an agent. Let's say you manage to sign with one of the few literary agents who represent short story collections. If the collection gets shopped around to publishers for several months and no one bites, your agent may suggest retooling the work into a novel. Agents suggest changes—some bigger than others—and not all writers think their work is malleable. It's all a matter of what you're writing and how you feel about it.

BEFORE YOU SUBMIT YOUR NONFICTION BOOK

- Formulate a concrete idea for your book. Sketch a brief outline, making sure you'll have enough material for a book-length manuscript.
- Research works on similar topics to understand the competition and determine how your book is unique.
- Write sample chapters. This will help you estimate how much time you'll need to complete the work and determine whether or not your writing will need editorial help. You will also need to include a few sample chapters in the proposal itself.
- Publish completed chapters in journals and/or magazines. This validates your work to agents and provides writing samples for later in the process.
- Polish your nonfiction book proposal so you can refer to it while drafting a query letter—and so you'll be prepared when agents contact you.
- Brainstorm three to four subject categories that best describe your material.
- Use the Internet and resources like *Guide to Literary Agents* to construct a list of agents who are open to new writers and looking for your category of nonfiction.
- Rank your list. Research agent websites and narrow your list further, according to your preferences.
- Write your query. Give an agent an excellent first impression by describing your premise and your experience professionally and succinctly.
- Educate yourself about the business of agents so you can act on any offer.

ASSESSING CREDIBILITY

Many people wouldn't buy a used car without at least checking the odometer, and savvy shoppers would consult the blue books, take a test drive, and even ask for a mechanic's opinion. Much like the shrewd car shopper, you want to obtain the best possible agent for your writing, so you should research the business of agents before sending out query letters. Understanding how agents operate will help you find an agent appropriate for your work, as well as alert you about the types of agents to avoid.

Many writers take for granted that any agent who expresses interest in their work is trustworthy. They'll sign a contract before asking any questions and simply hope everything will turn out all right. We often receive complaints from writers regarding agents *after* they have lost money or have work bound by contract to an ineffective agent. If writers put the same amount of effort into researching agents as they did writing their full manuscripts, they would save themselves unnecessary angst.

The best way to educate yourself is to read all you can about agents and other authors. Organizations such as the Association of Authors' Representatives (AAR, www.aaronline.org), the National Writers Union (NWU, www.nwu.org), American Society of Journalists and Authors (ASJA, www.asja.org), and Poets & Writers, Inc. (www.pw.org) all have informational material on finding and working with an agent.

The magazine *Publishers Weekly* (www.publishersweekly.com) covers publishing news affecting agents and others in the publishing industry. The Publishers Lunch newsletter (www.publishersmarketplace.com) comes free via e-mail every workday and offers news on agents and editors, job postings, recent book sales, and more.

The Internet also has a wide range of sites where you can learn basic information about preparing for your initial contact, as well as specific details on individual agents. You can find online forums and listservs that keep authors connected and allow them to share experiences they've had with different editors and agents. Keep in mind, however, that not everything printed on the Web is fact; you may come across a writer who is bitter because an agent rejected his manuscript. Your best bet is to use the Internet only to *supplement* your other research.

Once you've established what your resources are, it's time to see which agents meet your criteria. Below are some of the key items to pay attention to when researching agents.

LEVEL OF EXPERIENCE

Through your research, you will discover the need to be wary of some agents. Anybody can go to the neighborhood copy center and order business cards that say "literary agent," but that title doesn't mean she can sell your book. She may lack the proper connections with others in the publishing industry, and an agent's reputation with editors can be a major strength or weakness.

Agents who have been in the business awhile have a large number of contacts and carry the most clout with editors. They know the ins and outs of the industry and are often able to take more calculated risks. However, veteran agents can be too busy to take on new clients or might not have the time to help develop an author. Newer agents, on the other hand, may be hungrier, as well as more open to unpublished writers. They probably have a smaller client list and are able to invest the effort to make your book a success.

If it's a new agent without a track record, be aware that you're taking more of a risk signing with her than with a more established agent. However, even a new agent should not be new to publishing. Many agents were editors before they were agents, or they worked at an agency as an assistant. This experience is crucial for making contacts in the publishing industry, and learning about rights and contracts. The majority of listings in this book explain how long the agent has been in business, as well as what she did before becoming an agent. After an agent has offered representation, you could ask her to name a few editors off the top of her head who she thinks may be interested in your work and why they sprang to mind. Has she sold to them before? Do they publish books in your genre?

If an agent has no contacts in the business, she has no more clout than you do. Without publishing prowess, she's just an expensive mailing service. Anyone can make photocopies, slide them into an envelope, and address them to "Editor." Unfortunately, without a contact name and a familiar return address on the envelope, or a phone call from a trusted colleague letting an editor know a wonderful submission is on its way, your work will land in the slush pile with all the other submissions that don't have representation. You can do your own mailings with higher priority than such an agent could.

PAST SALES

Agents should be willing to discuss their recent sales with you: how many, what type of books, and to what publishers. Keep in mind, though, that some agents consider this information confidential. If an agent does give you a list of recent sales, you can call the publishers' contracts department to ensure the sale was actually made by that agent. While it's true that even top agents are not able to sell every book they represent, an inexperienced agent who proposes too many inappropriate submissions will quickly lose her standing with editors.

You can also unearth details of recent sales on your own. Nearly all of the listings in this book offer the titles and authors of books with which the agent has worked. Some of them also note to which publishing house the book was sold. Again, you can call the publisher and confirm the sale. If you don't have the publisher's information, simply check to see if it's available on Amazon. You can also check your local library or bookstore to see if they carry the book. You may want to be wary of the agent if her books are nowhere to be found or are only available through the publisher's website. Distribution is a crucial component to getting published, and you want to make sure the agent has worked with competent publishers.

TYPES OF FEES

Becoming knowledgeable about the different types of fees agents may charge is vital to conducting effective research. Most agents make their living from the commissions they receive after selling their clients' books, and these are the agents we've listed. Be sure to ask about any expenses you don't understand so you have a clear grasp of what you're paying for. Here are some types of fees you may encounter in your research:

Office Fees

Occasionally, an agent will charge for the cost of photocopies and postage made on your behalf. This is acceptable, so long as she keeps an itemized account of the expenses and you've agreed on a ceiling cost. The agent should ask for office expenses only after agreeing to represent the writer. These expenses should be discussed up front, and the writer should receive a statement accounting for them. This money is sometimes returned to the author upon sale of the manuscript. Be wary if there is an upfront fee amounting to hundreds of dollars, which is excessive.

Reading Fees

Agencies that charge reading fees often do so to cover the cost of additional readers or the time spent reading that could have been spent selling. Agents also claim that charging reading fees cuts down on the number of submissions they receive. This practice can save the agent time and may allow her to consider each manuscript more extensively. Whether such promises are kept depends upon the honesty of the agency. You may pay a fee and never receive a response from the agent, or you may pay someone who never submits your manuscript to publishers.

Officially, the Association of Authors' Representatives' (AAR) Canon of Ethics prohibits members from directly or indirectly charging a reading fee, and the Writers Guild of America (WGA) does not allow WGA signatory agencies to charge a reading fee to WGA members, as stated in the WGA's Artists' Manager Basic Agreement. A signatory may charge you a fee if you are not a member, but most signatory agencies do not charge a reading fee as an across-the-board policy.

WARNING SIGNS! BEWARE OF:

- Excessive typos or poor grammar in an agent's correspondence.
- A form letter accepting you as a client and praising generic things about your manuscript that could apply to any work. A good agent doesn't take on a new client very often, so when she does, it's a special occasion that warrants a personal note or phone call.
- Unprofessional contracts that ask you for money up front, contain clauses you haven't discussed, or are covered with amateur clip-art or silly borders.
- Rudeness when you inquire about any points you're unsure of. Don't employ any business partner who doesn't treat you with respect.
- Pressure, by way of threats, bullying, or bribes. A good agent is not desperate to represent more clients. She invites worthy authors but leaves the final decision up to them.
- Promises of publication. No agent can guarantee you a sale. Not even the top agents sell everything they choose to represent. They can only send your work to the most appropriate places, have it read with priority, and negotiate you a better contract if a sale does happen.
- A print-on-demand book contract or any contract offering no advance. You can sell your own book to an e-publisher anytime you wish without an agent's help. An agent should pursue traditional publishing routes with respectable advances.
- Reading fees from $25–$500 or more. The fee is usually nonrefundable, but sometimes agents agree to refund the money if they take on a writer as a client or if they sell the writer's manuscript. Keep in mind, however, that a payment for a reading fee does not ensure representation.
- No literary agents who charge reading fees are listed in this book. It's too risky of an option for writers, plus those who don't charge such fees have a stronger incentive to sell your work. After all, they don't make a dime until they make a sale. If you find that a literary agent listed in this book charges a reading fee, please contact the editor at amy.jones@fwmedia.com.

Critique Fees

Sometimes a manuscript will interest an agent, but the agent will point out areas requiring further development and offer to critique it for an additional fee. Like reading fees, payment of a critique fee does not ensure representation. When deciding if you will benefit from having someone critique your manuscript, keep in mind that the quality and quantity of comments vary from agent to agent. The critique's usefulness will depend on the agent's knowledge of the market. Also be aware that agents who spend a significant portion of their time commenting on manuscripts will have less time to actively market work they already represent.

In other cases, the agent may suggest an editor who understands your subject matter or genre, and has some experience getting manuscripts into shape. Occasionally, if your story is exceptional, or your ideas and credentials are marketable but your writing needs help, you will work with a ghostwriter or co-author who will either share a percentage of your commission or work with you at an agreed-upon cost per hour.

An agent may refer you to editors she knows, or you may choose an editor in your area. Many editors do freelance work and would be happy to help you with your writing project. Of course, before entering into an agreement, make sure you know what you'll be getting for your money. Ask the editor for writing samples, references, or critiques he's done in the past. Make sure you feel comfortable working with him before you give him your business.

An honest agent will not make any money for referring you to an editor. We strongly advise writers not to use critiquing services offered through an agency. Instead, try hiring a freelance editor or joining a writer's group until your work is ready to be submitted to agents who don't charge fees.

CRAFTING A QUERY

How to write a stand-out letter that gets agents' attention.

Kara Gebhart Uhl

Think of the hours, days, months, years you've spent writing your book. The thought you've put into plot, character development, scene setting, and backstory. The words you've kept. The words you've cut. The joy and frustration you've felt as you channeled Oscar Wilde: "I spent all morning putting in a comma and all afternoon taking it out."

And then you finish. You write "The End." You have a celebratory drink. You sleep.

But as any aspiring author knows, you haven't truly reached "The End." In terms of publishing, you've only just begun. And the next chapter in your publishing journey is your query. It's imperative you treat this chapter with as much attention to detail as you did to all the chapters in your book. Because a good query is your golden ticket. Your charmed demo tape. Your "in."

A query is a short, professional way of introducing yourself to an agent. If you're frustrated by this step, consider: Agents receive hundreds of submissions every month. Often they read these submissions on their own time—evenings, weekends, on their lunch break. Given the number of writers submitting—and the number of agents reading—it would simply be impossible for agents to ask for and read entire book manuscripts from every aspiring author. Instead, a query is a quick way for you to, first and foremost, pitch your book. But it's also a way to pitch yourself. If an agent is intrigued by your query, she may ask for a partial (say, the first three chapters of your manuscript). Or she may ask for the entire thing.

Remember all the time you've invested in your book. Take your time crafting your query. Yes, it's another step in a notoriously slow process. But it's necessary. Have you ever seen pictures of slush piles—those piles of unread queries on many well-known agents' desks? Imagine the size of those slush piles if they held full manuscripts instead of one-page query letters. Thinking of it this way, query letters begin to make more sense. And a well-crafted query just might help land all your well-placed commas into the public's hands.

Here we share with you the basics of a query, including its three parts and a detailed list of dos and don'ts.

PART I: THE INTRODUCTION

Whether you're submitting a 100-word picture book or a 90,000-word novel, you must be able to sum up the most basic aspects of your book in one sentence. Agents are busy. And they constantly receive submissions for types of work they don't represent. So up front they need to know that, after reading your first paragraph, the rest of your query is going to be worth their time.

An opening sentence designed to "hook" an agent is fine—if it's good and if it works. But this is the time to tune your right brain down and your left brain up—agents desire professionalism and queries that are short and to the point. Err on the side of formality with only a touch of whimsy. Tell the agent, in as few words as possible, what you've written, including title, genre, and length.

In the intro, you must also connect with the agent. Simply sending one hundred identical query letters out to "Dear Agent" won't get you published. Instead, your letter should be addressed not only to a specific agency but to a specific agent within that agency. (And double, triple, quadruple check that the agent's name is spelled correctly.)

When asked for submission tips, agents always mention the importance of making your letter personal. A good author-agent relationship is like a good marriage. It's important that both sides invest the time to find a good fit that meets their needs. So how do you connect with an agent you don't know personally? Research.

1. Make a Connection Based on a Book the Agent Already Represents

Most agencies have websites that list who and what they represent. Research those sites. Find a book similar to yours and explain that, because such-and-such book has a similar theme or tone, you think your book would be a great fit. In addition, many agents will list specific genres/categories they're looking for, either on their websites or in interviews. If your book is a match, state that.

2. Make a Connection Based on an Interview You Read

Search agents' names online and read any and all interviews they've given. Perhaps they mentioned a love for X and your book is all about X. Mention the specific interview. Prove that you've invested as much time researching them as they're about to spend researching you.

3. Make a Connection Based on a Conference You Both Attended

Was the agent you're querying the keynote speaker at a writing conference you were recently at? If so, mention it, and comment on an aspect of his speech you liked. Even better, did you meet the agent in person? Mention it, and if there's something you can say to jog her memory about the meeting, say it. Better yet, did the agent specifically ask you to send your manuscript? Mention it.

Finally, if you're being referred to a particular agent by an author the agent represents—that's your opening sentence. That referral is guaranteed to get your query placed at the top of the stack.

PART II: THE PITCH

Here's where you really get to sell your manuscript—but in only three to ten sentences. Consider a book's jacket flap and its role in convincing readers to plunk down $24.95 to buy what's in between those flaps. Like a jacket flap, you need to hook an agent in the confines of a very limited space. What makes your story interesting and unique? Is your story about someone's disappearance? Fine, but there are hundreds of stories about missing persons. Is your story about a teenager who has disappeared, and her frantic family and friends who are looking for her? Again, fine, but this story, too, already exists—in many forms. Is your story about a teenager who has disappeared, but her frantic family and friends who are looking for her don't realize that she ran away after finding out she was kidnapped as a baby and her biological parents are waiting for her in a secret place? *Now* you have a hook.

Practice your pitch. Read it out loud, not only to family and friends, but to people willing to give you honest, intelligent criticism. If you belong to a writing group, workshop your pitch. Share it with members of an online writing forum. Know anyone in the publishing industry? Share it with them. We're not talking about querying magazines here; we're talking about querying an agent who could become a lifelong partner. Spend time on your pitch. Write your pitch, put it aside for a week, then look at it again. Perfect it. Turn it into jacket-flap material so detailed, exciting, and clear that it would be near impossible to read your pitch and not want to read more. Use active verbs. Don't send a query simply because you finished a book. Send a query because you finished your pitch and you are ready to begin the next chapter of your publishing journey.

PART III: THE BIO

If you write fiction for adults or children, unless you're a household name or you've recently been a guest on some very big TV or radio shows, an agent is much more interested in your pitch than in who you are. If you write nonfiction, who you are—more specifically, your platform and publicity—is much more important. Regardless, these are key elements that must be present in every bio:

1. Publishing Credits

If you're submitting fiction, focus on your fiction credits—previously published works and short stories. That said, if you're submitting fiction and all your previously published work is nonfiction—articles, essays, etc.—that's still fine and good to mention. Don't be overly long about it. Mention your publications in bigger magazines or well-known literary journals. If you've never had anything published, don't say you lack official credits. Simply skip this altogether.

2. Contests and Awards

If you've won many, focus on the most impressive ones and those that most directly relate to your work. Don't mention contests you entered and weren't named in. Also, feel free to leave titles and years out.

3. MFAS

If you've earned or are working toward a master of fine arts in writing, say so and state the program. Don't mention English or journalism degrees, or online writing courses.

4. Large, Recognized Writing Organizations

Agents don't want to hear about your book club or the small critique group you meet with once a week. And they really don't want to hear about the online writing forum you belong to. But if you're a member of something like the Romance Writers of America (RWA), the Mystery Writers of America (MWA), the Society of Children's Book Writers and Illustrators (SCBWI), the Society of Professional Journalists (SPJ), the American Medical Writers, etc., say so. This shows you're serious about what you do and you're involved in groups that can aid with publicity and networking.

5. Platform and Publicity

If you write nonfiction, who you are and how you're going to help sell the book once it's published become very important. Why are you the best person to write it? What do you have now—public speaking engagements, an active website or blog, substantial cred in your industry—that will help you sell this book?

Finally, be cordial. Thank the agent for taking the time to read your query and consider your manuscript. Ask if you may send more, in the format she desires (partial, full, etc.).

Think back to the time you spent writing your book. The first draft wasn't your final. Don't fret too much over rejection slips. A line agents seemingly love to use on rejections is this: "Unfortunately, this isn't a right fit for me at this time, but I'm sure another agent will feel differently." It has merit. Your book—and query—can be good and still garner a rejection, for a myriad of reasons. Be patient. Keep pitching. And in the meantime, start writing that next book.

DOS AND DON'TS FOR QUERIES

DO:

- Keep the tone professional.
- Query a specific agent at a specific agency.
- Proofread. Double-check the spelling of the agency and the agent's name.
- Keep the query concise, limiting the overall length to one page (single-spaced, twelve-point type in a commonly used font).
- Focus on the plot, not your bio, when pitching fiction.
- Pitch agents who represent the type of material you write.
- Check an agency's submission guidelines to see how to query—for example, via e-mail or snail mail—and whether or not to include a SASE.
- Keep pitching, despite rejections.

DON'T:

- Include personal info not directly related to the book. For example, stating that you're a parent doesn't make you more qualified than someone else to write a children's book.
- Say how long it took you to write your manuscript. Some best-selling books took ten years to write—others, six weeks. An agent doesn't care how long it took—an agent only cares if it's good. Same thing goes with drafts—an agent doesn't care how many drafts it took you to reach the final product.
- Mention that this is your first novel or, worse, the first thing you've ever written. If you have no other publishing credits, don't advertise that fact. Don't mention it at all.
- State that your book has been edited by peers or professionals. Agents expect manuscripts to be edited, no matter how the editing was done.
- Bring up scripts or film adaptations—you're querying an agent about publishing a book, not making a movie.
- Mention any previous rejections.
- State that the story is copyrighted with the U.S. Copyright Office or that you own all rights. You already own all rights. You wrote it.

- Rave about how much your family and friends loved it. What matters is that the agent loves it.
- Send flowers or anything else except a self-addressed stamped envelope (and only if the SASE is required), if sending through snail mail.
- Follow up with a phone call. After the appropriate time has passed (many agencies say how long it will take to receive a response), follow up in the manner you queried—via e-mail or snail mail. And know that "no responses" do happen. After one follow-up and no response, cross the agent off your list.

KARA GEBHART UHL (pleiadesbee.com) writes and edits from Fort Thomas, KY.

1 SAMPLE QUERY 1: LITERARY FICTION

Agent's Comments: Jeff Kleinman (Folio Literary Management)

From: Garth Stein
To: Jeff Kleinman
Subject: Query: "The Art of Racing in the Rain" 1

Dear Mr. Kleinman:

2 Saturday night I was participating in a fundraiser for the King County Library System out here in the Pacific Northwest, and I met your client Layne Maheu. He spoke very highly of you and suggested that I contact you.

3 I am a Seattle writer with two published novels. I have recently completed my third novel, *The Art of Racing in the Rain*, and I find myself in a difficult situation: My new book is narrated by a dog, and my current agent 4 told me that he cannot (or will not) sell it for that very reason. Thus, I am seeking new representation.

5 *The Art of Racing in the Rain* is the story of Denny Swift, a race car driver who faces profound obstacles in his life, and ultimately overcomes them by applying the same techniques that have made him successful on the track. His story is narrated by his "philosopher dog," Enzo, who, having a nearly human soul (and an obsession with opposable thumbs), believes he will return as a man in his next lifetime.

6 My last novel, *How Evan Broke His Head and Other Secrets*, won a 2006 Pacific Northwest Booksellers Association Book Award, and since the award ceremony a year ago, I have given many readings, workshops, and lectures promoting the book. When time has permitted, I've read the first chapter from *The Art of Racing in the Rain*. Audience members have been universally enthusiastic and vocal in their response, and the first question asked is always: "When can I buy the book about the dog?" Also very positive.

7 I'm inserting, below, a short synopsis of *The Art of Racing in the Rain*, and my biography. Please let me know if the novel interests you; I would be happy to send you the manuscript.

Sincerely,
Garth Stein

1 Putting the word *Query* and the title of the book on the subject line of an e-mail often keeps your e-mail from falling into the spam folder. 2 One of the best ways of starting out correspondence is figuring out your connection to the agent. 3 The author has some kind of track record. Who's the publisher, though? Were these both self-published novels, or were there reputable publishers involved? (I'll read on, and hope I find out.) 4 This seems promising, but also know this kind of approach can backfire, because we agents tend to be like sheep—what one doesn't like, the rest of us are wary of, too (or, conversely, what one likes, we all like). But in this case getting in the "two published novels" early is definitely helpful. 5 The third paragraph is the key pitch paragraph and Garth gives a great description of the book—he sums it up, gives us a feel for what we're going to get. This is the most important part of your letter. 6 Obviously it's nice to see the author's winning awards. Also good: The author's not afraid of promoting the book. 7 The end is simple and easy—it doesn't speak of desperation, or doubt, or anything other than polite willingness to help.

2 SAMPLE QUERY 2: YOUNG ADULT

Agent's Comments: Ted Malawer (Upstart Crow Literary)

Dear Mr. Malawer:

I would like you to represent my 65,000-word contemporary teen novel *My Big Nose & Other Natural Disasters.*

1 Seventeen-year-old Jory Michaels wakes up on the first day of summer vacation with her same old big nose, no passion in her life (in the creative sense of the word), and all signs still pointing to her dying a virgin. Plus, her mother is busy roasting a chicken for Day #6 of the Dinner For Breakfast Diet.

2 In spite of her driving record (it was an accident!), Jory gets a job delivering flowers and cakes to Reno's casinos and wedding chapels. She also comes up with a new summer goal: saving for a life-altering nose job. She and her new nose will attract a fabulous boyfriend. Nothing like the shameless flirt Tyler Briggs, or Tom who's always nice but never calls. Maybe she'll find someone kind of like Gideon at the Jewel Café, except better looking and not quite so different. Jory survives various summer disasters like doing yoga after sampling Mom's Cabbage Soup Diet, Enforced Mother Bonding With Crazy Nose-Obsessed Daughter Night, and discovering Tyler's big secret. But will she learn to accept herself and maybe even find her passion in the creative (AND romantic!) sense of the word?

3 I have written for *APPLESEEDS, Confetti, Hopscotch, Story Friends, Wee Ones Magazine,* the *Deseret News, Children's Playmate,* and Blooming Tree Press' *Summer Shorts* anthology. I won the Utah Arts Council prize for *Not-A-Dr. Logan's Divorce Book*. My novels *Jungle Crossing* and *Going Native!* each won first prize in the League of Utah Writers contest. I currently serve as an SCBWI Regional Advisor.

4 I submitted *My Big Nose & Other Natural Disasters* to Krista Marino at Delacorte because she requested it during our critique at the summer SCBWI conference (no response yet).

Thank you for your time and attention. I look forward to hearing from you.

Sincerely,
Sydney Salter Husseman

1 With hundreds and hundreds of queries each month, it's tough to stand out. Sydney, however, did just that. First, she has a great title that totally made me laugh. Second, she sets up her main character's dilemma in a succinct and interesting way. In one simple paragraph, I have a great idea of who Jory is and what her life is about—the interesting tidbits about her mother help show the novel's sense of humor, too. 2 Sydney's largest paragraph sets up the plot and the conflict, and introduces some exciting potential love interests and misadventures that I was excited to read about. Again, Sydney really shows off her fantastic sense of humor, and she leaves me hanging with a question that I needed an answer to. 3 She has writing experience and has completed other manuscripts that were prize worthy. Her SCBWI involvement—while not a necessity—shows me that she has an understanding of and an interest in the children's publishing world. 4 The fact that an editor requested the manuscript is always a good sign. That I knew Krista personally and highly valued her opinion was, as Sydney's main character Jory would say, "The icing on the cake."

3 SAMPLE QUERY 3: NONFICTION (SELF-HELP)

Agent's Comments: Michelle Wolfson (Wolfson Literary Agency)

Dear Ms. Wolfson:

1 Have you ever wanted to know the best day of the week to buy groceries or go out to dinner? Have you ever wondered about the best time of day to send an e-mail or ask for a raise? What about the best time of day to schedule a surgery or a haircut? What's the best day of the week to avoid lines at the Louvre? What's the best day of the month to make an offer on a house? What's the best time of day to ask someone out on a date? 2

My book, *Buy Ketchup in May and Fly at Noon: A Guide to the Best Time to Buy This, Do That, and Go There*, has the answers to these questions and hundreds more.

3 As a longtime print journalist, I've been privy to readership surveys that show people can't get enough of newspaper and magazine stories about the best time to buy or do things. This book puts several hundreds of questions and answers in one place—a succinct, large-print reference book that readers will feel like they need to own. Why? Because it will save them time and money, and it will give them valuable information about issues related to health, education, travel, the workplace, and more. In short, it will make them smarter, so they can make better decisions. 4

Best of all, the information in this book is relevant to anyone, whether they live in Virginia or the Virgin Islands; Portland, Oregon, or Portland, Maine. In fact, much of the book will find an audience in Europe and Australia.

5 I've worked as a journalist since 1984. In 1999, the Virginia Press Association created an award for the best news writing portfolio in the state—the closest thing Virginia had to a reporter-of-the-year award. I won it that year and then again in 2000. During the summer of 2007, I left newspapering to pursue book projects and long-form journalism.

6 I saw your name on a list of top literary agents for self-help books, and I read on your website that you're interested in books that offer practical advice. *Buy Ketchup in May and Fly at Noon* offers plenty of that. Please let me know if you'd like to read my proposal.

Sincerely,
Mark Di Vincenzo

1 I tend to prefer it when authors jump right into the heart of their book, the exception being if we've met at a conference or have some other personal connection. Mark chose clever questions for the opening of the query. All of those questions are, in fact, relevant to my life—with groceries, dinner, e-mail, and a raise—and yet I don't have a definitive answer to them. 2 He gets a little more offbeat and unusual with questions regarding surgery, the Louvre, buying a house, and dating. This shows a quirkier side to the book and also the range of topics it is going to cover, so I know right away there is going to be a mix of useful and quirky information on a broad range of topics. 3 By starting with "As a long time print journalist," Mark immediately establishes his credibility for writing on this topic. 4 This helps show that there is a market for this book and establishes the need for such a book. 5 Mark's bio paragraph offers a lot of good information. 6 It's nice when I feel like an author has sought me out specifically and thinks we would be a good fit.

4 SAMPLE QUERY 4: WOMEN'S FICTION

Agent's Comments: Elisabeth Weed (Weed Literary)

Dear Ms. Weed:

1 Natalie Miller had a plan. She had a goddamn plan. Top of her class at Dartmouth. Even better at Yale Law. Youngest aide ever to the powerful Senator Claire Dupris. Higher, faster, stronger. This? Was all part of the plan. True, she was so busy ascending the political ladder that she rarely had time to sniff around her mediocre relationship with Ned, who fit the three Bs to the max: basic, blond, and boring, and she definitely didn't have time to mourn her mangled relationship with Jake, her budding rock star ex-boyfriend.

The lump in her right breast that Ned discovers during brain-numbingly bland morning sex? That? Was most definitely not part of the plan. And Stage IIIA breast cancer? Never once had Natalie jotted this down on her to-do list for conquering the world. When her (tiny-penised) boyfriend has the audacity to dump her on the day after her diagnosis, Natalie's entire world dissolves into a tornado of upheaval, and she's left with nothing but her diary to her ex-boyfriends, her mornings lingering over *The Price Is Right*, her burnt-out stubs of pot that carry her past the chemo pain, and finally, the weight of her life choices—the ones in which she might drown in if she doesn't find a buoy.

2 *The Department of Lost and Found* is a story of hope, of resolve, of digging deeper than you thought possible until you find the strength not to crumble, and ultimately, of making your own luck, even when you've been dealt an unsteady hand.

3 I'm a freelance writer and have contributed to, among others, *American Baby, American Way, Arthritis Today, Bride's, Cooking Light, Fitness, Glamour, InStyle Weddings, Men's Edge, Men's Fitness, Men's Health, Parenting, Parents, Prevention, Redbook, Self, Shape, Sly, Stuff, USA Weekend, Weight Watchers, Woman's Day, Women's Health,* and ivillage.com, msn.com, and women.com. I also ghostwrote *The Knot Book of Wedding Flowers.*

If you are interested, I'd love to send you the completed manuscript. Thanks so much! Looking forward to speaking with you soon.

Allison Winn Scotch

1 The opening sentence reads like great jacket copy, and I immediately know who our protagonist is and what the conflict for her will be. (And it's funny, without being silly.) 2 The third paragraph tells me where this book will land: upmarket women's fiction. (A great place to be these days!) 3 This paragraph highlights impressive credentials. While being able to write nonfiction does not necessarily translate over to fiction, it shows me that she is someone worth paying more attention to. And her magazine contacts will help when it comes time to promote the book.

5 SAMPLE QUERY 5: MAINSTREAM/COMEDIC FICTION

Agent's Comments: Michelle Brower (Folio Literary Management)

Dear Michelle Brower:

1 "I spent two days in a cage at the SPCA until my parents finally came to pick me up. The stigma of bringing your undead son home to live with you can wreak havoc on your social status, so I can't exactly blame my parents for not rushing out to claim me. But one more day and I would have been donated to a research facility."

Andy Warner is a zombie.

After reanimating from a car accident that killed his wife, Andy is resented by his parents, abandoned by his friends, and vilified by society. Seeking comfort and camaraderie in Undead Anonymous, a support group for zombies, Andy finds kindred souls in Rita, a recent suicide who has a taste for consuming formaldehyde in cosmetic products, and Jerry, a 21-year-old car crash victim with an artistic flair for Renaissance pornography.

2 With the help of his new friends and a rogue zombie named Ray, Andy embarks on a journey of personal freedom and self-discovery that will take him from his own casket to the SPCA to a media-driven, class-action lawsuit for the civil rights of all zombies. And along the way, he'll even devour a few Breathers.

Breathers is a contemporary dark comedy about life, or undeath, through the eyes of an ordinary zombie. In addition to *Breathers*, I've written three other novels and more than four dozen short stories—a dozen of which have appeared in small press publications. Currently, I'm working on my fifth novel, also a dark comedy, about fate.

Enclosed is a two-page synopsis and the first chapter of *Breathers*, with additional sample chapters or the entire manuscript available upon request. I appreciate your time and interest in considering my query and I look forward to your response.

Sincerely,
Scott G. Browne

1 What really draws me to this query is the fact that it has exactly what I'm looking for in my commercial fiction—story and style. Scott includes a brief quote from the book that manages to capture his sense of humor as an author and his uniquely relatable main character (hard to do with someone who's recently reanimated). I think this is a great example of how query letters can break the rules and still stand out in the slush pile. I normally don't like quotes as the first line, because I don't have a context for them, but this quote both sets up the main concept of the book *and* gives me a sense of the character's voice. This method won't necessarily work for most fiction, but it absolutely is successful here. 2 The letter quickly conveys that this is an unusual book about zombies, and being a fan of zombie literature, I'm aware that it seems to be taking things in a new direction. I also appreciate how Scott conveys the main conflict of his plot and his supporting cast of characters—we know there is an issue for Andy beyond coming back to life as a zombie, and that provides momentum for the story.

WHAT AGENTS ARE LOOKING FOR IN THE IDEAL CLIENT

by Carly Watters

An "ideal client" means something different to every agent, but we have a lot of things in common. We're looking for a talented individual with something unique to say, a voice to say it with, the patience to execute it properly and the marketing wherewithal to share it with the world. Is that too much to ask? Well, agents don't take this business lightly. What might be a writing hobby for some is a passionate career endeavor for us.

The modern publishing business requires a lot of authors, which is why our agency started a literary branding division. Agents must know that potential clients are ready for the challenge and can see the big picture—and we want to know at the querying stage. Here's what agents look for in an ideal client who can thrive in today's marketplace. It's about more than the right project; it's about the right overall package and fit.

CREATIVE BRAND LONGEVITY

One-off projects are risky business. Agents spend a lot of energy and time launching new authors so we need to know you're in it for the long run. We need to know you have plenty of ideas, the energy to pursue them, and talent to complete them. Publishing is a strange business to market in because a launch is different for every author. We can't repackage the same promotional plan for everyone like you would in other industries. Each unique book requires unique attention and with publishers' lists very full each season you need your agent as your advocate to help build a brand that will last a long time. Editors move publishing houses, books get delayed, writers switch genres, but the one thing that stays the same is your solid relationship with your agent who understands your compelling creative vision.

DIGITAL LITERACY

Do you have a website? Do you know how to manage it? Do you understand the basics of social media marketing? Are you very active on at least 1 platform? If you answered no to any of these questions you're potentially a risky client prospect because much of the marketing falls to authors now. I need to know you can handle yourself out there in the wild west of the world wide web. As the Director of Literary Branding at PSLA I can coach you, but as any coach knows your pupil must have talent and the drive to build on existing, inherent skills. Agents don't get paid to coach though—we get paid to sell books for you—so we don't want to spend our days helping you set up your website. We assume you've done all of this. Some writers take to it like wildfire, which is a thrill to see because their sales and reputation blossom because of it. But some don't and we assume even if you don't like it that you understand why you must do it.

MARKET AWARENESS

> *"If you want to be a writer, you must do two things above all others: read a lot and write a lot." - Stephen King*

You'll notice that King says read before write and I'm in complete agreement. Reading not only improves your craft, but it also introduces you to things like category, genre, audience, and your contemporaries. I say contemporaries because you have to read what's being published right now and you have to be cognizant about how those books are being marketed, positioned, and sold. Networking with other authors either online or at events (festivals, writers conferences etc.) is key to building a brand for yourself within your own industry. Are you known for being in a certain group of writers? Just running with a certain crowd can help you when the time comes to ask for blurb endorsements. Not to mention a better understanding of how to get published in that category. Every genre has its own expectations.

FLEXIBLE, COOPERATIVE RELATIONSHIP BUILT ON TRUST

We all know how much noise is out there on the internet. It's loud out there. There are blogs about agents, good and bad, and firstly you have to do your research to know which are the ones worth submitting to. That ideal fit goes both ways between author and agent. What I love about my job is that the relationship between an author and an agent is a special one. I am genuinely friends with some clients, with others it's less personal and more business partnership and I hear from them when necessary. However, there is always trust and an understanding that I have their best interests in mind. The ideal client knows that and chooses me to represent them based on the fact that they think we can build that trust over a long period of time. We have long conversations about ambition, goals, and strategic steps. But ultimately they must know that the relationship we have is between the two of us and taking things to air out on Twitter isn't the way to do it. Writers get lots of advice from other writer friends, but you should always bring it back to your agent before going forth—that's the trust we're looking for.

SUPREME TALENT

I've written quite a bit about marketing and positioning. Those are crucial to the publishing business. However, you get absolutely nowhere in this industry without the talent to back it all up. At the end of the day the book stands alone on the shelf. It needs to be able to support all those marketing endeavors, promotional pushes, and agent advocacy. My reputation is on the line every time I sign up a new client and pitch a new project. I'm looking for that creative longevity I spoke about in point one, but also the talent longevity to support a long career. This industry is not for the faint hearted. The path to getting an agent is hard, but it doesn't get any easier after that. Every stage with every subsequent book is hard: Did you get favorable reviews? How did the sell-in go to bookstores? Did you get nominated for any awards? Did your book sub-rights sell? There are ups and downs that can feel emotionally draining, but the one thing that must hold steadfast is the talent that keeps your career going. Our agency gets thousands of queries a month. I request material from 1.5% of the batch and end up signing 0.02% per year. (Yes, I've done the math.) It's a sliver of the total pie, but all that said I do sign up new clients and I am actively looking for new writers. They just have to be extraordinarily special. Not just talented, but have something new to say about the world and a fresh way of telling it. Talent includes things like innovative subject matter, unique voice, interesting structure, lightening-fast pacing, and reflecting on human nature in a way that can stop time. Show me a book that has a great hook but not enough finesse and a book that has supreme talent but some gaps in the plot and I'll always choose the latter. I can coach a skilled writer, but I'm not a creative writing instructor so I won't be teaching you the craft.

Carly Watters is a VP and Senior Literary Agent at the P.S. Literary Agency. Carly began her publishing career in London at the Darley Anderson Literary, TV and Film Agency. Since joining PSLA in 2010 Carly has had great success launching new authors domestically and abroad. Never without a book on hand she reads across categories which is reflected in the genres she represents at PSLA. Representing debuts and bestsellers, Carly is drawn to emotional, well-paced fiction, with a great voice and characters that readers can get invested in; and platform-driven nonfiction.

CRAFTING THE PERFECT SYNOPSIS

by Kaitlyn Johnson

While writing queries and books is no leisurely picnic, the synopsis is often the most complicated submission material a writer can attempt. Everything else can be perfect—pitch, query, voice, and pages—but it's the synopsis that tells where the story goes, if the plot is fully fleshed out, or if the ending is left dangling without reason. If something in this document foreshadows intense editing, problematic theming, or unresolved endings, it could mean a pass. That's where crafting the synopsis correctly comes into play.

FORMATTING BASICS

The industry standard for synopses is a document that is one to two pages in length. Single-spacing is only acceptable if the entire document fits on one page. However, the rules change upon hitting the second page. If the synopsis exceeds one page, the writer must double space and ensure they don't exceed two pages. If the synopsis is longer than two pages after applying the double-space format, it's too long. It's as simple as that.

Like the manuscript and query letter, stick to regular margins and fonts: Times New Roman, 12 size font, and one-inch margins. Remember, some houses or agencies have their own guidelines, so always check their websites to double check. While one editor asks for two pages, another may ask for six. Do your research.

But don't panic if this feels complicated! No one expects a synopsis to be perfect. Going over a couple lines isn't a big deal, but breaking limits by page lengths is a fast way to rejection. Style guides are set for a reason; don't give the agent a reason to say no before they even get to your manuscript pages.

TIPS & TRICKS

Something not often discussed is how to deal with introducing a new character in a synopsis. Always place the name in ALL CAPS when a character makes their first appearance. This tactic draws the eye and alerts the reader that they haven't met this person yet.

Make an attempt to include these first introductions somewhere within the first two-to-three fully-formed paragraphs. If someone pops up near the end of the book, it may be seen as a general red flag that the plot hasn't been seamless throughout.

Obviously, there are outliers, but these late additions can usually be fixed by eliminating a name altogether. If a new character only appears in one scene toward the end, thereby barely influencing the plot, forego the name. They can simply be "a soldier," a "nobleman," a "messenger," etc. Remember, the more names a reader is forced to remember, the more plot details might slip from their heads. Focus in on the big players: the protagonist, antagonist, supporting characters, and/or love interest.

STRUCTURE

Always write the synopsis in chronological order. This isn't the blurb on the back cover of a book, and it's not the same as the query, either. The synopsis can cover a basic three-step structure: Set-up, Confrontation, and Resolution. The best way to grab a reader is by highlighting the facts unique to the story and giving characters a sense of agency.

STEP 1: Set-up

When crafting your first paragraph, here's what does not work.

1. **A summary of the world rules/history:** Don't begin with the book's own "In the beginning was light..." scenario and don't start off with "My story is about...". Instead, focus on concise details to save space. Explaining a country/city was overrun and colonized so-and-so years ago is fine, but it should be contained in one short sentence and not a sprawling run-on. In addition, give only the worldbuilding/history that is absolutely essential to the main plot. Hold off on subplot explanations.
2. **A character list:** Don't include what characters look like, their purpose in the story, their motivations, etc. The agent doesn't need character descriptions to understand the plot. Save these discoveries for the page.
3. **The Query Letter itself:** Do not simply repeat the blurb from the query. Usually, the agent reads the synopsis shortly after reading the query, and this sort of repetition may show the writer didn't do their research or doesn't know how to explain their own story in detail.

Here's what does work when beginning a synopsis. Use the first paragraph to describe the opening scene—explain what the reader will be walking in to on page one. Establish the main character's name, age, and the gender they identify as. This helps create a picture of "who" they are to the story. Avoid including any secondary characters who appear only for that scene and disappear for the remainder of the novel. Instead, use those who are key to the central plot.

STEP 2: Confrontation

Step 2 gets more internal with character and external with plot. Meaning, the main characters' development—their reasoning and motivations—plays a more dominant role. Call it the "getting to know you" section, AKA the Journey. Here, readers see bonding or flirting, and often a lot of "so tell me about yourself" moments. This will all lead up to the "Inciting Event." For example, something suddenly goes wrong in the trip and provides the characters with an obstacle (i.e. a rockslide on the path, attack from an unknown assailant, or betrayal by one of those close to the protagonist).

This moment is different from the event in your opening scene. The beginning establishes why the characters are compelled into the plot—examples here could be they are forcibly removed from their homeland, they see their family die, or their power/magic is revealed. That's set-up, not the journey.

The middle inciting event drives the book to its final outcome. It defines pacing, controls character growth, and establishes a climax or high point to the center of the story.

STEP 3: Resolution

Here, the reader faces the story's darkest/deepest moment, a "rock bottom" for the characters. Explain how the moment is overcome and what the protagonist must do to move onward in the journey. Then comes the moment for the final climax and eventual ending. Sometimes, these are one and the same, while at other times they can be two interlocking scenes. For example, a final battle is the climax, but the true ending is when the victor is crowned as king, not the fighting itself.

FILLER BITS

Tying major plot points together is just as important as describing the events themselves. Writers often want to include every scene of the story in a step-by-step method. Every crawl or trip or laugh is important—it's their "baby" after all. But to an agent, no two moments are equal.

This is where filler bits come into play—the parts connecting the beginning to the middle or the middle to the end. No more than one-to-two short paragraphs should be spent on these.

Here's a visual aid: Beginning > 1-to-2 paragraph connections > Middle/Inciting Event > 1-to-2 paragraph connections > Final Climax/Ending.

For filler bits, use concrete details vital to understanding how the reader moves from one section to another. Overdoing these elements or adding too many world-specific terms can lead to confusion, so use them sparingly. Names often aren't as important as actions.

VOICE & POVS

In the synopsis, always maintain an active third person. Avoid using passive voice—such as "there was an obstacle" versus "an obstacle lay in the road"; "he had stared out the window" versus "he stared out the window"; "snow was falling slowly" versus "the snow fell slowly"—as it drags pacing and gives the writing a monotone quality.

For writers who use multiple POVs, choose a dominant voice. Most stories have one or two, usually love interests or mortal enemies or hero and sidekick. Determine who drives the plot the most. It's often easier to write the synopsis from the eyes of one character while mentioning the others' role/impact alongside this main figure.

Dueling timelines throw a wrench in this tactic. There are a couple options to tackling those stories: focus on the separation by character—as in, take the main character in the main timeline and present their journey, proving how the other timeline affects it in significant moments; the writer could also split the synopsis in two—describe events of the first timeline on the first page and the second timeline on the second page, using the last paragraph to reveal how they intersect.

Whether through one or multiple POVs, every story has subplots. These are details, hints, or characters that don't play a major role in the current story's main plot. This can include emotional drive/consequences from secondary or tertiary characters, justification for character actions, or locations that appear in the journey but don't impact the bigger picture. Avoid using up space for these moments. The synopsis should focus on main characters influencing the main plot, with backup from secondary characters only when necessary.

ENDINGS

Endings in a synopsis are mandatory. That doesn't mean an agent will actually read the ending. Some prefer to leave it unspoiled while others believe it's necessary before requesting more pages. Regardless, it must be included.

A query leaves the finale as a wonderful secret, but the synopsis is the exact opposite. Cutting off the document with subtle comments like, "They enter the castle, intent on fighting the beast," won't cut it. That statement says nothing about the true ending: the outcome of the battle! If a character dies, if unrequited love is announced, or if the reader is faced with a cliffhanger, those details must be disclosed.

Endings are necessary for agents to know if they feel connected to the entirety of the work. If they enter the pages with details already in mind, it's all the better when a writer has the power to change their opinion, to surprise them by making them enjoy something they'd previously disliked.

Another reason for endings in the synopsis is to prove the writer knows how to offer closure. Especially with novels that are intended for a series, the first book should be strong enough to satisfy despite the storyline continuing onward. No story should "depend" on a sequel for strength or entertainment, and the synopsis is a way to determine if the writer achieved this goal.

Remember, it's fine if a synopsis comes across stiff or to-the-point. Voice is key within the query and manuscript pages, but the synopsis acts as a quick summary to outline the need-to-know elements of your story. An agent doesn't expect perfection; they simply desire clarity and honesty.

After receiving a BA in Writing, Literature, and Publishing from Emerson College, Kaitlyn Johnson refused to leave the concept of nightly homework behind. As well as being a junior agent for Corvisiero Literary Agency, she is also a freelance editor at her own company, K. Johnson Editorial, and has worked as a copyeditor for academic publisher codeMantra, a YA editor for Accent Press, and a Conference Assistant for GrubStreet, Boston. She has written various articles for *Writer's Digest* and has had a flash fiction story published in the anthology *A Box of Stars Beneath the Bed.*

LANDING THE SIX-FIGURE DEAL

What Makes Your Proposal Hot

by SJ Hodges

It's the question every first-time author wants to ask:

"If I sell my book, will the advance even cover my rent?"

Authors, I am happy to tell you that, yes, the six-figure book deal for a newbie still exists—even if you're not a celebrity with your own television show! As a ghostwriter, I work with numerous authors and personalities to develop both nonfiction and fiction proposals, and I've seen unknown first-timers land life-changing deals even in a down economy. Is platform the ultimate key to their success? You better believe it's a huge consideration for publishers, but here's the good news: Having a killer platform is only one element that transforms a "nice deal" into a "major deal."

You still have to ensure the eight additional elements of your proposal qualify as major attractions. Daniela Rapp, editor at St. Martin's Press explains, "In addition to platform, authors need to have a fantastic, original idea. They have to truly be an expert in their field and they must be able to write." So how do you craft a proposal that conveys your brilliance, your credentials, your talent and puts a couple extra zeroes on your check?

ONE: NARRATIVE OVERVIEW

Before you've even written word one of your manuscript, you are expected to, miraculously, summarize the entirety of your book in such a compelling and visceral way that a publisher or agent will feel as if they are reading *The New York Times* review. Sound impossible? That's because it is.

That's why I'm going to offer two unorthodox suggestions. First, consider writing the first draft of your overview after you've created your table of contents and your chapter outlines. You'll know much more about the content and scope of your material even if you're not 100 percent certain about the voice and tone. That's why you'll take another pass after you complete your sample chapters. Because then you'll be better acquainted with the voice of your book which brings me to unorthodox suggestion number two... treat your overview as literature.

I believe every proposal component needs to be written "in voice" especially because your overview is the first page the editor sees after the title page. By establishing your voice on the page immediately, your proposal becomes less of a sales document and more of a page-turner. Remember, not everyone deciding your fate works in marketing and sales. Editors still have some buying power and they are readers, first and foremost.

TWO: TABLE OF CONTENTS AND CHAPTER OUTLINES

Television writers call this "breaking" a script. This is where you break your book or it breaks you. This is where you discover if what you plan to share with the world actually merits 80,000 words and international distribution.

Regardless of whether you're writing fiction or nonfiction, this element of your proposal must take your buyer on a journey (especially if it's nonfiction) and once more, I'm a big fan of approaching this component with creativity particularly if you're exploring a specific historical time period, plan to write using a regional dialect, rely heavily on "slanguage," and especially if the material is highly technical and dry.

This means you'll need to style your chapter summaries and your chapter titles as a form of dramatic writing. Think about the arc of the chapters, illuminating the escalating conflict, the progression towards a resolution, in a cinematic fashion. Each chapter summary should end with an "emotional bumper," a statement that simultaneously summarizes and entices in the same way a television show punches you in the gut before they cut to a commercial.

Is it risky to commit to a more creative approach? Absolutely. Will it be perfect the first time you write it? No. The fifth time you write it? No. The tenth time? Maybe. But the contents and chapter summary portion of your proposal is where you really get a chance to show off your skills as an architect of plot and structure and how you make an editor's job much, much easier. According to Lara Asher, acquisitions editor at Globe Pequot Press, it is the single most important component of your proposal. "If I can't easily understand what a book is trying to achieve then I can't present it to my colleagues," Asher says. "It won't make it through the acquisitions process."

THREE: YOUR AUTHOR BIO

Your author bio page must prove that you are more than just a pro, that you are recognized by the world at large as "the definitive expert" on your topic, that you have first-hand experience tackling the problems and implementing your solutions, and that you've seen positive results not only in your personal life but in the lives of others. You have to have walked the walk and talked the talk. You come equipped with a built-in audience, mass media attention, and a strong social network. Your bio assures your buyer that you are the right writer exploring the right topic at the right time.

FOUR: YOUR PLATFORM

Platform, platform, platform. Sit through any writing conference, query any agent, lunch with any editor and you'll hear the "P" word over and over again. What you won't hear is hard-and-fast numbers about just how large this platform has to be in order to secure a serious offer. Is there an audience-to-dollar-amount ratio that seems to be in play? Are publishers paying per head?

"I haven't found this to be the case," says Julia Pastore, former editor for Random House. "It's easier to compel someone to 'Like' you on Facebook or follow you on Twitter than it is to compel them to plunk down money to buy your book. Audience engagement is more important than the sheer number of social media followers."

With that said, if you're shooting for six-figures, publishers expect you'll have big numbers and big plans. Your platform will need to include:

Cross-promotional partnerships

These are organizations or individuals that already support you, are already promoting your brand, your products or your persona. If you host a show on HGTV or Nike designed a tennis racket in your honor, they definitely qualify. If, however, you're not rolling like an A-lister just yet, you need to brainstorm any and every possible connection you have to organizations with reach in the 20,000+ range. Maybe your home church is only 200 people but the larger association serves 40,000 and you often write for their newsletter. Think big. Then think bigger.

Specific, verifiable numbers proving the loyalty of your audience

"Publishers want to see that you have direct contact with a loyal audience," says Maura Teitelbaum, an agent at Folio Literary Management. This means having a calendar full of face-to-face speaking engagements, a personal mailing list, extensive database and verifiable traffic to your author website.

But how much traffic does there need to be? How many public appearances? How many e-mails in your Constant Contact newsletter? Publishers are loathe to quote concrete numbers for "Likes" and "Followers" so I'll stick my neck out and do it instead. At a minimum, to land a basic book deal, meaning a low five-figure sum, you'll need to prove that you've got 15,000-20,000 fans willing to follow you into hell and through high water.

For a big six-figure deal, you'll need a solid base of 100,000 rabid fans plus access to hundreds of thousands more. If not millions. Depressed yet? Don't be. Because we live in a time when things as trivial as Angry Oranges or as important as scientific TED talks can go viral and propel a writer out of obscurity in a matter of seconds. It is only your job to become part of the conversation. And once your foot is in the door, you'll be able to gather...

Considerable media exposure

Publishers are risk averse. They want to see that you're a media darling achieving pundit status. Organize and present all your clips, put together a DVD demo reel of your on-air appearances and be able to quote subscriber numbers and demographics about the publications running your articles or features about you.

Advance praise from people who matter

Will blurbs really make a difference in the size of your check? "I would include as many in a proposal as possible," says Teitelbaum. "Especially if those people are willing to write letters of commitment saying they will promote the book via their platform. That shows your efforts will grow exponentially."

FIVE: PROMOTIONAL PLANS

So what is the difference between your platform and your promotional plan? Your promotional plan must demonstrate specifically how you will activate your current platform and the expected sales results of that activation. These are projections starting three to six months before your book release date and continuing for one year after its hardcover publication. They want your guarantee to sell 15,000 books within that first year.

In addition, your promotional plan also issues promises about the commitments you are willing to make in order to promote the book to an even wider market. This is your expansion plan. How will you broaden your reach and who will help you do it? Publishers want to see that your goals are ambitious but doable.

Think about it this way. If you own a nail salon and you apply for a loan to shoot a movie, you're likely to be rejected. But ask for a loan to open your second salon and your odds get much better. In other words, keep your promotional plans in your wheelhouse while still managing to include:

- Television and radio appearances
- Access to print media
- A massive social media campaign
- Direct e-mail solicitations
- E-commerce and back-of-room merchandising
- New joint partnerships
- Your upcoming touring and speaking schedule with expected audience

You'll notice that I did not include hiring a book publicist as a requirement. Gone are the days when an advance-sucking, three-month contract with a book publicist makes any difference. For a six-figure author, publishers expect there is a team in place: a powerful agent, a herd of assistants and a more generalized media publicist already managing the day-to-day affairs of building your brand, growing your audience. Hiring a book publicist at the last minute is useless.

SIX: YOUR MARKET ANALYSIS

It would seem the odds against a first-time author hitting the jackpot are slim but that's where market analysis provides a glimmer of hope. There are actually markets considered more desirable to publishers. "Broader is generally better for us," says Rapp. "Niche generally implies small. Not something we [St. Martin's Press] can afford to do these days. Current affairs books, if they are explosive and timely, can work. Neuroscience is hot. Animal books (not so much animal memoirs) still work. Military books sell."

"The health and diet category will always be huge," says Asher. "But in a category like parenting which is so crowded, we look for an author tackling a niche topic that hasn't yet been covered."

Niche or broad, your market analysis must position your book within a larger context, addressing the needs of the publishing industry, the relevant cultural conversations happening in the zeitgeist, your potential audience and their buying power, and the potential for both domestic and international sales.

SEVEN: YOUR C.T.A.

Choose the books for your Competitive Title Analysis not only for their topical similarities but also because the author has a comparable profile and platform to your own. Says Pastore, "It can be editorially helpful to compare your book to *Unbroken* by Hillenbrand, but unless your previous book was also a bestseller, this comparison won't be helpful to our sales force."

Limit your C.T.A. to five or six solid offerings then get on BookScan and make sure none of the books sold fewer than 10,000 copies. "Higher sales are preferable," says Rapp. "And you should leave it to the publisher to decide if the market can hold one more title or not. We always do our own research anyway, so just because the book is not mentioned in your line-up doesn't mean we won't know about it."

EIGHT: SAMPLE CHAPTERS

Finally, you have to/get to prove you can … write. Oh yeah, that!

This is the fun part, the pages of your proposal where you really get to shine. It is of upmost importance that these chapters, in harmony with your overview and chapter summaries, allow the beauty, wisdom and/or quirkiness of your voice to be heard. Loud and clear.

"Writing absolutely matters and strong sample chapters are crucial." Pastore explains, "An author must be able to turn their brilliant idea into engaging prose on the page."

Approach the presentation of these chapters creatively. Consider including excerpts from several different chapters and not just offering the standard Introduction, Chapter One and Two. Consider the inclusion of photographs to support the narrative, helping your editor put faces to names. Consider using sidebars or box quotes from the narrative throughout your proposal to build anticipation for the actual read.

NINE: YOUR ONE-PAGER

Lastly, you'll need a one-pager, which is a relatively new addition to the book proposal format. Publishers now expect an author to squeeze a 50- or 60-page proposal down to a one-page summary they can hand to their marketing and sales teams. In its brevity, the one-pager must provide your buyer with "a clear vision of what the book is, why it's unique, why you are the best person to write it, and how we can reach the audience," says Pastore. And it must do that in fewer than 1,000 words. There is no room to be anything but impressive.

And if you're shooting for that six-figure deal, impressive is what each component of your book proposal must be. Easy? No. But still possible? Yes.

SJ HODGES is an 11-time published playwright, ghostwriter and editor. Her most recent book, a memoir co-authored with Animal Planet's "Pit Boss" Shorty Rossi was purchased by Random House/Crown, hit #36 on the Amazon bestseller list and went into its 3rd printing less than six weeks after its release date. As a developmental editor, SJ has worked on books published by Vanguard Press, Perseus Book Group and St. Martin's Press. SJ is a tireless advocate for artists offering a free listing for jobs, grants and fellowships at her Facebook page: facebook.com/constantcreator. She can be reached through her website: sjhodges.com.

THE 9 KEY ELEMENTS OF A SUCCESSFUL NONFICTION BOOK PROPOSAL

by Brian A. Klems

So you have a nonfiction book idea—maybe you even have some of it written—and you're ready to take that idea outside of your small, quiet writing space, and launch it into the world of agents and publishers. The idea is so good, in fact, that it'll land you that vacation home you've always wanted (or, at least, net you a nice enough advance that you can stay for a week at a reasonably priced AirBnB not far from that dream home). There's only one problem: You know how to write the book, but you don't know how to sell the book.

That's where the nonfiction book proposal comes into play. The nonfiction book proposal is what sells your idea to those who can get your work published and help you earn money from it. Here I'm going to walk you through the basic essentials needed to start a proposal, the nine key elements successful nonfiction book proposals should include, and examples of what those key elements should look like, sharing examples from my own successful proposal for *Oh Boy, You're Having a Girl: A Dad's Survival Guide to Raising Daughters* (Adams Media, Simon & Schuster). My proposal helped land me an agent, land me a book deal and land my book in brick and mortar stores, as well as online retailers. Before we dive in, let's start with several basic things you need to understand:

What is a Nonfiction Book Proposal?

A nonfiction book proposal is a document that focuses on key elements that help show prospective agents and publishers your idea, why there's a market for it and why you are the right person to write it.

What Do You Need to Have Before Writing a Nonfiction Book Proposal?

- A great idea – something of interest to specific people
- Platform – How you reach those specific people
- More Platform – (Yes, this is that important)

What is the Biggest Difference Between Selling Nonfiction and Fiction?

When you are trying to sell fiction or memoir, you need to have a completed manuscript. You don't need that with nonfiction (yay!)—you just need a great idea and a few sample chapters.

One of the most important concepts to remember when thinking in terms of a nonfiction book proposal is that it's idea-driven, which is why you don't need the entire manuscript completed and edited before pitching it to agents. The idea should be strong enough to appeal to a specific audience. And in your proposal, you'll not only show why it's a great idea, you'll also show why your audience needs this book and, equally as important, why you're the right person to write it.

THE 9 KEY ELEMENTS OF A NONFICTION BOOK PROPOSAL

The nine key elements of a nonfiction book proposal are as follows:

1. Title Page
2. The Hook Page (Overview)
3. Target Audience
4. Competitive Titles
5. Marketing Plan
6. Author Bio
7. Chapter outline/Table of Contents
8. Chapter by Chapter Summary
9. Sample Chapters

Each of these sections plays a pivotal role in helping you sell your idea. There are proper ways to handle each section, and below I'll walk you through each one and provide examples from my own successful proposal.

Section 1. The Title Page

The Title Page includes the bare-bone basics of your concept: your book's tentative title, your name and your logline. A logline is a one-sentence description that sums up your book. Often in nonfiction books, you'll see a variation of the logline appear just after the title (often after a colon). My title page looked like this:

Title: Oh Boy, You're Having a Girl

Author: Brian A. Klems

Logline: A Dad's humorous survival guide to having and raising daughters.

You'll see that the publisher merged the title and a variation of my logline (*Oh Boy, You're Having a Girl: A Dad's Survival Guide to Raising Daughters*). If you can't sum your concept up in one sentence, you're not ready to write your proposal.

Section 2. The Hook (or Overview)

The Hook, which is sometimes referred to as the Overview, answers these two specific questions: Why do people need your book and why are you qualified to write it? You're not trying to explain everything about your concept in the Hook, you're trying to show an agent or publisher why people will need or want it. Think of the back of your book jacket. Novels tell a mini version of their story. Nonfiction books make a sales pitch.

The Hook it typically between 400-600 words. Here's the Hook section from my proposal (which actually turned into the Introduction in my book):

> First off, my condolences. If you're a guy and you've opened this book, you either have a daughter, are on the verge of having a daughter or are in the delivery room hoping that the sweet bundle of job that just emerged from your wife somehow, someway, spontaneously grows a penis. I am here to tell you: That almost never happens.
>
> One thing is certainly clear—you're in trouble. You've spent all your life being a guy, developing skills like chest-bumping and growing a mustache, all of which provide zero education on how to raise a girl. In fact, your friends, who are acutely aware of how little you know about girls, are probably still unclear as to how you landed a wife. They definitely won't believe you when you tell them that you "wowed her" by finishing third in your legacy fantasy baseball league. (They also will remind you that your team, "The Man-Eating Sweater Vests," actually finished fifth.)

> I'm going to be honest with you, things don't look pretty. You don't realize it yet, but you're starting down a path that will crush your soul with tiptoeing ballet shoes and drown your spirit in make-believe tea. You are going to schedule emergency eye doctor appointments to confirm (or deny) that you are suffering from a rare condition that allows you to see only shades of pink. And, worst of all, you'll spend every second of every hour of every day trying to convince your wife that the outside of your house is in dire need of a 17-foot-wide moat filled with alligators and fire-breathing dragons. (NOTE: I've read that doing this increases your property value and saves you on homeowners insurance.)
>
> But before you start to panic and say something crazy to your wife like "Are you sure this baby is mine?" or "I liked the way LeBron handled his exit from Cleveland," hear me out. Raising a daughter is one of the biggest challenges you will ever experience as a guy, and it's one you can't take lightly. Trust me, I know.
>
> Believe me, I've lived through it and, so far, I've survived it. And I want to help you survive it too. I've learned a lot throughout my first five years of having daughters. I hope through my experiences, advice and wisdom, you'll see that you are not alone and you'll learn to rise to the challenge when your daughter requires help naming of all the Disney princesses or asks you, in front of your softball buddies, "Dad, where are your boobs?" (Trust me, this will happen.)
>
> While you are certainly in trouble now, the good news is that by the end of this book, you'll be moderately less in trouble. You won't feel nearly as terrified as you did when the doctor uttered those six life-changing words, "Oh boy, you're having a girl!" In fact, you will start to feel a bit relieved. You may even start to feel lucky that you have daughters—after all, they are called "Daddy's Girls" for a reason.
>
> But I'd still consider building that moat.

In my Hook, I aimed to give the agent a sense of my voice on top of answering the question of why dads (my audience) will need this book (raising daughters is hard) and why I'm qualified to write it (I had three daughters in the span of five years). Look specifically at the fifth paragraph, as that's the key to my entire hook. I used a few paragraphs to set it up, then hammer home the why and the why me.

Section 3. Target Audience

In your Target Audience section, you want to explain who your potential readers are. You don't want to be too broad—it's best to be specific as possible. Here's *Oh Boy*'s Target Audience paragraph:

> Nearly 4 million babies are born in the U.S. each year and, according to United States Census Bureau, 49% of them are girls. This book is written for the men whom those

girls will eventually call dad. It is also written for moms looking to laugh and relate to the experiences their counterparts will go through, as well as grandparents and friends who are looking for the perfect baby shower gift.

Because *Oh Boy* has a rather large target audience, I was able to pull in specific numbers (49% of 4 million) while also attributing it (United States Census Bureau) while keeping it brief. I also made sure to alert the agent that I view this as a gift book as well, broadening the market. Make sure your Target Audience section pulls in any numbers it can, even if it's as simple as noting that the book is written for women ages 18-25.

Section 4. Competitive titles

In the Competitive Titles section of your proposal, your goal is to present 3-5 books that are similar to yours—in other words, books that may also be purchased by your target audience. What you're ultimately showcasing here is that there is a market for your book. To do this effectively, you want to pick bestselling and popular books in your category. If you show agents books that bombed, they're just going to assume yours will bomb too (because the evidence says the market for books like that are weak).

Also, your goal isn't to bash these books or speak negatively of them (after all, an agent you pitch may have represented one of them). Your priority is to make the agent/publisher think that your book is the next logical book in that progression—the next bestseller. Here's an example of one comparative title for *Oh Boy* and how I set it apart:

Comparative Title: *8 Simple Rules for Dating My Teenage Daughter*

W. Bruce Cameron takes on the task of raising daughters during their teenage years, looking at the challenges dads face with typical teenage girls, and dishing advice on how to survive this time of your life. Plus, he does it with such hilarity that you'll forget your life is, for the time being, in chaos.

Oh Boy is a reboot of this concept, only it focuses on a dad's role in raising daughters during the very early years (from birth to age 5). With its own brand of humor, it'll tackle everything from naming your daughter (I can't believe my wife rejected the name Megatron) to surviving tea parties, potty training, Disney princess life and more.

Section 5. Marketing Plan

Your proposal's Marketing Plan isn't just a section based on pie-in-the-sky dream marketing scenarios. It's designed to be a realistic view of marketing and promotional items that you will accomplish to help raise awareness of your book. You shouldn't say, "I plan to launch a website," you should say "I am building a website to launch six months before the release of the book, focused on (FILL IN THE BLANK)." Hopefully you see the difference in the approach.

This section also focuses on your platform—which is essential for all nonfiction book writers. A platform is your ability to reach potential readers and buyers of your book. Having a weak platform is like standing on home plate at a Major League Baseball ballpark with mostly empty seats, yelling "I have a new book out." No matter how loud you scream it, there's no one to hear it. Having an excellent platform is like having a sell-out crowd, where everyone is anxiously waiting in anticipation of what you have to say. Potential platform items you should consider including are your social media audiences (particularly if they reach five-figures in size), groups you belong to who would let you speak or market to them, magazines that will let you guest post (and promote your book in the process) and anything else that will reach your target audience.

For *Oh Boy*, I focused on a few key items:

- I had a parenting blog that registered 40,000 pageviews per month.
- I spoke at a dozen writing conferences all over the country where I could promote my book.
- I made a list of local and regional parenting magazines (print and online) throughout the country and provided a plan to reach out to all of them, offering to write an article for free (so long as they promoted my book at the end of the article). If they weren't interested in an article, I would offer a free copy of my book for them to give away as a promotion on their social media channels.

Many magazines took me up on at least one of these offers, but it all stemmed from putting together that list (a pro-active move) and reaching out to them (and actionable item). So when planning out your marketing section, think in terms of what you can accomplish on your own (without the help of a publisher).

Section 6. Author Bio

The Author Bio section is where you brag about yourself. Why are you the expert to write this book? What are your credentials? Do you have awards in your field? Do you have connections in your field? Anything that proves you're the expert should be included in here. Here's an abbreviated version of my bio for my proposal:

> BRIAN A. KLEMS is a writer, editor, husband, perennial fantasy sports underachiever, and father of three girls. He's a proud graduate of the E.W. Scripps journalism school at Ohio University. He writes an award-winning parenting blog, TheLifeOfDad.com, for the Cincinnati Enquirer, which was named one of the Best Parent Blogs in Ohio by Moms Trusted. His writing has appeared in dozens of print and online periodicals, including *Southern MOMentum, Family Friendly Cincinnati, OC Fam-*

ily, and more. You can find him on Twitter @BrianKlems, on his parenting blog, or at Great American Ballpark with his daughters cheering on his beloved Cincinnati Reds.

By including these items, I established that not only am I an expert (because I have three daughters), but also that others think I'm an expert on it too (I was picked up by a large metropolitan newspaper and won awards by groups that value parent-advice blogs).

When writing your bio do not hold back. As uncomfortable as many of us are about bragging on our accomplishments, this is no time to be modest: celebrate you right here.

Section 7. Chapter outline/Table of Contents

The Chapter Outline/Table of Contents is pretty straight forward, as it shows the tentative table of contents for your book. This allows the agent to envision, without having to read a full manuscript, the direction of your book. Below is the original table of contents for *Oh Boy*, so you can see how simple it is to put this section together:

Oh Boy, You're Having a Girl: A Dad's Survival Guide to Having Daughters will have a brief introduction followed by 15 chapters:

Introduction

A short introduction spelling out the trouble you are in, why you need help and why I'm the guy to deliver it to you in this book.

CHAPTER I. It's a Girl (& You Can't Name Her Megatron)

CHAPTER II. Get Used to Pink

CHAPTER III. Your Friends Will Give You a Hard Time

CHAPTER IV. Disney is Going To Ruin Your Life

CHAPTER V. She Can't JUST Wear Baseball Jerseys

CHAPTER VI. Questions You Never Expected to Be Asked

CHAPTER VII. Dora is Your New Best Friend

CHAPTER VIII. Get Used to Fashion Shows

CHAPTER IX. Goodbye Fantasy Sports League Championship

CHAPTER X. She's Sick: She Can Have Whatever She Wants

CHAPTER XI. Planning Ahead for Future Bankruptcy

CHAPTER XII. Diaper-to-Potty-Training-to-Public-Bathroom (Meltdown) Breakdown

CHAPTER XIII. Ballet isn't a Sport

CHAPTER XIV. How to Handle Her First Crush (Preschool Edition)

CHAPTER XV. Why Having Daughters is Really the Best

If I had to do it over again, I would have worked harder to make each chapter title focus on a takeaway, as some titles, in retrospect, aren't as strong as they could have been. But these held together well enough as a guide for agents to get an idea of what to expect, and that's ultimately the goal you're aiming to achieve.

Section 8. Chapter by Chapter Summary

The Chapter by Chapter Summary section allows you to elaborate on the chapter titles from your table of contents in a paragraph or two (preferably no more than two). The key here is to show not just what's in the chapter, but, more important, what the takeaway is for the reader. If there isn't a takeaway—an element that causes the reader to learn something that he or she can apply to their life (or, at the minimum, make him or her more intelligent about the topic), then you'll have to rethink that potential chapter of your book. Here's a look at the chapter from *Oh Boy* on Disney's influence on a dad's life:

> **CHAPTER IV.** Disney is Going to Ruin Your Life
>
> When you have daughters, princesses sneak their way into everything, and not just movies. *Oh no!* They show up on cups, on plates, on bedsheets and blankets. They even show up in your favorite board games—It's not Yahtzee, it's PRINCESS YAHTZEE! It's not Clue, it's PRINCESS CLUE! Thanks a lot Disney! But even though princesses have never been high on the "things you care about" list, now the number one thing you care about is *your* little princess. Use these strategies to become a Disney princess pro that will not only impress your daughter, but will also make you the envy of all her princess friends!

9. Sample Chapters

Finally, you'll close out your nonfiction book proposal with three to five sample chapters of your book. These sample chapters help the agent or publisher get a clear idea of what the book will be like, how it will be written and why they can trust you to deliver on the promises you've made earlier in the proposal.

With most nonfiction titles I recommend including the first several chapters. Only choose others if you have a strong, thoughtful reason to do so. For *Oh Boy* I attached the first three chapters, as I believed those were the most pivotal chapters in establishing what I aimed to accomplish with the book. They showed not only the stories and takeaways that I planned to weave throughout the entire manuscript, but also displayed the voice of my writing so agents could decide whether they enjoyed my humor sensibilities or not. For example:

OK, so I'm not going to share my sample chapters—that'd take up too much real estate here. But I hope you consider grabbing a copy of the book and studying them, as they are pretty close to what I submitted in my proposal. Plus you can consider it a business expense and write it off! It's like Kramer said in *Seinfeld*: You just write it off!

Remember, the number one reason a nonfiction concept doesn't sell is because the proposed idea is like thousands of others before it: nothing compelling sets it apart. The second reason is a lack-luster nonfiction book proposal. If you have a great idea and include these key elements in your proposal, you'll give your book the best chance you can to succeed.

And when you find success and sell that first book, start working on the next book. After all, that future vacation home is going to need some really cool furniture for when you host friends.

Brian A. Klems is a freelance writer, editor, speaker and author of the Amazon bestselling humor parenting book, *Oh Boy, You're Having a Girl: A Dad's Survival Guide to Raising Daughters*. He can be reached on Twitter @BrianKlems.

THE AGENT QUERY TRACKER

Submit smarter and follow up faster with these simple spreadsheets to revolutionize your record-keeping.

Tyler Moss

Everyone knows the real magic of writing comes from time spent in the chair, those sessions in which your fingertips flitting across the keyboard can barely keep pace with the electric current sparking through your brain.

Those in-between periods, full of administrative tasks—the querying, the tracking of payments, the day-to-day doldrums that occupy the interstitial moments of a writer's life—become an afterthought. But when such responsibilities are given short shrift, the inevitable result is disorganization—which at best can impede creativity and at worst can have dire consequences. Missed payments, embarrassing gaffes (querying the same agent twice, or realizing you have no record of where your previous agent submitted your last novel), and incomplete records come tax time are entirely avoidable headaches.

Still, organized record-keeping takes work. Which is why we decided to do it for you.

This does not have to mean you're about to start spending more time on these tasks—in fact, quite the opposite. Once you invest in a standard process up front, each future action will require little more than filling out a few cells in a spreadsheet. (Learn to love them as I have for their clean, quadrilateral beauty.)

You can use the simple guides on the following pages to customize forms of your own, whether you're querying an agent, tracking the places your agent is submitting, or working on your freelancing career between projects.

AGENT QUERY TRACKER

AGENT	**Example:** Booker M. Sellington		
AGENCY	The Booker M. Sellington Agency		
E-MAIL	BMS@bmsagency.com		
DATE QUERIED	8/1/16		
MATERIALS SENT	Query, Synopsis, first 10 pages		
DATE FOLLOWED UP	9/1/16		
RESPONSE	Request for additional materials		
ADDITIONAL MATERIALS REQUESTED	Full manuscript		
DATE FOLLOWED UP	10/15/16		
RESPONSE	Offer of representation		
NOTES	Specializes in thrillers		

Few writers hit the jackpot and manage to land a literary agent on their first query. As this process can take weeks or months, and as agency guidelines vary widely, it can be helpful to keep a detailed record of whom you have contacted, what agency they work for, what materials you've sent in, and the specifics of their responses. Customize your own tracker starting from these column headings:

- **AGENT, AGENCY & E-MAIL:** Where you are sending your query
- **POLICY AGAINST QUERYING MULTIPLE AGENTS AT AGENCY:** [Optional Field] Some agencies have a no-from-one-agent-means-no-from-the-whole-agency policy; noting this saves you time and embarrassment, particularly at larger firms where multiple reps might seem like a potential fit
- **DATE QUERIED & MATERIALS SENT:** When and what you submitted, always following guidelines (query letter, first ten pages, synopsis, proposal, etc.)
- **"NO RESPONSE MEANS NO" POLICY:** [Optional Field] Agents who specify in their guidelines that no response equates to a rejection, meaning you shouldn't follow up
- **DATE FOLLOWED UP:** In the event of no response and excluding those with the policy noted above
- **RESPONSE:** A rejection, a request to see more, or any constructive feedback
- **ADDITIONAL MATERIALS REQUESTED & DATE SENT:** Typically a full or partial manuscript is requested if your query garners interest

- **DATE FOLLOWED UP:** For a full or partial, follow up after at least four weeks if there's no response (unless you have an offer for representation elsewhere, in which case you'll follow up immediately to request a decision or withdraw your manuscript from consideration)
- **RESPONSE:** The agent's final feedback or response
- **NOTES:** Any helpful info on your interaction with the agent or agency, or feedback that could be addressed before additional querying (e.g., "The protagonist often behaves erratically and inconsistently," or "The manuscript could use a proofread")

If you opt to forgo seeking representation and instead are submitting directly to publishers that accept unagented submissions, then I suggest you make a separate spreadsheet to track that information, swapping the headings **AGENT** and **AGENCY** for **ACQUIRING EDITOR** and **IMPRINT/PUBLISHER**, respectively.

ORGANIZE YOUR QUERIES

Both versions of the tracker are available for download at writersdigest.com/GLA-18.

AGENT SUBMISSIONS TO PUBLISHER TRACKER

IMPRINT/PUBLISHER	**Example:** Pendant Publishing		
ACQUIRING EDITOR	Elaine Benes		
DATE SENT	8/1/16		
DATE FOLLOWED UP	9/1/16		
RESPONSE	Pass		
EDITOR'S COMMENTS	Says a "book about nothing" is not right for their Spring 2018 lineup		
ADDITIONAL NOTES	Suggests changes to plot in which the judge sentences protagonist to be the antagonist's butler		

After signing with an agent, it's critical to stay in close communication as she sends your manuscript to publishers. Such records allow you to stay involved in the direction of your career, gather essential data about the imprints your agent believes you'd be best suited for, and pinpoint commonalities or contradictions in feedback. And if you must someday sever ties with your agent, you'll have what you need to help your new representation pick up right where your old representation left off. Keep record of the following details:

- **IMPRINT/PUBLISHER, ACQUIRING EDITOR & DATE SENT:** The details of exactly where and when your agent submitted your manuscript
- **DATE FOLLOWED UP:** Date on which your agent followed up with the acquiring editor if you did not receive an initial response
- **RESPONSE:** Accepted, rejected, revise-and-resubmit request
- **EDITOR'S COMMENTS:** A one-line description highlighting any relevant feedback received
- **ADDITIONAL NOTES:** Miscellaneous information about the publisher, editor or the overall interaction between agent and publishing house

PRO TIP: SAVE SPREADSHEETS TO GOOGLE DRIVE

Recently I read a news story in which a writer in New Orleans ran into his burning home to save the manuscripts of two completed novels stored on his computer—the only place he had them saved. Luckily, he weathered the blaze and escaped with laptop in hand. Though we can admire his dedication to his work, there are any number of digital-age options that could've prevented this horrible scenario—among them, Google Drive.

The system is ideal for uploading a fresh document of your manuscript every time you make changes, storing files online in addition to on your computer (Google Drive has an online storage function similar to services such as Dropbox and Microsoft OneDrive).

Google Drive allows you to create documents, spreadsheets, slide shows, and more, all of which can be accessed from anywhere—laptop, tablet, smartphone—by logging into a free Google account. Such items are easily shared with your co-author, agent, or publicist for more efficient record keeping or file sharing. It's also a great place to create and modify the trackers from this article.

Simply log in to your account at google.com/drive (or create one for free), hit the New button in the top left corner of the interface and click on Google Sheets. This will open a new window with a clean spreadsheet, where you can then begin entering the appropriate column headings. Title the spreadsheet by clicking "Untitled spreadsheet" at the top of the page. Once complete, you'll be able to open up your Freelance Payment Tracker or Agent Query Tracker on any device with an Internet connection—far from flames or flood.

FREELANCE PITCH TRACKER

SUBJECT	**Example:** Essay about meeting Stephen King in the waiting room at the dentist		
PUBLICATION	*Writer's Digest*		
EDITOR	Tyler Moss		
E-MAIL	wdsubmissions@ fwmedia.com		
PITCH SUBMITTED	8/1/16		
FOLLOW UP	8/15/16		
RESULT	Accepted		
DEADLINE	10/15/16		
NOTES	$0.50 cents/word for 600 words		

For freelance writers, ideas are currency—but they don't exist in a vacuum. Once you've brainstormed a solid premise and started to pitch potential markets, the resulting interactions can quickly clutter your in-box. Avoid losing track by recording your pitches in a spreadsheet with the following column headings:

- **SUBJECT:** One-line description of your story idea
- **PUBLICATION:** Name of magazine, website, or newspaper you pitched to
- **EDITOR & E-MAIL:** Where you sent your pitch
- **PITCH SUBMITTED:** When the query was sent
- **FOLLOW UP:** The date on which you plan to follow up if you haven't received a response (typically two weeks later, unless the submission guidelines specify otherwise)
- **RESULT:** Accepted, rejected, asked to rework
- **DEADLINE:** If accepted, date story is due
- **NOTES:** Additional info, based on your interactions with the editor (e.g., "Publication pays too little," or "Editor rejected pitch, but encouraged pitching again soon")

In addition to keeping track of irons currently in the fire, this spreadsheet is invaluable for later looking up contact info of editors you haven't e-mailed in a while.

If you want to track submissions to literary journals, simply switch out the column headings **SUBJECT** and **PUBLICATION** with **STORY TITLE** and **JOURNAL**, respectively, ax the **FOLLOW UP** column (journals tend to operate on slower, more sporadic schedules, sometimes without full-time staff), and replace the **DEADLINE** column with **READING FEE** (so you can evaluate and track any submission expenses where applicable).

ORGANIZE YOUR FREELANCE LIFE

Find both the freelance pitch and journal versions of this pitch tracker available for download at writersdigest.com/GLA-18.

FREELANCE PAYMENT TRACKER

ARTICLE HEADLINE	Example: Tongue Tied		
PUBLICATION/URL	*Ball & String Magazine*		
PAYMENT	$500		
DATE PUBLISHED	July 2016		
TOTAL WORDS	1,000		
$/WORD	$0.40 cents/word		
INVOICE #	#2014-1		
INVOICE SUBMITTED	8/12/16		
PAID	8/30/16		

When you've been commissioned to write a piece, it's vital to document the status of your payment. Not only will it keep you from missing a check, but it's incredibly useful for noting what a publication has paid you in the past and comparing the rates of different publications for which you freelance—which can help you prioritize your time by targeting the most lucrative outlets. It's also a lifesaver come April 15.

As depicted in the example spreadsheet above, you can use the following column headings to trace the path of your payments:

- **HEADLINE:** Title of the finished, published piece
- **PUBLICATION/URL:** Outlet that published the article and, if applicable, the URL where the article can be found online
- **PAYMENT:** Total payment received for work
- **DATE PUBLISHED:** Date article went live online, or issue month if for a print magazine or journal
- **TOTAL WORDS & $/WORD:** Length of the piece and amount you were paid per word, found by dividing the total payment by the total number of words (a common standardization for freelance payment rates)

- **INVOICE # & SUBMITTED:** Unique number of the invoice you submitted for this particular article (if applicable), and date on which it was submitted
- **PAID:** Date on which you received the payment, most commonly via check or direct deposit

Of course, you can also use this same basic format to develop a spreadsheet that covers advances, royalties, speaking honoraria, etc. Use the basic format outlined here to construct your own customized version.

TYLER MOSS is the editor-in-chief of *Writer's Digest*. Follow him on Twitter @tjmoss11.

WORKING WITH A PUBLICIST

by Cris Freese

So you found an agent, and he landed you the publishing contract of your dreams. Okay, if you've picked up this book, it's more likely that you're dreaming of that day on the near horizon.

Regardless, you're going to find yourself with three champions when that dream comes true. Two of them are oft-discussed—your agent and your editor—and you'll undoubtedly read plenty of articles about developing a strong, working relationship with them. But your third advocate is just as important, and less discussed—your publicist.

As the former editor of *Guide to Literary Agents*, I found myself often working with publicists to secure interviews with authors (particularly debut authors!), asking for guest posts, and combing through advanced reading copies. That is, publicists sought out places where they could get their client exposure.

And, as you'll see, publicists are tireless workers, doing their best to secure that interview, byline, or mention that piques the interest of readers enough to pick up the book in a bookstore or read description copy on Amazon—and maybe sell some copies!

I sat down with four publicists—two working with traditional, large publishers, and two working for marketing agencies—to talk about their jobs, how authors can help themselves, and more.

MEET THE PUBLICISTS

Katie Bassel is a Publicity Manager at St. Martin's Press.
Julia Borcherts is a publicist for Kaye Publicity.
Jordan Rodman is a publicity manager for Alfred A. Knopf & Pantheon.
Sara Wigal is a senior book publicist at JKS Communications.

How did you get started as a publicist?

Sara Wigal: When I was in my early twenties I hopped around between a few editorial jobs and also thinking I might want to be an agent. I went to the Publishing graduate program at Emerson College to sort out what would really be the best career arc for me, and, while studying for my M.A., I took a Marketing course with Beth Ineson [now the Executive Director of NEIBA]. What I learned in that class really resonated with me, and I started to feel like I had more direction, and that something more on the PR side of things would probably be a good fit for what I found most interesting, work-wise. When I saw a job opening with Open Book Publicity I jumped at the chance to start working in literary publicity while still finishing my degree. I was a radio publicist, meaning that I helped put authors on radio shows, and I really loved both the principals at my company, as well as the radio producers and hosts I got to work with (let alone the authors!). I did that for quite a few years before I had another opportunity to become a comprehensive publicist at my current firm, JKS Communications, where I've been able to grow into a larger role and learn so much about our industry and how to best serve authors on a broad scale.

Katie Bassel: I started my career in Corporate Sales & Marketing for the St. Louis Cardinals. When I made the move to New York, I sought out a job in publishing. The skill-set was similar, I'm a Journalism major, and I've always been a reader and lover of books, so the switch was easy!

Julia Borcherts: I met Dana Kaye in the early 2000s when we were both studying fiction writing at Columbia College Chicago. She was working as a book critic; I was writing features for Chicago publications and producing and hosting literary events, so our paths crossed often, especially after she founded Kaye Publicity. In 2014, she needed to replace a publicist and we talked about how my skills (and my interest in books) would translate to that role. I had long admired the way she managed her business and I knew that I could learn so much from her.

Jordan Rodman: While in college, I spent a summer interning in NYC for Barbara Jones, the brilliant Executive Editor at Henry Holt. I didn't know anything at all about publishing (had no idea how to even pronounce Knopf). She recommended I look into jobs in publicity, because as a publicist, you are able to be close to both the books as well as the authors and are able to think creatively and have much more than a traditional desk job.

At her recommendation, I attended the NYU Summer Publishing Institute and went on informational interviews at many publishing houses. I told everyone I knew (and strangers) that I wanted to work with books (a bank teller I spoke with set me up for an interview with her cousin in publishing). Eventually, I got my dream starting job as a Publicity Assistant at Pantheon and Knopf.

Can you describe what you feel is your primary goal as a publicist for writers?

KB: Book media!

JR: I want to place media coverage, create partnerships, and execute stellar events, all with the end goal of driving buzz and word of mouth about my books and authors. I want people to go up to their friends and family and say: "I just read Sweetbitter by Stephanie Danler and you literally have to stop everything you are doing and read it immediately, like right now." Or something along those lines.

SW: I like to tell all my clients that I have my dream job—I help people learn about good books. The mechanism for that, of course, is by helping authors to get media attention ... as well as events opportunities, and because I work for a comprehensive firm, we also do a lot of digital marketing. Basically my job is to find and focus on a lot of different ways to get an author's brand out there and growing in the public sphere. Hopefully the authors I work with find a readership that keeps them writing and creating art for many years to come.

JB: The bottom line is to help move the needle on book sales, but we also look at the writer's goals. Is the main objective to become established as an expert in a certain field for speaking opportunities or a tenure-track academic position? Is it to improve the odds that a debut novel will attract enough fans for the publisher to invest in a series? To potentially land a more lucrative deal for the next book? To mobilize the fan base from the author's established social media platforms in the cultural conversation arena? Knowing the answers to those questions helps us to customize our strategy.

What goes into finding places for an author to write guest posts, sign books, speak, participate in an interview/Q&A, etc.?

JB: The first question we ask ourselves is, "Who is the target audience for this book and where does that audience go to get their news—and entertainment recommendations?" Newspapers and magazines? Pop culture websites? Morning drive-time radio programs? Mom-centric lifestyle publications? YouTube book reviewers and other social media influencers?

The other piece is the author's brand—where does the author as a person intersect with the characters or themes in the books they write? That can provide possibilities to introduce the author to new readers who'd connect to the themes in the author's books due to shared interests. For example, an athlete who's written a memoir about competing in the Olympics could contribute a "conditioning tips" piece to a fitness publication or participate in an interview for a sports-themed radio show or podcast—both audiences could also be interested in reading that memoir. On the other hand, a rom-com novelist could write a humorous guest post about their own nuptials for a wedding magazine—and someone reading that piece might also be drawn to a lighthearted romance novel with a built-in happily-ever-after.

We do attend conferences and festivals and ask our clients for feedback on those they've attended to get a sense of whether the experience offsets the time and expense involved. Are there opportunities to connect with readers, industry professionals and influencers? Are the panels well-attended? Is there good traffic and interaction at the signing tables?

For events at venues without a built-in audience, such as a library or bookstore, we want to make sure that the author can mobilize their own fan base to attend and buy books there, rather than relying on the venue to drum up an audience (which won't happen). Many writers already have a relationship with a favorite bookstore or library branch so if that place is convenient for their friends, family and fans, we usually start there. If the author has a local connection (hometown, current residence) we can pitch local media and position the event as a news hook.

KB: This may seem obvious, but I always consider where the author lives, where the author was born, and where the book is set when I compile my list of outlets to pitch. Those are three key markets to go after for interviews and reviews. And they're usually the most receptive too, for obvious reasons!

If I'm working with a debut author, I seek out all the debut author opportunities available (Goodreads' Debut Author Snapshot, *Writer's Digest*'s Breaking In, etc.).

When it comes to signings, I work in collaboration with our Author Events Department. I let them know which authors I plan to tour and where I plan to send them, and they seek out requests from the indies and chains across the country. Once I know which stores are interested in hosting an event, I give them a call and we get to planning! The goal is to always also book media in each tour city to support the event, but that is becoming harder and harder as regional newspaper staffs grow smaller in size.

JR: Step one is thinking about all of the possible audiences who might be interested in the book you are publicizing. There are always more ways into a story than you might initially think. Next, you match those audiences with the media outlets that cater to them and place content. For events, you think about metros that make sense for the publication and in-conversation partners, big-mouths, influencers, and like-minded brands that can help get the word out.

SW: Media and event list building is a never-ending job! Most publicists will have a solid base of contacts, but if you work comprehensively and not with a certain niche, as I do, then you will always have more research to do and can't rely on that base only. Finding new media outlets that cover the specific angles I'm working on, especially in any emerging genres, involves a lot of reading news, googling, and watching other author coverage vigilantly. Quite a bit of in-person networking helps this too—I meet media at conferences and often through my personal social life that end up being good places for coverage. How you approach these contacts is key to whether you can create lasting media relationships—a good publicist spends time learning how each journalist wants to communicate and what their beat is before blasting them with a million requests. That takes a lot of time.

Do you primarily field requests for authors, or are you seeking out places?

KB: For fiction, there's hardly any fielding of requests. For nonfiction, I do usually receive a handful of worthwhile requests. To give two examples: I recently worked on the publicity campaigns for *The Wife Between Us* (women's commercial fiction) and *Gold Dust Woman* (a bio of Stevie Nicks). For *The Wife Between Us*, I'd say 95 percent of the reviews and interviews secured were due to my efforts, and 5 percent due either to the co-authors' connections or requests to my inbox. For *Gold Dust Woman*, however, I'd say it was closer to 50-50!

SW: As a publicist at a private firm, the majority of coverage comes from my team and myself pitching the media (and not the media coming to me). I have contacts I've known for years and they do come to me when they need certain things, but the majority of the work is to go after it, not to wait for it to roll in! When it does knock on my door, I'm on cloud nine.

JB: The primary focus of every campaign is on outreach we generate, although as an author becomes more established, the incoming media requests and speaking opportunities do multiply and we love to facilitate those as well. Since we customize each campaign to what is unique about that author and book, we are always actively researching interesting new opportunities.

JR: I am always actively seeking out! As they say, nothing comes to those who wait!

What should an author expect from their publicist?

JR: An author should expect a publicist to be their ally. To spread the word about the author's work to all of their contacts. To think innovatively about their book, and to help the author see new ways into their writing that they might not have known themselves. To be the author's spirit guide through the publishing process.

SW: That's a loaded question! There's so much to say here, but I think one of the important things about the author/publicist relationship that I want to express is that truly the best campaigns are run when I am able to work in partnership with the author. Mutual respect for one another's professionalism, expertise, and time is really key—an author should expect that a qualified publicist will work their hardest to satisfy the goals of their individual campaign.

KB: I put this question out to a few of my colleagues, and these were the most popular responses!

- That we read your book!
- That we know what's best for your book, and who to pitch.
- That we are taking advantage of all opportunities for your book.

JB: The scope of the campaign should be outlined in the proposal and the publicist should provide regular written updates of their activities on the author's behalf and the outcomes of those efforts. The publicist should collaborate with the author's in-house team. They should listen to the author's ideas and be honest in their assessments of those ideas. And they should provide expert guidance for any questions the author has about their campaign and their career.

What should an author not expect from their publicist?

SW: Oprah appearances and coverage from *The New York Times*. Those are the top two requests every publicist rolls their eyes at. Not because no one ever gets them, but because it's such a given that if a book merits the attention of those major players, of course the publicist will go for it. The author truly doesn't even need to ask—publicists are possibly even more excited than authors when we land a big "gain" like that! Authors should work with publicists they can trust to do what's best for them, and not every book is a fit for those types of outlets. That doesn't make them un-newsworthy or inferior—it just means that how audience factors into the news coverage might not lead to those specific places having interest in that book. But other places will, and we can focus on using time effectively to reach those media contacts.

KB: Same for this one! I put this question out to a few of my colleagues, and these were the most popular responses.

- That we be actively pitching your book to the media three, four, five months post-publication. (Most all of the pitching magic, and interest, happens in the months or weeks leading up to publication.)
- That we book media that is unrealistic for your book. (Not every book will be reviewed in the *New York Times* or on NPR.)
- That we find a bookseller for your event a week before it's to take place. (Impossible.)

JB: Guaranteed results are not possible—publicity is earned coverage; advertising and "advertorials" are paid coverage. A publicist should also not be hired with the expectation of making an author 'famous' or to implement a to-do list of directives issued by an author. And, while a publicist should respond to questions in a timely manner and to be available if an emergency occurs—say, a touring author's plane is grounded due to weather and they may be late for a signing—an author shouldn't expect the publicist to be on call 24/7 unless it's outlined in the contract.

JR: An author should be respectful of a publicist's time. Publicist's manage their time working on many different projects. That doesn't mean they do not have the time and energy to work on your book, but it means that if you send your publicist fifteen emails a day, they will use the time they have allotted to pitching your book to instead craft responses to all of your emails. Also, a publicist is not a therapist, respect boundaries.

Is your role different depending on if you're working with an experienced, multi-published author versus a debut author? If so, how?

KB: Sometimes, sometimes not. Debut authors are often easier to pitch because reviewers want to be the first to sing their praises and lift their careers. If an author has published, say, twenty books, it's exceedingly difficult to get reviewers to pay attention to this latest release. We've gone back to the well too many times, so to speak!

JB: The basics are the same but with a debut author, it's more about introducing a fresh new voice into the conversation. There is often more education involved as well—working to maximize their online presence, coaching them for successful media appearances, showing them ways to promote their book that are engaging rather than obnoxious. If the debut author is already established on another platform—perhaps they're a popular blogger or a sought-after public speaker—then we'd want to look at mobilizing that audience to read the book, too.

For an experienced author, a publicist can determine patterns that have been successful in previous campaigns—which types of outlets provide recurring coverage, what works well to mobilize that audience, where the reader base could be expanded. The experienced author is likely to offer insight into that as well. It's also possible to capitalize on their strengths—and to have links to lively broadcast interviews, well-written guest posts and starred reviews from their previous campaigns.

But there are also certain types of coverage that will already have been used up—the hometown paper won't review every single book in a series; the pop culture magazine won't repeat the same author in their annual holiday gift guide; the alumni magazine won't profile the same graduate twice. So the publicist has to look for ways to expand into new areas for potential coverage and to take note of any exciting new developments in the life of the author or noteworthy angles in their latest book that would appeal to readers and media outlets.

SW: A debut author has so many more questions about how the publishing industry works, so for a lot of those campaigns we build in time for those explanations and some of the necessary coaching that helps them understand vital components of the process. A more veteran author often has a more mature understanding of how their campaign will run and what to expect, so things may run a bit differently for that author because need less preparation.

JR: Yes! With debut authors, I make sure to explain the entire publishing process to them so they are aware of all the ways I can help and what exactly it is that I will need from them.

I still do a lot of handholding with multipublished authors, but less about process.

Is there anything a writer can do to make your job easier?

SW: Of course! Going back to that partnering concept, when my clients are responsive to email and also willing to think creatively with me, that makes my job so much easier. When I send over media requests and can get a response quickly, it helps snag opportunities faster, which means less back-and-forth and also downsizes the possibility for missed coverage because we missed a deadline or something like that. Authors who are willing to let me use my expertise to guide them tend to have smoother campaigns—essentially they're paying for consultancy, and letting me have a bit of free rein usually results in a more magical set of media results at the day's end. Publicity work is pretty grueling at times (we tend to work some of the longer hours in this industry) but the payoff of what we can accomplish for an author feels incredible, and often the client is a big part in making that happen.

KB: Say "yes" to all opportunities, big and small. Reply to emails with some speed. But above all, trust your publicist is doing everything she/he can for your book. There will be periods of "quiet" during the road to publication, but that doesn't mean we've forgotten about you! Quite the opposite. It means we're following up, and trying to get answers, so we can share the good news with you. And we do share good news, right away (!), when we have it. That's the best part of the job.

JB: Authors should also advise their publicist of every opportunity that comes their way directly. The publicist can then give them advice on how to maximize that coverage or avoid conflict with coverage already in the works. No publicist wants an author to post a guest column two months before their book's launch—no one will remember the book by the time they can actually buy it—or to find out that the essay they just pitched the *New York Times* has already been given away to an old high school classmate's blog that currently has 12 followers.

Also, writers should begin making inquiries to publicists earlier than they might think—an ideal campaign timeline usually starts about five or six months ahead of the book launch. There isn't much point in hiring a publicist until after the contract is signed with the publishing house but once that happens and the book has gone through its initial round of edits, that's a good time to think about bringing a publicist on board.

JR: Pro-tips for authors re: publicists: Merge all your thoughts and ideas into one email a day if possible. Phone calls are great to get a lot done at once, but please make sure there is a reason for it. Be kind to your publicist. Trust their judgement, realize they have experience and are professionals. They are the person in your corner and want to help you. Help them help you. Provide your publicist with all media connections, big mouths, and influencers that you have connections with. Flowers/wine/gifts can never hurt

What's the most important thing that an about-to-be-published or just-published author can do?

SW: Connect with other writers! No man is an island and the ones that try to be are often stilted in their ability to grow in their craft and in their brand reach. There's this mythology still of the lone writer in an ivory tower, hacking away at a typewriter and then producing the perfect manuscript that' goes straight through to publication and becomes a bestseller. That's truly not the case—friends are first "beta readers" for authors and getting a writing community to rally around you is the best way an author can get the best version of their book started… but it's also the first group of people that will buy the book, show up to bookstore readings, and tell their own networks about the book too.

KB: Leverage any and all connections, even if they seem small and insignificant. And don't be shy about it (this is the time to call in favors!), or wait until the eleventh hour to do so. Being active on social media is becoming more and more important, too, with the rise of bookstagrammers, and book bloggers taking to twitter and facebook to share their reviews. Even some news outlets look for authors with large social presences when making decisions about who to invite onto their shows.

JR: Gather a list of all of their media connections and big mouths and give it to their publicist. Work on increasing their social media footprint. Tell every person they know (or don't know) about their forthcoming book. Brainstorm related op-ed ideas. Befriend Oprah + Terry Gross.

JB: Right now, it's to create and maintain a newsletter program through a professional-looking, easy-to-use service such as Mailchimp and offer incentives for readers to sign up (such as an early excerpt available nowhere else). In the newsletter, the author should offer exclusive content that does not appear on other platforms. This is something we find to be a crucial asset for authors for connecting to readers and one of our prime marketing initiatives is to help them create and grow that reach organically. It used to be that social media followings were important, but nowadays, none of us controls what those followers see—what shows up in our feeds is at the mercy of algorithms, sponsored content placements, people deleting their accounts and so many other factors outside our control. You don't "own" your Twitter followers or your Facebook friends—if that platform shuts down tomorrow, your audience there is gone. With a newsletter, you own your following and it's guaranteed that your email will appear in everyone's inbox. And by reaching out every month or two and providing worthwhile, newsletter-only content when you do, they'll look forward to opening it up.

What's the most difficult job about your role?

JR: I honestly love my job so much it is hard to say. To be able to promote incredible books and authors is an honor rather than a job. It can be difficult in this current political climate to compete with the news cycle, and I find that to be frustrating. I just want people to know that books are one of the most important ways to learn and cope and move forward and they house powerful ideas that can change the way we see the world and interact with humans, regardless of whether or not their subject directly relates to politics.

SW: Setting expectations. For example, sometimes I will get a pretty big piece of coverage, but if the author isn't familiar with that outlet, he or she may not be appreciative, and ask after other dream "gains" that just aren't within reach for whatever reason (we're past deadline, they don't cover that genre, etc., I am talking about really legitimate reasons why an outlet would decline an author). There are radio shows and online magazines with literally millions of listeners/viewers each week that I've had authors sort of shrug off because they personally might not be familiar with the outlet. The thing is, there is such an abundance of media out there now because of the internet that you never really could know every single media outlet … even publicists find new outlets! Helping authors understand that their personal experience of the media is not necessarily universal is a challenge. It's true that not all media outlets are the same, so I provide circulation and/or social media reach to help an author understand what the coverage means in terms of the exposure they are receiving, and it can be hard to set expectations properly if they are focused on specific places for coverage that might not be reasonable, or the best fit for the book.

JB: Finding the time to stay on top of what's happening in the publishing industry, measuring patterns in media coverage, exploring what platforms are trending with different people, looking into technologies and innovations that could benefit writers, discovering what new conversations are happening in the world of writing and books—but these topics are so fascinating and so important that I make the time to delve into them.

KB: When you put all of your heart and soul into pitching a book and/or an author you adore, and, for whatever reason, it just doesn't resonate with the media or the buying public. It can be very disheartening.

Cris Freese is a former editor of *Guide to Literary Agents*, a freelance writer, and literary intern with Corvisiero Literary. Follow him on Twitter @crisfreese.

PITCH PARTY

Everything You Should Know About Twitter Pitch Parties

by Cris Freese

Everyone is going to tell you that you should be on social media now to promote your book if you're a published author. But if you're a writer who's currently querying, there's a couple of reasons that you should join Twitter.

The first reason is that you get to be a part of a conversation and interact with literary agents, published authors, and other writers. Take a look at writers and agents currently talking on Twitter—it's a true community. People promoting other people's books, offering writing and querying advice, discussing current events, and more.

The second reason? There's a legitimate chance you could find an editor or publisher.

With the creation of Twitter pitch parties, you have an opportunity to pitch your completed and unpublished manuscript without having to write a query letter. Granted, you still have to condense your story into a compelling idea that's fewer than 280 characters. But it's a great opportunity.

If you're going to participate, you'll want to take a step back and get the lay of the land. Here are a couple of helpful guidelines to follow, no matter what the party:

1. **Read the guidelines!** I've tried to summarize the most important bits of several major pitch parties. However, I can't cover everything in this article. You'll want to make sure you know how many times you can pitch and what the timeframe for each competition is.
2. **Check the hashtags.** And I don't mean the competition hashtags. Use suggested hashtags for age categories (if you're pitching a book for an audience younger than the adult audience) and genres. This will be the easiest way for an agent to find your

pitch—they're going to be looking for genres they represent, after all.

3. **Study the competitions.** The great thing about Twitter: Everything stays out there! I'd suggest going back to previous competitions by searching for the hashtag and your genre. See what agents Liked and requested. (This is how agents get your attention, letting you know they'd like you to query them!) This will give you a good feel for what agents are looking for and what's hot. But remember: Trends last only so long, and you're looking at things that are now (probably) a year old.
4. **Use all your characters!** And I don't mean in the pitch itself. I mean the hashtag, your author title, and, perhaps most importantly, potential comps. It can help further clarify your tweet if you add comp titles for your manuscript. The best, and most character-efficient, way to do this is [Title] + [Title] in your tweet.
5. **Research the agents and editors.** There's no reason to participate in a pitch party if there are agents you don't match up with—or there's only one agent you're really looking for. Just query that agent, the old-fashioned way.

And while it's not a guideline, it's a friendly reminder that only interested agents or editors should be Liking tweets. Feel free to support fellow writers by retweet tweets, but keep your finger away from the Like button!

Now, down to the pitch parties themselves. Here are eight major pitch parties that you should take a look at and consider adding to your calendar (just be sure to look up the dates on their websites!):

- **#PBPitch (http://www.pbpitch.com/):** In this Twitter pitch party exclusive to picture books, you'll have a 12-hour window to pitch your manuscript on Twitter twice—once in the morning and once in the evening. Having two times where you can pitch gives agents a larger window to find your pitch; it also gives you the opportunity to try a different approach if your first attempt doesn't snag any coveted Likes.
- **#PitMad (http://pitchwars.org/pitmad/):** Founded by Brenda Drake, #PitMad has grown like crazy over the past few years. It's one of the most widely viewed pitch parties on Twitter by agents and editors. Because of that, you'll have the chance to pitch your manuscript up to three times over the course of the allotted time. The official website suggests you break it up every four hours, and tweet a different pitch. Drake and Heather Cashman continually add sub-hashtags to the list of available hashtags, making it easier for industry professionals to find the manuscripts they're interested. So, when you're tweeting, be sure to include the age category and/or genre of your project (#YA for young adult, #MG for middle-grade, #H for horror, #LF for literary fiction, and so forth). Check out their official website for a list of genres and subgenres.

- **#AdPit (https://heidinorrod.wordpress.com/adpit/):** With a six-hour pitch time, plus the opportunity to pitch six times over that time period, this is a pitch party with plenty of chances to catch an agent's eye. With every pitch, you should also include either an #A for Adult or #NA for New Adult, plus any of the relevant genre hashtags. Bonus: You can get two bonus opportunities to pitch with the addition of media pitches. A media pitch makes use of Twitter's media feature (images), and you can use up to forty-five words, plus the title of your manuscript and age range and genre. Check out their website for a sample!
- **#KidPit (https://heidinorrod.wordpress.com/kidpit/):** From the same creator as #AdPit, #KidPit gives you the opportunity to pitch the following categories: board books, picture books, easy reader/chapter books, middle-grade, and young adult novels. See the #AdPit entry for rules and stipulations. You can identify your tweet with #BB for board book, #PB for picture book, #CB for chapter books or early readers, #MG for middle-grade, and #YA for young adult.
- **#Pit2Pub (https://www.kristinvanrisseghem.com/pit2pub):** This pitch party is like any other, except it's only publishers who are participating by Liking tweets. As an author, you're only allowed to pitch once (per manuscript) every two hours during the 12-hour time period. Be sure to check out the website for publishers who are participating. Since these are publishers looking at these tweets, you'll really want to make sure you do research beforehand to see if there's one particular one you're shooting for. Of course, if that's the case, then why not just try and query them directly?
- **#RevPit (http://www.reviseresub.com/annual-contest/how-to-submit):** Off of Twitter, this is known as Revise & Resub—a common term that some writers may be familiar with. Known from the query process, "revise and resubmit" is when agents aren't offering representation, but have taken enough interest in your manuscript to offer true, personalized feedback. There's something special about your writing, but it's not quite there yet. By revising and resubmitting, you're getting another chance at potential representation. Originally founded by a group of editors, this pitch party supports authors with editing-focused chats and mini-events throughout the year. While you won't be pitching directly on Twitter, this event is still worth looking into. By entering, you have the chance to win five weeks of editing of your full manuscript. The website recommends that you spend time with at least one beta reader before submitting. You can only submit one time, and you'll pick two choices of editors, with one alternate. When submitting, be sure to also have your query letter polished and ready to go!
- **#SFFPit (http://dankoboldt.com/sffpit/):** Completely dedicated to those writing science-fiction and fantasy (but still open to picture book, middle-grade, young adult,

new adult and adult authors!), this contest is held twice a year. Founded by Dan Koboldt, the editor of the upcoming WD Book, *Putting the Science in Fiction*, you'll have a 10-hour window to pitch your manuscript via Twitter. And you get one tweet per hour, or 10 pitches total! The website includes a list of subgenres for science-fiction and fantasy, so you'll want to check out additional hashtags, like #SO for space opera and #PA for post-apocalyptic science-fiction.

- **#DVpit (http://dvpit.com/index):** Hosted and moderated by literary agent Beth Phelan, #DVPit is massive—and important. This event was created to showcase pitches from marginalized voices that have been historically underrepresented in publishing. Since the first #DVpit in April 2016, more than 60 authors have signed with agents and more than 20 book deals have been contracted as a direct result of this event. This event actually hosts two separate contests on back-to-back days: one for children's and teen fiction and nonfiction, and the other for adult fiction and nonfiction. You'll have a 12-hour window to pitch, but you're limited to just six pitches per project.

This list is certainly not the end-all-be-all for Twitter pitch parties. More ones—reputable ones—will crop up over the course of the next year.

And there are also pitch contests, which are an entirely separate entity, but still valuable. Be sure to check out pitch contests, like Pitch Wars, where you'll often find an online community and a hashtag to follow on Twitter. The kinds of conversations writers, agents and editors are exchanging there are invaluable as you seek to break out.

Cris Freese is a former editor of *Guide to Literary Agents*, a freelance writer, and literary intern with Corvisiero Literary. Follow him on Twitter @crisfreese.

THE LIFE OF AGENT-AUTHORS

by Cris Freese

It's safe to say that the majority of querying authors probably find literary agents to be intimidating. After all, there's a long history of agents being seen as "gatekeepers" to the world of publishing.

But, today, are agents really all that different from the writers they represent?

A quick peek at their Twitter handles shows character and personality, but also a deep respect for the craft, the marketplace, the authors they represent and the writers they hope to represent. And a whole bunch of .gifs, with a few corgis thrown in there, too.

One thing every agent is: tuned in. They know what good writing is, and they're passionate about their careers—and their authors. And they know how to help their writers, and get them published.

They're part of an ongoing literary conversation, and they're accessible. Oftentimes, literary agents are, in fact, writers themselves.

To give you a better idea of the literary world, and pull back the curtain, so to speak, I asked a few literary agents who double as writers to sit down and talk about their career, their relationships with clients and editors, advice, and more.

MEET THE AGENTS

Paula Munier is a Senior Literary Agent and Content Strategist at Talcott Notch Literary Services. She is the author of *A Borrowing of Bones*, *The Writer's Guide to Beginnings*, *Writing with Quiet Hands*, *Plot Perfect*, *Fixing Freddie*, and *5-Minute Mindfulness*.

Rena Rossner is a Literary Agent at the Deborah Harris Agency. She is the author of *Eating the Bible*.

Eric Smith is a Literary Agent at P.S. Literary. He is the author of *The Geek's Guide to Dating*, *Inked*, *Branded*, and *The Girl and the Grove*. He is the editor of the anthology *Welcome Home*.

Lauren Spieller is an Associate Literary Agent at Triada US. She is the author of *Your Destination is on the Left*.

Kari Sutherland is a Literary Agent at the Bradford Literary Agency. She is the co-author of The Menagerie series.

Were you an agent or author first? What drove you to both careers?

Eric Smith: I was an author first, but I initially started my publishing career working at an actual publishing house! I worked at Quirk Books for five years, before diving into the agenting life. While I was at Quirk, I had two books published in 2013 and 2015, and eventually took the leap into agenting in late 2015.

So, neither of those things really came first. But I do agent and write at the same time these days, and I like to think my experience as an author brings something to the table for my clients. I've been through it myself, so I can talk to them about what to expect.

I've always wanted to write, since I was a little kid. Didn't really matter what career I found myself in. As for agenting, I wanted a chance to help publish the sort of books I was passionate about. I wanted to work on even more YA books, on unusual literary fiction, odd pop-culture and non-fiction projects… the stuff I like to read the most.

It just happened to work out this way, the writing and agenting at the same time. And I'm really grateful that I get to make my life all about books.

Lauren Spieller: Technically I was a writer first, but I had only written about half of my first book when I started researching what to do with it when I finished. That's when I discovered the publishing industry, and the job of a literary agent. I very quickly realized it was my dream job, and since then writing and working in publishing have gone hand in hand.

Paula Munier: I was a writer first, and always. I sold my first story to *Cosmopolitan* magazine when I was still in college. Later I worked as a reporter and editor for newspapers and magazines, and from there I got my first job in book publishing, as managing editor for Prima Publishing (now part of Crown). I segued from production to acquisitions, acquiring fiction and nonfiction for a number of houses over the course of fifteen years. I kept writing all along—everything from jacket copy to full-length projects, even a memoir.

When I became an agent, it was at the invitation of my own agent, Gina Panettieri of Talcott Notch Literary. She expected me to keep on writing, as I always had. And so I did, using my experience as a writer and an editor to help my clients navigate the sometimes challenging waters of book publishing.

Rena Rossner: I was a reader first and foremost, but that quickly turned me into a writer. I was winning writing contests already in elementary school. I always knew that writing would be a part of my life, and I think I started dreaming about being a published author when I was about eight. In college I studied at Johns Hopkins' Writing Seminars program, and my plan was to go to NYC after graduation and to either make it big as a journalist or to get a job in publishing. But life took a different turn and I met my husband, moved to Canada, got a Masters Degree in History, moved to Israel, had five kids…so that NYC dream never really materialized. But I never stopped writing. I worked in journalism, grant writing, art direction, publicity and marketing, I edited books and academic articles…and I hated all of it. After I had my fifth kid I decided that I should be a stay at home mom—that lasted about three months. I was bored out of my mind. But I only wanted to go back to work if I could do something that I really wanted to do. My husband asked me what that was—and without hesitation I said "I want to work as a literary agent at The Deborah Harris Agency"—Jerusalem's only literary agency (and Israel's premiere literary agency). My husband said, "So what are you waiting for?" He was right. I put my big girl panties on and wrote to Deborah, said I'd do anything to work for her, and she wrote me back 5 minutes later and asked me to come in for an interview. The next day she offered me a job. I think that a lot of people think that working in publishing has to follow some kind of set route—but I've met more people in publishing who've had unconventional career paths into the business than you'd expect. We're here and we're proud!

Kari Sutherland: I was an editor first, then an author, now an agent. I think a love of books, of writing and exploring characters and delving into new worlds is what drew me to all three careers. Editors and agents both get to discover and foster talent, too, guiding an author through the process of publishing.

Do you feel as if being a published author gives you extra perspective when working with writers?

PM: As a writer, I must face the blank page just as my clients do. I understand the physical, mental, and emotional demands of writing—and the toll meeting those demands can take. I'm there to listen, advise, read, edit, cheer, nudge, counsel, console, and congratulate. I'm intimately familiar with the process—from idea and outline and draft after draft to publication and promotion. I know the pleasures and the perils that color the work of writer, the editor, and the publisher—and that gives me that extra perspective, methinks.

ES: I like to think it does. On the creative side of things, I'm a pretty heavy editorial agent, and since I also like writing stories, I hope my insight on character, dialogue, story… I hope it helps. Then again, all the writers I represent are infinitely better writers than I am, so I guess it's up to them to take or leave that kind of advice. But as an author there's another level to all that, and that's the marketing, publicity, and sales side of the business. I've been through all of that with every book, and I know what to expect for my writers. We're able to have really frank conversations about what they should be doing, what the publisher should be doing, and the like. And I think it makes me a little more sensitive to everything, also being a writer.

LS: I like to think that writing and agenting are two sides of the same coin. I have an editorial eye born of being a writer myself that helps me prepare manuscripts for submission, but I also speak writer, so I understand how important their work is to them, and how stressful publishing can be. That empathy, paired with my love of my clients' books, makes me a passionate advocate.

KS: Yes, absolutely. I know the agony of sending your work off and wanting a response right away, even though that's implausible, and enjoying getting positive responses along with suggested feedback. I try to keep my writers updated so they know if I haven't had a chance to dive into their revision yet or when they can expect notes. My feedback always includes aspects I enjoyed as well as what elements I'd like them to tackle in a revision.

RR: Absolutely. I always tell my authors this. My debut novel—The Sisters of the Winter Wood—is the third book I queried with my third agent. My first two books went to acquisitions at major houses and didn't make it through. It took me about ten years to get my publishing deal (with a cookbook I published in five languages along the way—it's called Eating the Bible and it came out first with Skyhorse) so I feel like there's pretty much nothing I haven't already experienced and I think it really helps me empathize with my authors. I also think it makes me a better editorial agent, and I love helping my authors plot and smooth out sentences. I love having my hands involved in every aspect of the craft.

How do you balance your writing time versus working for/with your authors?

LS: I do my best writing in the morning, before the work day starts. I also love writing retreats, so I sneak a few of those in every year as well. But I'll be honest—my clients always come first, even if that means putting my own writing aside for a few days (don't tell my agent!).

RR: My clients always come first unless I have a deadline—but even then, I still spend most of my day working as an agent. If I have a revision due for my own work and the turnaround is a week, then that might change, but I have a hard time sitting in a chair and doing the same thing for ten hours straight anyway (don't we all?) so I find that having more than one thing to do at a time helps motivate me because I can go back and forth between the projects. I don't think I could ever just write full time—I'd be bored out of my mind. I've always been a Nanowrimo kind of author—I have to force myself to write 500 to 1,000 words a day or I'll never get anything done—and that writing usually happens late at night after I've already done everything else I need to do, my kids are asleep, the house is quiet, the bats are flitting around outside my window…you get the picture.

ES: I don't. Work life balance? What is that, even? Okay, but really, I can't really focus on my own writing when I know that I have work to do on my clients' books. My parents raised me to understand the importance of crushing guilt. It's something I embrace. This approach maybe disappoints my agent (all apologies to the great Dawn Frederick), but I have to take care of my babies first.

PM: Like most of my clients, I have a day job, and I do my writing in my so-called spare time. Being an agent is for all intents and purposes running your own business, and so the hours are long. We live in a 24/7 world now more than ever, and with clients and colleagues in several time zones across the continent and around the world, I'm often on the job early in the morning and also late at night. (Not long ago I had one client say to me "oh, you're an early bird like me" and another say "oh, you're a night owl like me" on the same day.) But just as I manage to squeeze in time to cook and walk the dog and do yoga, I also manage to squeeze in time to write.

KS: I don't write as much anymore, that's for sure! But I tend to save my writing time for late, late at night or weekends, after my agenting work is done for the day.

Do you ever feel inspired from working with clients?

RR: More like intimidated? Ha! I often read my clients' work and bemoan the fact that I will never be as talented.

ES: Oh, only every single day.

LS: Absolutely. I represent hard-working, conscientious people who are passionate about what they do. What's more inspiring than that?

PM: Always. Since I was a writer and an editor first, I already knew a lot of writers when I became an agent. They all inspired me. Many of them were my friends. And some of them became my clients as well. All of my clients inspire me, and I hope I inspire them…to write, to revise, and, most important, to persist.

KS: I'm inspired by their passion and creativity, but everyone's style is different, so I focus on my own voice when I'm writing.

Do you write in the genres you represent? What do you prefer to write most?

ES: I do! I write young adult fantasy and contemporary, and I mostly work on Young Adult books. I read YA, I write YA, so representing YA only makes sense. It's easier to work on what you know, in my opinion.

LS: My debut and sophomore novels are both YA contemporaries, which I do represent, but I tend to look for stories that are different from mine when it comes to style, voice, and the sorts of questions the narratives are asking. As for my own writing preferences, I dabble in a little bit of everything, but right now I'm loving contemporary, realistic stories about teen girls.

PM: I represent many kinds of projects, a reflection no doubt of my history in acquisition and my own eclectic reading tastes. I admit to a soft spot for crime fiction, which I also write. I like writing nonfiction, too.

KS: I co-wrote a middle grade fantasy series with my sister before I became an agent, which definitely falls in a category I represent. But nowadays most of my writing is novelizations of children's movies. That work allows me to access my creative side—building out relationships and highlighting themes as well as exploring my love of language—without as much of the time-consuming side of muddling through plot twists (leaving me brain-space to help my authors with that on their stories!). It's the perfect balance for me at the moment.

RR: My first love will always be Fantasy and Science Fiction, though I do love History and Poetry as well, and that's certainly where my own work falls—at the intersection of all those elements, and that's definitely what I love to represent. But I also work with YA contemporary novels in a big way, and have sold quite a lot of Middle Grade recently. I love horror and a good thriller/mystery. And I'll never not want to read a good literary/upmarket novel. Many of my authors were poets first and I also represent a good amount of novels in verse (my own debut novel is written partially in prose and partially in verse.) And I'm a foodie. I will always look at cookbooks and want to represent them. Like definitely calls to like. It took me two novels to have the courage to write fantasy—I love the genre so much and have so much respect for it that I had no idea what I could possibly add—until I did, and now I know that's where I really belong as a writer. But good writing on the sentence level will grab me every time—no matter the genre, and I think that all my authors have that in common, and that it comes from me having started out as a poet.

How do you prep authors for the experience of working with an editor, when you've been through it yourself?

KS: They get at least one round of revision notes from me before we submit to publishers, so they have firsthand experience! I always caution them that edit letters can be long or short (mine tend towards the long side and are packed with questions), and that if they have any concerns about any feedback it is always best to discuss them with the editor. Oftentimes what an editor is reacting to is something that the author didn't convey fully on the page, so if the author can explain what she was intending, they can come up with a way to strengthen or rework that element.

PM: I've been both the editor and the writer, having sat on both sides of the table. I have enormous respect for good editors, because I know how smart and skilled and insightful and talented the good ones are—not to mention overworked and underpaid. A good editor is the one person who can help you figure out how to take your work to the next level. I tell my debut authors that what they're getting when they sign their first contract is a master class in publishing, taught by their editor. Because now they're not only going to be writers, but authors. And that's a whole new ballgame.

LS: My authors are all very savvy, so there hasn't been a ton of "preparing" needed, but I always let them know that the editor—like their agent—is ultimately here to help them make their story the best version of itself it can be. That means that while it's important to always be open to revision and new ideas, they also need to keep their eye on the goals they set out to achieve when they first started writing the manuscript. In other words, make the manuscript the best it can be while staying true to their voice and their story.

RR: That's a hard question because every editor works differently. Sometimes you have to wait six months for your notes, and they will be extensive. Sometimes you get them within a month and they're not—or they are! Some of that has to do with the manuscript and some of that has to do with the editor. But I definitely can say things like: "When they ask you to make changes they really mean it! Respond to every comment they make not just in the notes but by actually changing the text. They may not give up until you do. Trust me, I know." (And I see my own editor out there reading this and laughing! Hi Nivia!) So, there's that.

ES: We just have very honest conversations about it. How it's okay to push back. That in the end, it's their story, but to choose their battles.

What do you wish you would've known when you began down your literary career?

LS: I wish I'd known that sometimes the journey is the best part. I've always been a very results-driven, goal-oriented person, and while that's served me well, I also think it can get in the way of enjoying the little things along the way. Some of the greatest joys of both my writing and my agenting life thus far have been the small things: finishing a chapter that I struggled with. Meeting a new writing friend. Reading a client's revision, and marveling at how wonderful it is. Reading a craft article that changed how I think about character. None of those were goals I set out to achieve, but when I look back, those are the memories that really stand out.

PM: I don't know. For me, this has been a very engaging, mostly enjoyable, and always enlightening journey. I love words and I love stories and I love books and I love people involved in words and stories and books. I've been lucky enough to spend my working life in all their company. And I hope to continue to do so for a long, long time...

RR: Hmmm. I don't know if I would have wanted to know that it would take me ten years to get published! That might have been really discouraging. But if I could look back at past me and give myself advice it would be two things: 1. Ask Deborah Harris for a job way earlier than you did, and 2. Never to stop reading fantasy. When I was in college I had this whole highbrow stage where I thought I should only be reading "real" literary fiction, both great works of literature and new works from emerging literary authors. And while I'm grateful certainly to my teachers who introduced me to diverse works of literature—I was definitely not just reading white men, it took me years to find my way back to fantasy and sci-fi—my true loves—and realize that there is just as much incredible literary fiction happening in those spaces. Maybe then I would have been writing fantasy ten years ago, and not have had to go through all these growing pains. At the same time, I wouldn't be the person I am today. I'm not big on regrets. The person I am today is a really happy person, I'm living the dream. I love my job (Both my jobs! As Agent and Author) with all my heart. And I wouldn't have it any other way.

KS: Write/acquire what you love regardless of whether it's "trending" or not. Everything comes back around and a well-written story will stand on its own.

ES: To be patient. Publishing is a game of patience, truly. There's no rush. Take your time, do things right, and if it takes a while to find that agent or write that book… it's okay. Deep breaths, writer friends. You got this.

What piece of advice do you treasure most as an author? As an agent?

RR: Actually I think it's the same advice: don't compare yourself to others. That's the hardest thing as both an agent and an author. The drive to always be comparing oneself to others—"How many six figure deals did they make? Why aren't I making the same kinds of deals?" Is really parallel to—"Why does it seem like all the authors around me are getting six figure deals and I'm not?" or "Why isn't my book getting the publicity/attention that their book is getting?" and "Why didn't I get a starred review?"—and the answer to both of those things is that you need to just keep your head down and keep doing your thing. You know what you're good at and that's all that matters. Every path to publication is different, and there are books that are successful without ever having made any kind of list, and books that sold for really small amounts of money and got no starred reviews that hit the New York Times best-seller list—and that applies to both agents and authors. We just have to believe in our work—in the things we write and the authors we represent. We do the best we can—and that's usually pretty great! The rest really isn't up to us.

ES: It's a piece of advice that I think applies to both in a big way. And that's always keep working on the next thing. If you're a writer, and you're busy pitching around your latest manuscript, or you have an agent who is pitching you to publishers…

don't stop. Always be pushing ahead and working on the next project, so you have something ready to go when that other book gets sold, get an agent, or, in the worst case, doesn't land someplace. You want to be ready. Same with the agenting. You're pitching around projects, working with clients, and all that great stuff... but always keep an eye out for the next thing. Read those queries actively. Read books that get pitched your way. Head to conferences. Be open. Don't get stuck with nothing to work on. All this of course, unless you need a break. Self-care is important. Don't run yourself into the ground.

LS: As an author, the best advice I've ever been given is to read. Read, read, read! And not just the types of stories you write, though you should read those too! It's important to read all types of stories—be they novels, short stories, or narrative essays—because that's how you grow as a storyteller. You never know where inspiration—or a great writing lesson—will come from. It's also a wonderful way to "refill the well," or replenish your creative energy. I'm also going to cheat here, and give one more piece of writerly advice, which is this: surround yourself with supportive people. Your community will celebrate you when you're up, but more importantly, they'll lift you up when you're down. Publishing can be a tough road, so make sure you're on the journey with people you care about and that care about you. The best advice I got as an agent has probably been to only take on projects that I am passionate about. I live by that advice, and it makes my job an absolute joy and privilege.

PM: As an author: Writers write. It's that simple—and that complicated. That said, I have more than 1000 books on writing, and have written three on writing myself. But there's still always more to learn. As an agent: I heard literary agent Jason Yarn tell a writer this when we were both on a panel at a conference early in my career as an agent: "Publishers want work that is 95 percent there. So, I can only take on work that is 90 percent there. I can help you get to 95 percent." This was important for me to hear, as I was still thinking like an editor, and taking on work that was only 60 to 75 percent there—instead of 90 percent.

KS: As an author, I remind myself of the tip to let the first draft be a draft—get it all down and go back later rather than editing as I go. As an agent, I am grateful for the advice to speak to authors before signing them as clients. It is important to know that an author and I would work well together and communication is the founding block of any relationship.

Cris Freese is a former editor of *Guide to Literary Agents*, a freelance writer, and literary intern with Corvisiero Literary. Follow him on Twitter @crisfreese.

THRILLERS TODAY

by Cris Freese

You'll often hear in the publishing world that by the time you try to jump on a hot trend, it's too late. Vampires. Zombies. The dog as the narrator or protagonist. The trend's time in the limelight is over.

Yet, some trends have become more than that. They've developed into their own genre.

Take the thriller, for example. What once started slowly has erupted into a full-fledged genre that so many writers want to partake in. And now, we're seeing the off-shoots of those genres. Medical thrillers. Spy thrillers. Domestic thrillers.

Some of these plots and ideas are well told and recycled—they've been around for ages. Others are new, with fresh voices.

One thing is for sure: Thrillers are here to stay; and they're continually evolving with the publishing landscape.

If you're one of those writers that's chasing a thrill, we pulled together a trio of literary agents who specialize in thrillers to talk about sub-genres, standout submissions, weaknesses, overused tropes, and what's coming on the horizon. Hopefully you'll find the inspiration to thrill your own audience!

MEET THE AGENTS

Stacey Donaghy is the founder of Donaghy Literary Group.

Dee Mura is the founder of Dee Mura Literary.

Michelle Richter is an associate agent at Fuse Literary.

When it comes down to the sub-genres of thrillers, it can get messy—and confusing. In the types of thrillers you represent, what really stands out to you?

Dee Mura: The most confusing part is that many elements of one sub-genre can cross over to another. And others that are harder to define are placed into a general "suspense" category or "modern detective" category.

Despite all this, there are definitely elements that stand out. Specifically, I find that an intriguing premise with a well-thought-out plot can culminate into a compelling story. Add that to a storyline punctuated with excitement and imagination, and I know that readers, editors, including myself will be in for a treat.

Michelle Richter: Characters I want to spend lots of time with or figure out how they tick. I love an unreliable narrator, and lots of twists. Unusual skills or jobs are a plus, as are underrepresented voices like people of color, LGBT, or disabled people in the lead rather than just a sidekick role.

Stacey Donaghy: A strong voice and writing that immediately draws me in as a reader. Also, pacing and the ability to drive the plot forward by sharing enough information to keep the reader engaged without giving too much away. I love a surprising twist.

What are you seeing a demand for in the current marketplace?

MR: Women with secrets that come to haunt them, psychological thrillers, domestic suspense. Also, CIA/FBI espionage thrillers that echo aspects of shows like *The Americans* and *Homeland* and *The Blacklist*. But don't write to the trends, because they'll likely move on by the time you do.

DM: The broader categories appear to be more popular than the niche categories, such as political, legal, medical, military, and psychological. Currently the most popular demand is for general suspense. Espionage and historical are also popular.

SD: Psychological thrillers/suspense and especially those with an unreliable narrator.

What about a submission inspires confidence that you'll be able to find the work a home with a publisher?

DM: When I look at a submission, I like to have a visual idea of the bigger picture and what the story is about. What helps to create that visual is a thought-provoking title and a great tag line. It also helps to include compelling characters that come to life within the first few pages. If this happens for me, then I am confident it will happen for a prospective publisher.

MR: A unique hook and strong plotting, and the feeling that a thriller reader could easily imagine themselves in the main character's shoes. Good pacing is crucial too.

SD: When the writing is really something special, a story that has grabbed hold of me almost immediately, and has not let me go. A story that has surprised me, as I tend to be hard to surprise and a bit suspicious so often find myself disengaged having already discovered the big reveal before the halfway point. A new spin on a great formula.

What are the most common weaknesses in your submission pile?

MR: Lack of originality and lack of, well, thrills. Not enough happening in the beginning to hook me or keep me turning the pages.

DM: a) An implausible storyline. b) Unimaginative dialogue. c) Too many coincidences—often because the writer doesn't take care to find more creative alternatives. d) Confusing timelines. e) Not enough conflict. f) Weak subplots or too many subplots and characters to keep track of. g) Characters that are flat, boring, or too perfect. h) Wives and bosses that fall into generic stereotypes. i) An antagonist that isn't smart or strong enough to compete with the protagonist.

SD: When a writer is not clear about the genre and adds a number of genres to one story. Sending in a submission for a genre that I do not represent and prefacing the query with "I know you do not represent…" Queries with numerous errors. Also submitting stories that are currently published, unfortunately, that train has left the station. Unless the sales have broken the ceiling and the story is on key best-seller lists, it is extremely hard to sell a published story, so it is usually a hard pass for me. Also, queries that fail to hook, similar to elevator pitches, you need to hook the agent and standout amongst hundreds of others. If there is no hook, I rarely move onto the sample pages.

Are there any particular plot structures or premises that are overplayed in thrillers?

SD: Military and terrorism based thrillers are one of the reasons that I have narrowed my preference to psychological. Although psychological thrillers have always been my first choice, I did find that my inbox was loaded with the aforementioned and all of the premises were very similar.

DM: Not for me, as long as the writer can come up with an imaginative retake, or an old theme with a new twist.

MR: Amnesia. Untrustworthy (homicidal?) spouses. Returning to hometowns where everyone hates or distrusts the main character, usually because a parent or aunt or grandparent is sick or dead.

What's the best thriller you've read recently? What makes it stand out?

DM: While not a die-hard thriller, I just read *Robicheaux*, by James Lee Burke. You don't have to read any of the other books in the Robicheaux series to appreciate this one. It completely stands out on its own on many levels. First, we have Burke's mastery of prose and dialogue. Then there are constant surprises at every twist and turn, plus a colorful array of enjoyable and hateful characters throughout. Robicheaux with all his flaws and demons has an inherent goodness and a constant quest for truth and justice.

SD: *The Woman in the Window*, by A.J. Finn. The writing is stunning and the voice is incredible. The pacing is superb! The second the story opened, I was riveted and knew that this one was something special. The main character is hard to turn away from, she is well spoken, intelligent and a total mess. The author used a common disorder/phobia and built the story around this, making the main character a victim and hostage to her circumstances.

I won't say any more about the story except read it! This is hands-down one of the best psychological thrillers I have read in years.

MR: *IQ*, by Joe Ide, because its main character was unlike any I'd seen before, and *Jar of Hearts*, by Jennifer Hillier, for twist after twist that kept me reeling.

What part of the craft of writing do you find that yet-to-be-published thriller writers need to work on most?

SD: Read, read, and read some more, especially in the genre that you plan to write in. Read stories by best-selling authors in your genre area, read as many as you can. Pay attention to the things that make these stories work. Although every writer approaches their story differently, you'll notice the pacing, and approach to suspense are similar.

Psychological suspense/thriller must be driven by the big reveal at the end, but along the way, the writer must drop enough tidbits and add enough twists to keep the reader engaged without giving away the big reveal.

Also, write every day, to hone your craft.

MR: Starting the book in the right place seems to trip up many writers. Many great thrillers start in media res— not in backstory, waiting for something to happen. Grip the reader with action yet make them care about the person it's happening to.

DM: The most prevalent areas a writer needs to pay more attention to are believable plots and sub-plots. Imaginative and fully developed characters and supporting characters are a close second. All this helps move the story forward.

Where do you see the thriller genre evolving next?

MR: An embrace of retro themes and enemies—noir, Russian villains, and Hitchcock vibes—with modern protagonists.

DM: I love where we've come from and I equally enjoy where we're going. For example, I'm a history buff, so I'll always enjoy something from the past brought forward. But I'm also a futurist, so anything related to advanced technology, biologics, climate change, politics, and the threat to democracy could provide excellent themes for the thriller genre.

SD: I am not sure what's next but I do think that psychological thrillers will continue to be a genre that is sought after, as it has been for years and years. There are so many ways a writer can approach this sub-genre, the psyche is a powerful thing, a good storyteller and writer knows how to take advantage of that and add their own spin. One only has to look as far as the news, their imagination things others fear and even the DSM-5 to come up with a different spin.

Cris Freese is a former editor of *Guide to Literary Agents*, a freelance writer, and literary intern with Corvisiero Literary. Follow him on Twitter @crisfreese.

DEBUT AUTHORS TELL ALL

by Cris Freese

It was time for a little bit of a change with this year's Debut Authors Tell-All feature. You can probably already tell it's different because of this opening paragraph!

Over the past two years of putting together this feature, I've found a number of authors who I thought had impressive credentials, a story I wanted to feature, and a book that I thought looked good. Yet they didn't have an agent.

Of course, *Guide to Literary Agents* is all about helping you find a literary agent. And it will remain that way. But, in constructing this feature this year, I felt it prudent to show that you can get published without a literary agent. And it can end up coming out a nice product. So sprinkled in amongst the debut authors this year are a few authors who chose to publish without a literary agent.

And that doesn't make them a failure or "less-than." It just means they chose to get published via a different route. And just because they don't have an agent now, doesn't mean they won't land an agent in the future.

Historical Fiction

Clarissa Harwood (www.clarissaharwood.com): *Impossible Saints* (January 2018, Pegasus Books); Laura Crockett, TriadaUS Literary Agency

Quick Take: In 1907 England, Lilia Brooke, an agnostic militant suffragette, believes marriage to a clergyman is a fate worse than death. Paul Harris, a quiet, intellectual Anglican priest, is well aware that falling in love with Lilia is incompatible with his ambition to become the next cathedral dean. Lilia and Paul must decide which compromises they're willing to make and whether their love is worth fighting for. **Writes From:** London, Ontario, Canada. **Pre-Book:** I'm a part-time university instructor with a PhD in

Nineteenth-Century British Literature. I've taught everything from academic writing to children's literature. **Time Frame:** *Impossible Saints* took about twenty years from conception to publication, but I was a graduate student when I first had the idea and didn't have time to write, so another ten years passed before I was able to focus on the novel. The first draft took me a little over a year, but I've written so many drafts since then that I've lost count. I gave up on it several times and wrote other books, but I kept coming back to it. **Enter the Agent:** I started querying agents in 2008, shortly after I finished the first draft of *Impossible Saints*. I knew very little about the publishing industry at the time, and I didn't realize that the novel wasn't ready. I queried agents for three different novels and received hundreds of rejections before I signed with Laura in 2014. I had no connections to anyone in the industry, so mine is a "slush pile" success story! **Biggest Surprise:** I assumed that as soon as I had an agent, the publishing offers would start pouring in! The truth is that every step of the publishing process involves a lot of waiting. In my case, the novel that snagged my agent was not the one that was published. Laura and I worked together on three novels before the offer from Pegasus came in for *Impossible Saints*. **What I Did Right:** I researched agents and agencies carefully and followed their query guidelines. I'm always surprised to hear that many people don't do this! I also showed my work to trusted critique partners and beta readers and used their feedback to make it better. **What I Wish I Would Have Done Differently:** I wish I had waited longer and learned more about the publishing industry before starting to query agents. I wish I hadn't assumed I knew how to write because I had a PhD in Literature and taught academic writing. This seems to be a common pitfall among writers: just because we are literate and even experts in the field we're writing about doesn't mean we know how to tell a story that will keep readers turning pages. **Platform:** I use Twitter most of the time and Facebook occasionally. Because I work at home, I like to think of Twitter as my office "water cooler" and chat with my colleagues there during my lunch break. **Advice for Writers:** Never give up! Also, be willing to take constructive criticism. It's impossible to be objective about your own writing. Finally, don't be afraid to take a chance on a new agent as I did, especially if she is part of an established agency or is mentored by an established agent. **Next Up:** I've written a companion novel to *Impossible Saints* with some of the same characters. I'm fascinated by the way two people can view the same situation or relationship in completely different ways, so I've taken the villain of *Impossible Saints* and made him the hero of his own story!

Women's Fiction

Luke Allnutt (www.lukeallnutt.com): *We Own The Sky* (February 2018, Trapeze); Juliet Mushens, Caskie Mushens

Quick Take: Rob Coates can't believe his luck. There is Anna, his incredible wife, and most precious of all, Jack, their son, who makes every day an extraordinary adventure. Rob feels like he's won the lottery of life. Or rather—he did. Until the day it all changes when Anna becomes convinced there is something wrong with Jack. **Writes From:** Prague. **Pre-Book:** I work as a journalist, based in the Czech Republic. **Time Frame:** About three years. **Enter the Agent:** I submitted to agents in 2015 and got some rejections and two revise-and-resubmit requests—one of them from my agent, Juliet Mushens. We spoke on the phone and then, over the next nine months, I did a complete overhaul. I resubmitted the book to Juliet in 2016 and she took me on as a client. **Biggest Surprise:** How long everything takes, from getting the book deal to the book coming out. Also, just how many people at the publishing house, across different departments, have read the book. Naively, I thought it would just be the editor. **What I Did Right:** Not being afraid to go back to the drawing board and completely rewrite the book, even though I was cutting lots of material I loved. **What I Wish I Would Have Done Different:** Had faith in my writing earlier in my life. **Platform:** Just Twitter really, although I'm not very good at it. **Advice for Writers:** Never give up. Understand, very early on, that not everyone will like your book. We all like different kinds of books and that goes for editors and agents too. It's good to develop a thick skin. **Next Up:** I'm writing a second novel about a comedian who goes blind. My father was blind from birth, so it's a subject matter that's always interested me. I want to present a realistic portrait of what it's like to be blind, as portrayals of blind people are often a little clichéd: blind person as all-seeing sage, for example. My current novel, *We Own The Sky*, is quite sad so I wanted to write something a little funnier.

Romantic Suspense

Kelli Clare (kelliclare.com): *Hidden* (June 2018, SparkPress); No Literary Agent

Quick Take: Soon after meeting a mysterious Englishman, a small-town Connecticut art teacher learns that a society of assassins has targeted her lineage. *Hidden* is a sensual tale of death and survival, family intrigue, and absolute love. **Writes From:** Northwest Ohio. **Pre-Book:** I'm a former human resource executive, contributing writer for an online women's publication, and progressive voice for a global coalition of bloggers focused on issues involving women, children, and world hunger. **Time Frame:** I started writing *Hidden* in January 2016 and ended the year with a final manuscript. I spent about four months on the first draft, six months revising with the help of a developmental editor, and the last few months fine-tuning with editors from my publishing house. **Enter the Agent:** When I began this journey, I had a strong desire to learn the workings of the industry first hand, and since I'd received offers from a few independent presses, I chose to consult rather than sign with an agent. I was fortunate enough to find a terrific agent willing to work with me that way. Once this particular experience is complete, I'll query for formal representation with future projects. **Biggest Surprise:** I was pleasantly surprised by how much I loved the involved research. For instance, I really enjoyed researching and learning to fire the same weapon handled by *Hidden*'s protagonist. **What I Did Right:** I tossed out the rules and my outline and wrote the story the way it demanded to be told. I believe we're storytellers, not just writers, and I never allowed myself to lose that idea. **What I Wish I Would Have Done Different:** I don't believe in regret. Every misstep has been an essential part of my journey; those mistakes represent growth. But if there were things I wish I'd done differently, it would be tossing out that formulaic outline sooner and less worrying about market trends. **Platform:** I can be found online at kelliclare.com and on Twitter (@KellideClare), Facebook (/KellideClare), and Instagram (kellideclare). **Advice for Writers:** Be authentic when you write—we're all wonderfully unique individuals so let that shine—and find your tribe, as they say. The best writing tribes will encourage you, challenge you, and support your personal and professional development in a manner beyond your wildest dreams. I'd be remiss if I didn't give a well-deserved shout out to one of mine, the Women's Fiction Writers Association community. **Next Up:** The story that begins in *Hidden* continues over three books. I'm currently working on revisions for the second book of the trilogy.

Romantic Comedy

Leslie Cohen: *This Love Story Will Self-Destruct* (January 2018, Gallery Books); Andrew Blauner, Blauner Books

Quick Take: *This Love Story Will Self-Destruct* is a romantic comedy set in New York City over the span of ten years (think *When Harry Met Sally*, but circa now!). It's a classic love story in many ways but it takes a lot of fun/unusual twists. It's told from the alternating perspectives of two characters, Eve and Ben. Eve is a bit of a neurotic mess and Ben is extremely logical. Will they fall in love despite their differences, or will the whole thing go down in flames? **Writes From:** I write at the New York Society Library on 79th Street in NYC. Sometimes from my mother's apartment, depending on whether she has snacks. **Pre-Book:** I wrote a music column for a newspaper in Colorado, previewing/ reviewing concerts in the area. I got to interview famous musicians and go to shows for free and it was just like *Almost Famous* (in my head) (in reality it was substantially less cool). Then I moved back to New York, which is where I'm from, and worked in publishing at a few different literary agencies. **Time Frame:** About a year. I had written and re-written three books before this one that were ultimately rejected, so when I got to this one, I was some combination of frustrated and fired up. I knew exactly what I wanted to write and went full-speed ahead without much sleep or sanity. **Enter the Agent:** Well, I was working in publishing at the time, so naturally I met my agent while standing in line at the grocery store. I had a head of lettuce in my hands. Uncharacteristically, I was planning to make a salad for dinner. Lesson learned: decide not to get pizza delivered for once and your whole life can change! **Biggest Surprise:** Reading responses to the book and seeing how many people loved it exactly the way I wanted it to be loved. It's the best part and the reason to keep going, despite the difficulties at times. **What I Did Right:** I used to want to read every rejection letter and every critique, but I try to shield myself more these days. I discovered that too much information can be dangerous in my hands. I've also learned not to take each person's opinions too seriously, to take the advice that feels true to me and then leave the rest behind. **What I Wish I Would Have Done Different:** Since I was working in publishing while writing a novel, I was informed about what books were selling, what was appealing to agents, and how the business operated in general. I wish that I had worried less about trying to find the perfect "hook" because at the end of the day, it's just about finding the right editor who loves your book and the marketing can be sorted out later. **Platform:** I don't have much of a "platform" per se. I prefer hiding under my couch, but sometimes I make jokes on Twitter and then send myself into a shame spiral about whether or not they're funny. **Advice for Writers:** Take every victory, no matter how small, and run with it. Have faith that the victories will get bigger over time. Don't waste time questioning how talented you are. Assume that you have enough talent to get by, and then supplement it with tons of hard work. **Next Up:** I'm working on my second novel, which is darker and more dysfunctional than my first, but still a fun ride.

Family Drama

Mira T. Lee (miratlee.com): *Everything Here Is Beautiful* (January 2018, Pamela Dorman Books); Susan Golomb, Writers House

Quick Take: *Everything Here Is Beautiful* is a cross-cultural family drama about two sisters, and how their lifelong bond is put to the test as the younger struggles with a difficult mental illness. Tackling themes of identity, immigration, parenthood, and belonging, this heartwrenching novel is ultimately about the sacrifices we make for the ones we love most, and how tricky it can be to find the right balance between duty to others and remaining true to ourselves. **Writes From:** small, dark spaces in Cambridge, MA. **Pre-Book:** I wrote short stories for seven years before I attempted my novel. At various points in my life, I was also a graphic designer, drummer, biology graduate student, and salsa dancing fanatic. **Time Frame:** From the time that I told myself, "I'm going to try to write a book" it took me two and half years to get through four drafts. With the fourth draft, I found my agent, spent another month editing, after which the book was sold at auction. Another year of edits, another year of pre-pub waiting. From conception to pub date: 5 years. **Enter the Agent:** I queried six agents with my second draft. I thought it was "good enough," and that they'd see that I, and the novel, had "potential." It was a huge mistake. Mostly, I think I wanted the manuscript out of my own hands, but I should've searched harder for good readers rather than sending the work out to agents. A few of these agents were people I had some tenuous connection with through personal acquaintances, so the manuscript did get read, and I received some positive feedback, but no takers. As they say, you only get one chance to make a first impression. I worked on the book for another year, queried four agents with my fourth draft, and at that point had three takers. Going to New York to meet with them was one of the greatest highlights of this journey. **Biggest Surprise:** I knew it would be difficult to put my work out there for the entire world to pass judgment, but I didn't think I'd be affected by other people's opinions as much as I have been. Putting a novel out into the world is an act of total exposure, and it leaves you completely vulnerabie. You have to develop a really thick skin, and learn to stay grounded and true to yourself. **What I Did Right:** After receiving a handful of (mostly kind) rejections, I stopped querying with my second draft. I spent another year revising the manuscript—that was critical. I once heard the advice, "when you think it's done, revise for another year." I say that's about right. **What I Wish I Would Have Done Different:** I wish I'd approached the whole notion of publication with fewer expectations. That way, everything would've been icing on the cake! **Platform:** I like Facebook, I tolerate Twitter, I don't do Instagram, though probably I should. **Advice for Writers:** First timers, don't censor yourself, and don't think about the marketplace. Write what you care about passionately. **Next Up:** The ideas are swirling around…

Coming of Age

Rhiannon Navin (rhiannonnavin.com): *Only Child* (February 2018, Knopf); Jeff Kleinman, Folio Literary Management

Quick Take: Six-year old Zach Taylor survives a shooting at his elementary school by hiding in the closet of his first-grade classroom, but his older brother Andy's is one of the nineteen lives taken during the shooting rampage. While his family and their community quickly begin to unravel as they grapple with their grief, Zach retreats into his super-secret hideout and loses himself in a world of books and art. Ultimately it is little Zach, who, with his honesty and optimism and stubbornness, manages to lead his family and their community to a path towards compassion and forgiveness and a chance to heal, together. **Writes From:** My kitchen table in New Rochelle, NY. **Pre-Book:** In my pre-writing life I was a stay-at-home mom of three, ahem, lively children, which of course is still job number one now. In the life before that, I worked for several large advertising agencies in New York and Duesseldorf, Germany. **Time Frame:** It took me about a year to write *Only Child*. It was my first foray into the world of writing and I began scribbling the first few scenes in one of my kids' school notebooks. About a third of the way into my story I realized I should probably find some form of sounding board for my writing. I needed to know—was it worth neglecting piles and piles of dirty laundry and dishes? I found my perfect sounding board in the form of an amazing writing coach (who calls herself the Unkind Editor, so I knew she'd be perfect.) She helped me through the process of completing several drafts and she has been by my side throughout my publishing journey. **Enter the Agent:** I did a ton of homework researching agents. There were spreadsheets and wish lists. In the end, I only queried one agent, Jeff Kleinman from Folio. Go big or go home, I thought. Jeff responded within hours and his enthusiasm for my story blew me away. **Biggest Surprise:** Just how quickly Jeff secured a book deal for *Only Child*. Or book deals I should say. The first offer came from Mantle in the UK, followed quickly by offers in the US (Knopf) and other countries around the world. Never in a million years would I have expected such a response. The other big surprise was the waiting. After the fast and furious accepting of offers (accompanied by much champagne!) came…a long time of nothing. I didn't realize it would be another year plus before I'd get to see my book on the shelves. **What I Did Right:** Definitely trusting in the experience of the many experts I had in my camp, Jeff of course, and my wonderful editors, Carole Baron at Knopf and Sam Humphreys at Mantle, and the whole team at the publishers'. Everything about the publishing journey was new to me and I had a lot of learning to do. But I continued to trust my instincts, too, which allowed me to write the story in the first place. When it came down to certain questions during the editing process (would a six-year old really think or say something like that?) I relied on my gut for answers. **What I Wish I Would Have Done Different:** I wish I had immediately kept writing after handing *Only Child* off to Jeff. I let too much time go by initially and that messed with my head. I'm back into the swing of things now, but I wish I had started sooner. **Platform:** I enjoy actually connecting and having conversations with my readers. My website is my main platform and I am thrilled whenever I receive an email from a reader with comments or questions. I answer them all. I love small events (libraries, book clubs) that allow me to have a real exchange. I hang out on Facebook and Twitter, but I get overwhelmed a lot. It's such a time-suck—you go on "real quick" and before you know it, hours have gone by! **Advice for Writers:** I'm not sure I'm really in a position to give writers advice, since I'm so new to writing. But I imagine that writing with a certain expectation, an agenda could present an obstacle to really focusing on the story itself. If you worry about how it will be received before you've written it, if you daydream about the reviews you will receive, you will probably do the story a disservice. **Next Up:** Got something brewing I'm excited about, but I'd rather not talk about it yet in case I jinx it, if that's OK.

Romantic Suspense

Sharon Wray (www.sharonwray.com): *Every Deep Desire* (March 2018, Sourcebooks); Deidre Knight & Kristy Hunter, The Knight Agency

Quick Take: *Every Deep Desire* is the first in the romantic suspense Deadly Force Series about a group of ex-Green Berets and smart, sexy women who redeem Shakespeare's greatest love stories. *Every Deep Desire,* about an ex-Green Beret and the wife he abandoned and has returned for, is a retelling of *Romeo and Juliet.* **Writes From:** Virginia. **Pre-Book:** I am a research librarian and a former wedding gown designer. I'm also married to my high school sweetheart and am a mother of teenage twins. **Time Frame:** This book, my ninth manuscript, was rewritten a number of times. The last version (a complete rewrite) took me 11 months. **Enter the Agent:** It took me six years and six manuscripts to get an agent. I think of those years as the Great Query Wars. I queried and was rejected by so many agents that I lost count. But, because I'd been persistent, I'd gotten to the point where the agents who rejected me always asked to see my next project. After rejecting multiple projects, Deidre Knight offered representation on a very early version of this book. **Biggest Surprise:** Even though I'd signed with an agent, it took me another six years to sell. I'm a slow writer and needed the time and editorial feedback my agent gave me to get to the point where I could sell. **What I Did Right:** I accepted constructive criticism and was always open to making changes. I also took a lot of craft classes and read craft books. In fact, I still do. I think learning how to write well is going to be a lifelong job. **What I Wish I Would Have Done Different:** Even though this is something I can't change, I wish I was a faster writer. I've tried everything to pick up my speed—from experimenting with different plot outline processes to setting up structured writing hours—but nothing has made me faster. I'm slow and plodding and have to put in the hours to get the story out. I'm hoping that as I finish more and more books that I'll speed up. Although, I'm not holding my breath. **Platform:** I've always loved to blog and have built up a following with different series that didn't rely on having a published book available. As a librarian and readers advisor, I publish a bi-annual middle grade & young adult book list of books read by my tween and teenage reading army. It's not a bestseller list, just a cumulative list of books (new and old) that they love. I also publish a weekly series called The Hungry {Romance} Writer which showcases super-easy yet healthy recipes for really busy people and families. I have a few other ongoing series, all of them tied into writing but not necessarily about romance novels. All of these blog posts have helped me build my email/newsletter list. I also use Instagram and Facebook. I struggle with Twitter and haven't touched Tumblr. I think the advice about doing what you love is true. I love to blog and take photos so my blog and Instagram are where I prefer to be. **Advice for Writers:** This doesn't come from me. It comes from a 1941 speech by Winston Churchill. (And for writers, Churchill's enemy refers to our own self-doubt): "Never give in—never, never, never, never, in nothing great or small, large or petty, never give in except to convictions of honour and good sense. Never yield to force; never yield to the apparently overwhelming might of the enemy."

Nonfiction: Self-Help

Julia Samuel (www.griefworks.co.uk): *Grief Works* (March 2018, Viking Penguin); Felicity Rubinstein, Lutyens and Rubinstein

Quick Take: *Grief Works* is a compassionate guide that will support, inform and engage anyone who is grieving, from the 'expected' death of a parent to the sudden and unexpected death of a small child, and provides clear advice for those seeking to comfort the bereaved. **Writes From:** I write at home mainly, on the sofa in my sitting room, computer on my lap. I can write anywhere, I surprise myself in finding the train a good place to write. **Pre-Book:** Worked as a psychotherapist and trainer. **Time Frame:** 8 months. **Enter the Agent:** She contacted me after hearing a radio recording I did of Desert Island Discs. **Biggest Surprise:** The level of emails and messages I receive from people who have read my book—and how enriching it is meeting people who have read it and found it helpful. **What I Did Right:** I kept my expectations low, but my hopes high. I worked hard at promoting it, accepted every invitation I could. **What I Wish I Would Have Done Different:** I wish I could have worried less, and enjoyed the whole process more. **Platform:** No, nothing special about my platform—people bought the book, and often bought more than one copy because they wanted to give it to friends and family. Sometimes I would sign 5 or 6 copies for one person. **Advice for Writers:** Keep writing, don't worry about the grammar, or even the content, get words on the page every day, and then edit. I was helped enormously by the encouragement of a freelance editor, who told me to keep writing, and that I had a voice. **Next Up:** I am writing a new book about how we transition and adapt through the lifespan—the same format of case studies and reflections. With the same agent and editor at Viking Penguin. The title at the moment is Life Works.

Urban Fantasy

Carolyn M. Walker (https://carolynmwalker.wordpress.com/): *Immortal Descent* (April 2018, Astrea Press/Clean Reads); No Literary Agent

Quick Take: For centuries, the truth about immortality has remained a secret but now that secret is about to break free. When Ethan West falls victim to a paranormal attack, he quickly learns the world is full of dark secrets—including the truth about his own rare soul. Now he's become a savior and a target overnight, facing a fate that's impossible to outrun. **Writes From:** In short, I write from the heart. I write what comes to me and oftentimes the story evolves on its own, like it's alive. I'm inspired by the smallest things—a sound, a smell, a memory. For me, writing is an art that moves me and I'm the artist who paints the pictures. **Pre-Book:** I was busy being a young mom, going to college, and trying to figure out what I wanted to be when I grew up. I'd always loved writing and found creative ways to weave it into my professional life. That's why I decided to become a professional copywriter and copy editor. For years before writing my first novel, I worked as a copywriter and marketing consultant. Before that I was a travel agent! **Time Frame:** Almost two years. **Enter the Agent:** I actually don't have an agent yet! I'd love to have one, so I can share my excitement with a professional who can help me get more of my work out there! I'm infinitely passionate about both the craft of writing and the business of it, so I'm seeking an agent who is just as passionate about getting quality work in front of the right readers! **Biggest Surprise:** The publication process in general! I was aware that the path to publication wasn't going to be easy. I knew I had to pull my weight and make this happen, as much as the professionals helping me get out there. Even with this mindset going into it, I never could have prepared for how complex it was! I'm an avid researcher and stubborn do-it-yourselfer, but no amount of research could have prepared me for the process itself. There are so many variables and moving pieces at play! You have to have thick skin, steadfast professionalism, and an open mind to get through it with grace! Indeed a surpise! I've learned so much and grown with each step. **What I Did Right:** Regarding writing: I kept a clear mindset. If I let myself, I can be the queen of digressing. So, I had to keep myself focused and confident—clear in my goals. I won't say I wasn't without doubts, but I didn't allow myself to stay there. I kept telling myself that I could do this. A writer can be their own worst enemy. Many times, I had to separate my writer self from my reader self. This helped me to edit more objectively and ensure I had the most polished work I could stand behind. I also read every piece of my work aloud. That is such a wonderful editing tool! Your work sounds so different when read aloud! Regarding publication: I did my homework! I am a planner and an organizer and that helped me a lot! I didn't go into the process completely blind, so I had some sort of idea of expectations. I followed instructions to the T and made sure my end of everything was thorough. As an author, your success has a lot to do with how much care you put into things. I care about the work I create and the people I work with, and that makes all the difference. **What I Wish I Would Have Done Different:** If I could go back, I would have had more beta readers. I didn't really take too much advantage of this and I wish I had. I think those outside opinions are so valuable in those early stages of writing. Good beta readers who care will tell you the truth and point out things you might otherwise be writing-blind to. It's worth taking advantage of having a team of beta readers! **Platform:** Online: I'm a positive person and I try to inspire others. I'm a lover of quotes because another's words can be worth their weight in gold. I try to infuse this into my platform online. I've even got a motto I throw around every so often: "Mind over matter, pen over paper." I'm about positivity and engagement. I want people to know I'm a real person and we are all in this crazy thing called life, together. That's the message I try to convey with as much grace as possible. I'm very active on Facebook, Twitter and my blog (I'm still working on Instagram). When writing: I primarily use an older version of Microsoft Word (2010 edition). I also use notepad a lot for side notes, ideas, pointers, you name it. Sometimes I handwrite out details too. I'm all over the place but there is a definite method to the madness and it always come together in the end. **Advice for Writers:** Believe in yourself. So many people say keep writing and don't stop—just do it. I say believe. What good is something if you don't believe in it? Believe you have what it takes and that will propel you to do the rest. Even when every part of you screams to stop or give up, and you're tired of it all, believe. Imagine you've already finished. Imagine you've reached others with your amazing work and allow yourself to feel the words within. If you can do that, you are on your way. If not, consider what that means. If you can't find it in you to believe in your own work, why should anyone else? That's the truth! **Next Up:** I'm working on the second installment in the Immortal Series. I plan on it being a trilogy. I also have an own voices literary work I've begun, and a young adult conspiracy thriller underway. I typically write adult fiction, but I'm especially excited for the young adult project because with today's teens and young adults being more politically inclined, opinionated, and informed than ever, my story will be very relevant. Outside of all these exciting upcoming works, I've got a box full of other great ideas at the ready when the time comes.

Science Fiction

David Pedreira (www.davidpedreira.com): *Gunpowder Moon* (February 2018, Harper Voyager); David Fugate, Launchbooks Literary Agency

Quick Take: *Gunpowder Moon* is a near-future science fiction thriller about the first murder on the Moon—and how that murder will lead to a full lunar war if a U.S. mining chief and his crew can't figure out who did it, and why. It's a gritty, realistic look at the frontier days of lunar colonization, and it has mystery and military sci-fi elements to it. **Writes From:** Florida. In between fishing, golfing, and diving. **Pre-Book:** I actually started out as a writer. I spent about ten years as a reporter for daily newspapers including *The (Annapolis) Capital*, *The Tampa Tribune*, and the *St. Petersburg Times*. I've also served as a corporate communications director for technology companies, and I currently co-own a legal and executive recruiting company. **Time Frame:** It took about a year to draft the original manuscript. But once you land an agent and a book deal, there's more work to come. Agents typically suggest a few changes before submitting the novel to publishing houses, and once you have a publisher, there will be several rounds of editing. It's a long process, but it leads to a stronger book. **Enter the Agent:** I read *The Martian* by Andy Weir. After a few chapters, I realized that Weir's agent might like my book. While they tell very different stories, both novels are near-future, hard science fiction thrillers set in our solar system. I did a little research, learned that the agent in question was David Fugate, and sent him a query letter. He asked for a few sample chapters, and things moved on from there. **Biggest Surprise:** How slowly things progress in publishing. From landing an agent to seeing the book in print, it took a little more than two years. Apparently, that's a pretty common timeline. **What I Did Right:** I finally figured out that when you're looking for an agent, you have to cast a narrow net. Querying every agent within your novel's larger genre won't get it done. You need to target agents who represent your kind of book. An agent who likes cyberpunk, for example, isn't likely to respond to an alien invasion epic. So you have to dig a little deeper and find an agent who represents stories that come from the same world as yours. **What I Wish I Would Have Done Different:** I would have written my first novel ten years ago! **Platform:** My platform is pretty standard. I have an author website and I mostly use Facebook and Twitter to put out information about my writing endeavors. I've also moved into writing op-eds about space and politics, and I'm trying to show up at as many book fairs and conventions as possible. **Advice for Writers:** Read a lot and write a lot, and don't be afraid to edit your work. That's basically it. **Next Up:** We're finalizing a contract on a TV/movie deal for *Gunpowder Moon*, which we'll be announcing soon, and I'm working on a few different ideas for a next novel.

Psychological Thriller

Wendy Heard (www.wendyheard.com): *Hunting Annabelle* (December 2018, MIRA Books); Lauren Spieller, Triada US

Quick Take: Sean struggles to control his murderous impulses as he desperately searches for his kidnapped girlfriend before she falls victim to a killer even more dangerous than he. Pitched as *Dexter* meets *Gone Girl*, *Hunting Annabelle* is a psychological thriller set in the 1980s. **Writes From:** Los Angeles, CA—I am a rare native Angeleno. **Pre-Book:** I like to outline in four acts, which splits act 2 into 2A and 2B. This organization really helps me delineate the sections of the story, which I think of as set up and launch; climbing uphill to the midpoint; everything falling apart; and climax and conclusion. Of course, I didn't invent this. I use *Save the Cat*, *Anatomy of Story* and other plotting and outlining tools. *Hunting Annabelle* was research-intensive, and I spent months on pre-writing research. **Time Frame:** *Hunting Annabelle* was written over a period of two years if you include agent and editor rewrites. **Enter the Agent:** I found her on www.manuscriptwishlist.com. My project seemed a good fit for her, but I knew her excellent reputation and queried her without much hope of a reply. To my delight, she was excited about the project and had some brilliant ideas for revision. I love how editorial Lauren is, and I cannot recommend her enough to any querying writers. She's smart and talented, and she herself is an author, so she sees projects from all angles. **Biggest Surprise:** My biggest surprise was a pleasant one: I was shocked by my editor's love for this book. She has been such a cheerleader of my work; I would never have dared hope for this type of enthusiasm. **What I Did Right:** Before I queried, I sent my book through a number of rounds of revisions with critique partners. I examined it critically against my beat sheet after each revision to make sure I was still hitting my beats. I revised a query letter with the help of critique partners, and I sent out small batches of queries rather than papering the town with a first version. **What I Wish I Would Have Done Different:** I wish I had established my current prewriting practices earlier on. I spent too many years writing with no outline, which left readers unsatisfied and made it hard for me to know why certain parts lagged or felt unsatisfying. I know authors who can write this way successfully, but I was definitely not one of them. **Platform:** I'm on Twitter a lot, and I'm also active on Instagram. I've met a lot of great bloggers and reviewers on the latter, but I feel I connect to potential readers and fellow authors more personally on the former. I have a website I built through Squarespace, which is a great tool for making a professional-looking site without much experience. I do use Facebook as well, but I'm not as experienced on that platform. **Advice for Writers:** I would advise writers to embrace critique, work hard on improving their writing with each project, and settle in; publishing is a slow and steady journey. It's easy to despair when you hear stories about people publishing their very first novel, about books going straight to auction, about books getting snatched up in hours. I've heard those stories too, but most published authors got there by being persistent, humble, flexible, by working their asses off—and with a little luck. **Next Up:** I'm writing the second in a two-book deal. I can't release much information about it, since it's still in developmental phases (this is a nice way of saying the Scrivener file is open and nagging at me as I type this), but I can't wait to share it with the world!

Cozy Mystery

Debra Sennefelder (www.DebraSennefelder.com): *The Uninvited Corpse* (March 2018, Kensington Publishing); Blue Ridge Literary Agency

Quick Take: Leaving behind a series of high profile failures, newly divorced food blogger Hope Early thought things were finally on the upswing. Her schedule is already jam packed with recipe testing and shameless plugs for her blog as she rushes off to attend a spring garden tour in the charming town of Jefferson, Connecticut. Unfortunately, it isn't the perfectly arranged potted plants that grab her attention—it's the bloody body of a reviled real estate agent who is her sister's business rival. With a second murder and her sister a suspect, Hope has no choice but to uncover the murderer before she's taken offline permanently. **Writes From:** Newtown, CT. **Pre-Book:** I worked in customer service for a nonfiction publisher. **Time Frame:** About ten months to complete three drafts of the book before it was ready to submit. **Enter the Agent:** I was referred by a friend who was also represented by the agency. I then sent the agent a synopsis and the first three chapters of the manuscript. **Biggest Surprise:** I've been pursuing publication for a while and I have many friends who are published so I was prepared for navigating the world of traditional publishing. Though, seeing how long everything took in traditional publishing was still surprising. Looking back, I now really understand. Many departments are involved with publishing and they're juggling hundreds of books each year. **What I Did Right:** I began building my reader base early. When I signed my three-book contract in December 2016, I began my author Facebook page and newsletter in January 2017 and have been continually building both organically. I'd already had a website in place by the time I received the offer. I also connected with other authors in the agency and out of that I gained promotional opportunities while my debut novel was in pre-order status. **What I Wish I Would Have Done Different:** I would have begun my author Facebook page earlier because I found many readers were very interested in the journey from unpublished to published. **Platform:** For just over a period of a year I didn't have any books to sell. What I had was a debut book available for pre-order so I had to be creative with staying in front of readers. I shared about the journey of what happens between the sale and promotion. I primarily use Facebook and Instagram along with a monthly newsletter. **Advice for Writers:** I would advise writers to set their own deadlines so they are prepared for the deadlines their publishers will set for them in their contract. Also, I would encourage writers not to give up. It's easy to throw in the towel because rejections are hard but finally making that sale is so amazing. **Next Up:** I sold a second series to my publisher, The Resale Boutique Mystery series, and the first book in that series releases in January 2019. The second Food Blogger book releases in April 2019.

Nonfiction

Emma Byrne (https://www.emmabyrne.net): *Swearing is Good for You, the Amazing Science of Bad Language* (January 2018, W.W. Norton); Carrie Plitt, Felicity Brown Associates

Quick Take: Swearing kills pain, bonds social groups, and has helped to unlock the structure of the brain. Bad language and great science meet in this gloriously uplifting look at why (and how) we swear. **Writes From:** Home, or the British Library most often. Also trains, cars, buses, airplanes, the hairdresser, the queue at the supermarket. Any chance I can snatch really! **Pre-Book:** I'm a researcher in artificial intelligence. **Time Frame:** The idea first came about in 2013, when I put together a fifteen-minute broadcast on BBC Radio 4. After that, I wrote a proposal that I submitted to a few agents. The first rightly pointed out all the rough edges, the second wanted me to do something quite 'Malcolm Gladwell' (I'm not Malcolm Gladwell!) Carrie just 'got' the book that I wanted to write straight away, helped me hone it, and in March 2015 I was signed to Profile Books. In November 2015 I was signed to W W Norton, and in March 2016 my daughter was born! I managed to finish the complete manuscript before I went into labor, with the unflagging support of my editor, Rebecca Gray. Then there was a hiatus while I took care of my newborn before I came to do final edits. I think the final touches were done in spring of 2017 and we launched last November. It seems like a long time in retrospect, but I was learning so much at each stage! **Enter the Agent:** Carrie had a fantastic profile on her page of the agency's website. I knew straight away that she had the amazing blend of terrific industry savvy, supportive ambition for her authors, and was looking for something like the book I really wanted to write. It was a great fit! **Biggest Surprise:** Just how kind, supportive, generous, and talented people are in publishing! I don't know if I'm unusually lucky with my representation and my publishers, but I've had such an opportunity to grow thanks to their hard work and support. The sales process was a crash course in selling myself (which doesn't come naturally to me, like so many people.) The editing process was a masterclass in writing. The publicity round has given me opportunities to write for publications, and appear in venues, that I would never have dreamed I'd get chance to do. **What I Did Right:** Kept going through the self-doubt and the time pressure. That endurance is something that I feel justifiably proud of. It's so easy to succumb to the voice that says, 'I can't do this!' Some days nothing goes right. I will never again underestimate the tenacity of anyone who has made it into print. **What I Wish I Would Have Done Different:** I wish I'd realized how much time I'd be spending on publicity. It's a really nice problem to have, but I haven't quite figured out how to balance promoting *Swearing is Good for You* and writing the proposal for book two. **Platform:** Nothing particularly special. I tweet, but I wouldn't say I'm 'on brand.' One minute it's robots, then it's funny toddlers, then it's neuroscience, then it's politics! My website is a bit more organized: I use it as a repository of links to public appearances, broadcasts, and my other writing. I really should be more disciplined about keeping it up to date. Mainly I do a lot of personal appearances—I'm lucky, living in the UK means that I can appear at a literary festival or a science festival pretty much every weekend. I spend a lot of time on trains these days. I've also been lucky enough to do some great radio and podcasts. Audio broadcasting is by far the most fun part of publicity for me. I've spoken to people on four continents without leaving my home city. One day I spoke to people in Canada and New Zealand and was still home in time for dinner! **Advice for Writers:** You will doubt yourself. You will be rejected. Your book will not be universally loved. That's normal. Don't give up. **Next Up:** Something that sits in the intersection of AI and neuroscience, looking at why we're not in any danger of being replaced by machines for some time to come.

Military Science Fiction

Michael Mammay (MichaelMammay.com): *Planetside* (July 2018, Harper Voyager); Lisa Rodgers, JABberwocky

Quick Take: A seasoned military officer on a routine investigation on a distant space station orbiting a war-ravaged planet discovers a deadly conspiracy that threatens the galaxy. The answers are planetside, in the combat zone. If he can survive it long enough to find them. **Writes From:** Georgia. **Pre-Book:** I was an officer in the United States Army for 27 years. I recently retired from that, and now I teach high school English. You know... standard English teacher career path. **Time Frame:** I started writing the book in November, 2014 and started querying in November, 2015. But I wasn't writing that whole time, as I had a pretty serious injury and was on bed rest part of the time. As to how long it took...I finished page proofs in February, 2018, so I've been working on the book in some form for a while. But in the original form that got my agent? A bit less than a year. **Enter the Agent:** I got into a contest called Pitch Wars, where I did another revision of my book along with my mentor, Dan Koboldt (now my critique partner.) I got almost no love in the agent round (one request) so I started querying all the Sci-Fi agents at the beginning of November, 2015. It went slow at first. I got a bunch of rejections, and almost no requests. Sometime in February that all changed. I got a partial request from an agent that turned into a full overnight, and an offer a couple days later. That spurred other agents to request, and I signed with Lisa the first week of March, 2016. In the end I sent out 32 queries, got five partial requests, four of which became full requests, and two of which became offers. **Biggest Surprise:** How good an editor my agent is. I queried a good book. Lisa immediately gave me notes that blew me away (I wrote an entire blog post about it on my website.) In total we did two rounds of edits before we went on submission in June, 2016. Like I said, the book was good. She made it much, much better. I didn't think that was possible, but when she gave me the notes, I immediately knew she was right. **What I Did Right:** Two things. First, I found good critique partners early on in my writing life. People who tell me the truth about my work, even when it hurts. People who make me a better writer. Second, every time I sent something out into the world, I believed it was the best thing I could create. That gave me peace. When I queried, it was the best thing I could write at the time. When we went on submission, it was the best thing I could write at the time. Knowing it was my best work, I didn't worry about it as much. I put my best foot forward, and someone was either going to offer on it or they weren't. I'd done my part, and there was nothing else I could do. Having that attitude made querying and being on submission bearable. I controlled what I could control, and that was writing the best book I could write. **What I Wish I Would Have Done Different:** This is a tough one, because there's not much. I don't spend a lot of time thinking about this sort of thing. I guess if I had to say one thing, I'd say I should have been writing more while I was on submission, though that thought might be influenced by the fact that I'm currently on deadline for book two and not finished. Honestly, knowing myself, I was never going to get much writing done during that time. I find that I need a defined goal, and at the time I didn't know what book two would be, since book one hadn't sold. **Platform:** I just use my website and twitter, where I have a decent following. I've done a lot of mentoring of aspiring writers in contests, which is definitely part of who I am as a writer. **Advice for Writ-**

ers: Two things. First, find your tribe. Find good critique partners who help you develop as a writer, but more than that, find other writers who support you and lift you up on the bad days. Writing is a lonely pursuit. You need other people. I know it's hard to put yourself out there, but it's so worth it. And bonus, when you become a debut, those same people will support you through that new stress, too. Second, put your best work forward and then don't worry about it. Write the best book you can, send it to agents, and get to work on whatever is next. They're either going to love it or they aren't. But if you put your best work out there, you've already controlled everything you can control. There's nothing left to worry about. **Next Up:** As I write this, my April 8th deadline for my currently untitled book two is about two weeks away. So there's that. Book two is a sequel, though book one was originally written as a stand-alone, and can be read that way. After I finish that it's full steam ahead on promotion for book one's release, intermingled with starting a new book I've been dreaming up in a slightly different part of the genre. It's still science fiction, but a little less on the military side. You'll be able to find me at NYC Comicon, in October, and Atomacon in Charleston, SC, in late November.

Historical Women's Fiction

Diane Byington (www.dianebyington.com): *Who She Is* (March 2018, Red Adept Publishing); No Literary Agent

Quick Take: In 1967, sixteen-year-old Faye wants to run the Boston Marathon, but women aren't allowed to register for the race. She decides to do it anyway, but while training, strange memories that are related to running begin to surface. She must solve the mystery of her life while keeping her eyes on the finish line. **Writes From:** Boulder, Colorado, and Tavares, Florida. **Pre-Book:** I have had a varied career: college professor, yoga instructor, executive coach, and psychotherapist. I love to do a variety of things. **Time Frame:** The first draft was finished in six months. The rewriting took seven years. **Enter the Agent:** I decided to publish with a small publisher rather than to struggle to find an agent. I'm not sorry I did it this way. **Biggest Surprise:** My biggest surprise was how important reviews are to an author's success. I didn't realize before I published that I needed reviews. Now I make a point to post a review for every book I read. I picture the author smiling when s/he checks and finds out there's another review. **What I Did Right:** I had three offers from different small publishers. I chose the one I thought would be best for me and my work, and I'm very pleased with how it turned out. **What I Wish I Would Have Done Different:** Being a debut author is a major learning experience, whether you are published by a small press or one of the Big 5. I wish I had started preparing for the book launch months earlier. **Platform:** I'm learning how to use my author Facebook account and Twitter, and I'm beginning to love Instagram. I understand how important social media is. I'm not an expert yet, but I will be before I'm done. Also, my book uses song titles from the 1960s as chapter headings. I'm posting a different song on social media every day, and I love revisiting this music. Other people seem to like it, too. **Advice for Writers:** Realize that there are many ways to get published. You can self-publish, publish with a small press, or go for the big guys. The point is to get your book in front of readers and see what happens. Keep an open mind as you go about the process of deciding what's best for you and your book. **Next Up:** I have a time travel book almost ready to go. An historian finds old journals of Nikola Tesla's in which he describes his experiments in time travel. She decides to follow in his footsteps and go back into her life to redo a mistake she's always regretted. It's a fun, suspenseful read.

Picture Book

Tina Cho (www.tinamcho.com): *Rice from Heaven: The Secret Mission to Feed North Koreans* (August 2018, Little Bee Books); Adria Goetz, Martin Literary Agency

Quick Take: Yoori, a South Korean girl, helps her father with a secret kindness mission to send rice in balloons over the border to impoverished families in North Korea, based on real events. **Writes From:** Pyeongtaek, South Korea. **Pre-Book:** I am an elementary teacher and have taught in the U.S. and now at an international school in South Korea. I also did freelance writing for educational and children's markets. **Time Frame:** I wrote the first draft eight days after I participated in the rice balloon launch with a church group. That took only a day to write. However, almost a year later and 17 drafts, the book sold. **Enter the Agent:** The short answer: Twitter. I simply responded to the tweet of another agent at the agency. The long answer: I had submitted to many agents and was getting personal feedback, even had a personal phone call with one that didn't work out. Then you know that phrase, "when it rains, it pours"? Two agents had requested my manuscripts, and then I saw an interesting tweet from another agent I follow on Twitter. She announced there was a new agent at her agency, someone who would specialize in the Christian market. I started researching her. My stories weren't specifically written for the Christian market, but they could be tweaked to lean that way. I queried Adria with two stories I thought she'd like, one of which was Rice from Heaven. The next day she said to send them over. About three weeks later, she emailed saying she had read my stories that same day and hadn't been able to stop thinking about them. Then she asked for THE CALL. So that weekend after working out time zones in which to call, she offered representation. I signed the contract December 5th, 2017, after first querying her on October 30th. I'm so thankful to God for connecting Adria and me. **Biggest Surprise:** My biggest surprise was receiving F&G's of my book the day before Valentine's Day. I was surprised my publisher mailed them to me in Korea! Another surprise is being included in this interview for Children's Writer! **What I Did Right:** When I was told to make my manuscript more lyrical and dreamy, I sought the help of mentor texts and my three critique groups. The picture book that made the biggest impact was Jane Yolen's *Owl Moon.* I don't own it, so I listened to it on YouTube and wrote down every word. (Being in another country, I can't just check it out from my local library.) I studied it and her poetic techniques. I also made my own *How to Write a Lyrical Picture Book 101* by studying blog posts from other authors and ReFoReMo (Reading for Research Month). You can read my long post about that here: https://groggorg.blogspot.kr/2017/06/how-to-write-lyrical-picture-book-self.html. Other things that helped me on my journey were being a part of SCBWI, Julie Hedlund's 12x12 for a couple years, taking picture book classes, attending webinars, participating in critique groups, and participating in the online kidlit community on Facebook. **Platform:** I'm on Facebook daily and involved in many kidlit groups. I participate with Twitter & Pinterest weekly, and I'm slowly learning how to use Instagram for writers. **Advice for Writers:** Be involved in critique groups and in the online kidlit community. You learn so much from each other. Reading blogs and articles is giving yourself a mini writing course. Take time to learn the craft of writing well. Revise, revise, and revise some more. Save money to take courses or to pay for critiques from editors. It's worth it to experience their expertise. Lastly, be patient. The writing journey is long and slow. **Next Up:** *Korean Celebrations*, a nonfiction picture book about Korean holidays, will be published by Tuttle Fall 2018. I also have another picture book scheduled for January 2020, which hasn't been announced yet. Currently, my work-in-progress involves other picture books with Korean themes: Korean granny divers called haenyeo, a Korean princess, and a MG novel about North Korean escapees.

Cris Freese is a former editor of *Guide to Literary Agents*, a freelance writer, and literary intern with Corvisiero Literary. Follow him on Twitter @crisfreese.

LITERARY AGENTS

Literary agents listed in this section do not charge for reading or considering your manuscript or book proposal. It's the goal of an agent to find salable manuscripts: Her income depends on finding the best publisher for your manuscript.

Since an agent's time is better spent meeting with editors, she will have little or no time to critique your writing. Agents who don't charge fees must be selective and often prefer to work with established authors, celebrities, or those with professional credentials in a particular field.

SUBHEADS

Each agency listing is broken down into subheads to make locating specific information easier. In the first section, you'll find contact information for each agency. Additional information in this section includes the size of each agency, its willingness to work with new or unpublished writers, and its general areas of interest.

MEMBER AGENTS: Agencies comprised of more than one agent list member agents and their individual specialties. This information will help you determine the appropriate person to whom you should send your query letter.

REPRESENTS: This section allows agencies to specify what nonfiction and fiction subjects they represent. Make sure you query only those agents who represent the type of material you write.

Look for the key icon to quickly learn an agent's areas of specialization. In this portion of the listing, agents mention the specific subject areas they're currently seeking as well as those subject areas they do not consider.

HOW TO CONTACT: Most agents open to submissions prefer an initial query letter that briefly describes your work. You should send additional material only if the agent requests it. In this section, agents also mention if they accept queries by fax or e-mail, if they consider simultaneous submissions, and how they prefer to obtain new clients.

TERMS: Provided here are details of an agent's commission, whether a contract is offered and for how long, and what additional office expenses you might have to pay if the agent agrees to represent you. Standard commissions range from 10–15 percent for domestic sales and 15–25 percent for foreign or dramatic sales (with the difference going to the co-agent who places the work).

RECENT SALES: Some agencies have chosen to list recent book sales in their listing. To get to know an agency better, investigate these published titles and learn about writing styles that the agency has bonded with.

WRITERS CONFERENCES: A great way to meet an agent is at a writers conference. Here agents list the conferences they usually attend. For more information about a specific conference, check the Conferences section.

TIPS: In this section, agents offer advice and additional instructions for writers.

SPECIAL INDEX

LITERARY AGENTS SPECIALTIES INDEX: This index organizes agencies according to the subjects they are interested in receiving. This index should help you compose a list of agents specializing in your areas. Cross-referencing categories and concentrating on agents interested in two or more aspects of your manuscript might increase your chances of success.

A+B WORKS

Website: http://aplusbworks.com. **Contact:** Amy Jameson, Brandon Jameson. Estab. 2004.

Amy began her career in New York with esteemed literary agency Janklow & Nesbit Associates, where she launched Shannon Hale's career.

MEMBER AGENTS Amy Jameson (middle grade and young adult).

REPRESENTS Novels. **Considers these fiction areas:** middle grade, young adult.

HOW TO CONTACT Query via online submission form. "Due to the high volume of queries we receive, we can't guarantee a response." Accepts simultaneous submissions.

DOMINICK ABEL LITERARY AGENCY, INC.

146 W. 82nd St., #1A, New York NY 10024. (212)877-0710. **Fax:** (212)595-3133. **E-mail:** agency@dalainc.com. **Website:** dalainc.com. **Contact:** Dominick Abel. "The agency represents authors of fiction (especially mysteries and suspense novels), narrative nonfiction, and business books. It is a full-service agency, with co-agents in all major countries and in Hollywood. Among the agency's clients are *New York Times* bestselling writers as well as winners of Edgar, Malice Domestic, Shamus, Anthony, Dilys, Bram Stoker, and other awards." Estab. 1975. Member of AAR. Represents 50 clients.

REPRESENTS Fiction, novels. **Considers these nonfiction areas:** business, true crime. **Considers these fiction areas:** action, adventure, crime, detective, mystery, police.

HOW TO CONTACT Query via e-mail. No attachments. "If you wish to submit fiction, describe what you have written and what market you are targeting (you may find it useful to compare your work to that of an established author). Include a synopsis of the novel and the first two or three chapters. If you wish to submit nonfiction, you should, in addition, detail your qualifications for writing this particular book. Identify the audience for your book and explain how your book will be different from and better than already published works aimed at the same market." Accepts simultaneous submissions. Responds in 2-3 weeks.

ADAMS LITERARY

7845 Colony Rd., C4 #215, Charlotte NC 28226. (704)542-1440. **Fax:** (704)542-1450. **E-mail:** info@adamsliterary.com. **Website:** www.adamsliterary.com. **Contact:** Tracey Adams, Josh Adams. Adams Literary is a full-service literary agency exclusively representing children's and young adult authors and artists. Estab. 2004. Member of AAR. Other memberships include SCBWI and WNBA.

MEMBER AGENTS Tracey Adams, Josh Adams, Lorin Oberweger.

REPRESENTS Considers these fiction areas: middle grade, picture books, young adult.

Represents "the finest children's book and young adult authors and artists."

HOW TO CONTACT Submit through online form on website only. Send e-mail if that is not operating correctly. All submissions and queries should first be made through the online form on website. Will not review—and will promptly recycle—any unsolicited submissions or queries received by mail. Before submitting work for consideration, review complete guidelines online, as the agency sometimes shuts off to new submissions. Accepts simultaneous submissions. Responds in 6 weeks if interested. "While we have an established client list, we do seek new talent—and we accept submissions from both published and aspiring authors and artists."

TERMS Agent receives 15% commission on domestic sales; 20% on foreign sales. Offers written contract.

RECENT SALES *The Cruelty*, by Scott Bergstrom (Feiwel & Friends); *The Little Fire Truck*, by Margery Cuyler (Christy Ottaviano); *Unearthed*, by Amie Kaufman and Meagan Spooner (Disney-Hyperion); *A Handful of Stars*, by Cynthia Lord (Scholastic); *Under Their Skin*, by Margaret Peterson Haddix (Simon & Schuster); *The Secret Horses of Briar Hill*, by Megan Shepherd (Delacorte); *The Secret Subway*, by Shana Corey (Schwartz & Wade); *Impyrium*, by Henry Neff (HarperCollins).

TIPS "Guidelines are posted (and frequently updated) on our website."

BRET ADAMS LTD. AGENCY

Bret Adams, Ltd., 448 W. 44th St., New York NY 10036. (212)765-5630. **Fax:** (212)265-2212. **Website:** bretadamsltd.net. A full service boutique theatrical agency representing playwrights, directors, and designers. Member of AAR.

MEMBER AGENTS Bruce Ostler; Mark Orsini; Alexis Williams.

REPRESENTS Theatrical stage play, stage plays. **Considers these script areas:** stage plays, theatrical stage play.

- Handles theatre projects. No books. Cannot accept unsolicited material.

HOW TO CONTACT Use the online submission form. Because of this agency's submission policy and interests, it's best to approach with a professional recommendation from a client. Accepts simultaneous submissions.

THE AHEARN AGENCY, INC.

2021 Pine St., New Orleans LA 70118. (504)861-8395. **Fax:** (504)866-6434. **E-mail:** pahearn@aol.com. **Website:** www.ahearnagency.com. **Contact:** Pamela G. Ahearn. Estab. 1992. Other memberships include MWA, RWA, ITW. Represents 30 clients.

- Prior to opening her agency, Ms. Ahearn was an agent for 8 years and an editor with Bantam Books.

REPRESENTS Novels. **Considers these fiction areas:** crime, detective, romance, suspense, thriller.

- Handles general adult fiction, specializing in women's fiction and suspense. Does not deal with any nonfiction, poetry, juvenile material or science fiction.

HOW TO CONTACT Query with SASE or via e-mail. Please send a one-page query letter stating the type of book you're writing, word length, where you feel your book fits into the current market, and any writing credentials you may possess. Please do not send ms pages or synopses if they haven't been previously requested. If you're querying via e-mail, send no attachments unless requested. Accepts simultaneous submissions. Responds in 2 months on submissions, 4 months on queries. Obtains most new clients through recommendations from others, solicitations, conferences.

TERMS Agent receives 15% commission on domestic sales; 20% commission on foreign sales. Offers written contract, binding for 1 year; renewable by mutual consent.

RECENT SALES *Paper Ghosts*, by Julia Heaberlin; *The Secret of Flirting*, by Sabrina Jeffries; *Mister Tender's Girl*, by Carter Wilson; *Married at Midnight*, by Gerri Russell; *The Ripper's Shadow*, by Laura Joh Rowland; *The Husband Hunter's Guide to London*, by Kate Moore; *Just a Breath Away*, by Carlene Thompson.

WRITERS CONFERENCES Romance Writers of America, Thrillerfest, Bouchercon.

TIPS "Be professional! Always send in exactly what an agent/editor asks for—no more, no less. Keep query letters brief and to the point, giving your writing credentials and a very brief summary of your book. If 1 agent rejects you, keep trying—there are a lot of us out there!"

AITKEN ALEXANDER ASSOCIATES

291 Gray's Inn Rd., Kings Cross, London WC1X 8QJ United Kingdom. (020)7373-8672. **Fax:** (020)7373-6002. **E-mail:** reception@aitkenalexander.co.uk. **E-mail:** submissions@aitkenalexander.co.uk. **Website:** www.aitkenalexander.co.uk. Estab. 1976.

MEMBER AGENTS Gillon Aitken; Clare Alexander (literary, commercial, memoir, narrative nonfiction, history); Matthew Hamilton (literary fiction, suspense, music, politics, and sports); Gillie Russell (middle grade, young adult); Mary Pachnos; Anthony Sheil; Lucy Luck (quality fiction and nonfiction); Lesley Thorne; Matias Lopez Portillo; Shruti Debi; Leah Middleton.

REPRESENTS Nonfiction, novels. **Considers these nonfiction areas:** creative nonfiction, memoirs, music, politics, sports. **Considers these fiction areas:** commercial, literary, mainstream, middle grade, suspense, thriller, young adult.

- "We specialize in literary fiction and nonfiction." Does not represent illustrated children's books, poetry, or screenplays.

HOW TO CONTACT "If you would like to submit your work to us, please e-mail your covering letter with a short synopsis and the first 30 pages (as a Word document) to submissions@aitkenalexander.co.uk indicating if there is a specific agent who you would like to consider your work. Although every effort is made to respond to submissions, if we have not responded within three months please assume that your work is not right for the agency's list. Please note that the Indian Office does not accept unsolicited submissions." Accepts simultaneous submissions. Obtains most new clients through recommendations from others, solicitations.

RECENT SALES *A Country Row, A Tree*, by Jo Baker (Knopf); *Noonday*, by Pat Barker (Doubleday); *Beatlebone*, by Kevin Barry (Doubleday); *Spill Simmer Falter Wither*, by Sara Baume (Houghton Mifflin).

ALIVE LITERARY AGENCY

7680 Goddard St., Suite 200, Colorado Springs CO 80920. (719)260-7080. **Fax:** (719)260-8223. **E-mail:** info@aliveliterary.com. **E-mail:** submissions@aliveliterary.com. **Website:** www.aliveliterary.com. **Contact:** Rick Christian. Alive is the largest, most influential literary agency for inspirational content and authors. Estab. 1989. Member of AAR. Other memberships include Authors Guild.

MEMBER AGENTS Rick Christian president (blockbusters, bestsellers); Andrea Heinecke (thoughtful/inspirational nonfiction, women's fiction/nonfiction, popular/commercial nonfiction & fiction); Bryan Norman (popular nonfiction, biography/memoir/autobiography, spiritual growth, inspirational, literary); Lisa Jackson (popular nonfiction, biography/memoir/autobiography, spiritual growth, inspirational, literary, women's nonfiction).

REPRESENTS Nonfiction, fiction, novels, short story collections, novellas. **Considers these nonfiction areas:** autobiography, biography, business, child guidance, economics, health, how-to, humor, inspirational, memoirs, parenting, popular culture, politics, religious, self-help, women's issues, young adult. **Considers these fiction areas:** adventure, contemporary issues, family saga, historical, humor, inspirational, literary, mainstream, mystery, religious, romance, satire, sports, suspense, thriller, young adult.

This agency specializes in inspirational fiction, Christian living, how-to, and commercial nonfiction. Actively seeking inspirational, literary and mainstream fiction, inspirational nonfiction, and work from authors with established track records and platforms. Does not want to receive poetry, scripts, or dark themes.

HOW TO CONTACT "Because all our agents have full client loads, they are only considering queries from authors referred by clients and close contacts. Please refer to our guidelines at http://aliveliterary.com/submissions. Authors referred by an Alive client or close contact are invited to send proposals to submissions@aliveliterary.com." Your submission should include a referral (name of referring Alive client or close contact in the e-mail subject line. In the e-mail, please describe your personal or professional connection to the referring individual), a brief author biography (including recent speaking engagements, media appearances, social media platform statistics, and sales histories of your books), a synopsis of the work for which you are seeking agency representation (including the target audience, sales and marketing hooks, and comparable titles on the market), and the first 3 chapters of your manuscript. Alive will respond to queries meeting the above guidelines within 8-10 weeks.

TERMS Agent receives 15% commission on domestic sales. Offers written contract; two-month notice must be given to terminate contract.

TIPS Rewrite and polish until the words on the page shine. Endorsements, a solid platform, and great connections may help, provided you can write with power and passion. Hone your craft by networking with publishing professionals, joining critique groups, and attending writers' conferences.

AMBASSADOR LITERARY AGENCY

P.O. Box 50358, Nashville TN 37205. (615)370-4700. **E-mail:** info@ambassadoragency.com. **Website:** www.ambassadorspeakers.com/acp/index.aspx. **Contact:** Wes Yoder. Represents 25-30 clients.

Prior to becoming an agent, Mr. Yoder founded a music artist agency in 1973; he established a speakers bureau division of the company in 1984.

REPRESENTS Nonfiction, novels. **Considers these nonfiction areas:** inspirational, religious, spirituality. **Considers these fiction areas:** contemporary issues, religious.

"Ambassador's Literary department represents a select list of best-selling authors and writers who are published by the leading religious and general market publishers in the United States and Europe."

HOW TO CONTACT Authors should e-mail a short description of their ms with a request to submit their work for review. Official submission guidelines will be sent if we agree to review a ms. Direct all inquiries and submissions to info@ambassadoragency.com. Accepts simultaneous submissions.

BETSY AMSTER LITERARY ENTERPRISES

607 Foothill Blvd. #1061, La Canada Flintridge CA 91012. **E-mail:** b.amster.assistant@gmail.com (for adult titles); b.amster.kidsbooks@gmail.com (for children's and young adult). **Website:** www.amsterlit.com; www.cummingskidlit.com. **Contact:** Betsy Amster (adult); Mary Cummings (children's and young

adult). Estab. 1992. Member of AAR. Represents more than 75 clients.

Prior to opening her agency, Ms. Amster was an editor at Pantheon and Vintage for 10 years and served as editorial director for the Globe Pequot Press for 2 years. Prior to joining the agency, Mary Cummings served as education director at the Loft Literary Center in Minneapolis for 14 years, overseeing classes, workshops, and conferences. She curated the annual Festival of Children's Literature and selected judges for the McKnight Award in Children's Literature.

REPRESENTS Nonfiction, novels, juvenile books. **Considers these nonfiction areas:** autobiography, biography, business, child guidance, cooking, creative nonfiction, cultural interests, decorating, design, foods, gardening, health, history, horticulture, how-to, interior design, investigative, medicine, memoirs, money, multicultural, parenting, popular culture, psychology, science, self-help, sociology, travel, women's issues, young adult. **Considers these fiction areas:** crime, detective, family saga, juvenile, literary, middle grade, multicultural, mystery, picture books, police, suspense, thriller, women's, young adult.

"Betsy Amster is actively seeking strong narrative nonfiction, particularly by journalists; outstanding literary fiction; witty, intelligent commercial women's fiction; character-driven mysteries and thrillers that open new worlds to us; high-profile self-help, psychology, and health, preferably research-based; and cookbooks and food narratives by West Coast–based chefs and food writers with an original viewpoint and national exposure. Does not want to receive poetry, romances, western, science fiction, action/adventure, screenplays, fantasy, techno-thrillers, spy capers, apocalyptic scenarios, or political or religious arguments. Mary Cummings is actively seeking great read-aloud picture books and middle-grade novels with strong story arcs, a spunky central character, and warmth, humor, or quirky charm as well as picture-book biographies and lyrically written children's nonfiction on science, nature, mindfulness, and social awareness."

HOW TO CONTACT "For adult fiction or memoirs, please embed the first 3 pages in the body of your e-mail. For nonfiction, please embed the overview of your proposal. For children's picture books, please embed the entire text in the body of your e-mail. For longer middle-grade and YA fiction and nonfiction, please embed the first 3 pages." Accepts simultaneous submissions. Responds in 1 month to queries; 2 months to mss. Obtains most new clients through recommendations from others, solicitations, and conferences.

TERMS Agent receives 15% commission on domestic sales; 20% commission on foreign sales. Offers written contract, binding for 1 year; three-month notice must be given to terminate contract. Charges for photocopying, postage, messengers, galleys/books used in submissions to foreign and film agents and to magazines for first serial rights. (Please note that it is rare to incur much in the way of expenses now that most submissions are made by e-mail.)

RECENT SALES **Betsy Amster**: *Kachka: A Return to Russian Cooking*, by Bonnie Frumkin Morales with Deena Prichep (Flatiron); *It Takes One to Tango*, by Winifred Reilly (Touchstone); *Good Trouble*, by Christopher Noxon (Abrams); *The Lost Gutenberg*, by Margaret Leslie Davis (Avery). **Mary Cummings**: *Where is My Balloon?*, by Ariel Bernstein (Paula Wiseman Books/Simon & Schuster); *When Numbers Met Letters*, by Lois Barr (Holiday House); *Do Not Go in There!*, by Ariel Horn (Macmillan/Imprint); *Bike and Trike*, by Elizabeth Verdick (Paula Wiseman Books/Simon & Schuster).

THE ANDERSON LITERARY AGENCY

(917)363-6829. **E-mail:** giles@andersonliteraryagency.com. **Website:** www.andersonliteraryagency.com. **Contact:** Giles Anderson. Estab. 2000.

Owner and founder Giles Anderson started the agency in 2000 after working several years at The Waxman Literary Agency, Zephyr Press, and The Carnegie Council for Ethics in International Affairs.

MEMBER AGENTS Giles Anderson.

"Over time my interests have increasingly turned to books that help us understand people, ideas and the possibility of change. From an examination of the religious beliefs of a Founder to the science of motivation, I'm looking for books that surprise, inform and inspire."

HOW TO CONTACT Send query via e-mail. Accepts simultaneous submissions.

RECENT SALES *Mindset: The New Psychology of Sucess*, by Carol S. Dweck, Ph.D.; *9 Things Successful People Do Differently*, by Heidi Grant Halverson; *Reality-Based Leadership*, by CY Wakeman.

APONTE LITERARY AGENCY

E-mail: agents@aponteliterary.com. **Website:** aponteliterary.com. **Contact:** Natalia Aponte. Member of AAR. Signatory of WGA.

MEMBER AGENTS Natalia Aponte (any genre of mainstream fiction and nonfiction, but she is especially seeking women's novels, historical novels, supernatural and paranormal fiction, fantasy novels, political and science thrillers); Victoria Lea (any category, especially interested in women's fiction, science fiction and speculative fiction).

REPRESENTS Novels. **Considers these fiction areas:** fantasy, historical, paranormal, science fiction, supernatural, thriller, women's.

Actively seeking women's novels, historical novels, supernatural and paranormal fiction, fantasy novels, political and science thrillers, science fiction and speculative fiction. In nonfiction, will look at any genre with commercial potential.

HOW TO CONTACT E-query. Accepts simultaneous submissions. Responds in 6 weeks if interested.

RECENT SALES *The Nightingale Bones*, by Ariel Swan; *An Irish Doctor in Peace and At War*, by Patrick Taylor; *Siren's Treasure*, by Debbie Herbert.

⊘ ARCADIA

31 Lake Place N., Danbury CT 06810. **E-mail:** arcadialit@gmail.com. **Contact:** Victoria Gould Pryor. Member of AAR.

REPRESENTS Nonfiction. **Considers these nonfiction areas:** biography, current affairs, health, history, medicine, popular culture, psychology, science.

We're not seeking new clients at this time.

HOW TO CONTACT No unsolicited submissions.

⊘ THE AUGUST AGENCY, LLC

Website: www.augustagency.com. **Contact:** Cricket Freemain, Jeffery McGraw. Estab. 2004. Represents 25-40 clients.

Before opening The August Agency, Ms. Freeman was a freelance writer, magazine editor and independent literary agent. Mr. McGraw worked as an editor for HarperCollins and publicity manager for Abrams.

MEMBER AGENTS Jeffery McGraw, Cricket Freeman.

REPRESENTS Novels. **Considers these nonfiction areas:** art, biography, business, current affairs, history, memoirs, popular culture, politics, sociology, true crime, Creative nonfiction, narrative nonfiction, academic works,. **Considers these fiction areas:** crime, mainstream.

"At this time, we are not accepting the following types of submissions:self-published works, screen plays, children's books, genre fiction, romance, horror, westerns, fantasy, science fiction, poetry, short story collections."

HOW TO CONTACT **Currently closed to submissions.**

THE AXELROD AGENCY

55 Main St., P.O. Box 357, Chatham NY 12037. (518)392-2100. **E-mail:** steve@axelrodagency.com. **Website:** www.axelrodagency.com. **Contact:** Steven Axelrod. Member of AAR. Represents 15-20 clients.

Prior to becoming an agent, Mr. Axelrod was a book club editor.

MEMBER AGENTS Steven Axelrod, representation; Lori Antonson, subsidiary rights.

REPRESENTS Novels. **Considers these fiction areas:** crime, mystery, new adult, romance, women's.

This agency specializes in women's fiction and romance.

HOW TO CONTACT Query via e-mail. Accepts simultaneous submissions. Obtains most new clients through recommendations from others.

TERMS Agent receives 15% commission on domestic sales; 20% commission on foreign sales. No written contract.

WRITERS CONFERENCES RWA National Conference.

AZANTIAN LITERARY AGENCY

E-mail: queries@azantianlitagency.com. **Website:** www.azantianlitagency.com. **Contact:** Jennifer Azantian. Estab. 2014.

Prior to establishing ALA, Ms. Azantian was with the Sandra Dijkstra Literary Agency.

REPRESENTS Novels. **Considers these fiction areas:** fantasy, horror, middle grade, science fiction, urban fantasy, young adult.

Stories that explore meaningful human interactions against fantastic backdrops, underrepresented voices, obscure retold fairy tales, quirky middle grade, modernized mythologies, psychological horror, literary science fiction, historical fantasy, magical realism, internally consistent epic fantasy, and spooky stories for younger readers.

HOW TO CONTACT During open submission windows only: send your query letter, 1-2 page synopsis, and first 10-15 pages all pasted in an e-mail (no attachments). Please note in the e-mail subject line if your work was requested at a conference, is an exclusive submission, or was referred by a current client. Accepts simultaneous submissions. Responds within 6 weeks. Please check the submissions page of the agency website before submitting to make sure Ms. Azantian is currently open to queries.

BARONE LITERARY AGENCY

385 North St., Batavia OH 45103. (513)732-6740. **Fax:** (513)297-7208. **E-mail:** baroneliteraryagency@roadrunner.com. **Website:** www.baroneliteraryagency.com. **Contact:** Denise Barone. Represents Cathy Bennett, Rebekah Purdy, Michele Barrow-Belisle, Angharad Jones, Denise Gwen, Laurie Albano, Robert E. Hoxie, Rhonda Vincent, Anna Snow, Jennifer Petersen Fraser, and Yvette Geer. Estab. 2010. Member of AAR. Signatory of WGA. Member of RWA. Represents 11 clients.

REPRESENTS Nonfiction, fiction, novels. **Considers these nonfiction areas:** memoirs, theater, young adult. **Considers these fiction areas:** action, adventure, cartoon, comic books, commercial, confession, contemporary issues, crime, detective, erotica, ethnic, experimental, family saga, fantasy, feminist, frontier, gay, glitz, hi-lo, historical, horror, humor, inspirational, juvenile, lesbian, literary, mainstream, metaphysical, military, multicultural, multimedia, mystery, new adult, New Age, occult, paranormal, plays, police, psychic, regional, religious, romance, satire, science fiction, spiritual, sports, supernatural, suspense, thriller, translation, urban fantasy, war, westerns, women's, young adult.

Actively seeking adult contemporary romance. Does not want textbooks.

HOW TO CONTACT "Please send a query letter via e-mail. If I like your query letter, I will ask for the first 3 chapters and a synopsis as attachments." Accepts simultaneous submissions. "I make every effort to respond within 4 months." Obtains new clients by queries/submissions via e-mail only.

TERMS Agency receives 15% commission on domestic sales; 20% on foreign sales. Offers written contract.

RECENT SALES *The Beekeeper*, by Robert E. Hoxie (Six Gun Pictures); *All The Glittering Bones*, by Anna Snow (Entangled Publishing); *Devon's Choice*, by Cathy Bennett (Clean Reads); *Molly's Folly*, by Denise Gwen (Clean Reads); *In Deep*, by Laurie Albano (Solstice Publishing).

WRITERS CONFERENCES Annual Conference of Romance Writers of America, Orlando, Florida, 2017; Lori Foster's Readers and Authors' Get-Together, West Chester, Ohio; A Weekend with the Authors, Nashville, Tennessee; Willamette Writers' Conference, Portland, Oregon.

TIPS "The best writing advice I ever got came from a fellow writer, who wrote, 'Learn how to edit yourself,' when signing her book to me."

BAROR INTERNATIONAL, INC.

P.O. Box 868, Armonk NY 10504. **E-mail:** heather@barorint.com. **Website:** www.barorint.com. **Contact:** Danny Baror; Heather Baror-Shapiro. Represents 300 clients.

MEMBER AGENTS Danny Baror; Heather Baror-Shapiro.

REPRESENTS Fiction. **Considers these fiction areas:** fantasy, literary, science fiction, young adult, adult fiction, commerical.

This agency represents authors and publishers in the international market. Currently representing commercial fiction, literary titles, science fiction, young adult, and more.

HOW TO CONTACT Submit by e-mail or mail (with SASE); include a cover letter and a few sample chapters Accepts simultaneous submissions.

LORELLA BELLI LITERARY AGENCY (LBLA)

54 Hartford House, 35 Tavistock Crescent, Notting Hill, London England W11 1AY United Kingdom. (44)(207)727-8547. **Fax:** (44)(870)787-4194. **E-mail:** info@lorellabelliagency.com. **Website:** www.lorellabelliagency.com. **Contact:** Lorella Belli. Estab. 2002. Membership includes AAA (this is the British Association of Authors Agents), Crime Writers' Association, Romantic Novelists Association, The Book Society, Women in Publishing.

REPRESENTS Nonfiction, fiction, novels, juvenile books. **Considers these nonfiction areas:** autobiography, biography, cooking, current affairs, diet/nutrition, history, memoirs, multicultural, popular culture, psychology, science, self-help, sports, translation, travel, true crime, women's issues, young adult. **Considers these fiction areas:** action, adventure, commercial, contemporary issues, crime, detective, family saga, feminist, historical, inspirational, literary, mainstream, multicultural, mystery, new adult, police, romance, suspense, thriller, women's, young adult.

This agency handles adult fiction, adult nonfiction, and YA. Does not want to receive children's picture books, fantasy, science fiction, screenplays, short stories, poetry, academic, or specialist books.

HOW TO CONTACT E-query. Do not send a proposal or ms before it's requested. Please send an initial brief query via e-mail. Accepts simultaneous submissions.

TERMS Agent receives 15% commission on domestic sales; 20% commission on foreign sales.

RECENT SALES Follow us on Twitter and Facebook to see all sales.

THE BENT AGENCY

19 W. 21st St., #201, New York NY 10010. **E-mail:** info@thebentagency.com. **E-mail:** Please see website. **Website:** www.thebentagency.com. **Contact:** Jenny Bent. Estab. 2009. Member of AAR.

Prior to forming her own agency, Ms. Bent was an agent and vice president at Trident Media Group.

MEMBER AGENTS Jenny Bent (adult fiction, including women's fiction, romance, and crime/suspense; she particularly likes novels with magical or fantasy elements that fall outside of genre fiction; young adult and middle-grade fiction; memoir; humor); Nicola Barr (literary and commercial fiction for adults and children, and nonfiction in the areas of sports, popular science, popular culture, and social and cultural history); Molly Ker Hawn (young adult and middle-grade books, including contemporary, historical, fantasy, science fiction, thrillers, and mystery); Gemma Cooper (all ages of children's and young adult books, including picture books; likes historical, contemporary, thrillers, mystery, humor, and science fiction); Louise Fury (children's fiction: picture books, literary middle-grade, and all young adult; adult fiction: speculative fiction, suspense/thriller, commercial fiction, and all subgenres of romance including erotic; nonfiction: cookbooks and pop culture); Sarah Manning (commercial and accessible literary adult fiction and nonfiction in the area of memoir, lifestyle, and narrative nonfiction); Beth Phelan (young adult, thrillers, suspense and mystery, romance and women's fiction, literary and general fiction, cookbooks, lifestyle, and pets/animals); Victoria Cappello (commercial and literary adult fiction as well as narrative nonfiction); Heather Flaherty (young adult and middle-grade fiction: all genres; select adult fiction: upmarket fiction, women's fiction, and female-centric thrillers; select nonfiction: pop culture, humorous, and social media–based projects, as well as teen memoir).

REPRESENTS Nonfiction, novels, short story collections, juvenile books. **Considers these nonfiction areas:** animals, cooking, creative nonfiction, foods, juvenile nonfiction, popular culture, women's issues, young adult. **Considers these fiction areas:** adventure, commercial, crime, erotica, fantasy, feminist, historical, horror, humor, juvenile, literary, mainstream, middle grade, multicultural, mystery, new adult, picture books, romance, short story collections, suspense, thriller, women's, young adult.

HOW TO CONTACT "Tell us briefly who you are, what your book is, and why you're the one to write it. Then include the first 10 pages of your material in the body of your e-mail. We respond to all queries; please resend your query if you haven't had a response within 4 weeks." Accepts simultaneous submissions.

RECENT SALES *Caraval*, by Stephanie Garber (Flatiron); *Rebel of the Sands*, by Alwyn Hamilton (Viking Children's/Penguin BFYR); *The Square Root of Summer*, by Harriet Reuter Hapgood (Roaring Brook/Macmillan); *Dirty Money*, by Lisa Renee Jones (Simon & Schuster); *True North*, by Liora Blake (Pocket Star).

BIDNICK & COMPANY

E-mail: bidnick@comcast.net. **Website:** www.publishersmarketplace.com/members/bidnick. **Contact:** Carole Bidnick. Estab. 1997.

Prior to becoming an agent, Ms. Bidnick was a founding member of Collins Publishers and vice president of HarperCollins, San Francisco.

REPRESENTS Nonfiction. **Considers these nonfiction areas:** cooking.

- This agency specializes in cookbooks and commercial nonfiction.

HOW TO CONTACT Send queries via e-mail only. Accepts simultaneous submissions.

RECENT SALES *Burma Superstar Cookbook*, by Desmond Tan and Kate Leahy (Ten Speed); *The Healthiest Diet on the Planet*, by Dr. John McDougall and Mary McDougall (Harper One); *The Road to Sparta*, by Dean Karnazes (Rodale); *The Bold Dry Garden*, by Johanna Silver (Timber Press); *Foreign Cinema Cookbook*, by Gayle Pirie and John Clark (Abrams); *Crave*, by Christine O'Brien (St. Martin's Press) The Bloated Belly Whisperer by Tamara Duker Freuman (St. Martin's Press.)

VICKY BIJUR LITERARY AGENCY

27 W. 20th St., Suite 1003, New York NY 10011. **E-mail:** queries@vickybijuragency.com. **Website:** www.vickybijuragency.com. Estab. 1988. Member of AAR.

- Vicky Bijur worked at Oxford University Press and with the Charlotte Sheedy Literary Agency. Books she represents have appeared on *the New York Times Bestseller List*, in the *New York Times* Notable Books of the Year, *Los Angeles Times* Best Fiction of the Year, *Washington Post* Book World Rave Reviews of the Year.

MEMBER AGENTS Vicky Bijur; Alexandra Franklin.

REPRESENTS Nonfiction, novels. **Considers these nonfiction areas:** memoirs. **Considers these fiction areas:** commercial, literary, mystery, new adult, thriller, women's, young adult, Campus novels, coming-of-age.

- "We are not the right agency for screenplays, picture books, poetry, self-help, science fiction, fantasy, horror, or romance."

HOW TO CONTACT "Please send a query letter of no more than 3 paragraphs on what makes your book special and unique, a very brief synopsis, its length and genre, and your biographical information, along with the first 10 pages of your manuscript. Please let us know in your query letter if it is a multiple submission, and kindly keep us informed of other agents' interest and offers of representation. If sending electronically, paste the pages in an e-mail as we don't open attachments from unfamiliar senders. If sending by hard copy, please include an SASE for our response. If you want your material returned, include an SASE large enough to contain pages and enough postage to send back to you." Accepts simultaneous submissions. "We generally respond to all queries within 8 weeks of receipt."

RECENT SALES *That Darkness*, by Lisa Black; *Long Upon the Land*, by Margaret Maron; *Daughter of Ashes*, by Marcia Talley.

DAVID BLACK LITERARY AGENCY

335 Adams St., Suite 2707, Brooklyn NY 11201. (718)-852-5500. **Fax:** (718)852-5539. **Website:** www.davidblackagency.com. **Contact:** David Black, owner. Estab. 1989. Member of AAR. Represents 150 clients.

MEMBER AGENTS David Black; Jenny Herrera; Gary Morris; Joy E. Tutela (narrative nonfiction, memoir, history, politics, self-help, investment, business, science, women's issues, GLBT issues, parenting, health and fitness, humor, craft, cooking and wine, lifestyle and entertainment, commercial fiction, literary fiction, MG, YA); Susan Raihofer (commercial fiction and nonfiction, memoir, pop culture, music, inspirational, thrillers, literary fiction); Sarah Smith (memoir, biography, food, music, narrative history, social studies, literary fiction).

REPRESENTS Nonfiction, novels. **Considers these nonfiction areas:** biography, business, cooking, crafts, gay/lesbian, health, history, humor, inspirational, memoirs, music, parenting, popular culture, politics, science, self-help, sociology, sports, women's issues. **Considers these fiction areas:** commercial, literary, middle grade, thriller, young adult.

HOW TO CONTACT "To query an individual agent, please follow the specific query guidelines outlined in the agent's profile on our website. Not all agents are currently accepting unsolicited queries. To query the agency, please send a 1-2 page query letter describing your book, and include information about any previously published works, your audience, and your platform." Do not e-mail your query unless an agent specifically asks for an e-mail. Accepts simultaneous submissions. Responds in 2 months to queries.

RECENT SALES Some of the agency's best-selling authors include: Erik Larson, Stuart Scott, Jeff Hobbs, Mitch Albom, Gregg Olsen, Jim Abbott, and John Bacon.

JUDY BOALS, INC.

262 W. 38th St., #1207, New York NY 10018. (212)500-1424. **Fax:** (212)500-1426. **Website:** www.judyboals.com. **Contact:** Judy Boals. "Serving and supporting

the artistry of our clients with a positive and holistic business practice."

HOW TO CONTACT Query by referral or invitation only. Accepts simultaneous submissions.

BOND LITERARY AGENCY

4340 E. Kentucky Ave., Suite 471, Denver CO 80246. (303)781-9305. **E-mail:** queries@bondliteraryagency.com. **Website:** www.bondliteraryagency.com. **Contact:** Sandra Bond. The agency is small, with a select list of writers. Represents adult and young adult fiction, both literary and commercial, including mysteries and women's fiction. Nonfiction interests include narrative, history, science and business.

Prior to her current position, Ms. Bond worked with agent Jody Rein and was the program administrator at the University of Denver's Publishing Institute.

MEMBER AGENTS Sandra Bond, agent (fiction: adult commercial and literary, mystery/thriller/suspense, women's, historical, young adult; nonfiction: narrative, history, science, business);
Becky LeJeune, associate agent (fiction: horror, mystery/thriller/suspense, science fiction/fantasy, historical, general fiction, young adult).

REPRESENTS Nonfiction, fiction, novels, juvenile books. **Considers these nonfiction areas:** business, history, juvenile nonfiction, popular culture, science, young adult. **Considers these fiction areas:** commercial, crime, detective, family saga, fantasy, historical, horror, juvenile, literary, mainstream, middle grade, multicultural, mystery, police, science fiction, suspense, thriller, urban fantasy, women's, young adult.

Agency does not represent romance, poetry, young reader chapter books, children's picture books, or screenplays.

HOW TO CONTACT Please submit query by e-mail (absolutely no attachments unless requested). No unsolicited mss. "They will let you know if they are interested in seeing more material. No phone calls, please." Accepts simultaneous submissions.

TERMS No Fees

RECENT SALES *The Past is Never*, by Tiffany Quay Tyson; *Cold Case: Billy the Kid*, by W.C. Jameson; *Women in Film: The Truth and the Timeline*, by Jill S. Tietjen and Barbara Bridges; Books 7 & 8 in the Hiro Hattori Mystery Series, by Susan Spann.

BOOK CENTS LITERARY AGENCY, LLC

121 Black Rock Turnpike, Suite #499, Redding Ridge CT 06876. **E-mail:** cw@bookcentsliteraryagency.com. **Website:** www.bookcentsliteraryagency.com. **Contact:** Christine Witthohn. "It is our goal not only to assist our clients in selling their creative work(s), but to also assist them with growing their writing careers and helping them reach their targeted audiences. We will make it our mission to work hard and be diligent, and to keep the lines of communication open with the authors we represent. We are not an agency whose main interest is in acquiring large numbers of clients. Rather, we are looking to find quality authors with fresh and creative voices who are not afraid to write what they love. We aggressively sell and license our clients' titles in all formats in both domestic and foreign markets. We concentrate on print, digital, audio, dramatic, large print, serial, multimedia, and graphic, as well as other rights and licenses. We also collaborate with our authors on marketing and promotional ideas, assist in implementing branding strategies, and help our authors reach their targeted audience(s)." Estab. 2005. Member of AAR. RWA, MWA, SinC, KOD.

REPRESENTS Novels. **Considers these nonfiction areas:** cooking, gardening, travel, women's issues. **Considers these fiction areas:** commercial, mainstream, multicultural, mystery, paranormal, romance, suspense, thriller, urban fantasy, women's, young adult.

Actively seeking upmarket fiction, commercial fiction (particularly if it has crossover appeal), women's fiction (emotional and layered), romance (single title or category), mainstream mystery/suspense, thrillers (particularly psychological), and young adult. For a detailed list of what this agency is currently searching for, visit the website. Does not want to receive third party submissions, previously published titles, short stories/novellas, erotica, inspirational, historical, science fiction/fantasy, horror/pulp/slasher thrillers, middle-grade, children's picture books, poetry, or screenplays. Does not want stories with priests/nuns, religion, abuse of children/animals/elderly, rape, or serial killers.

HOW TO CONTACT Submit via form on website. Does not accept mail or e-mail submissions.

TIPS Sponsors the International Women's Fiction Festival in Matera, Italy. See www.womensfictionfestival.com for more information. Ms. Witthohn is also the U.S. rights and licensing agent for leading French publisher Bragelonne, German publisher Egmont, and Spanish publisher Edebe.

BOOKENDS LITERARY AGENCY

Website: www.bookendsliterary.com. **Contact:** Jessica Faust, Kim Lionetti, Jessica Alvarez, Moe Ferrara, Tracy Marchini, Rachel Brooks, Natascha Morris, Beth Campbell, James McGowan. "Since opening its doors in 1999, BookEnds Literary Agency has never strayed from our original goal: achieving dreams and doing what we love. Representing fiction and nonfiction for adults and children alike, BookEnds agents continue to live their dreams while helping authors achieve theirs. First opened as a book packaging company, we were originally looking to take our own fresh and fun ideas and find just the right people to create the books publishers and readers were looking for. Over time, we missed working on fiction and seeing what could come from an author's imagination as well as an author's platform. So not 2 years after opening its doors, BookEnds changed its literary status to agency." Estab. 1999. Member of AAR. RWA, MWA, SCBWI, SFWA. Represents 50+ clients.

MEMBER AGENTS Jessica Faust (women's fiction, mysteries, thrillers, suspense); Kim Lionetti (romance, women's fiction, young adult); Jessica Alvarez (romance, women's fiction, mystery, suspense, thrillers, and nonfiction); Beth Campbell (fantasy, science fiction, young adult, suspense, romantic suspense, and mystery); Moe Ferrara (middle-grade, young adult, and adult: romance, science fiction, fantasy, horror); Tracy Marchini (picture book, middle-grade, and young adult: fiction and nonfiction); Rachel Brooks (young adult, romance, women's fiction, cozy mysteries); Natascha Morris (young adult, middle grade, picture book).

REPRESENTS Nonfiction, novels, juvenile books. **Considers these nonfiction areas:** art, business, creative nonfiction, ethnic, how-to, inspirational, juvenile nonfiction, money, self-help, women's issues, young adult, picture book, middle grade. **Considers these fiction areas:** adventure, comic books, crime, detective, erotica, fantasy, gay, historical, horror, juvenile, lesbian, mainstream, middle grade, multicultural, mystery, paranormal, picture books, police, romance, science fiction, supernatural, suspense, thriller, urban fantasy, women's, young adult.

"BookEnds is currently accepting queries from published and unpublished writers in the areas of romance, mystery, suspense, science fiction and fantasy, horror, women's fiction, picture books, middle-grade, and young adult. In nonfiction we represent titles in the following areas: current affairs, reference, business and career, parenting, pop culture, coloring books, general nonfiction, and nonfiction for children and teens." BookEnds does not represent short fiction, poetry, screenplays, or techno-thrillers.

HOW TO CONTACT Visit website for the most up-to-date guidelines and current preferences. BookEnds agents accept all submissions through their personal Query Manager forms. These forms are accessible on the agency website under Submissions. Accepts simultaneous submissions. "Our response time goals are 6 weeks for queries and 12 weeks on requested partials and fulls."

THE BOOK GROUP

20 W. 20th St., Suite 601, New York NY 10011. (212)803-3360. **E-mail:** submissions@thebookgroup.com. **Website:** www.thebookgroup.com. The Book Group is a full service literary agency located in the heart of Manhattan. Launched in 2015 by publishing industry veterans. The Book Group shares a singular passion: to seek out and cultivate writers, and to serve as their champions throughout their careers. "We represent a wide range of distinguished authors, including critically acclaimed and bestselling novelists, celebrated writers of children's literature, and award-winning historians, food writers, memoirists and journalists." Estab. 2015. Member of AAR. Signatory of WGA.

MEMBER AGENTS Julie Barer; Faye Bender; Brettne Bloom (fiction: literary and commercial fiction, select young adult; nonfiction, including cookbooks, lifestyle, investigative journalism, history, biography, memoir, and psychology); Elisabeth Weed (upmarket fiction, especially plot-driven novels with a sense of place); Rebecca Stead (innovative forms, diverse voices, and open-hearted fiction for children, young adults, and adults); Dana Murphy (story-driven fiction with a strong sense of place, narrative nonfiction/essays with a pop-culture lean, and YA with an honest voice).

REPRESENTS **Considers these nonfiction areas:** biography, cooking, history, investigative, memoirs, psychology. **Considers these fiction areas:** commercial, literary, mainstream, women's, young adult.

Please do not send poetry or screenplays.

HOW TO CONTACT Send a query letter and 10 sample pages to submissions@thebookgroup.com, with the first and last name of the agent you are querying in the subject line. All material must be in the body of the e-mail, as the agents do not open attachments. "If we are interested in reading more, we will get in touch with you as soon as possible." Accepts simultaneous submissions.

RECENT SALES *This Is Not Over*, by Holly Brown; *Perfect Little World*, by Kevin Wilson; *City of Saints & Thieves*, by Natalie C. Anderson; *The Runaway Midwife*, by Patricia Harman; *Always*, by Sarah Jio; *The Young Widower's Handbook*, by Tom McAllister.

BOOKS & SUCH LITERARY MANAGEMENT

52 Mission Circle, Suite 122, PMB 170, Santa Rosa CA 95409. **E-mail:** representation@booksandsuch.com. **Website:** www.booksandsuch.com. **Contact:** Janet Kobobel Grant, Wendy Lawton, Rachel Kent, Rachelle Gardner, Cynthia Ruchti. Estab. 1996. CBA, American Christian Fiction Writers Represents 250 clients.

Prior to founding the agency, Ms. Grant was an editor for Zondervan and managing editor for Focus on the Family. Ms. Lawton was an author, sculptor, and designer of porcelain dolls and became an agent in 2005. Ms. Ruchti has written 21 books—both fiction and nonfiction—and was president of ACFW. Now she serves as ACFW's professional relations liaison (since 2011) and became an agent in 2017. Ms. Kent has worked as an agent for ten years and is a graduate of UC Davis majoring in English. Ms. Gardner worked as an editor at NavPress, at General Publishing Group in rights and marketing, and at Fox Broadcasting Company as special programming coordinator before becoming an agent in 2007.

REPRESENTS Nonfiction, fiction, novels, juvenile books. **Considers these nonfiction areas:** autobiography, biography, business, cooking, creative nonfiction, cultural interests, current affairs, foods, health, inspirational, juvenile nonfiction, memoirs, parenting, popular culture, religious, self-help, spirituality, true crime, women's issues, young adult. **Considers these fiction areas:** adventure, commercial, crime, family saga, frontier, historical, inspirational, juvenile, literary, mainstream, middle grade, mystery, religious, romance, spiritual, suspense, women's, young adult.

This agency specializes in general and inspirational fiction and nonfiction, and in the Christian booksellers market. Actively seeking well-crafted material that presents Judeo-Christian values, even if only subtly.

HOW TO CONTACT Query via e-mail only; no attachments. Accepts simultaneous submissions. Responds in 1 month to queries. "If you don't hear from us asking to see more of your writing within 30 days after you have sent your e-mail, please know that we have read and considered your submission but determined that it would not be a good fit for us." Obtains most new clients through recommendations from others, conferences.

TERMS Agent receives 15% commission on domestic sales; 20% commission on foreign sales. Offers written contract; two-month notice must be given to terminate contract. No additional charges.

RECENT SALES A full list of this agency's clients (and the awards they have won) is on the agency website.

WRITERS CONFERENCES Mount Hermon Christian Writers Conference, American Christian Fiction Writers Conference, San Francisco Writers Conference.

TIPS "Our agency highlights personal attention to individual clients that includes coaching on how to thrive in a rapidly changing publishing climate, grow a career, and get the best publishing offers possible."

BOOKSTOP LITERARY AGENCY

67 Meadow View Rd., Orinda CA 94563. (925)254-2664. **E-mail:** info@bookstopliterary.com. **Website:** www.bookstopliterary.com. Represents authors and illustrators of books for children and young adults. Estab. 1984.

REPRESENTS Nonfiction, fiction, novels, short story collections, juvenile books, poetry books. **Considers these nonfiction areas:** juvenile nonfiction, young adult. **Considers these fiction areas:** hi-lo, middle grade, picture books, plays, poetry, young adult.

"Special interest in Hispanic, Asian-American, African-American, and multicultural writers. Also seeking quirky picture books; clever adventure/mystery novels; eye-opening nonfiction; heartfelt middle-grade; unusual teen romance."

HOW TO CONTACT Send: cover letter, entire ms for picture books; first 10 pages of novels; proposal and sample chapters OK for nonfiction. E-mail submissions: Paste cover letter and first 10 pages of ms into body of e-mail, send to info@bookstopliterary.com. Send sample illustrations only if you are an illustrator. Illustrators: send postcard or link to online portfolio. Do not send original artwork. Accepts simultaneous submissions.

TERMS Agent receives 15% commission on domestic sales. Offers written contract, binding for 1 year.

⊘ GEORGES BORCHARDT, INC.

136 E. 57th St., New York NY 10022. (212)753-5785. **Website:** www.gbagency.com. Estab. 1967. Member of AAR. Represents 200+ clients.

MEMBER AGENTS Anne Borchardt, Georges Borchardt, Valerie Borchardt, Samantha Shea.

REPRESENTS Nonfiction, fiction, novels, short story collections, novellas. **Considers these nonfiction areas:** art, biography, creative nonfiction, current affairs, history, investigative, literature, memoirs, philosophy, politics, religious, science, true crime, women's issues.

This agency specializes in literary fiction and outstanding nonfiction.

HOW TO CONTACT No unsolicited submissions. Obtains most new clients through recommendations from others.

TERMS Agent receives 15% commission on domestic sales; 20% commission on foreign sales. Offers written contract.

RECENT SALES *The Relive Box and Other Stories*, by T.C. Boyle; *Nutshell*, by Ian McEwan; *What It Means When a Man Falls From the Sky*, by Lesley Nneka Arimah.

BRADFORD LITERARY AGENCY

5694 Mission Center Rd., #347, San Diego CA 92108. (619)521-1201. **E-mail:** queries@bradfordlit.com. **Website:** www.bradfordlit.com. **Contact:** Laura Bradford, Natalie Lakosil, Sarah LaPolla, Monica Odom. "The Bradford Literary Agency is a boutique agency which offers a full range of representation services to authors who are both published and pre-published. Our mission at the Bradford Literary Agency is to form true partnerships with our clients and build long-term relationships that extend from writing the first draft through the length of the author's career." Estab. 2001. Member of AAR. RWA, SCBWI, ALA Represents 130 clients.

MEMBER AGENTS Laura Bradford (romance [historical, romantic suspense, paranormal, category, contemporary, erotic], mystery, women's fiction, thrillers/suspense, middle grade & YA); Natalie Lakosil (children's literature [from picture book through teen and New Adult], romance [contemporary and historical], cozy mystery/crime, upmarket women's/general fiction and select children's nonfiction); Sarah LaPolla (YA, middle grade, literary fiction, science fiction, magical realism, dark/psychological mystery, literary horror, and upmarket contemporary fiction); Monica Odom (nonfiction by authors with demonstrable platforms in the areas of: pop culture, illustrated/graphic design, food and cooking, humor, history and social issues; narrative nonfiction, memoir, literary fiction, upmarket commercial fiction, compelling speculative fiction and magic realism, historical fiction, alternative histories, dark and edgy fiction, literary psychological thrillers, and illustrated/picture books).

REPRESENTS Nonfiction, fiction, novels, juvenile books. **Considers these nonfiction areas:** biography, cooking, creative nonfiction, cultural interests, foods, history, humor, juvenile nonfiction, memoirs, parenting, popular culture, politics, self-help, women's issues, women's studies, young adult. **Considers these fiction areas:** commercial, crime, ethnic, gay, historical, juvenile, lesbian, literary, mainstream, middle grade, multicultural, mystery, new adult, paranormal, picture books, romance, science fiction, thriller, women's, young adult.

Laura Bradford does not want to receive poetry, screenplays, short stories, westerns, horror, new age, religion, crafts, cookbooks, gift books. Natalie Lakosil does not want to receive inspirational novels, memoir, romantic suspense, adult thrillers, poetry, screenplays. Sarah LaPolla does not want to receive nonfiction, picture books, inspirational/spiritual novels, romance, or erotica. Monica Odom does not want to receive genre romance, erotica, military, poetry, or inspirational/spiritual works.

HOW TO CONTACT Accepts e-mail queries only; For submissions to Laura Bradford or Natalie Lakosil, send to queries@bradfordlit.com. For submissions to Sarah LaPolla, send to sarah@bradfordlit.com. For submissions to Monica Odom, send to Monica@bradfordlit.com. The entire submission must appear in the body of the e-mail and not as an attachment. The subject line should begin as follows: "QUERY: (the title of the ms or any short message that is important should follow)." For fiction: e-mail a query letter along with the first chapter of ms and a synopsis. Include the genre and word count in your query letter. Nonfiction: e-mail full nonfiction proposal including a query letter and a sample chapter. Accepts simultaneous submissions. Responds in 4 weeks to queries; 10 weeks to mss. Obtains most new clients through queries.

TERMS Agent receives 15% commission on domestic sales; 25% commission on foreign sales. Offers written contract. Charges for extra copies of books for foreign submissions.

RECENT SALES Sold 115 titles in the last year, including *Snowed In With Murder*, by Auralee Wallace (St. Martin's); *All the Secrets We Keep*, by Megan Hart (Montlake); *The Notorious Bargain*, by Joanna Shupe (Avon); *Allegedly*, by Tiffany Jackson (Katherine Tegen Books); *Wives of War*, by Soraya Lane (Amazon); *The Silver Gate*, by Kristin Bailey (Katherine Tegen Books); *Witchtown*, by Cory Putman Oakes (Houghton Mifflin Harcourt); *Under Her Skin*, by Adriana Anders (Sourcebooks); *The Fixer*, by HelenKay Dimon (Avon); *Too Hard To Forget*, by Tessa Bailey (Grand Central); *In A Daze Work*, by Siobhan Gallagher (Ten Speed); *Piper Morgan Makes A Splash*, by Stephanie Faris (Aladdin); *The Star Thief*, by Lindsey Becker (Little, Brown); *Vanguard*, by Ann Aguirre (Feiwel & Friends); *Gray Wolf Island*, by Tracey Neithercott (Knopf); *Single Malt*, by Layla Reyne (Carina Press); *Whiskey Sharp: Unraveled*, by Lauren Dane (HQN).

WRITERS CONFERENCES RWA National Conference, Romantic Times Booklovers Convention.

BRANDT & HOCHMAN LITERARY AGENTS, INC.

1501 Broadway, Suite 2310, New York NY 10036. (212)840-5760. **Fax:** (212)840-5776. **Website:** brandthochman.com. **Contact:** Gail Hochman. Member of AAR. Represents 200 clients.

MEMBER AGENTS Gail Hochman (works of literary fiction, idea-driven nonfiction, literary memoir and children's books); Marianne Merola (fiction, nonfiction and children's books with strong and unique narrative voices); Bill Contardi (voice-driven young adult and middle grade fiction, commercial thrillers, psychological suspense, quirky mysteries, high fantasy, commercial fiction and memoir); Emily Forland (voice-driven literary fiction and nonfiction, memoir, narrative nonfiction, history, biography, food writing, cultural criticism, graphic novels, and young adult fiction); Emma Patterson (fiction from dark, literary novels to upmarket women's and historical fiction; narrative nonfiction that includes memoir, investigative journalism, and popular history; young adult fiction); Jody Kahn (literary and upmarket fiction; narrative nonfiction, particularly books related to sports, food, history, science and pop culture—including cookbooks, and literary memoir and journalism); Henry Thayer (nonfiction on a wide variety of subjects and fiction that inclines toward the literary). The e-mail addresses and specific likes of each of these agents is listed on the agency website.

REPRESENTS Nonfiction, novels. **Considers these nonfiction areas:** biography, cooking, current affairs, foods, health, history, memoirs, music, popular culture, science, sports, narrative nonfiction, journalism. **Considers these fiction areas:** fantasy, historical, literary, middle grade, mystery, suspense, thriller, women's, young adult.

No screenplays or textbooks.

HOW TO CONTACT "We accept queries by e-mail and regular mail; however, we cannot guarantee a response to e-mailed queries. For queries via regular mail, be sure to include a SASE for our reply. Query letters should be no more than 2 pages and should include a convincing overview of the book project and information about the author and his or her writing credits. Address queries to the specific Brandt & Hochman agent whom you would like to consider your work. Agent e-mail addresses and query preferences may be found at the end of each agent profile on the 'Agents' page of our website." Accepts simultaneous submissions. Obtains most new clients through recommendations from others.

TERMS Agent receives 15% commission on domestic sales; 20% commission on foreign sales.

RECENT SALES This agency sells 40-60 new titles each year. A full list of their hundreds of clients is on the agency website.

TIPS "Write a letter which will give the agent a sense of you as a professional writer—your long-term interests as well as a short description of the work at hand."

THE BRATTLE AGENCY

P.O. Box 380537, Cambridge MA 02238. (617)721-5375. **E-mail:** christopher.vyce@thebrattleagency.com. **E-mail:** submissions@thebrattleagency.com. **Website:** thebrattleagency.com. **Contact:** Christopher Vyce. Member of AAR. Signatory of WGA.

Prior to being an agent, Mr. Vyce worked for the Beacon Press in Boston as an acquisitions editor.

REPRESENTS Nonfiction, fiction. **Considers these nonfiction areas:** art, biography, cultural interests, history, literature, popular culture, politics, sports, race studies, American studies. **Considers these fiction areas:** literary, graphic novels.

HOW TO CONTACT Query by e-mail. Include cover letter, brief synopsis, brief CV. Accepts simultaneous submissions. Responds to queries in 72 hours. Responds to approved submissions in 6-8 weeks.

BARBARA BRAUN ASSOCIATES, INC.

7 E. 14th St., #19F, New York NY 10003. **Fax:** (212)604-9023. **E-mail:** bbasubmissions@gmail.com. **Website:** www.barbarabraunagency.com. **Contact:** Barbara Braun. Member of AAR. Authors Guild, PEN Center USA

REPRESENTS Nonfiction, novels. **Considers these nonfiction areas:** architecture, art, biography, design, film, history, photography, politics, psychology, women's issues, social issues, cultural criticism, fashion, narrative nonfiction. **Considers these fiction areas:** commercial, historical, literary, multicultural, mystery, thriller, women's, young adult, Art-related fiction.

"Our fiction is strong on stories for women, art-related fiction, historical and multicultural stories, and to a lesser extent mysteries and thrillers. We are interested in narrative nonfiction and current affairs books by journalists, as well as YA literature." Does not represent poetry, science fiction, fantasy, horror, or screenplays.

HOW TO CONTACT "We no longer accept submissions by regular mail. Please send all queries via e-mail, marked 'Query' in the subject line. Your query should include: a brief summary of your book, word count, genre, any relevant publishing experience, and the first 5 pages of your manuscript pasted into the body of the e-mail. (No attachments—we will not open these.)" Accepts simultaneous submissions.

TERMS Agent receives 15% commission on domestic sales; 20% commission on foreign sales. No reading fees.

TIPS "Our clients' books are represented throughout Europe, Asia, and Latin America by various subagents. We are also active in selling motion picture rights to the books we represent, and work with various Hollywood agencies."

BRESNICK WEIL LITERARY AGENCY

115 W. 29th St., Third Floor, New York NY 10001. (212)239-3166. **Fax:** (212)239-3165. **E-mail:** query@bresnickagency.com. **Website:** bresnickagency.com. **Contact:** Paul Bresnick.

Prior to becoming an agent, Mr. Bresnick spent 25 years as a trade book editor.

MEMBER AGENTS Paul Bresnick; Susan Duff (women's health, food and wine, fitness, humor, memoir); Lisa Kopel (narrative nonfiction, memoir, pop culture, and both commercial and literary fiction); Matthew MiGangi (music, American history, sports, politics, weird science, pop/alternative culture, video games, and fiction).

REPRESENTS Nonfiction, novels. **Considers these nonfiction areas:** foods, health, history, humor, memoirs, music, popular culture, politics, science, sports, women's issues, fitness, pop/alternative culture, video games. **Considers these fiction areas:** commercial, literary.

Matthew DiGangi does not represent YA, middle grade, or books for children.

HOW TO CONTACT Electronic submissions only. For fiction, submit query and 2 chapters. For nonfiction, submit query with proposal. Accepts simultaneous submissions.

M. COURTNEY BRIGGS

Derrick & Briggs, LLP, 100 N. Broadway Ave., 28th Floor, Oklahoma City OK 73102. (405)235-1900. **Fax:** (405)235-1995. **Website:** www.derrickandbriggs.com. "M. Courtney Briggs combines her primary work as a literary agent with expertise in intellectual property, entertainment law, and estates and probate. Her clients are published authors (exclusively), theatres, and a variety of small businesses and individuals."

RICK BROADHEAD & ASSOCIATES LITERARY AGENCY

47 St. Clair Ave. W., Suite 501, Toronto ON M4V 3A5 Canada. (416)929-0516. **E-mail:** info@rbaliterary.com. **E-mail:** submissions@rbaliterary.com. **Website:** www.rbaliterary.com. **Contact:** Rick Broadhead, president. The agency's clients include accomplished journalists, historians, scholars, physicians, television personalities, bloggers, creators of popular websites, successful business executives, and experts in their respective fields. Estab. 2002. Membership includes Authors Guild. Represents 125 clients.

With an MBA from the Schulich School of Business, one of the world's leading business schools, Rick Broadhead is one of the few literary agents in the publishing industry with a business and entrepreneurial background, one that benefits his clients at every step of the book development and contract negotiation process.

REPRESENTS Nonfiction. **Considers these nonfiction areas:** biography, business, current affairs, environment, health, history, humor, medicine, military, popular culture, politics, science, self-help, relationships, pop science, security/intelligence, natural history.

The agency is actively seeking compelling proposals from experts in their fields, journalists, and authors with relevant credentials and an established media platform (TV, web, radio, print experience/exposure). Does not want to receive fiction, screenplays, children's or poetry at this time.

HOW TO CONTACT Query with e-mail. Include a brief description of your project, your credentials, and contact information. Accepts simultaneous submissions.

TIPS "Books rarely sell themselves these days, so I look for authors who have a 'platform' (media exposure/experience, university affiliation, recognized expertise, etc.). Remember that a literary agent has to sell your project to an editor, and then the editor has to sell your project internally to his/her colleagues (including the marketing and sales staff), and then the publisher has to sell your book to the book buyers at the chains and bookstores. You're most likely to get my attention if you write a succinct and persuasive query letter that demonstrates your platform/credentials, the market potential of your book, and why your book is different."

CURTIS BROWN, LTD.

10 Astor Place, New York NY 10003. (212)473-5400. **Fax:** (212)598-0917. **Website:** www.curtisbrown.com. Represents authors and illustrators of fiction, nonfiction, picture books, middle grade, young adult. Member of AAR. Signatory of WGA.

MEMBER AGENTS Noah Ballard (literary debuts, upmarket thrillers, narrative nonfiction, always looking for honest and provocative new writers); Tess Callero (young adult, upmarket commercial women's fiction, mysteries/ thrillers, romance, nonfiction: pop culture, business, cookbooks, humor, biography, self-help, and food narrative projects); Ginger Clark (science fiction, fantasy, paranormal romance, literary horror, and young adult and middle grade fiction); Kerry D'Agostino (literary and commercial fiction, as well as narrative nonfiction and memoir); Katherine Fausset (literary fiction, upmarket commercial fiction, journalism, memoir, popular science, and narrative nonfiction); Holly Frederick; Peter Ginsberg, president; Elizabeth Harding, vice president (represents authors and illustrators of juvenile, middle-grade and young adult fiction); Ginger Knowlton, executive vice president (authors and illustrators of children's books in all genres—picture book, middle grade, young adult fiction and nonfiction); Timothy Knowlton, CEO; Jonathan Lyons (biographies, history, science, pop culture, sports, general narrative nonfiction, mysteries, thrillers, science fiction and fantasy, and young adult fiction); Sarah Perillo (middle grade fiction and commercial fiction for adults, nonfiction:history, politics, science, pop culture, and humor, and is especially fond of anything involving animals or food); Laura Blake Peterson, vice president (memoir and biography, natural history, literary fiction, mystery, suspense, women's fiction, health and fitness, children's and young adult, faith issues and popular culture); Steven Salpeter (literary fiction, fantasy, graphic novels, historical fiction, mysteries, thrillers, young adult, narrative nonfiction, gift books, history, humor, and popular science); Maureen Walters, senior vice president (working primarily in women's fiction and nonfiction projects on subjects as eclectic as parenting & child care, popular psychology, inspirational/motivational volumes as well as a few medical/nutritional books); Mitchell Waters (literary and commercial fiction and nonfiction, including mystery, history, biography, memoir, young adult, cookbooks, self-help and popular culture); Monika Woods (plot-driven literary novels, non-fiction that is creatively critical, unique perspectives, a great cookbook, and above all, original prose).

REPRESENTS Nonfiction, fiction, novels, short story collections, juvenile books. **Considers these nonfiction areas:** biography, computers, cooking, current affairs, ethnic, health, history, humor, juvenile nonfiction, memoirs, popular culture, psychology, religious, science, self-help, spirituality, sports. **Considers these fiction areas:** fantasy, horror, humor, juvenile, literary, mainstream, middle grade, mystery, paranormal, picture books, religious, romance, spiritual, sports, suspense, thriller, women's, young adult.

HOW TO CONTACT Please refer to the "Agents" page on the website for each agent's submission guidelines. Accepts simultaneous submissions. Responds in 3 weeks to queries; 5 weeks to mss. Obtains most new clients through recommendations from others, solicitations, conferences.

TERMS Agent receives 15% commission on domestic sales; 20% on foreign sales. Offers written contract. 75-day notice must be given to terminate contract. Charges for some postage (overseas, etc.).

RECENT SALES This agency prefers not to share information on specific sales.

CURTIS BROWN (AUST) PTY LTD

P.O. Box 19, Paddington NSW 2021 Australia. (+61) (2)9361-6161. **Fax:** (+61)(2)9360-3935. **E-mail:** reception@curtisbrown.com.au. **E-mail:** submission@curtisbrown.com.au. **Website:** www.curtisbrown.com.au.

"Prior to joining Curtis Brown, most of our agents worked in publishing or the film/theatre industries in Australia and the United Kingdom."

MEMBER AGENTS Fiona Inglis (managing director/agent); Tara Wynne (agent); Pippa Masson (agent); Clare Forster (agent); Grace Heifetz (agent).

"We are Australia's oldest and largest literary agency representing a diverse range of Australian and New Zealand writers and Estates."

HOW TO CONTACT "Please refer to our website for information regarding ms submissions, permissions, theatre rights requests, and the clients and Estates we represent. We are not currently looking to represent poetry, short stories, stage/screenplays, picture books, or translations. We do not accept e-mailed or faxed submissions. No responsibility is taken for the receipt or loss of mss." Accepts simultaneous submissions.

BROWNE & MILLER LITERARY ASSOCIATES

52 Village Place, Hinsdale IL 60521. (312) 922-3063. **E-mail:** mail@browneandmiller.com. **Website:** www.browneandmiller.com. **Contact:** Danielle Egan-Miller, president. Founded in 1971 by Jane Jordan Browne, Browne & Miller Literary Associates is the Chicago area's leading literary agency. Danielle Egan-Miller became president of the agency in 2003 and has since sold hundreds of books with a heavy emphasis on commercial adult fiction. Her roster includes several New York Times best-selling authors and numerous prize- and award-winning writers. She loves a great story well told. Estab. 1971. Member of AAR. RWA, MWA, Authors Guild.

Prior to joining the agency as Jane Jordan Browne's partner, Danielle Egan-Miller worked as an editor.

REPRESENTS Nonfiction, fiction, novels. **Considers these fiction areas:** commercial, crime, detective, erotica, family saga, historical, inspirational, literary, mainstream, mystery, police, religious, romance, suspense, thriller, women's, Christian/inspirational fiction.

Browne & Miller is most interested in literary and commercial fiction, women's fiction, women's historical fiction, literary-leaning crime fiction, dark suspense/domestic suspense, romance of most subgenres including time travel, Christian/inspirational fiction by established authors, and a wide range of platform-driven nonfiction by nationally-recognized author-experts. "We do not represent children's books of any kind; we do not represent horror, science fiction or fantasy, short stories, poetry, original screenplays,or articles."

HOW TO CONTACT Query via e-mail only; no attachments. Do not send unsolicited mss. Accepts simultaneous submissions.

ANDREA BROWN LITERARY AGENCY, INC.

E-mail: andrea@andreabrownlit.com; caryn@andreabrownlit.com; lauraqueries@gmail.com; jennifer@andreabrownlit.com; kelly@andreabrownlit.com; jennL@andreabrownlit.com; jamie@andreabrownlit.com; jmatt@andreabrownlit.com; kathleen@andreabrownlit.com; lara@andreabrownlit.com; soloway@

andreabrownlit.com. **Website:** www.andreabrownlit.com. Member of AAR.

Prior to opening her agency, Ms. Brown served as an editorial assistant at Random House and Dell Publishing and as an editor with Knopf.

MEMBER AGENTS Andrea Brown (president); Laura Rennert (executive agent); Caryn Wiseman (senior agent); Jennifer Laughran (senior agent); Jennifer Rofé (senior agent); Kelly Sonnack (senior agent); Jamie Weiss Chilton (senior agent); Jennifer Mattson (agent); Kathleen Rushall (agent); Lara Perkins (associate agent, digital manager); Jennifer March Soloway (associate agent).

REPRESENTS Juvenile books. **Considers these nonfiction areas:** juvenile nonfiction, young adult, narrative. **Considers these fiction areas:** juvenile, middle grade, picture books, young adult, middle-grade, all juvenile genres.

Specializes in all kinds of children's books—illustrators and authors. 98% juvenile books. Considers: nonfiction, fiction, picture books, young adult.

HOW TO CONTACT For picture books, submit a query letter and complete ms in the body of the e-mail. For fiction, submit a query letter and the first 10 pages in the body of the e-mail. For nonfiction, submit proposal, first 10 pages in the body of the e-mail. Illustrators: submit a query letter and 2-3 illustration samples (in jpeg format), link to online portfolio, and text of picture book, if applicable. "We only accept queries via e-mail. No attachments, with the exception of jpeg illustrations from illustrators." Visit the agents' bios on our website and choose only one agent to whom you will submit your e-query. Send a short e-mail query letter to that agent with "QUERY" in the subject field. Accepts simultaneous submissions. "If we are interested in your work, we will certainly follow up by e-mail or by phone. However, if you haven't heard from us within 6 to 8 weeks, please assume that we are passing on your project." Obtains most new clients through referrals from editors, clients and agents. Check website for guidelines and information.

TERMS Agent receives 15% commission on domestic sales; 25% commission on foreign sales. Offers written contract.

RECENT SALES *The Scorpio Races*, by Maggie Stiefvater (Scholastic); *The Future of Us*, by Jay Asher; *Triangles*, by Ellen Hopkins (Atria); *Crank*, by Ellen Hopkins (McElderry/S&S); *Burned*, by Ellen Hopkins (McElderry/S&S); *Impulse*, by Ellen Hopkins (McElderry/S&S); *Glass*, by Ellen Hopkins (McElderry/S&S); *Tricks*, by Ellen Hopkins (McElderry/S&S); *Fallout*, by Ellen Hopkins (McElderry/S&S); *Perfect*, by Ellen Hopkins (McElderry/S&S); *The Strange Case of Origami Yoda*, by Tom Angleberger (Amulet/Abrams); *Darth Paper Strikes Back*, by Tom Angleberger (Amulet/Abrams); *Becoming Chloe*, by Catherine Ryan Hyde (Knopf); Sasha Cohen autobiography (HarperCollins); *The Five Ancestors*, by Jeff Stone (Random House); *Thirteen Reasons Why*, by Jay Asher (Penguin); *Identical*, by Ellen Hopkins (S&S).

WRITERS CONFERENCES SCBWI, Asilomar; Maui Writers' Conference, Southwest Writers' Conference, San Diego State University Writers' Conference, Big Sur Children's Writing Workshop, William Saroyan Writers' Conference, Columbus Writers' Conference, Willamette Writers' Conference, La Jolla Writers' Conference, San Francisco Writers' Conference, Hilton Head Writers' Conference, Pacific Northwest Conference, Pikes Peak Conference.

TRACY BROWN LITERARY AGENCY

P.O. Box 772, Nyack NY 10960. **Fax:** (914)931-1746. **E-mail:** tracy@brownlit.com. **Contact:** Tracy Brown. Estab. 2003. Represents 35 clients.

Prior to becoming an agent, Mr. Brown was a book editor for 25 years.

REPRESENTS Nonfiction. **Considers these nonfiction areas:** biography, current affairs, health, history, psychology, travel, women's issues.

Specializes in thorough involvement with clients' books at every stage of the process from writing to proposals to publication. Actively seeking serious nonfiction. Does not want to receive young adult, science fiction, or romance.

HOW TO CONTACT Submit outline/proposal, synopsis, and author bio. Accepts simultaneous submissions. Responds in 2 weeks to queries. Obtains most new clients through referrals.

TERMS Agent receives 15% commission on domestic sales. Agent receives 20% commission on foreign sales. Offers written contract.

SHEREE BYKOFSKY ASSOCIATES, INC.

P.O. Box 706, Brigantine NJ 08203. **E-mail:** shereebee@aol.com. **Website:** www.shereebee.com. **Con-**

tact: Sheree Bykofsky. Sheree Bykofsky is the author or coauthor of more than 30 books, including *The Complete Idiot's Guide to Getting Published, 5th Edition*. As an adjunct professor, she teaches publishing at Rosemont College, NYU, and offers her all-day preconference pitch workshop at writers conferences, libraries, and other venues around the country. Janet Rosen is the former president of the NYC chapter of the Women's National Book Association. Her writing has appeared in *Glamour, Publishers Weekly, Paper,* and other print and online publications. Estab. 1991. Member of AAR. Author's Guild, Atlantic City Chamber of Commerce, PRC Council Represents 1,000+ clients.

Prior to opening her agency, Sheree Bykofsky served as executive editor of the Stonesong Press and managing editor of Chiron Press. Janet Rosen worked as associate book editor at *Glamour* and as the senior books and fiction editor at *Woman* before turning to agenting at Sheree Bykofsky Associates, where she represents a range of nonfiction and a limited amount of fiction.

MEMBER AGENTS Sheree Bykofsky, Janet Rosen.

REPRESENTS Nonfiction, novels, scholarly books. **Considers these nonfiction areas:** Americana, animals, anthropology, architecture, art, autobiography, biography, business, child guidance, cooking, crafts, creative nonfiction, cultural interests, current affairs, dance, decorating, diet/nutrition, design, economics, education, environment, ethnic, film, foods, gardening, gay/lesbian, government, health, history, hobbies, how-to, humor, inspirational, language, law, literature, medicine, memoirs, metaphysics, military, money, multicultural, music, New Age, parenting, philosophy, photography, popular culture, politics, psychology, recreation, regional, religious, science, self-help, sex, sociology, software, spirituality, sports, technology, theater, translation, travel, true crime, war, women's issues, creative nonfiction. **Considers these fiction areas:** commercial, contemporary issues, crime, detective, literary, mainstream, mystery, women's. **Considers these script areas:** Dramatic rights represented by Joel Gotler.

This agency is seeking nonfiction, both prescriptive and narrative, and some fiction. Prescriptive nonfiction: primarily health and business. Narrative nonfiction: pop culture, biography, history, popular and social science, language, music, cities, medicine, fashion, military, and espionage. Fiction: women's commercial fiction (with a literary quality) and mysteries. Does not want to receive poetry, children's, screenplays, westerns, science fiction, or horror.

HOW TO CONTACT Query via e-mail to submitbee@aol.com. "We only accept e-queries. We respond only to those queries in which we are interested. No attachments, snail mail, or phone calls, please. We do not open attachments." Fiction: one-page query, one-page synopsis, and first three pages of ms in body of the e-mail. Nonfiction: one-page query in the body of the e-mail. Currently we are focusing much more on our nonfiction portfolio. Accepts simultaneous submissions. Responds in 1 month to requested mss. Obtains most new clients through referrals but still reads all submissions closely.

TERMS Agent receives 15% commission on domestic sales. Agent receives 15% commission on foreign sales, plus international co-agent receives another 10%. Offers written contract, binding for 1 year. Charges for international postage.

RECENT SALES *Virtual Billions: The Genius, the Drug Lord, and the Ivy League Twins Behind the Rise of Bitcoin* by Eric Geissinger (Prometheus Books), *Thank You, Teacher: Grateful Students Tell the Stories of the Teachers Who Changed Their Lives* by Holly and Bruce Holbert (New World Library), *The Type B Manager: Leading Successfully in a Type A World* by Victor Lipman (Prentice Hall), *Let the Story Do the Work: The Art of Storytelling for Business Success* by Esther Choy (Amacom), *Convicting Avery: The Bizarre Laws and Broken System Behind "Making a Murderer"* by Michael D. Cicchini (Prometheus Books), *The Curious Case of Kiryas Joel: The Rise of a Village Theocracy and the Battle to Defend the Separation of Church and State* by Louis Grumet with John Caher (Chicago Review Press), *Cells are the New Cure* by Robin L. Smith, M.D. and Max Gomez, Ph.D.; dozens of international sales

WRITERS CONFERENCES Truckee Meadow Community College Keynote, ASJA Writers Conference, Asilomar, Florida Suncoast Writers' Conference, Whidbey Island Writers' Conference, Florida First Coast Writers' Festival, Agents and Editors Conference, Columbus Writers' Conference, Southwest Writers' Conference, Willamette Writers' Conference, Dorothy Canfield Fisher Conference, Maui Writers'

Conference, Pacific Northwest Writers' Conference, IWWG.

KIMBERLEY CAMERON & ASSOCIATES

1550 Tiburon Blvd., #704, Tiburon CA 94920. (415)789-9191. **Website:** www.kimberleycameron.com. **Contact:** Kimberley Cameron. Member of AAR. Signatory of WGA.

Kimberley Cameron & Associates (formerly The Reece Halsey Agency) has had an illustrious client list of established writers, including Aldous Huxley, Upton Sinclair, William Faulkner, and Henry Miller.

MEMBER AGENTS Kimberley Cameron; Elizabeth Kracht (temporarily closed to submissions); Amy Cloughley (literary and upmarket fiction, women's, historical, narrative nonfiction, travel or adventure memoir); Mary C. Moore (fantasy, science fiction, upmarket "book club," genre romance, thrillers with female protagonists, and stories from marginalized voices); Lisa Abellera (currently closed to unsolicited submissions); Douglas Lee, douglas@kimberlycameron.com (only accepting submissions via conference and in-person meetings in the Bay Area); Dorian Maffei (only open to submissions requested through Twitter pitch parties, conferences, or #MSWL).

REPRESENTS Considers these nonfiction areas: animals, environment, health, memoirs, science, spirituality, travel, true crime, narrative non-fiction. **Considers these fiction areas:** commercial, fantasy, historical, literary, mystery, romance, science fiction, thriller, women's, young adult, LGBTQ.

"We are looking for a unique and heartfelt voice that conveys a universal truth."

HOW TO CONTACT Prefers queries via site. Only query one agent at a time. For fiction, fill out the correct submissions form for the individual agent and attach the first 50 pages and a synopsis (if requested) as a Word doc or PDF. For nonfiction, fill out the correct submission form of the individual agent and attach a full book proposal and sample chapters (includes the first chapter and no more than 50 pages) as a Word doc or PDF. Accepts simultaneous submissions. Obtains new clients through recommendations from others, solicitations.

CYNTHIA CANNELL LITERARY AGENCY

54 W. 40th St., New York NY 10018. (212)396-9595. **Website:** www.cannellagency.com. **Contact:** Cynthia Cannell. "The Cynthia Cannell Literary Agency is a full-service literary agency in New York City active in both the national and the international publishing markets. We represent the authors of literary fiction as well as memoir, biography, historical fiction, popular science, self-improvement, spirituality, and nonfiction on contemporary issues." Estab. 1997. Member of AAR. Women's Media Group and the Authors Guild

Prior to forming the Cynthia Cannell Literary Agency, Ms. Cannell was the vice president of Janklow & Nesbit Associates for 12 years.

REPRESENTS Nonfiction, fiction. **Considers these nonfiction areas:** biography, current affairs, memoirs, self-help, spirituality.

Does not represent screenplays, children's books, illustrated books, cookbooks, romance, category mystery, or science fiction.

HOW TO CONTACT "Please query us with an e-mail or letter. If querying by e-mail, send a brief description of your project with relevant biographical information including publishing credits (if any) to info@cannellagency.com. Do not send attachments. If querying by conventional mail, enclose an SASE." Responds if interested. Accepts simultaneous submissions.

RECENT SALES Check the website for an updated list of authors and sales.

CAPITAL TALENT AGENCY

1330 Connecticut Ave. NW, Suite 271, Washington DC 20036. (202)429-4785. **Fax:** (202)429-4786. **E-mail:** literary.submissions@capitaltalentagency.com. **Website:** capitaltalentagency.com/html/literary.shtml. **Contact:** Cynthia Kane. Estab. 2014. Member of AAR. Signatory of WGA.

Prior to joining CTA, Ms. Kane was involved in the publishing industry for more than 10 years. She has worked as a development editor for different publishing houses and individual authors and has seen more than 100 titles to market.

MEMBER AGENTS Cynthia Kane; Roger Yoerges; Michelle Muntifering; J. Fred Shiffman.

REPRESENTS Nonfiction, fiction, movie scripts, stage plays.

HOW TO CONTACT "We accept submissions only by e-mail. We do not accept queries via postal mail or fax. For fiction and nonfiction submissions, send a query letter in the body of your e-mail. Please note that while we consider each query seriously, we are unable to respond to all of them. We endeavor to respond within 6 weeks to projects that interest us." Accepts simultaneous submissions. 6 weeks

CATALYST FOR THE ARTS

(818)597-8335. **Fax:** (818)597-1443. **E-mail:** cftaharrison@gmail.com. **Website:** www.catalystforthearts.com/. **Contact:** Harvey E. Harrison. Estab. 1996.

REPRESENTS Nonfiction, fiction, novels, juvenile books, movie scripts, feature film, TV scripts, episodic drama, sitcom, animation. Video and New Media, motion pictures. **Considers these nonfiction areas:** anthropology, inspirational, juvenile nonfiction, law, literature, metaphysics, military, philosophy, religious, sex, spirituality. **Considers these fiction areas:** action, adventure, cartoon, crime, detective, literary, metaphysical, New Age, poetry, religious, spiritual. **Considers these script areas:** action, adventure, animation, cartoon, comedy, crime, detective, documentary, episodic drama, ethnic, feature film, feminist, frontier, historical, movie scripts, multimedia, mystery, religious, romantic comedy, romantic drama, sitcom, TV movie of the week.

HOW TO CONTACT Accepts simultaneous submissions.

TIPS "We do not accept or review query or literary material except by known referral. We seek to see innovative, compelling online video such as that at Burning Shorts www.burningshorts.com, as well as innovative, compelling digital media in all forms of expression."

CHALBERG & SUSSMAN

115 W. 29th St., Third Floor, New York NY 10001. (917)261-7550. **Website:** www.chalbergsussman.com. Member of AAR. Signatory of WGA.

Prior to her current position, Ms. Chalberg held a variety of editorial positions, and was an agent with The Susan Golomb Literary Agency. Ms. Sussman was an agent with Zachary Shuster Harmsworth. Ms. James was with The Aaron Priest Literary Agency.

MEMBER AGENTS Terra Chalberg; Rachel Sussman (narrative journalism, memoir, psychology, history, humor, pop culture, literary fiction); Nicole James (plot-driven fiction, psychological suspense, uplifting female-driven memoir, upmarket self-help, and lifestyle books); Lana Popovic (young adult, middle grade, contemporary realism, speculative fiction, fantasy, horror, sophisticated erotica, romance, select nonfiction, international stories).

REPRESENTS Nonfiction, fiction, novels. **Considers these nonfiction areas:** history, humor, memoirs, popular culture, psychology, self-help, narrative journalism. **Considers these fiction areas:** erotica, fantasy, horror, literary, middle grade, romance, science fiction, suspense, young adult, contemporary realism, speculative fiction.

HOW TO CONTACT To query by e-mail, please contact one of the following: terra@chalbergsussman.com, rachel@chalbergsussman.com, nicole@chalbergsussman.com, lana@chalbergsussman.com. To query by regular mail, please address your letter to one agent and include SASE. Accepts simultaneous submissions.

RECENT SALES The agents' sales and clients are listed on their website.

CHASE LITERARY AGENCY

11 Broadway, Suite 1010, New York NY 10004. (212)477-5100. **E-mail:** farley@chaseliterary.com. **Website:** www.chaseliterary.com. **Contact:** Farley Chase. "After starting out at *The New Yorker*, I moved to The New Press and later became an editor at Talk Miramax Books. I spent 8 years as a literary agent at the Waxman Literary Agency, and I founded Chase Literary Agency in 2012. I live in NYC with my wife and dog and am a graduate of Macalester College. Over my more than 13 years as a literary agent and 19 years in publishing, I've been fortunate to work with distinguished authors of fiction and nonfiction. They include winners of the Pulitzer Prize, MacArthur Fellows, Members of Congress, Olympic Gold Medalists, and members of the Baseball Hall of Fame."

MEMBER AGENTS Farley Chase.

REPRESENTS Nonfiction, fiction, novels. **Considers these nonfiction areas:** agriculture, Americana, animals, anthropology, archeology, architecture, autobiography, biography, business, creative nonfiction, cultural interests, current affairs, design, education, environment, ethnic, film, foods, gay/lesbian, health, history, how-to, humor, inspirational, investigative, juvenile nonfiction, language, law, literature, medicine, memoirs, metaphysics, military, money, multicultural, music, philosophy, popular culture, politics, recreation, regional, satire, science, sex, sociology, sports, technology, translation, travel, true crime, war, women's issues, women's studies. **Considers these fiction areas:** commercial, historical, literary, mystery.

No romance, science fiction, or young adult.

HOW TO CONTACT E-query farley@chaseliterary.com. If submitting fiction, please include the first few pages of the ms with the query. "I do not response to queries not addressed to me by name. I'm keenly interested in both fiction and nonfiction. In fiction, I'm looking for both literary or commercial projects in either contemporary or historical settings. I'm open to anything with a strong sense of place, voice, and, especially plot. I don't handle science fiction, romance, supernatural or young adult. In nonfiction, I'm especially interested in narratives in history, memoir, journalism, natural science, military history, sports, pop culture, and humor. Whether by first-time writers or long time journalists, I'm excited by original ideas, strong points of view, detailed research, and access to subjects which give readers fresh perspectives on things they think they know. I'm also interested in visually-driven and illustrated books. Whether they involve photography, comics, illustrations, or art I'm taken by creative storytelling with visual elements, four color or black and white." Accepts simultaneous submissions.

RECENT SALES *Devil in the Grove: Thurgood Marshall, the Groveland Boys, and the Dawn of a New America* by Gilbert King (Harper); *Heads in Beds: A Reckless Memoir of Hotels, Hustles, and So-Called Hospitality*, by Jacob Tomsky (Doubleday); *And Every Day Was Overcast*, by Paul Kwiatowski (Black Balloon); *The Badlands Saloon*, by Jonathan Twingley (Scribner).

CHENEY ASSOCIATES, LLC

78 Fifth Ave., 3rd Floor, New York NY 10011. (212)277-8007. **Fax:** (212)614-0728. **E-mail:** submissions@cheneyliterary.com. **Website:** www.cheneyliterary.com. **Contact:** Elyse Cheney; Adam Eaglin; Alex Jacobs; Alice Whitwham.

Prior to her current position, Ms. Cheney was an agent with Sanford J. Greenburger Associates.

MEMBER AGENTS Elyse Cheney; Adam Eaglin (literary fiction and nonfiction, including history, politics, current events, narrative reportage, biography, memoir, and popular science); Alexander Jacobs (narrative nonfiction [particularly in the areas of history, science, politics, and culture], literary fiction, crime, and memoir); Alice Whitwham (literary and commercial fiction, as well as voice-driven narrative nonfiction, cultural criticism, and journalism).

REPRESENTS Nonfiction, novels. **Considers these nonfiction areas:** biography, cultural interests, current affairs, history, memoirs, politics, science, narrative nonfiction, narrative reportage. **Considers these fiction areas:** commercial, crime, family saga, historical, literary, short story collections, suspense, women's.

HOW TO CONTACT Query by e-mail or snail mail. For a snail mail responses, include a SASE. Include up to 3 chapters of sample material. Do not query more than one agent. Accepts simultaneous submissions.

RECENT SALES *The Love Affairs of Nathaniel P.*, by Adelle Waldman (Henry Holt & Co.); *This Town*, by Mark Leibovich (Blue Rider Press); *Thunder & Lightning*, by Lauren Redniss (Random House).

THE CHUDNEY AGENCY

72 N. State Rd., Suite 501, Briarcliff Manor NY 10510. (914)465-5560. **E-mail:** steven@thechudneyagency.com. **Website:** www.thechudneyagency.com. **Contact:** Steven Chudney. Estab. 2001. SCBWI

Prior to becoming an agent, Mr. Chudney held various marketing and sales positions with major publishers.

REPRESENTS Novels, juvenile books. **Considers these nonfiction areas:** humor. **Considers these fiction areas:** commercial, family saga, gay, historical, juvenile, lesbian, literary, middle grade, picture books, regional, suspense, thriller, young adult.

"At this time, the agency is only looking for author/illustrators (one individual), who can both write and illustrate wonderful picture books. The author/illustrator must really know and understand the prime audience's needs and wants of the child reader! Storylines should be engaging, fun, with a hint of a life lessons and cannot be longer than 800 words. With chapter books, middle grade and teen novels, I'm primarily looking for quality, contemporary literary fiction: novels that are exceedingly well-written, with wonderful settings and developed, unforgettable characters. I'm looking for historical fiction that will excite me, young readers, editors, and reviewers, and will introduce us to unique characters in settings and situations, countries, and eras we haven't encountered too often yet in children's and teen literature." Does not want most fantasy and no science fiction.

HOW TO CONTACT No snail mail submissions. Queries only. Submission package info to follow should we be interested. For children's picture books, we only want author/illustrator projects. Submit a pdf with full text and at least 5-7 full-color illustrations. Accepts simultaneous submissions. Responds if interested in 2-3 weeks to queries.

⊘ CINE/LIT REPRESENTATION

P.O. Box 802918, Santa Clarita CA 91380. (661)513-0268. **Contact:** Mary Alice Kier. Member of AAR.

MEMBER AGENTS Mary Alice Kier, Anna Cottle.

HOW TO CONTACT Not currently accepting queries for representation. Note this agency's specialized nature. Accepts simultaneous submissions.

CK WEBBER ASSOCIATES

E-mail: carlie@ckwebber.com. **Website:** ckwebber.com. **Contact:** Carlisle Webber. "CK Webber Associates is a literary agency open to commercial fiction for people ages 8 and up. Our mission is to develop long-term careers for writers in a variety of genres. Our prime directive is outstanding fiduciary and editorial services for our clients." Member of AAR. Signatory of WGA.

Ms. Webber's professional publishing experience includes an internship at Writers House and work with the Roger Williams Agency and the Jane Rotrosen Agency. She is also a graduate of the Columbia Publishing Course and holds a Professional Certificate in Editing from UC Berkeley.

REPRESENTS Novels, juvenile books. **Considers these fiction areas:** action, adventure, commercial, contemporary issues, crime, detective, family saga, fantasy, feminist, horror, literary, mainstream, middle grade, mystery, new adult, romance, science fiction, suspense, thriller, westerns, women's, young adult.

"We are currently not accepting nonfiction (including memoir), picture books, easy readers, early chapter books, poetry, scripts, novellas, or short story collections."

HOW TO CONTACT Accepts queries via e-mail only. To submit your work for consideration, please send a query letter, synopsis, and the first 30 pages or 3 chapters of your work, whichever is more, to carlie@ckwebber.com and put the word "query" in the subject line of your e-mail. Please include your materials in the body of your e-mail. Blank emails that include an attachment will be deleted unread. Accepts simultaneous submissions.

WM CLARK ASSOCIATES

54 W. 21st St., Suite 809, New York NY 10010. (212)675-2784. **E-mail:** general@wmclark.com. **Website:** www.wmclark.com. **Contact:** William Clark. Estab. 1997. Member of AAR.

Prior to opening WCA, Mr. Clark was an agent at the William Morris Agency.

REPRESENTS Nonfiction, novels. **Considers these nonfiction areas:** architecture, art, autobiography, biography, creative nonfiction, cultural interests, current affairs, dance, design, economics, ethnic, film, foods, history, inspirational, interior design, literature, memoirs, music, popular culture, politics, religious, science, sociology, technology, theater, translation, travel. **Considers these fiction areas:** historical, literary.

William Clark represents a wide range of titles across all formats to the publishing, motion picture, television, and multimedia fields. Offering individual focus and a global reach, we move quickly and strategically on behalf of domestic and international clients ranging from authors of award-winning, best-selling narrative nonfiction, to authors in translation, chefs, musicians, and artists. The agency undertakes to discover, develop, and market today's most interesting content and the talent that creates it, and forge sophisticated and innovative plans for self-promotion, reliable revenue streams, and an enduring creative career. Agency does not represent screenplays or respond to screenplay pitches. "It is advised that before querying you become familiar with the kinds of books we handle by browsing our Book List, which is available on our website."

HOW TO CONTACT Accepts queries via online query form only. "We will endeavor to respond as soon as possible as to whether or not we'd like to see a proposal or sample chapters from your manuscript." Responds in 1-2 months to queries.

TERMS Agent receives 15% commission on domestic sales; 20% commission on foreign sales. Offers written contract.

WRITERS CONFERENCES London Book Fair, Frankfurt Book Fair.

TIPS "Translation rights are sold directly in the German, Italian, Spanish, Portuguese, Latin American, French, Dutch, and Scandinavian territories; and through corresponding agents in China, Bulgaria, Czech Republic, Latvia, Poland, Hungary, Russia, Japan, Greece, Israel, Turkey, Korea, Taiwan, Vietnam, and Thailand."

FRANCES COLLIN, LITERARY AGENT

P.O. Box 33, Wayne PA 19087-0033. **E-mail:** queries@francescollin.com. **Website:** www.francescollin.com. The agency represents the Estates of John Williams (*Stoner, Butcher's Crossing, Augustus*) and Esther Forbes (*Johnny Tremain*), among others. Fran Collin is the trustee for the estate of Rachel Carson (*Silent Spring*). Clients include Nadine Darling, Kirsten Kaschock, Wendy Sparrow/Wendy Laine, Christopher Merkner, Matthew Jakubowski, Barbara Hambly, Vonda N. McIntyre, Marilyn Hacker, Caroline Stevermer, Ana Veciana-Suarez, the Estate of Robert Bright and the Estate of Hal Borland. Formerly the Marie Rodell-Frances Collin Literary Agency. Celebrating 69 years as an agency! Estab. 1948. Member of AAR. Represents 50 clients.

Sarah Yake has been with the agency since 2005 and handles foreign and sub-rights as well as her own client list. She holds an M.A. in English Literature and has been a sales rep for a major publisher and a bookstore manager. She currently teaches in the Rosemont College Graduate Publishing Program.

MEMBER AGENTS Frances Collin; Sarah Yake.

REPRESENTS Nonfiction, fiction, novels. **Considers these nonfiction areas:** architecture, art, autobiography, biography, creative nonfiction, cultural interests, dance, environment, history, literature, memoirs, popular culture, science, sociology, travel, women's issues, women's studies. **Considers these fiction areas:** adventure, commercial, experimental, feminist, historical, juvenile, literary, middle grade, multicultural, science fiction, women's, young adult.

Actively seeking authors who are invested in their unique visions and who want to set trends not chase them. "I'd like to think that my authors are unplagiarizable by virtue of their distinct voices and styles." Does not want previously self-published work. Query with new mss only, please.

HOW TO CONTACT "We ask that writers send a traditional query e-mail describing the project and copy and paste the first 5 pages of the manuscript into the body of the e-mail. We look forward to hearing from you at queries@francescollin.com. Please send queries to that e-mail address. Any queries sent to another e-mail address within the agency will be deleted unread." Accepts simultaneous submissions. Responds in 1-4 weeks for initial queries, longer for full mss.

COMPASS TALENT

(646)376-7747. **Website:** www.compasstalent.com. **Contact:** Heather Schroder. Founded by Heather Schroder after over 25 years as an agent at ICM Partners, Compass is dedicated to working with authors to shape their work and guide their careers through each stage of the publication process. Member of AAR. Signatory of WGA.

REPRESENTS **Considers these nonfiction areas:** cooking, creative nonfiction, foods, memoirs. **Considers these fiction areas:** commercial, literary, mainstream.

HOW TO CONTACT This agency is currently closed to unsolicited submissions. Accepts simultaneous submissions.

RECENT SALES A full list of agency clients is available on the website.

DON CONGDON ASSOCIATES INC.

110 William St., Suite 2202, New York NY 10038. (212)645-1229. **Fax:** (212)727-2688. **E-mail:** dca@doncongdon.com. **Website:** doncongdon.com. Estab. 1983. Member of AAR.

MEMBER AGENTS Cristina Concepcion (crime fiction, narrative nonfiction, political science, journalism, history, books on cities, classical music, biography, science for a popular audience, philosophy, food and wine, iconoclastic books on health and human relationships, essays, and arts criticism); Michael Congdon (commercial and literary fiction, suspense, mystery, thriller, history, military history, biography, memoir, current affairs, and narrative nonfiction [adventure, medicine, science, and nature]); Katie Grimm (literary fiction, historical, women's fiction, short story collections, graphic novels, mysteries, young adult, middle-grade, memoir, science, academic); Katie Kotchman (business [all areas], narrative nonfiction [particularly popular science and social/cultural issues], self-help, success, motivation, psychology, pop culture, women's fiction, realistic young adult, literary fiction, and psychological thrillers); Maura Kye-Casella (narrative nonfiction, cookbooks, women's fiction, young adult, self-help, and parenting); Susan Ramer (literary fiction, upmarket commercial fiction [contemporary and historical], narrative nonfiction, social history, cultural history, smart pop culture [music, film, food, art], women's issues, psychology and mental health, and memoir).

REPRESENTS Nonfiction, novels, short story collections. **Considers these nonfiction areas:** art, biography, business, cooking, creative nonfiction, cultural interests, current affairs, film, foods, history, humor, literature, medicine, memoirs, military, multicultural, music, parenting, philosophy, popular culture, politics, psychology, science, self-help, sociology, sports, women's issues, young adult. **Considers these fiction areas:** crime, hi-lo, historical, literary, middle grade, mystery, short story collections, suspense, thriller, women's, young adult.

Susan Ramer: "Not looking for romance, science fiction, fantasy, espionage, mysteries, politics, health/diet/fitness, self-help, or sports." Katie Kotchman: "Please do not send her screenplays or poetry."

HOW TO CONTACT "For queries via e-mail, you must include the word 'query' and the agent's full name in your subject heading. Please also include your query and sample chapter in the body of the e-mail, as we do not open attachments for security reasons. Please query only one agent within the agency at a time. If you are sending your query via regular mail, please enclose a SASE for our reply. If you would like us to return your materials, please make sure your postage will cover their return." Accepts simultaneous submissions.

RECENT SALES This agency represents many best-selling clients such as David Sedaris and Kathryn Stockett.

THE DOE COOVER AGENCY

P.O. Box 668, Winchester MA 01890. (781)721-6000. **E-mail:** info@doecooveragency.com. **Website:** www.doecooveragency.com. Represents 150+ clients.

MEMBER AGENTS **Doe Coover** (general nonfiction, including business, cooking/food writing, history, biography, health, and science); **Colleen Mohyde** (literary fiction and commercial fiction, general nonfiction); **Frances Kennedy**.

REPRESENTS Nonfiction, novels. **Considers these nonfiction areas:** creative nonfiction. **Considers these fiction areas:** commercial, literary.

The agency specializes in narrative nonfiction, particularly biography, business, cooking and food writing, health, history, popular science, social issues, gardening, and humor; literary and commercial fiction. The agency does not represent poetry, screenplays, romance, fantasy, science fiction, or unsolicited children's books.

HOW TO CONTACT Accepts queries by e-mail only. Check website for submission guidelines. No unsolicited mss. Accepts simultaneous submissions. Responds within 6 weeks. Responds only if additional material is required. Obtains most new clients through solicitation and recommendation.

TERMS Agent receives 15% commission on domestic sales, 10% of original advance commission on foreign sales. No reading fees.

RECENT SALES *Lessons from a Grandfather* by Jacques Pepin (Houghton Mifflin Harcourt), *Lift Off* by Donovan Livingston (Speigel & Grau), *World Food* by James Oseland (Ten Speed Press), *Biography of Garry Trudeau* by Steven Weinberg (St. Martin's Press), *A Welcome Murder* by Robin Yocum (Prometheus Books).

JILL CORCORAN LITERARY AGENCY

2150 Park Place, Suite 100, El Segundo CA 90245. **Website:** jillcorcoranliteraryagency.com. **Contact:** Jill Corcoran. Estab. 2013.

MEMBER AGENTS Jill Corcoran, Adah Nuchi, Silvia Arienti, Eve Porinchak.

REPRESENTS Nonfiction, novels, juvenile books. **Considers these nonfiction areas:** business, how-to, juvenile nonfiction, true crime, young adult. **Considers these fiction areas:** commercial, crime, juvenile, middle grade, picture books, romance, young adult.

Actively seeking picture books, middle-grade, young adult, crime novels, psyhcological suspense, and true crime. Does not want to receive screenplays, chapbooks, or poetry.

HOW TO CONTACT Please go online to the agency submissions page and submit to the agent you feel would best represent your work. Accepts simultaneous submissions.

CORVISIERO LITERARY AGENCY

275 Madison Ave., at 40th, 14th Floor, New York NY 10016. (646)856-4032. **Fax:** (646)217-3758. **E-mail:** consult@corvisieroagency.com. **Website:** www.corvisieroagency.com. **Contact:** Marisa A. Corvisiero, Founder, Senior Agent, Attorney. "We are a boutique literary agency founded by Marisa A Corvisiero, Esq. This agency is a place where authors can find professional and experienced representation." *Does not accept unsolicited mss.* Estab. 2012.

MEMBER AGENTS Marisa A. Corvisiero, senior agent and literary attorney (contemporary romance, thrillers, adventure, paranormal, urban fantasy, science fiction, MG, YA, picture books, Christmas themes, time travel, space science fiction, nonfiction, self-help, science, business); Saritza Hernandez, senior agent (all kinds of romance, GLBT, YA, erotica); Doreen Thistle (do not query); Cate Hart (YA, fantasy, magical realism, MG, mystery, fantasy, adventure, historical romance, LGBTQ, erotic, history, biography); Veronica Park (dark or edgy YA/NA, Commercial adult, adult romance and romantic suspense, and funny and/or current/controversial nonfiction); Kelly Peterson (MG, fantasy, paranormal, sci-fi, YA, steampunk, historical, dystopian, sword and sorcery, romance, historical romance, adult, fantasy, romance); Justin Wells; Kaitlyn Johnson (upper MG, YA, NA, and Adult; fantasy, urban fantasy, romance, historical fiction, contemporary, LGBTQ); Kortney Price (MG, YA, and Adult; fantasy, steampunk, science fiction, mystery, thriller, contemporary); Jennifer Haskin (Fiction only, YA, NA, fantasy, sci-fi, dystopian, steampunk, thriller, LGBTQ, romance, dark).

REPRESENTS Nonfiction, fiction, novels, juvenile books. **Considers these nonfiction areas:** biography, business, cooking, crafts, current affairs, diet/nutrition, economics, foods, gardening, history, how-to, interior design, law, medicine, memoirs, metaphysics, money, parenting, politics, science, self-help, spirituality, travel, women's issues, young adult. **Considers these fiction areas:** action, adventure, erotica, family saga, fantasy, feminist, gay, historical, humor, juvenile, lesbian, metaphysical, middle grade, multicultural, mystery, new adult, New Age, occult, paranormal, picture books, psychic, religious, romance, science fiction, spiritual, suspense, thriller, urban fantasy, women's, young adult, magical realism, steampunk, dystopian, sword and sorcery. **Considers these script areas:** action, adventure, family saga, fantasy, romantic comedy, romantic drama, science fiction, suspense, teen.

HOW TO CONTACT Accepts submissions via QueryManager. Include query letter, 5 pages of complete and polished ms, and a 1-2 page synopsis. For nonfiction, include a proposal instead of the synopsis. Each agent profile on website has a button for direct submissions. Accepts simultaneous submissions.

WRITERS CONFERENCES SCWC (San Diego); AuthorPreneur Workshop Charlotte; NJ Fiction Writers; Muse and the Marketplace; RT Convention; LI Romance Writers; BEA; DFW Fort Worth; Thrillerfest NYC; RWA; Writers Digest NYC; AuthorPreneur Workshop Red Bank; SCWC (Los Angeles); NJ Romance Writers.

CREATIVE BOOK SERVICES

111 W. 19th St., Sixth Floor, New York NY 10011. (212)226-1936. **E-mail:** bob.mecoy@gmail.com. **Contact:** Bob Mecoy, owner. Estab. 2001.

REPRESENTS Nonfiction, novels. **Considers these nonfiction areas:** art, autobiography, biography, business, cooking, creative nonfiction, current affairs, foods, history, investigative, juvenile nonfiction, literature, memoirs, military, sports, technology, war, young adult. **Considers these fiction areas:** action, adventure, cartoon, comic books, crime, detective, fantasy, literary, mainstream, mystery, new adult, romance, science fiction, sports, urban fantasy, war.

Actively seeking fiction (literary, crime, science fiction/fantasy, romance), nonfiction (true crime, finance, adventure, memoir, literary), and graphic novels of all stripes.

HOW TO CONTACT Query with sample chapters and synopsis. Accepts simultaneous submissions.

CREATIVE MEDIA AGENCY, INC.

(212)812-1494. **E-mail:** paige@cmalit.com. **Website:** www.cmalit.com. **Contact:** Paige Wheeler. Creative Media Agency, Inc. is a New York City-based literary agency. Founded in 1997, we focus on representing professional writers in a variety of genres and subject matters, and cultivating the evolving agent-author relationship. With over 20 years of experience, we work to discover authors and nurture long-standing careers every step of the way. Our goal is to go beyond simply selling an author's book. From the first contract to the final sales figures, CMA has every detail covered: editorial work, marketing and publicity plans, royalties, and foreign rights. We have tailored our agency to meet an author's every need to get them performing the best in their field. CMA has represented New York Times and USA Today best sellers, as well as winners of the RITA, Edgar, Agatha, Anthony, Shamus, and other major awards. In addition to established authors, we welcome many first-time authors pursuing publication and a career in writing. Estab. 1997. Member of AAR. WMG, RWA, MWA, Authors Guild. Represents about 30 clients.

After starting out as an editor for Harlequin Books in NY and Euromoney Publications in London, Paige repped writers, producers, and celebrities as an agent with Artists Agency, until she formed Creative Media Agency in 1997. In 2006 she co-created Folio Literary Management and grew that company for 8 years into a successful mid-sized agency. In 2014 she decided to once again pursue a boutique approach, and she relaunched CMA.

REPRESENTS Nonfiction, fiction, novels. **Considers these nonfiction areas:** biography, business, creative nonfiction, diet/nutrition, health, inspirational, memoirs, money, parenting, popular culture, self-help, travel, women's issues, prescriptive nonfiction, narrative nonfiction. **Considers these fiction areas:** commercial, crime, detective, historical, inspirational, mainstream, middle grade, mystery, new adult, romance, suspense, thriller, women's, young adult, general fiction.

Fiction: All commercial and upscale (think book club) fiction, as well as women's fiction, romance (all types), mystery, thrillers, inspirational/Christian and psychological suspense. I enjoy both historical fiction as well as contemporary fiction, so do keep that in mind. I seem to be especially drawn to a story if it has a high concept and a fresh, unique voice. Nonfiction: I'm looking for both narrative nonfiction and prescriptive nonfiction. I'm looking for books where the author has a huge platform and something new to say in a particular area. Some of the areas that I like are lifestyle, relationship, parenting, business/entrepreneurship, food-subsistence-homesteading topics, popular/trendy reference projects and women's issues. I'd like books that would be a good fit on the *Today* show. Does not want to receive children's books, science fiction, fantasy, or academic nonfiction.

HOW TO CONTACT E-query. Write "query" in your e-mail subject line. For fiction, paste in the first 5 pages of the ms after the query. For nonfiction, paste in an extended author bio as well as the marketing section of your book proposal after the query. Accepts simultaneous submissions. Responds in 4-6 weeks.

CREATIVE TRUST, INC.

210 Jamestown Park Dr., Suite 200, Brentwood TN 37027. (615)297-5010. **Fax:** (615)297-5020. **E-mail:** info@creativetrust.com. **Website:** www.creativetrust.com.

REPRESENTS Nonfiction, novels, movie scripts. multimedia, other. **Considers these nonfiction areas:** memoirs.

HOW TO CONTACT "Creative Trust Literary Group does not accept unsolicited manuscripts or book proposals from unpublished authors. We do accept unsolicited inquiries from previously published authors under the following requisites; email inquiries only, which must not be accompanied by attachments of any kind, to info@creativetrust.com. Please indicate 'Literary Submission' in your subject line. Due to the volume of queries we receive, we are not able to respond except to request additional materials." Accepts simultaneous submissions.

RICHARD CURTIS ASSOCIATES, INC.

200 E. 72nd St., Suite 28J, New York NY 10021. (212)772-7363. **Fax:** (212)772-7393. **Website:** www.curtisagency.com. Member of AAR. RWA, MWA, ITW, SFWA. Represents 100 clients.

Prior to becoming an agent, Mr. Curtis authored blogs, articles, and books on the publishing business and help for authors.

REPRESENTS Nonfiction, fiction, novels, juvenile books. **Considers these nonfiction areas:** biography, business, current affairs, dance, gay/lesbian, health, history, how-to, investigative, literature, military, music, politics, psychology, science, sports, theater, true crime, war, women's issues, young adult. **Considers these fiction areas:** commercial, fantasy, romance, science fiction, thriller, young adult.

Actively seeking nonfiction (but no memoir), women's fiction (especially contemporary), thrillers, science fiction, middle-grade, and young adult. Does not want screenplays.

HOW TO CONTACT Use submission procedure on website. "We also read one-page query letters accompanied by SASE." Accepts simultaneous submissions.

TERMS Agent receives 15% commission on domestic sales; 25% commission on foreign sales. Offers written contract. Charges for photocopying, express mail, international freight, book orders.

RECENT SALES Sold 100 titles in the last year, including *The Library*, by D.J. MacHale; *Tylers of Texas*, by Janet Dailey; and *Death of an Heir*, by Philip Jett.

D4EO LITERARY AGENCY

7 Indian Valley Rd., Weston CT 06883. (203)544-7180. **Fax:** (203)544-7160. **Website:** www.d4eoliteraryagency.com. **Contact:** Bob Diforio. Estab. 1990.

Prior to opening his agency, Mr. Diforio was a publisher.

MEMBER AGENTS Bob Diforio; Joyce Holland; Pam Howell; Quressa Robinson; Kelly Van Sant.

REPRESENTS Nonfiction, novels. **Considers these nonfiction areas:** biography, business, health, history, humor, money, psychology, science, sports. **Considers these fiction areas:** adventure, detective, erotica, juvenile, literary, mainstream, middle grade, mystery, new adult, romance, sports, thriller, young adult.

HOW TO CONTACT Each of these agents has a different submission e-mail and different tastes regarding how they review material. See all on their individual agent pages on the agency website. Responds in 1 week to queries if interested. Obtains most new clients through recommendations from others.

TERMS Offers written contract, binding for 2 years; automatic renewal unless 60 days notice given prior to renewal date. Charges for photocopying and submission postage.

LAURA DAIL LITERARY AGENCY, INC.

121 W. 27th St., Suite 1201, New York NY 10001. (212)239-7477. **E-mail:** literary@ldlainc.com. **E-mail:** queries@ldlainc.com. **Website:** www.ldlainc.com. Member of AAR.

MEMBER AGENTS Laura Dail; Tamar Rydzinski; Elana Roth Parker.

REPRESENTS Nonfiction, fiction, novels, juvenile books. **Considers these nonfiction areas:** biography, cooking, creative nonfiction, current affairs, government, history, investigative, juvenile nonfiction, memoirs, multicultural, popular culture, politics, psychology, sociology, true crime, war, women's studies, young adult. **Considers these fiction areas:** commercial, contemporary issues, crime, detective, ethnic, fantasy, feminist, gay, historical, juvenile, lesbian, mainstream, middle grade, multicultural, mystery, picture books, thriller, women's, young adult.

Specializes in women's fiction, literary fiction, young adult fiction, as well as both practical and idea-driven nonfiction. "Due to the volume of queries and mss received, we apologize for not answering every e-mail and letter. None of us handles children's picture books or chapter books. No New Age. We do not handle screenplays or poetry."

HOW TO CONTACT "If you would like, you may include a synopsis and no more than 10 pages. If you are mailing your query, please be sure to include a self-addressed, stamped envelope; without it, you may not hear back from us. To save money, time and trees, we prefer queries by e-mail to queries@ldlainc.com. We get a lot of spam and are wary of computer viruses, so please use the word 'Query' in the subject line and include your detailed materials in the body of your message, not as an attachment." Accepts simultaneous submissions. Responds in 2-4 weeks.

DANIEL LITERARY GROUP

601 Old Hickory Blvd., #56, Brentwood TN 37027. **E-mail:** greg@danielliterarygroup.com. **E-mail:** submissions@danielliterarygroup.com. **Website:** www.danielliterarygroup.com. **Contact:** Greg Daniel. Represents 45 clients.

Prior to becoming an agent, Mr. Daniel spent 10 years in publishing—6 at the executive level at Thomas Nelson Publishers.

REPRESENTS Nonfiction. **Considers these nonfiction areas:** autobiography, biography, business, child guidance, current affairs, economics, environment, film, health, history, how-to, humor, inspirational, medicine, memoirs, parenting, popular culture, religious, satire, self-help, sports, theater, women's issues, women's studies.

"We take pride in our ability to come alongside our authors and help strategize about where they want their writing to take them in both the near and long term. Forging close relationships with our authors, we help them with such critical factors as editorial refinement, branding, audience, and marketing." The agency is open to submissions in almost every popular category of nonfiction, especially if authors are recognized experts in their fields. No fiction, screenplays, poetry, children's, or short stories.

HOW TO CONTACT Query via e-mail only. Submit publishing history, author bio, key selling points; no attachments. Check the agency's online Submissions Guidelines before querying or submitting, as they do change. Please do not query via telephone. Accepts simultaneous submissions. Responds in 2-3 weeks to queries.

DARHANSOFF & VERRILL LITERARY AGENTS

133 W. 72nd St., Room 304, New York NY 10023. (917)305-1300. **E-mail:** submissions@dvagency.com. **Website:** www.dvagency.com. "We are most interested in literary fiction, narrative nonfiction, memoir, sophisticated suspense, and both fiction and nonfiction for younger readers. Please note we do not represent theatrical plays or film scripts." Member of AAR.

MEMBER AGENTS Liz Darhansoff; Chuck Verrill; Michele Mortimer; Eric Amling.

REPRESENTS Nonfiction, novels. **Considers these nonfiction areas:** creative nonfiction, juvenile nonfiction, memoirs, young adult. **Considers these fiction areas:** literary, middle grade, suspense, young adult.

HOW TO CONTACT Send queries via e-mail. Accepts simultaneous submissions.

RECENT SALES A full list of clients is available on their website.

CAROLINE DAVIDSON LITERARY AGENCY

5 Queen Anne's Gardens, London W4 1TU United Kingdom. (44)(0)(20)8995-5768. **Fax:** (44)(0)(20)8994-2770. **E-mail:** enquiries@cdla.co.uk. **Website:** www.cdla.co.uk. **Contact:** Ms. Caroline Davidson. AAA

REPRESENTS Nonfiction, fiction. **Considers these nonfiction areas:** agriculture, archeology, architecture, art, biography, cooking, cultural interests, current affairs, design, environment, foods, gardening, health, history, medicine, politics, psychology, science, astronomy, climate change, ecology, global warming, home life, linguistics, natural history, reference, rual life, water supplies.

Does not want chick lit, romance, erotica, crime and thrillers, science fiction, fantasy, poetry, individual short stories, children's, young adult, misery memoirs and fictionalised autobiography, conspiracy theories, educational textbooks, local history, occult, PhD theses, self-help, 'sob stories,' unfortunate personal experiences, painful lives, true crime, and war stories.

HOW TO CONTACT Send preliminary letter with CV and detailed well thought-out book proposal/synopsis and/or first 50 pages and last 10 pages of novel in hard copy only. No e-mail submissions will be accepted or replied to. No reply without large SASE with correct return postage. No reading fee. Please refer to website for further information. CDLA does not acknowledge or reply to e-mail inquiries. No telephone inquiries.

LIZA DAWSON ASSOCIATES

121 W. 27th St., Suite 1201, New York NY 10001. (212)465-9071. **Website:** www.lizadawsonassociates.com. **Contact:** Caitie Flum. Member of AAR. MWA, Women's Media Group. Represents 50+ clients.

Prior to becoming an agent, Ms. Dawson was an editor for 20 years, spending 11 years at William Morrow as vice president and 2 years at Putnam as executive editor. Ms. Blasdell was a senior editor at HarperCollins and Avon. Ms. Johnson-Blalock was an assistant at Trident Media Group. Ms. Flum was the coordinator for the Children's Book of the Month club.

MEMBER AGENTS Liza Dawson, queryliza@lizadawsonassociates.com (plot-driven literary and popular fiction, historical, thrillers, suspense, history, psychology [both popular and clinical], politics, narrative nonfiction, and memoirs); Caitlin Blasdell, querycaitlin@lizadawsonassociates.com (science fiction, fantasy [both adult and young adult], parenting, business, thrillers, and women's fiction); Hannah Bowman, queryhannah@lizadawsonassociates.com (commercial fiction [especially science fiction and fantasy, young adult] and nonfiction in the areas of mathematics, science, and spirituality); Monica Odom, querymonica@lizadawsonassociates.com (nonfiction in the areas of Social Studies, including topics of: identity, race, gender, sexual orientation, socioeconomics, civil rights and social justice, advice/relationships, self-help/self-reflection, how-to, crafting/creativity, food and cooking, humor, pop culture, lifestyle, fashion & beauty, biography, memoir, narrative, business, politics and current affairs, history, science and literary fiction and upmarket fiction, Illustrators with demonstrable platforms, preferably author/illustrators, working on nonfiction, graphic memoirs or graphic novels); Caitie Flum, querycaitie@lizadawsonassociates.com (commercial fiction, especially historical, women's fiction, mysteries, crossover fantasy, young adult, and middle-grade; nonfiction in the areas of theater, current affairs, and pop culture).

REPRESENTS Nonfiction, novels. **Considers these nonfiction areas:** agriculture, Americana, animals, anthropology, archeology, architecture, art, autobiography, biography, business, computers, cooking, creative nonfiction, cultural interests, current affairs, environment, ethnic, film, gardening, gay/lesbian, history, humor, investigative, juvenile nonfiction, memoirs, multicultural, parenting, popular culture, politics, psychology, religious, science, sex, sociology, spirituality, theater, travel, true crime, women's issues, women's studies, young adult. **Considers these fiction areas:** action, adventure, commercial, contemporary issues, crime, detective, ethnic, family saga, fantasy, feminist, gay, historical, horror, humor, juvenile, lesbian, mainstream, middle grade, multicultural, mystery, new adult, police, romance, science fiction, supernatural, suspense, thriller, urban fantasy, women's, young adult.

This agency specializes in readable literary fiction, thrillers, mainstream historicals, women's fiction, young adult, middle-grade, academics, historians, journalists, and psychology.

HOW TO CONTACT Query by e-mail only. No phone calls. Each of these agents has their own specific submission requirements, which you can find online at the agency's website. Obtains most new clients through recommendations from others, conferences, and queries.

TERMS Agent receives 15% commission on domestic sales; 20% commission on foreign sales. Offers written contract.

THE JENNIFER DE CHIARA LITERARY AGENCY

299 Park Ave., 6th Floor, New York NY 10171. (212)739-0803. **E-mail:** jenndec@aol.com. **Website:** www.jdlit.com. **Contact:** Jennifer De Chiara. Estab. 2001.

MEMBER AGENTS Jennifer De Chiara, jenndec@aol.com (fiction interests include literary, commercial, women's fiction [no bodice-rippers, please], chick-lit, mystery, suspense, thrillers, funny/quirky picture books, middle-grade, and young adult; nonfiction interests include celebrity memoirs and biographies, LGBT, memoirs, books about the arts and performing arts, behind-the-scenes-type books, and books about popular culture); Stephen Fraser, fraserstephena@gmail.com (one-of-a-kind picture books; strong chapter book series; whimsical, dramatic, or humorous middle-grade; dramatic or high-concept young adult; powerful and unusual nonfiction on a broad range of topics; Marie Lamba, marie.jdlit@gmail.com (young adult and middle-grade fiction, along with general and women's fiction and some memoir; interested in established illustrators and picture book authors); Roseanne Wells, queryroseanne@gmail.com (picture book, middle grade, young adult, select literary fiction, narrative nonfiction, select memoir, science (popular or trade, not academic), history, religion (not inspirational or Christian market), travel, humor, food/cooking, and similar subjects); Victoria Selvaggio, vickiaselvaggio@gmail.com (board books, picture books, chapter books, middle-grade, young adult, new adult, and adult; interested in nonfiction and fiction in all genres); Damian McNicholl, damianmcnichollvarney@gmail.com (accessible literary fiction, memoir, narrative nonfiction [especially biography, investigative journalism, cultural, legal, and LGBT]); Alexandra Weiss, alexweiss.jdlit@gmail.com (voice-driven young adult in all genres, silly and smart middle-grade fiction, chapter books, fiction and nonfiction picture books, especially science-based stories, select literary fiction); Cari Lamba, cari.jdlit.@gmail.com (middle-grade fiction, especially contemporary and quirky, fiction and nonfiction picture books, commercial fiction, mysteries, cozies, and foodie novels); David Laurell, dclaurell@gmail.com (celebrity memoir, pop culture, television, broadcasting, all genres of entertainment and sports, inspirational, collecting and strong character-driven fiction).

REPRESENTS Nonfiction, fiction, novels, juvenile books. **Considers these nonfiction areas:** art, autobiography, biography, child guidance, cooking, creative nonfiction, cultural interests, current affairs, dance, film, foods, gay/lesbian, health, history, humor, investigative, juvenile nonfiction, literature, memoirs, multicultural, parenting, philosophy, popular culture, politics, psychology, religious, science, self-help, sex, spirituality, technology, theater, travel, true crime, war, women's issues, women's studies, young adult. **Considers these fiction areas:** commercial, contemporary issues, crime, ethnic, family saga, fantasy, feminist, gay, historical, horror, humor, inspirational, juvenile, lesbian, literary, mainstream, middle grade, multicultural, mystery, new adult, New Age, paranormal, picture books, science fiction, suspense, thriller, urban fantasy, women's, young adult.

HOW TO CONTACT Each agent has their own e-mail submission address and submission instructions; check the website for the current updates, as policies do change. Accepts simultaneous submissions. Obtains most new clients through recommendations from others, conferences, query letters.

TERMS Agent receives 15% commission on domestic sales. Offers written contract.

DEFIORE & COMPANY

47 E. 19th St., 3rd Floor, New York NY 10003. (212)925-7744. **Fax:** (212)925-9803. **E-mail:** info@defliterary.com, submissions@defliterary.com. **Website:** www.defliterary.com. Member of AAR. Signatory of WGA.

Prior to becoming an agent, Mr. DeFiore was publisher of Villard Books (1997-1998), editor-in-chief of Hyperion (1992-1997), editorial director of Delacorte Press (1988-1992), and an editor at St. Martin's Press (1984-88).

MEMBER AGENTS **Brian DeFiore** (popular nonfiction, business, pop culture, parenting, commercial fiction); **Laurie Abkemeier** (memoir, parenting, business, how-to/self-help, popular science); **Matthew Elblonk** (young adult, popular culture, narrative nonfiction); **Caryn Karmatz-Rudy** (popular fiction, self-help, narrative nonfiction); **Adam Schear** (commercial fiction, humor, young adult, smart thrillers, historical fiction, quirky debut literary novels, popular science, politics, popular culture, current events); **Meredith Kaffel Simonoff** (smart upmarket women's fiction, literary fiction [especially debut], literary thrillers, narrative nonfiction, nonfiction about science and tech, sophisticated pop culture/humor books); **Rebecca Strauss** (literary and commercial fiction, women's fiction, urban fantasy, romance, mystery, young adult, memoir, pop culture, select nonfiction); **Lisa Gallagher** (fiction and nonfiction); **Nicole Tourtelot** (narrative and prescriptive nonfiction, food, lifestyle, wellness, pop culture, history, humor, memoir, select young adult and adult fiction); **Ashely Collom** (women's fiction, children's and young adult, psychological thrillers, memoir, politics, photography, cooking, narrative nonfiction, LGBT issues, feminism, occult); **Miriam Altshuler** (adult literary and commercial fiction, narrative nonfiction, middle-grade, young adult, memoir, narrative nonfiction, self-help, family sagas, historical novels); **Reiko Davis** (adult literary and upmarket fiction, narrative nonfiction, young adult, middle-grade, memoir).

REPRESENTS Nonfiction, novels, short story collections, juvenile books, poetry books. **Considers these nonfiction areas:** autobiography, biography, business, child guidance, cooking, economics, foods, gay/lesbian, how-to, inspirational, money, multicultural, parenting, photography, popular culture, politics, psychology, religious, science, self-help, sex, sports, technology, travel, women's issues, young adult. **Considers these fiction areas:** comic books, commercial, ethnic, feminist, gay, lesbian, literary, mainstream, middle grade, mystery, paranormal, picture books, poetry, romance, short story collections, suspense, thriller, urban fantasy, women's, young adult.

"Please be advised that we are not considering dramatic projects at this time."

HOW TO CONTACT Query with SASE or e-mail to submissions@defliterary.com. "Please include the word 'query' in the subject line. All attachments will be deleted; please insert all text in the body of the e-mail. For more information about our agents, their individual interests, and their query guidelines, please visit our 'About Us' page on our website." Accepts simultaneous submissions. Obtains most new clients through recommendations from others.

TERMS Agent receives 15% commission on domestic sales. Agent receives 20% commission on foreign sales. Offers written contract; 10-day notice must be given to terminate contract. Charges clients for photocopying and overnight delivery (deducted only after a sale is made).

JOELLE DELBOURGO ASSOCIATES, INC.

101 Park St., Montclair NJ 07042. (973)773-0836. **E-mail:** joelle@delbourgo.com. **E-mail:** submissions@delbourgo.com. **Website:** www.delbourgo.com. **Contact:** Joelle Delbourgo. "We are a boutique agency representing a wide range of nonfiction and fiction. Nonfiction: narrative, research-based and prescriptive nonfiction, including history, current affairs, education, psychology and personal development, parenting, science, business and economics, diet and nutrition, and cookbooks. Adult and young adult commercial and literary fiction, some middle grade.

We do not represent plays, screenplays, poetry and picture books." Estab. 1999. Member of AAR. Represents more than 500 clients.

Prior to becoming an agent, Ms. Delbourgo was an editor and senior publishing executive at HarperCollins and Random House. She began her editorial career at Bantam Books where she discovered the Choose Your Own Adventure series. Joelle Delbourgo brings more than three decades of experience as an editor and agent. Prior to joining the agency, Jacqueline Flynn was Executive Editor at Amacom for more than 15 years.

MEMBER AGENTS Joelle Delbourgo; Jacqueline Flynn.

REPRESENTS Nonfiction, fiction, novels. **Considers these nonfiction areas:** Americana, animals, anthropology, archeology, autobiography, biography, business, child guidance, cooking, creative nonfiction, current affairs, dance, decorating, diet/nutrition, design, economics, education, environment, film, gardening, gay/lesbian, government, health, history, how-to, humor, inspirational, interior design, investigative, juvenile nonfiction, literature, medicine, memoirs, military, money, multicultural, music, parenting, philosophy, popular culture, politics, psychology, science, self-help, sex, sociology, spirituality, sports, translation, travel, true crime, war, women's issues, women's studies. **Considers these fiction areas:** adventure, commercial, contemporary issues, crime, detective, fantasy, feminist, juvenile, literary, mainstream, middle grade, military, mystery, new adult, New Age, romance, science fiction, thriller, urban fantasy, women's, young adult.

"We are former publishers and editors with deep knowledge and an insider perspective. We have a reputation for individualized attention to clients, strategic management of authors' careers, and creating strong partnerships with publishers for our clients." Do not send scripts, picture books, poetry.

HOW TO CONTACT It's preferable if you submit via e-mail to a specific agent. Query 1 agent only. No attachments. Put the word "Query" in the subject line. "While we do our best to respond to each query, if you have not received a response in 60 days you may consider that a pass. Please do not send us copies of self-published books unless requested. Let us know if you are sending your query to us exclusively or if this is a multiple submission. For nonfiction, let us know if a proposal and sample chapters are available; if not, you should probably wait to send your query when you have a completed proposal. For fiction and memoir, embed the *first* 10 pages of manuscript into the e-mail after your query letter. Please no attachments. If we like your first pages, we may ask to see your synopsis and more manuscript. Please do not cold call us or make a follow-up call unless we call you." Accepts simultaneous submissions.

TERMS Agent receives 15% commission on domestic sales and 20% commission on foreign sales as well as television/film adaptation when a co-agent is involved. Offers written contract. Charges clients for postage and photocopying.

RECENT SALES *Prison 865: The Search for Hitler's Death Camp Guards in America*, by Debbie Cenziper (Hachette Books); *Hushed in Death*, by Stephen P. Kelly (Pegasus); *Hypersext: Keeping Our Children Safe in a Sexualized World*, by Jillian P. Roberts PhD with Sara Au (Quarto); *The Griffins of Castle Cary*, by Heather Shumaker (Simon & Schuster Children's); *Biscuit: 50 California-Style Recipes*, by Michael Volpatt (Running Press); *Husbands and Other Sharp Objects*, by Marilyn Simon Rothstein (Lake Union).

WRITERS CONFERENCES Unicorn Conference.

TIPS "Do your homework. Do not cold call. Read and follow submission guidelines before contacting us. Do not call to find out if we received your material. No e-mail queries. Treat agents with respect, as you would any other professional, such as a doctor, lawyer or financial advisor."

SANDRA DIJKSTRA LITERARY AGENCY

1155 Camino del Mar, PMB 515, Del Mar CA 92014. **E-mail:** queries@dijkstraagency.com. **Website:** www.dijkstraagency.com. The Dijkstra Agency was established over 35 years ago and is known for guiding the careers of many best-selling fiction and non-fiction authors, including Amy Tan, Lisa See, Maxine Hong Kingston, Chitra Divakaruni, Eric Foner, Marcus Rediker, and many more. "We handle nearly all genres, except for poetry." Please see www.dijkstraagency.com for each agent's interests. Member of AAR. Authors Guild, Organization of American Historians, RWA. Represents 200+ clients.

MEMBER AGENTS President: Sandra Dijkstra (adult only). Acquiring Associate agents: Elise Capron (adult only); Jill Marr (adult only); Thao Le (adult and YA); Roz Foster (adult and YA); Jessica Watterson (subgenres of adult romance, and women's fiction); Suzy Evans (adult and YA); Jennifer Kim (adult and YA).

REPRESENTS Nonfiction, fiction, novels, short story collections, juvenile books, scholarly books. **Considers these nonfiction areas:** Americana, animals, anthropology, art, biography, business, creative nonfiction, cultural interests, current affairs, design, economics, environment, ethnic, gardening, government, health, history, juvenile nonfiction, literature, memoirs, multicultural, parenting, popular culture, politics, psychology, science, self-help, sports, true crime, women's issues, women's studies, young adult, narrative. **Considers these fiction areas:** commercial, contemporary issues, detective, family saga, fantasy, feminist, historical, horror, juvenile, literary, mainstream, middle grade, multicultural, mystery, new adult, romance, science fiction, short story collections, sports, suspense, thriller, urban fantasy, women's, young adult.

HOW TO CONTACT "Please see guidelines on our website, www.dijkstraagency.com. Please note that we only accept e-mail submissions. Due to the large number of unsolicited submissions we receive, we are only able to respond those submissions in which we are interested." Accepts simultaneous submissions. Responds to queries of interest within 6 weeks.

TERMS Works in conjunction with foreign and film agents. Agent receives 15% commission on domestic sales and 20% commission on foreign sales. Offers written contract. No reading fee.

TIPS "Remember that publishing is a business. Do your research and present your project in as professional a way as possible. Only submit your work when you are confident that it is polished and ready for prime-time. Make yourself a part of the active writing community by getting stories and articles published, networking with other writers, and getting a good sense of where your work fits in the market."

DONAGHY LITERARY GROUP

(647)527-4353. **E-mail:** stacey@donaghyliterary.com. **Website:** www.donaghyliterary.com. **Contact:** Stacey Donaghy. "Donaghy Literary Group provides full-service literary representation to our clients at every stage of their writing career. Specializing in commercial fiction, we seek middle grade, young adult, new adult and adult novels." RWA, PACLA.

Prior to opening her agency, Ms Donaghy served as an agent at the Corvisiero Literary Agency. And before this, she worked in training and education; acquiring and editing academic materials for publication and training. Ms. Noble interned for Jessica Sinsheimer of Sarah Jane Freymann Literary Agency. Ms. Miller previously worked in children's publishing with Scholastic Canada and also interned with Bree Ogden during her time at the D4EO Agency. Ms. Ayers-Barnett is a former Associate Editor for Pocket Books, Acquisitions Editor for Re.ad Publishing, and a freelance book editor for New York Book Editors.

MEMBER AGENTS Stacey Donaghy (women's fiction, romantic suspense, LGBTQ, Diverse and #Ownvoice, thriller, mystery, contemporary romance, and YA); Valerie Noble (historical, science fiction and fantasy [think Kristin Cashore and Suzanne Collins] for young adults and adults); Sue Miller (YA, urban fantasy, contemporary romance); Amanda Ayers Barnett (mystery/thrillers and middle-grade, young adult, new adult and women's fiction).

REPRESENTS Fiction, novels, juvenile books. **Considers these fiction areas:** commercial, contemporary issues, crime, detective, ethnic, family saga, fantasy, feminist, gay, historical, horror, juvenile, lesbian, literary, mainstream, middle grade, multicultural, mystery, new adult, paranormal, police, psychic, romance, science fiction, sports, supernatural, suspense, thriller, urban fantasy, women's, young adult.

HOW TO CONTACT Visit agency website for "new submission guidelines" Do not e-mail agents directly. This agency only accepts submissions through the QueryManager database system. Accepts simultaneous submissions. Time may vary depending on the volume of submissions.

TERMS Agent receives 15% commission on domestic sales; 20% commission on foreign sales. Offers written contract, 30-day notice must be given to terminate contract.

WRITERS CONFERENCES Romantic Times Booklovers Convention, Windsor International Writers Conference, OWC Ontario Writers Conference, SoCal Writers Conference, WD Toronto Writer's Workshop.

TIPS "Only submit to one DLG agent at a time, we work collaboratively and often share projects that may be better suited to another agent at the agency."

JIM DONOVAN LITERARY

5635 SMU Blvd., Suite 201, Dallas TX 75206. **E-mail:** jdliterary@sbcglobal.net. **Contact:** Melissa Shultz, agent. Estab. 1993. Represents 34 clients.

MEMBER AGENTS Jim Donovan (history—particularly American, military and Western; biography; sports; popular reference; popular culture; fiction—literary, thrillers and mystery); Melissa Shultz (all subjects listed above [like Jim], along with parenting and women's issues).

REPRESENTS Nonfiction, fiction, novels. **Considers these nonfiction areas:** biography, current affairs, health, history, investigative, literature, military, parenting, popular culture, science, sports, war, women's issues. **Considers these fiction areas:** action, adventure, commercial, crime, detective, frontier, historical, mainstream, multicultural, mystery, police, suspense, thriller, war, westerns.

This agency specializes in commercial fiction and nonfiction. "Does not want to receive poetry, children's, sci-fi, fantasy, short stories, memoir, inspirational or anything else not listed above."

HOW TO CONTACT "For nonfiction, I need a well-thought-out query letter telling me about the book: What it does, how it does it, why it's needed now, why it's better or different than what's out there on the subject, and why the author is the perfect writer for it. For fiction, the novel has to be finished, of course; a short (2- to 5-page) synopsis—not a teaser, but a summary of all the action, from first page to last—and the first 30-50 pages is enough. This material should be polished to as close to perfection as possible." Accepts simultaneous submissions. Responds in 2 weeks to queries; 1 month to mss. Obtains most new clients through recommendations from others.

TERMS Agent receives 15% commission on domestic sales. Agent receives 20% commission on foreign sales. Offers written contract, binding for 1 year; 30-day notice must be given to terminate contract. This agency charges for things such as overnight delivery and manuscript copying. Charges are discussed beforehand.

RECENT SALES *The Road to Jonestown*, by Jeff Guinn (S&S); *The Earth Is All That Lasts*, by Mark Gardner (HarperCollins); *As Good as Dead*, by Stephen Moore (NAL); *James Monroe*, by Tim McGrath (NAL); *The Greatest Fury*, by William C. Davis (NAL); *The Hamilton Affair*, by Elizabeth Cobbs (Arcade); *Resurrection Pass*, by Kurt Anderson (Kensington).

TIPS "Get published in short form—magazine reviews, journals, etc.—first. This will increase your credibility considerably, and make it much easier to sell a full-length book."

DOYEN LITERARY SERVICES, INC.

Website: www.barbaradoyen.com. **Contact:** B.J. Doyen, President.

HOW TO CONTACT Not accepting submissions. Accepts simultaneous submissions.

DREISBACH LITERARY MANAGEMENT

P.O. Box 5379, El Dorado Hills CA 95762. (916)804-5016. **E-mail:** verna@dreisbachliterary.com. **Website:** www.dreisbachliterary.com. **Contact:** Verna Dreisbach. Currently not accepting submissions. Estab. 2007. Member of AAR. Signatory of WGA.

REPRESENTS Nonfiction. **Considers these nonfiction areas:** biography, business, economics, health, history, memoirs, multicultural, parenting, science, technology, travel, true crime, women's issues.

DUNHAM LITERARY, INC.

110 William St., Suite 2202, New York NY 10038. (212)929-0994. **E-mail:** query@dunhamlit.com. **Website:** www.dunhamlit.com. **Contact:** Jennie Dunham. Estab. 2000. Member of AAR. SCBWI Represents 50 clients.

Prior to opening her agency, Ms. Dunham worked as a literary agent for Russell & Volkening. The Rhoda Weyr Agency is now a division of Dunham Literary, Inc.

MEMBER AGENTS Jennie Dunham, Bridget Smith, Leslie Zampetti.

REPRESENTS Nonfiction, fiction, novels, short story collections, juvenile books. **Considers these nonfiction areas:** anthropology, archeology, art, biography, creative nonfiction, cultural interests, environment, gay/lesbian, health, history, language, literature, medicine, memoirs, multicultural, parenting, popular culture, politics, psychology, science, sociology, technology, women's issues, women's studies, young adult. **Considers these fiction areas:** family saga, fantasy, feminist, gay, historical, humor, juvenile, lesbian, literary, mainstream, middle grade, multicultural, mystery, picture books, science fiction, short story collections, sports, urban fantasy, women's, young adult.

Does not want Westerns, genre romance, poetry.

HOW TO CONTACT E-mail queries preferred, with all materials pasted in the body of the e-mail. Attachments will not be opened. Paper queries are also accepted. Please include a SASE for response and return of materials. Please include the first 5 pages with the query. Accepts simultaneous submissions. Responds in 4 weeks to queries; 2 months to mss. Obtains most new clients through recommendations from others, solicitations.

TERMS Agent receives 15% commission on domestic sales; 20% commission on foreign sales.

RECENT SALES *The Bad Kitty Series*, by Nick Bruel (Macmillan); *The Christmas Story*, by Robert Sabuda (Candlewick); *The Gollywhopper Games* and Sequels, by Jody Feldman (HarperCollins); *Foolish Hearts*, by Emma Mills (Macmillan); *Learning Not To Drown*, by Anna Shinoda (Simon & Schuster); *Gangster Nation*, by Tod Goldberg (Counterpoint); *A Shadow All of Light*, by Fred Chappell (Tor).

DUNOW, CARLSON, & LERNER AGENCY

27 W. 20th St., Suite 1107, New York NY 10011. (212)645-7606. **E-mail:** mail@dclagency.com. **Website:** www.dclagency.com. Member of AAR.

MEMBER AGENTS Jennifer Carlson (narrative nonfiction writers and journalists covering current events and ideas and cultural history, as well as literary and upmarket commercial novelists); Henry Dunow (quality fiction–literary, historical, strongly written commercial–and with voice-driven nonfiction across a range of areas–narrative history, biography, memoir, current affairs, cultural trends and criticism, science, sports); Erin Hosier (nonfiction: popular culture, music, sociology and memoir); Betsy Lerner (nonfiction writers in the areas of psychology, history, cultural studies, biography, current events, business; fiction: literary, dark, funny, voice driven); Yishai Seidman (broad range of fiction: literary, postmodern, and thrillers; nonfiction: sports, music, and pop culture); Amy Hughes (nonfiction in the areas of history, cultural studies, memoir, current events, wellness, health, food, pop culture, and biography; also literary fiction); Eleanor Jackson (literary, commercial, memoir, art, food, science and history); Julia Kenny (fiction—adult, middle grade and YA—and is especially interested in dark, literary thrillers and suspense); Edward Necarsulmer IV (strong new voices in teen & middle grade as well as picture books); Stacia Decker; Arielle Datz (fiction—adult, YA, or middle-grade—literary and commercial, nonfiction—essays, unconventional memoir, pop culture, and sociology).

REPRESENTS Nonfiction, fiction, novels, short story collections. **Considers these nonfiction areas:** art, biography, creative nonfiction, cultural interests, current affairs, foods, health, history, memoirs, music, popular culture, psychology, science, sociology, sports. **Considers these fiction areas:** commercial, literary, mainstream, middle grade, mystery, picture books, thriller, young adult.

HOW TO CONTACT Query via snail mail with SASE, or by e-mail. E-mail preferred, paste 10 sample pages below query letter. No attachments. Will respond only if interested. Accepts simultaneous submissions. Responds in 4-6 weeks if interested.

RECENT SALES A full list of agency clients is on the website.

DYSTEL, GODERICH & BOURRET LLC

1 Union Square W., Suite 904, New York NY 10003. (212)627-9100. **Fax:** (212)627-9313. **Website:** www.dystel.com. Estab. 1994. Member of AAR. Other membership includes SCBWI. Represents 600+ clients.

MEMBER AGENTS Jane Dystel; Miriam Goderich, miriam@dystel.com (literary and commercial fiction as well as some genre fiction, narrative nonfiction, pop culture, psychology, history, science, art, business books, and biography/memoir); Stacey Glick, sglick@dystel.com (adult narrative nonfiction including memoir, parenting, cooking and food, psychology, science, health and wellness, lifestyle, current events, pop culture, YA, middle grade, children's nonfiction, and select adult contemporary fiction); Michael Bourret, mbourret@dystel.com (middle grade and young adult fiction, commercial adult fiction, and all sorts of nonfiction, from practical to narrative; he's especially interested in food and cocktail related books, memoir, popular history, politics, religion (though not spirituality), popular science, and current events); Jim McCarthy, jmccarthy@dystel.com (literary women's fiction, underrepresented voices, mysteries, romance, paranormal fiction, narrative nonfiction, memoir, and paranormal nonfiction); Jessica Papin, jpapin@dystel.com (plot-driven literary and smart commercial fiction, and narrative non-fiction across a range of subjects, including history, medicine, science, economics and women's issues); Lauren Abramo, labramo@dystel.com (humorous middle grade and contemporary YA on the children's side, and upmarket commercial fiction and well-paced literary fiction on the adult side; adult narrative nonfiction, especially pop culture, psychology, pop science, reportage, media, and contemporary culture; in nonfiction, has a strong preference for interdisciplinary approaches, and in all categories she's especially interested in underrepresented voices); John Rudolph, jrudolph@dystel.com (picture book author/illustrators, middle grade, YA, select commercial fiction, and narrative nonfiction—especially in music, sports, history, popular science, "big think", performing arts, health, business, memoir, military history, and humor); Sharon Pelletier, spelletier@dystel.com (smart commercial fiction, from upmarket women's fiction to domestic suspense to literary thrillers, and strong contemporary romance novels; compelling nonfiction projects, especially feminism and religion); Michael Hoogland, mhoogland@dystel.com (thriller, SFF, YA, upmarket women's fiction, and narrative nonfiction); Erin Young, eyoung@dystel.com (YA/MG, literary and intellectual commercial thrillers, memoirs, biographies, sport and science narratives); Amy Bishop, abishop@dystel.com (commercial and literary women's fiction, fiction from diverse authors, historical fiction, YA, personal narratives, and biographies); Kemi Faderin, kfaderin@dystel.com (smart, plot-driven YA, historical fiction/non-fiction, contemporary women's fiction, and literary fiction).

REPRESENTS **Considers these nonfiction areas:** animals, art, autobiography, biography, business, cooking, cultural interests, current affairs, ethnic, foods, gay/lesbian, health, history, humor, inspirational, investigative, medicine, memoirs, metaphysics, military, New Age, parenting, popular culture, politics, psychology, religious, science, sports, women's issues, women's studies. **Considers these fiction areas:** commercial, ethnic, gay, lesbian, literary, mainstream, middle grade, mystery, paranormal, romance, suspense, thriller, women's, young adult.

"We are actively seeking fiction for all ages, in all genres." No plays, screenplays, or poetry.

HOW TO CONTACT Query via e-mail and put "Query" in the subject line. "Synopses, outlines or sample chapters (say, one chapter or the first 25 pages of your manuscript) should either be included below the cover letter or attached as a separate document. We won't open attachments if they come with a blank e-mail." Accepts simultaneous submissions. Responds in 6 to 8 weeks to queries; within 8 weeks to mss. Obtains most new clients through recommendations from others, solicitations, conferences.

TERMS Agent receives 15% commission on domestic sales; 19% commission on foreign sales. Offers written contract.

WRITERS CONFERENCES Backspace Writers' Conference, Pacific Northwest Writers' Association, Pike's Peak Writers' Conference, Writers League of Texas, Love Is Murder, Surrey International Writers Conference, Society of Children's Book Writers and Illustrators, International Thriller Writers, Willamette Writers Conference, The South Carolina Writers Workshop Conference, Las Vegas Writers Conference, Writer's Digest, Seton Hill Popular Fiction, Romance Writers of America, Geneva Writers Conference.

TIPS "DGLM prides itself on being a full-service agency. We're involved in every stage of the publishing process, from offering substantial editing on mss and proposals, to coming up with book ideas for authors looking for their next project, negotiating contracts and collecting monies for our clients. We follow a book from its inception through its sale to a publisher, its publication, and beyond. Our commitment to our writers does not, by any means, end when we have collected our commission. This is one of the many things that makes us unique in a very competitive business."

EBELING & ASSOCIATES

898 Pioneer Rd, Lyons CO 80540. (303)823-6963. **E-mail:** michael@ebelingagency.com. **Website:** www.ebelingagency.com. **Contact:** Michael Ebeling. Estab. 2000. Represents 6 clients.

Prior to becoming an agent, Mr. Ebeling established a career in the publishing industry through long-term author management. He has expertise in sales, platform building, publicity and marketing.

REPRESENTS Nonfiction. **Considers these nonfiction areas:** business, health, New Age, parenting, self-help, spirituality, commercial.

Does not want to receive fiction, poetry or children's lit.

HOW TO CONTACT Accepts e-mail submissions and proposals only. Include a brief statement of the purpose and premise of your book, your contact information, proposal, 1-2 page description of the book, biography, promotion plan, TOC, significant aspects of your platform, introduction and 1-2 sample chapters, current status of ms, and any other relevant information. Accepts simultaneous submissions. Responds in 6-8 weeks to queries.

RECENT SALES A partial list of clients and recent sales are available on their website.

EDEN STREET LITERARY

P.O. Box 30, Billings NY 12510. **E-mail:** info@edenstreetlit.com. **E-mail:** submissions@edenstreetlit.com. **Website:** www.edenstreetlit.com. **Contact:** Liza Voges. Eden Street represents over 40 authors and author-illustrators of books for young readers from preschool through young adult. Their books have won numerous awards over the past 30 years. Eden Street prides themselves on tailoring services to each client's goals, working in tandem with them to achieve literary, critical, and commercial success. Welcomes the opportunity to work with additional authors and illustrators. This agency gives priority to members of SCBWI. Member of AAR. Signatory of WGA. Represents over 40 clients.

REPRESENTS Nonfiction, fiction, novels, juvenile books. **Considers these fiction areas:** juvenile, middle grade, picture books, young adult.

HOW TO CONTACT E-mail a picture book ms or dummy; a synopsis and 3 chapters of a MG or YA novel; a proposal and 3 sample chapters for nonfiction. Accepts simultaneous submissions. Responds only to submissions of interest.

RECENT SALES *Dream Dog*, by Lou Berger; *Biscuit Loves the Library*, by Alyssa Capucilli; *The Scraps Book*, by Lois Ehlert; *Two Bunny Buddies*, by Kathryn O. Galbraith; *Between Two Worlds*, by Katherine Kirkpatrick.

JUDITH EHRLICH LITERARY MANAGEMENT, LLC

146 Central Park W., 20E, New York NY 10023. (646)505-1570. **Fax:** (646)505-1570. **E-mail:** jehrlich@judithehrlichliterary.com. **Website:** www.judithehrlichliterary.com. Judith Ehrlich Literary Management LLC, established in 2002 and based in New York City, is a full service agency. "We represent nonfiction and fiction, both literary and commercial for the mainstream trade market. Our approach is very hands on, editorial, and constructive with the primary goal of helping authors build successful writing careers." Special areas of interest include compelling narrative nonfiction, outstanding biographies and memoirs, lifestyle books, works that reflect our changing culture, women's issues, psychology, science, social issues, current events, parenting, health, history, business, and prescriptive books offering fresh information and advice. "We also seek and represent stellar commercial and literary fiction, including romance and other women's fiction, historical fiction, literary mysteries, and select thrillers. Our agency deals closely with all major and independent publishers. When appropriate, we place our properties with foreign agents and co-agents at leading film agencies in New York and Los Angeles." Estab. 2002. Member of the Author's Guild and the American Society of Journalists and Authors.

Prior to her current position, Ms. Ehrlich was a senior associate at the Linda Chester Agency and is an award-winning journalist; she is the co-author of *The New Crowd: The Changing of the Jewish Guard on Wall Street* (Little, Brown).

MEMBER AGENTS Judith Ehrlich, jehrlich@judithehrlichliterary.com (upmarket, literary and quality commercial fiction, nonfiction: narrative, women's, business, prescriptive, medical and health-related topics, history, and current events).

REPRESENTS Nonfiction, fiction, novels, short story collections, juvenile books. **Considers these nonfiction areas:** animals, art, autobiography, biography, business, creative nonfiction, cultural interests, current affairs, diet/nutrition, health, history, how-to, humor, inspirational, investigative, juvenile nonfiction, memoirs, parenting, photography, popular culture, politics, psychology, science, self-help, sociology, true crime, women's issues, young adult. **Considers these fiction areas:** adventure, commercial, contemporary issues, crime, detective, family saga, historical, humor, juvenile, literary, middle grade, mystery, picture books, short story collections, suspense, thriller, women's, young adult.

Does not want to receive novellas, poetry, textbooks, plays, or screenplays.

HOW TO CONTACT E-query, with a synopsis and some sample pages. The agency will respond only if interested. Accepts simultaneous submissions.

RECENT SALES Fiction: *The Bicycle Spy*, by Yona Zeldis McDonough (Scholastic); *The House on Primrose Pond*, by Yona McDonough (NAL/Penguin); *You Were Meant for Me*, by Yona McDonough (NAL/Penguin); *Echoes of Us: The Hybrid Chronicles*, Book 3 by Kat Zhang (HarperCollins); *Once We Were: The Hybrid Chronicles* Book 2, by Kat Zhang (HarperCollins). Nonfiction: *Listen to the Echoes: The Ray Bradbury Interviews (Deluxe Edition)*, by Sam Weller (Hat & Beard Press); *What are The Ten Commandments?*, by Yona McDonough (Grosset & Dunlap); *Little Author in the Big Woods: A Biography of Laura Ingalls Wilder*, by Yona McDonough (Christy Ottaviano Books/Henry Holt); *Ray Bradbury: The Last Interview: And Other Conversations*, by Sam Weller (Melville House); *Who Was Sojourner Truth?*, by Yona McDonough (Grosset & Dunlap); *Power Branding: Leveraging the Success of the World's Best Brands*, by Steve McKee (Palgrave Macmillan); *Confessions of a Sociopath: A Life Spent Hiding in Plain Sight*, by M.E. Thomas (Crown); *Luck and Circumstance: A Coming of Age in New York* and *Hollywood* and *Points Beyond*, by Michael Lindsay-Hogg (Knopf).

EINSTEIN LITERARY MANAGEMENT

27 W. 20th St., No. 1003, New York NY 10011. (212)221-8797. **E-mail:** info@einsteinliterary.com. **E-mail:** submissions@einsteinliterary.com. **Website:** http://einsteinliterary.com. **Contact:** Susanna Einstein. Estab. 2015. Member of AAR. Signatory of WGA.

Prior to her current position, Ms. Einstein was with LJK Literary Management and the Einstein Thompson Agency.

MEMBER AGENTS Susanna Einstein, Susan Graham, Shana Kelly.

REPRESENTS Nonfiction, fiction, novels, short story collections, juvenile books. **Considers these nonfiction areas:** cooking, creative nonfiction, memoirs, blog-to-book projects. **Considers these fiction areas:** comic books, commercial, crime, fantasy, historical, juvenile, literary, middle grade, mystery, picture books, romance, science fiction, suspense, thriller, women's, young adult.

"As an agency we represent a broad range of literary and commercial fiction, including upmarket women's fiction, crime fiction, historical fiction, romance, and books for middle-grade children and young adults, including picture books and graphic novels. We also handle non-fiction including cookbooks, memoir and narrative, and blog-to-book projects. Please see agent bios on the website for specific information about what each of ELM's agents represents." Does not want poetry, textbooks, or screenplays.

HOW TO CONTACT Please submit a query letter and the first 10 double-spaced pages of your manuscript in the body of the e-mail (no attachments). Does not respond to mail queries or telephone queries or queries that are not specifically addressed to this agency. Accepts simultaneous submissions. Responds in 6 weeks if interested.

THE LISA EKUS GROUP, LLC

57 North St., Hatfield MA 01038. (413)247-9325. **Fax:** (413)247-9873. **E-mail:** info@lisaekus.com. **Website:** www.lisaekus.com. **Contact:** Sally Ekus. This agency specializes in cookbooks, health and wellness, and culinary narrative. Estab. 1982. Member of AAR.

MEMBER AGENTS Lisa Ekus; Sally Ekus.

REPRESENTS Nonfiction. **Considers these nonfiction areas:** cooking, diet/nutrition, foods, health, how-to, humor, women's issues, occasionally health/well-being and women's issues; humor; lifestyle.

"Please note that we do not handle fiction, poetry, or children's books. If we receive a query for titles in these categories, please understand that we do not have the time or resources to respond."

HOW TO CONTACT "For more information about our literary services, visit http://lisaekus.com/services/literary-agency. Submit a query via e-mail or through our contact form on the website. You can also submit complete hard copy proposal with title page, proposal contents, concept, bio, marketing, TOC, etc. Include SASE for the return of materials." Accepts simultaneous submissions. Responds in 4-6 weeks.

RECENT SALES "Please see the regularly updated client listing on our website."

TIPS "Please do not call. No phone queries."

EMPIRE LITERARY

115 W. 29th St., 3rd Floor, New York NY 10001. (917)213-7082. **E-mail:** abarzvi@empireliterary.com. **E-mail:** queries@empireliterary.com. **Website:** www.empireliterary.com. Estab. 2013. Member of AAR. Signatory of WGA.

MEMBER AGENTS Andrea Barzvi; Carrie Howland; Kathleen Schmidt; Penny Moore.

REPRESENTS Nonfiction, novels. **Considers these nonfiction areas:** diet/nutrition, health, memoirs, popular culture. **Considers these fiction areas:** literary, middle grade, women's, young adult.

HOW TO CONTACT Please only query one agent at a time. "If we are interested in reading more we will get in touch with you as soon as possible." Accepts simultaneous submissions.

FELICIA ETH LITERARY REPRESENTATION

555 Bryant St., Suite 350, Palo Alto CA 94301-1700. **E-mail:** feliciaeth.literary@gmail.com. **Website:** eth-literary.com. **Contact:** Felicia Eth. Member of AAR.

Worked as agent in NY at Writers House Inc. Prior to that worked in the movie business, Warner Bros NY. and Palomar Pictures for Story Dept.

REPRESENTS Nonfiction, fiction, novels. **Considers these nonfiction areas:** animals, creative nonfiction, cultural interests, current affairs, foods, history, investigative, memoirs, parenting, popular culture, psychology, science, sociology, travel, women's issues. **Considers these fiction areas:** contemporary issues, historical, literary, mainstream, suspense.

This agency specializes in high-quality fiction (preferably mainstream/contemporary) and provocative, intelligent, and thoughtful nonfiction on a wide array of commercial subjects. "The agency does not represent genre ficiton, including romance novels, sci fi and fantasy, westerns, anime and graphic novels, mysteries."

HOW TO CONTACT For fiction: Please write a query letter introducing yourself, your book, your writing background. Don't forget to include degrees you may have, publishing credits, awards and endorsements. Please wait for a response before including sample pages. "We only consider material where the manuscript for which you are querying is complete, unless you have previously published." For nonfiction: A query letter is best, introducing idea and what you have written already (proposal, manuscript?). "For writerly nonficiton (narratives, bio, memoir) please let us know if you have a finished manuscript. Also it's important you include information about yourself, your background and expertise, your platform and notoriety, if any. We do not ask for exclusivity in most instances but do ask that you inform us if other agents are considering the same material." Accepts simultaneous submissions. Responds in ideally 2 weeks for query, a month if more.

TERMS Agent receives 15% commission on domestic sales; 20% commission on foreign and film sales. Charges clients for photocopying and express mail service

RECENT SALES *Bumper Sticker Philosophy*, by Jack Bowen (Random House); *Boys Adrift*, by Leonard Sax (Basic Books); *The Memory Thief*, by Emily Colin (Ballantine Books); *The World is a Carpet*, by Anna Badkhen (Riverhead).

WRITERS CONFERENCES "Wide array—from Squaw Valley to Mills College."

MARY EVANS INC.

242 E. Fifth St., New York NY 10003. (212)979-0880. **Fax:** (212)979-5344. **E-mail:** info@maryevansinc.com. **Website:** maryevansinc.com. Member of AAR.

MEMBER AGENTS Mary Evans (progressive politics, alternative medicine, science and technology, social commentary, American history and culture); Julia Kardon (literary and upmarket fiction, narrative nonfiction, journalism, and history); Tom Mackay (nonfiction that uses sport as a platform to explore other issues and playful literary fiction).

REPRESENTS Nonfiction, novels. **Considers these nonfiction areas:** creative nonfiction, cultural interests, history, medicine, politics, science, technology, social commentary, journalism. **Considers these fiction areas:** literary, upmarket.

No screenplays or stage plays.

HOW TO CONTACT Query by mail or e-mail. If querying by mail, include a SASE. If querying by e-mail, put "Query" in the subject line. For fiction: Include the first few pages, or opening chapter of your novel as a single Word attachment. For nonfiction: Include your book proposal as a single Word attachment. Accepts simultaneous submissions. Responds within 4-8 weeks.

EVATOPIA, INC.

8447 Wilshire Blvd., Suite 401, Beverly Hills CA 90211. **E-mail:** submissions@evatopia.com. **Website:** www.evatopia.com. **Contact:** Margery Walshaw. Evatopia supports writers through consulting, literary management, and publishing services. Estab. 2004. BAFTA, IBPA, NetGalley Represents 15 clients.

Prior to becoming an agent, Ms. Walshaw was a writer and publicist for the entertainment industry.

MEMBER AGENTS Mary Kay (story development); Jamie Davis (story editor); Jill Jones (story editor).

REPRESENTS Nonfiction, fiction, novels, juvenile books, movie scripts, feature film, TV movie of the week. **Considers these fiction areas:** crime, detective, fantasy, juvenile, new adult, paranormal, romance, supernatural, thriller, women's, young adult, Projects aimed at women, teens and children. **Considers these script areas:** action, contemporary issues, detective, movie scripts, romantic drama, supernatural, TV movie of the week, projects aimed at women, teens and children. REPRESENTS Screenplays and novels; provides self-publishing support to novelists.

"All of our staff members have strong writing and entertainment backgrounds, making us sympathetic to the needs of our clients."

HOW TO CONTACT Submit via online submission form at www.evatopiaentertainment.com. Accepts simultaneous submissions. Obtains most new clients through recommendations.

TERMS Agent receives 15% commission on domestic sales. Agent receives 15% commission on foreign sales. Offers written contract; 30-day notice must be given to terminate contract.

TIPS "Remember that you only have 1 chance to make that important first impression. Make your loglines original and your synopses concise. The secret to a screenwriter's success is creating an original story and telling it in a manner that we haven't heard before."

FAIRBANK LITERARY REPRESENTATION

P.O. Box Six, Hudson NY 12534-0006. (617)576-0030. **E-mail:** queries@fairbankliterary.com. **Website:** www.fairbankliterary.com and www.publishersmarketplace.com/members/SorcheFairbank/. **Contact:** Sorche Elizabeth Fairbank. A small, selective agency and member of AAR, the Author's Guild, the Agents Round Table, PEN, and Grub Street's Literary Advisory Council, Fairbank Literary Representation is happily in its fifteenth year. Clients range from first-time authors to international best-sellers, prize winning-journalists to professionals at the top of their fields. They can be found with all the major publishers, as well as in the New York Times, Harper's, the Atlantic, the New Yorker, Granta, Best American Short Stories, and more. Our tastes tend toward literary and international fiction; the occasional mystery or thriller with a firm sense of place; BIG memoir that goes beyond the me-moir; topical or narrative non-fiction with a strong interest in women's voices, global perspectives, and class and race issues; children's picture Books & Middle Grade from illustrator/artists only; quality lifestyle books (food, wine, and design); pop culture; craft; and gift and humor books. We are most likely to pick up works that are of social or cultural significance, newsworthy, or that cause us to take great delight in the words, images or ideas on the page. Lately we have been doing extremely well in the humor/gift/pop culture category, international fiction, and children's picture books by illustrator artists, and we'd love to take on more projects in those categories. Above all, we look for a fresh voice, approach, story, or idea. Estab. 2002. Member of AAR. Author's Guild, the Agents Round Table, and Grub Street's Literary Advisory Council.

MEMBER AGENTS Sorche Fairbank (narrative nonfiction, commercial and literary fiction, memoir, food and wine); Matthew Frederick, matt@fairbankliterary.com (scout for sports nonfiction, architecture, design).

REPRESENTS Nonfiction, novels, short story collections. **Considers these nonfiction areas:** agriculture, animals, architecture, art, autobiography, biography, cooking, crafts, creative nonfiction, cultural interests, current affairs, decorating, diet/nutrition, design, environment, ethnic, foods, gardening, gay/lesbian, government, hobbies, horticulture, how-to, humor, interior design, investigative, juvenile nonfiction, law, memoirs, photography, popular culture, politics, science, sociology, sports, technology, true crime, women's issues, women's studies. **Considers these fiction areas:** commercial, feminist, literary, mainstream, mystery, picture books, short story collections, sports, suspense, thriller, women's, International voices. Southern voices.

"I tend to gravitate toward literary fiction and narrative nonfiction, with a strong interest in women's issues and women's voices, international voices, class and race issues, and projects that simply teach me something new about the greater world and society around us. We have a good reputation for working closely and developmentally with our authors and love what we do." Actively seeking literary fiction, international and culturally diverse voices, narrative nonfiction, topical subjects (politics, current affairs), history, sports, humor, architecture/design and humor/pop culture. Also looking for picture books by artist authors only. Does not want to receive romance, screenplays, poetry, science fiction or fantasty, young adult, or children's works unless by an artist author.

HOW TO CONTACT Query by e-mail queries@fairbankliterary.com or by mail with SASE. Accepts simultaneous submissions. Obtains most new clients through recommendations from others, solicitations, conferences, ideas generated in-house.

TERMS Agent receives 15% commission on domestic sales; 20% commission on foreign sales. Offers written contract, binding for 12 months; 45-day notice must be given to terminate contract.

RECENT SALES 3-book deal for Terry Border for picture books to Philomel; 2-book deal for Lisa Currie, *Surprise Yourself* and a 2nd book scheduled for 2019 to Marian Lizzi at Tarcher Perigee; scratch & sniff spin-off and an early reader adaptation of Terry Border's best-selling *Peanut Butter & Cupcake* to Grosset and Dunlap/Penguin; 4-book deal for Matthew Frederick for his best-selling *101 Things I Learned Series* moving to Crown.

TIPS "Be professional from the very first contact. There shouldn't be a single typo or grammatical flub in your query. Show me that you know your audience—and your competition. Have the writing and/or proposal at the very, very best it can be before starting the querying process. Don't assume that if someone likes it enough they'll 'fix' it. The biggest mistake new writers make is starting the querying process before they—and the work—are ready. Take your time and do it right."

LEIGH FELDMAN LITERARY

E-mail: assistant@lfliterary.com. **E-mail:** query@lfliterary.com. **Website:** http://lfliterary.com. **Contact:** Leigh Feldman. Estab. 2014. Member of AAR. Signatory of WGA.

During her 25 years as a literary agent based in New York City, Leigh Feldman has established herself as an invaluable partner to the writers she represents, and is highly respected by her peers in the industry. Her agency, Leigh Feldman Literary, is the culmination of experiences and lessons learned from her 20-plus years at Darhansoff, Verrill, Feldman Literary Agency and Writer's House. In that time, Feldman has represented National Book Award winners and bestsellers of literary fiction, historical fiction, memoir, middle grade, and young adult. No matter the writer or the category, Feldman only represents books she believes in, that captivate her, and that she can best serve with her passion and tenacity. Leigh Feldman Literary is a full service literary agency.

REPRESENTS Nonfiction, fiction, novels, short story collections. **Considers these nonfiction areas:** creative nonfiction, memoirs. **Considers these fiction areas:** contemporary issues, family saga, feminist, gay, historical, lesbian, literary, multicultural, short story collections, women's, young adult.

Does not want mystery, thriller, romance, paranormal, sci-fi.

HOW TO CONTACT E-query. "Please include 'query' in the subject line. Due to large volume of submissions, we regret that we can not respond to all queries individually. Please include the first chapter or the first 10 pages of your manuscript (or proposal) pasted after your query letter. I'd love to know what led you to query me in particular, and please let me know if you are querying other agents as well." Accepts simultaneous submissions.

RECENT SALES List of recent sales and best known sales are available on the agency website.

THE FIELDING AGENCY, LLC

1550G Tiburon Blvd., #528, Tiburon CA 94920. **E-mail:** wlee@fieldingagency.com. **Website:** www.fieldingagency.com. **Contact:** Whitney Lee. "The Fielding Agency is a full-service literary agency that represents a select number of authors domestically and also handles the foreign rights for titles on behalf of many prominent literary agencies."

REPRESENTS Nonfiction, fiction, juvenile books.

HOW TO CONTACT Accepts simultaneous submissions.

DIANA FINCH LITERARY AGENCY

116 W. 23rd St., Suite 500, New York NY 10011. (917)544-4470. **E-mail:** diana.finch@verizon.net. **Website:** dianafinchliteraryagency.blogspot.com. **Contact:** Diana Finch. A boutique agency in Manhattan's Chelsea neighborhood. "Many of the agency's clients are journalists, and I handle book-related magazine assignments as well as book deals. I am the Chair of the AAR's International Committee, attend

overseas book fairs, and actively handle foreign rights to my clients' work." Estab. 2003. Member of AAR. Represents approximately 40 active clients clients.

Seeking to represent books that change lives. Prior to opening her own agency in 2003, Ms. Finch worked at Ellen Levine Literary Agency for 18 years. She started her publishing career in the editorial department at St. Martin's Press.

REPRESENTS Nonfiction, fiction, novels, scholarly books. **Considers these nonfiction areas:** autobiography, biography, business, child guidance, computers, cultural interests, current affairs, dance, diet/nutrition, economics, environment, ethnic, film, government, health, history, how-to, humor, investigative, juvenile nonfiction, law, medicine, memoirs, military, money, music, parenting, photography, popular culture, politics, psychology, satire, science, self-help, sex, sports, technology, theater, translation, true crime, war, women's issues, women's studies, young adult. **Considers these fiction areas:** action, adventure, contemporary issues, crime, detective, ethnic, fantasy, historical, literary, mainstream, middle grade, multicultural, new adult, police, science fiction, sports, thriller, urban fantasy, young adult.

For news about the agency and agency clients, see the agency Facebook page at https://www.facebook.com/DianaFinchLitAg/. "Does not want romance or children's picture books."

HOW TO CONTACT This agency prefers submissions via its online form. Accepts simultaneous submissions. Obtains most new clients through recommendations from others.

TERMS Agent receives 15% commission on domestic sales; 20% commission on foreign sales. Offers written contract. "I charge for overseas postage, galleys, and books purchased, and try to recoup these costs from earnings received for a client, rather than charging outright."

RECENT SALES *The Journeys of the Trees*, by Zach St George (W. W. Norton); *Owls of the Eastern Ice*, by Jonathan Slaght (FSG/Scientific American); *Uncolor: on toxins in personal products*, by Ronnie Citron-Fink (Island Press); *Cutting School* by Professor Noliwe Rooks (The New Press); *Merchants of Men*, by Loretta Napoleoni (Seven Stories Press); *Beyond $15*, by Jonathan Rosenblum (Beacon Press); *The Age of Inequality*, by the Editors of In These Times (Verso Books); *Seeds of Resistance*, by Mark Schapiro (Hot Books/Skyhorse).

WRITERS CONFERENCES Washington Writers Conference; Writers Digest NYC Conference; CLMP/New School conference, and others on an individual basis.

TIPS "Do as much research as you can on agents before you query. Have someone critique your query letter before you send it. It should be only 1 page and describe your book clearly—and why you are writing it—but also demonstrate creativity and a sense of your writing style."

FINEPRINT LITERARY MANAGEMENT

207 W. 106th St., Suite 1D, New York NY 10025. (212)279-1282. **Website:** www.fineprintlit.com. Estab. 2007. Member of AAR.

MEMBER AGENTS Peter Rubie, CEO, peter@fineprintlit.com (nonfiction interests include narrative nonfiction, popular science, spirituality, history, biography, pop culture, business, technology, parenting, health, self help, music, and food; fiction interests include literate thrillers, crime fiction, science fiction and fantasy, military fiction and literary fiction, middle grade and boy-oriented YA fiction); Stephany Evans, stephany@fineprintlit.com (nonfiction: health and wellness, spirituality, lifestyle, food and drink, sustainability, running and fitness, memoir, and narrative nonfiction; fiction interests include mystery/crime, women's fiction, from literary to commercial to romance); Laura Wood, laura@fineprintlit.com (serious nonfiction, especially in the areas of science and nature, along with substantial titles in business, history, religion, and other areas by academics, experienced professionals, and journalists; select genre fiction only (no poetry, literary fiction or memoir) in the categories of science fiction & fantasy and mystery); June Clark, june@fineprintlit.com (nonfiction projects in the areas of entertainment, self-help, parenting, reference/how-to books, food and wine, style/beauty, and prescriptive business titles); Jacqueline Murphy, jacqueline@fineprintlit.com.

REPRESENTS Nonfiction, fiction, novels, short story collections. **Considers these nonfiction areas:** biography, business, cooking, cultural interests, current affairs, diet/nutrition, environment, foods, health, history, how-to, humor, investigative, medicine, memoirs, music, parenting, popular culture, psychology, science, self-help, spirituality, technology, travel, women's issues, fitness, lifestyle. **Considers these fiction areas:** commercial, crime, fantasy, historical, literary, mainstream, middle grade, mystery, romance, science fiction, suspense, thriller, women's, young adult.

HOW TO CONTACT E-query. For fiction, send a query, synopsis, bio, and 30 pages pasted into the e-mail. No attachments. For nonfiction, send a query only; proposal requested later if the agent is interested. Accepts simultaneous submissions. Obtains most new clients through recommendations from others, solicitations.

TERMS Agent receives 15% commission on domestic sales; 20% commission on foreign sales.

JAMES FITZGERALD AGENCY

118 Waverly Place, #1B, New York NY 10011. **E-mail:** submissions@jfitzagency.com. **Website:** www.jfitzagency.com. **Contact:** James Fitzgerald. "As an agency, we primarily represent books that reflect the popular culture of today being in the forms of fiction, nonfiction, graphic and packaged books. In order to have your work considered for possible representation, the following information must be submitted. Please submit all information in English even if your manuscript is in another language."

Prior to his current position, Mr. Fitzgerald was an editor at St. Martin's Press and Doubleday.

MEMBER AGENTS James Fitzgerald; Dylan Lowy.

REPRESENTS Nonfiction, fiction, novels, juvenile books, scholarly books. graphic novles, packaged books. **Considers these nonfiction areas:** Americana, animals, anthropology, art, autobiography, biography, business, cooking, cultural interests, current affairs, diet/nutrition, environment, ethnic, film, foods, gay/lesbian, government, history, humor, inspirational, investigative, literature, memoirs, multicultural, music, photography, popular culture, politics, regional, religious, science, technology, true crime, war, women's issues, young adult. **Considers these fiction areas:** action, adventure, cartoon, comic books, crime, detective, fantasy, frontier, historical, humor, juvenile, literary, mainstream, middle grade, mystery, picture books, science fiction, sports, supernatural, suspense, thriller, translation, war, westerns, young adult.

HOW TO CONTACT Query via e-mail or snail mail. This agency's online submission guidelines page explains all the elements they want to see when you submit a nonfiction book proposal. Accepts simultaneous submissions.

RECENT SALES A full and diverse list of titles are on this agency's website.

FLANNERY LITERARY

1140 Wickfield Ct., Naperville IL 60563. **E-mail:** jennifer@flanneryliterary.com. **Website:** flanneryliterary.com. **Contact:** Jennifer Flannery. "Flannery Literary is a Chicago-area literary agency representing writers of books for children and young adults because the most interesting, well-written, and time-honored books are written with young people in mind." Estab. 1992. Represents 40 clients.

REPRESENTS Nonfiction, fiction, novels, juvenile books. **Considers these nonfiction areas:** juvenile nonfiction, young adult. **Considers these fiction areas:** juvenile, middle grade, new adult, picture books, young adult.

This agency specializes in children's and young adult fiction and nonfiction. It also accepts picture books. 100% juvenile books. Actively seeking middle grade and young adult novels. Fewer picturebooks. None that rhyme, please

HOW TO CONTACT Query by e-mail only. "Multiple queries are fine, but please inform us. Please no attachments. If you're sending a query about a novel, please embed in the e-mail the first 5-10 pages; if it's a picture book, please embed the entire text in the e-mail. We do not open attachments unless they have been requested." Accepts simultaneous submissions. Responds in 2-4 weeks to queries; 1 month to mss. Obtains new clients through referrals and queries.

TERMS Agent receives 15% commission on domestic sales; 20% commission on foreign sales. Offers written contract, binding for life of book in print.

TIPS "Write an engrossing, succinct query describing your work. We are always looking for a fresh new voice."

FLETCHER & COMPANY

78 Fifth Ave., 3rd Floor, New York NY 10011. **E-mail:** info@fletcherandco.com. **Website:** www.fletcherandco.com. **Contact:** Christy Fletcher. Today, Fletcher & Co. is a full-service literary management and production company dedicated to writers of upmarket nonfiction as well as commercial and literary fiction. Estab. 2003. Member of AAR.

MEMBER AGENTS Christy Fletcher (referrals only); Melissa Chinchillo (select list of her own authors); Rebecca Gradinger (literary fiction, up-market commercial fiction, narrative nonfiction, self-help, memoir, Women's studies, humor, and pop culture); Gráinne Fox (literary fiction and quality commercial authors, award-winning journalists and food writers, American voices, international, literary crime, upmarket fiction, narrative nonfiction); Lisa Grubka (fiction—literary, upmarket women's, and young adult; and nonfiction — narrative, food, science, and more); Sylvie Greenberg (literary fiction, business, sports, science, memoir and history); Donald Lamm (history, biography, investigative journalism, politics, current affairs, and business); Todd Sattersten (business books); Eric Lupfer; Sarah Fuentes; Veronica Goldstein; Mink Choi; Erin McFadden.

REPRESENTS Nonfiction, novels. **Considers these nonfiction areas:** biography, business, creative nonfiction, current affairs, foods, history, humor, investigative, memoirs, popular culture, politics, science, self-help, sports, women's studies. **Considers these fiction areas:** commercial, crime, literary, women's, young adult.

HOW TO CONTACT Send queries to info@fletcherandco.com. Please do not include e-mail attachments with your initial query, as they will be deleted. Address your query to a specific agent. No snail mail queries. Accepts simultaneous submissions.

RECENT SALES *The Profiteers*, by Sally Denton; *The Longest Night*, by Andrea Williams; *Disrupted: My Misadventure in the Start-Up Bubble*, by Dan Lyons; *Free Re-Fills: A Doctor Confronts His Addiction*, by Peter Grinspoon, M.D.; *Black Man in a White Coat: A Doctor's Reflections on Race and Medicine*, by Damon Tweedy, M.D.

FOLIO LITERARY MANAGEMENT, LLC

The Film Center Building, 630 Ninth Ave., Suite 1101, New York NY 10036. (212)400-1494. **Fax:** (212)967-0977. **Website:** www.foliolit.com. Member of AAR. Represents 100+ clients.

Prior to creating Folio Literary Management, Mr. Hoffman worked for several years at another agency; Mr. Kleinman was an agent at Graybill & English.

MEMBER AGENTS Claudia Cross (romance novels, commercial women's fiction, cooking and food writing, serious nonfiction on religious and spiritual topics); Scott Hoffman (literary and commercial fiction, journalistic or academic nonfiction, narrative nonfiction, pop culture books, business, history, politics, spiritual or religious-themed fiction and nonfiction, sci-fi/fantasy literary fiction, heartbreaking memoirs, humorous nonfiction); Jeff Kleinman (book-club fiction (not genre commercial, like mysteries or romances), literary fiction, thrillers and suspense novels, narrative nonfiction, memoir); Dado Derviskadic (nonfiction: cultural history, biography, memoir, pop science, motivational self-help, health/nutrition, pop culture, cookbooks; fiction that's gritty, introspective, or serious); Frank Weimann (biography, business/investing/finance, history, religious, mind/body/spirit, health, lifestyle, cookbooks, sports, African-American, science, memoir, special forces/CIA/FBI/mafia, military, prescriptive nonfiction, humor, celebrity; adult and children's fiction); Michael Harriot (commercial non-fiction (both narrative and prescriptive) and fantasy/science fiction); Erin Harris (book club, historical fiction, literary, narrative nonfiction, psychological suspense, young adult); Katherine Latshaw (blogs-to-books, food/cooking, middle grade, narrative and prescriptive nonfiction); Annie Hwang (literary and upmarket fiction with commercial appeal; select nonfiction: popular science, diet/health/fitness, lifestyle, narrative nonfiction, pop culture, and humor); Erin Niumata (fiction: commercial women's fiction, romance, historical fiction, mysteries, psychological thrillers, suspense, humor; nonfiction: self-help, women's issues, pop culture and humor, pet care/pets, memoirs, and anything blogger); Ruth Pomerance (narrative nonfiction and commercial fiction); Marcy Posner (adult: commercial women's fiction, historical fiction, mystery, biography, history, health, and lifestyle, commercial novels, thrillers, narrative nonfiction; children's: contemporary YA and MG, mystery series for boys, select historical fiction and fantasy); Jeff Silberman (narrative nonfiction, biography, history, politics, current affairs, health, lifestyle, humor, food/cookbook, memoir, pop culture, sports, science, technology; commercial, literary, and book club fiction); Steve Troha; Emily van Beek (YA, MG, picture books), Melissa White (general nonfiction, literary and commercial fiction, MG, YA); John Cusick (middle grade, picture books, YA); Jamie Chambliss.

REPRESENTS Nonfiction, novels. **Considers these nonfiction areas:** animals, art, biography, business, cooking, creative nonfiction, economics, environment, foods, health, history, how-to, humor, inspirational, memoirs, military, parenting, popular culture, politics, psychology, religious, satire, science, self-help, technology, war, women's issues, women's studies. **Considers these fiction areas:** commercial, fantasy, horror, literary, middle grade, mystery, picture books, religious, romance, thriller, women's, young adult.

No poetry, stage plays, or screenplays.

HOW TO CONTACT Query via e-mail only (no attachments). Read agent bios online for specific submission guidelines and e-mail addresses, and to check if someone is closed to queries. "All agents respond to queries as soon as possible, whether interested or not. If you haven't heard back from the individual agent within the time period that they specify on their bio page, it's possible that something has gone wrong, and your query has been lost–in that case, please e-mail a follow-up."

TIPS "Please do not submit simultaneously to more than one agent at Folio. If you're not sure which of us is exactly right for your book, don't worry. We work closely as a team, and if one of our agents gets a query that might be more appropriate for someone else, we'll always pass it along. It's important that you check each agent's bio page for clear directions as to how to submit, as well as when to expect feedback."

FOUNDRY LITERARY + MEDIA

33 W. 17th St., PH, New York NY 10011. (212)929-5064. **Fax:** (212)929-5471. **Website:** www.foundrymedia.com.

MEMBER AGENTS Peter McGuigan, pmsubmissions@foundrymedia.com (smart, offbeat voices in all genres of fiction and nonfiction); Yfat Reiss Gendell, yrgsubmissions@foundrymedia.com (practical nonfiction: health and wellness, diet, lifestyle, how-to, and parenting; range of narrative nonfiction that includes humor, memoir, history, science, pop culture, psychology, and adventure/travel stories; unique commercial fiction, including young adult fiction, that touch on her nonfiction interests, including speculative fiction, thrillers, and historical fiction); Chris Park, cpsubmissions@foundrymedia.com (memoirs, narrative nonfiction, sports books, Christian nonfiction and character-driven fiction); Hannah Brown Gordon, hbgsubmissions@foundrymedia.com (stories and narratives that blend genres, including thriller, suspense, historical, literary, speculative, memoir, pop-science, psychology, humor, and pop culture); Brandi Bowles, bbsubmissions@foundrymedia.com (nonfiction list ranges from cookbooks to prescriptive books, science, pop culture, and real-life inspirational stories; high-concept novels that feature strong female bonds and psychological or scientific themes); Kirsten Neuhaus, knsubmissions@foundrymedia.com (platform-driven narrative nonfiction, in the areas of memoir, business, lifestyle (beauty/fashion/relationships), current events, history and stories with strong female voices, as well as smart fiction that appeals to a wide market); Jessica Regel, jrsubmissions@foundrymedia.com (young adult and middle grade books, as well as a select list of adult general fiction, women's fiction, and adult nonfiction); Anthony Mattero, amsubmissions@foundrymedia.com (smart, platform-driven nonfiction particularly in the genres of pop culture, humor, music, sports, and pop-business); Peter Steinberg, pssubmissions@foundrymedia.com (narrative nonfiction, commercial and literary fiction, memoir, health, history, lifestyle, humor, sports, and young adult); Roger Freet, rfsubmissions@foundrymedia.com (narrative and idea-driven nonfiction clients in the areas of religion, spirituality, memoir, and cultural issues by leading scholars, pastors, historians, activists and musicians); Adriann Ranta, arsubmissions@foundrymedia.com (accepts all genres and age groups; loves gritty, realistic, true-to-life narratives; women's fiction and nonfiction; accessible, pop nonfiction in science, history, and craft; and smart, fresh, genre-bending works for children).

REPRESENTS Considers these nonfiction areas: creative nonfiction, current affairs, diet/nutrition, health, history, how-to, humor, medicine, memoirs, music, parenting, popular culture, psychology, science, sports, travel. **Considers these fiction areas:** commercial, historical, humor, literary, middle grade, suspense, thriller, women's, young adult.

HOW TO CONTACT Target one agent only. Send queries to the specific submission e-mail of the agent. For fiction: send query, synopsis, author bio, first 3 chapters—all pasted in the e-mail. For nonfiction, send query, sample chapters, TOC, author bio (all pasted). "We regret that we cannot guarantee a response to every submission we receive. If you do not receive a response within 8 weeks, your submission is not right for our lists at this time." Accepts simultaneous submissions.

TIPS "Consult website for each agent's submission instructions."

FOX LITERARY

110 W. 40th St., Suite 2305, New York NY 10018. **E-mail:** submissions@foxliterary.com. **Website:** foxliterary.com. Fox Literary is a boutique agency which represents commercial fiction, along with select works of literary fiction and nonfiction that have broad commercial appeal.

MEMBER AGENTS Diana Fox.

REPRESENTS Nonfiction, fiction, novels, short story collections, juvenile books, scholarly books. graphic novels. **Considers these nonfiction areas:** autobiography, biography, creative nonfiction, cultural interests, film, gay/lesbian, health, history, juvenile nonfiction, language, law, literature, medicine, memoirs, multicultural, parenting, philosophy, popular culture, psychology, recreation, science, self-help, sex, sociology, spirituality, women's issues, women's studies, young adult, mind/body/spirit. **Considers these fiction areas:** action, adventure, comic books, commercial, confession, contemporary issues, crime, detective, erotica, fantasy, feminist, gay, historical, juvenile, lesbian, literary, mainstream, middle grade, multicultural, mystery, new adult, paranormal, romance, science fiction, short story collections, spiritual, suspense, thriller, urban fantasy, women's, young adult, general.

HOW TO CONTACT E-mail query and first 5 pages in body of e-mail. E-mail queries preferred. For snail mail queries, must include an e-mail address for response and no response means no. Do not send SASE. No e-mail attachments. Accepts simultaneous submissions.

LYNN C. FRANKLIN ASSOCIATES, LTD.

1350 Broadway, Suite 2015, New York NY 10018. (212)868-6311. **E-mail:** agency@franklinandsiegal.com. **Website:** www.publishersmarketplace.com/members/LynnCFranklin/. **Contact:** Lynn Franklin, president; Claudia Nys, foreign rights.

REPRESENTS Nonfiction. **Considers these nonfiction areas:** biography, current affairs, memoirs, psychology, self-help, spirituality, alternative medicine.

Primary interest lies in nonfiction (memoir, biography, current affairs, spirituality, psychology/self-help, alternative medicine, etc.).

HOW TO CONTACT Query via e-mail to agency@franklinandsiegal.com. No unsolicited mss. No attachments. For nonfiction, query letter with short outline and synopsis. For fiction, query letter with short synopsis and a maximum of 10 sample pages (in the body of the e-mail). Accepts simultaneous submissions.

JEANNE FREDERICKS LITERARY AGENCY, INC.

221 Benedict Hill Rd., New Canaan CT 06840. (203)972-3011. **Fax:** (203)972-3011. **E-mail:** jeanne.fredericks@gmail.com. **Website:** www.jeannefredericks.com. **Contact:** Jeanne Fredericks. "The Jeanne Fredericks Literary Agency specializes in representing quality adult nonfiction by experts in their fields. We particularly enjoy working with authors who communicate important new information that will make a positive difference in the lives of a sizable population. We are more likely to represent authors who understand the importance of having a marketing platform and have already secured media placements and significant social media followings." Estab. 1997. Member of AAR. Other memberships include Authors Guild. Represents 100+ clients.

Prior to opening her agency in 1997, Ms. Fredericks was an agent and acting director with the Susan P. Urstadt, Inc. Agency. Previously she was the editorial director of Ziff-Davis Books and managing editor and acquisitions editor at Macmillan Publishing Company.

REPRESENTS Nonfiction. **Considers these nonfiction areas:** Americana, animals, autobiography, biography, child guidance, cooking, decorating, diet/nutrition, environment, foods, gardening, health, history, how-to, interior design, medicine, parenting, photography, psychology, self-help, women's issues.

This agency specializes in quality adult nonfiction by authorities in their fields. "We do not handle: fiction, true crime, juvenile, textbooks, poetry, essays, screenplays, short stories, science fiction, pop culture, guides to computers and software, politics, horror, pornography, books on overly depressing or violent topics, romance, teacher's manuals, or memoirs."

HOW TO CONTACT Query first by e-mail, then send outline/proposal, 1-2 sample chapters, if requested and after you have consulted the submission guidelines on the agency website. If you do send requested submission materials, include the word "Requested" in the subject line. Accepts simultaneous submissions. Responds in 3-5 weeks to queries; 2-4 months to mss.

Obtains most new clients through recommendations from others, solicitations, conferences.

TERMS Agent receives 15% commission on domestic sales; 25% commission on foreign sales with co-agent. Offers written contract, binding for 9 months; 2-month notice must be given to terminate contract. Charges client for photocopying of whole proposals and mss, overseas postage, expedited mail services. Almost all submissions are made electronically so these charges rarely apply.

RECENT SALES *Coming to Our Senses About Concussion*, by Elizabeth Sandel, M.D. (Harvard University Press); *The Autoimmune Disease Handbook*, by Julius Birnbaum, M.D. (Johns Hopkins University Press); *The Secret Language of Cells*, by Jonathan Lieff, M.D. (BenBella Books); *How to Build Your Own Tiny Home*, by Roger Marshall (Taunton Press); *Yoga Therapy*, by Larry Payne, PH.D.,Terra Gold, D.O.M., and Eden Goldman, D.C. (Basic Health/Turner); *The Creativity Cure*, by Carrie Alton, M.D. and Alton Barron, M.D. (Scribner); *For Sale—American Paradise*, by Willie Drye (Lyons); *Lilias! Yoga*, by Lilias Folan (Skyhorse); *Horse Stories*, by Sharon Smith (Lyons).

WRITERS CONFERENCES Harvard Medical School CME Course in Publishing, Connecticut Authors and Publishers Association-University Conference, ASJA Writers' Conference, BookExpo America, Garden Writers' Association Annual Symposium.

TIPS "Be sure to research competition for your work and be able to justify why there's a need for your book. I enjoy building an author's career, particularly if he/she is professional, hardworking, and courteous, and actively involved in establishing a marketing platform. Aside from 25 years of agenting experience, I've had 10 years of editorial experience in adult trade book publishing that enable me to help an author polish a proposal so that it's more appealing to prospective editors. My MBA in marketing also distinguishes me from other agents."

GRACE FREEDSON'S PUBLISHING NETWORK

7600 Jericho Turnpike, Suite 300, Woodbury NY 11797. (516)931-7757. **Fax:** (516)931-7759. **E-mail:** gfreedson@gmail.com. **Contact:** Grace Freedson. . The Publishing Network is a Literary Agency and Book Packager. "In addition, we consult on a number of Publishing concerns including peer evaluation and content review; ghost writing and contracts." Estab. 2000. Member of AAR. Women's Media Group; Author's Guild Represents 100 clients.

Prior to becoming an agent, Ms. Freedson was a managing editor and director of acquisition for Barron's Educational Series.

REPRESENTS Nonfiction, scholarly books. **Considers these nonfiction areas:** animals, business, child guidance, computers, cooking, crafts, creative nonfiction, current affairs, diet/nutrition, economics, education, environment, foods, gardening, health, history, hobbies, horticulture, how-to, humor, inspirational, interior design, juvenile nonfiction, language, law, medicine, memoirs, metaphysics, money, multicultural, parenting, philosophy, popular culture, psychology, recreation, regional, satire, science, self-help, sports, technology, true crime, war, women's issues, women's studies. **Considers these script areas:** Test Preparation.

"In addition to representing many qualified authors, I work with publishers as a packager of unique projects—mostly series." Actively seeking true crime and science for the general reader. Does not want to receive fiction.

HOW TO CONTACT Query with SASE. Submit synopsis, SASE. Responds in 2-6 weeks to queries. Obtains most new clients through recommendations from others.

TERMS Agent receives 15% commission on domestic sales. Offers written contract; 30-day notice must be given to terminate contract.

RECENT SALES *If He's So Great Why Do I Feel So Bad*, by Avery Neal (Citadel); *Southern Appalachian Cooking: New and Traditional Recipes*, by John Tullock (Countryman Press); *Mad City: The True Story of the Campus Murders that America Forgot*, by Dr. Michael Arntfield (Little A).

WRITERS CONFERENCES BookExpo of America.

TIPS "At this point, I am only reviewing proposals on nonfiction topics by credentialed authors with platforms."

FRESH BOOKS LITERARY AGENCY

E-mail: matt@fresh-books.com. **Website:** www.fresh-books.com. **Contact:** Matt Wagner.

Prior to becoming an agent, Mr. Wagner was with Waterside Productions.

REPRESENTS Nonfiction. **Considers these nonfiction areas:** art, business, computers, cooking, creative nonfiction, diet/nutrition, design, education, health, hobbies, how-to, photography, recreation, satire, science, self-help, true crime, popular science, technology, fitness, gadgets, social media, career development, leadership, personal finance,.

- "I'm looking for new and established authors writing narrative non-fiction, lifestyle and reference titles, including: popular science, technology, health, fitness, photography, design, computing, gadgets, social media, career development, education, business, leadership, personal finance, how-to, and humor." Does not want fiction, children's books, poetry, or screenplays.

HOW TO CONTACT Plain text e-mail query (with no attachments) to matt@fresh-books.com. Accepts simultaneous submissions.

TERMS Agent receives 15% commission on domestic sales; 20% commission on foreign sales.

RECENT SALES *The Photographer's Black and White Handbook*, by Harold Davis (Monacelli); *Machine Learning For Dummies*, by John Paul Mueller and Luca Massaron (Wiley); *How to Get a Meeting with Anyone*, by Stu Heinecke (Ben Bella); *Born to Eat*, by Wendy Jo Peterson and Leslie Schilling (Skyhorse).

SARAH JANE FREYMANN LITERARY AGENCY

(212)362-9277. **E-mail:** sarah@sarahjanefreymann.com. **E-mail:** submissions@sarahjanefreymann.com. **Website:** www.sarahjanefreymann.com. **Contact:** Sarah Jane Freymann, Steve Schwartz.

MEMBER AGENTS Sarah Jane Freymann (nonfiction: spiritual, psychology, self-help, women/men's issues, books by health experts [conventional and alternative], cookbooks, narrative non-fiction, natural science, nature, memoirs, cutting-edge journalism, travel, multicultural issues, parenting, lifestyle, fiction: literary, mainstream YA); Jessica Sinsheimer, jessica@sarahjanefreymann.com; Steven Schwartz, steve@sarahjanefreymann.com (popular fiction [crime, thrillers, and historical novels], world and national affairs, business books, self-help, psychology, humor, sports and travel).

REPRESENTS Nonfiction, fiction, novels. **Considers these nonfiction areas:** business, cooking, creative nonfiction, current affairs, health, humor, memoirs, multicultural, parenting, psychology, science, self-help, spirituality, sports, travel, women's issues, men's issues, nature, journalism, lifestyle. **Considers these fiction areas:** crime, historical, literary, mainstream, thriller, young adult, Popular fiction.

HOW TO CONTACT Query via e-mail. No attachments. Below the query, please paste the first 10 pages of your work. Accepts simultaneous submissions.

TERMS Charges clients for long distance, overseas postage, photocopying. 100% of business is derived from commissions on ms sales.

FREDRICA S. FRIEDMAN AND CO., INC.

857 Fifth Ave., New York NY 10065. (212)639-9455. **E-mail:** info@fredricafriedman.com. **E-mail:** submissions@fredricafriedman.com. **Website:** www.fredricafriedman.com. **Contact:** Ms. Chandler Smith.

- Prior to establishing her own literary management firm, Ms. Friedman was the Editorial Director, Associate Publisher and Vice President of Little, Brown & Co., a division of Time Warner, and the first woman to hold those positions.

REPRESENTS Nonfiction, fiction.

- Does not want poetry, plays, screenplays, children's picture books, sci-fi/fantasy, or horror.

HOW TO CONTACT Submit e-query, synopsis; be concise, and include any pertinent author information, including relevant writing history. If you are a fiction writer, submit the first 10 pages of your manuscript. Keep all material in the body of the e-mail. Accepts simultaneous submissions. Responds in 6 weeks.

REBECCA FRIEDMAN LITERARY AGENCY

E-mail: brandie@rfliterary.com. **Website:** www.rfliterary.com. Estab. 2013. Member of AAR. Signatory of WGA.

- Prior to opening her own agency in 2013, Ms. Friedman was with Sterling Lord Literistic from 2006 to 2011, then with Hill Nadell Agency.

MEMBER AGENTS Rebecca Friedman (commercial and literary fiction with a focus on literary novels of suspense, women's fiction, contemporary romance, and young adult, as well as journalistic nonfiction and memoir); Susan Finesman, susan@rfliterary.com (fiction, cookbooks, and lifestyle); Abby Schulman, abby@rfliterary.com (YA and nonfiction related to health, wellness, and personal development); Brandie Coonis, brandie@rfliterary.com (MG, YA, SFF, and writers that defy genre).

REPRESENTS Nonfiction, fiction, novels. **Considers these nonfiction areas:** cooking, health, memoirs, young adult, journalistic nonfiction. **Considers these fiction areas:** commercial, family saga, fantasy, feminist, frontier, gay, historical, horror, literary, middle grade, mystery, new adult, romance, science fiction, suspense, thriller, women's, young adult.

HOW TO CONTACT Please submit your brief query letter and first chapter (no more than 15 pages, double-spaced). No attachments. Accepts simultaneous submissions. Tries to respond in 6-8 weeks.

RECENT SALES A complete list of agency authors is available online.

THE FRIEDRICH AGENCY

19 W. 21st St., Suite 201, New York NY 10010. (212)317-8810. **E-mail:** mfriedrich@friedrichagency.com; lcarson@friedrichagency.com; kwolf@friedrichagency.com. **Website:** www.friedrichagency.com. **Contact:** Molly Friedrich; Lucy Carson; Kent D. Wolf. Estab. 2006. Member of AAR. Signatory of WGA. Represents 50+ clients.

Prior to her current position, Ms. Friedrich was an agent at the Aaron Priest Literary Agency.

MEMBER AGENTS Molly Friedrich, founder and agent (open to queries); Lucy Carson, TV/film rights director and agent (open to queries); Kent D. Wolf, foreign rights director and agent (open to queries).

REPRESENTS Nonfiction, fiction, novels, short story collections. **Considers these nonfiction areas:** autobiography, biography, creative nonfiction, memoirs, true crime, young adult. **Considers these fiction areas:** commercial, detective, family saga, feminist, literary, multicultural, short story collections, suspense, women's, young adult.

HOW TO CONTACT Query by e-mail only. Please query only 1 agent at this agency. Accepts simultaneous submissions. Responds in 2-4 weeks.

RECENT SALES *W is For Wasted*, by Sue Grafton; *Olive Kitteridge*, by Elizabeth Strout. Other clients include Frank McCourt, Jane Smiley, Esmeralda Santiago, Terry McMillan, Cathy Schine, Ruth Ozeki, Karen Joy Fowler, and more.

FULL CIRCLE LITERARY, LLC

San Diego CA **Website:** www.fullcircleliterary.com. **Contact:** Stefanie Von Borstel. "Full Circle Literary is a full-service literary agency, offering a full circle approach to literary representation. Our team has diverse experience in book publishing including editorial, marketing, publicity, legal and rights, which we use collectively to build careers book by book. We work with both award-winning veteran and debut writers and artists and our team has a knack for finding and developing new and diverse talent. Learn more about our agency and submission guidelines by visiting our website." This agency goes deeply into depth about what they are seeking and submission guidelines on their agency website. Estab. 2005. Member of AAR. Society of Children's Books Writers & Illustrators, Authors Guild. Represents 100+ clients.

MEMBER AGENTS Stefanie Sanchez Von Borstel; Adriana Dominguez; Taylor Martindale Kean; Lilly Ghahremani.

REPRESENTS **Considers these nonfiction areas:** how-to, multicultural, women's issues, young adult. **Considers these fiction areas:** literary, middle grade, multicultural, young adult.

Actively seeking nonfiction and fiction projects that offer new and diverse viewpoints, and literature with a global or multicultural perspective. "We are particularly interested in books with a Latino or Middle Eastern angle."

HOW TO CONTACT Online submissions only via submissions form online. Please complete the form and submit cover letter, author information and sample writing. For sample writing: fiction please include the first 10 ms pages. For nonfiction, include a proposal with 1 sample chapter. Accepts simultaneous submissions. "Due to the high volume of submissions, please keep in mind we are no longer able to personally respond to every submission. However, we read every submission with care and often share for a second read within the office. If we are interested, we will contact you by email to request additional materials (such as a complete manuscript or additional manuscripts). Please keep us updated if there is a change in the status of your project, such as an offer of representation or book contract." If you have not heard from us in 6-8 weeks, your project is not right for our agency at the current time and we wish you all the best with your writing. Obtains most new clients through recommendations from others and conferences.

TERMS Agent receives 15% commission on domestic sales; 25% commission on foreign sales. Offers written contract which outlines responsibilities of the author and the agent.

FUSE LITERARY

Foreword Literary, Inc. dba FUSE LITERARY, P.O. Box 258, La Honda CA 94020. **E-mail:** info@fuseliterary.com. **E-mail:** query[firstnameofagent]@fuseliterary.com. **Website:** www.fuseliterary.com. **Contact:** Contact each agent directly via e-mail. Fuse Literary is a full-service, hybrid literary agency based in San Francisco with offices in New York, Chicago, Dallas, North Dakota and Vancouver. "We blend the tried-and-true methods of traditional publishing with the brash new opportunities engendered by digital publishing, emerging technologies, and an evolving author-agent relationship. Fuse manages a wide variety of clients, from bestsellers to debut authors, working with fiction and nonfiction for children and adults worldwide. We combine technical efficiency with outside-the-covers creative thinking so that each individual client's career is specifically fine-tuned for them. We are not an agency that sells a book and then washes our hands of the project. We realize that our ongoing success directly results from that of our clients, so we remain at their side to cultivate and strategize throughout the many lives of each book, both before and after the initial sale. Innovations, such as our Short Fuse client publishing program, help bridge the gaps between books, growing and maintaining the author's fan base without lag. The partners launched Fuse following tenures at established agencies, bringing with them experience in writing, teaching, professional editing, book marketing, blogging and social media, running high-tech companies, and marketing new technologies. A boutique, collaborative agency, Fuse provides each client with the expertise and forward vision of the group. We pride ourselves on our flexibility and passion for progression in an ever-changing publishing environment. We believe that the agency of the future will not just react to change but will actively create change, pushing markets and advancing formats to provide authors with the best possible outlets for their art." Estab. 2013. RWA, SCBWI. Represents 100+ clients.

Each agent at Fuse had a specific set of interests and jobs prior to becoming a member of Team Fuse. Laurie ran a multi-million dollar publicity agency. Michelle was an editor at a St. Martins Press. Emily worked in the contracts department at Simon & Schuster. Gordon ran a successful independent editing business. Tricia worked in the video game industry. Connor worked in talent management. Carlisle is a youth librarian. Margaret taught English. Check each agent's bio on our website for more specific information.

MEMBER AGENTS Laurie McLean (only accepting referral inquiries and submissions requested at conferences or online events); Gordon Warnock, querygordon@fuseliterary.com (fiction: high-concept commercial fiction, literary fiction (adults through YA), graphic novels (adults through MG); nonfiction: memoir (adult, YA, NA, graphic), cookbooks/food narrative/food studies, illustrated/art/photography (especially graphic nonfiction), political and current events, pop science, pop culture (especially punk culture and geek culture), self-help, how-to, humor, pets, business and career); Connor Goldsmith, queryconnor@fuseliterary.com (fiction: sci-fi/fantasy/horror, thrillers, and upmarket commercial fiction with a unique and memorable hook; books by and about people from marginalized perspectives, such as LGBT people and/or racial minorities; nonfiction (from recognized experts with established platforms): history (particularly of the ancient world), theater, cinema, music, television, mass media, popular culture, feminism and gender studies, LGBT issues, race relations, and the sex industry); Michelle Richter, querymichelle@fuseliterary.com (primarily seeking fiction, specifically book club reads, literary fiction, and mystery/suspense/thrillers; for nonfiction, seeking fashion, pop culture, science/medicine, sociology/social trends, and economics); Emily S. Keyes, queryemily@fuseliterary.com (picture books, middle grade and young adult children's books, plus select commercial fiction, including fantasy & science fiction, women's fiction, new adult fiction, pop culture and humor); Tricia Skinner, querytricia@fuseliterary.com (Romance: science fiction, futuristic, fantasy, military/special ops, medieval historical; brand new relationships; diversity); Margaret Bail, querymargaret@fuseliterary.com (adult fiction in the genres of romance [no Christian or inspirational, please], science fiction [soft sci-fi rather than hard], mystery, thrillers, action adventure, historical fiction [not a fan of WWII era], and fantasy. In nonfiction, memoirs with a unique hook, and cookbooks with a strong platform); Carlisle Webber, querycarlisle@fuseliterary.com (high-concept commercial fiction in middle grade, young adult, and adult; dark thrillers, mystery, horror, dark women's fiction, dark pop/mainstream fiction; especially interested in diverse authors and their stories).

REPRESENTS Nonfiction, fiction, novels, juvenile books, scholarly books, poetry books. **Considers these nonfiction areas:** autobiography, biography, business, child guidance, computers, cooking, crafts, creative nonfiction, cultural interests, current affairs, dance, decorating, diet/nutrition, design, economics, education, environment, ethnic, film, foods, gardening, gay/lesbian, government, health, history, hobbies, horticulture, how-to, humor, inspirational, interior design, investigative, juvenile nonfiction, language, law, literature, medicine, memoirs, metaphysics, money, multicultural, music, New Age, parenting, philosophy, photography, popular culture, politics, psychology, recreation, regional, satire, science, self-help, sex, sociology, software, spirituality, sports, technology, theater, travel, true crime, women's issues, women's studies, young adult, celebrity. **Considers these fiction areas:** action, adventure, cartoon, comic books, commercial, confession, contemporary issues, crime, detective, erotica, ethnic, experimental, family saga, fantasy, feminist, frontier, gay, glitz, hi-lo, historical, horror, humor, inspirational, juvenile, lesbian, literary, mainstream, metaphysical, middle grade, multicultural, multimedia, mystery, new adult, New Age, occult, paranormal, picture books, plays, poetry, poetry in translation, police, psychic, regional, romance, satire, science fiction, spiritual, sports, supernatural, suspense, thriller, urban fantasy, westerns, women's, young adult. "We are committed to expanding storytelling into a wide variety of formats other than books, including video games, movies, television shows, streaming videos, enhanced ebooks, VR, etc."

HOW TO CONTACT E-query an individual agent. Check the website to see if any individual agent has closed themselves to submissions, as well as for a description of each agent's individual submission preferences. (You can find these details by clicking on each agent's photo.) Usually responds in 4-6 weeks, but sometimes more if an agent is exceptionally busy. Check each agent's bio/submissions page on the website. Only accepts e-mailed queries that follow our online guidelines.

TERMS "We earn 15% on negotiated deals for books and with our co-agents earn between 20-30% on foreign translation deals depending on the territory; 20% on TV/Movies/Plays; other multimedia deals are so new there is no established commission rate. The author has the last say, approving or not approving all deals." After the initial 90-day period, there is a 30-day termination of the agency agreement clause. No fees.

RECENT SALES Seven-figure and six figure deals for NYT bestseller Julie Kagawa (YA); six-figure deal for debut Melissa D. Savage (MG); six-figure deal for Kerry Lonsdale (suspense); two six-figure audio deals for fantasy author Brian D. Anderson; *First Watch*, by Dale Lucas (fantasy); *This Is What a Librarian Looks Like*, by Kyle Cassidy (photo essay); *A Big Ship at the Edge of the Universe*, by Alex White (sci-fi); Runebinder Chronicles, by Alex Kahler (YA); *Perceptual Intelligence*, by Dr. Brian Boxler Wachler (science); *The Night Child*, by Anna Quinn (literary); *Pay Day*, by Kellye Garrett (mystery); Breakup Bash Series, by Nina Crespo (romance); *America's Next Reality Star*, by Laura Heffernan (women's fiction); *Losing the Girl*, by MariNaomi (graphic novel); *Maggie and Abby's Neverending Pillow Fort*, by Will Taylor (MG); *Idea Machine*, by Jorjeana Marie (how-to).

WRITERS CONFERENCES Agents from this agency attend many conferences. A full list of their appearances is available on the agency website.

THE G AGENCY, LLC

P.O. Box 374, Bronx NY 10471. **E-mail:** gagencyquery@gmail.com. **Website:** www.publishersmarketplace.com/members/jeffg/. **Contact:** Jeff Gerecke. Estab. 2012. Member of AAR.

MEMBER AGENTS Jeff Gerecke.

REPRESENTS Nonfiction, fiction. **Considers these nonfiction areas:** biography, business, computers, history, military, money, popular culture, technology. **Considers these fiction areas:** historical, mainstream, military, mystery, suspense, thriller, war.

- Does not want screenplays, sci-fi/fantasy or romance.

HOW TO CONTACT E-mail submissions required. Please do attach sample chapters or proposal. Enter "QUERY" along with the title in the subject line of e-mails. "I cannot guarantee replies to every submission. If you do not hear from me the first time, you may send me one reminder. I encourage you to make multiple submissions but want to know that is the case if I ask for a manuscript to read." Accepts simultaneous submissions.

RECENT SALES *The Race for Paradise*, by Paul Cobb (Oxford UP); *Barles Story*, by Else Poulsen (Greystone); *Weed Land*, by Peter Hecht (Univ of Calif Press); *Nothin' But Blue Skies*, by Edward McClelland

(Bloomsbury); *Tear Down*, by Gordon Young (Univ of Calif Press).

TIPS "I am interested in commercial and literary fiction, as well as serious nonfiction and pop culture. My focus as an agent has always been on working with writers to shape their work for its greatest commercial potential. I provide lots of editorial advice in sharpening manuscripts and proposals before submission. I've been a member of the Royalty Committee of the Association of Authors Representatives since its founding and am always keen to challenge publishers for their willfully obscure royalty reporting. Also I have recently taken over the position of Treasurer of the A.A.R. My publishing background includes working at the University of California Press so I am always intrigued by academic subjects which are given a commercial spin to reach an audience outside academia. I've also worked as a foreign scout for publishers like Hodder & Stoughton in England and Wilhelm Heyne in Germany, which gives me a good sense of how American books can be successfully translated overseas."

GALLT AND ZACKER LITERARY AGENCY

273 Charlton Ave., South Orange NJ 07079. (973)761-6358. **Website:** www.galltzacker.com. **Contact:** Nancy Gallt, Marietta Zacker. "At the Gallt and Zacker Literary Agency we represent people, not projects. We aim to bring to life stories and artwork that help young readers throughout the world become life-long book enthusiasts and to inspire and entertain readers of all ages." Estab. 2000. Represents 80 clients.

Ms. Gallt was subsidiary rights director of the children's book division at Morrow, Harper and Viking. Ms. Zacker started her career as a teacher, championing children's and YA books, then worked in the children's book world, bookselling, marketing, and editing. Ms. Camacho held positions in foreign rights, editorial, marketing, and operations at Penguin Random House, Dorchester, Simon and Schuster, and Writers House literary agency before venturing into agenting at Prospect Agency. Ms. Phelan got her start at Scott Waxman Agency and Morhaim Literary then spent four years as an agent with The Bent Agency.

MEMBER AGENTS Nancy Gallt; Marietta Zacker; Linda Camacho; Beth Phelan.

REPRESENTS Nonfiction, fiction, novels, juvenile books, scholarly books, poetry books. **Considers these fiction areas:** juvenile, middle grade, picture books, young adult.

"Books for children and young adults." Actively seeking author, illustrators, author/illustrators who create books for young adults and younger readers.

HOW TO CONTACT Submit through online submission form on agency website. No e-mail queries, please. Accepts simultaneous submissions. Obtains new clients through submissions, conferences and recommendations from others.

TERMS Agent receives 15% commission on domestic sales; 20% commission on foreign sales. Offers written contract; 30-day notice must be given to terminate contract.

RECENT SALES Rick Riordan's Books (Hyperion); *Trace*, by Pat Cummings (Harper); *What Gloria Heard*, illustrated by Daria Peoples (Bloomsbury); *Gondra's Treasure*, illustrated by Jennifer Black Reinhardt (Clarion/HMH); *Caterpillar Summer*, by Gillian McDunn (Bloomsbury); *It Wasn't Me*, by Dana Alison Levy (Delacorte/Random House); *Namesake*, by Paige Britt (Scholastic); *The Turning*, by Emily Whitman (Harper); *Rot*, by Ben Clanton (Simon & Schuster). *The Year They Fell*, by David Kreizman (Imprint/Macmillan); *Manhattan Maps*, by Jennifer Thermes (Abrams); *The Moon Within*, by Aida Salazar (Scholastic); *Artist in Space*, by Dean Robbins (Scholastic); *Lucy McGee*, by Mary Amato (Holiday House); *Where Are You From?*, by Yamile Saied Méndez (Harper); *The Artist*, by Selina Alko (Scholastic).

TIPS "Writing and illustrations stand on their own, so submissions should tell the most compelling stories possible—whether visually, in narrative, or both."

KAREN GANTZ LITERARY MANAGEMENT AND ATTORNEY AT LAW

(212)734-3619. **E-mail:** karen@karengantzlit.com. **Website:** www.karengantzlit.com. **Contact:** Karen Gantz.

Prior to her current position, Ms. Gantz practiced law at two law firms, wrote two cookbooks, *Taste of New York* (Addison-Wesley) and *Superchefs* (John Wiley & Sons). She also participated in a Presidential Advisory Committee on Intellectual Property, U.S. Department of Commerce.

REPRESENTS Nonfiction.

Actively seeking nonfiction.

HOW TO CONTACT Accepting queries and summaries by e-mail only. Check the website for complete submission information, because it is intricate and specific. Accepts simultaneous submissions. Responds in 4-8 weeks to queries.

RECENT SALES *Nevertheless*, by Alec Baldwin (Harper); *The Magic of Math: Solving for X and Figuring Out Why*, by Arthur Benjamin (Basic Books); *The Nixon Effect: How His Presidency has Changed American Politics*, by Douglas Schoen (Encounter Books).

THE GARAMOND AGENCY, INC.

1840 Columbia Rd. NW, #503, Washington DC 20009. **E-mail:** query@garamondagency.com. **Website:** www.garamondagency.com. The Garamond Agency represents authors of idea-driven nonfiction. Covering history and science to current affairs and narrative nonfiction, our eclectic list brings big ideas and important voices to print. We are a full-service literary agency, representing writers, scholars, and journalists. Other memberships include Author's Guild.

MEMBER AGENTS Lisa Adams; David Miller.

REPRESENTS Nonfiction. **Considers these nonfiction areas:** anthropology, archeology, biography, business, creative nonfiction, current affairs, economics, environment, government, history, law, medicine, parenting, politics, psychology, science, sociology, sports, technology, women's issues.

No proposals for children's or young adult books, fiction, poetry, or memoir.

HOW TO CONTACT "Queries sent by e-mail may not make it through the spam filters on our server. Please e-mail a brief query letter only, we do not read unsolicited manuscripts submitted by e-mail under any circumstances. See our website." Accepts simultaneous submissions.

RECENT SALES *Firepower*, by Paul Lockhart (Basic Books); *The Emancipation of Priscilla Joyner*, by Carole Emberton (W. W. Norton); *Every Drop of Blood*, by Edward Achorn (Grove Atlantic); *Reinventing Capitalism*, by Viktor Mayer-Schoenberger and Thomas Ramge (Basic Books); *Occupying Boston*, by Serena Zabin (Houghton Mifflin Harcourt; *No Reason to Give Thanks*, by David Silverman (Bloomsbury); *Bird of Paradox*, by Jack Davis (Norton); *Downhill From Here*, by Katherine S. Newman (Metropolitan Books); *Free and Equal*, by Jeremy Popkin (Basic Books). See website for other clients.

TIPS "Query us first if you have any questions about whether we are the right agency for your work."

MAX GARTENBERG LITERARY AGENCY

912 N. Pennsylvania Ave., Yardley PA 19067. (215)295-9230. **Website:** www.maxgartenberg.com. **Contact:** Anne Devlin (nonfiction). Estab. 1954. Represents 100 clients.

MEMBER AGENTS Anne G. Devlin (current events, education, politics, true crime, women's issues, sports, parenting, biography, environment, narrative nonfiction, health, lifestyle, and celebrity).

REPRESENTS Nonfiction, juvenile books, scholarly books, textbooks. **Considers these nonfiction areas:** animals, art, biography, current affairs, education, film, gardening, government, health, history, how-to, military, money, music, psychology, science, sports, true crime, women's issues.

HOW TO CONTACT Writers desirous of having their work handled by this agency may query by e-mail to agdevlin@aol.com. Accepts simultaneous submissions. Responds in 2 weeks to queries; 6 weeks to mss.

TERMS Agent receives 15% commission on sales.

RECENT SALES *The Enlightened College Applicant*, by Andrew Belasco (Rowman and Littlefield); *Beethoven for Kids: His Life and Music*, by Helen Bauer (Chicago Review Press); *Portrait of a Past Life Skeptic*, by Robert L. Snow (Llewellyn Books); *Beyond Your Baby's Checkup*, by Luke Voytas, MD (Sasquatch Books); *Unorthodox Warfare: The Chinese Experience*, by Ralph D. Sawyer (Westview Press); *Encyclopedia of Earthquakes and Volcanoes*, by Alexander E. Gates (Facts on File); *Pandas!: Step Into Reading*, by David Salomon (Random House Children's Bookss).

TIPS "We have recently expanded to allow more access for new writers."

GELFMAN SCHNEIDER / ICM PARTNERS

850 7th Ave., Suite 903, New York NY 10019. **E-mail:** mail@gelfmanschneider.com. **Website:** www.gelfmanschneider.com. **Contact:** Jane Gelfman, Deborah Schneider. Member of AAR. Represents 300+ clients.

MEMBER AGENTS Deborah Schneider (all categories of literary and commercial fiction and nonfiction); Jane Gelfman; Heather Mitchell (particularly interested in narrative nonfiction, historical fiction and young debut authors with strong voices); Penelope Burns, penelope.gsliterary@gmail.com (literary and commercial fiction and nonfiction, as well as a variety of young adult and middle grade).

REPRESENTS Nonfiction, fiction, juvenile books. **Considers these nonfiction areas:** creative nonfiction, popular culture. **Considers these fiction areas:** commercial, fantasy, historical, literary, mainstream, middle grade, mystery, science fiction, suspense, women's, young adult.

"Among our diverse list of clients are novelists, journalists, playwrights, scientists, activists & humorists writing narrative nonfiction, memoir, political & current affairs, popular science and popular culture nonfiction, as well as literary & commercial fiction, women's fiction, and historical fiction." Does not currently accept screenplays or scripts, poetry, or picture book queries.

HOW TO CONTACT Query. Check Submissions page of website to see which agents are open to queries and further instructions. Accepts simultaneous submissions.

TERMS Agent receives 15% commission on domestic sales; 20% commission on foreign sales; 15% commission on film sales. Offers written contract. Charges clients for photocopying and messengers/couriers.

THE GERNERT COMPANY

136 E. 57th St., New York NY 10022. (212)838-7777. **E-mail:** info@thegernertco.com. **Website:** www.thegernertco.com. "Our client list is as broad as the market; we represent equal parts fiction and nonfiction." Estab. 1996.

MEMBER AGENTS Sarah Burnes (literary fiction and nonfiction; children's fiction); Stephanie Cabot (represents a variety of genres, including crime/thrillers, commercial and literary fiction, latte lit, and nonfiction); Chris Parris-Lamb (nonfiction, literary fiction); Seth Fishman (looking for the new voice, the original idea, the entirely breathtaking creative angle in both fiction and nonfiction); Alia Hanna Habib (narrative nonfiction, literary fiction, and culinary titles); Will Roberts (smart, original thrillers with distinctive voices, compelling backgrounds, and fast-paced narratives); Erika Storella (nonfiction projects that make an argument, narrate a history, and/or provide a new perspective); Sarah Bolling (literary fiction, smart genre fiction —particularly sci-fi— memoir, pop culture, and style); Julia Eagleton (literary fiction and nonfiction: science, politics, nature, and memoir); Anna Worrall (smart women's literary and commercial fiction, psychological thrillers, and narrative nonfiction); Ellen Coughtrey (women's literary and commercial fiction, historical fiction, narrative nonfiction and smart, original thrillers, plus. well-written Southern Gothic anything); Jack Gernert (stories about heroes—both real and imagined); Libby McGuire (distinctive storytelling in both fiction and nonfiction, across a wide range of genres). At this time, Courtney Gatewood and Rebecca Gardner are closed to queries. See the website to find out the tastes of each agent.

REPRESENTS Nonfiction, novels. **Considers these fiction areas:** commercial, crime, fantasy, historical, literary, middle grade, science fiction, thriller, women's, young adult.

HOW TO CONTACT Please send us a query letter by e-mail to info@thegernertco.com describing the work you'd like to submit, along with some information about yourself and a sample chapter if appropriate. Please indicate in your letter which agent you are querying. Please do not send e-mails directly to individual agents. It's our policy to respond to your query only if we are interested in seeing more material, usually within 4-6 weeks. See company website for more instructions. Accepts simultaneous submissions. Obtains most new clients through recommendations from others, solicitations.

RECENT SALES *Partners*, by John Grisham; *The River Why*, by David James Duncan; *The Thin Green Line*, by Paul Sullivan; *A Fireproof Home for the Bride*, by Amy Scheibe; *The Only Girl in School*, by Natalie Standiford.

GHOSH LITERARY

E-mail: submissions@ghoshliterary.com. **Website:** www.ghoshliterary.com. **Contact:** Anna Ghosh. Member of AAR. Signatory of WGA.

Prior to opening her own agency, Ms. Ghosh was previously a partner at Scovil Galen Ghosh.

REPRESENTS Nonfiction, fiction.

"Anna's literary interests are wide and eclectic and she is known for discovering and developing writers. She is particularly interested in literary narratives and books that illuminate some aspect of human endeavor or the natural world. Anna does not typically represent genre fiction but is drawn to compelling storytelling in most guises."

HOW TO CONTACT E-query. Please send an e-mail briefly introducing yourself and your work. Although no specific format is required, it is helpful to know the following: your qualifications for writing your book, including any publications and recognition for your work; who you expect to buy and read your book; similar books and authors. Accepts simultaneous submissions.

GLASS LITERARY MANAGEMENT

138 W. 25th St., 10th Floor, New York NY 10001. (646)237-4881. **E-mail:** alex@glassliterary.com; rick@glassliterary.com. **Website:** www.glassliterary.com. **Contact:** Alex Glass or Rick Pascocello. Mr. Glass is a generalist and takes submissions for virtually all kinds of fiction and nonfiction (except children's picture books). Estab. 2014. Member of AAR. Signatory of WGA.

MEMBER AGENTS Alex Glass; Rick Pascocello.

REPRESENTS Nonfiction, novels.

- Represents general fiction, mystery, suspense/thriller, juvenile fiction, biography, history, mind/body/spirit, health, lifestyle, cookbooks, sports, literary fiction, memoir, narrative nonfiction, pop culture. "We do not represent picture books for children."

HOW TO CONTACT "Please send your query letter in the body of an e-mail and if we are interested, we will respond and ask for the complete manuscript or proposal. No attachments." Accepts simultaneous submissions.

RECENT SALES *100 Days of Cake*, by Shari Goldhagen; *The Red Car*, by Marcy Dermansky; *The Overnight Solution*, by Dr. Michael Breus; *So That Happened: A Memoir*, by Jon Cryer; *Bad Kid*, by David Crabb; *Finding Mr. Brightside*, by Jay Clark; *Strange Animals*, by Chad Kultgen.

GLOBAL LION INTELLECTUAL PROPERTY MANAGEMENT

P.O. Box 669238, Pompano Beach FL 33066. **E-mail:** queriesgloballionmgt@gmail.com. **Website:** www.globallionmanagement.com. **Contact:** Peter Miller. Estab. 2013. Member of AAR. Signatory of WGA.

- Prior to his current position, Mr. Miller was formerly the founder of previously PMA Literary & Film Management Inc. of New York.

- "I look for cutting-edge authors of both fiction and nonfiction with global marketing and motion picture/television production potential."

HOW TO CONTACT E-query. Global Lion Intellectual Property Management. Inc. accepts exclusive submissions only. "If your work is under consideration by another agency, please do not submit it to us." Below the query, paste a one page synopsis, a sample of your book (20 pages is fine), a short author bio, and any impressive social media links.

BARRY GOLDBLATT LITERARY LLC

320 7th Ave. #266, Brooklyn NY 11215. **E-mail:** query@bgliterary.com. **Website:** www.bgliterary.com. **Contact:** Barry Goldblatt; Jennifer Udden. Estab. 2000. Member of AAR. Signatory of WGA.

MEMBER AGENTS Barry Goldblatt; Jennifer Udden, query.judden@gmail.com (speculative fiction of all stripes, especially innovative science fiction or fantasy; contemporary/erotic/LGBT/paranormal/historical romance; contemporary or speculative YA; select mysteries, thrillers, and urban fantasies).

REPRESENTS Fiction. **Considers these fiction areas:** fantasy, middle grade, mystery, romance, science fiction, thriller, young adult.

- "Please see our website for specific submission guidelines and information on our particular tastes."

HOW TO CONTACT "E-mail queries can be sent to query@bgliterary.com and should include the word 'query' in the subject line. To query Jen Udden specifically, e-mail queries can be sent to query.judden@gmail.com. Please know that we will read and respond to every e-query that we receive, provided it is properly addressed and follows the submission guidelines below. We will not respond to e-queries that are addressed to no one, or to multiple recipients. Your e-mail query should include the following within the body of the e-mail: your query letter, a synopsis of the book, and the first 5 pages of your manuscript. We will not open or respond to any e-mails that have attachments. If we like the sound of your work, we will request more from you. Our response time is 4 weeks on queries, 6-8 weeks on full manuscripts. If you haven't heard from us within that time, feel free to check in via e-mail." Accepts simultaneous submissions. Obtains clients through referrals, queries, and conferences.

TERMS Agent receives 15% commission on domestic sales; 20% on foreign and dramatic sales. Offers written contract. 60 days notice must be given to terminate contract.

RECENT SALES *Trolled*, by Bruce Coville; *Grim Tidings*, by Caitlin Kittridge; *Max at Night*, by Ed Vere.

TIPS "We're a hands-on agency, focused on building an author's career, not just making an initial sale. We don't care about trends or what's hot; we just want to sign great writers."

FRANCES GOLDIN LITERARY AGENCY, INC.

214 W. 29th St., Suite 410, New York NY 10001. (212)777-0047. **Fax:** (212)228-1660. **Website:** www.goldinlit.com. Estab. 1977. Member of AAR.

MEMBER AGENTS Frances Goldin, founder/president; Ellen Geiger, vice president/principal (nonfiction: history, biography, progressive politics, photography, science and medicine, women, religion and serious investigative journalism; fiction: literary thriller, and novels in general that provoke and challenge the status quo, as well as historical and multicultural works. Please no New Age, romance, how-to or right-wing politics); Matt McGowan, agent/rights director, mm@goldinlit.com, (literary fiction, essays, history, memoir, journalism, biography, music, popular culture & science, sports [particularly soccer], narrative nonfiction, cultural studies, as well as literary travel, crime, food, suspense and sci-fi); Sam Stoloff, vice president/principal, (literary fiction, memoir, history, accessible sociology and philosophy, cultural studies, serious journalism, narrative and topical nonfiction with a progressive orientation); Ria Julien, agent/counsel; Nina Cochran, literary assistant.

REPRESENTS Nonfiction, novels. **Considers these nonfiction areas:** biography, creative nonfiction, cultural interests, foods, history, investigative, medicine, memoirs, music, philosophy, photography, popular culture, politics, science, sociology, sports, travel, women's issues, crime. **Considers these fiction areas:** historical, literary, mainstream, multicultural, suspense, thriller.

"We are hands on and we work intensively with clients on proposal and manuscript development." "Please note that we do not handle screenplays, romances or most other genre fiction, and hardly any poetry. We do not handle work that is racist, sexist, ageist, homophobic, or pornographic."

HOW TO CONTACT There is an online submission process you can find online. Responds in 4-6 weeks to queries.

IRENE GOODMAN LITERARY AGENCY

27 W. 24th St., Suite 700B, New York NY 10010. **E-mail:** miriam.queries@irenegoodman.com, barbara.queries@irenegoodman.com, rachel.queries@irenegoodman.com, kim.queries@irenegoodman.com, victoria.queries@irenegoodman.com, irene.queries@irenegoodman.com, brita.queries@irenegoodman.com. **E-mail:** submissions@irenegoodman.com. **Website:** www.irenegoodman.com. **Contact:** Brita Lundberg. Estab. 1978. Member of AAR. Represents 150 clients.

MEMBER AGENTS Irene Goodman, Miriam Kriss, Barbara Poelle, Rachel Ekstrom, Kim Perel, Brita Lundberg, Victoria Marini.

REPRESENTS Nonfiction, fiction, novels, juvenile books. **Considers these nonfiction areas:** animals, autobiography, cooking, creative nonfiction, cultural interests, current affairs, decorating, diet/nutrition, design, foods, health, history, how-to, humor, interior design, juvenile nonfiction, memoirs, parenting, politics, science, self-help, women's issues, young adult, parenting, social issues, francophilia, anglophilia, Judaica, lifestyles, cooking, memoir. **Considers these fiction areas:** action, crime, detective, family saga, historical, horror, middle grade, mystery, romance, science fiction, suspense, thriller, urban fantasy, women's, young adult.

Commercial and literary fiction and nonfiction. No screenplays, poetry, or inspirational fiction.

HOW TO CONTACT Query. Submit synopsis, first 10 pages pasted into the body of the email. E-mail queries only! See the website submission page. No e-mail attachments. Query 1 agent only. Accepts simultaneous submissions. Responds in 2 months to queries. Consult website for each agent's submission guidelines.

TERMS Agent receives 15% commission.

TIPS "We are receiving an unprecedented amount of e-mail queries. If you find that the mailbox is full, please try again in two weeks. E-mail queries to our personal addresses will not be answered. E-mails to our personal inboxes will be deleted."

DOUG GRAD LITERARY AGENCY, INC.

156 Prospect Park West, #3L, Brooklyn NY 11215. (718)788-6067. **E-mail:** query@dgliterary.com.

Website: www.dgliterary.com. **Contact:** Doug Grad. Throughout Doug's editorial career, he was always an author's advocate—the kind of editor authors wanted to work with because of his keen eye, integrity, and talent for developing projects. He was also a skillful negotiator, sometimes to the chagrin of literary agents. For the last 10 years, he has been bringing those experiences to the other side of the table in offering publishers the kind of high-quality commercial fiction and nonfiction that he himself was proud to publish. He has sold award-winning and bestselling authors. Estab. 2008. Member of AAR. Signatory of WGA. Represents 50+ clients.

Prior to being an agent, Doug Grad spent 22 years as an editor at imprint at 4 major publishing houses—Simon & Schuster, Random House, Penguin, and HarperCollins.

MEMBER AGENTS Doug Grad (narrative nonfiction, military, sports, celebrity memoir, thrillers, mysteries, cozies, historical fiction, music, style, business, home improvement, cookbooks, science and theater).

REPRESENTS Nonfiction, fiction, novels. **Considers these nonfiction areas:** Americana, autobiography, biography, business, cooking, creative nonfiction, current affairs, diet/nutrition, design, film, government, history, humor, investigative, language, military, music, popular culture, politics, science, sports, technology, theater, travel, true crime, war. **Considers these fiction areas:** action, adventure, commercial, crime, detective, historical, horror, literary, mainstream, military, mystery, police, romance, science fiction, suspense, thriller, war, young adult.

Does not want fantasy, young adult, or children's picture books.

HOW TO CONTACT Query by e-mail first. No sample material unless requested; no printed submissions by mail. Accepts simultaneous submissions. Due to the volume of queries, it's impossible to give a response time.

RECENT SALES *The Next Greatest Generation*, by Joseph L. Galloway and Marvin J. Wolf (Thomas Nelson); *Game Face: A Lifetime of Hard-Learned Lessons On and Off the Basketball Court*, by Bernard King with Jerome Preisler (Da Capo); Dan Morgan thriller series, by Leo Maloney (Kensington); Cajun Country cozy mystery series, by Ellen Byron (Crooked Lane); *Please Don't Feed the Mayor* and *Alaskan Catch*, by Sue Pethick (Kensington).

GRAHAM MAW CHRISTIE LITERARY AGENCY

37 Highbury Place, London England N5 1QP United Kingdom. **E-mail:** enquiries@grahammawchristie.com. **E-mail:** submissions@grahammawchristie.com. **Website:** www.grahammawchristie.com. Association of Authors' Agents. Represents 50 clients.

Jane Graham Maw was a publishing director at HarperCollins, where she worked in rights, publicity and editorial. She later worked as a ghostwriter. She therefore has an insider knowledge of both the publishing industry and the pleasures and pitfalls of authorships. Jennifer Christie has been a literary agent for 13 years. She previously worked in advertising, PR and journalism, giving her a keen marketing focus and honed editorial skills. She has also worked as a ghostwriter and a child counsellor.

MEMBER AGENTS Jane Graham Maw; Jennifer Christie.

REPRESENTS Nonfiction. **Considers these nonfiction areas:** biography, business, child guidance, cooking, crafts, cultural interests, current affairs, diet/nutrition, foods, gardening, health, history, hobbies, how-to, humor, inspirational, memoirs, parenting, philosophy, popular culture, psychology, science, self-help, sex, women's issues.

"We aim to make the publishing process easier and smoother for authors. We work hard to ensure that publishing proposals are watertight before submission. We aim for collaborative relationships with publishers so that we provide the right books to the right editor at the right time. We represent ghostwriters as well as authors." Does not want to receive fiction, poetry, plays or screenwriters.

HOW TO CONTACT E-queries only. This agency only accepts nonfiction. Query with a one-page summary of the topic, a detailed chapter-by-chapter outline, your qualifications for writing the book, your social media and online profile, a note on the market and competing titles, how you could help promote and sell the book, a sample chapter, your contact details. Aims to respond within 3-4 weeks to queries. Recommendations, approaches and submissions.

TERMS Agent receives 15% commission on domestic sales; 20% commission on foreign sales. Offers written contract; 90-day notice must be given to terminate contract.

WRITERS CONFERENCES London Book Fair, Frankfurt Book Fair.

TIPS "UK clients only!"

SANFORD J. GREENBURGER ASSOCIATES, INC.

55 Fifth Ave., New York NY 10003. (212)206-5600. **Fax:** (212)463-8718. **Website:** www.greenburger.com.

"Large enough to be a full service agency, including international rights, but small enough to manage and service clients personally, SJGA works closely with authors to edit and fine-tune proposals, refine concepts and ensure that the best work reaches editors. The agents freely share information and expertise, creating a collaborative partnership unique to the industry. The combined result is reflected in the numerous successes of the agency's authors (including Dan Brown, Patrick Rothfuss, and Robin Preiss Glasser)." Member of AAR. Represents 500 clients.

MEMBER AGENTS Matt Bialer, querymb@sjga.com (fantasy, science fiction, thrillers, and mysteries as well as a select group of literary writers, and also loves smart narrative nonfiction including books about current events, popular culture, biography, history, music, race, and sports); Brenda Bowen, querybb@sjga.com (literary fiction, writers and illustrators of picture books, chapter books, and middle-grade and teen fiction); Faith Hamlin, fhamlin@sjga.com (receives submissions by referral); Heide Lange, queryhl@sjga.com (receives submissions by referral); Daniel Mandel, querydm@sjga.com (literary and commercial fiction, as well as memoirs and nonfiction about business, art, history, politics, sports, and popular culture); Rachael Dillon Fried, rfried@sjga.com (both fiction and nonfiction authors, with a keen interest in unique literary voices, women's fiction, narrative nonfiction, memoir, and comedy); Stephanie Delman, sdelman@sjga.com (literary/upmarket contemporary fiction, psychological thrillers/suspense, and atmospheric, near-historical fiction); Ed Maxwell, emaxwell@sjga.com (expert and narrative nonfiction authors, novelists and graphic novelists, as well as children's book authors and illustrators).

REPRESENTS Nonfiction, fiction, novels, juvenile books. **Considers these nonfiction areas:** art, biography, business, creative nonfiction, current affairs, ethnic, history, humor, memoirs, music, popular culture, politics, sports. **Considers these fiction areas:** commercial, crime, family saga, fantasy, feminist, historical, literary, middle grade, multicultural, mystery, picture books, romance, science fiction, thriller, women's, young adult.

HOW TO CONTACT E-query. "Please look at each agent's profile page for current information about what each agent is looking for and for the correct email address to use for queries to that agent. Please be sure to use the correct query e-mail address for each agent." Agents may not respond to all queries; will respond within 6-8 weeks if interested. Obtains most new clients through recommendations from others.

TERMS Agent receives 15% commission on domestic sales; 20% commission on foreign sales. Charges for photocopying and books for foreign and subsidiary rights submissions.

RECENT SALES *Origin*, by Dan Brown; *Sweet Pea and Friends: A Sheepover*, by John Churchman and Jennifer Churchman; *Code of Conduct*, by Brad Thor.

THE GREENHOUSE LITERARY AGENCY

E-mail: submissions@greenhouseliterary.com. **Website:** www.greenhouseliterary.com. **Contact:** Sarah Davies. Estab. 2008. Member of AAR. Other memberships include SCBWI. Represents 50 clients.

Before launching Greenhouse, Sarah Davies had an editorial and management career in children's publishing spanning 25 years; for 5 years prior to launching the Greenhouse she was Publishing Director of Macmillan Children's Books in London, and published leading authors from both sides of the Atlantic.

MEMBER AGENTS Sarah Davies, vice president (fiction and nonfiction by North American authors, chapter books through to middle grade and young adult); Polly Nolan, agent (fiction by UK, Irish, Commonwealth–including Australia, NZ and India–authors, plus European authors writing in English, author/illustrators (texts under 1,000 words) to young fiction series, through middle grade and young adult).

REPRESENTS Juvenile books. **Considers these nonfiction areas:** juvenile nonfiction, young adult. **Considers these fiction areas:** juvenile, young adult.

"We represent authors writing fiction and nonfiction for children and teens. The agency has offices in both the US and UK, and the agency's commission structure reflects this—taking

15% for sales to both US and UK, thus treating both as 'domestic' market." All genres of children's and YA fiction. Very occasionally, a nonfiction proposal will be considered. Does not want to receive picture books texts (ie, written by writers who aren't also illustrators) or short stories, educational or religious/inspirational work, pre-school/novelty material, screenplays. Represents novels and some nonfiction. Considers these fiction areas: juvenile, chapter book series, middle grade, young adult. Does not want to receive poetry, picture book texts (unless by author/illustrators) or work aimed at adults; short stories, educational or religious/inspirational work, pre-school/novelty material, or screenplays.

HOW TO CONTACT Query 1 agent only. Put the target agent's name in the subject line. Paste the first 5 pages of your story after the query. Accepts simultaneous submissions.

TERMS Agent receives 15% commission on domestic sales; 25% commission on foreign sales. Offers written contract. This agency occasionally charges for submission copies to film agents or foreign publishers.

RECENT SALES *The Preacher Woods*, by Ashley Elston (Disney-Hyperion); *The Science of Breakable Things*, by Tae Keller (Random House); *We Speak in Storms*, by Natalie Lund (Philomel); *When We Wake*, by Elle Cosimano; *Secrets of Topsea* by Kir Fox & M. Shelley Coats; *The Bigfoot Files*, by Lindsay Eagar (Candlewick); *Wanted: Women Mathematicians*, by Tami Lewis Brown & Debbie Loren Dunn (Disney-Hyperion); *Fake*, by Donna Cooner (Scholastic).

WRITERS CONFERENCES Bologna Children's Book Fair, ALA and SCBWI conferences, BookExpo America.

TIPS "Before submitting material, authors should visit the Greenhouse Literary Agency website and carefully read all submission guidelines."

KATHRYN GREEN LITERARY AGENCY, LLC

157 Columbus Ave., Suite 510, New York NY 10023. (212)245-4225. **E-mail:** query@kgreenagency.com. **Website:** www.kathryngreenliteraryagency.com. **Contact:** Kathy Green. Estab. 2004. Other memberships include Women's Media Group.

Prior to becoming an agent, Ms. Green was a book and magazine editor.

REPRESENTS Nonfiction, fiction, novels, short story collections, juvenile books. **Considers these nonfiction areas:** autobiography, biography, business, cooking, cultural interests, current affairs, diet/nutrition, foods, history, how-to, humor, inspirational, investigative, memoirs, parenting, popular culture, psychology, satire, science, spirituality, sports, true crime, women's issues, young adult. **Considers these fiction areas:** commercial, crime, detective, family saga, historical, humor, juvenile, literary, mainstream, middle grade, multicultural, mystery, police, romance, satire, suspense, thriller, women's, young adult.

"Considers all types of fiction but particularly like historical fiction, cozy mysteries, young adult and middle grade. For nonfiction, I am interested in memoir, parenting, humor with a pop culture bent, and history. Quirky nonfiction is also a particular favorite." Does not want to receive science fiction, fantasy, children's picture books, screenplays, or poetry.

HOW TO CONTACT Query by e-mail. Send no attachments unless requested. Do not send queries via regular mail. Responds in 4 weeks. "Queries do not have to be exclusive; however if further material is requested, please be in touch before accepting other representation." Accepts simultaneous submissions. Obtains most new clients through recommendations from others, solicitations, conferences.

TERMS Agent receives 15% commission on domestic sales; 20% commission on foreign sales.

RECENT SALES *Jigsaw Jungle*, by Kristin Levine; *Jane, Anonymous*, by Laurie Faria, Stolarz; *To Woo a Wicked Widow*, by Jenna Jaxon.

GREGORY & COMPANY AUTHORS' AGENTS

David Higham Associates, Waverley House, 7–12 Noel St., London W1F 8GQ England. 020 7434 5900. **E-mail:** laura@gregoryandcompany.co.uk; sara@gregoryandcompany.co.uk; info@gregoryandcompany.co.uk. **E-mail:** maryjones@gregoryandcompany.co.uk. **Website:** www.gregoryandcompany.co.uk. **Contact:** Laura Darpetti. Interested in all types of fiction–particularly literary, up-market commercial, up-market women's fiction, thrillers, mysteries, suspense and crime fiction. No children's books, poetry or original scripts for theatre, film or TV. Estab. 1987. Other memberships include AAA. Represents 60 clients.

MEMBER AGENTS Jane Gregory (English language and Film and TV sales); Claire Morris (Translation rights sales); Stephanie Glencross and Mary Jones (Editorial); Sara Langham (Editorial Assistant); Laura Darpetti (Rights Assistant).

REPRESENTS Fiction, novels. **Considers these fiction areas:** commercial, crime, detective, historical, literary, mystery, police, suspense, thriller, women's.

"As a British agency, we do not generally take on American authors as there are many US based agents who would do this better!" Actively seeking well-written, accessible novels. Does not want to receive horror, science fiction, fantasy, mind/body/spirit, children's books, screenplays, plays, short stories, or poetry.

HOW TO CONTACT Submit outline of the complete plot, the first three chapters or up to 50 pages by e-mail or by post together with publishing history, and a brief author biography. Send submissions to Mary Jones, submissions editor: maryjones@gregoryandcompany.co.uk. If by post, include a SASE. Accepts simultaneous submissions. Allow 3 or 4 weeks for a response. Returns materials only with SASE. Obtains most new clients through recommendations from others.

TERMS Agent receives 15% commission on domestic sales and 20% commission on foreign sales. Offers written contract; 1-month notice must be given to terminate contract. Charges clients for photocopying of whole typescripts and copies of book for submissions.

GREYHAUS LITERARY

3021 20th St., Pl. SW, Puyallup WA 98373. **E-mail:** scott@greyhausagency.com. **E-mail:** submissions@greyhausagency.com. **Website:** www.greyhausagency.com. **Contact:** Scott Eagan, member RWA. Greyhaus Literary Agency focuses exclusively in the print romance and women's fiction genres. Please take the time to review all guidelines found on the website before submitting. Estab. 2003. Member of AAR. Signatory of WGA.

REPRESENTS Novels. **Considers these fiction areas:** new adult, romance, women's.

Greyhaus only focuses on romance and women's fiction. Please review submission information found on the website to know exactly what Greyhaus is looking for. Stories should be 75,000-120,000 words in length or meet the word count requirements for Harlequin found on its website. Does not want fantasy, single title inspirational, young adult or middle grade, picture books, memoirs, biographies, erotica, urban fantasy, science fiction, screenplays, poetry, authors interested in only e-publishing or self-publishing.

HOW TO CONTACT Submissions to Greyhaus can be done in one of three ways: 1) A standard query letter via email. If using this method, do not attach documents or send anything else other than a query letter. 2) Use the Submission Form found on the website on the Contact page. Or 3) send a query, the first 3 pages and a synopsis of no more than 3-5 pages (and a SASE), using a snail mail submission. Accepts simultaneous submissions. Responds in up to 3 months.

TERMS Agent receives 15% commission.

JILL GRINBERG LITERARY MANAGEMENT

392 Vanderbilt Ave., Brooklyn NY 11238. (212)620-5883. **E-mail:** info@jillgrinbergliterary.com. **Website:** www.jillgrinbergliterary.com. "Our authors are novelists, historians, and scientists; memoirists and journalists; illustrators and musicians, cultural critics and humanitarians. They are passionate about what they write. They have strong, authentic voices, whether they are writing fiction or writing nonfiction. They are brilliant storytellers. Our authors have won the American Book Award, the National Book Award and the Pulitzer Prize, as well as the Printz Award and Newbery Honor award. They appear on The New York Times and international bestseller lists. We don't make a habit of dividing our list by category—our authors transcend category. Our authors write for every audience, picture book to adult. They are not easily boxed or contained within any neat, singular label. They often cross categories, are 'genre busting.' We love books, but we take on authors. Our authors are career authors. We are deeply invested in their careers and in making every book count. We are committed to developing ongoing relationships with writers and have represented a good number of our authors for 10 years plus. We understand the importance of the author–publisher connection and put great focus on matching our authors to the right editors and publishers. We fiercely advocate for our authors while maintaining a strong network of top editors and publishers. We have many years of publicity and marketing experience between us, and we give tremendous thought to positioning. Every project requires a tailored, per-

sonalized plan. Every author is a unique. Every author has a different path." Estab. 1999. Member of AAR.

Prior to her current position, Ms. Grinberg was at Anderson Grinberg Literary Management.

MEMBER AGENTS Jill Grinberg; Cheryl Pientka; Katelyn Detweiler; Sophia Seidner.

REPRESENTS Nonfiction, fiction, novels. **Considers these nonfiction areas:** biography, creative nonfiction, current affairs, ethnic, history, language, literature, memoirs, parenting, popular culture, politics, science, sociology, spirituality, sports, travel, women's issues, young adult. **Considers these fiction areas:** fantasy, historical, juvenile, literary, mainstream, middle grade, multicultural, picture books, romance, science fiction, women's, young adult.

"We do not accept unsolicited queries for screenplays."

HOW TO CONTACT "Please send queries via e-mail to info@jillgrinbergliterary.com–include your query letter, addressed to the agent of your choice, along with the first 50 pages of your ms pasted into the body of the e-mail or attached as a doc. or docx. file. We also accept queries via mail, though e-mail is preferred. Please send your query letter and the first 50 pages of your ms by mail, along with a SASE, to the attention of your agent of choice. Please note that unless a SASE with sufficient postage is provided, your materials will not be returned. As submissions are shared within the office, please only query one agent with your project." Accepts simultaneous submissions.

TIPS "We prefer submissions by electronic mail."

JILL GROSJEAN LITERARY AGENCY

1390 Millstone Rd., Sag Harbor NY 11963. (631)725-7419. **E-mail:** jilllit310@aol.com. **Contact:** Jill Grosjean. Estab. 1999.

Prior to becoming an agent, Ms. Grosjean managed an independent bookstore. She also worked in publishing and advertising.

REPRESENTS Novels. **Considers these fiction areas:** historical, literary, mainstream, mystery, women's.

Actively seeking literary novels and mysteries. Does not want serial killer, science fiction or YA novels.

HOW TO CONTACT E-mail queries preferred, no attachments. No cold calls, please. Accepts simultaneous submissions, though when manuscript requested, requires exclusive reading time. Accepts simultaneous submissions. Responds in 1 week to queries; month to mss. Obtains most new clients through recommendations and through recommendations and solicitations.

TERMS Agent receives 15% commission on domestic sales; 20% commission on foreign and film sales.

RECENT SALES *The Gold Pawn*, by L.A. Chandlar (Kensington Books); *Caught in Time*, by Julie McEwain (Pegasus Books); *A Murder in Time*, by Julie McEwain (Pegasus Books); *A Twist in Time*, by Julie McEwain (Pegasus Books); *The Silver Gun*, by LA Chandlar (Kensington Books); *The Edison Effect*, by Bernadette Pajer (Poison Pen Press); *Threading the Needle*, by Marie Bostwick (Kensington Publishing); *Tim Cratchit's Christmas Carol: A Novel of Scrooge's Legacy*, by Jim Piecuch (Simon & Schuster); *The Lighterman's Curse*, by Loretta Marion (Crooked Lane Books).

WRITERS CONFERENCES Thrillerfest, Texas Writer's League, Book Passage Mystery's Writer's Conference, Writer's Market Conference.

LAURA GROSS LITERARY AGENCY

E-mail: assistant@lg-la.com. **Website:** www.lg-la.com. Estab. 1988. Represents 30 clients.

Prior to becoming an agent, Ms. Gross was an editor and ran a reading series.

REPRESENTS Nonfiction, novels.

"I represent a broad range of both fiction and nonfiction writers. I am particularly interested in history, politics, and current affairs, and also love beautifully written literary fiction and intelligent thrillers."

HOW TO CONTACT Queries accepted online via online form on LGLA Submittable site. No e-mail queries. "On the submission form, please include a concise but substantive cover letter. You may include the first 6,000 words of your manuscript in the form as well. We will request further sample chapters from you at a later date, if we think your work suits our list." There may be a delay of several weeks in responding to your query. Accepts simultaneous submissions.

TERMS Agent receives 15% commission on domestic sales; 20% commission on foreign sales. Offers written contract.

THE JOY HARRIS LITERARY AGENCY, INC.

1501 Broadway, Suite 2310, New York NY 10036. (212)924-6269. **Fax:** (212)540-5776. **E-mail:** contact@

joyharrisliterary.com. **E-mail:** submissions@joyharrisliterary.com. **Website:** joyharrisliterary.com. **Contact:** Joy Harris. Estab. 1990. Member of AAR. Represents 100+ clients.

MEMBER AGENTS Joy Harris (literary fiction, strongly-written commercial fiction, narrative nonfiction across a broad range of topics, memoir and biography); Adam Reed (literary fiction, science and technology, and pop culture); Elizabeth Trout.

REPRESENTS Nonfiction, fiction. **Considers these nonfiction areas:** art, biography, creative nonfiction, memoirs, popular culture, science, technology. **Considers these fiction areas:** commercial, literary.

"We are not accepting poetry, screenplays, genre fiction, or self-help submissions at this time."

HOW TO CONTACT Please e-mail all submissions, comprised of a query letter, outline or sample chapter, to submissions@joyharrisliterary.com. Accepts simultaneous submissions. Obtains most new clients through recommendations from clients and editors.

TERMS Agent receives 15% commission on domestic sales; 20% commission on foreign sales. Charges clients for some office expenses.

RECENT SALES *Smash Cut*, by Brad Gooch; *The Other Paris*, by Luc Sante; *The Past*, by Tessa Hadley; *In A Dark Wood*, by Joseph Luzzi.

HARTLINE LITERARY AGENCY

123 Queenston Dr., Pittsburgh PA 15235-5429. (412)829-2483. **E-mail:** jim@hartlineliterary.com. **Website:** www.hartlineliterary.com. **Contact:** James D. Hart. Many of the agents at this agency are generalists. This agency also handles inspirational and Christian works. Estab. 1992. ACFW Represents 400 clients.

Jim Hart was a production journalist for 20 years; Joyce Hart was the Vice President of Marketing at Whitaker House Publishing.

MEMBER AGENTS Jim Hart, principal agent (jim@hartlineliterary.com); Joyce Hart, founder (joyce@hartlineliterary.com); Diana Flegal (diana@hartlineliterary.com); Linda Glaz (linda@hartlineliterary.com); Cyle Young (cyle@hartlineliterary.com).

REPRESENTS Nonfiction, fiction, novels, novellas, juvenile books, scholarly books. **Considers these nonfiction areas:** Americana, autobiography, biography, business, child guidance, creative nonfiction, cultural interests, current affairs, diet/nutrition, health, history, how-to, inspirational, investigative, juvenile nonfiction, memoirs, multicultural, music, parenting, philosophy, popular culture, politics, psychology, recreation, religious, self-help, spirituality, travel, true crime, women's issues, young adult. **Considers these fiction areas:** action, adventure, commercial, contemporary issues, crime, detective, family saga, fantasy, frontier, historical, humor, inspirational, literary, mystery, new adult, religious, romance, science fiction, suspense, thriller, urban fantasy, westerns, women's, young adult.

"This agency specializes in the Christian bookseller market." We also represent general market, but no graphic sex or language. Actively seeking adult fiction, all genres, self-help, social issues, Christian living, parenting, marriage, business, biographies, narrative nonfiction, creative nonfiction. Does not want to receive erotica, gay/lesbian, horror, graphic violence.

HOW TO CONTACT E-query preferred, USPS to the Pittsburgh office. Target one agent only. "All e-mail submissions sent to Hartline Agents should be sent as a MS Word doc attached to an e-mail with 'submission: title, authors name and word count' in the subject line. A proposal is a single document, not a collection of files. Place the query letter in the email itself. Do not send the entire proposal in the body of the e-mail or send PDF files." Further guidelines online. Accepts simultaneous submissions. Responds in 2 months to queries; 3 months to mss. Obtains most new clients through recommendations from others, and at conferences.

TERMS Agent receives 15% commission on domestic sales. Offers written contract.

WRITERS CONFERENCES ACFW; Oregon Christian Writers; Realm Makers; Blue Ridge Mountain Christian Writers; Florida Christian Writers; Write to Publish; Mount Hermon Conference; Taylor's Professional Writing Conference; Maranatha Christian Writers Conference; Write His Answer Christian Conferences.

TIPS Please follow the guidelines on our web site www.hartlineliterary for the fastest response to your proposal. E-mail proposals only.

ANTONY HARWOOD LIMITED

103 Walton St., Oxford OX2 6EB United Kingdom. (44)(018)6555-9615. **E-mail:** mail@antonyharwood.com. **Website:** www.antonyharwood.com. **Contact:**

Antony Harwood; James Macdonald Lockhart; Jo Williamson. Estab. 2000. Represents 52 clients.

Prior to starting this agency, Mr. Harwood and Mr. Lockhart worked at publishing houses and other literary agencies.

MEMBER AGENTS Antony Harwood, James Macdonald Lockhart, Jo Williamson (children's).

REPRESENTS Nonfiction, novels. **Considers these nonfiction areas:** Americana, animals, anthropology, archeology, architecture, art, autobiography, biography, business, child guidance, computers, cooking, current affairs, design, economics, education, environment, ethnic, film, gardening, gay/lesbian, government, health, history, horticulture, how-to, humor, language, memoirs, military, money, multicultural, music, parenting, philosophy, photography, popular culture, psychology, recreation, regional, science, self-help, sex, sociology, software, spirituality, sports, technology, translation, travel, true crime, war, women's issues, women's studies. **Considers these fiction areas:** action, adventure, cartoon, comic books, confession, crime, detective, erotica, ethnic, experimental, family saga, fantasy, feminist, frontier, gay, hi-lo, historical, horror, humor, lesbian, literary, mainstream, military, multicultural, multimedia, mystery, occult, picture books, plays, police, regional, religious, romance, satire, science fiction, spiritual, sports, suspense, thriller, translation, war, westerns, young adult, gothic.

HOW TO CONTACT "We are happy to consider submissions of fiction and nonfiction in every genre and category except for screenwriting and poetry. If you wish to submit your work to us for consideration, please send a covering letter, brief outline and the opening 50 pages by e-mail. If you want to post your material to us, please be sure to enclose an SAE or the cost of return postage." Replies if interested. Accepts simultaneous submissions. Responds in 2 months to queries.

TERMS Agent receives 15% commission on domestic sales; 20% commission on foreign sales.

JOHN HAWKINS & ASSOCIATES, INC.

80 Maiden Ln., Suite 1503, New York NY 10038. (212)807-7040. **E-mail:** jha@jhalit.com. **Website:** www.jhalit.com. **Contact:** Moses Cardona (rights and translations); Annie Kronenberg (permissions); Warren Frazier, literary agent; Anne Hawkins, literary agent; William Reiss, literary agent. John Hawkins & Associates, Inc. is one of the oldest literary agencies in this country, originally founded in 1893 by Paul Revere Reynolds. Four agents carry on in what we think is our traditional manner. We are editorially-minded lovers of the written word who are tough and aggressive deal makers for our clients. Estab. 1893. Member of AAR. The Author Guild Represents 100+ clients.

MEMBER AGENTS Moses Cardona, moses@jhalit.com (commercial fiction, suspense, business, science, and multicultural fiction); Warren Frazier, frazier@jhalit.com (fiction; nonfiction, specifically technology, history, world affairs and foreign policy); Anne Hawkins, ahawkins@jhalit.com (thrillers to literary fiction to serious nonfiction; interested in science, history, public policy, medicine and women's issues).

REPRESENTS Nonfiction, fiction, novels, short story collections, novellas, juvenile books. **Considers these nonfiction areas:** biography, business, history, medicine, politics, science, technology, women's issues. **Considers these fiction areas:** commercial, historical, literary, multicultural, suspense, thriller.

HOW TO CONTACT Query. Include the word "Query" in the subject line. For fiction, include 1-3 chapters of your book as a single Word attachment. For nonfiction, include your proposal as a single attachment. E-mail a particular agent directly if you are targeting one. Accepts simultaneous submissions. Responds in 1 month to queries. Obtains most new clients through recommendations from others.

TERMS Agent receives 15% commission on domestic sales; 20% commission on foreign sales. Charges clients for photocopying.

RECENT SALES *Forty Rooms*, by Olga Grushin; *A Book of American Martyrs*, by Joyce Carol Oates; *City on Edge*, by Stefanie Pintoff; *Cold Earth*, by Ann Cleeves; *The Good Lieutenant*, by Whitney Terrell; *Grief Cottage*, by Gail Godwin.

HELEN HELLER AGENCY INC.

4-216 Heath St. W., Toronto ON M5P 1N7 Canada. (416)489-0396. **E-mail:** info@helenhelleragency.com. **Website:** www.helenhelleragency.com. **Contact:** Helen Heller. Represents 30+ clients.

Prior to her current position, Ms. Heller worked for Cassell & Co. (England), was an editor for Harlequin Books, a senior editor for Avon Books, and editor-in-chief for Fitzhenry & Whiteside.

MEMBER AGENTS Helen Heller, helen@helenhelleragency.com (thrillers and front-list general fiction); Sarah Heller, sarah@helenhelleragency.com (front list commercial YA and adult fiction, with a particular interest in high concept historical fiction); Barbara Berson, barbara@helenhelleragency.com (literary fiction, nonfiction, and YA).

REPRESENTS Nonfiction, novels. **Considers these fiction areas:** commercial, crime, historical, literary, mainstream, thriller, young adult.

HOW TO CONTACT E-mail info@helenhelleragency.com. Submit a brief synopsis, publishing history, author bio, and writing sample, pasted in the body of the e-mail. No attachments with e-queries. Accepts simultaneous submissions. Responds within 3 months if interested. Accepts simultaneous submissions. Obtains most new clients through recommendations from others, solicitations.

TIPS "Whether you are an author searching for an agent, or whether an agent has approached you, it is in your best interest to first find out who the agent represents, what publishing houses has that agent sold to recently and what foreign sales have been made. You should be able to go to the bookstore, or search online and find the books the agent refers to. Many authors acknowledge their agents in the front or back or their books."

RICHARD HENSHAW GROUP

145 W. 28th St., 12th Floor, New York NY 10001. (212)414-1172. **E-mail:** submissions@henshaw.com. **Website:** www.richardhenshawgroup.com. **Contact:** Rich Henshaw. Member of AAR.

Prior to opening his agency, Mr. Henshaw served as an agent with Richard Curtis Associates, Inc.

REPRESENTS Novels. **Considers these fiction areas:** fantasy, historical, horror, literary, mainstream, mystery, police, romance, science fiction, thriller, young adult.

"We specialize in popular fiction and nonfiction and are affiliated with a variety of writers' organizations. Our clients include *New York Times* bestsellers and recipients of major awards in fiction and nonfiction." "We only consider works between 65,000-150,000 words." "We do not represent children's books, screenplays, short fiction, poetry, textbooks, scholarly works or coffee-table books."

HOW TO CONTACT "Please feel free to submit a query letter in the form of an e-mail of fewer than 250 words to submissions@henshaw.com address." No snail mail queries. Accepts simultaneous submissions. Obtains most new clients through recommendations from others, solicitations, conferences.

TERMS Agent receives 15% commission on domestic sales; 20% commission on foreign sales. No written contract. Charges clients for photocopying and book orders.

TIPS "While we do not have any reason to believe that our submission guidelines will change in the near future, writers can find up-to-date submission policy information on our website. Always include a SASE with correct return postage."

HERMAN AGENCY

350 Central Park W., Apt. 41, New York NY 10025. (212)749-4907. **E-mail:** ronnie@hermanagencyinc.com; katia.hermanagency@gmail.com. **E-mail:** katia.hermanagencyinc@gmail.com. **Website:** www.hermanagencyinc.com. **Contact:** Ronnie Ann Herman or Katia Herman. "We are a small boutique literary agency that represents authors and artists for the children's book market. We are only accepting submissions for picture books, middle grade, graphic novels." Estab. 1999. SCBWI Represents 19 clients.

Ronnie Ann Herman was an art director, associate publisher and V.P. at Random House and Grosset & Dunlap/Penguin. Ronnie is also an author of numerous picture books, under the name R.H. Herman.

MEMBER AGENTS Ronnie Ann Herman, Katia Herman.

REPRESENTS Juvenile books. **Considers these nonfiction areas:** juvenile nonfiction. **Considers these fiction areas:** juvenile, middle grade, picture books.

Specializes in childrens' books of all genres. Actively seeking author/artist picture books and illustrated readers, series, middle grade. Does not want YA or adult books.

HOW TO CONTACT Submit via e-mail only. Accepts simultaneous submissions. Responds in 8 weeks. If you have not had a response from us within this period, please understand that that means we are not able to represent your work. Obtains very few clients.

TERMS Agent receives 15% commission. Exclusive contract.

TIPS "Check our website to see if you belong with our agency."

THE JEFF HERMAN AGENCY, LLC

P.O. Box 1522, Stockbridge MA 01262. (413)298-0077. **E-mail:** jeff@jeffherman.com. **Contact:** Jeffrey H. Herman. Specializes in all areas of adult nonfiction. Estab. 1987. Represents 100 clients.

Prior to opening his agency, Mr. Herman served as a public relations executive.

MEMBER AGENTS Deborah Levine, vice president (nonfiction book doctor); Jeff Herman.

REPRESENTS Nonfiction, scholarly books, textbooks. **Considers these nonfiction areas:** Americana, animals, biography, business, child guidance, computers, crafts, creative nonfiction, cultural interests, current affairs, diet/nutrition, economics, education, ethnic, government, health, history, hobbies, how-to, humor, inspirational, investigative, law, medicine, memoirs, metaphysics, military, money, multicultural, New Age, parenting, popular culture, politics, psychology, regional, religious, science, self-help, sex, sociology, software, spirituality, technology, travel, true crime, war, women's issues, women's studies, popular reference.

This agency specializes in adult nonfiction.

HOW TO CONTACT Query by e-mail. Accepts simultaneous submissions.

TERMS Agent receives 15% commission on domestic sales. Offers written contract.

RECENT SALES Have agented more than 1,000 titles.

JULIE A. HILL AND ASSOCIATES, LLC

12997 Caminito Del Pasaje, Del Mar CA 92014. (858)259-2595. **Fax:** (858)259-2777. **E-mail:** hillagent@aol.com. **Website:** www.publishersmarketplace/members/hillagent. **Contact:** Julie Hill.

MEMBER AGENTS Julie Hill, agent and principal.

REPRESENTS Nonfiction. **Considers these nonfiction areas:** architecture, art, biography, health, memoirs, New Age, self-help, technology, travel, women's issues, technology books, both for professionals and laypersons. **Considers these script areas:** psychic.

Specialties of the house are memoir, health, self-help, art, architecture, business/technology, both literary and reference travel. NOTE: We also do contract and sale consulting for authors who are working unagented. Consulting inquiries welcome.

HOW TO CONTACT E-query or query via snail mail with SASE. Accepts simultaneous submissions. Responds in 4-6 weeks to queries. Obtains most new clients through recommendations from other authors, editors, and agents.

HILL NADELL LITERARY AGENCY

6442 Santa Monica Blvd., Suite 201, Los Angeles CA 90038. (310)860-9605. **E-mail:** queries@hillnadell.com. **Website:** www.hillnadell.com. Represents 100 clients.

MEMBER AGENTS Bonnie Nadell (nonfiction books include works on current affairs and food as well as memoirs and other narrative nonfiction; in fiction, she represents thrillers along with upmarket women's and literary fiction); Dara Hyde (literary and genre fiction, narrative nonfiction, graphic novels, memoir and the occasional young adult novel).

REPRESENTS Nonfiction, novels. **Considers these nonfiction areas:** biography, current affairs, environment, government, health, history, language, literature, medicine, popular culture, politics, science, technology, biography; government/politics, narrative. **Considers these fiction areas:** literary, mainstream, thriller, women's, young adult.

HOW TO CONTACT Send a query and SASE. If you would like your materials returned, please include adequate postage. To submit electronically: Send your query letter and the first 5-10 pages to queries@hillnadell.com. No attachments. Due to the high volume of submissions the agency receives, it cannot guarantee a response to all e-mailed queries. Accepts simultaneous submissions.

TERMS Agent receives 15% commission on domestic and film sales; 20% commission on foreign sales. Charges clients for photocopying and foreign mailings.

HOLLOWAY LITERARY

P.O. Box 771, Cary NC 27512. **E-mail:** submissions@hollowayliteraryagency.com. **Website:** hollowayliteraryagency.com. **Contact:** Nikki Terpilowski. A full-service boutique literary agency located in Raleigh, NC. Estab. 2011. Member of AAR. Signatory of WGA. International Thriller Writers and Romance Writers of America Represents 26 clients.

MEMBER AGENTS Nikki Terpilowski (romance, women's fiction, Southern fiction, historical fiction, cozy mysteries, lifestyle no-fiction (minimalism, homesteading, southern, etc.) commercial, upmarket/book club fiction, African-American fiction of all types, literary); Rachel Burkot (young adult contemporary, women's fiction, upmarket/book club fiction, contemporary romance, Southern fiction, nonfiction).

REPRESENTS Nonfiction, fiction, movie scripts, feature film. **Considers these nonfiction areas:** Americana, environment, humor, narrative nonfiction, New Journalism, essays. **Considers these fiction areas:** action, adventure, commercial, contemporary issues, crime, detective, ethnic, family saga, fantasy, glitz, historical, inspirational, literary, mainstream, metaphysical, middle grade, military, multicultural, mystery, new adult, New Age, regional, romance, short story collections, spiritual, suspense, thriller, urban fantasy, war, women's, young adult. **Considers these script areas:** action, adventure, biography, contemporary issues, ethnic, romantic comedy, romantic drama, teen, thriller, TV movie of the week.

"Note to self-published authors: While we are happy to receive submissions from authors who have previously self-published novels, we do not represent self-published works. Send us your unpublished manuscripts only." Nikki is open to submissions and is selectively reviewing queries for cozy mysteries with culinary, historical or book/publishing industry themes written in the vein of Jaclyn Brady, Laura Childs, Julie Hyzy and Lucy Arlington; women's fiction with strong magical realism similar to Meena van Praag's *The Dress Shop of Dreams*, Sarah Addison Allen's *Garden Spells, Season of the Dragonflies* by Sarah Creech and Mary Robinette Kowal's Glamourist Series. She would love to find a wine-themed mystery series similar to Nadia Gordon's Sunny McCoskey series or Ellen Crosby's Wine County Mysteries that combine culinary themes with lots of great Southern history. Nikki is also interested in seeing contemporary romance set in the southern US or any wine county or featuring a culinary theme, dark, edgy historical romance, gritty military romance or romantic suspense with sexy Alpha heroes and lots of technical detail. She is also interested in acquiring historical fiction written in the vein of Alice Hoffman, Lalita Tademy and Isabel Allende. Nikki is also interested in espionage, military, political and AI thrillers similar to Tom Clancy, Robert Ludlum, Steve Berry, Vince Flynn, Brad Thor and Daniel Silva. Nikki has a special interest in non-fiction subjects related to governance, politics, military strategy and foreign relations; food and beverage, mindfulness, southern living and lifestyle. Does not want horror, true crime or novellas.

HOW TO CONTACT Send query and first 15 pages of ms pasted into the body of e-mail to submissions@hollowayliteraryagency.com. In the subject header write: (Insert Agent's Name)/Title/Genre. Holloway Literary does accept submissions via mail (query letter and first 50 pages). Expect a response time of at least 3 months. Include e-mail address, phone number, social media accounts, and mailing address on your query letter. Accepts simultaneous submissions. Responds in 6-8 weeks. If the agent is interested, he/she'll respond with a request for more material.

RECENT SALES A list of recent sales are listed on the agency website's "news" page.

HORNFISCHER LITERARY MANAGEMENT

Austin TX **E-mail:** queries@hornfischerlit.com. **Website:** www.hornfischerlit.com. **Contact:** Jim Hornfischer, president.

Prior to becoming a literary agent in 1993, Mr. Hornfischer held editorial positions at HarperCollins and McGraw-Hill in New York.

REPRESENTS Nonfiction.

Hornfischer Literary Management, L.P., is a literary agency with a strong track record handling a broad range of serious and commercial nonfiction.

HOW TO CONTACT E-mail queries only. Responds if interested. Accepts simultaneous submissions. Obtains most new clients through referrals from clients, reading books and magazines, pursuing ideas with New York editors.

TERMS Agent receives 15% commission on domestic sales; 25% commission on foreign sales. Offers written contract.

TIPS "When you query agents and send out proposals, present yourself as someone who's in command of his material and comfortable in his own skin. Too many writers have a palpable sense of anxiety and insecurity. Take a deep breath and realize that—if you're good—someone in the publishing world will want you."

HSG AGENCY

37 W. 28th St., 8th Floor, New York NY 10001. **E-mail:** channigan@hsgagency.com; jsalky@hsgagency.com; jgetzler@hsgagency.com; sroberts@hsgagency.com; leigh@hsgagency.com. **Website:** hsgagency.com. **Contact:** Carrie Hannigan; Jesseca Salky; Josh Getzler; Soumeya Roberts; Leigh Eisenman. Hannigan Salky Getzler (HSG) Agency is a boutique literary agency, formed by Carrie Hannigan, Jesseca Salky and Josh Getzler in 2011. "Our agents have over 40 years combined experience in the publishing industry and represent a diverse list of best-selling and award-winning clients. HSG is a full-service literary agency that through collaborative and client-focused representation manages all aspects of an author's career, from manuscript shaping, to sale and publication, subsidiary rights management, marketing and publicity strategy, and beyond. Our diverse and skilled team represents all types of fiction and non-fiction, for both adults and children, and has strong relationships with every major publisher as well as familiarity with independent and start-up publishers offering a different approach to publishing. Our clients have access to the resources and expertise of every member of our agency team, which includes in-house lawyers and contracts professionals, foreign rights managers, and royalty and accounting specialists. Most importantly, our worth is measured by the success of our clients, and so you will find in each HSG agent not only a staunch advocate but a career-long ally." Estab. 2011. Member of AAR. Signatory of WGA.

Prior to opening HSG Agency, Ms. Hannigan, Ms. Salky. and Mr. Getzler were agents at Russell & Volkening.

MEMBER AGENTS Carrie Hannigan (children's books, illustrators, YA and MG); Jesseca Salky (literary and mainstream fiction); Josh Getzler (foreign and historical fiction; both women's fiction, straight-ahead historical fiction, and thrillers and mysteries); Soumeya Roberts (literary fiction and narrative nonfiction); Leigh Eisenman (literary and upmarket fiction, foodie/cookbooks, health and fitness, lifestyle, and select narrative nonfiction).

REPRESENTS Nonfiction, fiction, novels, short story collections, juvenile books. **Considers these nonfiction areas:** animals, business, cooking, creative nonfiction, cultural interests, current affairs, diet/nutrition, education, environment, foods, gardening, health, history, hobbies, humor, literature, memoirs, money, multicultural, music, parenting, photography, popular culture, politics, psychology, science, self-help, sports, women's issues, women's studies, young adult. **Considers these fiction areas:** adventure, commercial, contemporary issues, crime, detective, ethnic, experimental, family saga, fantasy, feminist, historical, humor, juvenile, literary, mainstream, middle grade, multicultural, mystery, picture books, science fiction, suspense, thriller, translation, women's, young adult.

Carrie Hannigan: In the kidlit world, right now Carrie is looking for humorous books and books with warmth, heart and a great voice in both contemporary and fantasy. She is also open to graphic novels and nonfiction. Jesseca Salky: Jesseca is looking for literary fiction submissions that are family stories (she loves a good mother/daughter tale), have a strong sense of place (where the setting feels like its own character), or a daring or unique voice (think Jamie Quatro), as well as upmarket fiction that can appeal to men and women and has that Tropper/Hornby/Matt Norman quality to it. Josh Getzler: Josh is particularly into foreign and historical fiction; both women's fiction (your Downton Abbey/Philippa Gregory Mashups), straight ahead historical fiction (think Wolf Hall or The Road to Wellville); and thrillers and mysteries (The Alienist, say; or Donna Leon or Arianna Franklin). He'd love a strong French Revolution novel. In nonfiction, he's very interested in increasing his list in history (including micro-histories), business, and political thought–but not screeds. Soumeya Roberts: In fiction, Soumeya is seeking literary and upmarket novels and collections, and also represents realistic young-adult and middle-grade. She likes books with vivid voices and compelling, well-developed story-telling, and is particularly interested in fiction that reflects on the post-colonial world and narratives by people of color. In nonfiction, she is primarily looking for idea-driven or voice-forward memoirs, personal essay collections, and approachable narrative nonfiction of all stripes. Leigh Eisenman: Leigh seeks submissions in the areas of literary and upmarket commercial fiction for adults, and is particularly drawn to: flawed protagonists she can't help but fall in love with (Holden Caulfield was her first crush); stories that take place in contemporary New York, but also any well-defined, vivid setting; explorations of relationships (including journeys of self-discovery); and of course, excellent writing. On the nonfiction side, Leigh is interested in cookbooks, food/travel-related works, health and fitness, lifestyle, humor/gift, and select narrative nonfiction. Please note that we do not represent screenplays, romance fiction, or religious fiction.

HOW TO CONTACT Please send a query letter and the first 5 pages of your ms (within the e-mail–no attachments please) to the appropriate agent for your book. If it is a picture book, please include the entire ms. If you were referred to us, please mention it in the first line of your query. Please note that we do not represent screenplays, romance fiction, or religious fiction. If Carrie and Jesseca have not responded to your query within 10 weeks of submission, please consider this a pass. Due to the volume of queries Leigh receives, she will only respond to those in which she's interested.Soumeya will not be accepting new unsolicited queries until May 1, 2018. All queries received during that time will be deleted. All agents are open to new clients.

RECENT SALES *A Spool of Blue Thread*, by Anne Tyler (Knopf); *Blue Sea Burning*, by Geoff Rodkey (Putnam); *The Partner Track*, by Helen Wan (St. Martin's Press); *The Thrill of the Haunt*, by E.J. Copperman (Berkley); *Aces Wild*, by Erica Perl (Knopf Books for Young Readers); *Steve & Wessley: The Sea Monster*, by Jennifer Morris (Scholastic); *Infinite Worlds*, by Michael Soluri (Simon & Schuster).

HUDSON AGENCY

3 Travis Lane, Montrose New York 10548. (914)737-1475. **Website:** www.hudsonagency.net. **Contact:** Sue Giordano. Signatory of WGA. Represents 20+ clients.

MEMBER AGENTS Sue Giordano (partner/agent); Pat Giordano (partner/producer); Leif Giordano (agent/creative consultant); Michele Dickinson (agent).

REPRESENTS TV scripts, TV movie of the week, animation.

"Our mission is to work with fresh talent from all over the globe on projects that will become classics, touching the hearts and minds of people now and in the years to come. With over a thousand contacts in the business, we have earned the reputation of being hard working, pleasantly persistent agents who follow through."

ICM PARTNERS

65 E. 55th St., New York NY 10022. (212)556-5600. **Website:** www.icmtalent.com. **Contact:** Literary Department. Member of AAR. Signatory of WGA.

REPRESENTS Nonfiction, fiction, novels.

HOW TO CONTACT Accepts simultaneous submissions.

INKLINGS LITERARY AGENCY

3419 Virginia Beach Blvd. #183, Virginia Beach VA 23452. **E-mail:** michelle@inklingsliterary.com. **E-mail:** query@inklingsliterary.com. **Website:** www.inklingsliterary.com. Inklings Literary Agency is a full service, hands-on literary agency seeking submissions from established authors as well as talented new authors. "We represent a broad range of commercial and literary fiction as well as memoirs and true crime. We are not seeking short stories, poetry, screenplays, or children's picture books." Estab. 2013. RWA, SinC, HRW.

"We offer our clients interactive representation for their work, as well as developmental guidance for their author platforms, working with them as they grow. With backgrounds in book selling, business, marketing, publicity, contract negotiation, as well as editing and writing, and script work, we work closely with our clients to build their brands and their careers." The face of publishing is ever-changing, and bending and shifting with the times and staying ahead of the curve are key for Michelle and her agency, Inklings Literary Agency. The agents of Inklings Literary Agency all strictly adhere to the AAR's code of ethics.

MEMBER AGENTS Michelle Johnson, michelle@inklingsliterary.com (in adult and YA fiction, contemporary, suspense, thriller, mystery, horror, fantasy — including paranormal and supernatural elements within those genres), romance of every level, nonfiction in the areas of memoir and true crime); Dr. Jamie Bodnar Drowley, jamie@inklingsliterary.com (new adult fiction in the areas of romance [all subgenres], fantasy [urban fantasy, light sci-fi, steampunk], mystery and thrillers—as well as young adult [all subgenres] and middle grade stories); Naomi Davis, naomi@inklingsliterary.com (romance of any variety—including paranormal, fresh urban fantasy, general fantasy, new adult and light sci-fi; young adult in any of those same genres; memoirs about living with disabilities, facing criticism, and mental illness); Whitley Abell, whitley@inklingsliterary.com (young adult, middle grade, and select upmarket women's fiction); Alex Barba, alex@inklingsliterary.com (YA fiction).

REPRESENTS Nonfiction, fiction, novels, juvenile books. **Considers these nonfiction areas:** cooking, creative nonfiction, diet/nutrition, gay/lesbian, memoirs, true crime, women's issues. **Considers these fiction areas:** action, adventure, commercial, contemporary issues, crime, detective, erotica, ethnic, fantasy, feminist, gay, historical, horror, juvenile, lesbian, mainstream, metaphysical, middle grade, military, multicultural, multimedia, mystery, new adult, New Age, occult, paranormal, police, psychic, regional, romance, science fiction, spiritual, sports, supernatural, suspense, thriller, urban fantasy, war, women's, young adult.

HOW TO CONTACT E-queries only. To query, type "Query (Agent Name)" plus the title of your novel in the subject line, then please send your query letter, short synopsis, and first 10 pages pasted into the body of the e-mail to query@inklingsliterary.com. Check the agency website to make sure that your targeted agent is currently open to submissions. Accepts simultaneous submissions. For queries, no response in 3 months is considered a rejection.

TERMS Agent takes 15% domestic, 20% subsidiary commission. Charges no fees.

INKWELL MANAGEMENT, LLC

521 Fifth Ave., Suite 2600, New York NY 10175. (212)922-3500. **Fax:** (212)922-0535. **E-mail:** info@inkwellmanagement.com. **E-mail:** submissions@inkwellmanagement.com. **Website:** www.inkwellmanagement.com. Represents 500 clients.

MEMBER AGENTS Stephen Barbara (select adult fiction and nonfiction); William Callahan (nonfiction of all stripes, especially American history and memoir, pop culture and illustrated books, as well as voice-driven fiction that stands out from the crowd); Michael V. Carlisle; Catherine Drayton (bestselling authors of books for children, young adults and women readers); David Forrer (literary, commercial, historical and crime fiction to suspense/thriller, humorous nonfiction and popular history); Alexis Hurley (literary and commercial fiction, memoir, narrative nonfiction and more); Nathaniel Jacks (memoir, narrative nonfiction, social sciences, health, current affairs, business,religion, and popular history, as well as fiction—literary and commercial, women's, young adult, historical, short story, among others); Jacqueline Murphy; (fiction, children's books, graphic novels and illustrated works, and compelling narrative nonfiction); Richard Pine; Eliza Rothstein (literary and commercial fiction, narrative nonfiction, memoir, popular science, and food writing); David Hale Smith; Kimberly Witherspoon; Jenny Witherell; Charlie Olson; Liz Parker (commercial and upmarket women's fiction and narrative, practical, and platform-driven nonfiction); George Lucas; Lyndsey Blessing; Claire Draper; Kate Falkoff; Claire Friedman; Michael Mungiello; Jessica Mileo; Corinne Sullivan; Maria Whelan.

REPRESENTS Novels. **Considers these nonfiction areas:** biography, business, cooking, creative nonfiction, current affairs, foods, health, history, humor, memoirs, popular culture, religious, science. **Considers these fiction areas:** commercial, crime, historical, literary, middle grade, picture books, romance, short story collections, suspense, thriller, women's, young adult.

HOW TO CONTACT "In the body of your e-mail, please include a query letter and a short writing sample (1-2 chapters). We currently accept submissions in all genres except screenplays. Due to the volume of queries we receive, our response time may take up to 2 months. Feel free to put 'Query for [Agent Name]: [Your Book Title]' in the e-mail subject line." Accepts simultaneous submissions. Obtains most new clients through recommendations from others.

TERMS Agent receives 15% commission on domestic sales; 20% commission on foreign sales. Offers written contract.

TIPS "We will not read mss before receiving a letter of inquiry."

INTERNATIONAL TRANSACTIONS, INC.

P.O. Box 97, Gila NM 88038-0097. (845)373-9696. **E-mail:** Info@internationaltransactions.us. **Website:** www.intltrans.com. **Contact:** Peter Riva. Since 1975, the company has specialized in international idea and intellectual property brokerage catering to multi-national, multi-lingual, licensing and rights' representation of authors and publishers as well as producing award-winning TV and other media. They have been responsible for over 40 years of production, in both media and product, resulting in excess of $1.6 billion in retail sales and several international historic events (the memorabilia of which are on permanent display in national institutions in America, Germany, and France as well as touring internationally). In 2000 by JoAnn Collins BA, RN joined the company and acts as an Associate Editor specializing in women's voices and issues. In 2013 they created an imprint, published by Skyhorse Publishing, called Yucca Publishing which featured over 40 new and independent voices–exciting additions to the book world. In 2015 they created an imprint, Horseshoe Books, to facilitate out-of-print backlist titles to re-enter the marketplace. Estab. 1975.

MEMBER AGENTS Peter Riva with Sandra Riva (part-time); JoAnn Collins (women's fiction, medical fiction).

REPRESENTS Nonfiction, fiction, novels, short story collections, juvenile books, scholarly books. illustrated books, anthologies. **Considers these nonfiction areas:** Americana, anthropology, archeology, architecture, art, autobiography, biography, business, computers, cooking, cultural interests, current affairs, diet/nutrition, design, environment, ethnic, film, foods, gay/lesbian, government, health, history, humor, inspirational, investigative, language, law, literature, medicine, memoirs, military, multicultural, music, photography, popular culture, politics, religious, satire, science, self-help, sports, technology, translation, true crime, war, women's issues, women's studies, young adult. **Considers these fiction areas:** action, adventure, commercial, crime, detective, erotica, experimental, family saga, feminist, gay, historical, humor, inspirational, lesbian, literary, mainstream, middle grade, military, multicultural, mystery, new adult, picture books, police, satire, science fiction, spiritual, sports, suspense, thriller, translation, war, westerns, women's, young adult, chick lit.

"We specialize in large and small projects, helping qualified authors perfect material for publication." Actively seeking intelligent, well-written innovative material that breaks new ground. Does not want to receive material influenced by TV (too much dialogue); a rehash of previous successful novels' themes, or poorly prepared material. Does not want to be sent any material being reviewed by others.

HOW TO CONTACT In 2018, we will be extremely selective of new projects. First, e-query with an outline or synopsis. E-queries only. Put "Query: [Title]" in the e-mail subject line. Submissions or emails received without these conditions met are automatically discarded. Responds in 3 weeks to queries if interested; 5 weeks to ms after follow-up request. Obtains most new clients through recommendations from others.

TERMS Agent receives 15% (25%+ on illustrated books) commission on domestic sales; 20% commission on foreign sales and media rights. Offers written contract; 100-day notice must be given to terminate contract. No additional fees, ever.

RECENT SALES Averaging 20+ book placements per year.

TIPS "'Book'—a published work of literature. That last word is the key. Not a string of words, not a book of (TV or film) 'scenes,' and never a stream of consciousness unfathomable by anyone outside of the writer's coterie. A writer should only begin to get 'interested in getting an agent' if the work is polished, literate and ready to be presented to a publishing house. Anything less is either asking for a quick rejection or is a thinly disguised plea for creative assistance—which is often given but never fiscally sound for the agents involved. Writers, even published authors, have difficulty in being objective about their own work. Friends and family are of no assistance in that process either. Writers should attempt to get their work read by the most unlikely and stern critic as part of the editing process, months before any agent is approached. In another matter: the economics of our job have changed as well. As the publishing world goes through the transition to e-books (much as the music industry went through the change to downloadable music)—a transition we expect to see at 95% within 10 years—everyone is nervous and wants 'assured bestsellers' from which to eke out a living until they know what the new e-world will continue to bring. This makes the sales rate and, especially, the advance royalty rates, plummet. Hence, our ability to take risks and take on new clients' work is increasingly perilous financially for us and all agents."

JABBERWOCKY LITERARY AGENCY

49 W. 45th St., 12th Floor, New York NY 10036. **Website:** www.awfulagent.com. **Contact:** Joshua Bilmes.

Estab. 1990. Other memberships include SFWA. Represents 80 clients.

MEMBER AGENTS Joshua Bilmes; Eddie Schneider; Lisa Rodgers.

REPRESENTS Nonfiction, fiction, novels, novellas, juvenile books. **Considers these nonfiction areas:** autobiography, biography, business, cooking, current affairs, economics, film, foods, gay/lesbian, government, health, history, humor, language, law, literature, medicine, money, music, popular culture, politics, satire, science, sociology, sports, technology, theater, war, women's issues, women's studies, young adult. **Considers these fiction areas:** action, adventure, contemporary issues, crime, detective, ethnic, family saga, fantasy, feminist, gay, glitz, historical, horror, humor, juvenile, lesbian, literary, mainstream, middle grade, mystery, new adult, paranormal, police, psychic, regional, romance, satire, science fiction, sports, supernatural, thriller, women's, young adult.

This agency represents quite a lot of genre fiction (science fiction & fantasy), romance, and mystery; and is actively seeking to increase the amount of nonfiction projects. It does not handle children's or picture books. Book-length material only—no poetry, articles, or short fiction.

HOW TO CONTACT "We are currently open to unsolicited queries. No e-mail, phone, or fax queries, please. Query with SASE. Please check our website, as there may be times during the year when we are not accepting queries. Query letter only; no manuscript material unless requested." Accepts simultaneous submissions. Responds in 3-6 weeks to queries. Obtains most new clients through solicitations, recommendation by current clients.

TERMS Agent receives 15% commission on domestic sales; 20% commission on foreign sales. Offers written contract, binding for 1 year. Charges clients for book purchases, photocopying, international book/ms mailing.

RECENT SALES *Alcatraz #5* by Brandon Sanderson; *Aurora Teagarden*, by Charlaine Harris; *The Unnoticeables*, by Robert Brockway; *Messenger's Legacy*, by Peter V. Brett; *Slotter Key*, by Elizabeth Moon. Other clients include Tanya Huff, Simon Green, Jack Campbell, Myke Cole, Marie Brennan, Daniel Jose Older, Jim Hines, Mark Hodder, Toni Kelner, Ari Marmell, Ellery Queen, Erin Tettensor, and Walter Jon Williams.

TIPS "In approaching with a query, the most important things to us are your credits and your biographical background to the extent it's relevant to your work. I (and most agents) will ignore the adjectives you may choose to describe your own work."

JANKLOW & NESBIT ASSOCIATES

285 Madison Ave., 21st Floor, New York NY 10017. (212)421-1700. **Fax:** (212)355-1403. **E-mail:** info@janklow.com. **E-mail:** submissions@janklow.com. **Website:** www.janklowandnesbit.com. Estab. 1989.

MEMBER AGENTS Morton L. Janklow; Anne Sibbald; Lynn Nesbit; Luke Janklow; PJ Mark (interests are eclectic, including short stories and literary novels. His nonfiction interests include journalism, popular culture, memoir/narrative, essays and cultural criticism); Paul Lucas (literary and commercial fiction, focusing on literary thrillers, science fiction and fantasy; also seeks narrative histories of ideas and objects, as well as biographies and popular science); Emma Parry (nonfiction by experts, but will consider outstanding literary fiction and upmarket commercial fiction); Kirby Kim (formerly of WME); Marya Spence; Allison Hunter; Melissa Flashman; Stefanie Lieberman.

REPRESENTS Nonfiction, fiction.

HOW TO CONTACT Be sure to address your submission to a particular agent. For fiction submissions, send an informative cover letter, a brief synopsis and the first 10 pages. "If you are sending an e-mail submission, please include the sample pages in the body of the e-mail below your query. For nonfiction submissions, send an informative cover letter, a full outline, and the first 10 pages of the ms. If you are sending an e-mail submission, please include the sample pages in the body of the e-mail below your query. For picture book submissions, send an informative cover letter, full outline, and include a picture book dummy and at least one full-color sample. If you are sending an e-mail submission, please attach a picture book dummy as a PDF and the full-color samples as JPEGs or PDFs." Accepts simultaneous submissions. Due to the volume of submissions received, please note that we cannot respond to every query. We shall contact you if we wish to pursue your submission. Obtains most new clients through recommendations from others.

TIPS "Please send a short query with first 10 pages or artwork."

J DE S ASSOCIATES, INC.

9 Shagbark Rd., Norwalk CT 06854. (203)838-7571. **E-mail:** jdespoel@aol.com. **Website:** www.jdesassociates.com. **Contact:** Jacques de Spoelberch. Estab. 1975.

Prior to opening his agency, Mr. de Spoelberch was an editor with Houghton Mifflin. And launched International Literary Management for the International Management Group.

REPRESENTS Novels. **Considers these nonfiction areas:** biography, business, cultural interests, current affairs, economics, ethnic, government, health, history, law, medicine, metaphysics, military, New Age, politics, self-help, sociology, sports, translation. **Considers these fiction areas:** crime, detective, frontier, historical, juvenile, literary, mainstream, mystery, New Age, police, suspense, westerns, young adult.

HOW TO CONTACT "Brief queries by regular mail and e-mail are welcomed for fiction and nonfiction, but kindly do not include sample proposals or other material unless specifically requested to do so." Accepts simultaneous submissions. Responds in 2 months to queries. Obtains most new clients through recommendations from authors and other clients.

TERMS Agent receives 15% commission on domestic sales; 20% commission on foreign sales. Charges clients for foreign postage and photocopying.

RECENT SALES Joshilyn Jackson's new novel *A Grown-Up Kind of Pretty* (Grand Central); Margaret George's final Tudor historical *Elizabeth I* (Penguin); the fifth in Leighton Gage's series of Brazilian thrillers *A Vine in the Blood* (Soho); Genevieve Graham's romance *Under the Same Sky* (Berkley Sensation); Hilary Holladay's biography of the early Beat Herbert Huncke, *American Hipster* (Magnus); Ron Rozelle's *My Boys and Girls Are In There: The 1937 New London School Explosion* (Texas A&M); the concluding novel in Dom Testa's YA science fiction series, *The Galahad Legacy* (Tor); and Bruce Coston's new collection of animal stories *The Gift of Pets* (St. Martin's Press).

THE CAROLYN JENKS AGENCY

30 Cambridge Park Dr. Unit 3140, Cambridge MA 02140. (617)233-9130. **E-mail:** carolynjenks@comcast.net. **Website:** www.carolynjenksagency.com. **Contact:** Carolyn Jenks. "We are a boutique agency, with famous authors as well as debut novelists. We engage in manuscript and filmscript development on special projects." Estab. 1987. Signatory of WGA. Represents 48 clients.

Began publishing career working at Scribner's Subsidiary Rights Dept., managing editor Ballantine Books, Literary agent subcontractor William Morris Agency, Partner Kurt Hellmer LIterary Agency. established Jenks Agency in NYC in the 1960's. Theatre, television and film acting career began in Chicago.

REPRESENTS Nonfiction, fiction, novels, short story collections, novellas, feature film, episodic drama, documentary, miniseries, theatrical stage play. **Considers these nonfiction areas:** animals, autobiography, biography, creative nonfiction, cultural interests, current affairs, education, environment, film, gay/lesbian, history, juvenile nonfiction, literature, memoirs, politics, theater, women's issues, women's studies. **Considers these fiction areas:** contemporary issues, crime, detective, ethnic, family saga, fantasy, feminist, gay, historical, lesbian, literary, mainstream, mystery, short story collections, thriller, women's. **Considers these script areas:** autobiography, biography, contemporary issues, detective, documentary, episodic drama, ethnic, family saga, feature film, feminist, gay, historical, lesbian, mainstream, mystery, romantic drama, suspense, theatrical stage play, thriller.

HOW TO CONTACT Please submit a one page query including a brief bio via the form on the agency website. Queries are reviewed on a rolling basis, and we will follow up directly with the author if there is interest. No cold calls.

TERMS Offers written contract, 1-3 years depending on the project. Standard agency commissions. No fees.

RECENT SALES *Snafu*, by Miryam Sivan, Cuidano Press; *The Land of Forgotten Girls*, by Erin Kelly, Harper Collins; *The Christos Mosaic*, by Vincent Czyz, Blank Slate Press; *A Tale of Two Maidens*, by Anne Echols, Bagwyn Books; *Esther*, by Rebecca Kanner, Simon and Schuster; *Magnolia City*, by Duncan Alderson, Kensington Books.

TIPS E-mail contact only. Do not query for more than one property at a time. Response within two weeks unless otherwise notified.

JERNIGAN LITERARY AGENCY

P.O. Box 741624, Dallas TX 75374. (972)722-4838. **E-mail:** jerniganliterary@gmail.com. **Contact:** Barry Jernigan. Estab. 2010. Represents 45 clients.

Prior to becoming an agent, spent many years in the book department at the William Morris Agency.

MEMBER AGENTS Barry Jernigan (eclectic tastes in nonfiction and fiction; nonfiction interests include women's issues, gay/lesbian, ethnic/cultural, memoirs, true crime; fiction interests include mystery, suspense and thriller).

REPRESENTS Nonfiction, fiction, novels, movie scripts, feature film. **Considers these nonfiction areas:** biography, business, child guidance, current affairs, education, ethnic, health, history, how-to, memoirs, military, psychology, self-help, true crime. **Considers these fiction areas:** historical, mainstream, mystery, romance, thriller.

HOW TO CONTACT E-mail your query with a synopsis, brief bio and the first few pages embedded (no attachments). "We do not accept unsolicited manuscripts. We accept submissions via e-mail only. No snail mail accepted." Accepts simultaneous submissions. Responds in 2 weeks to queries; 6 weeks to mss. Obtains new clients through conferences and word of mouth.

TERMS Agent receives 15% commission.

JET LITERARY ASSOCIATES

941 Calle Mejia, #507, Santa Fe NM 87501. (505)780-0721. **E-mail:** etp@jetliterary.com. **Website:** www.jetliterary.wordpress.com. **Contact:** Liz Trupin-Pulli. Estab. 1975.

MEMBER AGENTS Liz Trupin-Pulli (adult fiction/nonfiction; romance, mysteries, parenting); Jim Trupin (adult fiction/nonfiction, military history, pop culture).

REPRESENTS Nonfiction, fiction, novels, short story collections.

"JET was founded in New York in 1975, so we bring a wealth of knowledge and contacts, as well as quite a bit of expertise to our representation of writers." JET represents the full range of adult fiction and nonfiction. Does not want to receive YA, sci-fi, fantasy, horror, poetry, children's, how-to, illustrated or religious books.

HOW TO CONTACT Only an e-query should be sent at first. Accepts simultaneous submissions. Responds in 1 week to queries; 8-12 weeks to mss. Obtains most new clients through recommendations from others, solicitations, conferences.

TERMS Agent receives 15% commission on domestic sales; 10% commission on foreign sales, while foreign agent receives 10%. Offers written agency contract, binding for 3 years. This agency charges for reimbursement of mailing and any photocopying.

TIPS "Do not write cute queries; stick to a straightforward message that includes the title and what your book is about, why you are suited to write this particular book, and what you have written in the past (if anything), along with a bit of a bio."

LAWRENCE JORDAN LITERARY AGENCY

231 Lenox Ave., Suite One, New York NY 10027. (212)662-7871. **Fax:** (212)865-7171. **E-mail:** ljlagency@aol.com. **Contact:** Lawrence Jordan, president.

Prior to opening his agency, Mr. Jordan served as an editor with Doubleday & Co.

REPRESENTS Novels.

This agency specializes in general adult fiction and nonfiction. Handles spiritual and religious books, mystery novels, action suspense, thrillers, biographies, autobiographies, and celebrity books. Does not want to receive poetry, movie scripts, stage plays, juvenile books, fantasy novels, or science fiction.

HOW TO CONTACT Online submissions only. Please note that the agency takes on only a few new clients each year. Accepts simultaneous submissions.

TERMS Agent receives 15% commission on domestic sales; 20% commission on foreign and film sales. Charges for long-distance calls, photocopying, foreign submission costs, postage, cables, messengers.

KELLER MEDIA INC.

578 Washington Blvd., No. 745, Marina del Rey CA 90292. (800) 278-8706. **Website:** www.kellermedia.com. **Contact:** Wendy Keller, senior agent; Megan Close Zavala, literary agent; Elise Howard, query manager. Keller Media has made more than 1,500 deals; has 17 *New York Times* best sellers and 9 international best sellers. Estab. 1989. Member of the National Speakers Association.

Prior to becoming an agent, Ms. Keller was an award-winning journalist and worked for PR Newswire. Prior to her agenting career, Ms. Close Zavala read, reviewed, edited, rejected, and selected thousands of book and script projects for agencies, film companies, and publishing companies. She uses her background in entertainment and legal affairs in negotiating the best deals for her clients and in helping them think outside of the box.

REPRESENTS Nonfiction. **Considers these nonfiction areas:** archeology, autobiography, biography, business, child guidance, crafts, creative nonfiction, current affairs, diet/nutrition, economics, environment, film, foods, gardening, health, history, hobbies, how-to, inspirational, investigative, literature, money, music, parenting, popular culture, politics, psychology, science, self-help, sociology, technology, true crime, women's issues, relationships, pop culture, pop psychology, management, career, entrepreneurship, and personal finance.

"All of our authors are highly credible experts, who have or want to create a significant platform in media, academia, politics, paid professional speaking, syndicated columns, and/or regular appearances on radio/TV." Does not want (and absolutely will not respond to) scripts, teleplays, screenplays, poetry, juvenile, science fiction, fantasy, anything religious or overtly political, picture books, illustrated books, young adult, science fiction, fantasy, first-person stories of mental or physical illness, wrongful incarceration, abduction by aliens, books channeled by aliens, demons, or dead celebrities ("we wish we were kidding!").

HOW TO CONTACT "We look forward to working with talented writers who are offering something new and exciting and/or fresh takes on pre-existing subject matter. To query, please review our current screening criteria on our website. Please do not mail us anything unless requested to do so by a staff member." Accepts simultaneous submissions. Responds in 7 days or less. Obtains most new clients through referrals.

TERMS Agent receives 15% commission on domestic sales; 20% commission on foreign, dramatic, sponsorship, appearance fees, audio, and merchandising deals; 30% on speaking engagements we book for the author.

RECENT SALES Check online for latest sales.

TIPS "Don't send a query to any agent (including us) unless you're certain they handle the type of book you're writing. 90% of all rejections happen because what someone offered us doesn't fit our established, advertised, printed, touted and shouted guidelines. Be organized! Have your proposal in order before you query. Never make apologies for 'bad writing' or sloppy content. Please just get it right before you waste your 1 shot with us. Have something new, different or interesting to say and be ready to dedicate your whole heart to marketing it. Marketing is everything in publishing these days."

NATASHA KERN LITERARY AGENCY

White Salmon WA 98672. **E-mail:** via website. **Website:** www.natashakern.com. **Contact:** Natasha Kern. Estab. 1986. Other memberships include RWA, MWA, SinC, The Authors Guild, and American Society of Journalists and Authors. Represents 40 clients.

Prior to opening her agency, Ms. Kern worked in publishing in New York. This agency has sold more than 1,500 books.

REPRESENTS Fiction, novels. **Considers these nonfiction areas:** investigative journalism. **Considers these fiction areas:** commercial, historical, inspirational, mainstream, multicultural, mystery, romance, suspense, women's, Only Inspirational fiction in these genres.

"This agency specializes in inspirational fiction." Inspirational fiction in a broad range of genres including: suspense and mysteries, historicals, romance, and contemporary novels. By referral only. Does not represent horror, true crime, erotica, children's books, short stories or novellas, poetry, screenplays, technical, photography or art/craft books, cookbooks, travel, or sports books. No nonfiction.

HOW TO CONTACT This agency is currently closed to unsolicited fiction and nonfiction submissions. Submissions only via referral. Obtains new clients by referral only.

TERMS Agent receives 15% commission on domestic sales; 20% commission on foreign sales; 15% commission on film sales.

WRITERS CONFERENCES RWA National Conference; ACFW Conference.

TIPS "Your chances of being accepted for representation will be greatly enhanced by going to our website first. Our idea of a dream client is someone who participates in a mutually respectful business relationship, is clear about needs and goals, and communicates about career planning. If we know what you need and want, we can help you achieve it. A dream client has a storytelling gift, a commitment to a writing career, a desire to learn and grow, and a passion for excellence. We want clients who are expressing their own unique voice and truly have something of their own to communicate. This client understands that many people have to work together for a book to succeed and that everything in publishing takes far longer than one imagines. Trust and communication are truly essential."

HARVEY KLINGER, INC.

300 W. 55th St., Suite 11V, New York NY 10019. (212)581-7068. **E-mail:** queries@harveyklinger.com. **Website:** www.harveyklinger.com. **Contact:** Harvey Klinger. Always interested in considering new clients, both published and unpublished. Estab. 1977. Member of AAR. PEN Represents 100 clients.

MEMBER AGENTS Harvey Klinger, harvey@harveyklinger.com; David Dunton, david@harveyklinger.com (popular culture, music-related books, literary fiction, young adult, fiction, and memoirs); Andrea Somberg, andrea@harveyklinger.com (literary fiction, commercial fiction, romance, sci-fi/fantasy, mysteries/thrillers, young adult, middle grade, quality narrative nonfiction, popular culture, how-to, self-help, humor, interior design, cookbooks, health/fitness); Wendy Silbert Levinson, wendy@harveyklinger.com (literary and commercial fiction, occasional children's YA or MG, wide variety of nonfiction); Rachel Ridout, rachel@harveyklinger.com (children's MG and YA).

REPRESENTS Nonfiction, fiction, novels, juvenile books. **Considers these nonfiction areas:** autobiography, biography, business, child guidance, cooking, crafts, creative nonfiction, cultural interests, current affairs, diet/nutrition, foods, gay/lesbian, health, history, how-to, investigative, literature, medicine, memoirs, money, music, popular culture, psychology, science, self-help, sociology, spirituality, sports, technology, true crime, women's issues, women's studies, young adult. **Considers these fiction areas:** action, adventure, commercial, contemporary issues, crime, detective, erotica, family saga, fantasy, gay, glitz, historical, horror, juvenile, lesbian, literary, mainstream, middle grade, mystery, new adult, police, romance, suspense, thriller, women's, young adult.

This agency specializes in big, mainstream, contemporary fiction and nonfiction. Great debut or established novelists and in nonfiction, authors with great ideas and a national platform already in place to help promote one's book. No screenplays, poetry, textbooks or anything too technical.

HOW TO CONTACT Use online e-mail submission form on the website, or query with SASE via snail mail. No phone or fax queries. Don't send unsolicited mss or e-mail attachments. Make submission letter to the point and as brief as possible. Accepts simultaneous submissions. Responds in 2-4 weeks to queries, if interested. Obtains most new clients through recommendations from others.

TERMS Agent receives 15% commission on domestic sales; 25% commission on foreign sales. Offers written contract. Charges for photocopying mss and overseas postage for mss.

RECENT SALES *Land of the Afternoon Sun*, by Barbara Wood; *I Am Not a Serial Killer*, by Dan Wells; *Me, Myself and Us*, by Brian Little; *The Secret of Magic*, by Deborah Johnson; *Children of the Mist*, by Paula Quinn. Other clients include George Taber, Terry Kay, Scott Mebus, Jacqueline Kolosov, Jonathan Maberry, Tara Altebrando, Alex McAuley, Eva Nagorski, Greg Kot, Justine Musk, Michael Northrup, Nina LaCour, Ashley Kahn, Barbara De Angelis, Robert Patton, Augusta Trobaugh, Deborah Blum, Jonathan Skariton.

KNEERIM & WILLIAMS

90 Canal St., Boston MA 02114. **Website:** www.kwlit.com. Also located in Santa Fe, NM, with affiliated office in NYC. This agency has an affiliated agent in Santa Fe, NM. Estab. 1990.

Prior to becoming an agent, Mr. Williams was a lawyer; Ms. Kneerim was a publisher and editor; Ms. Flynn was pursuing a Ph.D. in history; Ms. Savarese was a publishing executive.

MEMBER AGENTS Katherine Flynn, kflynn@kwlit.com (history, biography, politics, current affairs, adventure, nature, pop culture, science, and psychology for nonfiction and particularly loves exciting narrative nonfiction; literary and commercial fiction with urban or foreign locales, crime novels, insight into women's lives, biting wit, and historical settings); Jill Kneerim, jill@kwlit.com (narrative history; big ideas; sociology; psychology and anthropology; biography; women's issues; and good writing); John Taylor ("Ike") Williams, jtwilliams@kwblit.com (biography, history, politics, natural science, and anthropology); Carol Franco, carolfranco@comcast.net (business; nonfiction; distinguished self-help/how-to); Lucy Cleland, lucy@kwlit.com (literary/commercial fiction, Y/A novels, history, narrative); Carolyn Savarese, carolyn@kwlit.com (riveting narratives in science, technology and medicine; unknown history; big think subjects; memoir; lifestyle and design, literary fiction and short stories); Hope Denekamp (agency manager); Emma Hamilton (literary fiction).

- Actively seeking distinguished authors, experts, professionals, intellectuals, and serious writers.

HOW TO CONTACT E-query an individual agent. Send no attachments. Put "Query" in the subject line. Accepts simultaneous submissions. Obtains most new clients through recommendations from others.

THE KNIGHT AGENCY

232 W. Washington St., Madison GA 30650. **E-mail:** deidre.knight@knightagency.net. **E-mail:** submissions@knightagency.net. **Website:** http://knightagency.net/. **Contact:** Deidre Knight. The Knight Agency is a full-service literary agency with a focus on genre-based adult fiction, YA, MG and select nonfiction projects. With 9 agents and a full-time support staff, our agency strives to give our clients individualized attention. "Our philosophy emphasizes building the author's entire career, from editorial, to marketing, to subrights and social media. TKA has earned a reputation for discovering vivid, original works, and our authors routinely land bestsellers on the New York Times, USA Today, Publishers Weekly, Los Angeles Times, Barnes & Noble Bestseller and Amazon.com Hot 100 lists. Awards received by clients include the RITA, the Hugo, the Newberry Medal, Goodreads Choice Award, the Lambda, the Christy, and Romantic Times' Reviewer Choice Awards, to name only a few." Estab. 1996. Member of AAR. SCWBI, WFA, SFWA, RWA Represents 200+ clients.

MEMBER AGENTS Deidre Knight (romance, women's fiction, erotica, commercial fiction, inspirational, m/m fiction, memoir and nonfiction narrative, personal finance, true crime, business, popular culture, self-help, religion, and health); Pamela Harty (romance, women's fiction, young adult, business, motivational, diet and health, memoir, parenting, pop culture, and true crime); Elaine Spencer (romance (single title and category), women's fiction, commercial "book-club" fiction, cozy mysteries, young adult and middle grade material); Lucienne Diver (fantasy, science fiction, romance, suspense and young adult); Nephele Tempest (literary/commercial fiction, women's fiction, fantasy, science fiction, romantic suspense, paranormal romance, contemporary romance, historical fiction, young adult and middle grade fiction); Melissa Jeglinski (romance [contemporary, category, historical, inspirational], young adult, middle grade, women's fiction and mystery); Kristy Hunter (romance, women's fiction, commercial fiction, young adult and middle grade material), Travis Pennington (young adult, middle grade, mysteries, thrillers, commercial fiction, and romance [nothing paranormal/fantasy in any genre for now]).

REPRESENTS Nonfiction, fiction, novels. **Considers these nonfiction areas:** autobiography, business, creative nonfiction, cultural interests, current affairs, diet/nutrition, design, economics, ethnic, film, foods, gay/lesbian, health, history, how-to, inspirational, interior design, investigative, juvenile nonfiction, literature, memoirs, military, money, multicultural, parenting, popular culture, politics, psychology, self-help, sociology, technology, travel, true crime, women's issues, young adult. **Considers these fiction areas:** commercial, crime, erotica, fantasy, gay, historical, juvenile, lesbian, literary, mainstream, middle grade, multicultural, mystery, new adult, paranormal, psychic, romance, science fiction, thriller, urban fantasy, women's, young adult.

- Actively seeking Romance in all subgenres, including romantic suspense, paranormal romance, historical romance (a particular love of mine), LGBT, contemporary, and also category romance. Occasionally I represent new adult. I'm also seeking women's fiction with vivid voices, and strong concepts (think me before you). Further seeking YA and MG, and select nonfiction in the categories of personal development, self-help, finance/business, memoir, parenting and health. Does not want to receive screenplays, short stories, poetry, essays, or children's picture books.

HOW TO CONTACT E-queries only. "Your submission should include a one page query letter and the first five pages of your manuscript. All text must be contained in the body of your e-mail. Attachments will not be opened nor included in the consideration of your work. Queries must be addressed to a specific agent. Please do not query multiple agents." Accepts simultaneous submissions. Responds in 1-2 weeks on queries, 6-8 weeks on submissions.

TERMS Simple agency agreement with open-ended commitment. 15% commission on all domestic sales, 20% on foreign and film.

LINDA KONNER LITERARY AGENCY

10 W. 15th St., Suite 1918, New York NY 10011. **E-mail:** ldkonner@cs.com. **Website:** www.lindakonnerliteraryagency.com. **Contact:** Linda Konner. Represents approximately 50 authors of adult nonfiction. Estab. 1996. Member of AAR. Other memberships include ASJA and Authors Guild. Represents 50 clients.

REPRESENTS Nonfiction. **Considers these nonfiction areas:** business, cooking, diet/nutrition, foods, health, how-to, medicine, money, parenting, popular culture, psychology, science, self-help, women's issues, biography (celebrity), African American and Latino issues, relationships, popular science.

This agency specializes in health, self-help, and how-to books. Authors/co-authors must be top experts in their field with a substantial media and/ or social media platform. Prescriptive (self-help) books written by recognized experts in their field with a large social media following and/or national profile via traditional media and speaking engagements. Does not want fiction, children's, YA, illustrated books.

HOW TO CONTACT Query by e-mail (or snail mail with SASE) with synopsis and author bio, including size of social media following, size of website following, appearances in traditional media (print/TV/radio) and frequency/size of speaking engagements. Prefers to read materials exclusively for 2 weeks. Accepts simultaneous submissions. Responds within 2 weeks. Obtains most new clients through recommendations from others, occasional solicitation among established authors/journalists.

TERMS Agent receives 15% commission on domestic sales; 25% commission on foreign sales. Offers written contract. Charges one-time fee for domestic expenses; additional expenses may be incurred for foreign sales.

RECENT SALES *Defusing the Alzheimer's Time Bomb*, by Jamie Tyrone and Marwan Sabbagh, MD (W Publishing/Harper Collins); *The Reducetarian Cookbook*, by Brian Kateman (Center Street/ Hachette); *Mead: The Libations, Legends and Lore*, by Fred Minnick (Running Press/ Hachette); *Get Money*, by Kristin Wong (Hachette Books).

WRITERS CONFERENCES ASJA Writers Conference, Harvard Medical School's "Publishing Books, Memoirs, and Other Creative Nonfiction" Annual Conference.

STUART KRICHEVSKY LITERARY AGENCY, INC.

6 E. 39th St., Suite 500, New York NY 10016. (212)725-5288. **Fax:** (212)725-5275. **Website:** www.skagency.com. Member of AAR.

MEMBER AGENTS Stuart Krichevsky, query@skagency.com (emphasis on narrative nonfiction, literary journalism and literary and commercial fiction); Ross Harris, rhquery@skagency.com (voice-driven humor and memoir, books on popular culture and our society, narrative nonfiction and literary fiction); David Patterson, dpquery@skagency.com (writers of upmarket narrative nonfiction and literary fiction, historians, journalists and thought leaders); Mackenzie Brady Watson, mbwquery@skagency.com (narrative nonfiction, science, history, sociology, investigative journalism, food, business, memoir, and select upmarket and literary YA fiction); Hannah Schwartz, hsquery@skagency; Laura Usselman, luquery@skagency.com.

REPRESENTS Nonfiction, novels. **Considers these nonfiction areas:** business, creative nonfiction, foods, history, humor, investigative, memoirs, popular culture, science, sociology, memoir. **Considers these fiction areas:** commercial, contemporary issues, literary, young adult.

HOW TO CONTACT Please send a query letter and the first few (up to 10) pages of your ms or proposal in the body of an e-mail (not an attachment) to one of the e-mail addresses. No attachments. Responds if interested. Accepts simultaneous submissions. Obtains most new clients through recommendations from others, solicitations.

KT LITERARY, LLC

9249 S. Broadway, #200-543, Highlands Ranch CO 80129. **E-mail:** contact@ktliterary.com. **E-mail:** katequery@ktliterary.com, saraquery@ktliterary.com, reneequery@ktliterary.com, hannahquery@ktliterary.com, hilaryquery@ktliterary.com. **Website:** www.ktliterary.com. **Contact:** Kate Schafer Testerman, Sara Megibow, Renee Nyen, Hannah Fergesen, Hilary Harwell. KT Literary is a full-service literary agency operating out of Highlands Ranch, in the suburbs of Denver, Colorado, where every major publishing house is merely an e-mail or phone call away. We believe in the power of new technology to connect writers to readers, and authors to editors. We bring over a decade of experience in the New York publishing scene, an extensive list of contacts, and a lifetime love of reading to the foothills of the Rocky Mountains. Estab. 2008. Member of AAR. Other agency memberships include SCBWI, YALSA, ALA, SFWA and RWA. Represents 75 clients.

MEMBER AGENTS Kate Testerman (middle grade and young adult); Renee Nyen (middle grade and young adult); Sara Megibow (middle grade, young adult, romance, science fiction and fantasy); Hannah Fergesen (middle grade, young adult and speculative fiction); and Hilary Harwell (middle grade and young adult). Always LGBTQ and diversity friendly!

REPRESENTS Fiction. **Considers these fiction areas:** fantasy, middle grade, romance, science fiction, young adult.

Kate is looking only at young adult and middle grade fiction, especially #OwnVoices, and selective nonfiction for teens and tweens. Sara seeks authors in middle grade, young adult, romance, science fiction, and fantasy. Renee is looking for young adult and middle grade fiction only. Hannah is interested in speculative fiction in young adult, middle grade, and adult. Hilary is looking for young adult and middle grade fiction only. "We're thrilled to be actively seeking new clients with great writing, unique stories, and complex characters, for middle grade, young adult, and adult fiction. We are especially interested in diverse voices." Does not want adult mystery, thrillers, or adult literary fiction.

HOW TO CONTACT "To query us, please select one of the agents at kt literary at a time. If we pass, you can feel free to submit to another. Please e-mail your query letter and the first 3 pages of your manuscript in the body of the e-mail to either Kate at katequery@ktliterary.com, Sara at saraquery@ktliterary.com, Renee at reneequery@ktliterary.com, Hannah at hannahquery@ktliterary.com, or Hilary at hilaryquery@ktliterary.com. The subject line of your e-mail should include the word 'Query' along with the title of your manuscript. Queries should not contain attachments. Attachments will not be read, and queries containing attachments will be deleted unread. We aim to reply to all queries within 4 weeks of receipt. For examples of query letters, please feel free to browse the About My Query archives on the KT Literary website. In addition, if you're an author who is sending a new query, but who previously submitted a novel to us for which we requested chapters but ultimately declined, please do say so in your query letter. If we like your query, we'll ask for the first 5 chapters and a complete synopsis. For our purposes, the synopsis should include the full plot of the book including the conclusion. Don't tease us. Thanks! We are not accepting snail mail queries or queries by phone at this time. We also do not accept pitches on social media." Accepts simultaneous submissions. Responds in 2-4 weeks to queries; 2 months to mss. Obtains most new clients through query slush pile.

TERMS Agent receives 15% commission on domestic sales; 20% commission on foreign sales. Offers written contract; 30-day notice must be given to terminate contract.

RECENT SALES *On the Wall*, by Carrie Harris; *The Last Sun*, by K.D. Edwards; *The Odds of Loving Grover Cleveland*, by Rebekah Crane; *Trail of Lightning*, by Rebecca Roanhorse; *Future Lost*, by Elizabeth Briggs; *The Summer of Jordi Perez*, by Amy Spalding; *What Goes Up*, by Wen Baragrey, and many more. A full list of clients and most recent sales are available on the agency website and some recent sales are available on Publishers Marketplace.

WRITERS CONFERENCES Various SCBWI conferences, ALA, BookExpo, Bologna, RWA, WonderCon, ComicCon.

THE LA LITERARY AGENCY

1264 North Hayworth Ave., Suite 10, Los Angeles CA 90046. (323)654-5288. **E-mail:** maureen@laliteraryagency.com. **E-mail:** ann@laliteraryagency.com. **Website:** www.laliteraryagency.com; www.labookeditor.com. **Contact:** Ann Cashman.

Prior to becoming an agent, Eric Lasher worked in broadcasting and publishing in New York and Los Angeles. Prior to opening the agency, Maureen Lasher worked in New York at Prentice-Hall, Liveright, and Random House. Please visit our websites for more information.

MEMBER AGENTS Ann Cashman, Eric Lasher, Maureen Lasher.

REPRESENTS Nonfiction, fiction, novels. **Considers these nonfiction areas:** Americana, animals, anthropology, archeology, art, autobiography, biography, business, child guidance, cooking, crafts, creative nonfiction, cultural interests, current affairs, education, government, health, history, investigative, literature, medicine, memoirs, multicultural, music, parenting, popular culture, politics, psychology, recreation, science, sociology, sports, technology, true crime, war, women's issues. **Considers these fiction areas:** action, adventure, commercial, confession, contemporary issues, crime, detective, family saga, feminist, historical, literary, mainstream, mystery, sports, suspense, thriller, war, westerns, women's.

HOW TO CONTACT Nonfiction: query letter and book proposal. Fiction: query letter and full ms as an attachment. Accepts simultaneous submissions.

RECENT SALES *The Fourth Trimester*, by Susan Brink (University of California Press); *Rebels in Paradise*, by Hunter Drohojowska-Philp (Holt); *La Cucina Mexicana*, by Marilyn Tausend (UC Press); *The Orpheus Clock*, by Simon Goodman (Scribner). Please visit the agency website for more information.

PETER LAMPACK AGENCY, INC.

The Empire State Building, 350 Fifth Ave., Suite 5300, New York NY 10118. (212)687-9106. **Fax:** (212)687-9109. **E-mail:** andrew@peterlampackagency.com. **Website:** www.peterlampackagency.com. **Contact:** Andrew Lampack. "The Peter Lampack Agency specializes in both commercial and literary fiction as well as nonfiction by recognized experts in a given field."

REPRESENTS Nonfiction, fiction, novels. **Considers these fiction areas:** action, adventure, commercial, crime, detective, literary, mainstream, mystery, police, suspense, thriller.

"This agency specializes in commercial fiction, and nonfiction by recognized experts." Actively seeking literary and commercial fiction in the following categories: adventure, action, thrillers, mysteries, suspense, and psychological thrillers. Does not want to receive horror, romance, science fiction, westerns, historical literary fiction, or academic material.

HOW TO CONTACT The Peter Lampack Agency no longer accepts material through conventional mail. E-queries only. When submitting, you should include a cover letter, author biography and a 1 or 2 page synopsis. Please do not send more than 1 sample chapter of your ms at a time. "Due to the extremely high volume of submissions, we ask that you allow 4-6 weeks for a response." Accepts simultaneous submissions. Obtains most new clients through referrals made by clients.

TERMS Agent receives 15% commission on domestic sales. Agent receives 20% commission on foreign sales.

RECENT SALES *The Rising Sea*, by Clive Cussler and Graham Brown; *Untitled Numa Files #16*, by Clive Cussler and Graham Brown; *Celtic Empire*, by Clive Cussler and Dirk Cussler; *Shadow Tyrants*, by Clive Cussler and Boyd Morrison; *Feast of Lies*, by Gerry Spence; *Untitled Isaac Bell #11*, by Clive Cussler; *The Gray Ghost*, by Clive Cussler and Robin Burcell; *Late Essays*, by J.M. Coetzee.

WRITERS CONFERENCES BookExpo America; Mystery Writers of America.

TIPS "Submit only your best work for consideration. Have a very specific agenda of goals you wish your prospective agent to accomplish for you. Provide the agent with a comprehensive statement of your credentials—educational and professional accomplishments."

THE STEVE LAUBE AGENCY

24 W. Camelback Rd., A-635, Phoenix AZ 85013. (602)336-8910. **E-mail:** krichards@stevelaube.com. **Website:** www.stevelaube.com. The Steve Laube Agency is committed to providing top quality guidance to authors. "Our years of experience and success brings a unique service to our clients. We focus primarily in the Christian marketplace and have put together an outstanding team of agents and a gallery of authors whose books continue to make an impact throughout the world." Estab. 2004. Represents 250+ clients.

Prior to becoming an agent, Mr. Laube worked over a decade as a Christian bookseller (honored as bookstore of the year in the industry) and 11 years as editorial director of nonfiction with Bethany House Publishers (named editor of the year). Also named Agent of the Year in 2009. Mrs. Murray was an accomplished novelist before becoming an agent. She was also named Agent of the Year in 2017. Mr. Balow was marketing director for the "Left Behind" series at Tyndale. Mr. Hostetler is an accomplished author with over 50 books in print. Combined the agency has over 100 years of experience in the industry.

MEMBER AGENTS Steve Laube (president), Tamela Hancock Murray, Dan Balow, Bob Hostetler.

REPRESENTS Nonfiction, fiction, novels. **Considers these nonfiction areas:** inspirational, religious, spirituality, Christian. **Considers these fiction areas:** fantasy, inspirational, religious, science fiction, Christian.

- Primarily serves the Christian market (CBA). Actively seeking Christian fiction and Christian nonfiction. Does not want to receive poetry or cookbooks.

HOW TO CONTACT Consult website for guidelines, because queries are sent to assistants, and the assistants' e-mail addresses may change. Submit proposal package, outline, 3 sample chapters, SASE. For e-mail submissions, attach as Word doc or PDF. Accepts simultaneous submissions. Responds in 6-8 weeks to queries. Obtains most new clients through recommendations from others, solicitations, conferences.

TERMS Agent receives 15% commission on domestic sales; 20% commission on foreign sales. Offers written contract; 30-day notice must be given to terminate contract.

RECENT SALES Averages closing a new book deal every two business days, often for multiple titles in a contract. Clients include Susan May Warren, Lisa Bergren, Lynette Eason, Deborah Raney, Elizabeth Camden, Allison Bottke, Ellie Kay, Karol Ladd, Stephen M. Miller, Nancy Pearcey, William Lane Craig, Elizabeth Goddard, Pamela Tracy, Kim Vogel Sawyer, Nadine Brandes, Mesu Andrews, Mary Hunt, Hugh Ross, Timothy Smith, Roseanna White, Bill & Pam Farrel, Carla Laureano, Stan Jantz, Ronie Kendig.

WRITERS CONFERENCES Mount Hermon Christian Writers' Conference; RealmMakers; American Christian Fiction Writers' Conference (ACFW).

LAUNCHBOOKS LITERARY AGENCY

E-mail: david@launchbooks.com. **Website:** www.launchbooks.com. **Contact:** David Fugate. Represents 45 clients.

- David Fugate has been an agent for over 25 years and has successfully represented more than 1,000 book titles. He left another agency to found LaunchBooks in 2005.

REPRESENTS Nonfiction, fiction, novels. **Considers these nonfiction areas:** animals, anthropology, autobiography, biography, business, computers, creative nonfiction, current affairs, diet/nutrition, economics, environment, film, health, history, how-to, humor, investigative, language, literature, medicine, memoirs, money, music, parenting, popular culture, politics, psychology, recreation, science, self-help, sex, sociology, sports, technology, travel. **Considers these fiction areas:** action, adventure, commercial, crime, fantasy, horror, humor, mainstream, military, paranormal, satire, science fiction, sports, suspense, thriller, urban fantasy, war, westerns, young adult.

- "We're looking for genre-breaking fiction. Do you have the next *The Martian*? Or maybe the next *Red Rising*, *Ready Player One*, or *Dark Matter*? We're on the lookout for fun, engaging, contemporary novels that appeal to a broad audience. In nonfiction, we're interested in a broad range of topics. Check www.launchbooks.com/submissions for a complete list."

HOW TO CONTACT Query via e-mail. Accepts simultaneous submissions. Responds in 1 week to queries; 4 weeks to mss. Obtains most new clients through recommendations from others, solicitations.

TERMS Agent receives 15% commission on domestic sales; 25% commission on foreign sales. Offers written contract; 30-day notice to terminate contract. Charges occur very seldom. This agency's agreement limits any charges to $50 unless the author gives a written consent.

RECENT SALES *Artemis* and *The Martian*, by Andy Weir (Random House); *Paradox Bound*, by Peter Clines (Crown);*Captivate*, by Vanessa Van Edwards (Portfolio); *Side Hustle*, by Chris Guillebeau (Crown); *The Art of Invisibility*, by Kevin Mitnick (Little, Brown); the 7-book series *Extinction Cycle*, by Nicholas Smith (Orbit); *A History of the United States in Five Crashes*, by Scott Nations (William Morrow); *Gunpowder Moon*, by Dave Pedreira (Voyager); *An Excess Male*, by Maggie Shen King (Voyager); *One of Us*, by Craig DiLouie (Orbit); *Betaball*, by Erik Malinowski (Atria).

SARAH LAZIN BOOKS

19 W. 21st St., Suite 501, New York NY 10010. (212)989-5757. **Fax:** (212)989-1393. **E-mail:** margaret@lazinbooks.com. **Website:** www.lazinbooks.com. **Contact:** Margaret Shultz. Estab. 1984. Member of AAR.

MEMBER AGENTS Sarah Lazin; Margaret Shultz.

REPRESENTS Nonfiction. **Considers these nonfiction areas:** autobiography, biography, business, current affairs, environment, history, investigative, memoirs, music, parenting, photography, popular culture, politics, women's studies.

HOW TO CONTACT "We accept submissions through referral only. We do not accept fiction submissions." Only accepts queries on referral.

TERMS Agent receives 15% commission on domestic sales; 20% commission on foreign sales.

SUSANNA LEA ASSOCIATES

28, rue Bonaparte, 75006 Paris France. **E-mail:** inquiries@susannalea.com. **E-mail:** ny@susannalea.com; london@susannalea.com; paris@susannalea.com. **Website:** www.susannalea.com. **Contact:** Submissions Department. 331 W. 20th St., New York NY 10011.

REPRESENTS Novels.

"Keeps list small; prefers to focus energies on a limited number of projects rather than spreading themselves too thinly. The company is currently developing new international projects—selective, yet broad in their reach, their slogan is: 'Published in Europe, Read by the World.'" Does not want to receive poetry, plays, screenplays, science fiction, educational text books, short stories or illustrated works.

HOW TO CONTACT To submit your work, please send the following by e-mail: a concise query letter, including your e-mail address, telephone number, any relevant information about yourself (previous publications, etc.), a brief synopsis, and the first 3 chapters and/or proposal. Accepts simultaneous submissions.

TIPS "Your query letter should be concise and include any pertinent information about yourself, relevant writing history, etc."

THE NED LEAVITT AGENCY

70 Wooster St., Suite 4F, New York NY 10012. (212)334-0999. **Website:** www.nedleavittagency.com. **Contact:** Ned Leavitt; Jillian Sweeney. Member of AAR. Represents 40+ clients.

MEMBER AGENTS Ned Leavitt, founder and agent; Britta Alexander, agent; Jillian Sweeney, agent.

REPRESENTS Novels.

"We are small in size, but intensely dedicated to our authors and to supporting excellent and unique writing."

HOW TO CONTACT This agency now only takes queries/submissions through referred clients. Do not cold query. Accepts simultaneous submissions.

TIPS "Look online for this agency's recently changed submission guidelines."

ROBERT LECKER AGENCY

4055 Melrose Ave., Montreal QC H4A 2S5 Canada. **E-mail:** robert.lecker@gmail.com. **Website:** www.leckeragency.com. **Contact:** Robert Lecker. RLA specializes in books about entertainment, music, popular culture, popular science, intellectual and cultural history, food, and travel. However, we are open to any idea that is original and well presented. We are also receptive to books written by academics that can attract a broad range of readers. Usually, we are able to make a decision regarding your submission within two weeks. Estab. 2013. PACLA Represents 50 clients.

Prior to becoming an agent, Mr. Lecker was the cofounder and publisher of ECW Press and professor of English literature at McGill University. He has 30 years of experience in book and magazine publishing.

MEMBER AGENTS Robert Lecker (popular culture, music); Mary Williams (travel, food, popular science).

REPRESENTS Nonfiction, novels. syndicated material. **Considers these nonfiction areas:** autobiography, biography, cooking, cultural interests, dance, diet/nutrition, ethnic, film, foods, how-to, language, literature, music, popular culture, science, technology, theater. **Considers these fiction areas:** action, adventure, crime, detective, erotica, literary, mainstream, mystery, police, suspense, thriller.

RLA specializes in books about popular culture, popular science, music, entertainment, food, and travel. The agency responds to articulate, innovative proposals within 2 weeks. We do not represent children's literature, screenplays, poetry, self-help books, or spiritual guides.

HOW TO CONTACT E-query. In the subject line, write: "New Submission QUERY." Accepts simultaneous submissions. Responds in 2 weeks to queries; 1 month to mss. Obtains most new clients through recommendations from others, conferences, interest in website.

TERMS Agent receives 15% commission on domestic sales; 15-20% commission on foreign sales. Offers written contract, binding for 1 year; 6-month notice must be given to terminate contract.

THE LESHNE AGENCY

New York NY **E-mail:** info@leshneagency.com. **E-mail:** submissions@leshneagency.com. **Website:** www.leshneagency.com. **Contact:** Lisa Leshne, agent and owner. "We are a full-service literary and talent management agency committed to the success of our clients over the course of their careers. We represent a select and growing number of writers, artists, and entertainers interested in building their brands, audience platforms, and developing long-term relationships via all forms of traditional and social media. We take a deeply personal approach by working closely with our clients to develop their best ideas for maximum impact and reach across print, digital and other formats, providing hands-on guidance and networking for lasting success." Estab. 2011. Member of AAR. Women's Media Group

Lisa Leshne has been in the media and entertainment business for over 25 years. Lisa's experience spans the broadest range of the industry. In 1991, she co-founded The Prague Post, the largest English-language newspaper in Central Europe, along with its book division and website, PraguePost.com. Lisa worked in Prague as the newspaper's Publisher for almost a decade. In 1999, she moved to Manhattan to work for Accenture as a Senior Consultant in the Entertainment & Media Group. She later worked in strategy and business development for Dow Jones, and was Executive Director, International, for WSJ.com, the Wall Street Journal Online, responsible for digital business operations in Europe and Asia, where she oversaw advertising, marketing and circulation. Lisa also served as VP, Strategy and Business Development, for Ink2, an industry leader in the print-on-demand industry and the owner of Cardstore.com. Lisa worked for a year after 9/11 at the Partnership for New York City's Financial Recovery Fund, evaluating grant applications and providing strategic advice to small businesses destroyed in the World Trade Center attacks. Prior to founding The Leshne Agency in 2011, she was a literary agent at LJK Literary.

MEMBER AGENTS Lisa Leshne, agent and owner; Sandy Hodgman, director of foreign rights.

REPRESENTS Nonfiction, fiction, novels. **Considers these nonfiction areas:** business, creative nonfiction, cultural interests, health, how-to, humor, inspirational, memoirs, parenting, politics, science, self-help, sports, women's issues. **Considers these fiction areas:** commercial, middle grade, young adult.

An avid reader of blogs, newspapers and magazines in addition to books, Lisa is most interested in narrative and prescriptive nonfiction, especially on social justice, sports, health, wellness, business, political and parenting topics. She loves memoirs that transport the reader into another person's head and give a voyeuristic view of someone else's extraordinary experiences. Lisa also enjoys literary and commercial fiction and some young adult and middle-grade books that take the reader on a journey and are just plain fun to read. Wants "authors across all genres. We are interested in narrative, memoir, and prescriptive nonfiction, with a particular interest in sports, wellness, business, political and parenting topics. We will also look at truly terrific commercial fiction and young adult and middle grade books."

HOW TO CONTACT The Leshne Agency is seeking new and existing authors across all genres. "We are especially interested in narrative; memoir; prescriptive nonfiction, with a particular interest in sports, health, wellness, business, political and parenting topics; and truly terrific commercial fiction, young adult and middle-grade books. We are not interested in screenplays; scripts; poetry; and picture books. If your submission is in a genre not specifically listed here, we are still open to considering it, but if your submission is for a genre we've mentioned as not being interested in, please don't bother sending it to us. All submissions should be made through the Authors.me portal by clicking on this link: https://app.authors.me/#submit/the-leshne-agency." Accepts simultaneous submissions.

LEVINE GREENBERG ROSTAN LITERARY AGENCY, INC.

307 Seventh Ave., Suite 2407, New York NY 10001. (212)337-0934. **Fax:** (212)337-0948. **E-mail:** submit@lgrliterary.com. **Website:** www.lgrliterary.com. Member of AAR. Represents 250 clients.

Prior to opening his agency, Mr. Levine served as vice president of the Bank Street College of Education.

MEMBER AGENTS Jim Levine (nonfiction, including business, science, narrative nonfiction, social and political issues, psychology, health, spirituality, parenting); Stephanie Rostan (adult and YA fiction; nonfiction, including parenting, health & wellness, sports, memoir); Melissa Rowland; Daniel Greenberg (nonfiction: popular culture, narrative nonfiction, memoir, and humor; literary fiction); Victoria Skurnick; Danielle Svetcov (nonfiction); Lindsay Edgecombe (narrative nonfiction, memoir, lifestyle and health, illustrated books, as well as literary fiction); Monika Verma (nonfiction: humor, pop culture, memoir, narrative nonfiction and style and fashion titles; some young adult fiction (paranormal, historical, contemporary)); Kerry Sparks (young adult and middle grade; select adult fiction and occasional nonfiction); Tim Wojcik (nonfiction, including food narratives, humor, pop culture, popular history and science; literary fiction); Arielle Eckstut (no queries); Sarah Bedingfield (literary and upmarket commercial fiction, Epic family dramas, literary novels with notes of magical realism, darkly gothic stories, psychological suspense).

REPRESENTS Nonfiction, novels. **Considers these nonfiction areas:** business, creative nonfiction, health, history, humor, memoirs, parenting, popular culture, science, spirituality, sports. **Considers these fiction areas:** commercial, literary, mainstream, middle grade, suspense, young adult.

HOW TO CONTACT E-query to submit@lgrliterary.com, or online submission form. "If you would like to direct your query to one of our agents specifically, please feel free to name them in the online form or in the email you send." Cannot respond to submissions by mail. Do not attach more than 50 pages. "Due to the volume of submissions we receive, we are unable to respond to each individually. If we would like more information about your project, we'll contact you within 3 weeks (though we do get backed up on occasion!)." Accepts simultaneous submissions. Obtains most new clients through recommendations from others.

TERMS Agent receives 15% commission on domestic sales; 20% commission on foreign sales. Offers written contract. Charges clients for out-of-pocket expenses—telephone, fax, postage, photocopying—directly connected to the project.

RECENT SALES **Notorious RBG**, by Irin Carmon and Shana Knizhnik; **Pogue's Basics: Life**, by David Pogue; **Invisible City**, by Julia Dahl; **Gumption**, by Nick Offerman; **All the Bright Places**, by Jennifer Niven.

WRITERS CONFERENCES ASJA Writers' Conference.

TIPS "We focus on editorial development, business representation, and publicity and marketing strategy."

PAUL S. LEVINE LITERARY AGENCY

1054 Superba Ave., Venice CA 90291. (310)450-6711. **Fax:** (310)450-0181. **E-mail:** paul@paulslevinelit.com. **Website:** www.paulslevinelit.com. **Contact:** Paul S. Levine. Paul S. Levine "wears two hats"–he is a lawyer (www.paulslevine.com) and a literary agent (www.paulslevinelit.com). Mr. Levine has practiced entertainment law for over 35 years, specializing in the representation of writers, producers, actors, directors, composers, musicians, artists, authors, photographers, galleries, publishers, developers, production companies and theatre companies in the fields of motion pictures, television, interactive multimedia, live stage, recorded music, concerts, the visual arts, publishing, and advertising. In 1998, Mr. Levine opened the Paul S. Levine Literary Agency, specializing in the representation of book authors and the sale of motion picture and television rights in and to books. Since starting his literary agency, Mr. Levine has sold over 100 adult, young adult, and children's fiction and nonfiction books to at least 50 different publishers and has had many books developed as movies-for-television, television series, and feature films. Estab. 1992. Other memberships include the State Bar of California. Represents over 100 clients.

MEMBER AGENTS Paul S. Levine (children's and young adult fiction and nonfiction, adult fiction and nonfiction except sci-fi, fantasy, and horror); Loren R. Grossman (archeology, art/photography, architecture, child guidance/parenting, coffee table books,gardening, education/academics, health/medicine/science/technology, law, religion, memoirs, sociology).

REPRESENTS Nonfiction, fiction, novels, TV movie of the week, episodic drama, sitcom, animation, documentary, miniseries, syndicated material, variety show. comic books; graphic novels. **Considers these nonfiction areas:** architecture, art, autobiography, biography, business, child guidance, cooking, crafts, creative nonfiction, current affairs, decorating, diet/nutrition, design, education, foods, gardening, gay/lesbian, health, history, how-to, humor, inspirational, interior design, investigative, juvenile nonfiction, law, medicine, memoirs, money, music, New Age, parenting, philosophy, photography, popular culture, politics, psychology, recreation, religious, satire, science, self-help, sex, sociology, spirituality, sports, technology, travel, true crime, women's issues, women's studies, young adult. **Considers these fiction areas:** adventure, ethnic, mainstream, mystery, romance, thriller, young adult.

Does not want to receive science fiction, fantasy, or horror.

HOW TO CONTACT E-mail preferred; "snail mail" with SASE is also acceptable. Send a 1-page, single-spaced query letter. In your query letter, note your target market, with a summary of specifics on how your work differs from other authors' previously published work. Accepts simultaneous submissions. Responds in 1 day to queries; 6-8 weeks to mss. Obtains most new clients through conferences, referrals, giving classes and seminars, and listings on various websites and in directories.

TERMS Agent receives 15% commission on domestic sales. Offers written contract. Charges for postage and actual, out-of-pocket costs only.

WRITERS CONFERENCES Willamette Writers Conference; San Francisco Writers Conference; Santa Barbara Writers Conference; Chicago Writers Conference; Atlanta Writers Conference; West Coast Writers Conferences; and many others.

TIPS "Write good, sellable books."

LEVY CREATIVE MANAGEMENT

425 E. 58th St., Suite 37F, New York NY 10022. (212)687-6463. **Fax:** (212)661-4839. **E-mail:** info@levycreative.com. **Website:** www.levycreative.com. **Contact:** Sari S. Schorr. Handles illustration, ms/illustration packages. Represents 15 illustrators. International Artist Management Agency headquartered in New York City, one of the leading Artist Management & Illustration agencies representing a small grouping of only award-winning artists. Estab. 1996. Member of AAR. Signatory of WGA.

Currently open to illustrators seeking representation. Open to both new and established illustrators.

HOW TO CONTACT For first contact, see submission guidelines on website. Accepts simultaneous submissions. Responds only if interested. Finds illustrators through recommendations from others, word of mouth, competitions.

TERMS Offers written contract. Advertising costs are split: 75% paid by illustrators; 25% paid by rep.

LIMELIGHT CELEBRITY MANAGEMENT LTD.

10 Filmer Mews, 75 Filmer Rd., London SW6 7JF United Kingdom. (44)(0)207-384-9950. **E-mail:** mail@limelightmanagement.com. **Website:** www.limelightmanagement.com. **Contact:** Fiona Lindsay. Estab. 1991. Other memberships include AAA.

Prior to becoming an agent, Ms. Lindsay was a public relations manager at the Dorchester and was working on her law degree.

MEMBER AGENTS Fiona Lindsay.

REPRESENTS **Considers these nonfiction areas:** art, autobiography, business, foods, gardening, health, history, politics, science, self-help, travel, antiques, drink, entertainment. **Considers these fiction areas:** crime, historical, literary, mystery, suspense, thriller, women's.

"We are always looking for exciting new authors and read all work submitted. We endeavour to respond within 8 to 10 weeks of receipt, but this time scale is not always possible due to the volume of submissions we receive." This agency will consider women's fiction, as well.

HOW TO CONTACT All work should be typed with double spacing. Ensure that the word "Submission" is clearly marked in the subject line and that any attachments include the title of your work. E-mail a brief synopsis and the first 3 chapters only as a Word or Open Document attachment. Only handles film and TV scripts for existing clients. Accepts simultaneous submissions. Obtains most new clients through recommendations from others.

TERMS Agent receives 15% commission on domestic sales; 25% commission on foreign sales; 10-20% commission on TV and radio deals.

LITERARY AND CREATIVE ARTISTS, INC.

3543 Albemarle St., N.W., Washington DC 20008-4213. (202)362-4688. **Fax:** (202)362-8875. **E-mail:** lca9643@lcadc.com. **Website:** www.lcadc.com. **Contact:** Muriel Nellis. Member of AAR. Other memberships include Authors Guild, American Bar Association, American Booksellers Association.

MEMBER AGENTS Prior to becoming an agent, Mr. Powell was in sales and contract negotiation.

REPRESENTS **Considers these nonfiction areas:** autobiography, biography, business, cooking, economics, foods, government, health, how-to, law, medicine, memoirs, philosophy, politics.

- "Actively seeking quality projects by authors with a vision of where they want to be in 10 years and a plan of how to get there." We do not handle poetry, or purely academic/technical work.

HOW TO CONTACT Query via e-mail first and include a synopsis. No attachments. We do not accept unsolicited mss, faxed mss, mss sent by e-mail, or mss on computer disk. Accepts simultaneous submissions. Responds in 3 weeks to queries; 1 week to mss. Obtains new clients through recommendations from others.

TERMS Agent receives 15% commission on domestic sales; 25% commission on foreign sales. Offers written contract. Charges clients for long-distance phone/fax, photocopying, shipping.

TIPS "If you are an unpublished author, join a writers group, even if it is on the Internet. You need good honest feedback. Don't send a manuscript that has not been read by at least five people. Don't send a manuscript cold to any agent without first asking if they want it. Try to meet the agent face to face before signing. Make sure the fit is right."

LITERARY MANAGEMENT GROUP, INC.

P.O. Box 41004, Nashville TN 37204. (615)812-4445. **E-mail:** brucebarbour@literarymanagementgroup.com. **Website:** literarymanagementgroup.com. **Contact:** Bruce R. Barbour. Literary Management Group provides intellectual property development and management consulting, literary representation and book packaging services to publishers, authors and clients. Specializes in adult nonfiction content with a distinctive Christian worldview; specifically from the Evangelical perspective. Estab. 1996. Represents 100+ clients.

- Prior to becoming an agent, Mr. Barbour held executive positions at several publishing houses, including Revell, Barbour Books, Thomas Nelson, and Random House.

REPRESENTS Nonfiction. **Considers these nonfiction areas:** business, child guidance, current affairs, diet/nutrition, health, history, how-to, inspirational, money, parenting, psychology, religious, self-help, spirituality, Christian living; spiritual growth; women's and men's issues; prayer; devotional; meditational; Bible study; marriage; business; family/parenting.

- Does not want to receive gift books, poetry, children's books, short stories, or juvenile/young adult fiction. No unsolicited mss or proposals from unpublished authors.

HOW TO CONTACT E-mail proposal as an attachment. Consult website for submission guidelines. Accepts simultaneous submissions. "We acknowledge receipt and review proposals within 4 weeks."

TERMS Agent receives 15% commission on domestic sales.

LITERARY SERVICES, INC.

P.O. Box 888, Barnegat NJ 08005. **E-mail:** jwlitagent@msn.com. **E-mail:** john@literaryservicesinc.com. **Website:** www.literaryservicesinc.com. **Contact:** John Willig. Celebrating 25 years of representing award-winning authors, our purpose has remained steadfast: to work honestly and creatively with writers to enhance the value of their work and careers. Being "of service" to our clients goes beyond securing a great deal and publisher to championing their work through the publishing process and helping to achieve positive outcomes- for the author and publisher. We're fortunate to represent many talented and hard working authors but always enjoy discovering new talent with unique research, creative approaches and an engaging writer's voice. Estab. 1991. Other memberships include Author's Guild. Represents 90 clients.

- "I started working in publishing in 1977 as a sales representative ('college traveler') in academic publishing and then marketing manager before becoming an editor; shifted to professional/subscription-based publishing as a senior editor and then became an executive editor for business professional and trade books for Prentice Hall/Simon & Schuster. In 1976 I graduated from Brown University and have always been an avid reader with a broad range of interests."

MEMBER AGENTS John Willig (business, personal growth, history, health and lifestyle, science and technology, politics, psychology, current events, food and travel, reference and gift books, true crime, humor, historical fiction).

REPRESENTS Nonfiction. **Considers these nonfiction areas:** Americana, architecture, art, autobiography, biography, business, child guidance, cooking, crafts, creative nonfiction, current affairs, decorating, diet/nutrition, design, economics, environment, foods, gardening, health, history, hobbies, how-to, humor, inspirational, interior design, language, literature, medicine, military, money, parenting, popular culture, politics, psychology, recreation, regional, science, self-help, sex, sociology, spirituality, sports, technology, travel, true crime, war, women's issues. **Considers these fiction areas:** historical, literary, mystery, translation.

Works primarily with nonfiction and historical fiction authors. "Our publishing experience and 'inside' knowledge of how companies and editors really work sets us apart from many agencies; our specialties are noted above, but we are open to unique research, creative and contrarian approaches, and fresh presentations with expert advice in all nonfiction topic areas. Whether non-fiction topics or historical fiction, I'm especially interested in writers 'shining a light' on new research, perspectives, events or stories. Actively seeking science, history, current events, health, lifestyle topics, psychology, business, food and travel, story and research-driven narratives. Does not want to receive fiction (except historical fiction - literary or thriller), children's books, science fiction, religion, or memoirs.

HOW TO CONTACT Query with SASE. For starters, a one-page outline sent via e-mail is acceptable. See our website and our Submissions section to learn more about our questions. Do not send a ms unless requested. Accepts simultaneous submissions. Thankfully, obtains most new clients through recommendations from others, solicitations, writer's conferences.

TERMS Agent receives 15% commission on domestic sales; 15% commission on foreign sales. Offers written contract. This agency charges an administrative fee for copying, postage, etc.

RECENT SALES Sold 25 titles in the last year including *Winning the Brain*, by Matthew May; *The Amazing Cell*, by Josh Rappaport; *John Lennon vs. The U.S.A.*, by Leon Wildes; *Life After the Diagnosis*, by Steven Pantilant; *The Future Workplace Experience*, by Jeanne Meister; *Amazing Stories of the Space Age*, by Rod Pyle; *The Art of Opportunity*, by Parker Lee; *The Little Book of Inner Peace*, by Ashley Davis Bush; *The Fearless Path to Emotional Healing*, by Leah Guy; *Thriving in the Gig Economy*, by Marion McGovern; *The Doha Experiment*, by Gary Wasserstein etc. A full listing of new and award-winning books is presented on our agency website.

WRITERS CONFERENCES ASJA; Writer's Digest Conference (NYC); Thrillerfest.

TIPS "Be focused. In all likelihood, your work is not going to be of interest to 'a very broad audience' or 'every parent,' so I appreciate when writers research and do some homework, i.e., positioning, special features and benefits of your work. Be a marketer. How have you tested your ideas and writing (beyond your inner circle of family and friends)? Have you received any key awards for your work or endorsements from influential persons in your field? What steps, especially social media and speaking, have you taken to increase your presence in the market?"

LKG AGENCY

60 Riverside Blvd., #1101, New York NY 10069. **E-mail:** query@lkgagency.com. **E-mail:** mgya@lkgagency.com (MG/YA); nonfiction@lkgagency.com (nonfiction). **Website:** lkgagency.com. **Contact:** Lauren Galit; Caitlen Rubino-Bradway. The LKG Agency was founded in 2005 and is based on the Upper West Side of Manhattan. "We are a boutique literary agency that specializes in middle grade and young adult fiction, as well as nonfiction, both practical and narrative, with a particular interest in women-focused how-to. We invest a great deal of care and personal attention in each of our authors with the aim of developing long-term relationships that last well beyond the sale of a single book." Estab. 2005.

MEMBER AGENTS Lauren Galit (nonfiction, middle grade, young adult); Caitlen Rubino-Bradway (middle grade and young adult, some nonfiction).

REPRESENTS Nonfiction, juvenile books. **Considers these nonfiction areas:** animals, child guidance, creative nonfiction, diet/nutrition, design, health, how-to, humor, juvenile nonfiction, memoirs, parenting, popular culture, psychology, women's issues, young adult. **Considers these fiction areas:** middle grade, young adult.

"The LKG Agency specializes in nonfiction, both practical and narrative, as well as middle grade and young adult fiction." Actively seeking parenting, beauty, celebrity, dating & relationships, entertainment, fashion, health, diet & fitness, home & design, lifestyle, memoir, narrative, pets, psychology, women's focused, middle grade & young adult fiction. Does not want history, biography, true crime, religion, picture books, spirituality, screenplays, poetry any fiction other than middle grade or young adult.

HOW TO CONTACT For nonfiction submissions, please send a query letter to nonfiction@lkgagency.com, along with a TOC and 2 sample chapters. The TOC should be fairly detailed, with a paragraph or 2 overview of the content of each chapter. Please also make sure to mention any publicity you have at your disposal. For middle grade and young adult submissions, please send a query, synopsis, and the three (3) chapters, and address all submissions to mgya@lkgagency.com. On a side note, while both Lauren and Caitlen consider young adult and middle grade, Lauren tends to look more for middle grade, while Caitlen deals more with young adult fiction. Please note: due to the high volume of submissions, we are unable to reply to every one. If you do not receive a reply, please consider that a rejection. Accepts simultaneous submissions.

STERLING LORD LITERISTIC, INC.

115 Broadway, New York NY 10006. (212)780-6050. **Fax:** (212)780-6095. **E-mail:** info@sll.com. **Website:** www.sll.com. Estab. 1987. Member of AAR. Signatory of WGA.

MEMBER AGENTS Philippa Brophy (represents journalists, nonfiction writers and novelists, and is most interested in current events, memoir, science, politics, biography, and women's issues); Laurie Liss (represents authors of commercial and literary fiction and nonfiction whose perspectives are well developed and unique); Sterling Lord; Peter Matson (abiding interest in storytelling, whether in the service of history, fiction, the sciences); Douglas Stewart (primarily fiction for all ages, from the innovatively literary to the unabashedly commercial); Neeti Madan (memoir, journalism, popular culture, lifestyle, women's issues, multicultural books and virtually any intelligent writing on intriguing topics); Robert Guinsler (literary and commercial fiction (including YA), journalism, narrative nonfiction with an emphasis on pop culture, science and current events, memoirs and biographies); Jim Rutman; Celeste Fine (expert, celebrity, and corporate clients with strong national and international platforms, particularly in the health, science, self-help, food, business, and lifestyle fields); Martha Millard (fiction and nonfiction, including well-written science fiction and young adult); Mary Krienke (literary fiction, memoir, and narrative nonfiction, including psychology, popular science, and cultural commentary); Jenny Stephens (nonfiction: cookbooks, practical lifestyle projects, transportive travel and nature writing, and creative nonfiction; fiction: contemporary literary narratives strongly rooted in place); Alison MacKeen (idea-driven research books: social scientific, scientific, historical, relationships/parenting, learning and education, sexuality, technology, the life-cycle, health, the environment, politics, economics, psychology, geography, and culture; literary fiction, literary nonfiction, memoirs, essays, and travel writing); John Maas (serious nonfiction, specifically business, personal development, science, self-help, health, fitness, and lifestyle); Sarah Passick (commercial nonfiction in the celebrity, food, blogger, lifestyle, health, diet, fitness and fashion categories).

REPRESENTS Nonfiction, fiction. **Considers these nonfiction areas:** biography, business, cooking, creative nonfiction, current affairs, economics, education, foods, gay/lesbian, history, humor, memoirs, multicultural, parenting, popular culture, politics, psychology, science, technology, travel, women's issues, fitness. **Considers these fiction areas:** commercial, juvenile, literary, middle grade, picture books, science fiction, young adult.

HOW TO CONTACT Query via snail mail. "Please submit a query letter, a synopsis of the work, a brief proposal or the first 3 chapters of the manuscript, a brief bio or resume, and SASE for reply. Original artwork is not accepted. Enclose sufficient postage if you wish to have your materials returned to you. We do not respond to unsolicited e-mail inquiries." Accepts simultaneous submissions.

TERMS Agent receives 15% commission on domestic sales; 20% commission on foreign sales. Offers written contract.

LOWENSTEIN ASSOCIATES INC.

115 E. 23rd St., Floor 4, New York NY 10010. (212)206-1630. **E-mail:** assistant@bookhaven.com. **Website:** www.lowensteinassociates.com. **Contact:** Barbara Lowenstein. Member of AAR.

MEMBER AGENTS Barbara Lowenstein, president (nonfiction interests include narrative nonfiction, health, money, finance, travel, multicultural, popular culture, and memoir; fiction interests include literary fiction and women's fiction); Mary South (literary fiction and nonfiction on subjects such as neuroscience, bioengineering, women's rights, design, and digital humanities, as well as investigative journalism, essays, and memoir).

REPRESENTS Nonfiction, fiction, novels, short story collections. **Considers these nonfiction areas:** autobiography, biography, business, creative nonfiction, cultural interests, health, humor, literature, memoirs, money, multicultural, popular culture, science, technology, travel, women's issues. **Considers these fiction areas:** commercial, literary, middle grade, science fiction, women's, young adult.

Barbara Lowenstein is currently looking for writers who have a platform and are leading experts in their field, including business, women's issues, psychology, health, science and social issues, and is particularly interested in strong new voices in fiction and narrative nonfiction. Does not want westerns, textbooks, children's picture books and books in need of translation.

HOW TO CONTACT "For fiction, please send us a 1-page query letter, along with the first 10 pages pasted in the body of the message by e-mail to assistant@bookhaven.com. If nonfiction, please send a 1-page query letter, a table of contents, and, if available, a proposal pasted into the body of the e-mail. Please put the word 'QUERY' and the title of your project in the subject field of your e-mail and address it to the agent of your choice. Please do not send an attachment as the message will be deleted without being read and no reply will be sent." Accepts simultaneous submissions. Will respond if interested. Obtains most new clients through recommendations from others, solicitations, conferences.

TERMS Agent receives 15% commission on domestic sales; 20% commission on foreign sales. Offers written contract. Charges for large photocopy batches, messenger service, international postage.

TIPS "Know the genre you are working in and read!"

ANDREW LOWNIE LITERARY AGENCY, LTD.

36 Great Smith St., London SW1P 3BU England. (44) (207)222-7574. **Fax:** (44)(207)222-7576. **E-mail:** lownie@globalnet.co.uk; david.haviland@andrewlownie.co.uk. **Website:** www.andrewlownie.co.uk. **Contact:** Andrew Lownie (nonfiction); David Haviland (fiction). The Andrew Lownie Literary Agency Ltd is one of the UK's leading boutique literary agencies with some 200 nonfiction and fiction authors and is actively building its fiction list through new agent David Haviland. Its authors regularly win awards and appear in the bestseller lists. It prides itself on its personal attention to its clients and specialises both in launching new writers and taking established writers to a new level of recognition. According to Publishers Marketplace, Andrew Lownie has been the top selling non-fiction agent in the world for the last few years. He has also been shortlisted for 'Agent of the Year' at the British Bookseller Awards many times. Estab. 1988. Society of Authors Represents 200 clients.

Prior to becoming an agent, Mr. Lownie was a journalist, bookseller, publisher and a former director of the Curtis Brown Agency. He is a critically acclaimed writer and President of the Biographers Club, a judge of several nonfiction prizes and regularly speaks at festivals around the world. Mr. Haviland is a best-selling writer and has worked in advertising, script development, and was co-founder of Sirius Television.

REPRESENTS Nonfiction, fiction, novels. **Considers these nonfiction areas:** autobiography, biography, current affairs, government, history, humor, investigative, law, memoirs, military, popular culture, politics, true crime, war. **Considers these fiction areas:** action, adventure, commercial, contemporary issues, crime, detective, ethnic, experimental, family saga, feminist, frontier, gay, glitz, hi-lo, historical, horror, humor, inspirational, juvenile, lesbian, literary, mainstream, metaphysical, middle grade, military, multicultural, mystery, new adult, paranormal, police, romance, satire, science fiction, sports, supernatural, suspense, thriller, translation, war, westerns, women's, young adult.

This agent has wide publishing experience, extensive journalistic contacts, and a specialty in showbiz/celebrity memoir. Actively seeking showbiz memoirs, narrative histories, and biographies. No poetry, short stories, children's fiction, academic, or scripts.

HOW TO CONTACT Query by e-mail only. For nonfiction, submit outline and one sample chapter. For fiction, a synopsis and the first 3 chapters. Accepts simultaneous submissions. Responds in 1 week to queries; 1 month to mss. Obtains most new clients through recommendations from others and unsolicited through website.

TERMS Agent receives 15% commission on domestic sales; 20% commission on foreign sales. Offers written contract; 30-day notice must be given to terminate contract.

RECENT SALES Sells about fifty books a year, with over a dozen top 10 bestsellers including many number ones, as well as the memoirs of Queen Elizabeth II's press officer Dickie Arbiter, Lance Armstrong's masseuse Emma O'Reilly, actor Warwick Davis, Multiple Personality Disorder sufferer Alice Jamieson, round-the-world yachtsman Mike Perham, poker player Dave 'Devilfish' Ulliott, David Hasselhoff, Sam Faiers and Kirk Norcross from TOWIE, Spencer Matthews from Made in Chelsea, singer Kerry Katona. Other clients: Juliet Barker, Guy Bellamy, Joyce Cary estate, Roger Crowley, Patrick Dillon, Duncan Falconer, Cathy Glass, Timothy Good, Robert Hutchinson, Lawrence James, Christopher Lloyd, Sian Rees, Desmond Seward, Daniel Tammet, Casey Watson and Matt Wilven.

LR CHILDREN'S LITERARY

(312)659-8325. **E-mail:** submissions@lrchildrensliterary.com. **Website:** www.lrchildrensliterary.com. **Contact:** Loretta Caravette. "LR Children's Literary represents authors and illustrators of children's books. We are interested in all genres–picture books, easy readers and early chapter books, middle grade and YA. Please no fantasy for YA or Middle Grade." Member of AAR. Signatory of WGA.

REPRESENTS **Considers these fiction areas:** juvenile, middle grade, picture books, young adult.

"I am very interested in the easy readers and early chapter books. I will take on an author/illustrator combination."

HOW TO CONTACT E-query only. Alert this agent if you are contacting other agencies at the same time. If submitting young adult or middle grade, submit the first 3 chapters and a synopsis. If submitting a picture book, send no more than 2 mss. Illustrations (no more than 5MB) can be sent as .JPG or .PDF formats. Accepts simultaneous submissions. Responds in up to 6 weeks.

TIPS "No phone calls please."

DONALD MAASS LITERARY AGENCY

1000 Dean St., Suite 252, Brooklyn NY 11238. (212)727-8383. **E-mail:** query.dmaass@maassagency.com. **Website:** www.maassagency.com. Literary agency for professional novelists, all genres. Estab. 1980. Member of AAR. Other memberships include SFWA, MWA, RWA. Represents more than 200 clients.

Prior to opening his agency, Mr. Maass worked as an editor at Dell Publishing (New York) and as a reader at Gollancz (London). He is a past president of the Association of Authors' Representatives, Inc. (AAR).

MEMBER AGENTS Donald Maass (mainstream, literary, mystery/suspense, science fiction, romance, women's fiction); Jennifer Jackson (science fiction and fantasy for both adult and YA markets, thrillers that mine popular and controversial issues, YA that challenges traditional thinking); Cameron McClure (literary, mystery/suspense, urban, fantasy, narrative nonfiction and projects with multicultural, international, and environmental themes, gay/lesbian); Katie Shea Boutillier (women's fiction/book club, edgy/dark, realistic/contemporary YA, commercial-scale literary fiction, and celebrity memoir); Paul Stevens (science fiction, fantasy, horror, mystery, suspense, and humorous fiction, LBGT a plus); Jennie Goloboy (fun, innovative, diverse, and progressive science fiction and fantasy for adults); Caitlin McDonald (SF/F - YA/MG/Adult, genre-bending/cross-genre fiction, diversity); Michael Curry (science fiction and fantasy, near future thrillers).

REPRESENTS Nonfiction, fiction, novels, juvenile books. **Considers these nonfiction areas:** autobiography, biography, creative nonfiction, memoirs, popular culture, science. **Considers these fiction areas:** commercial, contemporary issues, crime, detective, ethnic, fantasy, feminist, gay, historical, horror, juvenile, lesbian, literary, mainstream, middle grade, military, multicultural, mystery, paranormal, police, regional, romance, science fiction, supernatural, suspense, thriller, urban fantasy, westerns, women's, young adult.

This agency specializes in commercial fiction, especially science fiction, fantasy, thrillers, suspense, women's fiction—for both the adult and YA markets. Does not want poetry, screenplays, picture books.

HOW TO CONTACT Query via e-mail only. All the agents have different submission addresses and instructions. See the website and each agent's online profile for exact submission instructions. Accepts simultaneous submissions.

TERMS Agency receives 15% commission on domestic sales; 20% commission on foreign sales.

RECENT SALES *The Aeronaut's Windlass*, by Jim Butcher (Penguin Random House); *City of Blades*, by Robert Jackson Bennett (Crown); *I am Princess X*, by Cherie Priest (Scholastic); *Treachery at Lancaster Gate*, by Anne Perry (Random House); *Marked in Flesh*, by Anne Bishop (Penguin Random House); *We Are the Ants*, by Shaun David Hutchinson (Simon & Schuster); *Binti*, by Nnedi Okorafor (DAW); *Ninefox Gambit*, by Yoon Ha Lee (Solaris); *The Far End of Happy*, by Kathryn Craft (Sourcebooks); *The Traitor Baru Cormorant*, by Seth Dickinson (Tor).

WRITERS CONFERENCES See each agent's profile page at the agency website for conference schedules.

TIPS "We are fiction specialists, also noted for our innovative approach to career planning. We are always open to submissions from new writers." Works with subagents in all principle foreign countries and for film and television.

GINA MACCOBY LITERARY AGENCY

P.O. Box 60, Chappaqua NY 10514. (914)238-5630. **E-mail:** query@maccobylit.com. **Website:** www.publishersmarketplace.com/members/ginamaccoby/. **Contact:** Gina Maccoby. Gina Maccoby is a New York literary agent representing authors of literary and upmarket fiction and narrative nonfiction for adults and children, including New York Times bestselling and award-winning titles. First and foremost she is captured by an engaging, compelling voice; across all forms she is looking for strong storytelling and fresh perspectives. Areas of interest in nonfiction include history, biography, current events, long-form journalism, and popular science. In fiction she is looking for upmarket novels, mysteries and thrillers, middle grade, and young adult. Gina served four terms on the Board of Directors of the Association of Authors' Representatives and is a member of both the Royalties and Contracts Committees. She belongs to SCBWI and is a long-time member of the Authors Guild. Prior to establishing her own agency in 1986, she was a literary agent at Russell & Volkening for 6 years where she handled her own clients as well as first serial, foreign and movie rights for the agency. Gina grew up mostly in Northern California and graduated with Honors from Harvard College. Estab. 1986. Member of AAR. AAR Board of Directors; Royalties and Ethics and Contracts subcommittees; Authors Guild, SCBWI.

REPRESENTS Nonfiction, fiction, novels, juvenile books. **Considers these nonfiction areas:** autobiography, biography, cultural interests, current affairs, ethnic, history, juvenile nonfiction, literature, popular culture, women's issues, women's studies, young adult. **Considers these fiction areas:** crime, detective, family saga, historical, juvenile, literary, mainstream, middle grade, multicultural, mystery, new adult, thriller, women's, young adult.

HOW TO CONTACT Query by e-mail only. Accepts simultaneous submissions. Owing to volume of submissions, may not respond to queries unless interested. Obtains most new clients through recommendations.

TERMS Agent receives 15% commission on domestic sales; 20-25% commission on foreign sales, which includes subagents commissions. May recover certain costs, such as purchasing books, shipping books overseas by airmail, legal fees for vetting motion picture contracts, bank fees for electronic funds transfers, overnight delivery services.

WRITERS CONFERENCES ThrillerFest PitchFest, Washington Independent Writers Conference, New England Crime Bake, Ridgefield Writers Conference, CLMP Literary Writers Conference.

⊘ MACGREGOR LITERARY INC.

P.O. Box 1316, Manzanita OR 97130. **E-mail:** submissions@macgregorliterary.com. **Website:** www.macgregorliterary.com. **Contact:** Chip MacGregor. Over the past ten years, MacGregor Literary has been one of the top 5 agencies in the US, in terms of the number of contracted books with traditional publishers. "We are not generally accepting unpublished authors except through conferences and referrals, with the occasional exception for a well-established authority." Estab. 2006. Member of AAR. Signatory of WGA. Represents 80 clients.

Prior to his current position, Mr. MacGregor was the senior agent with Alive Communications, an agency in Colorado. Most recently, he was an associate publisher with the Time-Warner Book Group (now Hachette Book Group), and helped put together their Center Street imprint.

MEMBER AGENTS Chip MacGregor (general nonfiction and memoir, select fiction); Amanda Luedeke (nonfiction, literary fiction, romance, and twenty-something/post college-aged hip lit); Brian Tibbetts (literary fiction, new adult titles, science fiction, fantasy, horror, art and music memoirs, natural foods, alternative healing, and sustainability issues).

REPRESENTS Nonfiction, fiction. **Considers these nonfiction areas:** business, creative nonfiction, cultural interests, current affairs, history, inspirational, memoirs, parenting, popular culture, politics, religious, self-help, spirituality, sports, true crime, women's issues. **Considers these fiction areas:** action, commercial, crime, detective, family saga, humor, inspirational, literary, mainstream, mystery, new adult, police, religious, romance, suspense, thriller, women's.

"My specialty has been in career planning with authors—finding commercial ideas, then helping authors bring them to market, and in the midst of that assisting the authors as they get firmly established in their writing careers. I'm probably best known for my work with spirituality books and memoir over the years, but I've done a fair amount of general nonfiction as well." Nonfiction from authors with a proven platform. Significant literary and thriller fiction. Does not want screenplays, westerns, erotica, paranormal fiction, children's books, YA fiction, art books, poetry.

HOW TO CONTACT MacGregor Literary is not currently accepting submissions except through referrals. Please do not query this agency without an invitation or referral. Accepts simultaneous submissions. Responds in 4-6 weeks to queries. Obtains most new clients through recommendations from others. Not looking to add unpublished authors except through referrals from current clients.

TERMS Agent receives 15% commission on domestic sales; 10% commission on foreign sales. Offers written contract.

RECENT SALES Fiction includes *New York Times* bestselling authors Rachel Hauck, Vincent Zandri, Davis Bunn, Oprah Network star Evelyn Lozada, thriller writers Susan Sleeman and Maegan Beaumont. Nonfiction includes former Space Shuttle Commander Scott Parazynski, Waylon Jennings' son and memoirist Terry Jennings, marriage author Sheila Wray Gregoire, Olympic Gold Medalist Mark Schultz's *Foxcatcher*, Navy SEAL writer Robert Vera.

WRITERS CONFERENCES BEA, RWA, ThrillerFest, Left Coast Crime, several west-coast writing conferences.

TIPS "Seriously consider attending a good writers' conference. It will give you the chance to be face-to-face with people in the industry. Also, if you're a novelist, consider joining one of the national writers' organizations. RWA, ACFW, MWA, ITW are wonderful groups for new as well as established writers and will help you make connections and become a better writer."

KIRSTEN MANGES LITERARY AGENCY

115 W. 29th St., Third Floor, New York NY 10001. **Website:** www.mangeslit.com. **Contact:** Kirsten Manges.

Prior to her current position, Ms. Manges was an agent at Curtis Brown.

REPRESENTS Novels.

HOW TO CONTACT Closed to submissions. Obtains most new clients through recommendations from others, solicitations.

CAROL MANN AGENCY

55 Fifth Ave., 18th Floor, New York NY 10003. (212)206-5635. **Fax:** (212)675-4809. **E-mail:** submissions@carolmannagency.com. **Website:** www.carolmannagency.com. **Contact:** Agnes Carlowicz. Member of AAR. Represents Roughly 200 clients.

MEMBER AGENTS Carol Mann (health/medical, religion, spirituality, self-help, parenting, narrative nonfiction, current affairs); Laura Yorke; Gareth Esersky; Myrsini Stephanides (nonfiction areas of interest: pop culture and music, humor, narrative nonfiction and memoir, cookbooks; fiction areas of interest: offbeat literary fiction, graphic works, and edgy YA fiction); Joanne Wyckoff (nonfiction areas of interest: memoir, narrative nonfiction,personal narrative, psychology, women's issues, education, health and wellness, parenting, serious self-help, natural history; also accepts fiction); Lydia Shamah (edgy, modern fiction and timely nonfiction in the areas of business, self-improvement, relationship and gift books, particularly interested in female voices and experiences); Tom Miller (narrative nonfiction, self-help/psychology, popular culture, body-mind-spirit, wellness, business, and literary fiction).

REPRESENTS Nonfiction, fiction, novels. **Considers these nonfiction areas:** anthropology, archeology, architecture, art, autobiography, biography, business, child guidance, cultural interests, current affairs, design, ethnic, government, health, history, humor, law, medicine, memoirs, money, music, parenting, popular culture, politics, psychology, self-help, sociology, sports, women's issues, women's studies. **Considers these fiction areas:** commercial, literary, young adult, graphic works. **Considers these script areas:** romantic drama.

Does not want to receive genre fiction (romance, mystery, etc.).

HOW TO CONTACT Please see website for submission guidelines. Accepts simultaneous submissions. Responds in 4 weeks to queries.

TERMS Agent receives 15% commission on domestic sales; 20% commission on foreign sales. Offers written contract.

MANSION STREET LITERARY MANAGEMENT

E-mail: querymansionstreet@gmail.com. **E-mail:** querymichelle@mansionstreet.com. **Website:** mansionstreet.com. **Contact:** Jean Sagendorph; Michelle Witte. Member of AAR. Signatory of WGA.

MEMBER AGENTS Jean Sagendorph, querymansionstreet@gmail.com (pop culture, gift books, cookbooks, general nonfiction, lifestyle, design, brand extensions), Michelle Witte, querymichelle@mansionstreet.com (young adult, middle grade, early readers, picture books (especially from author-illustrators), juvenile nonfiction).

REPRESENTS Nonfiction, novels. **Considers these nonfiction areas:** cooking, design, popular culture. **Considers these fiction areas:** juvenile, middle grade, young adult.

Jean is not interested in memoirs or medical/reference. Typically sports and self-help are not a good fit; also does not represent travel books. Michelle is not interested in fiction or nonfiction for adults.

HOW TO CONTACT Send a query letter and no more than the first 10 pages of your ms in the body of an e-mail. Query one specific agent at this agency. No attachments. You must list the genre in the subject line. If the genre is not in the subject line, your query will be deleted. Accepts simultaneous submissions. Responds in up to 6 weeks.

RECENT SALES *Shake and Fetch*, by Carli Davidson; *Bleed, Blister, Puke and Purge*, by J. Marin Younker; *Spectrum*, by Ginger Johnson; *I Left You a Present* and *Movie Night Trivia*, by Robb Pearlman; *Open Sesame!*, by Ashley Evanson; *Fox Hunt*, by Nilah Magruder; *ABC Now You See Me*, by Kim Siebold.

MANUS & ASSOCIATES LITERARY AGENCY, INC.

425 Sherman Ave., Suite 200, Palo Alto CA 94306. (650)470-5151. **Fax:** (650)470-5159. **E-mail:** manuslit@manuslit.com. **Website:** www.manuslit.com. **Contact:** Jillian Manus, Jandy Nelson, Penny Nelson. NYC address: 444 Madison Ave., 39th Floor, New York NY 10022. Member of AAR.

Prior to becoming an agent, Ms. Manus was associate publisher of two national magazines and director of development at Warner Bros. and Universal Studios; she has been a literary agent for 20 years.

MEMBER AGENTS Jandy Nelson (currently not taking on new clients); Jillian Manus, jillian@manuslit.com (political, memoirs, self-help, history, sports, women's issues, thrillers); Penny Nelson, penny@manuslit.com (memoirs, self-help, sports, nonfiction).

REPRESENTS Nonfiction, novels. **Considers these nonfiction areas:** cooking, history, inspirational, memoirs, politics, psychology, religious, self-help, sports, women's issues. **Considers these fiction areas:** thriller.

"Our agency is unique in the way that we not only sell the material, but we edit, develop concepts, and participate in the marketing effort. We specialize in large, conceptual fiction and nonfiction, and always value a project that can be sold in the TV/feature film market." Actively seeking high-concept thrillers, commercial literary fiction, women's fiction, celebrity biographies, memoirs, multicultural fiction, popular health, women's empowerment and mysteries. No horror, romance, science fiction, fantasy, western, young adult, children's, poetry, cookbooks, or magazine articles.

HOW TO CONTACT Snail mail submissions welcome. E-queries also accepted. For nonfiction, send a full proposal via snail mail. For fiction, send a query letter and 30 pages (unbound) if submitting via snail mail. Send only an e-query if submitting fiction via e-mail. If querying by e-mail, submit directly to one of the agents. Accepts simultaneous submissions. Responds in 3 months. Obtains most new clients through recommendations from others, solicitations, conferences.

TERMS Agent receives 15% commission on domestic sales; 20-25% commission on foreign sales. Offers written contract, binding for 2 years; 60-day notice must be given to terminate contract. Charges for photocopying and postage/UPS.

RECENT SALES *Nothing Down for the 2000s* and *Multiple Streams of Income for the 2000s*, by Robert Allen; *Missed Fortune 101*, by Doug Andrew; *Cracking the Millionaire Code*, by Mark Victor Hansen and Robert Allen; *Stress Free for Good*, by Dr. Fred Luskin and Dr. Ken Pelletier; *The Mercy of Thin Air*, by Ronlyn Domangue; *The Fine Art of Small Talk*, by Debra Fine; *Bone Men of Bonares*, by Terry Tamoff.

WRITERS CONFERENCES Maui Writers' Conference; San Diego State University Writers' Conference; Willamette Writers' Conference; BookExpo America; MEGA Book Marketing University.

TIPS "Research agents using a variety of sources."

DENISE MARCIL LITERARY AGENCY, LLC

483 Westover Rd., Stamford CT 06902. (203)327-9970. **E-mail:** dmla@denisemarcilagency.com; annemarie@denisemarcilagency.com. **E-mail:** dmla@denisemacilagency.com. **Website:** www.denisemarcilagency.com. **Contact:** Denise Marcil, Anne Marie O'Farrell. Address for Anne Marie O'Farrell: 86 Dennis St., Manhasset, NY 11030. Estab. 1977. Member of AAR. Women's Media Group

Prior to opening her agency, Ms. Marcil served as an editorial assistant with Avon Books and as an assistant editor with Simon & Schuster.

MEMBER AGENTS Denise Marcil (self-help and popular reference books such as wellness, health, women's issues); Anne Marie O'Farrell (books that convey and promote innovative, practical and cutting edge information and ideas which help people increase their self-awareness and fulfillment and maximize their potential in whatever area they choose; she is dying to represent a great basketball book).

REPRESENTS Nonfiction. **Considers these nonfiction areas:** business, cooking, diet/nutrition, education, health, how-to, New Age, psychology, self-help, spirituality, women's issues. **Considers these fiction areas:** commercial, suspense, thriller, women's.

"In nonfiction we are looking for self-help, personal growth, popular psychology, how-to, business, and popular reference; we want to represent books that help people's lives." Does not want fiction.

HOW TO CONTACT E-query. Accepts simultaneous submissions.

TERMS Agent receives 15% commission on domestic sales; 20% commission on foreign sales and film sales. Offers written contract, binding for 2 years.

RECENT SALES *Lilac Lane*, by Sherryl Woods; *Dr. Knox*, by Peter Spiegelman; *The Baby Book*, by William Sears, M.D. and Martha Sears, R.N.; Dr. Sears T5 Wellness Plan,by William Sears, M.D. and Erin Sears Basile; *The Allergy Book*, by Robert W. Sears, M.D. and William Sears, M.D.; Work that Works, by Geil Browning, Ph.D.; *Exponential Living*, by Sheri Riley;*The Girls of Ennismore and The Yellow House*, by Patricia Falvey; *Irresistible Force* and *Force Of Attraction*, by D.D. Ayres; *The Soldier's Forever Family*, by Gina Wilkins.

MARJACQ SCRIPTS LTD

Box 412, 19/12 Crawford St., London W1H 1PJ United Kingdom. (44)(207)935-9499. **Fax:** (44)(207)935-9115. **E-mail:** enquiries@marjacq.com. **E-mail:** subs@marjacq.com or (preferably) individual agent as shown on website. **Website:** www.marjacq.com. **Contact:** Submissions: individual agent. Business matters: Guy Herbert. Founded in 1974 by Jacqui Lyons and the late screenwriter and novelist George Markstein, Marjacq is a full-service literary agency with a diverse range of authors across both fiction and non-fiction for adults, young adults and children. We work closely with our authors at every stage of the process, from editorial guidance and negotiating deals, to long-term career management - including selling their work into as many languages as possible and seeking the best opportunities for adaptation to Film, TV and other media. We are a member of the Association of Authors' Agents (AAA). Estab. 1974. AAA Represents 120 clients.

Ms. Beaumont was an editor at Random House and an agent at UTA; Mr. Patterson was a film, TV, and theatre agent at Curtis Brown and sold rights at HarperCollins; Ms. Pelham worked as assistant to the late Gillon Aitken dealing with his very high profile clients; Ms. Pellegrino ran her own agency, and before that was at Rogers Coleridge and White; Ms. Sawicka worked as a rights executive in publishing.

MEMBER AGENTS Philip Patterson (thrillers, commercial fiction and nonfiction); Sandra Sawicka (commercial, genre, speculative and upmarket fiction); Diana Beaumont (commercial and accessible literary fiction and nonfiction); Imogen Pelham (literary fiction and nonfiction); Catherine Pellegrino (children's, middle grade and young adult).

REPRESENTS Nonfiction, fiction, novels, short story collections, novellas, juvenile books, scholarly books.

Actively seeking quality fiction, nonfiction, children's books, and young adult books. Does not want to receive stage plays or poetry.

HOW TO CONTACT Submit outline, synopsis, 3 sample chapters, bio, covering letter, SASE. "Do not bother with fancy bindings and folders. Keep synopses, bio, and covering letter short." Accepts simultaneous submissions. Responds in 4-6 weeks to mss. Don't send queries without sample. Obtains most new clients through recommendations from others, solicitations, conferences.

TERMS Agent receives 15% commission on direct book sales; 20% on foreign rights, film etc Offers written contract. Services include in-house business affairs consultant. No service fees other than commission. Recharges bank fees for money transfers.

RECENT SALES 3-book deal for Stuart McBride (HarperCollins UK) (repeated *Sunday Times* #1 bestseller); 3-book deal for Howard Linskey.

TIPS "Keep trying! If one agent rejects you, you can try someone else. Perseverance and self-belief are important, but do listen to constructive criticism. Be warned, few agents will give you advice as a non-client. We just don't have the time. Be aware of what is being published. If you show awareness of what other writers are doing in your field/genre, you might be able to see how your book fits in and why an editor/agent might be interested in taking it on. Take care with your submissions. Research the agency and pay attention to presentation: ALWAYS follow the specific agency submission guidelines. Doing so helps the agent assess your work. Join writers groups. Sharing your work is a good way to get constructive criticism. If you know anyone in the industry, use your contacts. A personal recommendation will get more notice than cold calling."

MARLENA AGENCY

278 Hamilton Ave., Princeton NJ 08540. (609)252-9405. **Fax:** (609)252-9408. **E-mail:** marlena@marlenaagency.com. **Website:** www.marlenaagency.com. Represents illustrators including Gerard Dubois, Linda Helton, Paul Zwolak, Serge Bloch, Hadley Hooper, Jean-François Martin, Pierre Mornet, Pep Montserrat, Tomasz Walenta, Istvan Orosz, Javier Jaen, Edmon de Haro, Scott Mckowen, Olimpia Zagnoli, Francesco Bongiorni, Lincoln Agnew, Frederic Benaglia, Natalya Balnova, Nate Kitch, Federico Jordan, Agata Endo Nowicka, Mariko Jesse and Carmen Segovia, Andre da Loba and others. Estab. 1990. Member of AAR. Signatory of WGA. Member of Society of Illustrators.

MEMBER AGENTS Staff includes Marlena Torzecka, Anna Pluskota, Tara Barry.

REPRESENTS We represent Illustrators for Picture Books, Books for Children and Book jackets for all genres.

Currently open to illustrators seeking representation. Open to both new and established illustrators.

HOW TO CONTACT For first contact, send tearsheets, photocopies, or e-mail low resolution samples only. Submission guidelines available for #10 SASE. Accepts simultaneous submissions. Finds illustrators through queries/solicitations, magazines and graphic design.

TERMS Exclusive representation required. Offers written contract.

TIPS "Be creative and persistent."

MARSAL LYON LITERARY AGENCY, LLC

PMB 121, 665 San Rodolfo Dr. 124, Solana Beach CA 92075. **E-mail:** jill@marsallyonliteraryagency.com, kevan@marsallyonliteraryagency.com, patricia@marsallyonliteraryagency.com, Deborah@marsallyonliteraryagency.com; shannon@marsallyonliteraryagency.com. **Website:** www.marsallyonliteraryagency.com. Query e-mails: jill@marsallyonliteraryagency.com; kevan@marsallyonliteraryagency.com; deborah@marsallyonliteraryagency.com; shannon@marsallyonliteraryagency.com; patricia@marsallyonliteraryagency.com. Estab. 2009. Represents See agency website for a client listing clients.

MEMBER AGENTS Kevan Lyon (women's fiction, with an emphasis on commercial women's fiction, young adult fiction and all genres of romance); Jill Marsal (all types of women's fiction, book club fiction, stories of family, friendships, relationships, secrets, and stories with strong emotion; mystery, cozy, suspense, psychological suspense, thriller; romance-contemporary, romantic suspense, historical, and category; nonfiction in the areas of current events, business, health, self-help, relationships, psychology, parenting, history, science, and narrative non-fiction); Patricia Nelson (literary fiction and commercial fiction, all types of women's fiction, contemporary and historical romance, young adult and middle grade fiction, LGBTQ fiction for both YA and adult); Deborah Ritchken (lifestyle books, specifically in the areas of food, design and entertaining; pop culture; women's issues; biography; and current events; her niche interest is projects about France, including fiction); Shannon Hassan (literary and commercial fiction, young adult and middle grade fiction, and select nonfiction).

REPRESENTS Nonfiction, fiction, novels, juvenile books. **Considers these nonfiction areas:** animals, biography, business, cooking, creative nonfiction, current affairs, diet/nutrition, foods, health, history, how-to, investigative, memoirs, multicultural, parenting, popular culture, politics, psychology, science, self-help, sports, true crime, women's issues, women's studies, young adult. **Considers these fiction areas:** commercial, juvenile, literary, mainstream, middle grade, multicultural, mystery, paranormal, romance, suspense, thriller, women's, young adult.

HOW TO CONTACT Query by e-mail. Query only one agent at this agency at a time. "Please visit our website to determine who is best suited for your work. Write 'query' in the subject line of your e-mail. Please allow up to several weeks to hear back on your query." Accepts simultaneous submissions. Query response time is generally up to 2 weeks and submission time varies by agent.

RECENT SALES All sales are posted on Publishers' Marketplace.

TIPS "Our agency's mission is to help writers achieve their publishing dreams. We want to work with authors not just for a book but for a career; we are dedicated to building long-term relationships with our authors and publishing partners. Our goal is to help find homes for books that engage, entertain, and make a difference."

THE EVAN MARSHALL AGENCY

1 Pacio Ct., Roseland NJ 07068-1121. (973)287-6216. **E-mail:** evan@evanmarshallagency.com. **Website:** www.evanmarshallagency.com, www.themarshallplan.net. **Contact:** Evan Marshall. Founded in 1987, the Evan Marshall Agency is a leading literary management firm specializing in adult and young-adult fiction. "We handle a wide-ranging roster of writers in numerous genres, from romance to mystery and thriller to literary fiction. We take pride in providing careful career guidance and strategizing to our clients. As a result, a number of our authors have been with us for nearly three decades, and our titles regularly hit national bestseller lists including Amazon, USA TODAY, Barnes & Noble, Publishers Weekly and the New York Times." The Evan Marshall Agency is a member of the Association of Authors' Representatives and adheres to its Code of Ethics. Evan Marshall is president of The Evan Marshall Agency. He is an award-winning literary agent specializing in fiction. Evan has held senior editorial positions at Houghton Mifflin, Ariel Books, New American Library, Everest House and Dodd, Mead, where he acquired national and international bestsellers. An expert on fiction writing, he has served as a contest judge for Wattpad and has been a NaNoWriMo Mighty Catalyst for Literary Righteousness. He authored the classic writing guide The Marshall Plan® for Novel Writing in 1998. It is now available as How To Write A Novel-The Marshall® Plan Software, co-created with Martha Jewett. The Marshall Plan® takes the frustration out of writing and delivers successful results fast. He is a graduate of Boston College. Evan is the author of ten traditionally published mystery novels in the Hidden Manhattan series and Jane Stuart series, called "Miss Marple lite" by Kirkus Reviews. Estab. 1987. Member of AAR. Novelists, Inc. Represents 50+ clients.

Prior to becoming an agent, Evan Marshall held senior editorial positions at Houghton Mifflin, Ariel Books, New American Library, Everest House and Dodd, Mead, where he acquired national and international bestsellers.

REPRESENTS Fiction, novels. **Considers these fiction areas:** action, adventure, crime, detective, erotica, ethnic, family saga, fantasy, feminist, frontier, gay, glitz, historical, horror, humor, inspirational, lesbian, literary, mainstream, military, multicultural, multimedia, mystery, new adult, New Age, occult, paranormal, police, psychic, regional, religious, romance, satire, science fiction, spiritual, sports, supernatural, suspense, thriller, translation, urban fantasy, war, westerns, women's, young adult, romance (contemporary, gothic, historical, regency).

"We represent all genres of adult and young-adult full-length fiction." Actively seeking high-quality adult and young-adult fiction in all genres. Does not want articles, children's books, essays, memoirs, nonfiction, novellas, poetry, screenplays, short stories, stage plays.

HOW TO CONTACT E-mail query letter, synopsis and first 3 chapters of novel within body of e-mail. Will request full manuscript if interested. Accepts simultaneous submissions. Responds in 1 week to queries if interested. Responds in 2 months to mss. Obtains new clients through queries and through recommendations from editors and current clients.

TERMS Agent receives 15% commission on domestic sales; 20% commission on foreign and film/TV sales. Offers written contract.

RECENT SALES *The Taster*, by V. S. Alexander (Kensington); *A Man for Honor*, by Emma Miller (Love Inspired); *The Devil's Wind*, by Steve Goble (Seventh Street); *The Maverick's Holiday Surprise*, by Karen Rose Smith (Harlequin); *Nemesis*, by Joe Yogerst (Blank Slate Press); *Echoes of the Haight*, by Max Tomlinson (Oceanview).

THE MARTELL AGENCY

1350 Avenue of the Americas, Suite 1205, New York NY 10019. **Fax:** (212)317-2676. **E-mail:** submissions@themartellagency.com. **Website:** www.themartellagency.com. **Contact:** Alice Martell.

REPRESENTS Nonfiction, fiction, novels. **Considers these nonfiction areas:** "big idea" books, business, current affairs, economics, health/diet, history, medicine, memoirs, multicultural, politics, personal finance, psychology, science for the general reader, self-help, women's issues.

Seeks the following subjects in fiction: literary and commercial, including mystery, suspense and thrillers. Does not want to receive romance, genre mysteries, genre historical fiction, science fiction or children's books.

HOW TO CONTACT E-query Alice Martell. This should include a summary of the project and a short biography and any information, if appropriate, as to why you are qualified to write on the subject of your book, including any publishing credits. Accepts simultaneous submissions.

MARTIN LITERARY AND MEDIA MANAGEMENT

914 164th St. SE, Suite B12, #307, Mill Creek WA 98012. **E-mail:** sharlene@martinlit.com. **Website:** www.martinlit.com. **Contact:** Sharlene Martin. "Please see our website at www.martinlit.com for company overview, testimonials, bios of literary managers." Estab. 2002.

Prior to becoming an agent, Ms. Martin worked in film/TV production and acquisitions.

MEMBER AGENTS Sharlene Martin (nonfiction); Clelia Gore (children's, middle grade, young adult); Adria Goetz (Christian books, lifestyle books, children and YA); Natalie Grazian (adult fiction).

REPRESENTS Nonfiction. **Considers these nonfiction areas:** autobiography, biography, business, child guidance, creative nonfiction, current affairs, economics, health, history, how-to, humor, inspirational, investigative, medicine, memoirs, parenting, popular culture, psychology, satire, self-help, true crime, war, women's issues, women's studies. **Considers these fiction areas:** adventure, contemporary issues, fantasy, feminist, historical, humor, literary, middle grade, science fiction, supernatural, suspense, urban fantasy, women's, young adult.

This agency has strong ties to film/TV. Sharlene Martin has an overall deal with ITV for unscripted television, Actively seeking nonfiction that is highly commercial and that can be adapted to film. "We are being inundated with queries and submissions that are wrongfully being submitted to us, which only results in more frustration for the writers. Please review our Submission Page on our website and direct your query accordingly."

HOW TO CONTACT Query via e-mail with MS Word only. No attachments on queries; place letter in body of e-mail. Accepts simultaneous submissions. Responds in 2 weeks to queries; 3-4 weeks to mss. Obtains most new clients through recommendations from others.

TERMS Agent receives 15% commission on domestic sales. We are exclusive for foreign sales to Taryn Fagerness Agency. Offers written contract, binding for 1 year; 1-month notice must be given to terminate contract. 99% of materials are sent electronically to minimize charges to author for postage and copying.

RECENT SALES *Taking My Life Back*, by Rebekah Gregory with Anthony Flacco; *Maximum Harm*, by Michele McPhee; *Breakthrough*, by Jack Andraka; *In the Matter of Nikola Tesla: A Romance of the Mind*, by Anthony Flacco; *Honor Bound: My Journey to Hell and Back with Amanda Knox*, by Raffaele Sollecito;

Impossible Odds: The Kidnapping of Jessica Buchanan and Dramatic Rescue by SEAL Team Six, by Jessica Buchanan, Erik Landemalm and Anthony Flacco; *Walking on Eggshells*, by Lisa Chapman; *Newtown: An American Tragedy*, by Matthew Lysiak; *Publish Your Nonfiction Book*, by Sharlene Martin and Anthony Flacco.

TIPS "Have a strong platform for nonfiction. Please don't call. (I can't tell how well you write by the sound of your voice.) I welcome e-mail. I'm very responsive when I'm interested in a query and work hard to get my clients' materials in the best possible shape before submissions. Do your homework prior to submission and only submit your best efforts. Please review our website carefully to make sure we're a good match for your work. If you read my book, *Publish Your Nonfiction Book: Strategies For Learning the Industry, Selling Your Book and Building a Successful Career* (Writer's Digest Books) you'll know exactly how to charm me."

MASSIE & MCQUILKIN

27 W. 20th St., Suite 305, New York NY 10011. **E-mail:** info@lmqlit.com. **Website:** www.lmqlit.com.

MEMBER AGENTS Laney Katz Becker, laney@lmqlit.com (book club fiction, upmarket women's fiction, suspense, thrillers and memoir); Ethan Bassoff, ethan@lmqlit.com (literary fiction, crime fiction, and narrative nonfiction in the areas of history, sports writing, journalism, science writing, pop culture, humor, and food writing); Jason Anthony, jason@lmqlit.com (commercial fiction of all types, including young adult, and nonfiction in the areas of memoir, pop culture, true crime, and general psychology and sociology); Will Lippincott, will@lmqlit.com (narrative nonfiction and nonfiction in the areas of politics, history, biography, foreign affairs, and health); Rob McQuilkin, rob@lmqlit.com (literary fiction; narrative nonfiction and nonfiction in the areas of memoir, history, biography, art history, cultural criticism, and popular sociology and psychology; Rayhane Sanders, rayhane@lmqlit.com (literary fiction, historical fiction, upmarket commercial fiction [including select YA], narrative nonfiction [including essays], and select memoir); Stephanie Abou (literary and upmarket commercial fiction (including select young adult and middle grade), crime fiction, memoir, and narrative nonfiction); Julie Stevenson (literary and upmarket fiction, narrative nonfiction, YA and children's books).

REPRESENTS Nonfiction, fiction, novels. **Considers these nonfiction areas:** art, biography, cultural interests, foods, health, history, humor, memoirs, popular culture, politics, psychology, science, sociology, sports, true crime, narrative nonfiction. **Considers these fiction areas:** commercial, contemporary issues, crime, literary, mainstream, middle grade, suspense, thriller, women's, young adult.

"Massie & McQuilkin is a full-service literary agency that focuses on bringing fiction and nonfiction of quality to the largest possible audience."

HOW TO CONTACT E-query preferred. Include the word "Query" in the subject line of your e-mail. Review the agency's online page of agent bios (lmqlit.com/contact.html), as some agents want sample pages with their submissions and some do not. If you have not heard back from the agency in 4 weeks, assume they are not interested in seeing more. Accepts simultaneous submissions. Obtains most new clients through recommendations from others, solicitations, conferences.

TERMS Agent receives 15% commission on domestic sales; 20% commission on foreign sales. Offers written contract; 30-day notice must be given to terminate contract. Only charges for reasonable business expenses upon successful sale.

RECENT SALES Clients include Roxane Gay, Peter Ho Davies, Kim Addonizio, Natasha Trethewey, David Sirota, Katie Crouch, Uwen Akpan, Lydia Millet, Tom Perrotta, Jonathan Lopez, Chris Hayes, Caroline Weber.

MARGRET MCBRIDE LITERARY AGENCY

P.O. Box 9128, La Jolla CA 92038. (858)454-1550. **E-mail:** staff@mcbridelit.com. **Website:** www.mcbrideliterary.com. The Margret McBride Literary Agency has been in business for almost 40 years and has successfully placed over 300 books with mainstream publishers such as Hachette, Hyperion, HarperCollins, Penguin Random House, Simon & Schuster, Rodale, Macmillan, John Wiley & Sons, Houghton Mifflin Harcourt, Workman and Thomas Nelson. We are always looking for new and interesting projects to get excited about. For information about submitting your work for our consideration, please see our website: www.mcbrideliterary.com." Estab. 1981. Member of AAR. Other memberships include Authors Guild.

Prior to opening her agency, Ms. McBride worked at Random House and Ballantine Books. Later, she became the Director of Publicity at Warner Books, and Director of Publicity, Promotions and Advertising for Pinnacle Books.

MEMBER AGENTS Margret McBride; Faye Atchison.

REPRESENTS Nonfiction, fiction, novels. **Considers these nonfiction areas:** autobiography, biography, business, cooking, creative nonfiction, cultural interests, current affairs, diet/nutrition, ethnic, foods, gay/lesbian, health, history, hobbies, how-to, inspirational, investigative, juvenile nonfiction, medicine, memoirs, money, multicultural, music, popular culture, psychology, science, self-help, sex, sociology, theater, travel, true crime, women's issues, young adult. **Considers these fiction areas:** action, adventure, comic books, commercial, confession, contemporary issues, crime, detective, family saga, feminist, historical, horror, juvenile, mainstream, multicultural, multimedia, mystery, new adult, paranormal, police, psychic, regional, supernatural, suspense, thriller, young adult.

This agency specializes in mainstream nonfiction and some commercial fiction. Actively seeking commercial nonfiction, business, health, self-help. Does not want screenplays, romance, poetry, or children's.

HOW TO CONTACT Please check our website, as instructions are subject to change. Only e-mail queries are accepted: staff@mcbridelit.com. In your query letter, provide a brief synopsis of your work, as well as any pertinent information about yourself. We recommend that authors look at book jacket copy of professionally published books to get an idea of the style and content that should be included in a query letter. Essentially, you are marketing yourself and your work to us, so that we can determine whether we feel we can market you and your work to publishers. There are detailed nonfiction proposal guidelines on our website, but we recommend author's get a copy of How to Write a Book Proposal by Michael Larsen for further instruction. **Please note: The McBride Agency will not respond to queries sent by mail, and will not be responsible for the return of any material submitted by mail.** Accepts simultaneous submissions. Responds within 8 weeks to queries; 6-8 weeks to requested mss. "You are welcome to follow up by phone or e-mail after 6 weeks if you have not yet received a response."

TERMS Agent receives 15% commission on domestic sales; 25% commission on translation rights sales (15% to agency, 10% to sub-agent). Charges for overnight delivery and photocopying.

RECENT SALES *Millennial Money*, by Grant Sabatier (Atria/Penguin Random House); *Nimble*, by Baba Prasad (Perigee/Penguin Random House—US and World rights excluding India); *Carefrontation*, by Dr. Arlene Drake (Regan Arts/Phaidon); *There Are No Overachievers*, by Brian Biro (Crown Business/Penguin Random House); *Cheech Is Not My Real Name*, by Richard Marin (Grand Central Books/Hachette); *Killing It!*, by Sheryl O'Loughlin (Harper Business/HarperCollins); *Scrappy*, by Terri Sjodin (Portfolio/Penguin Random House).

TIPS "E-mail queries only. Please don't call to pitch your work by phone."

E.J. MCCARTHY AGENCY

(415)383-6639. **E-mail:** ejmagency@gmail.com. **Website:** http://www.publishersmarketplace.com/members/ejmccarthy/. Signatory of WGA.

Prior to his current position, Mr. McCarthy was a former executive editor with more than 20 years book publishing experience (Bantam Doubleday Dell, Presidio Press, Ballantine/Random House).

REPRESENTS Considers these nonfiction areas: biography, history, memoirs, military, sports.

This agency specializes in nonfiction.

HOW TO CONTACT Query first by e-mail. Accepts simultaneous submissions.

RECENT SALES *One Bullet Away*, by Nathaniel Fick; *The Unforgiving Minute*, by Craig Mullaney; *The Sling And The Stone*, by Thomas X. Hammes; *The Heart and the First*, by Eric Greitens; *When Books Went to War*, by Molly Guptill Manning.

SEAN MCCARTHY LITERARY AGENCY

E-mail: submissions@mccarthylit.com. **Website:** www.mccarthylit.com. **Contact:** Sean McCarthy. Estab. 2013.

Prior to his current position, Sean McCarthy began his publishing career as an editorial intern at Overlook Press and then moved over to the Sheldon Fogelman Agency.

REPRESENTS Considers these nonfiction areas: juvenile nonfiction, young adult. **Considers these fiction areas:** juvenile, middle grade, picture books, young adult.

Sean is drawn to flawed, multifaceted characters with devastatingly concise writing in YA, and character-driven work or smartly paced mysteries/adventures in MG. In picture books, he looks more for unforgettable characters, offbeat humor, and especially clever endings. He is not currently interested in issue-driven stories or query letters that pose too many questions.

HOW TO CONTACT E-query. "Please include a brief description of your book, your biography, and any literary or relevant professional credits in your query letter. If you are a novelist: Please submit the first 3 chapters of your manuscript (or roughly 25 pages) and a 1-page synopsis in the body of the e-mail or as a Word or PDF attachment. If you are a picture book author: Please submit the complete text of your manuscript. We are not currently accepting picture book manuscripts over 1,000 words. If you are an illustrator: Please attach up to 3 JPEGs or PDFs of your work, along with a link to your website." Accepts simultaneous submissions.

MCCORMICK LITERARY

37 W. 20th St., New York NY 10011. (212)691-9726. **E-mail:** queries@mccormicklit.com. **Website:** mccormicklit.com. "McCormick Literary is an independent literary agency specializing in literary and commercial fiction and quality nonfiction, including memoir, history, narrative, biography, lifestyle, sports, self-help, and pop culture." Member of AAR. Signatory of WGA.

MEMBER AGENTS David McCormick; Pilar Queen (narrative nonfiction, practical nonfiction, and commercial women's fiction); Bridget McCarthy (literary and commercial fiction, narrative nonfiction, memoir, and cookbooks); Alia Hanna Habib (literary fiction, narrative nonfiction, memoir and cookbooks); Edward Orloff (literary fiction and narrative nonfiction, especially cultural history, politics, biography, and the arts); Daniel Menaker; Leslie Falk; Emma Borges-Scott.

REPRESENTS Nonfiction, novels. **Considers these nonfiction areas:** biography, cooking, history, memoirs, politics. **Considers these fiction areas:** literary, women's.

HOW TO CONTACT Snail mail queries only. Send an SASE. Accepts simultaneous submissions.

ANNE MCDERMID & ASSOCIATES, LTD

320 Front St. W., Suite 1105, Toronto ON M5V 3B6 Canada. (647)788-4016. **Fax:** (416)324-8870. **E-mail:** admin@mcdermidagency.com. **E-mail:** info@mcdermidagency.com. **Website:** www.mcdermidagency.com. **Contact:** Anne McDermid. Estab. 1996.

MEMBER AGENTS Anne McDermid, Martha Webb, Monica Pacheco, Chris Bucci.

REPRESENTS Novels.

The agency represents literary novelists and commercial novelists of high quality, and also writers of nonfiction in the areas of memoir, biography, history, literary travel, narrative science, and investigative journalism. "We also represent a certain number of children's and YA writers and writers in the fields of science fiction and fantasy."

HOW TO CONTACT Query via e-mail or mail with a brief bio, description, and first 5 pages of project only. Accepts simultaneous submissions. *No unsolicited manuscripts.* Obtains most new clients through recommendations from others.

MCINTOSH & OTIS, INC.

353 Lexington Ave., New York NY 10016. (212)687-7400. **Fax:** (212)687-6894. **E-mail:** info@mcintoshandotis.com. **Website:** www.mcintoshandotis.com. **Contact:** Elizabeth Winick Rubinstein. McIntosh & Otis has a long history of representing authors of adult and children's books. The children's department is a separate division. Estab. 1928. Member of AAR. Signatory of WGA. SCBWI

MEMBER AGENTS Elizabeth Winick Rubinstein, ewrquery@mcintoshandotis.com (literary fiction, women's fiction, historical fiction, and mystery/suspense, along with narrative nonfiction, spiritual/self-help, history and current affairs); Christa Heschke, CHquery@mcintoshandotis.com (picture books, middle grade, young adult and new adult projects); Adam Muhlig, AMquery@mcintoshandotis.com (music–from jazz to classical to punk–popular culture, natural history, travel and adventure, and sports).

REPRESENTS Considers these nonfiction areas: creative nonfiction, current affairs, history, popular culture, self-help, spirituality, sports, travel. **Considers these fiction areas:** fantasy, historical, horror, literary, middle grade, mystery, new adult, paranormal, picture books, romance, science fiction, suspense, urban fantasy, women's, young adult.

Actively seeking "books with memorable characters, distinctive voices, and great plots."

HOW TO CONTACT E-mail submissions only. Each agent has their own e-mail address for subs. For fiction: Please send a query letter, synopsis, author bio, and the first 3 consecutive chapters (no more than 30 pages) of your novel. For nonfiction: Please send a query letter, proposal, outline, author bio, and 3 sample chapters (no more than 30 pages) of the ms. For children's & young adult: Please send a query letter, synopsis and the first 3 consecutive chapters (not to exceed 25 pages) of the ms. Accepts simultaneous submissions. Obtains clients through recommendations from others, editors, conferences and queries.

TERMS Agent receives 15% commission on domestic sales; 20% on foreign sales.

WRITERS CONFERENCES Attends Bologna Book Fair, in Bologna Italy in April, SCBWI Conference in New York in February, and regularly attends other conferences and industry conventions.

MENDEL MEDIA GROUP, LLC

115 W. 30th St., Suite 209, New York NY 10001. (646)239-9896. **E-mail:** query@mendelmedia.com. **Website:** www.mendelmedia.com. The Mendel Media Group LLC is an independent literary agency in New York. We represent nonfiction writers in most subject areas, from biography and serious history to health and relationships. Our nonfiction clientele includes individual authors and institutions whose works, collections, archives, researchers and/or policy experts contribute to important public discussions and debates. We also represent more light-hearted nonfiction projects, when they suit the market particularly well. The agency's fiction writers principally write historical and contemporary multicultural fiction, contemporary thrillers and mainstream women's fiction. We help our clients develop their projects, and we market those projects to U.S., U.K., Australian and foreign language publishing houses. We negotiate all contracts to our clients' works and keep track of monies due them, and we serve as their champions and career advisors. Both critical and commercial success are as important to us as they are to our clients. We want writing to be the source of a significant portion of our individual clients' incomes. We also want our institutional clients' works to support their missions financially as well as intellectually. In addition, wherever possible and preferable we reserve and represent the subsidiary rights to our clients' properties, including magazine and newspaper serialization, translation and other foreign rights, film and television development, audio book, large-print, book club, electronic and merchandising rights. We always aim to multiply our clients' incomes by making strategic decisions about licensing and sub-licensing as many of those rights as possible. In accordance with the Canon of Ethics of the Association of Authors Representatives, we charge our clients no reading fees. We do not represent screenwriters, unless they are creating works derived from a literary work we have already developed and marketed. Estab. 2002. Member of AAR. Represents 60-90 clients.

Prior to becoming an agent, Mr. Mendel was an academic. "I taught American literature, Yiddish, Jewish studies, and literary theory at the University of Chicago and the University of Illinois at Chicago while working on my PhD in English. I also worked as a freelance technical writer and as the managing editor of a healthcare magazine. In 1998, I began working for the late Jane Jordan Browne, a long-time agent in the book publishing world."

REPRESENTS Nonfiction, fiction, novels. **Considers these nonfiction areas:** Americana, animals, anthropology, architecture, art, biography, business, child guidance, cooking, current affairs, dance, education, environment, ethnic, foods, gardening, gay/lesbian, government, health, history, how-to, humor, investigative, language, medicine, memoirs, military, money, multicultural, music, parenting, philosophy, popular culture, psychology, recreation, regional, religious, science, self-help, sex, sociology, software, spirituality, sports, travel, true crime, war, women's issues, women's studies, all narrative projects, and creative nonfiction. **Considers these fiction areas:** action, adventure, contemporary issues, crime, detective, erotica, ethnic, feminist, gay, glitz, historical, humor, inspirational, juvenile, lesbian, literary, mainstream, mystery, picture books, police, religious, romance, satire, sports, thriller, young adult, commercial and literary fiction.

"I am interested in major works of history, current affairs, biography, business, politics, economics, science, major memoirs, narrative nonfiction, and other sorts of general nonfiction." Actively seeking new, major or definitive work on a subject of broad interest, or a controversial, but authoritative, new book on a subject that affects many people's lives. "I also represent more light-hearted nonfiction projects, such as gift or novelty books, when they suit the market particularly well." Does not want "queries about projects written years ago that were unsuccessfully shopped to a long list of trade publishers by either the author or another agent. I am specifically not interested in reading poetry, original plays, or original film scripts."

HOW TO CONTACT You should e-mail your work to query@mendelmedia.com. We no longer accept or read submissions sent by mail, so please do not send inquiries by any other method. If we want to read more or discuss your work, we will respond to you by e-mail or phone. Fiction queries: If you have a novel you would like to submit, please paste a synopsis and the first twenty pages into the body of your email, below a detailed letter about your publication history and the history of the project, if it has been submitted previously to publishers or other agents. Please do not use attachments, as we will not open them. Nonfiction queries: If you have a completed nonfiction book proposal and sample chapters, you should paste those into the body of an e-mail, below a detailed letter about your publication history and the history of the project, if it has been submitted previously to any publishers or other agents. Please do not use attachments, as we will not open them. If we want to read more or discuss your work, we will call or e-mail you directly. If you do not receive a personal response within a few weeks, we are not going to offer representation. In any case, however, please do not call or email to inquire about your query. Accepts simultaneous submissions. Responds within a few weeks, if interested. Obtains most new clients through referrals.

TERMS Agent receives 15% commission on domestic sales; 20% commission on foreign sales.

WRITERS CONFERENCES BookExpo America; Frankfurt Book Fair; London Book Fair; RWA National Conference; Modern Language Association Convention; Jerusalem Book Fair.

TIPS "While I am not interested in being flattered by a prospective client, it does matter to me that she knows why she is writing to me in the first place. Is one of my clients a colleague of hers? Has she read a book by one of my clients that led her to believe I might be interested in her work? Authors of descriptive nonfiction should have real credentials and expertise in their subject areas, either as academics, journalists, or policy experts, and authors of prescriptive nonfiction should have legitimate expertise and considerable experience communicating their ideas in seminars and workshops, in a successful business, through the media, etc."

SCOTT MEREDITH LITERARY AGENCY

One Exchange Plaza, Suite 2002, 55 Broadway, New York NY 10006. (646)274-1970. **Fax:** (212)977-5997. **E-mail:** info@scottmeredith.com. **Website:** www.scottmeredith.com. **Contact:** Arthur Klebanoff, CEO. Adheres to the AAR canon of ethics. Represents 20 clients.

Prior to becoming an agent, Mr. Klebanoff was a lawyer.

REPRESENTS Textbooks.

This agency's specialty lies in category nonfiction publishing programs. Actively seeking category leading nonfiction. Does not want to receive first fiction projects.

HOW TO CONTACT Query with SASE. Submit proposal package, author bio. Accepts simultaneous submissions. Responds in 2 weeks to queries; 4 weeks to mss. Obtains most new clients through recommendations from others.

TERMS Agent receives 15% commission on domestic sales. Offers written contract.

THE STUART M. MILLER CO.

11684 Ventura Blvd., #225, Studio City CA 91604. (818)506-6067. **E-mail:** smmco@aol.com. **Contact:** Stuart Miller. Memberships include Signatory of WGA, DGA, Association of Talent Agents (ATA).

REPRESENTS Nonfiction, fiction, novels, scholarly books, movie scripts, feature film, TV scripts, TV movie of the week, animation, miniseries. **Considers these nonfiction areas:** autobiography, biography, business, computers, creative nonfiction, current affairs, government, health, history, literature, memoirs, military, politics, sports, true crime, war. **Considers**

these fiction areas: adventure, detective, historical, literary, mainstream, military, mystery, police, satire, short story collections, sports, suspense, thriller, war. **Considers these script areas:** action, adventure, animation, autobiography, biography, cartoon, comedy, crime, detective, feature film, historical, mainstream, miniseries, movie scripts, multimedia, mystery, police, romantic comedy, romantic drama, sports, teen, thriller.

HOW TO CONTACT For screenplays, query via e-mail, narrative outline (2-3 pages). For books, e-mail narrative outline (5-10 pages). Accepts simultaneous submissions. "If requests full screenplay or mss, requires reasonable exclusivity period." Responds in 5 days to queries; 2-3 weeks to screenplays and 4-6 weeks to mss.

TERMS Screenplays, teleplays—10%, All books and other underlying rights—15% Written contract, binding for 2 years for WGA, DGA members, 3 years for non-guild & authors.

RECENT SALES This agency prefers not to share information on specific sales.

TIPS "Always include an e-mail address with query letters. Agents are incredibly busy; make it easy to respond."

⊘ ROBIN MIZELL LTD.

OH **Contact:** Robin Mizell. This agency represented a limited number of authors and is not accepting any new clients. Estab. 2008.

HOW TO CONTACT Submissions are closed.

HOWARD MORHAIM LITERARY AGENCY

30 Pierrepont St., Brooklyn NY 11201. (718)222-8400. **Fax:** (718)222-5056. **E-mail:** info@morhaimliterary.com. **Website:** www.morhaimliterary.com. Member of AAR.

MEMBER AGENTS Howard Morhaim, howard@morhaimliterary.com; Kate McKean, kmckean@morhaimliterary.com; DongWon Song, dongwon@morhaimliterary.com; Kim-Mei Kirtland, kimmei@morhaimliterary.com.

REPRESENTS Considers these nonfiction areas: biography, business, cooking, crafts, creative nonfiction, design, economics, foods, health, humor, memoirs, parenting, self-help, sports. **Considers these fiction areas:** fantasy, historical, literary, middle grade, new adult, romance, science fiction, women's, young adult, LGBTQ young adult, magical realism, fantasy should be high fantasy, historical fiction should be no earlier than the 20th century.

> Kate McKean is open to many subgenres and categories of YA and MG fiction. Check the website for the most details. Actively seeking fiction, nonfiction, and young adult novels.

HOW TO CONTACT Query via e-mail with cover letter and 3 sample chapters. See each agent's listing for specifics. Accepts simultaneous submissions.

⊘ WILLIAM MORRIS ENDEAVOR ENTERTAINMENT

1325 Avenue of the Americas, New York NY 10019. (212)586-5100. **Fax:** (212)246-3583. **Website:** wmeentertainment.com. **Contact:** Literary Department Coordinator. Member of AAR.

REPRESENTS Novels.

HOW TO CONTACT This agency is generally closed to unsolicited literary submissions. Meet an agent at a conference, or query through a referral. Accepts simultaneous submissions.

TERMS Agent receives 15% commission on domestic sales; 20% commission on foreign sales.

MOVEABLE TYPE MANAGEMENT

244 Madison Ave., Suite 334, New York NY 10016. **E-mail:** achromy@movabletm.com. **Website:** www.movabletm.com. **Contact:** Adam Chromy. Estab. 2002.

REPRESENTS Nonfiction, fiction, novels. **Considers these nonfiction areas:** Americana, business, creative nonfiction, current affairs, film, foods, history, how-to, humor, literature, memoirs, military, money, music, popular culture, politics, psychology, satire, science, self-help, sex, sports, technology, theater, true crime, war, women's issues, women's studies. **Considers these fiction areas:** action, commercial, crime, detective, erotica, hi-lo, historical, literary, mainstream, mystery, romance, satire, science fiction, sports, suspense, thriller, women's.

> Mr. Chromy is a generalist, meaning that he accepts fiction submissions of virtually any kind (except juvenile books aimed for middle grade and younger) as well as nonfiction. He has sold books in the following categories: new adult, women's, romance, memoir, pop culture, young adult, lifestyle, horror, how-to, general fiction, and more.

HOW TO CONTACT E-queries only. Responds if interested. For nonfiction: Send a query letter in the body of an e-mail that precisely introduces your topic and approach, and includes a descriptive bio. For journalists and academics, please also feel free to include a CV. Fiction: Send your query letter and the first 10 pages of your novel in the body of an e-mail. Your subject line needs to contain the word "Query" or your message will not reach the agency. No attachments and no snail mail. Accepts simultaneous submissions.

RECENT SALES *The Wedding Sisters*, by Jamie Brenner (St. Martin's Press); *Rage*, by (AmazonCrossing); *Sons Of Zeus*, by Noble Smith (Thomas Dunne Books); *World Made By Hand And Too Much Magic*, by James Howard Kunstler (Grove/Atlantic Press); *Dirty Rocker Boys*, by Bobbie Brown (Gallery/S&S).

⊘ ERIN MURPHY LITERARY AGENCY

824 Roosevelt Trail, #290, Windham ME 04062. **Website:** emliterary.com. **Contact:** Erin Murphy, president; Ammi-Joan Paquette, senior agent; Tricia Lawrence, agent; Tara Gonzalez, associate agent. Estab. 1999.

REPRESENTS Juvenile books. **Considers these fiction areas:** middle grade, picture books, young adult.

Specializes in children's books only.

HOW TO CONTACT Accepts simultaneous submissions.

TERMS Agent receives 15% commission on domestic sales; 20-30% on foreign sales. Offers written contract. 30 days notice must be given to terminate contract.

TIPS Please do not submit to more than one agent at EMLA at a time.

JEAN V. NAGGAR LITERARY AGENCY, INC.

JVNLA, Inc., 216 E. 75th St., Suite 1E, New York NY 10021. (212)794-1082. **Website:** www.jvnla.com. **Contact:** Jennifer Weltz. Estab. 1978. Member of AAR. Other memberships include Women's Media Group, SCBWI, Pace University's Masters in Publishing Board Member. Represents 450 clients.

MEMBER AGENTS Jennifer Weltz (well-researched and original historicals, thrillers with a unique voice, wry dark humor, and magical realism; enthralling narrative nonfiction; voice driven young adult, middle grade); Alice Tasman (literary, commercial, YA, middle grade, and nonfiction in the categories of narrative, biography, music or pop culture); Ariana Philips (nonfiction both prescriptive and narrative).

REPRESENTS Nonfiction, fiction, novels, short story collections, novellas, juvenile books, scholarly books, poetry books.

This agency specializes in mainstream fiction and nonfiction and literary fiction with commercial potential as well as young adult, middle grade, and picture books. Does not want to receive screenplays.

HOW TO CONTACT "Visit our website to send submissions and see what our individual agents are looking for. No snail mail submissions please!" Accepts simultaneous submissions. Depends on the agent. No responses for queries unless the agent is interested.

TERMS Agent receives 15% commission on domestic sales; 20% commission on foreign sales. Offers written contract. Charges for overseas mailing, messenger services, book purchases, photocopying—all deductible from royalties received.

RECENT SALES *Mort(e)*, by Robert Repino; *The Paying Guests*, by Sarah Waters; *The Third Victim*, by Phillip Margolin; *Every Kind of Wanting*, by Gina Frangello; *The Lies They Tell*, by Gillian French; *Dietland*, by Sarai Walker; *Mr. Rochester*, by Sarah Shoemaker; *Not If I See You First*, by Eric Lindstrom.

TIPS "We recommend courage, fortitude, and patience: the courage to be true to your own vision, the fortitude to finish a novel and polish it again and again before sending it out, and the patience to accept rejection gracefully and wait for the stars to align themselves appropriately for success."

NELSON LITERARY AGENCY

1732 Wazee St., Suite 207, Denver CO 80202. (303)292-2805. **E-mail:** query@nelsonagency.com. **E-mail:** querykristin@nelsonagency.com; querydanielle@nelsonagency.com; queryjoanna@nelsonagency.com; queryqueressa@nelsonagency.com. **Website:** www.nelsonagency.com. **Contact:** Kristin Nelson, President. Kristin Nelson established Nelson Literary Agency, LLC, in 2002 and over the last decade of her career, she has represented over thirty-five *New York Times* bestselling titles and many *USA Today* bestsellers. Editors call her "a hard-working bulldog agent that will fight for you." When not busy selling books, she is quite sporty. She attempts to play tennis and golf. She also loves playing Bridge (where she is the youngest person in the club). On weekends, she and her husband can be found in the mountains hiking with their 12-year old rat terrier, Chutney. "I'm looking for a good story well told. How you tell that story doesn't need to fit in a neat little category. For specifics, check out the examples on the Submission Guidelines page, follow the clear directions posted there, then submit a query directly to." Estab. 2002. Member of AAR. RWA, SCBWI, SFWA. Represents 79 clients.

MEMBER AGENTS Danielle Burby; Joanna MacKenzie; Quressa Robinson.

REPRESENTS Fiction, novels. young adult, middle grade, literary commercial, upmarket women's fiction, single-title romance, science fiction, fantasy. **Considers these fiction areas:** commercial, fantasy, historical, horror, literary, mainstream, middle grade, romance, science fiction, suspense, thriller, urban fantasy, women's, young adult.

⊶ NLA specializes in representing commercial fiction and high-caliber literary fiction. "We represent many popular genre categories, including historical romance, steampunk, and all subgenres of YA." Regardless of genre, "we are actively seeking good stories well told." Does not want nonfiction, memoir, stage plays, screenplays, short story collections, poetry, children's picture books, early reader chapter books, or material for the Christian/inspirational market.

HOW TO CONTACT "Please visit our website and carefully read our submission guidelines. We do not accept any queries on Facebook or Twitter. Query by e-mail only. Write the word 'Query' in the e-mail subject line along with the title of your novel. Send no attachments, but please paste the first 10 pages of your novel in the body of the e-mail beneath your query letter." Accepts simultaneous submissions. Makes best efforts to respond to all queries within 3 weeks. Response to full mss requested can take up to 3 months.

TERMS Agent charges industry standard commission.

TIPS "If you would like to learn how to write an awesome pitch paragraph for your query letter or would like any info on how publishing contracts work, please visit Kristin's popular industry blog Pub Rants: http://nelsonagency.com/pub-rants/."

NEW LEAF LITERARY & MEDIA, INC.

110 W. 40th St., Suite 2201, New York NY 10018. (646)248-7989. **Fax:** (646)861-4654. **E-mail:** query@newleafliterary.com. **Website:** www.newleafliterary.com. "We are a passionate agency with a relentless focus on building our clients' careers. Our approach is big picture, offering a one-stop shop built without silos and access to a variety of services including international sales, film and television, and branding resources for all clients. Our aim is to challenge conformity and re-imagine the marketplace while equipping our clients with the tools necessary to navigate an evolving landscape and succeed." Estab. 2012. Member of AAR.

MEMBER AGENTS Joanna Volpe (women's fiction, thriller, horror, speculative fiction, literary fiction and historical fiction, young adult, middle grade, art-focused picture books); Kathleen Ortiz, Director of Subsidiary Rights and literary agent (new voices in YA and animator/illustrator talent); Suzie Townsend (new adult, young adult, middle grade, romance [all subgenres], fantasy [urban fantasy, science fiction, steampunk, epic fantasy] and crime fiction [mysteries, thrillers]); Pouya Shahbazian, Director of Film and Television (no unsolicited queries); Janet Reid, janet@newleafliterary.com; Jaida Temperly (all fiction: magical realism, historical fiction; literary fiction; stories that are quirky and fantastical; nonfiction: niche, offbeat, a bit strange; middle grade; JL Stermer (nonfiction, smart pop culture, comedy/satire, fashion, health & wellness, self-help, and memoir).

REPRESENTS Nonfiction, fiction, novels, novellas, juvenile books, poetry books. **Considers these nonfiction areas:** cooking, crafts, creative nonfiction, science, technology, women's issues, young adult. **Considers these fiction areas:** crime, fantasy, historical, horror, literary, mainstream, middle grade, mystery, new adult, paranormal, picture books, romance, thriller, women's, young adult.

HOW TO CONTACT Send query via e-mail. Please do not query via phone. The word "Query" must be in the subject line, plus the agent's name, i.e.–Subject: Query, Suzie Townsend. You may include up to 5 double-spaced sample pages within the body of the e-mail. No attachments, unless specifically requested. Include all necessary contact information. You will receive an auto-response confirming receipt of your query. "We only respond if we are interested in seeing your work." Responds only if interested. All queries read within 1 month.

RECENT SALES *Carve the Mark*, by Veronica Roth (HarperCollins); *Red Queen*, by Victoria Aveyard (HarperCollins); *Lobster is the Best Medicine*, by Liz

Climo (Running Press); *Ninth House*, by Leigh Bardugo (Henry Holt); *A Snicker of Magic*, by Natalie Lloyd (Scholastic).

DANA NEWMAN LITERARY

1800 Avenue of the Stars, 12th Floor, Los Angeles CA 90067. **E-mail:** dananewmanliterary@gmail.com. **Website:** dananewman.com. **Contact:** Dana Newman. Dana Newman Literary, LLC, is a boutique literary agency in Los Angeles. "Our deep expertise in working with content creators, from crafting proposals and polishing manuscripts through negotiating and managing contracts and protecting intellectual property rights, allows us to provide a sophisticated, innovative approach to our role as author advocates." Estab. 2009. Member of AAR. California State Bar. Represents 29 clients.

Prior to becoming an agent, Ms. Newman was an attorney in the entertainment industry for 14 years.

MEMBER AGENTS Dana Newman (narrative nonfiction, business, lifestyle, current affairs, parenting, memoir, pop culture, sports, health, literary, and upmarket fiction).

REPRESENTS Nonfiction, novels, short story collections. **Considers these nonfiction areas:** architecture, art, autobiography, biography, business, child guidance, cooking, creative nonfiction, cultural interests, current affairs, diet/nutrition, design, education, ethnic, film, foods, gay/lesbian, government, health, history, how-to, inspirational, interior design, investigative, language, law, literature, medicine, memoirs, money, multicultural, music, New Age, parenting, popular culture, politics, psychology, science, self-help, sociology, sports, technology, theater, travel, true crime, women's issues, women's studies. **Considers these fiction areas:** commercial, contemporary issues, family saga, feminist, historical, literary, multicultural, sports, women's.

Ms. Newman has a background as an attorney in contracts, licensing, and intellectual property law. She is experienced in digital content creation and distribution. "We are interested in practical nonfiction (business, health and wellness, psychology, parenting, technology) by authors with smart, unique perspectives and established platforms who are committed to actively marketing and promoting their books. We love compelling, inspiring narrative nonfiction in the areas of memoir, biography, history, pop culture, current affairs/women's interest, sports, and social trends. On the fiction side, we consider a very selective amount of literary fiction and women's upmarket fiction." Does not want religious, children's, poetry, horror, mystery, thriller, romance, or science fiction. Does not represent screenplays.

HOW TO CONTACT E-mail queries only. For both nonfiction and fiction, please submit a query letter including a description of your project and a brief biography. "If we are interested in your project, we will contact you and request a full book proposal (nonfiction) or a synopsis and the first 25 pages (fiction)." Accepts simultaneous submissions. "If we have requested your materials after receiving your query, we usually respond within 4 weeks." Obtains new clients through recommendations from others, queries, and submissions.

TERMS Obtains 15% commission on domestic sales; 20% on foreign sales. Offers 1 year written contract. Notice must be given 1 month prior to terminate a contract.

RECENT SALES *Climbing the Hill*, by Jaime Harrison and Amos Snead (Ten Speed Press); *Nora Murphy's Country House Style*, by Nora Murphy (Vendome Press); *Into the Abyss*, by Ginger Lerner-Wren (Beacon Press); *Native Advertising*, by Mike Smith (McGraw-Hill); *Breakthrough: The Making of America's First Woman President*, by Nancy L. Cohen (Counterpoint); *Just Add Water*, by Clay Marzo and Robert Yehling (Houghton Mifflin Harcourt); *A Stray Cat Struts*, by Slim Jim Phantom (St. Martin's Press); *Tuff Juice*, by Caron Butler and Steve Springer (Lyons Press).

HAROLD OBER ASSOCIATES

425 Madison Ave., New York NY 10017. (212)759-8600. **Fax:** (212)759-9428. **Website:** www.haroldober.com. **Contact:** Appropriate agent. Member of AAR. Represents 250 clients.

MEMBER AGENTS Phyllis Westberg; Craig Tenney (few new clients, mostly Ober backlist and foreign rights).

HOW TO CONTACT Submit concise query letter addressed to a specific agent with the first 5 pages of the ms or proposal and SASE. No fax or e-mail. Does not handle filmscripts or plays. Responds as promptly as possible. Obtains most new clients through recommendations from others.

TERMS Agent receives 15% commission on domestic sales; 20% commission on foreign sales. Charges clients for express mail/package services.

⊘ PARADIGM TALENT AND LITERARY AGENCY

140 Broadway, 26th Floor, New York NY 10005. (212)897-6400. **Fax:** (212)764-8941. **Website:** www.paradigmagency.com.

REPRESENTS Theatrical stage play, stage plays.

Paradigm Talent and Literary Agency is an Los-Angeles-based talent agency with additional offices in New York City, Nashville, and Monterey. The firm acquired Writers & Artists Group International in 2004. The acquisition of WAGI added both talent and agents to Paradigm's roster, bolstering its New York office with legit agents, representing playwrights and theatre directors.

HOW TO CONTACT Accepts simultaneous submissions. Responds only if interested.

ALLEN O'SHEA LITERARY AGENCY

615 Westover Rd., Stamford CT 06902. (203)359-9965. **Fax:** (203)357-9909. **E-mail:** marilyn@allenoshea.com; coleen@allenoshea.com. **Website:** www.allenoshea.com. **Contact:** Marilyn Allen. Women's Media Group.

Prior to becoming agents, both Ms. Allen and Ms. O'Shea held senior positions in publishing.

MEMBER AGENTS Marilyn Allen; Coleen O'Shea.

REPRESENTS Nonfiction. **Considers these nonfiction areas:** animals, autobiography, biography, business, cooking, crafts, creative nonfiction, current affairs, decorating, diet/nutrition, design, environment, film, foods, gardening, health, history, how-to, humor, inspirational, interior design, medicine, memoirs, military, money, New Age, parenting, popular culture, psychology, regional, science, self-help, sports, true crime, women's issues, women's studies.

This agency specializes in practical nonfiction, including health, cooking and cocktails, business, and pop culture. Looks for passionate clients with strong marketing platforms and new ideas coupled with writing talent. Actively seeking narrative nonfiction, health, popular science, cookbooks, and history writers; very interested in writers who have large media platforms and interesting topics. Does not want to receive fiction, poetry, textbooks, or children's books.

HOW TO CONTACT Query via e-mail or mail with SASE. Submit book proposal with sample chapters, competitive analysis, outline, author bio, and marketing page. No phone or fax queries. Accepts simultaneous submissions. Obtains most new clients through recommendations from others, conferences.

TERMS Agent receives 15% commission on domestic sales. Offers written contract, binding for 2 years; one-month notice must be given to terminate contract.

TIPS "Prepare a strong book proposal that includes an overview, sample chapter, a well-thought out marketing plan, a competitive analysis, and bio. We will consider your project when your proposal is ready." Thanks for the opportunity to review your work.

PARK LITERARY GROUP, LLC

270 Lafayette St., Suite 1504, New York NY 10012. (212)691-3500. **Fax:** (212)691-3540. **E-mail:** info@parkliterary.com. **E-mail:** queries@parkliterary.com. **Website:** www.parkliterary.com. Estab. 2005.

MEMBER AGENTS Theresa Park (plot-driven fiction and serious nonfiction); Abigail Koons (popular science, history, politics, current affairs and art, and women's fiction); Peter Knapp (children's and YA).

REPRESENTS Nonfiction, novels. **Considers these nonfiction areas:** art, current affairs, history, politics, science. **Considers these fiction areas:** juvenile, middle grade, suspense, thriller, women's, young adult.

The Park Literary Group represents fiction and nonfiction with a boutique approach: an emphasis on servicing a relatively small number of clients, with the highest professional standards and focused personal attention. Does not want to receive poetry or screenplays.

HOW TO CONTACT Please specify the first and last name of the agent to whom you are submitting in the subject line of the e-mail. All materials must be in the body of the e-mail. Responds if interested. For fiction submissions, please include a query letter with short synopsis and the first 3 chapters of your work. Accepts simultaneous submissions.

RECENT SALES This agency's client list is on their website. It includes bestsellers Nicholas Sparks, Soman Chainani, Emily Giffin, and Debbie Macomber.

PAVILION LITERARY MANAGEMENT

660 Massachusetts Ave., Suite 4, Boston MA 02118. (617)792-5218. **E-mail:** jeff@pavilionliterary.com. **Website:** www.pavilionliterary.com. **Contact:** Jeff Kellogg.

Prior to his current position, Mr. Kellogg was a literary agent with The Stuart Agency, and an acquiring editor with HarperCollins.

REPRESENTS Nonfiction, novels. **Considers these nonfiction areas:** creative nonfiction, memoirs, science. **Considers these fiction areas:** adventure, fantasy, juvenile, mystery, thriller.

HOW TO CONTACT No unsolicited submissions. If the agency has requested your submission: Query first by e-mail (no attachments). The subject line should specify fiction or nonfiction and include the title of the work. If submitting nonfiction, include a book proposal (no longer than 75 pages), with sample chapters. Accepts simultaneous submissions.

L. PERKINS AGENCY

5800 Arlington Ave., Riverdale NY 10471. (718)543-5344. **E-mail:** submissions@lperkinsagency.com. **Website:** lperkinsagency.com. Full service New York literary agency comprised of 6 agents with sub agents in 11 foreign countries and film associates. Specializes in romance (all types), science fiction, fantasy, horror, pop culture, thrillers, women's fiction, YA and middle grade, as well as literary fiction. Estab. 1987. Member of AAR. Represents 150 clients.

Ms. Perkins has been an agent for 25 years. She is also the author of *The Insider's Guide to Getting an Agent* (Writer's Digest Books), as well as 3 other nonfiction books. She has edited 25 erotic anthologies, and is also the founder and publisher of Riverdale Avenue Books, an award-winning hybrid publisher with 9 imprints.

MEMBER AGENTS Tish Beaty, ePub agent (erotic romance–including paranormal, historical, gay/lesbian/bisexual, and light-BDSM fiction; also, she seeks new adult and YA); Sandy Lu, sandy@lperkinsagency.com (fiction: she is looking for dark literary and commercial fiction, mystery, thriller, psychological horror, paranormal/urban fantasy, historical fiction, YA, historical thrillers or mysteries set in Victorian times; nonfiction: narrative nonfiction, history, biography, pop science, pop psychology, pop culture [music/theatre/film], humor, and food writing); Lori Perkins (not currently taking new clients); Leon Husock (science fiction & fantasy, as well as young adult and middle-grade); Rachel Brooks (picture books, all genres of young adult and new adult fiction, as well as adult romance—especially romantic suspense [NOTE: Rachel is currently closed to unsolicited submissions]); Maximilian Ximinez (fiction: science fiction, fantasy, horror, thrillers; nonfiction: popular science, true crime, arts and trends in developing fields and cultures).

REPRESENTS Nonfiction, fiction, novels, short story collections. **Considers these nonfiction areas:** autobiography, biography, business, creative nonfiction, cultural interests, current affairs, film, foods, gay/lesbian, history, how-to, humor, literature, memoirs, music, popular culture, psychology, science, sex, theater, true crime, women's issues, women's studies, young adult. **Considers these fiction areas:** commercial, crime, detective, erotica, fantasy, feminist, gay, historical, horror, lesbian, literary, middle grade, mystery, new adult, paranormal, picture books, romance, science fiction, short story collections, supernatural, thriller, urban fantasy, women's, young adult.

"Most of our clients write both fiction and nonfiction. This combination keeps our clients publishing for years. The founder of the agency is also a published author, so we know what it takes to write a good book." Actively seeking erotic romance, romance, young adult, middle grade, science fiction, fantasy, memoir, pop culture, thrillers. Does not want poetry, stand alone short stories or novellas, scripts, plays, westerns, textbooks.

HOW TO CONTACT E-queries only. Include your query, a 1-page synopsis, and the first 5 pages from your novel pasted into the e-mail, or your proposal. No attachments. Submit to only 1 agent at the agency. No snail mail queries. "If you are submitting to one of our agents, please be sure to check the submission status of the agent by visiting their social media accounts listed [on the agency website]." Accepts simultaneous submissions. Obtains most new clients through recommendations from others, solicitations, conferences.

TERMS Agent receives 15% commission on domestic sales; 20% commission on foreign sales. No written contract. Charges clients for photocopying.

RECENT SALES *Arena*, by Holly Jennings; *Taking the Lead*, by Cecilia Tan; *The Girl with Ghost Eyes*, by M. H. Boroson; *Silent Attraction*, by Lauren Brown.

WRITERS CONFERENCES Romantic Times; Romance Writers of America nationals; Rainbow Book Fair; NECON; Killercon; BookExpo America; World Fantasy Convention.

TIPS "Research your field and contact professional writers' organizations to see who is looking for what. Finish your novel before querying agents. Read my book, *An Insider's Guide to Getting an Agent*, to get a sense of how agents operate. Read agent blogs-agentinthemiddle.blogspot.com and ravenousromance.blogspot.com."

RUBIN PFEFFER CONTENT

648 Hammond St., Chestnut Hill MA 02467. **E-mail:** info@rpcontent.com. **Website:** www.rpcontent.com. **Contact:** Rubin Pfeffer. Rubin Pfeffer Content is a literary agency exclusively representing children's and young adult literature, as well as content that will serve educational publishers and digital developers. Working closely with authors and illustrators, RPC is devoted to producing long-lasting children's literature: work that exemplifies outstanding writing, innovative creativity, and artistic excellence. Estab. 2014. Member of AAR. Signatory of WGA.

Rubin has previously worked as the vice-president and publisher of Simon & Schuster Children's Books and as an independent agent at East West Literary Agency.

MEMBER AGENTS Melissa Nasson is an associate agent at Rubin Pfeffer Content and an attorney. She previously interned at Zachary Shuster Harmsworth, Perseus Books Group, and East-West Literary Agency before joining Rubin Pfeffer Content. Melissa also works as contracts director at Beacon Press.

REPRESENTS Considers these nonfiction areas: juvenile nonfiction, young adult. **Considers these fiction areas:** juvenile, middle grade, picture books, young adult.

High-quality children's fiction and nonfiction, including picture books, middle-grade, and young adult. No manuscripts intended for an adult audience.

HOW TO CONTACT Note: Rubin Pfeffer accepts submissions by referral only. Melissa Nasson is open to queries for picture books, middle-grade, and young adult fiction and nonfiction. To query Melissa, email her at melissa@rpcontent.com, include the query letter in the body of the email, and attach the first 50 pages as a Word doc or PDF. If you wish to query Rubin Pfeffer by referral only, specify the contact information of your reference when submitting. Authors/illustrators should send a query and a 1-3 chapter ms via e-mail (no postal submissions). The query, placed in the body of the e-mail, should include a synopsis of the piece, as well as any relevant information regarding previous publications, referrals, websites, and biographies. The ms may be attached as a .doc or a .pdf file. Specifically for illustrators, attach a PDF of the dummy or artwork to the e-mail. Accepts simultaneous submissions. Strives to respond within 6-8 weeks.

PIPPIN PROPERTIES, INC.

110 W. 40th St., Suite 1704, New York NY 10018. (212)338-9310. **E-mail:** info@pippinproperties.com. **Website:** www.pippinproperties.com. **Contact:** Holly McGhee. Pippin Properties, Inc. opened its doors in 1998, and for the past 17 years we have been privileged to help build careers for authors and artists whose work stands the test of time, many of whom have become household names in their own right such as Peter H. Reynolds, Kate DiCamillo, Sujean Rim, Doreen Cronin, Renata Liwska, Sarah Weeks, Harry Bliss, Kate & Jim McMullan, Katherine Applegate, David Small, and Kathi Appelt. We also love to launch new careers for amazing authors and artists such as Jason Reynolds, Anna Kang and Chris Weyant, and Jandy Nelson. Estab. 1998.

Prior to becoming an agent, Ms. McGhee was an editor for 7 years and in book marketing for 4 years.

MEMBER AGENTS Holly McGhee; Elena Giovinazzo; Sara Crowe; Larissa Helena. Although each of the agents take children's books, you can find in-depth preferences for each agent on the Pippin website.

REPRESENTS Juvenile books. **Considers these fiction areas:** middle grade, picture books, young adult.

"We are strictly a children's literary agency devoted to the management of authors and artists in all media. We are small and discerning in choosing our clientele."

HOW TO CONTACT If you are a writer who is interested in submitting a ms, please query us via e-mail, and within the body of that e-mail please include: the first chapter of your novel with a short synopsis of the work or the entire picture book ms. For illustrators interested in submitting their work, please send a query letter detailing your background in illustration and include links to website with a dummy or other examples of your work. Direct all queries to the agent whom you wish to query and please do not query more than one. No attachments, please. Accepts simultaneous submissions. Obtains most new clients through recommendations from others.

TERMS Agent receives 15% commission on domestic sales; 25% commission on foreign sales. Offers written contract; 30-day notice must be given to terminate contract.

TIPS "Please do not call after sending a submission."

PONTAS LITERARY & FILM AGENCY

Sèneca, 31, principal 08006, Barcelona Spain. (34) (93)218-2212. **E-mail:** submissions@pontas-agency.com. **Website:** www.pontas-agency.com. Founded in 1992 by Anna Soler-Pont, Pontas is a literary and film agency representing internationally a wide range of authors from all over the world. "All together we can read and write in several languages and our aim is to provide the best service to our clients. Pontas attends more than ten events annually between book fairs, literary festivals and film markets. At some of them, such as the Frankfurt Book Fair, we have been present every year since 1992 with no exception." Estab. 1992. Represents 70 clients.

REPRESENTS Fiction, novels. **Considers these fiction areas:** action, adventure, commercial, confession, contemporary issues, crime, detective, ethnic, experimental, family saga, feminist, frontier, gay, historical, horror, inspirational, lesbian, literary, mainstream, multicultural, mystery, regional, satire, thriller, translation, women's, young adult.

"At this moment in time, we are only looking for works of adult fiction written in English and French." Please defer to send any materials that do not match this requirement. Does not want original film screenplays, theatre plays, poetry, sci-fi, fantasy, romance, children's, illustrated.

HOW TO CONTACT When submitting work, include a brief cover letter with your name and title of your mss in the e-mail subject, a detailed synopsis of your plot, your biography, and the full work in PDF or Word format. Accepts simultaneous submissions. "Due to the enormous and increasing volume of submissions that we receive, we cannot guarantee a reply. If you do not receive a response 6 weeks from the date of your submission, you can assume we're not interested. It's also important to note that we don't provide specific reasons nor editorial feedback on the submissions received."

PRENTIS LITERARY

PMB 496 6830 NE Bothell Way, Kenmore WA 98028. **Website:** prentisliterary.com. **Contact:** Autumn Frisse, acquisitions; Terry Johnson, business manager. A boutique author focused agency with a devotion to words and the innovative voices that put those words to good use. The agency has always centered on finding books we are passionate about homes. When Linn Prentis was alive, this was her mission and long before she passed, it indeed has been ours as well. Many a time passion has lead us to love, champion and sell books that defy pat definition. While we obviously are seeking the commercially successful, we also demand good writing which we admire that sparks our passion. Represents 12-15 clients.

Trodayne Northern worked as an English teacher and Academic Advisor prior to being and agent. He also worked as both a fiction and nonfiction freelancer writer and editor. After coming to work for The Literary Group, Mr. Northern started working for Linn Prentis in 2010. Trodayne Northern, Leslie Varney and Terry Johnson took over the agency and rebranded the company after Linn's retirement and eventual passing.

REPRESENTS Nonfiction, fiction, novels. **Considers these nonfiction areas:** biography, current affairs, ethnic, gay/lesbian, humor, memoirs, popular culture, women's issues. **Considers these fiction areas:** adventure, ethnic, fantasy, gay, historical, horror, humor, lesbian, literary, mainstream, middle grade, mystery, paranormal, romance, science fiction, supernatural, thriller, urban fantasy, young adult.

Special interest in sci-fi and fantasy, but fiction is what truly interests us. Nonfiction projects have to be something we just can't resist. Actively seeking science fiction/fantasy, POC/intersectional, women's fiction, LBGTQ+, literary fiction, children's fiction, YA, MG, mystery, horror, romance, nonfiction/memoir. Please visit website for comprehensive list. Does not want to "receive books for little kids."

HOW TO CONTACT No phone or fax queries. No surface mail. For submission use our submission form posted on our submission page or e-mail acquisitions afrisse@prentisliterary.com. For other business business questions e-mail: tjohnson@prentisliterary.com. Accepts simultaneous submissions. Obtains most new clients through recommendations from others, solicitations.

TERMS Agent receives 15% commission on domestic sales; 20% commission on foreign sales. Offers written contract; 60-day notice must be given to terminate contract.

RECENT SALES Sales include The Relic Hunter: A Gina Miyoko Mystery NYT best selling author, Maya Bohnhoff, Substrate Phantoms for Jessica Reisman, Vienna for William Kirby; Hunting Ground, Frost Burned and Night Broken titles in two series for NY Times bestselling author Patricia Briggs (as well as a graphic novel *Homecoming*) and a story collection; with more coming; a duology of novels for A.M. Dellamonica whose first book, *Indigo Springs*, won Canada's annual award for best fantasy, as well as several books abroad for client Tachyon Publications.

AARON M. PRIEST LITERARY AGENCY

200 W. 41st St., 21st Floor, New York NY 10036. (212)818-0344. **Fax:** (212)573-9417. **E-mail:** info@aaronpriest.com. **Website:** www.aaronpriest.com. Estab. 1974. Member of AAR.

MEMBER AGENTS Aaron Priest, querypriest@aaronpriest.com (thrillers, commercial fiction, biographies); Lisa Erbach Vance, queryvance@aaronpriest.com (contemporary fiction, thrillers/suspense, international fiction, narrative nonfiction); Lucy Childs, querychilds@aaronpriest.com (literary and commercial fiction, memoir, edgy women's fiction); Mitch Hoffman, queryhoffman@aaronpriest.com (thrillers, suspense, crime fiction, and literary fiction, as well as narrative nonfiction, politics, popular science, history, memoir, current events, and pop culture).

REPRESENTS **Considers these nonfiction areas:** biography, current affairs, history, memoirs, popular culture, politics, science. **Considers these fiction areas:** commercial, contemporary issues, crime, literary, middle grade, suspense, thriller, women's, young adult.

⊶ Does not want to receive poetry, screenplays, horror or sci-fi.

HOW TO CONTACT Query one of the agents using the appropriate e-mail listed on the website. "Please do not submit to more than 1 agent at this agency. We urge you to check our website and consider each agent's emphasis before submitting. Your query letter should be about one page long and describe your work as well as your background. You may also paste the first chapter of your work in the body of the e-mail. Do not send attachments." Accepts simultaneous submissions. Responds in 4 weeks, only if interested.

TERMS Agent receives 15% commission on domestic sales.

PROSPECT AGENCY

551 Valley Rd., PMB 377, Upper Montclair NJ 07043. (718)788-3217. **Fax:** (718)360-9582. **Website:** www.prospectagency.com. "Prospect Agency focuses on adult and children's literature, and is currently looking for the next generation of writers and illustrators to shape the literary landscape. We are a small, personal agency that focuses on helping each client reach success through hands-on editorial assistance and professional contract negotiations. We also strive to be on the cutting edge of technologically. The agents here spend a lot of time forming personal relationships with authors and their work. Every agent here has incredibly strong editorial skills, and works directly with clients to balance the goals of selling individual books and managing a career." Estab. 2005. Member of AAR. Signatory of WGA. Represents 130+ clients.

MEMBER AGENTS Emily Sylvan Kim, esk@prospectagency.com (romance, women's, commercial, young adult, new adult); Rachel Orr, rko@prospectagency.com (picture books, illustrators, middle grade, young adult); Becca Stumpf, becca@prospectagency.com (young adult and middle grade [all genres, including fantasy/SciFi, literary, mystery, contemporary, historical, horror/suspense], especially MG and YA novels featuring diverse protagonists and life circumstances. Adult SciFi and Fantasy novels with broad appeal, upmarket women's fiction, smart, spicy romance novels); Carrie Pestritto, carrie@prospectagency.com (narrative nonfiction, general nonfiction, biography, and memoir; commercial fiction with a literary twist, women's fiction, romance, upmarket, historical fiction, high-concept YA and upper MG); Kirsten Carleton, kcarleton@prospectagency.com (upmarket speculative, thriller, and literary fiction for adult and YA).

REPRESENTS Nonfiction, fiction, novels, novellas, juvenile books, scholarly books, textbooks. **Considers these nonfiction areas:** biography, memoirs, popular culture, psychology. **Considers these fiction ar-**

eas: commercial, contemporary issues, crime, ethnic, family saga, fantasy, feminist, gay, historical, horror, humor, juvenile, lesbian, literary, mainstream, middle grade, multicultural, mystery, new adult, picture books, romance, science fiction, suspense, thriller, urban fantasy, women's, young adult.

"We're looking for strong, unique voices and unforgettable stories and characters."

HOW TO CONTACT All submissions are electronic and must be submitted through the portal at prospectagency.com/submissions. We do not accept any submissions through snail mail. Accepts simultaneous submissions. Obtains new clients through conferences, recommendations, queries, and some scouting.

TERMS Agent receives 15% on domestic sales, 20% on foreign sales sold directly and 25% on sales using a subagent. Offers written contract.

P.S. LITERARY AGENCY

2010 Winston Park Dr., 2nd Floor, Oakville ON L6H 5R7 Canada. **E-mail:** info@psliterary.com. **E-mail:** query@psliterary.com. **Website:** www.psliterary.com. **Contact:** Curtis Russell, principal agent; Carly Watters, senior agent; Maria Vicente, literary agent; Eric Smith; literary agent; Kurestin Armada, associate agent. The P.S. Literary Agency (PSLA) represents both fiction and nonfiction works to leading publishers in North America, Europe and throughout the World. "We maintain a small but select client list that receives our undivided attention and focused efforts. PSLA seeks to work with clients who are professional and committed to their goals. It is our desire to work with clients for the duration of their careers." Estab. 2005.

MEMBER AGENTS Curtis Russell (literary/commercial fiction, mystery, thriller, suspense, romance, young adult, middle grade, picture books, business, history, politics, current affairs, memoirs, health/wellness, sports, humor, pop culture, pop science, pop psychology); Carly Watters (upmarket/commercial fiction, women's fiction, book club fiction, literary thrillers, cookbooks, health/wellness, memoirs, humor, pop science, pop psychology); Maria Vicente (young adult, middle grade, illustrated picture books, graphic novels, pop culture, science, lifestyle, design); Kurestin Armada (magic realism, science fiction, fantasy, illustrated picture books, middle grade, young adult, graphic novels, romance, design, cookbooks, pop psychology, photography, nature, science); Eric Smith (young adult, new adult, literary/commercial fiction, cookbooks, pop culture, humor, essay collections).

REPRESENTS Nonfiction, fiction, novels, juvenile books. **Considers these nonfiction areas:** animals, art, autobiography, biography, business, child guidance, computers, cooking, crafts, creative nonfiction, cultural interests, current affairs, dance, decorating, diet/nutrition, design, economics, education, environment, ethnic, film, foods, gardening, gay/lesbian, government, health, history, hobbies, how-to, humor, inspirational, interior design, investigative, juvenile nonfiction, literature, medicine, memoirs, military, money, multicultural, music, New Age, parenting, philosophy, photography, popular culture, politics, psychology, recreation, satire, science, self-help, sex, spirituality, sports, technology, travel, true crime, war, women's issues, women's studies, young adult. **Considers these fiction areas:** action, adventure, comic books, commercial, crime, detective, erotica, ethnic, experimental, family saga, fantasy, feminist, gay, historical, horror, humor, inspirational, juvenile, lesbian, literary, mainstream, middle grade, multicultural, mystery, new adult, New Age, paranormal, picture books, police, romance, satire, science fiction, sports, supernatural, suspense, thriller, urban fantasy, women's, young adult.

Actively seeking both fiction and nonfiction. Seeking both new and established writers. Does not want to receive poetry or screenplays.

HOW TO CONTACT Query letters should be directed to query@psliterary.com. PSLA does not accept or respond to phone, paper, or social media queries. Responds in 4-6 weeks to queries/proposals. Obtains most new clients through solicitations.

TERMS Agent receives 15% commission on domestic sales; 25% commission on foreign sales. "We offer a written contract, with 30-days notice to terminate."

TIPS "Please review our website for the most up-to-date submission guidelines. We do not charge reading fees. We do not offer a critique service."

PUBLICATION RIOT GROUP

E-mail: submissions@priotgroup.com. **Website:** www.priotgroup.com. **Contact:** Donna Bagdasarian. Member of AAR. Signatory of WGA.

Prior to being an agent, Ms. Bagdasarian worked as an acquisitions editor. Previously, she worked for the William Morris and Maria Carvainis agencies.

REPRESENTS Nonfiction, novels. **Considers these nonfiction areas:** memoirs, popular culture, politics, science, sociology. **Considers these fiction areas:** ethnic, historical, literary, mainstream, thriller, women's.

"The company is a literary management company, representing their authors in all processes of the entertainment trajectory: from book development, to book sales, to subsidiary sales in the foreign market, television and film." Does not want science fiction and fantasy.

HOW TO CONTACT Currently closed to all submissions. Accepts simultaneous submissions.

RECENT SALES List of sales on agency website.

JOANNA PULCINI LITERARY MANAGEMENT

E-mail: info@jplm.com. **Website:** www.jplm.com. **Contact:** Joanna Pulcini. Currently not accepting submissions.

HOW TO CONTACT Do not query this agency until they open their client list. Accepts simultaneous submissions.

THE PURCELL AGENCY

E-mail: tpaqueries@gmail.com. **Website:** www.thepurcellagency.com. **Contact:** Tina P. Schwartz. This is an agency for authors of children's and teen literature. Estab. 2012. SCBWI Represents 42 clients.

MEMBER AGENTS Tina P. Schwartz, Kim Blair McCollum, Catherine Hedrick.

REPRESENTS Nonfiction, fiction, novels, juvenile books. **Considers these nonfiction areas:** biography, child guidance, creative nonfiction, gay/lesbian, juvenile nonfiction, multicultural, parenting, young adult. **Considers these fiction areas:** juvenile, middle grade, women's, young adult.

This agency also takes juvenile nonfiction for MG and YA markets. At this point, the agency is not considering fantasy, science fiction or picture book submissions.

HOW TO CONTACT Check the website to see if agency is open to submissions and for submission guidelines. Accepts simultaneous submissions.

RECENT SALES *Seven Suspects*, by Renee James; *A Kind of Justice*, by Renee James; *Adventures at Hound Hotel*, by Shelley Swanson Sateren; *Adventures at Tabby Towers*, by Shelley Swanson Sateren; *Keys to Freedom*, by Karen Meade.

QUEEN LITERARY AGENCY

30 E. 60th St., Suite 1004, New York NY 10022. (212)974-8333. **Fax:** (212)974-8347. **E-mail:** submissions@queenliterary.com. **Website:** www.queenliterary.com. **Contact:** Lisa Queen.

Prior to her current position, Ms. Queen was a former publishing executive and most recently head of IMG Worldwide's literary division.

REPRESENTS Novels. **Considers these nonfiction areas:** business, foods, psychology, science, sports. **Considers these fiction areas:** commercial, historical, literary, mystery, thriller.

Ms. Queen's specialties: "While our agency represents a wide range of nonfiction titles, we have a particular interest in business books, food writing, science and popular psychology, as well as books by well-known chefs, radio and television personalities, and sports figures."

HOW TO CONTACT E-query. Accepts simultaneous submissions.

RECENT SALES A full list of this agency's clients and sales is available on their website.

RED SOFA LITERARY

P.O. Box 40482, St. Paul MN 55104. (651)224-6670. **E-mail:** dawn@redsofaliterary.com laura@redsofaliterary.com; amanda@redsofaliterary.com; stacey@redsofaliterary.com; erik@redsofaliterary.com; liz@redsofaliterary.com. **Website:** www.redsofaliterary.com. **Contact:** Dawn Frederick, owner/literary agent; Laura Zats, literary agent; Amanda Rutter, associate literary agent; Stacey Graham, associate literary agent; Erik Hane, associate literary agent; Liz Rahn, subrights agent. Estab. 2008. Authors Guild and the MN Publishers Round Table Represents 125 clients.

Dawn: "Before publishing I was a bookseller in the independent, chain, and specialty stores. I ended up in MN due to my first publishing job, eventually becoming a literary agent at Sebastian Literary Agency. I have B.S. in Human Ecology and a M.S. in Information Sciences from an ALA accredited institution. I'm also the co-founder of the MN Publishing Tweet Up, the News chair for the Twin Cities Advisory Council for MPR, and a teaching artist at Loft Literary. I can be found on Twitter at @redsofaliterary." **Laura:** "I received my B.A. from graduated from Grinnell College with degrees in English and anthropology. She began working in the publishing industry in 2011, joining Red Sofa Literary in 2013. As an agent, she specializes in children's fiction, science fiction and fantasy, and romance. She is also one-half of the weekly publishing podcast, Print Run. In her free time, Laura serves on the board of the Minnesota Book Publishers' Roundtable, teaches classes on writing and publishing, and drinks a lot of tea. Connect with her on Twitter @LZats." **Amanda:** "I have no formal qualifications in literary—in fact, my degree subject was accounting. But my professional history includes acquisition editor for Strange Chemistry, freelance editor for Bubblecow and Wise Ink Publishing, and book blogger." Bree: "I have a Bachelors in philosophy, a masters in journalism with an emphasis in editing and I've been working in various areas of journalism for the past 9 years. I started agenting in 2011 (after having interned at a literary agency for a year)." **Stacey**: "I have Bachelors of Science degrees in History and Archaeology/Anthropology from Oregon State University. I am the author of four books and multiple short stories, a screenwriter, ghostwriter, and editor." **Erik:** "Along with working as an agent at Red Sofa, Erik Hane is a freelance editor and writer based in Minneapolis. Since graduating from Knox College and the Denver Publishing Institute in 2012, he has worked as an assistant editor at Oxford University Press and then as an acquiring editor at The Overlook Press, both in New York. This experience at both academic and commercial publishing houses means he's performed editorial work on everything from serious scientific nonfiction to literary novels." **Liz**: "Liz Rahn graduated from Concordia College with degrees in English Literature and History. She was in the 2015 class of the Denver Publishing Institute and does freelance editing in addition to her work with Red Sofa Literary."

MEMBER AGENTS Laura Zats; Amanda Rutter; Stacey Graham; Erik Hane; Liz Rahn.

REPRESENTS Nonfiction, fiction, novels, juvenile books. **Considers these nonfiction areas:** Americana, animals, anthropology, archeology, biography, crafts, creative nonfiction, cultural interests, current affairs, dance, environment, ethnic, film, gay/lesbian, government, health, history, hobbies, humor, investigative, juvenile nonfiction, literature, multicultural, music, popular culture, politics, recreation, satire, science, sociology, sports, true crime, war, women's issues, women's studies, young adult, extreme sports. **Considers these fiction areas:** action, adventure, commercial, contemporary issues, detective, erotica, ethnic, fantasy, feminist, gay, humor, juvenile, lesbian, literary, mainstream, middle grade, multicultural, mystery, picture books, romance, science fiction, suspense, thriller, urban fantasy, young adult.

Dawn Frederick: "I am always in search of a good work of nonfiction that falls within my categories (see my specific list at our website). I especially love pop culture, interesting histories, social sciences/advocacy, humor and books that are great conversation starters. As for fiction, I am always in search of good YA and MG titles. For YA I will go a little darker on the tone, as I enjoy a good gothic, contemporary or historical YA novel. For MG, I will always want something fun and lighthearted, but would love more contemporary themes too." **Laura Zats:** " Diverse YA of all kinds, I'm looking for all genres here, and am especially interested in settings or characters I haven't seen before and queer romantic relationships if there's a romance. Adult science fiction and fantasy.Please note I have an anthropology degree, I'm interested in well-drawn cultures and subverting traditional Chosen One, quest, and colonial narratives. I will fall on the floor and salivate if your writing reminds me of N.K. Jemisin or Nnedi Okorafor. No white dudes on quests, dreams, or Western ideas of Hell, please. Romance/erotica - I am looking for all settings and subgenres here. Must have verbal consent throughout and a twist to traditional romance tropes. If you send me the next The Hating Game, I will be the happiest agent in all the land. Please no rape, querying anything shorter than 60K, or shifters" **Amanda Rutter:** "Science fiction/fantasy, the non-YA ideas, young adult and middle grade–science fiction/fantasy." **Stacey Graham:** "Middle-grade with a great voice — especially funny and/or spooky, Nonfiction (MG/YA/Adult), Romance, and Mystery with a humorous bent." **Erik Hane**: "Literary fiction, Nonfiction [no memoirs]." These are the things we are not actively seeking: **Dawn:** "Memoirs, it seems everyone ignores this request. I also prefer to represent books that aren't overly sappy, overly romantic, or any type of didactic/moralistic."**Laura**: "Nonfiction, including memoir. Adult mystery/thriller/literary fiction. Fiction without quirky or distinctive hooks. Books that follow or fit in trends." **Amanda:** "I am definitely not a non-fiction person. I rarely read it myself, so wouldn't know where to start where to represent! Also, although I enjoy middle grade fiction and would be happy to represent, I won't take on picture books." **Stacey**: "At this time, I do not want to represent YA, fantasy, sci-fi, or romance." **Erik:** "I definitely don't want to represent fiction that sets out at the start to be 'genre.' I like reading it, but I don't think it's for me as an agent. Bring me genre elements, but I think I'd rather let the classification happen naturally. I also don't want memoir unless you've really, really got something unique and accessible. I also don't want to represent children's lit; that's another thing I really do love and appreciate but don't quite connect with professionally."

HOW TO CONTACT Query by e-mail or mail with SASE. No attachments, please. Submit full proposal (for nonfiction especially, for fiction it would be nice) plus 3 sample chapters (or first 50 pages) and any other pertinent writing samples upon request by the specific agent. Do not sent within or attached to the query letter. Pdf/doc/docx is preferred, no rtf documents please. Accepts simultaneous submissions. Obtains new clients through queries, also through recommendations from others, solicitations.

TERMS Agent receives 15% commission on domestic sales; 20% commission on foreign sales. Offers written contract.

WRITERS CONFERENCES Surrey Writers Conference, Writers Digest, SDSU Writer's Conference, WorldCon, CONvergence, SCWBI (regional conferences), FWA Conference, DFW Writers Conference, Northern Colorado Writers Conference, Horror World Convention, Loft Literary Conference, Madison Writers Workshop, Emerald City Writers Conference, Missouri Writers Guild, Pike's Peak Conference, Willamette Writers Conference, and more.

TIPS "Always remember the benefits of building an author platform, and the accessibility of accomplishing this task in today's industry. Most importantly, research the agents queried. Avoid contacting every literary agent about a book idea. Due to the large volume of queries received, the process of reading queries for unrepresented categories (by the agency) becomes quite the arduous task. Investigate online directories, printed guides (like *Writer's Market*), individual agent websites, and more, before beginning the query process. It's good to remember that each agent has a vision of what s/he wants to represent and will communicate this information accordingly. We're simply waiting for those specific book ideas to come in our direction."

REES LITERARY AGENCY

14 Beacon St., Suite 710, Boston MA 02108. (617)227-9014. **E-mail:** lorin@reesagency.com. **Website:** reesagency.com. Estab. 1983. Member of AAR. Represents more than 100 clients.

MEMBER AGENTS Ann Collette, agent10702@aol.com (fiction: literary, upscale commercial women's, crime [including mystery, thriller and psychological suspense], upscale western, historical, military and war, and horror; nonfiction: narrative, military and war, books on race and class, works set in Southeast Asia, biography, pop culture, books on film and opera, humor, and memoir); Lorin Rees, lorin@reesagency.com (literary fiction, memoirs, business books, self-help, science, history, psychology, and narrative nonfiction); Rebecca Podos, rebecca@reesagency.com (young adult and middle grade fiction, particularly books about complex female relationships, beautifully written contemporary, genre novels with a strong focus on character, romance with more at stake than "will they/won't they," and LGBTQ books across all genres).

REPRESENTS Novels. **Considers these nonfiction areas:** biography, business, film, history, humor, memoirs, military, popular culture, psychology, science, war. **Considers these fiction areas:** commercial, crime, historical, horror, literary, middle grade, mystery, suspense, thriller, westerns, women's, young adult.

HOW TO CONTACT Consult website for each agent's submission guidelines and e-mail addresses, as they differ. Accepts simultaneous submissions. Obtains most new clients through recommendations from others, conferences, submissions.

TERMS Agent receives 15% commission on domestic sales; 20% commission on foreign sales.

REGAL HOFFMANN & ASSOCIATES LLC

242 W. 38th St., Floor 2, New York NY 10018. (212)684-7900. **Fax:** (212)684-7906. **E-mail:** submissions@rhaliterary.com. **Website:** www.rhaliterary.com. Regal Hoffmann & Associates LLC, a full-service agency based in New York, was founded in 2002. We represent works in a wide range of categories, with an emphasis on literary fiction, outstanding thriller and crime fiction, and serious narrative nonfiction. Estab. 2002. Member of AAR. Represents 70 clients.

MEMBER AGENTS Claire Anderson-Wheeler (nonfiction: memoirs and biographies, narrative histories, popular science, popular psychology; adult fiction: primarily character-driven literary fiction, but open to genre fiction, high-concept fiction; all genres of young adult / middle grade fiction); Markus Hoffmann (international and literary fiction, crime, [pop] cultural studies, current affairs, economics, history, music, popular science, and travel literature); Joseph Regal (literary fiction, international thrillers, history, science, photography, music, culture, and whimsy); Stephanie Steiker (serious and narrative nonfiction, literary fiction, graphic novels, history, philosophy, current affairs, cultural studies, biography, music, international writing); Grace Ross (literary fiction, historical fiction, international narratives, narrative nonfiction, popular science, biography, cultural theory, memoir).

REPRESENTS Nonfiction, fiction, novels, short story collections, juvenile books, scholarly books. **Considers these nonfiction areas:** biography, creative nonfiction, current affairs, economics, history, investigative, juvenile nonfiction, literature, memoirs, music, psychology, science, translation, travel, women's issues, women's studies, young adult. **Considers these fiction areas:** literary, mainstream, middle grade, short story collections, thriller, women's, young adult.

> We represent works in a wide range of categories, with an emphasis on literary fiction, outstanding thriller and crime fiction, and serious narrative nonfiction. Actively seeking literary fiction and narrative nonfiction. Does not want romance, science fiction, poetry, or screenplays.

HOW TO CONTACT Query with SASE or via e-mail to submissions@rhaliterary.com. No phone calls. Submissions should consist of a 1-page query letter detailing the book in question, as well as the qualifications of the author. For fiction, submissions may also include the first 10 pages of the novel or one short story from a collection. Responds if interested. Accepts simultaneous submissions. Responds in 4-8 weeks.

TERMS Agent receives 15% commission on domestic sales; 20% commission on foreign sales. We charge no reading fees.

RECENT SALES *Wily Snare*, by Adam Jay Epstein; *Perfectly Undone*, by Jamie Raintree; *A Sister in My House*, by Linda Olsson; *This Is How It Really Sounds*, by Stuart Archer Cohen; *Autofocus*, by Lauren Gibaldi; *We've Already Gone This Far*, by Patrick Dacey; *A Fierce and Subtle Poison*, by Samantha Mabry; *The Life of the World to Come*, by Dan Cluchey; *Willful Disregard*, by Lena Andersson; *The Sweetheart*, by Angelina Mirabella.

TIPS "We are deeply committed to every aspect of our clients' careers, and are engaged in everything from the editorial work of developing a great book proposal or line editing a fiction manuscript to negotiating state-of-the-art book deals and working to promote and publicize the book when it's published. We are at the forefront of the effort to increase authors' rights in publishing contracts in a rapidly changing commercial environment. We deal directly with co-agents and publishers in every foreign territory and also work directly and with co-agents for feature film and television rights, with extraordinary success in both arenas. Many of our clients' works have sold in dozens of translation markets, and a high proportion of our books have been sold in Hollywood. We have strong relationships with speaking agents, who can assist in arranging author tours and other corporate and college speaking opportunities when appropriate."

⊘ THE AMY RENNERT AGENCY

1550 Tiburon Blvd., #302, Tiburon CA 94920. **E-mail:** queries@amyrennert.com. **Website:** www.publishersmarketplace.com/members/amyrennert/. **Contact:** Amy Rennert.

REPRESENTS Nonfiction, novels. **Considers these nonfiction areas:** biography, business, creative nonfiction, health, history, memoirs, money, sports. **Con-**

siders these fiction areas: literary, mainstream, mystery.

"The Amy Rennert Agency specializes in books that matter. We provide career management for established and first-time authors, and our breadth of experience in many genres enables us to meet the needs of a diverse clientele."

HOW TO CONTACT Amy Rennert is not currently accepting unsolicited submissions. Accepts simultaneous submissions.

TIPS "Due to the high volume of submissions, it is not possible to respond to each and every one. Please understand that we are only able to respond to queries that we feel may be a good fit with our agency."

THE LISA RICHARDS AGENCY

108 Upper Leeson St., Dublin 4 Ireland. (03)(531)637-5000. **Fax:** (03)(531)667-1256. **E-mail:** info@lisarichards.ie. **Website:** www.lisarichards.ie. Estab. 1989.

MEMBER AGENTS Faith O'Grady (literary).

REPRESENTS Nonfiction, fiction, juvenile books. **Considers these nonfiction areas:** biography, history, humor, memoirs, popular culture, self-help, sports, travel, narrative, lifestyle. **Considers these fiction areas:** commercial, literary, middle grade, young adult. **Considers these script areas:** comedy, general scripts.

"For fiction, I am always looking for exciting new writing–distinctive voices, original, strong storylines, and intriguing characters." Doesn't handle horror, science fiction, screenplays, or children's picture books.

HOW TO CONTACT Contact If sending fiction, please limit your submission to the first three or four chapters, and include a covering letter and an SASE if required. If sending nonfiction, please send a detailed proposal about your book, a sample chapter and a cover letter. Every effort will be made to respond to submissions within 3 months of receipt. Accepts simultaneous submissions.

RECENT SALES Clients include Arlene Hunt, Roisin Ingle, Declan Lynch, Kevin Rafter.

THE RIGHTS FACTORY

P.O. Box 499, Station C, Toronto ON M6J 3P6 Canada. (416)966-5367. **Website:** www.therightsfactory.com. "The Rights Factory is an international literary agency." Estab. 2004. Represents ~150 clients.

MEMBER AGENTS Sam Hiyate (President: fiction, nonfiction and graphic novel); Ali McDonald (Kidlit Agent: YA and children's literature of all kinds); Olga Filina (Associate Agent: commercial and historical fiction; great genre fiction in the area of romance and mystery; nonfiction in the field of business, wellness, lifestyle and memoir; and young adult and middle grade novels with memorable characters); Cassandra Rogers (Associate Agent: adult literary and commercial women's fiction; historical fiction; nonfiction on politics, history, science, and finance; humorous, heartbreaking and inspiring memoir); Lydia Moed (Associate Agent: science fiction and fantasy, historical fiction, diverse voices; narrative nonfiction on a wide variety of topics, including history, popular science, biography and travel); Natalie Kimber (Associate Agent: literary and commercial fiction and creative nonfiction in categories such as memoir, cooking, pop-culture, spirituality, and sustainability); Harry Endrulat (Associate Agent: children's literature, especially author/illustrators and Canadian voices); Haskell Nussbaum (Associate Agent: literature of all kinds); Anna Trader (Associate Agent: literary, general and women's fiction; nonfiction in self-help and memoir.

REPRESENTS Nonfiction, fiction, novels, short story collections, novellas, juvenile books. **Considers these nonfiction areas:** biography, business, cooking, environment, foods, gardening, gay/lesbian, health, history, inspirational, juvenile nonfiction, memoirs, money, music, parenting, popular culture, politics, science, self-help, spirituality, travel, women's issues, young adult. **Considers these fiction areas:** commercial, crime, family saga, fantasy, gay, hi-lo, historical, horror, juvenile, lesbian, literary, mainstream, middle grade, multicultural, mystery, new adult, paranormal, picture books, romance, science fiction, short story collections, suspense, thriller, urban fantasy, women's, young adult.

Plays, screenplays, textbooks.

HOW TO CONTACT There is a submission form on this agency's website. Accepts simultaneous submissions. Responds in 3-6 weeks.

ANGELA RINALDI LITERARY AGENCY

P.O. Box 7875, Beverly Hills CA 90212-7875. (310)842-7665. **Fax:** (310)837-8143. **E-mail:** info@rinaldiliterary.com. **Website:** www.rinaldiliterary.com. **Contact:** Angela Rinaldi. Member of AAR.

Prior to opening her agency, Ms. Rinaldi was an editor at NAL/Signet, Pocket Books and

Bantam, and the manager of book development for *The Los Angeles Times*.

REPRESENTS Nonfiction, novels. TV and motion picture rights (for clients only). **Considers these nonfiction areas:** biography, business, cooking, current affairs, health, memoirs, parenting, psychology, self-help, women's issues, women's studies, narrative nonfiction, food narratives, wine, lifestyle, relationships, wellness, personal finance. **Considers these fiction areas:** commercial, historical, literary, mainstream, mystery, suspense, thriller, women's, contemporary, gothic, women's book club fiction.

Actively seeking commercial and literary fiction, as well as nonfiction. For fiction, we do not want to receive humor, CIA espionage, drug thrillers, techno thrillers, category romances, science fiction, fantasy, horror/occult/paranormal, poetry, film scripts, magazine articles or religion. For nonfiction, please do not send us magazine articles, celebrity bios, or tell alls.

HOW TO CONTACT E-queries only. Include the word "Query" in the subject line. For fiction, please send a brief synopsis and paste the first 10 pages into an e-mail. Nonfiction queries should include a detailed cover letter, your credentials and platform information as well as any publishing history. Tell us if you have a completed proposal. Accepts simultaneous submissions. Responds in 2-4 weeks.

TERMS Agent receives 15% commission on domestic sales; 25% commission on foreign sales. Offers written contract.

ANN RITTENBERG LITERARY AGENCY, INC.

15 Maiden Lane, Suite 206, New York NY 10038. (212)684-6936. **E-mail:** info@rittlit.com. **Website:** www.rittlit.com. **Contact:** Ann Rittenberg, president. Estab. 1992. Member of AAR. Represents 30 clients.

MEMBER AGENTS Ann Rittenberg, Rosie Jonker.

REPRESENTS Nonfiction, fiction, novels, juvenile books. **Considers these nonfiction areas:** biography, history, literature, memoirs, popular culture, true crime. **Considers these fiction areas:** crime, detective, family saga, literary, mainstream, mystery, suspense, thriller, women's.

"We don't represent screenplays, poetry, plays, or self-help."

HOW TO CONTACT Query via e-mail or postal mail (with SASE). Submit query letter with 3 sample chapters pasted into the body of the e-mail. If you query by e-mail, we will only respond if interested. If you are making a simultaneous submission, you must tell us in your query. Accepts simultaneous submissions. Responds in 6-8 weeks. However, as noted above, if you don't receive a response to an emailed query, that means it was a pass. Obtains most new clients through referrals from established writers and editors.

TERMS Agent receives 15% commission on domestic sales, and 20% commission on foreign and film deals. This 20% is shared with co-agents. Offers written contract. No charges except for PDFs or finished books for foreign and film submissions.

RECENT SALES *Since We Fell*, by Dennis Lehane; *Your First Novel - Revised and Expanded Edition*, by Ann Rittenberg and Laura Whitcomb with Camille Goldin; *Paradise Valley*, by C.J. Box; *The Field Guide to Dumb Birds of North America*, by Matt Kracht; *Stay Hidden*, by Paul Doiron.

TIPS "Refrain from sending enormous bouquets of red roses. Elegant bouquets of peonies, tulips, ranunculus, calla lily, and white roses are acceptable."

RIVERSIDE LITERARY AGENCY

41 Simon Keets Rd., Leyden MA 01337. (413)772-0067. **Fax:** (413)772-0969. **E-mail:** rivlit@sover.net. **Website:** www.riversideliteraryagency.com. **Contact:** Susan Lee Cohen. Estab. 1990.

Worked at Viking Penguin before becoming an agent at Richard Curtis Associates, and then Sterling Lord Literistic. Founded RLA in 1990.

REPRESENTS Nonfiction, fiction.

This agency sells adult nonfiction and fiction, and has sold books in the categories of science, psychology, spirituality, health, memoir, pop culture, true crime, parenting, history/politics, and narrative.

HOW TO CONTACT E-query. Accepts simultaneous submissions. Obtains most new clients through referrals.

TERMS Agent receives 15% commission on domestic sales. Offers written contract. Charges clients for foreign postage, photocopying large mss, express mail deliveries, etc.

RLR ASSOCIATES, LTD.

420 Lexington Ave., Suite 2532, New York NY 10170. (212)541-8641. **E-mail:** website.info@rlrassociates.net. **Website:** www.rlrassociates.net. **Contact:** Scott Gould. Member of AAR. Represents 50 clients.

REPRESENTS Nonfiction, novels. **Considers these nonfiction areas:** biography, creative nonfiction, foods, history, humor, popular culture, sports. **Considers these fiction areas:** commercial, literary, mainstream, middle grade, picture books, romance, women's, young adult, genre.

"We provide a lot of editorial assistance to our clients and have connections." Does not want to receive screenplays.

HOW TO CONTACT Query by snail mail. For fiction, send a query and 1-3 chapters (pasted). For nonfiction, send query or proposal. Accepts simultaneous submissions. "If you do not hear from us within 3 months, please assume that your work is out of active consideration." Obtains most new clients through recommendations from others.

TERMS Agent receives 15% commission on domestic sales; 20% commission on foreign sales. Offers written contract.

RECENT SALES Clients include Shelby Foote, The Grief Recovery Institute, Don Wade, David Plowden, Nina Planck, Karyn Bosnak, Gerald Carbone, Jason Lethcoe, Andy Crouch.

TIPS "Please check out our website for more details on our agency."

BJ ROBBINS LITERARY AGENCY

5130 Bellaire Ave., North Hollywood CA 91607-2908. **E-mail:** robbinsliterary@gmail.com. **Website:** www.bjrobbinsliterary.com. **Contact:** (Ms.) BJ Robbins. Estab. 1992. Member of AAR.

Prior to becoming an agent, Robbins spent 15 years in publishing, starting in publicity at Simon & Schuster and later as Marketing Director and Senior Editor at Harcourt.

REPRESENTS Nonfiction, fiction. **Considers these nonfiction areas:** autobiography, biography, creative nonfiction, cultural interests, current affairs, ethnic, film, health, history, investigative, medicine, memoirs, multicultural, music, popular culture, psychology, science, sociology, sports, theater, travel, true crime, women's issues, women's studies. **Considers these fiction areas:** contemporary issues, crime, detective, ethnic, historical, literary, mainstream, multicultural, mystery, sports, suspense, thriller, women's.

"We do not represent screenplays, plays, poetry, science fiction, fantasy, westerns, romance, techno-thrillers, religious tracts, dating books or anything with the word 'unicorn' in the title."

HOW TO CONTACT E-query with no attachments. For fiction, okay to include first 10 pages in body of e-mail. Accepts simultaneous submissions. Only responds to projects if interested. Obtains most new clients through conferences, referrals.

TERMS Agent receives 15% commission on domestic sales; 20% commission on foreign sales. Offers written contract. No fees.

RECENT SALES *Shoot for the Moon: The Perilous Voyage of Apollo 11*, by James Donovan (Little, Brown); *Mongrels*, by Stephen Graham Jones (William Morrow); *Blood Brothers: The Story of the Strange Friendship between Sitting Bull and Buffalo Bill*, by Deanne Stillman (Simon & Schuster); *Reliance, Illinois*, by Mary Volmer (Soho Press), Mapping the Interior by Stephen Graham Jones (Tor).

THE ROBBINS OFFICE, INC.

405 Park Ave., 9th Floor, New York NY 10022. (212)223-0720. **Fax:** (212)223-2535. **Website:** www.robbinsoffice.com. **Contact:** Kathy P. Robbins, owner.

MEMBER AGENTS Kathy P. Robbins; David Halpern.

REPRESENTS Novels.

This agency specializes in selling serious nonfiction as well as commercial and literary fiction.

HOW TO CONTACT Accepts submissions by referral only. Do not cold query this market. Accepts simultaneous submissions.

TERMS Agent receives 15% commission on domestic, foreign, and film sales. Bills back specific expenses incurred in doing business for a client.

RODEEN LITERARY MANAGEMENT

3501 N. Southport #497, Chicago IL 60657. **E-mail:** info@rodeenliterary.com. **E-mail:** submissions@rodeenliterary.com. **Website:** www.rodeenliterary.com. **Contact:** Paul Rodeen. Estab. 2009. Member of AAR. Signatory of WGA.

Paul Rodeen established Rodeen Literary Management in 2009 after 7 years of experience with the literary agency Sterling Lord Literistic, Inc.

REPRESENTS Nonfiction, novels, juvenile books. illustrations, graphic novels. **Considers these fiction areas:** juvenile, middle grade, picture books, young adult, graphic novels, comics.

- Actively seeking "writers and illustrators of all genres of children's literature including picture books, early readers, middle-grade fiction and nonfiction, graphic novels and comic books, as well as young adult fiction and nonfiction." This is primarily an agency devoted to children's books.

HOW TO CONTACT Unsolicited submissions are accepted by e-mail only. Cover letters with synopsis and contact information should be included in the body of your e-mail. An initial submission of 50 pages from a novel or a longer work of nonfiction will suffice and should be pasted into the body of your e-mail. Accepts simultaneous submissions.

LINDA ROGHAAR LITERARY AGENCY, LLC

P.O. Box 3561, Amherst MA 01004. **E-mail:** contact@lindaroghaar.com. **Website:** www.lindaroghaar.com. **Contact:** Linda L. Roghaar. Member of AAR.

- Prior to opening her agency, Ms. Roghaar worked in retail bookselling for 5 years and as a publishers' sales rep for 15 years.

REPRESENTS Nonfiction.

- The Linda Roghaar Literary Agency represents authors with substantial messages and specializes in nonfiction. We sell to major, independent, and university presses. Does not want fiction.

HOW TO CONTACT We prefer e-queries. Please mention 'query' in the subject line, and do not include attachments. For queries by mail, please include an SASE. Accepts simultaneous submissions. Responds within 12 weeks if interested.

TERMS Agent receives 15% commission on domestic sales. Agent receives negotiable commission on foreign sales. Offers written contract.

THE ROSENBERG GROUP

23 Lincoln Ave., Marblehead MA 01945. (781)990-1341. **Fax:** (781)990-1344. **Website:** www.rosenberg-group.com. **Contact:** Barbara Collins Rosenberg. Estab. 1998. Member of AAR. Recognized agent of the RWA. Represents 25 clients.

- Prior to becoming an agent, Ms. Rosenberg was a senior editor for Harcourt.

REPRESENTS Nonfiction, novels, textbooks. college textbooks only. **Considers these nonfiction areas:** biography, current affairs, foods, music, popular culture, psychology, science, self-help, sports, women's issues, women's studies, women's health, wine/beverages. **Considers these fiction areas:** romance, women's, chick lit.

- Ms. Rosenberg is well-versed in the romance market (both category and single title). She is a frequent speaker at romance conferences. The Rosenberg Group is accepting new clients working in romance fiction (please see my Areas of Interest for specific romance subgenres); women's fiction and chick lit. Does not want to receive inspirational, time travel, futuristic or paranormal.

HOW TO CONTACT Query via snail mail. Your query letter should not exceed one page in length. It should include the title of your work, the genre and/or sub-genre; the manuscript's word count; and a brief description of the work. If you are writing category romance, please be certain to let her know the line for which your work is intended. Accepts simultaneous submissions. Obtains most new clients through recommendations from others, solicitations, conferences.

TERMS Agent receives 15% commission on domestic and foreign sales. Offers written contract; 1-month notice must be given to terminate contract. Charges maximum of $350/year for postage and photocopying.

RECENT SALES Sold 27 titles in the last year.

WRITERS CONFERENCES RWA National Conference; BookExpo America.

RITA ROSENKRANZ LITERARY AGENCY

440 West End Ave., #15D, New York NY 10024. (212) 873-6333. **E-mail:** rrosenkranz@mindspring.com. **Website:** www.ritarosenkranzliteraryagency.com. **Contact:** Rita Rosenkranz. Member of AAR. Represents 40 clients.

- Prior to opening her agency, Ms. Rosenkranz worked as an editor at major New York publishing houses.

REPRESENTS Nonfiction. **Considers these nonfiction areas:** agriculture, Americana, animals, anthropology, archeology, architecture, art, autobiography, biography, business, child guidance, computers, cooking, crafts, creative nonfiction, cultural interests, current affairs, dance, decorating, diet/nutrition, design, economics, education, environment, ethnic, film, foods, gardening, gay/lesbian, government, health, history, hobbies, horticulture, how-to, humor, inspirational, interior design, investigative, language, law, literature, medicine, memoirs, military, money, multicultural, music, New Age, parenting, philosophy, photography, popular culture, politics, psychology, regional, religious, satire, science, self-help, sex, software, spirituality, sports, technology, theater, true crime, war, women's issues, women's studies.

"This agency focuses on adult nonfiction, stresses strong editorial development and refinement before submitting to publishers, and brainstorms ideas with authors." Actively seeks authors who are well paired with their subject, either for professional or personal reasons.

HOW TO CONTACT Send query letter only (no proposal) via regular mail or e-mail. Submit proposal package with SASE only on request. No fax queries. Accepts simultaneous submissions. Responds in 2 weeks to queries. Obtains most new clients through directory listings, solicitations, conferences, word of mouth.

TERMS Agent receives 15% commission on domestic sales; 20% commission on foreign sales. Offers written contract, binding for 3 years; 3-month written notice must be given to terminate contract. Charges clients for photocopying. Makes referrals to editing services.

RECENT SALES *Mindshift: How Ordinary and Extraordinary People Have Transformed Their Lives Through Learning—And You Can Too*, by Barbara A. Oakley (Tarcher); *On the Verge: Experience the Stillness of Presence, the Pulse of Potential, and the Power of Being Fully Alive*, by Cara Bradley (New World Library); *Lost Science*, by Kitty Ferguson (Sterling); *Power to the Poet*, by Diane Luby Lane (Beyond Words/Atria).

TIPS "Identify the current competition for your project to make sure the project is valid. A strong cover letter is very important to help get to the next step."

ANDY ROSS LITERARY AGENCY

767 Santa Ray Ave., Oakland CA 94610. (510)238-8965. **E-mail:** andyrossagency@hotmail.com. **Website:** www.andyrossagency.com. **Contact:** Andy Ross. "I opened my literary agency in 2008. Prior to that, I was the owner of the legendary Cody's Books in Berkeley for 30 years. My agency represents books in a wide range of nonfiction genres including: narrative nonfiction, science, journalism, history, popular culture, memoir, and current events. I also represent literary, commercial, historical, crime, upmarket women's fiction, and YA fiction. For nonfiction, I look for writing with a strong voice, robust story arc, and books that tell a big story about culture and society by authors with the authority to write about their subject. In fiction, I like stories about real people in the real world. No vampires and trolls, thank you very much. I don't represent poetry, science fiction, paranormal, and romance. Authors I represent include: Daniel Ellsberg, Jeffrey Moussaieff Masson, Anjanette Delgado, Elisa Kleven, Tawni Waters, Randall Platt, Mary Jo McConahay, Gerald Nachman, Michael Parenti, Paul Krassner, Milton Viorst, and Michele Anna Jordan. I am a member of the Association of Author Representatives (AAR). Check out my website and blog." Estab. 2008. Member of AAR. Represents See website for client list. clients.

I was the owner of Cody's Books in Berkeley California for 30 years.

REPRESENTS Nonfiction, fiction, novels, juvenile books, scholarly books. **Considers these nonfiction areas:** anthropology, autobiography, biography, child guidance, cooking, creative nonfiction, cultural interests, current affairs, economics, education, environment, ethnic, gay/lesbian, government, history, investigative, juvenile nonfiction, language, law, literature, memoirs, military, parenting, philosophy, popular culture, politics, psychology, science, sociology, technology, war, women's issues, women's studies, young adult. **Considers these fiction areas:** commercial, contemporary issues, historical, juvenile, literary, middle grade, picture books, young adult.

"This agency specializes in general nonfiction, politics and current events, history, biography, journalism and contemporary culture as well as literary, commercial, and YA fiction." Does not want to receive poetry.

HOW TO CONTACT Queries should be less than half page. Please put the word "query" in the title header of the e-mail. In the first sentence, state the category of the project. Give a short description of the book and your qualifications for writing. Accepts simultaneous submissions. Responds in 1 week to queries.

TERMS Agent receives 15% commission on domestic sales; 20% commission on foreign sales or other deals made through a sub-agent. Offers written contract.

RECENT SALES See my website.

JANE ROTROSEN AGENCY LLC

85 Broad St., 28th Floor, New York NY 10004. (212)593-4330. **Fax:** (212)935-6985. **Website:** www.janerotrosen.com. Estab. 1974. Member of AAR. Other memberships include Authors Guild. Represents more than 100 clients.

MEMBER AGENTS Jane Rotrosen Berkey (not taking on clients); Andrea Cirillo, acirillo@janerotrosen.com (general fiction, suspense, and women's fiction); Annelise Robey, arobey@janerotrosen.com (women's fiction, suspense, mystery, literary fiction, and select nonfiction); Meg Ruley, mruley@janerotrosen.com (commercial fiction, including suspense, mysteries, romance, and general fiction); Christina Hogrebe, chogrebe@janerotrosen.com (young adult, new adult, book club fiction, romantic comedies, mystery, and suspense); Amy Tannenbaum, atannenbaum@janerotrosen.com (contemporary romance, psychological suspense, thrillers, and new adult, as well as women's fiction that falls into that sweet spot between literary and commercial, memoir, narrative and prescriptive non-fiction in the areas of health, business, pop culture, humor, and popular psychology); Rebecca Scherer rscherer@janerotrosen.com (women's fiction, mystery, suspense, thriller, romance, upmarket/literary-leaning fiction); Jessica Errera (assistant to Christina and Rebecca).

REPRESENTS Nonfiction, novels. **Considers these nonfiction areas:** business, health, humor, memoirs, popular culture, psychology, narrative nonfiction. **Considers these fiction areas:** commercial, literary, mainstream, mystery, new adult, romance, suspense, thriller, women's, young adult.

Jane Rotrosen Agency is best known for representing writers of commercial fiction: thrillers, mystery, suspense, women's fiction, romance, historical novels, mainstream fiction, young adult, etc. We also work with authors of memoirs, narrative and prescriptive nonfiction.

HOW TO CONTACT Check website for guidelines. Accepts simultaneous submissions. Obtains most new clients through recommendations from others.

TERMS Agent receives 15% commission on domestic sales; 20% commission on foreign sales. Offers written contract, binding for 3 years; 2-month notice must be given to terminate contract. Charges clients for photocopying, express mail, overseas postage, book purchase.

THE RUDY AGENCY

825 Wildlife Ln., Estes Park CO 80517. (970)577-8500. **E-mail:** mak@rudyagency.com; claggett@rudyagency.com. **Website:** www.rudyagency.com. **Contact:** Maryann Karinch. "We are a full-service agency, meaning that we partner with authors from proposal stage through implementation of a promotion plan (nonfiction) and provide guidance on manuscript development (nonfiction and fiction). We welcome both experienced, published authors and first-timers. We are a boutique agency; out clientele is limited to allow up to give proper attention to every client." Estab. 2004. Adheres to AAR canon of ethics. Represents 24 clients.

Prior to becoming an agent, Ms. Karinch was, and continues to be, an author of nonfiction books—covering the subjects of health/medicine and human behavior. Prior to that, she was in public relations and marketing: areas of expertise she also applies in her practice as an agent.

MEMBER AGENTS Maryann Karinch and Hilary Claggett (selected nonfiction).

REPRESENTS Nonfiction, fiction, novels, scholarly books. **Considers these nonfiction areas:** Americana, anthropology, archeology, architecture, autobiography, biography, business, child guidance, computers, cooking, creative nonfiction, cultural interests, current affairs, diet/nutrition, design, economics, education, environment, gay/lesbian, government, health, history, how-to, inspirational, investigative, law, literature, medicine, memoirs, military, money, parenting, popular culture, politics, psychology, science, self-help, sex, sociology, sports, technology, theater, true crime, war, women's issues, women's studies. **Considers these fiction areas:** action, adventure, commercial, contemporary issues, crime, erotica, feminist, gay, historical, inspirational, lesbian, literary, military, multicultural, sports, thriller, women's.

"We support authors from the proposal stage through promotion of the published work. We work in partnership with publishers to promote the published work and coach authors in their role in the marketing and public relations campaigns for the book." Actively seeking projects with social value, projects that open minds to new ideas and interesting lives, and projects that entertain through good storytelling. Does not want to receive poetry, screenplays, novellas, religion books, children's lit, and joke books.

HOW TO CONTACT "Query us. If we like the query, we will invite a complete proposal (or complete ms if writing fiction). No phone queries, please. We won't hang up on you, but it makes it easier if you send us a note first." Accepts simultaneous submissions. Responds in under 3 weeks to non-fiction proposals and 8 weeks to invited manuscripts. Obtains most new clients through recommendations from others, solicitations.

TERMS Agent receives 15% commission on domestic sales. Offers written contract, binding for 1 year.

RECENT SALES *Isadora Duncan's Neck*, by Tim Rayborn (Skyhorse); *Control the Conversation*, by James O. Pyle (Red Wheel/Weiser); *Unavailable Men*, by Marni Feuerman (New World Library).

TIPS "Present yourself professionally. Know what we need to see in a query and what a proposal for a work of non-fiction must contain before you contact us."

REGINA RYAN PUBLISHING ENTERPRISES, INC.

251 Central Park W., 7D, New York NY 10024. **E-mail:** https://app.authors.me/submit/regina-ryan-books. **Website:** www.reginaryanbooks.com. **Contact:** Regina Ryan. "We are a boutique agency that represents significant books of nonfiction, both adult and juvenile." Estab. 1976. Member of AAR.

Prior to becoming an agent, Ms. Ryan was an editor at Alfred A. Knopf, editor-in-chief of Macmillan Adult Trade, and a book producer.

REPRESENTS Nonfiction. **Considers these nonfiction areas:** Americana, animals, anthropology, archeology, architecture, autobiography, biography, business, child guidance, cooking, cultural interests, diet/nutrition, environment, foods, gardening, health, history, horticulture, medicine, parenting, popular culture, politics, psychology, recreation, science, self-help, sex, sports, travel, true crime, women's issues, women's studies, adult and juvenile nonfiction: narrative nonfiction; natural history (especially birds and birding); popular science, lifestyle, sustainability, mind-body-spirit;.

"We are always looking for new and exciting books in our areas of interest, including well-written narrative nonfiction, architecture, history, politics, natural history (especially birds), science (especially the brain), the environment, women's issues, parenting, cooking, psychology, health, wellness, diet, lifestyle, sustainability, popular reference, and leisure activities including sports, narrative travel, and gardening. We represent books that have something new and fresh to say, are well-written and that will, if possible, make the world a better place." Actively seeking narrative nonfiction, food related travel projects, brain science.

HOW TO CONTACT All queries must come through the following site https://app.authors.me/submit/regina-ryan-books. Accepts simultaneous submissions. "We try to respond in 4-6 weeks but only if we are interested in pursuing the project. If you don't hear from us in that time frame, it means that we are not interested." Obtains most new clients through internet submissions.

TERMS Agent receives 15% commission on domestic and foreign sales. Offers written contract. Charges clients for all out-of-pocket expenses (e.g., long distance calls, messengers, freight, copying) if it's more than just a nominal amount.

RECENT SALES *The Friendly Orange Glow: The Untold Story of the PLATO Learning System and the Dawn of Cyberculture*, by Brian Dear; *What's Wrong With My Weed?*, by David Deardorff and Kathryn Wadsworth; *Itch! Everything You Didn't Want to Know about What Makes You Scratch*, by Anita Sanchez; *Craft Wines*, by Richard Bender; *Hair: A Human History*, by Kurt Stenn; *Wildlife Spectacles: Mass Migrations, Mating Rituals, and Other Fascinating Animal Behaviors*, by Vladimir Dinets; *Connecting in the Land of Dementia*, by Deborah Shouse; *The Backyard Birdsong Guide*, by Donald Kroodsma.

TIPS "It's important to include an analysis of comparable books that have had good sales, as well as an analysis of competitive books, that explains why your proposed book is different. Both are essential."

SADLER CHILDREN'S LITERARY

(815)209-6252. **E-mail:** submissions.sadlerliterary@gmail.com. **Website:** www.sadlerchildrensliterary.com. **Contact:** Jodell Sadler. "Sadler Children's Literary is an independent literary agency, serving aspiring authors and illustrators and branding careers through active media and marketing management in the field of children's literature." Member of AAR. Signatory of WGA.

REPRESENTS Nonfiction, fiction, novels, juvenile books. **Considers these nonfiction areas:** creative nonfiction, juvenile nonfiction, young adult. **Considers these fiction areas:** juvenile, middle grade, picture books, young adult.

- Actively seeks picture book author-illustrators or illustrators interested in picture book writing, or illustrators of MG illustrated titles or graphic novels. Please place this in the subject line when you query. Does not want fantasy. "It's not for me. I'm open to KidLit categories from board books to YA novels. My particular focus is on picture books from author-illustrators."

HOW TO CONTACT "E-mail submissions only from conferences and events, including participation in webinars and webinar series courses at KidLitCollege. Your subject line should read 'Code provided—(Genre) Title_by_Author' and specifically addressed to me. I prefer a short letter: Hook (why my agency), pitch for you project, and bio (brief background and other categories you work in). All submissions in body of the e-mail, no attachments. Query and complete picture book text; first 10 pages for longer genre category. If you are an illustrator or author-illustrator, I encourage you to contact me, and please send a link to your online portfolio." Accepts simultaneous submissions. "I only obtain clients through writing conferences and SCBWI, Writer's Digest, and KidLitCollege.com webinars and events."

TERMS Standard rate. Provided on contract.

RECENT SALES *Snow Beast* and *Dog Adoption Day* (Roaring Brook Press, Macmillan, 2017, 2018) by author-illustrator, Phil Gosier; *Mr. McGinty's Monarchs* (Sleeping Bear Press, 2016) by Linda Vander Heyden.

THE SAGALYN AGENCY / ICM PARTNERS

Chevy Chase MD **E-mail:** info@sagalyn.com. **E-mail:** query@sagalyn.com. **Website:** www.sagalyn.com. Estab. 1980. Member of AAR.

MEMBER AGENTS Raphael Sagalyn; Brandon Coward; Abby Serino.

REPRESENTS Nonfiction. **Considers these nonfiction areas:** biography, business, creative nonfiction, economics, popular culture, science, technology.

- "Our list includes upmarket nonfiction books in these areas: narrative history, biography, business, economics, popular culture, science, technology."

HOW TO CONTACT Please send e-mail queries only. Accepts simultaneous submissions.

TIPS "We receive 1,000-1,200 queries a year, which in turn lead to 2 or 3 new clients. See our website for sales information and recent projects."

VICTORIA SANDERS & ASSOCIATES

440 Buck Rd., Stone Ridge NY 12484. (212)633-8811. **E-mail:** queriesvsa@gmail.com. **Website:** www.victoriasanders.com. **Contact:** Victoria Sanders. Estab. 1992. Member of AAR. Signatory of WGA. Represents 135 clients.

MEMBER AGENTS Victoria Sanders; Bernadette Baker-Baughman; Jessica Spivey.

REPRESENTS Nonfiction, fiction, novels, short story collections, juvenile books. **Considers these nonfiction areas:** autobiography, biography, cooking, cultural interests, current affairs, ethnic, film, foods, gay/lesbian, government, history, humor, law, literature, memoirs, music, parenting, popular culture, politics, psychology, satire, theater, translation, women's issues, women's studies. **Considers these fiction areas:** action, adventure, cartoon, comic books, contemporary issues, crime, detective, ethnic, family saga, feminist, gay, historical, humor, inspirational, juvenile, lesbian, literary, mainstream, middle grade, multicultural, multimedia, mystery, new adult, picture books, suspense, thriller, women's, young adult.

HOW TO CONTACT Authors who wish to contact us regarding potential representation should send a query letter with the first 3 chapters (or about 25 pages) pasted into the body of the message to queriesvsa@gmail.com. We will only accept queries via e-mail. Query letters should describe the project and the author in the body of a single, 1-page e-mail that does not contain any attached files. Important note: Please paste the first 3 chapters of your manuscript (or about 25 pages, and feel free to round up to a chapter break) into the body of your e-mail." Accepts simultaneous submissions. Responds in 1-4 weeks, although occasionally it will take longer. "We will not respond to e-mails with attachments or attached files."

TERMS Agent receives 15% commission on domestic sales; 20% commission on foreign/film sales. Offers written contract.

TIPS "Limit query to letter (no calls) and give it your best shot. A good query is going to get a good response."

SCHIAVONE LITERARY AGENCY, INC.

236 Trails End, West Palm Beach FL 33413-2135. (561)966-9294. **Fax:** (561)966-9294. **E-mail:** profschia@aol.com. **Website:** www.publishersmarketplace.com/members/profschia; www.schiavoneliteraryagencyinc.blogspot.com. **Contact:** Dr. James Schiavone, CEO, corporate offices in Florida; Jennifer DuVall, president, New York office. Estab. 1996. Other memberships include National Education Association. Represents 40+ clients.

Prior to opening his agency, Dr. Schiavone was a full professor of developmental skills at the City University of New York and author of 5 trade books and 3 textbooks. Jennifer DuVall has many years of combined experience in office management and agenting.

MEMBER AGENTS James Schiavone, profschia@aol.com; Jennifer DuVall, jendu77@aol.com.

REPRESENTS Nonfiction, fiction, novels, scholarly books. We specialize in Celebrity memoirs. **Considers these nonfiction areas:** biography, business, cooking, health, history, politics, science, sports, true crime. **Considers these fiction areas:** literary, mainstream, mystery, romance, suspense, thriller, young adult.

This agency specializes in celebrity biography and autobiography and memoirs. Actively seeking celebrity memoirs. Does not want to receive poetry.

HOW TO CONTACT "One-page e-mail queries only. Absolutely no attachments. Postal queries are not accepted. No phone calls. We do not consider poetry, short stories, anthologies or children's books. Celebrity memoirs only. No scripts or screen plays. We handle dramatic, film and TV rights, options, and screen plays for books we have agented. We are not interested in work previously published in any format (e.g., self-published; online; e-books; Print On Demand). E-mail queries may be addressed to any of the agency's agents." Accepts simultaneous submissions. Responds in 2 weeks to queries; 6 weeks to mss. Obtains most new clients through referrals.

TERMS Agent receives 15% commission on domestic sales; 20% commission on foreign sales. Offers written contract. No fees.

RECENT SALES Check website.

WRITERS CONFERENCES Key West Literary Seminar; South Florida Writers' Conference; Tallahassee Writers' Conference, Million Dollar Writers' Conference; Alaska Writers Conference; Utah writers conference.

TIPS "We prefer to work with established authors published by major houses in New York. We will consider marketable proposals from new/previously unpublished writers."

WENDY SCHMALZ AGENCY

402 Union St., #831, Hudson NY 12534. (518)672-7697. **E-mail:** wendy@schmalzagency.com. **Website:** www.schmalzagency.com. **Contact:** Wendy Schmalz. Estab. 2002. Member of AAR.

REPRESENTS Juvenile books. **Considers these nonfiction areas:** young adult, Many nonfiction subjects are of interest to this agency. **Considers these fiction areas:** middle grade, young adult.

Not looking for picture books, science fiction or fantasy.

HOW TO CONTACT Accepts only e-mail queries. Paste synopsis into the e-mail. Do not attach the ms or sample chapters or synopsis. Replies to queries only if they want to read the ms. If you do not hear from this agency within 2 weeks, consider that a no. Accepts simultaneous submissions. Obtains clients through recommendations from others.

TERMS Agent receives 15% commission on domestic sales; 20% on foreign sales; 25% for Asia.

SUSAN SCHULMAN LITERARY AGENCY LLC

454 W. 44th St., New York NY 10036. (212)713-1633. **E-mail:** susan@schulmanagency.com. **E-mail:** queries@schulmanagency.com. **Website:** www.publishersmarketplace.com/members/schulman/. **Contact:** Susan Schulman. "A literary agency specializes in representing foreign rights, motion picture, television and allied rights, live stage including commercial theater, opera and dance adaptations, new media rights including e-book and digital applications, and other subsidiary rights on behalf of North American publishers and independent literary agents. The agency also represents its own clients domestically and internationally in all markets. The agency has a particular interest in fiction and nonfiction books for, by and about women and women's issues and interests. The agency's areas of focus include: commercial and literary fiction and nonfiction, specifically narrative memoir, politics, economics, social issues, history, urban planning, finance, law, health, psychology, body/

mind/spirit, and creativity and writing." Estab. 1980. Member of AAR. Signatory of WGA. Other memberships include Dramatists Guild, Writers Guild of America, East, New York Women in Film, Women's Media Group, Agents' Roundtable, League of New York Theater Women.

REPRESENTS Nonfiction, fiction, novels, juvenile books, feature film, TV scripts, theatrical stage play. **Considers these nonfiction areas:** anthropology, archeology, architecture, art, biography, business, child guidance, cooking, creative nonfiction, current affairs, economics, ethnic, government, health, history, juvenile nonfiction, law, money, popular culture, politics, psychology, religious, science, spirituality, women's issues, women's studies, young adult. **Considers these fiction areas:** commercial, contemporary issues, juvenile, literary, mainstream, new adult, religious, women's, young adult. **Considers these script areas:** theatrical stage play.

"We specialize in books for, by and about women and women's issues including nonfiction self-help books, fiction, and theater projects. We also handle the film, television. and allied rights for several agencies as well as foreign rights for several publishing houses." Actively seeking new nonfiction. Considers plays. Does not want to receive poetry, television scripts or concepts for television.

HOW TO CONTACT "For fiction: query letter with outline and three sample chapters, resume and SASE. For nonfiction: query letter with complete description of subject, at least one chapter, resume and SASE. Queries may be sent via regular mail or e-mail. Please do not submit queries via UPS or Federal Express. Please do not send attachments with e-mail queries Please incorporate the chapters into the body of the e-mail." Accepts simultaneous submissions. Responds in less than 1 week generally to a full query and 6 weeks to a full ms. Obtains most new clients through recommendations from others, solicitations, conferences.

TERMS Agent receives 15% commission on domestic sales; 20% commission on foreign sales. Offers written contract; 30-day notice must be given to terminate contract.

RECENT SALES Sold 70 titles in the last year; hundreds of subsidiary rights deals.

WRITERS CONFERENCES Geneva Writers' Conference (Switzerland); Columbus Writers' Conference; Skidmore Conference of the Independent Women's Writers Group. Attends Frankfurt Book Fair, London Book Fair, and BEA annually.

TIPS "Keep writing!" Schulman describes her agency as "professional boutique, long-standing, eclectic."

THE SCIENCE FACTORY

Scheideweg 34C, 20253 Hamburg, Germany. +49 40 4327 4959 (Germany); +44 (0)207 193 7296 (Skype). **E-mail:** info@sciencefactory.co.uk. **Website:** www.sciencefactory.co.uk. **Contact:** Peter Tallack. Estab. 2008.

Prior to his current position, Mr. Tallack was a director of the UK agency Conville & Walsh, publishing director at Weidenfeld & Nicolson, and on the editorial staff of the science journal *Nature*.

MEMBER AGENTS Peter Tallack; Tisse Takagi (interested in a wide range of explanatory and narrative nonfiction, particularly science, biography, music, dance, food, and history).

"The Science Factory is a leading UK literary agency specializing in stimulating nonfiction written by public intellectuals, academics and journalists. Experience of dealing directly in all markets, media and languages across the world." Represents "a diverse range of authors covering all areas of nonfiction, including history, biography, memoir, politics, current affairs and travel as well as science." Actively seeking popular science nonfiction, particularly from public intellectuals, academics and journalists.

HOW TO CONTACT E-query to info@sciencefactory.co.uk. "In the subject line please include the word 'query' and the name of your project or your name. If you are attaching a file (sample chapter for fiction, or proposal for nonfiction), please name the file with your name (not ours). You can expect a 'no' very quickly, often within a few days. If we're interested, we often respond by email or by phone to let you know. We may then offer to represent you, or we may ask for additional information about you or your project. In any case, we will let you know where we stand within 2-4 weeks." Accepts simultaneous submissions.

TIPS The Science Factory is the trading name of The Science Factory Ltd. Registered Office (not address for general correspondence): The Courtyard, Shoreham

Road, Upper Beeding, Steyning, West Sussex BN44 3TN, UK. Registered in England and Wales: Company No. 06498410. German VAT Registration No. DE 274 9743 26.

SCOVIL GALEN GHOSH LITERARY AGENCY, INC.

276 Fifth Ave., Suite 708, New York NY 10001. (212)679-8686. **Fax:** (212)679-6710. **E-mail:** info@sgglit.com. **Website:** www.sgglit.com. **Contact:** Russell Galen. Estab. 1992. Member of AAR. Represents 300 clients.

MEMBER AGENTS Russell Galen, russellgalen@sgglit.com (novels that stretch the bounds of reality; strong, serious nonfiction books on almost any subject that teach something new; no books that are merely entertaining, such as diet or pop psych books; serious interests include science, history, journalism, biography, business, memoir, nature, politics, sports, contemporary culture, literary nonfiction, etc.); Jack Scovil, jackscovil@sgglit.com; Anna Ghosh, annaghosh@sgglit.com (nonfiction proposals on all subjects, including literary nonfiction, history, science, social and cultural issues, memoir, food, art, adventure, and travel; adult commercial and literary fiction); Ann Behar, annbehar@sgglit.com (juvenile books for all ages).

HOW TO CONTACT E-mail queries only. Note how each agent at this agency has their own submission e-mail. Accepts simultaneous submissions.

SECRET AGENT MAN

P.O. Box 1078, Lake Forest CA 92609-1078. (949)354-8411. **E-mail:** scott@secretagentman.net. **Website:** www.secretagentman.net. **Contact:** Scott Mortenson. Estab. 1999.

REPRESENTS Nonfiction, fiction, novels. **Considers these nonfiction areas:** Americana, autobiography, biography, business, computers, creative nonfiction, film, government, history, how-to, humor, inspirational, investigative, law, literature, memoirs, music, parenting, politics, religious, sex, software, technology, true crime. **Considers these fiction areas:** action, crime, detective, horror, literary, mainstream, mystery, paranormal, psychic, religious, science fiction, spiritual, supernatural, suspense, thriller, westerns.

Mystery, thriller, suspense, and detective fiction. Select nonfiction projects that interesting and/or thought-provoking. Does not want to receive scripts or screenplays.

HOW TO CONTACT Query via e-mail only; include sample chapters, synopsis and/or outline. Prefers to read the real thing rather than a description, but a synopsis helps with getting an overall feel of the MS. Accepts simultaneous submissions. Responds in 2-6 weeks. Obtains most new clients through recommendations from others.

SELECTIC ARTISTS

9 Union Square, #123, Southbury CT 06488. **E-mail:** christopher@selectricartists.com. **E-mail:** query@selectricartists.com. **Website:** www.selectricartists.com. **Contact:** Christopher Schelling. "Selectric Artists is an agency for literary and creative management founded and run by Christopher Schelling. Selectric's client list includes best-selling and critically-acclaimed authors in many genres, as well as a few New York pop-rock musicians. Schelling has been an agent for over twenty years and previously held executive editor positions at Dutton and HarperCollins." Estab. 2011.

REPRESENTS Nonfiction, fiction, novels, short story collections, juvenile books. **Considers these nonfiction areas:** autobiography, biography, creative nonfiction, gay/lesbian, humor, juvenile nonfiction, literature, memoirs, music, popular culture, young adult. **Considers these fiction areas:** commercial, fantasy, feminist, gay, historical, horror, humor, juvenile, lesbian, literary, mainstream, science fiction, short story collections, suspense, thriller, young adult.

HOW TO CONTACT E-mail only. Consult agency website for status on open submissions. Accepts simultaneous submissions.

LYNN SELIGMAN, LITERARY AGENT

400 Highland Ave., Upper Montclair NJ 07043. (973)783-3631. **E-mail:** seliglit@aol.com. **Contact:** Lynn Seligman. Estab. 1986. Women's Media Group Represents 35 clients.

Prior to opening her agency, Ms. Seligman worked in the subsidiary rights department of Doubleday and Simon & Schuster, and served as an agent with Julian Bach Literary Agency (which became IMG Literary Agency). Foreign rights are represented by Books Crossing Borders, Inc.

REPRESENTS Nonfiction, fiction, novels. **Considers these nonfiction areas:** animals, anthropology, art, biography, business, child guidance, cooking, creative nonfiction, cultural interests, current affairs, diet/nutrition, education, ethnic, film, foods, government, health, history, how-to, humor, language, medicine, memoirs, money, music, parenting, photography, popular culture, psychology, science, self-help, sociology, true crime, women's issues, young adult. **Considers these fiction areas:** commercial, ethnic, fantasy, feminist, historical, horror, humor, literary, mainstream, mystery, new adult, romance, science fiction, women's, young adult.

"This agency specializes in general nonfiction and fiction. I also do illustrated and photography books and have represented several photographers for books."

HOW TO CONTACT Query with SASE or via e-mail with no attachments. Prefers to read materials exclusively but if not, please inform. Answers written queries, but does not respond to e-mail queries if not appropriate for the agency. Accepts simultaneous submissions. Responds in 2 weeks to queries; 2 months to mss. Obtains new clients through referrals from other writers and editors as well as unsolicited queries.

TERMS Agent receives 15% commission on domestic sales; 25% commission on foreign sales. Charges clients for photocopying, unusual postage, express mail, telephone expenses (checks with author first).

SERENDIPITY LITERARY AGENCY, LLC

305 Gates Ave., Brooklyn NY 11216. **E-mail:** rbrooks@serendipitylit.com; info@serendipitylit.com. **Website:** www.serendipitylit.com; facebook.com/serendipitylit. **Contact:** Regina Brooks. Estab. 2000. Member of AAR. Signatory of WGA. Represents 150 clients.

Prior to becoming an agent, Ms. Brooks was an acquisitions editor for John Wiley & Sons, Inc. and McGraw-Hill Companies.

MEMBER AGENTS Regina Brooks; Dawn Michelle Hardy (nonfiction, including sports, pop culture, blog and trend, music, lifestyle and social science); Folade Bell (literary and commercial women's fiction, YA, literary mysteries & thrillers, historical fiction, African-American issues, gay/lesbian, Christian fiction, humor and books that deeply explore other cultures; nonfiction that reads like fiction, including blog-to-book or pop culture); Nadeen Gayle (romance, memoir, pop culture, inspirational/ religious, women's fiction, parenting, young adult, mystery and political thrillers, and all forms of nonfiction); Rebecca Bugger (narrative nonfiction, investigative journalism, memoir, inspirational self-help, religion/spirituality, international, popular culture, and current affairs; literary and commercial fiction); Christina Morgan (literary fiction, crime fiction, and narrative nonfiction in the categories of pop culture, sports, current events and memoir); Jocquelle Caiby (literary fiction, horror, middle grade fiction, and children's books by authors who have been published in the adult market, athletes, actors, journalists, politicians, and musicians).

REPRESENTS Nonfiction, fiction, novels. **Considers these nonfiction areas:** Americana, anthropology, architecture, art, autobiography, biography, business, cooking, creative nonfiction, cultural interests, current affairs, inspirational, interior design, memoirs, metaphysics, music, parenting, popular culture, religious, self-help, spirituality, sports, travel, true crime, women's issues, women's studies, young adult. **Considers these fiction areas:** commercial, gay, historical, lesbian, literary, middle grade, mystery, romance, thriller, women's, young adult, Christian.

HOW TO CONTACT Check the website, as there are online submission forms for fiction, nonfiction and juvenile. Website will also state if we're temporarily closed to submissions to any areas. Accepts simultaneous submissions. Obtains most new clients through conferences, referrals.

TERMS Agent receives 15% commission on domestic sales; 20% commission on foreign sales. Offers written contract; 2-month notice must be given to terminate contract. Charges clients for office fees, which are taken from any advance.

TIPS "See the books *Writing Great Books For Young Adults* and *You Should Really Write A Book: How To Write Sell And Market Your Memoir.* We are looking for high concept ideas with big hooks. If you get writer's block try possibiliteas.co, it's a muse in a cup."

SEVENTH AVENUE LITERARY AGENCY

2052-124th St., South Surrey BC Canada. (604)538-7252. **Fax:** (604)538-7252. **E-mail:** info@seventhavenuelit.com. **Website:** www.seventhavenuelit.com. **Contact:** Robert Mackwood, owner and principal agent. "We represent authors from many countries and have sold rights, with our sub-agents in translation, on all continents." Estab. 1987. PACLA: Professional Association of Canadian Literary Agents. Represents 50 clients.

REPRESENTS Nonfiction. **Considers these nonfiction areas:** autobiography, biography, business, computers, economics, health, history, medicine, science, sports, technology, travel.

Seventh Avenue Literary Agency is both a literary agency and personal management agency. (The agency was originally called Contemporary Management.) "We also own and operate a self-publishing business imprint, Brilliant Idea Books, designed to help entrepreneurs and business owners develop their own '$20 business card' to further enhance their brand." Fiction

HOW TO CONTACT Query with SASE. Submit outline, synopsis, 1 sample chapter (nonfiction), publishing history, author bio, table of contents with proposal or query. Provide full contact information. Let us know the submission history. No fiction. Accepts simultaneous submissions. Obtains most new clients through recommendations from others, some solicitations. Does not add many new clients.

WRITERS CONFERENCES Willamette Writers Conference; Surrey Writers Conference; Okanagan Writers Conference.

TIPS "If you want your material returned, please include an SASE with adequate postage; otherwise, material will be recycled. (U.S. stamps are not adequate; they do not work in Canada.)"

THE SEYMOUR AGENCY

475 Miner St., Canton NY 13617. (239) 398-8209. **E-mail:** nicole@theseymouragency.com; julie@theseymouragency.com. **Website:** www.theseymouragency.com. Member of AAR. Signatory of WGA. Other memberships include RWA, Authors Guild, RWA, ACFW, HWA, MWA, SCBWI.

MEMBER AGENTS Nicole Rescinti, nicole@theseymouragency.com; Julie Gwinn, julie@theseymouragency.com; Tina Wainscott, tina@theseymouragency.com; Jennifer Wills, jennifer@theseymouragency.com; Lesley Sabga, lesley@theseymourageency.com.

REPRESENTS Nonfiction, fiction, novels, juvenile books. **Considers these nonfiction areas:** business, child guidance, cooking, crafts, cultural interests, decorating, diet/nutrition, design, foods, gardening, gay/lesbian, health, history, hobbies, how-to, humor, inspirational, juvenile nonfiction, literature, memoirs, metaphysics, military, music, New Age, parenting, philosophy, photography, popular culture, politics, psychology, religious, self-help, sex, spirituality, sports, theater, travel, true crime, war, women's issues, women's studies, young adult, ; cookbooks; any well-written nonfiction that includes a proposal in standard format and 1 sample chapter. **Considers these fiction areas:** action, adventure, commercial, contemporary issues, erotica, ethnic, experimental, family saga, fantasy, feminist, frontier, gay, horror, humor, inspirational, lesbian, literary, mainstream, metaphysical, middle grade, military, multicultural, multimedia, mystery, new adult, New Age, occult, paranormal, picture books, police, religious, romance, science fiction, spiritual, sports, supernatural, suspense, thriller, translation, urban fantasy, war, westerns, women's, young adult.

HOW TO CONTACT Accepts e-mail queries. Check online for guidelines. Accepts simultaneous submissions. Responds in 1 month to queries; 3 months to mss.

TERMS Agent receives 12-15% commission on domestic sales.

DENISE SHANNON LITERARY AGENCY, INC.

20 W. 22nd St., Suite 1603, New York NY 10010. **E-mail:** info@deniseshannonagency.com. **E-mail:** submissions@deniseshannonagency.com. **Website:** www.deniseshannonagency.com. **Contact:** Denise Shannon. Estab. 2002. Member of AAR.

Prior to opening her agency, Ms. Shannon worked for 16 years with Georges Borchardt and International Creative Management.

REPRESENTS Nonfiction, novels. **Considers these nonfiction areas:** biography, business, health, narrative nonfiction, politics, journalism, social history. **Considers these fiction areas:** literary.

"We are a boutique agency with a distinguished list of fiction and nonfiction authors."

HOW TO CONTACT "Queries may be submitted by post, accompanied by a SASE, or by e-mail to submissions@deniseshannonagency.com. Please include a description of the available book project and a brief bio including details of any prior publications. We will reply and request more material if we are interested. We request that you inform us if you are submitting material simultaneously to other agencies." Accepts simultaneous submissions.

RECENT SALES *Mister Monkey*, by Francine Prose (Harper); *Hotel Solitaire*, by Gary Shteyngart (Random House); *White Flights*, by Jess Row (Graywolf Press); *The Underworld*, by Kevin Canty (Norton).

TIPS "Please do not send queries regarding fiction projects until a complete manuscript is available for review. We request that you inform us if you are submitting material simultaneously to other agencies."

KEN SHERMAN & ASSOCIATES

1275 N. Hayworth Ave., Suite 103, Los Angeles CA 90046. (310)273-8840. **E-mail:** kenshermanassociates@gmail.com. **E-mail:** ksasubmissions@gmail.com. **Website:** www.kenshermanassociates.com. **Contact:** Ken Sherman. Estab. 1989. BAFTA (British Academy of Film and Television Arts). Represents 35 clients.

Prior to opening his agency, Mr. Sherman was with The William Morris Agency, The Lantz Office and Paul Kohner, Inc. He has taught The Business of Writing For Film and Television and The Book Worlds at UCLA and USC. He also lectures extensively at writer's conferences and film festivals around the U.S. He is currently a Commissioner of Arts and Cultural Affairs in the City of West Hollywood, and is on the International Advisory Board of the Christopher Isherwood Foundation.

REPRESENTS Nonfiction, fiction, novels, movie scripts, feature film, TV scripts, TV movie of the week, miniseries. teleplays, life rights, film/TV rights to books and life rights. **Considers these nonfiction areas:** agriculture, Americana, animals, anthropology, art, biography, business, child guidance, computers, cooking, crafts, current affairs, education, ethnic, film, gardening, gay/lesbian, government, health, history, horticulture, how-to, humor, interior design, language, memoirs, military, money, multicultural, music, New Age, philosophy, photography, popular culture, psychology, recreation, regional, religious, science, self-help, sex, sociology, software, spirituality, sports, translation, travel, true crime, women's issues, young adult, creative nonfiction. **Considers these fiction areas:** action, adventure, commercial, crime, detective, family saga, gay, literary, mainstream, middle grade, mystery, police, romance, satire, science fiction, suspense, thriller, women's, young adult. **Considers these script areas:** action, adventure, autobiography, biography, comedy, detective, episodic drama, ethnic, family saga, fantasy, feature film, feminist, frontier, gay, historical, horror, inspirational, juvenile, lesbian, mainstream, miniseries, movie scripts, multimedia, mystery, police, regional, romantic comedy, romantic drama, science fiction, supernatural, suspense, thriller, TV movie of the week, We represent book, film, tv writers and often sell film and and tv rights to books and life rights.

HOW TO CONTACT Contact by referral only, please. Reports in approximately 1 month. Accepts simultaneous submissions. Obtains most new clients through recommendations from others.

TERMS Agent receives 15% commission on domestic and foreign sales; 10-15% commission on film sales. Offers written contract. Charges clients for reasonable office expenses (postage, photocopying, etc.).

WRITERS CONFERENCES Maui Writers' Conference; Squaw Valley Writers' Workshop; Santa Barbara Writers' Conference; Screenwriting Conference in Santa Fe; Aspen Summer Words Literary Festival including The Aspen Institute, the San Francisco Writer's Conference, Eugene International Film Festival, The Chautauqua Institute - Writer's Conference, La Jolla Writer's Conference, Central Coast Writer's Conference (California), etc.

WENDY SHERMAN ASSOCIATES, INC.

138 W. 25th St., Suite 1018, New York NY 10001. (212)279-9027. **E-mail:** submissions@wsherman.com. **Website:** www.wsherman.com. **Contact:** Wendy Sherman. "We are a well-established boutique agency with a focus on quality fiction and nonfiction in a wide range of subjects. We are a hands-on agency that offers access to the best editors and publishers in the business. Our collective and individual experience, and relationships throughout the industry make us consistently successful in managing literary careers for our clients." Estab. 1999. Member of AAR.

Prior to opening the agency, Ms. Sherman held positions as vice president, executive director, associate publisher, subsidiary rights director, and sales and marketing director for major publishers including Simon & Schuster and Henry Holt.

MEMBER AGENTS Wendy Sherman (women's fiction that hits that sweet spot between literary and mainstream, Southern voices, suspense with a well-developed protagonist, anything related to food, dogs, mothers and daughters).

REPRESENTS Nonfiction, fiction, novels, juvenile books. **Considers these nonfiction areas:** creative nonfiction, foods, humor, memoirs, parenting, popular culture, psychology, self-help, narrative nonfiction. **Considers these fiction areas:** mainstream, Mainstream fiction that hits the sweet spot between literary and commercial.

"We specialize in developing new writers, as well as working with more established writers. My experience as a publisher has proven to be a great asset to my clients." Does not want genre fiction, picture books.

HOW TO CONTACT Query via e-mail only. "We ask that you include your last name, title, and the name of the agent you are submitting to in the subject line. For fiction, please include a query letter and your first 10 pages copied and pasted in the body of the e-mail. We will not open attachments unless they have been requested. For nonfiction, please include your query letter and author bio. Due to the large number of e-mail submissions that we receive, we only reply to e-mail queries in the affirmative. We respectfully ask that you do not send queries to our individual e-mail addresses." Accepts simultaneous submissions. Obtains most new clients through recommendations from other writers.

TERMS Agent receives standard 15% commission. Offers written contract.

RECENT SALES *All is Not Forgotten*, by Wendy Walker; *Z, A Novel of Zelda Fitzgerald*, by Therese Anne Fowler; *The Charm Bracelet*, by Viola Shipman; *The Silence of Bonaventure Arrow*, by Rita Leganski; *Together Tea*, by Marjan Kamali; *A Long Long Time Ago and Essentially True*, by Brigid Pasulka; *Lunch in Paris*, by Elizabeth Bard; *The Rules of Inheritance*, by Claire Bidwell Smith; *Eight Flavors*, by Sarah Lohman; *How to Live a Good Life*, by Jonathan Fields; *The Essential Oil Hormone Solution*, by Dr. Mariza Snyder.

TIPS "The bottom line is: do your homework. Be as well prepared as possible. Read the books that will help you present yourself and your work with polish. You want your submission to stand out."

BEVERLEY SLOPEN LITERARY AGENCY

131 Bloor St. W., Suite 711, Toronto ON M5S 1S3 Canada. (416)964-9598. **E-mail:** beverly@slopenagency.ca. **Website:** www.slopenagency.com. **Contact:** Beverley Slopen. Represents 70 clients.

Prior to opening her agency, Ms. Slopen worked in publishing and as a journalist.

REPRESENTS Nonfiction, novels. **Considers these nonfiction areas:** anthropology, archeology, autobiography, biography, business, creative nonfiction, current affairs, economics, investigative, psychology, sociology, true crime. **Considers these fiction areas:** commercial, literary, mystery, suspense.

"This agency has a strong bent toward Canadian writers." Actively seeking serious nonfiction that is accessible and appealing to the general reader. Does not want to receive fantasy, science fiction, or children's books.

HOW TO CONTACT Query by e-mail. Returns materials only with SASE (Canadian postage only). To submit a work for consideration, e-mail a short query letter and a few sample pages. Submit only one work at a time. "If we want to see more, we will contact the writer by phone or e-mail." Accepts simultaneous submissions. Responds in 1 month to queries only if interested.

TERMS Agent receives 15% commission on domestic sales; 10% commission on foreign sales. Offers written contract, binding for 2 years; 3-month notice must be given to terminate contract.

TIPS "Please, no unsolicited manuscripts."

THE SLW AGENCY, LLC

520 N. Kingsbury Plaza, Suite 2907, Chicago IL 60654. (847)207-2075. **E-mail:** shariwenk@swenkagency.com. **Contact:** Shari Wenk. Representing sports celebrities and sports journalists in book publishing, social media, marketing strategies, publicity, and brand development.

REPRESENTS Nonfiction. **Considers these nonfiction areas:** sports.

"This agency specializes in representing books written by sports celebrities and sports journalists."

HOW TO CONTACT Query via e-mail, but note the agency's specific specialty. Accepts simultaneous submissions.

ROBERT SMITH LITERARY AGENCY, LTD.

12 Bridge Wharf, 156 Caledonian Rd., London NI 9UU England. (44)(207)278-2444. **Fax:** (44)(207)833-5680. **E-mail:** robert@robertsmithliteraryagency.com. **Website:** www.robertsmithliteraryagency.com. **Contact:** Robert Smith. Other memberships include AAA. Represents 40 clients.

Prior to becoming an agent, Mr. Smith was a book publisher (Ebury Press, Sidgwick & Jackson, Smith Gryphon).

REPRESENTS Nonfiction. syndicated material. **Considers these nonfiction areas:** autobiography, biography, business, cooking, cultural interests, current affairs, diet/nutrition, film, foods, health, history, inspirational, investigative, medicine, memoirs, military, music, popular culture, self-help, sports, theater, true crime, war, entertainment.

Actively seeking autobiographies.

HOW TO CONTACT Contact via e-mail or snail mail (with SASE), provide initially a synopsis of chapters, an overview of the whole book, a sample chapter (if one is available), a review of competitive books, your personal profile and details of any previous media coverage, which you or your book has received. Prefers to read materials exclusively; please specify exclusive or simultaneous submission. Responds to all submissions. Responds in 2 weeks to queries. Obtains most new clients through recommendations from others, direct approaches to prospective authors.

TERMS Agent receives 15% commission on domestic sales; 20% commission on foreign sales. Offers written contract, binding for 3 months; 3-month notice must be given to terminate contract. Charges clients for couriers, photocopying, overseas mailings of mss (subject to client authorization).

RECENT SALES *Shamed*, by Sarbjit Kaur Athwal; *Living with a Serial Killer*, by Delia Balmer; *The Ghosts of Happy Valley*, by Juliet Barnes.

MICHAEL SNELL LITERARY AGENCY

H. Michael Snell, Inc., P.O. Box 1206, Truro MA 02666-1206. (508)349-3718. **E-mail:** query@michaelsnellagency.com. **Website:** michaelsnellagency.com. **Contact:** Patricia Snell, Michael Snell. 32 Bridge Road (for UPS, FedEx only) "We will celebrate our 40th Anniversary in 2018. The agency has sold over 1,500 books since it opened. Both Patricia and Michael Snell offer a wide range of services: author representation, book development, and writing/editing support." Estab. 1977. Represents 300 clients.

Prior to opening his agency in 1978, Mr. Snell served as an editor at Wadsworth and Addison-Wesley for 13 years.

MEMBER AGENTS Michael Snell (business, leadership, entrepreneurship, pets, sports); Patricia Snell, (business, business communications, parenting, relationships, health).

REPRESENTS Nonfiction. **Considers these nonfiction areas:** animals, business, creative nonfiction, health, how-to, parenting, psychology, science, self-help, women's issues, women's studies, fitness.

This agency specializes in how-to, self-help, and all types of business, business leadership, entrepreneurship titles, as well as books for small-business owners. "We place a wide range of topics, from low-level how-to to professional and reference. We are especially interested in business management, communication, strategy, culture building, performance enhancement, marketing and sales, finance and investment, marketing and sales, career development, executive skills, leadership, and organization development." Actively seeking strong book proposals in any area of business where a clear need exists for a new book. Does not want to receive fiction, children's books, or complete mss (considers proposals only).

HOW TO CONTACT Query by mail with SASE, or e-mail. Visit the agency's website for proposal guidelines. "We only consider new clients on an exclusive basis." Responds in 1 week to queries; 2 weeks to mss. Obtains most new clients through unsolicited mss, word of mouth, *Literary Market Place*, *Guide to Literary Agents*.

TERMS Agent receives 15% commission on all sales, domestic and foreign.

RECENT SALES *Lead Right for Your Company Type*, by William Schneider AMACOM); *Excuse me: The Survival Guide to Modern Business Etiquette*, by Rosanne Thomas AMACOM); *Finding Peace When Your Heart is in Pieces*, by Paul Coleman (Adams Media); *Fix It: Solving 240 of Your Toughest Business Problems*, by Roger Connors (Random House/Portfolio); *Body Language Secrets to Win More Negotiations*, by Greg Williams (Career Press); *Career Courage*, by Katie Kelley (AMACOM); *The Supply Chain Revolution*, by Suman Sarkar (AMACOM).

TIPS "Visit the agency's website to view recent sales and publications and to review guidelines for writing a book proposal. Prospective authors can also download model book proposals at the website. The agency only considers new clients on an exclusive basis. Simultaneous queries are OK; multiple submissions are not."

SPECTRUM LITERARY AGENCY

320 Central Park W., Suite 1-D, New York NY 10025. (212)362-4323. **Fax:** (212)362-4562. **Website:** www.spectrumliteraryagency.com. **Contact:** Eleanor Wood, president. Estab. 1976. SFWA Represents 90 clients.

MEMBER AGENTS Eleanor Wood (referrals only; commercial fiction: science fiction, fantasy, suspense, as well as select nonfiction); Justin Bell (science fiction, mysteries, and select nonfiction).

REPRESENTS Novels. **Considers these fiction areas:** commercial, fantasy, mystery, science fiction, suspense.

HOW TO CONTACT Unsolicited mss are not accepted. Send snail mail query with SASE. "The letter should describe your book briefly and include publishing credits and background information or qualifications relating to your work, and the first 10 pages of your work. Our response time is generally 2-3 months." Responds in 1-3 months to queries. Obtains most new clients through recommendations from authors.

TERMS Agent receives 15% commission on domestic sales. Deducts for photocopying and book orders.

TIPS "Spectrum's policy is to read only book-length manuscripts that we have specifically asked to see. Unsolicited manuscripts are not accepted. The letter should describe your book briefly and include publishing credits and background information or qualifications relating to your work, if any."

SPEILBURG LITERARY AGENCY

E-mail: speilburgliterary@gmail.com. **Website:** speilburgliterary.com. **Contact:** Alice Speilburg. Speilburg Literary Agency represents authors in fiction and nonfiction. Our client list includes award-winning and debut authors, to whom we offer hands-on editorial attention and business management throughout their publishing careers. Estab. 2012. SCBWI; MWA; RWA.

MEMBER AGENTS Alice Speilburg worked for John Wiley & Sons and Howard Morhaim Literary Agency, before launching Speilburg Literary. She is a member of Romance Writers of America, Mystery Writers of America, and Society of Children's Book Writers and Illustrators, and she is a board member of Louisville Literary Arts. She represents novels and narrative nonfiction. Eva Scalzo has a B.A. in the Humanities from the University of Puerto Rico and a M.A. in Publishing and Writing from Emerson College. She has spent her career in scholarly publishing, working for Houghton Mifflin, Blackwell Publishing, John Wiley & Sons, and Cornell University in a variety of roles. Eva is looking to represent all subgenres of Romance, with the exclusion of inspirational romance, as well as Young Adult fiction.

REPRESENTS Nonfiction, fiction, novels. **Considers these nonfiction areas:** biography, cultural interests, health, history, investigative, music, popular culture, psychology, science, travel, women's issues, women's studies, young adult. **Considers these fiction areas:** adventure, commercial, detective, fantasy, feminist, historical, horror, mainstream, mystery, police, romance, science fiction, suspense, urban fantasy, westerns, women's, young adult.

Does not want picture books; screenplays; poetry.

HOW TO CONTACT In the subject line of your query e-mail, please include "Query [AGENT'S FIRST NAME]" followed by the title of your project. For fiction, please send the query letter and the first three chapters. For nonfiction, please send the query letter and a proposal, which should include a detailed TOC and a sample chapter. Accepts simultaneous submissions.

SPENCERHILL ASSOCIATES

8131 Lakewood Main St., Building M, Suite 205, Lakewood Ranch FL 34202. (941)907-3700. **E-mail:** submission@spencerhillassociates.com. **Website:** www.spencerhillassociates.com. **Contact:** Karen Solem, Nalini Akolekar, Amanda Leuck, Sandy Harding, and Ali Herring. Member of AAR.

Prior to becoming an agent, Ms. Solem was editor-in-chief at HarperCollins and an associate publisher.

MEMBER AGENTS Karen Solem; Nalini Akolekar; Amanda Leuck; Sandy Harding; Ali Herring.

REPRESENTS Fiction, novels, juvenile books. **Considers these fiction areas:** commercial, contemporary issues, crime, detective, erotica, family saga, feminist, gay, historical, inspirational, lesbian, literary, mainstream, middle grade, multicultural, mystery, new adult, paranormal, police, religious, romance, suspense, thriller, women's, young adult.

"We handle mostly commercial women's fiction, historical novels, romance (historical, contemporary, paranormal, urban fantasy), thrillers, and mysteries. We also represent Christian fiction only—no nonfiction." No nonfiction, poetry, children's picture books, or scripts.

HOW TO CONTACT "We accept electronic submissions only. Please send us a query letter in the body of an e-mail, pitch us your project and tell us about yourself: Do you have prior publishing credits? Attach the first three chapters and synopsis preferably in .doc, rtf or txt format to your email. Send all queries to submission@spencerhillassociates.com. Or submit through the QueryManager link on our website. We do not have a preference for exclusive submissions, but do appreciate knowing if the submission is simultaneous. We receive thousands of submissions a year and each query receives our attention. Unfortunately, we are unable to respond to each query individually. If we are interested in your work, we will contact you within 12 weeks." Accepts simultaneous submissions. Responds in approximately 12 weeks.

TERMS Agent receives 15% commission on domestic sales; 20% commission on foreign sales. Offers written contract; 3-month notice must be given to terminate contract.

RECENT SALES A full list of sales and clients is available on the agency website.

THE SPIELER AGENCY

27 W. 20 St., Suite 302, New York NY 10011. (212)757-4439, ext. 1. **Fax:** (212)333-2019. **Website:** thespieleragency.com. **Contact:** Joe Spieler. Represents 160 clients.

Prior to opening his agency, Mr. Spieler was a magazine editor.

MEMBER AGENTS Victoria Shoemaker, victoria@thespieleragency.com (environment and natural history, popular culture, memoir, photography and film, literary fiction and poetry, and books on food and cooking); John Thornton, john@thespieleragency.com (nonfiction); Joe Spieler, joe@thespieleragency.com (nonfiction and fiction and books for children and young adults); Helen Sweetland, helen@thespieleragency.com (children's from board books through young adult fiction; adult general-interest nonfiction, including nature, green living, gardening, architecture, interior design, health, and popular science).

REPRESENTS Nonfiction, novels, juvenile books. **Considers these nonfiction areas:** architecture, biography, cooking, environment, film, foods, gardening, health, history, memoirs, photography, popular culture, science, sociology, spirituality. **Considers these fiction areas:** literary, middle grade, New Age, picture books, thriller, young adult.

HOW TO CONTACT "Before submitting projects to the Spieler Agency, check the listings of our individual agents and see if any particular agent shows a general interest in your subject (e.g. history, memoir, YA, etc.). Please send all queries either by e-mail or regular mail. If you query us by regular mail, we can only reply to you if you include a SASE." Accepts simultaneous submissions. Cannot guarantee a personal response to all queries. Obtains most new clients through recommendations, listing in *Guide to Literary Agents*.

TERMS Agent receives 15% commission on domestic sales. Charges clients for messenger bills, photocopying, postage.

WRITERS CONFERENCES London Book Fair.

PHILIP G. SPITZER LITERARY AGENCY, INC

50 Talmage Farm Ln., East Hampton NY 11937. (631)329-3650. **Fax:** (631)329-3651. **E-mail:** lukas.ortiz@spitzeragency.com; annelise.spitzer@spitzeragency.com. **E-mail:** kim.lombardini@spitzeragency.com. **Website:** www.spitzeragency.com. **Contact:** Lukas Ortiz. Estab. 1969. Member of AAR.

Prior to opening his agency, Mr. Spitzer served at New York University Press, McGraw-Hill, and the John Cushman Associates Literary Agency.

MEMBER AGENTS Philip G. Spitzer; Anne-Lise Spitzer; Lukas Ortiz.

REPRESENTS Novels. **Considers these nonfiction areas:** biography, current affairs, history, politics, sports, travel. **Considers these fiction areas:** literary, mainstream, suspense, thriller.

This agency specializes in mystery/suspense, literary fiction, sports, and general nonfiction (no how-to).

HOW TO CONTACT E-mail query containing synopsis of work, brief biography, and a sample chapter (pasted into the e-mail). Be aware that this agency openly says their client list is quite full. Obtains most new clients through recommendations from others.

TERMS Agent receives 15% commission on domestic sales; 20% commission on foreign sales.

RECENT SALES *The Jealous Kind*, by James Lee Burke (Simon & Schuster); *The Ex*, by Alafair Burke (HarperCollins); *Townie*, by Andre Dubus III (Norton); *The Wrong Side of Goodbye*, by Michael Connelly (Little, Brown & Co); *The Emerald Lie*, Ken Bruen (Mysterious Press/Grove-Atlantic); *Terror in the City of Champions*, by Tom Stanton (Lyons Press); *The Brain Defense*, by Kevin Davis (Penguin Press); *The Silent Girls*, by Eric Rickstad (HarperCollins); *Assume Nothing*, Gar Anthony Haywood (Severn House); *The Hanged Man*, by Gary Inbinder (Norton); *Cold Black Earth*, by Sam Reaves (Thomas & Mercer); *Mexico*, by Josh Barkan (Hogarth).

WRITERS CONFERENCES London Bookfair, Frankfurt, BookExpo America, Bouchercon.

NANCY STAUFFER ASSOCIATES

P.O. Box 1203, Darien CT 06820. (203)202-2500. **E-mail:** nancy@staufferliterary.com. **Website:** www.publishersmarketplace.com/members/nstauffer. **Contact:** Nancy Stauffer Cahoon. Nancy Stauffer Associates is a boutique agency representing a small, select group of authors of the highest quality literary fiction and literary narrative nonfiction. Other memberships include Authors Guild.

"Over the course of my more than 20 year career, I've held positions in the editorial, marketing, business, and rights departments of The New York Times, McGraw-Hill, and Doubleday. Before founding Nancy Stauffer Associates, I was Director of Foreign and Performing Rights then Director, Subsidiary Rights, for Doubleday, where I was honored to have worked with a diverse range of internationally known and bestselling authors of all genres."

REPRESENTS **Considers these fiction areas:** literary.

We do not represent mysteries, romance, action adventure, historical fiction, or thrillers

HOW TO CONTACT Accepts simultaneous submissions. Obtains most new clients through referrals from existing clients.

TERMS Agent receives 15% commission on domestic sales.

RECENT SALES *You Don't Have To Say You Love Me*, by Sherman Alexie; *Our Souls At Night*, by Kent Haruf; *Bone Fire*, by Mark Spragg.

STIMOLA LITERARY STUDIO

308 Livingston Ct., Edgewater NJ 07020. **E-mail:** info@stimolaliterarystudio.com. **E-mail:** see submission page on website. **Website:** www.stimolaliterarystudio.com. **Contact:** Rosemary B. Stimola. "A full service literary agency devoted to representing authors and author/illustrators of fiction and nonfiction, pre-school through young adult, who bring unique and substantive contributions to the industry." Estab. 1997. Member of AAR. PEN, Authors Guild, ALA Represents 75 clients.

Prior to opening her agency, Rosemary Stimola was an independent children's bookseller. Erica Rand Silverman, Senior Agent, was a high school teacher and former senior agent at Sterling Lord Literistic.

MEMBER AGENTS Rosemary B. Stimola; Erica Rand Silverman; Allison Remcheck; Adriana Stimola.

REPRESENTS Juvenile books. **Considers these nonfiction areas:** cooking, foods, juvenile nonfiction, young adult. **Considers these fiction areas:** middle grade, picture books, young adult.

Actively seeking remarkable middle grade, young adult fiction, and debut picture book author/illustrators. No institutional books.

HOW TO CONTACT Query via e-mail as per submission guidelines on website. Author/illustrators of picture books may attach text and sample art. A PDF dummy is preferred. Accepts simultaneous submissions. Responds in 3 weeks to queries "we wish to pursue further;" 2 months to requested mss. While unsolicited queries are welcome, most clients come through editor, agent, client referrals.

TERMS Agent receives 15% commission on domestic sales; 20% (if subagents are employed) commission on foreign sales. Offers written contract, binding for all children's projects. 60 days notice must be given to terminate contract.

TIPS Agent is hands-on, no-nonsense. May request revisions. Does not line edit but may offer suggestions for improvement before submission. Well-respected by clients and editors. "A firm but reasonable deal negotiator."

STONESONG

270 W. 39th St. #201, New York NY 10018. (212)929-4600. **E-mail:** editors@stonesong.com. **E-mail:** submissions@stonesong.com. **Website:** stonesong.com. Member of AAR. Signatory of WGA.

MEMBER AGENTS Alison Fargis; Ellen Scordato; Judy Linden; Emmanuelle Morgen; Leila Campoli (business, science, technology, and self improvement); Maria Ribas (cookbooks, self-help, health, diet, home, parenting, and humor, all from authors with demonstrable platforms; she's also interested in narrative nonfiction and select memoir); Melissa Edwards (children's fiction and adult commercial fiction, as well as select pop-culture nonfiction); Alyssa Jennette (children's and adult fiction and picture books, and has dabbled in humor and pop culture nonfiction); Madelyn Burt (adult and children's fiction, as well as select historical nonfiction).

REPRESENTS Nonfiction, fiction, novels, juvenile books. **Considers these nonfiction areas:** architecture, art, biography, business, cooking, crafts, creative nonfiction, cultural interests, current affairs, dance, decorating, diet/nutrition, design, economics, foods, gay/lesbian, health, history, hobbies, how-to, humor, interior design, investigative, literature, memoirs, money, music, New Age, parenting, photography, popular culture, politics, psychology, science, self-help, sociology, spirituality, sports, technology, women's issues, young adult. **Considers these fiction areas:** action, adventure, commercial, confession, contemporary issues, ethnic, experimental, family saga, fantasy, feminist, gay, historical, horror, humor, juvenile, lesbian, literary, mainstream, middle grade, military, multicultural, mystery, new adult, New Age, occult, paranormal, regional, romance, satire, science fiction, supernatural, suspense, thriller, urban fantasy, women's, young adult.

Does not represent plays, screenplays, picture books, or poetry.

HOW TO CONTACT Accepts electronic queries for fiction and nonfiction. Submit query addressed to a specific agent. Include first chapter or first 10 pages of ms. Accepts simultaneous submissions.

RECENT SALES *Sweet Laurel*, by Laurel Gallucci and Claire Thomas; *Terrain: A Seasonal Guide to Nature at Home*, by Terrain; *The Prince's Bane*, by Alexandra Christo; *Deep Listening*, by Jillian Pransky; *Change Resilience*, by Lior Arussy; *A Thousand Words*, by Brigit Young.

STRACHAN LITERARY AGENCY

P.O. Box 2091, Annapolis MD 21404. **E-mail:** query@strachanlit.com. **Website:** www.strachanlit.com. **Contact:** Laura Strachan. Strachan Literary Agency is a boutique agency focused on literary fiction and narrative nonfiction: *Compelling stories, well told.* Estab. 1998.

REPRESENTS Nonfiction, fiction, novels, short story collections, juvenile books. **Considers these nonfiction areas:** anthropology, art, creative nonfiction, cultural interests, current affairs, literature, memoirs, travel, Narrative. **Considers these fiction areas:** feminist, literary, multicultural, short story collections, translation, young adult.

"This agency specializes in literary fiction and narrative nonfiction."

HOW TO CONTACT Please query with description of project and short biographical statement. Do not paste or attach sample pages. Accepts simultaneous submissions.

ROBIN STRAUS AGENCY, INC.

The Wallace Literary Agency, 229 E. 79th St., Suite 5A, New York NY 10075. (212)472-3282. **Fax:** (212)472-3833. **E-mail:** info@robinstrausagency.com. **Website:** www.robinstrausagency.com. **Contact:** Ms. Robin Straus. Estab. 1983. Member of AAR.

Prior to becoming an agent, Robin Straus served as a subsidiary rights manager at Random House and Doubleday. She began her career in the editorial department of Little, Brown.

REPRESENTS **Considers these nonfiction areas:** biography, cooking, creative nonfiction, current affairs, environment, foods, gay/lesbian, health, history, memoirs, multicultural, music, parenting, popular culture, politics, psychology, science, travel, women's issues, mainstream science. **Considers these fiction areas:** commercial, contemporary issues, fantasy, feminist, literary, mainstream, science fiction, translation, women's.

Does not represent juvenile, young adult, horror, romance, Westerns, poetry, or screenplays.

HOW TO CONTACT E-query only. No physical mail accepted. See our website for full submission instructions. Email us a query letter with contact information, an autobiographical summary, a brief synopsis or description of your book project, submission history, and information on competition. If you wish, you may also include the opening chapter of your manuscript (pasted). While we do our best to reply to all queries, you can assume that if you haven't heard from us after six weeks, we are not interested. Accepts simultaneous submissions.

TERMS Agent receives 15% commission on domestic sales; 20% commission on foreign sales. Offers written contract.

THE STRINGER LITERARY AGENCY LLC

P.O. Box 111255, Naples FL 34108. **E-mail:** mstringer@stringerlit.com. **Website:** www.stringerlit.com. **Contact:** Marlene Stringer. This agency focuses on commercial fiction for adults and teens. Estab. 2008. Member of AAR. Signatory of WGA. RWA, MWA, ITW, SBCWI Represents 50 clients.

REPRESENTS Fiction, novels. **Considers these fiction areas:** commercial, crime, detective, fantasy, historical, horror, mainstream, multicultural, mystery, new adult, paranormal, police, romance, science fiction, suspense, thriller, urban fantasy, women's, young adult, No space opera SF.

This agency specializes in fiction. "We are an editorial agency, and work with clients to make their manuscripts the best they can be in preparation for submission. We focus on career planning, and help our clients reach their publishing goals. We advise clients on marketing and promotional strategies to help them reach their target readership. Because we are so hands-on, we limit the size of our list; however, we are always looking for exceptional voices and stories that demand we read to the end. You never know where the next great story is coming from." This agency is seeking thrillers, crime fiction (not true crime), mystery, women's fiction, single title and category romance, fantasy (all subgenera), earth-based science fiction (no space opera, aliens, etc.), and YA/teen. Does not want to receive picture books, MG, plays, short stories, or poetry. This is not the agency for inspirational romance or erotica. No space opera. The agency is not seeking nonfiction as of this time (2016).

HOW TO CONTACT Electronic submissions through website submission form only. Please make sure your ms is as good as it can be before you submit. Agents are not first readers. For specific information on what we like to see in query letters, refer to the information at www.stringerlit.com under the heading "Learn." Accepts simultaneous submissions. "We strive to respond quickly, but current clients' work always comes first." Obtains new clients through referrals, submissions, conferences.

TERMS Standard commission. "We do not charge fees."

RECENT SALES *The Conqueror's Wife*, by Stephanie Thornton; *When I'm Gone*, by Emily Bleeker; *Magic Bitter, Magic Sweet*, by Charlie N. Holmberg; *Belle Chasse*, by Suzanne Johnson; *Chapel of Ease*, by Alex Bledsoe; *Wilds of the Bayou*, by Susannah Sandlin; *Summit Lake*, by Charlie Donlea; The Jane Doe Series, by Liana Brooks; *The Mermaid's Secret*, by Katie Schickel; *The Sutherland Scandals*, by Anna Bradley; *Fly By Night*, by Andrea Thalasinos; The Joe Gale Mystery Series, by Brenda Buchanan; The Kate Baer Series, by Shannon Baker; Los Nephilim Series, by T. Frohock; The Dragonsworn Series, by Caitlyn McFarland; *The Devious Dr. Jekyll*, by Viola Carr; *The Dragon's Price*, by Bethany Wiggins; The Otter Bite Romance Series, by Maggie McConnell; *Machinations*, by Haley Stone; Film Rights to *Wreckage*, by Emily Bleeker.

WRITERS CONFERENCES RWA National and various other conferences.

TIPS "If your ms falls between categories, or you are not sure of the category, query and we'll let you know if we'd like to take a look. We strive to respond as quickly as possible. If you have not received a response in the time period indicated on website, please re-query."

THE STROTHMAN AGENCY, LLC

63 E. 9th St., 10X, New York NY 10003. **E-mail:** info@strothmanagency.com. **E-mail:** strothmanagency@gmail.com. **Website:** www.strothmanagency.com. **Contact:** Wendy Strothman, Lauren MacLeod. The Strothman Agency, LLC is a highly selective literary agency operating out of New York and Nashville, TN dedicated to advocating for authors of significant books through the entire publishing cycle. Recent Strothman Agency authors have won the Pulitzer Prize for Biography, the National Book Critics Circle Award for Non-Fiction, the Lincoln Prize, and many other awards. Clients have appeared on New York Times bestsellers lists, on National Book Award Long Lists, and two were Finalists for the Pulitzer Prize in History. Estab. 2003. Member of AAR. Represents 100+ clients.

Prior to becoming an agent, Ms. Strothman was head of Beacon Press (1983-1995) and executive vice president of Houghton Mifflin's Trade & Reference Division (1996-2002).

MEMBER AGENTS Wendy Strothman (history, narrative nonfiction, narrative journalism, science and nature, and current affairs); Lauren MacLeod (young adult fiction and nonfiction, middle grade novels, as well as adult narrative nonfiction, particularly food writing, science, pop culture and history).

REPRESENTS Nonfiction, juvenile books. **Considers these nonfiction areas:** anthropology, archeology, business, cooking, cultural interests, current affairs, economics, environment, foods, government, history, investigative, juvenile nonfiction, language, law, literature, popular culture, politics, science, sociology, true crime, war, women's issues, women's studies, young adult. **Considers these fiction areas:** middle grade, young adult.

Specializes in history, science, biography, politics, narrative journalism, nature and the environment, current affairs, narrative nonfiction, business and economics, young adult fiction and nonfiction, and middle grade fiction and nonfiction. "The Strothman Agency seeks out scholars, journalists, and other acknowledged and emerging experts in their fields. We specialize in history, science, narrative journalism, nature and the environment, current affairs, narrative nonfiction, business and economics, young adult fiction and nonfiction, middle grade fiction and nonfiction. We are not signing up projects in romance, science fiction, picture books, or poetry."

HOW TO CONTACT Accepts queries only via e-mail. See submission guidelines online. Accepts simultaneous submissions. "All e-mails received will be responded to with an auto-reply. If we have not replied to your query within 6 weeks, we do not feel that it is right for us." Accepts simultaneous submissions. Obtains most new clients through recommendations from others.

TERMS Agent receives 15% commission on domestic sales; 20% commission on foreign sales. Offers written contract; 30-day notice must be given to terminate contract.

THE STUART AGENCY

260 W. 52 St., #25C, New York NY 10019. (212)586-2711. **E-mail:** andrew@stuartagency.com. **Website:** stuartagency.com. **Contact:** Andrew Stuart. The Stuart Agency is a full-service literary agency representing a wide range of high-quality nonfiction and fiction, from Pulitzer Prize winners and entertainment figures to journalists, public intellectuals, academics and novelists. Estab. 2002.

Prior to his current position, Mr. Stuart was an agent with Literary Group International for five years. Prior to becoming an agent, he was an editor at Random House and Simon & Schuster.

MEMBER AGENTS Andrew Stuart (history, science, narrative nonfiction, business, current events, memoir, psychology, sports, literary fiction); Christopher Rhodes, christopher@stuartagency.com (literary and upmarket fiction [including thriller and horror]; connected stories/essays [humorous and serious]; memoir; creative/narrative nonfiction; history; religion; pop culture; and art & design); Rob Kirkpatrick, rob@stuartagency.com (memoir, biography, sports, music, pop culture, current events, history, and pop science).

REPRESENTS Nonfiction, novels. **Considers these nonfiction areas:** art, business, creative nonfiction, current affairs, history, memoirs, popular culture, psychology, religious, science, sports. **Considers these fiction areas:** horror, literary, thriller.

HOW TO CONTACT Query via online submission form on the agency website. Accepts simultaneous submissions.

EMMA SWEENEY AGENCY, LLC

245 E 80th St., Suite 7E, New York NY 10075. **E-mail:** info@emmasweeneyagency.com. **E-mail:** queries@emmasweeneyagency.com. **Website:** www.emmassweeneyagency.com. Estab. 2006. Member of AAR. Other memberships include Women's Media Group. Represents 80 clients.

Prior to becoming an agent, Ms. Sweeney was director of subsidiary rights at Grove Press. Since 1990, she has been a literary agent. Ms. Sutherland Brown was an Associate Editor at St. Martin's Press/Thomas Dunne Books and a freelance editor. Ms. Watson attended Hunter College where she earned a BA in English (with a focus on Creative Writing) and a BA in Russian Language & Culture.

MEMBER AGENTS Emma Sweeney, president; Margaret Sutherland Brown (commercial and literary fiction, mysteries and thrillers, narrative nonfiction, lifestyle, and cookbook); Kira Watson (children's literature).

REPRESENTS Nonfiction, fiction, novels, juvenile books. **Considers these nonfiction areas:** biography, cooking, creative nonfiction, cultural interests, decorating, diet/nutrition, design, foods, gardening, history, how-to, interior design, juvenile nonfiction, literature, memoirs, popular culture, psychology, religious, science, sex, sociology, young adult. **Considers these fiction areas:** commercial, contemporary issues, crime, historical, horror, juvenile, literary, mainstream, middle grade, mystery, new adult, suspense, thriller, women's, young adult.

Does not want erotica.

HOW TO CONTACT "We accept only electronic queries, and ask that all queries be sent to queries@emmasweeneyagency.com rather than to any agent directly. Please begin your query with a succinct (and hopefully catchy) description of your plot or proposal. Always include a brief cover letter telling us how you heard about ESA, your previous writing credits, and a few lines about yourself. We cannot open any attachments unless specifically requested, and ask that you paste the first 10 pages of your proposal or novel into the text of your e-mail." Accepts simultaneous submissions.

STEPHANIE TADE LITERARY AGENCY

P.O. Box 235, Durham PA 18039. (610)346-8667. **E-mail:** submissions@stephanietadeagency.com. **Website:** stephanietadeagency.com. **Contact:** Stephanie Tade.

Prior to becoming an agent, Ms. Tade was an executive editor at Rodale Press. She was also an agent with the Jane Rotrosen Agency.

MEMBER AGENTS Stephanie Tade, president and principal agent; Colleen Martell, editorial director and associate agent (cmartell@stadeagency.com).

REPRESENTS Nonfiction, fiction.

Seeks prescriptive and narrative nonfiction, specializing in physical, emotional, psychological and spiritual wellness, as well as select commercial fiction.

HOW TO CONTACT Query by e-mail or mail with SASE. "When you write to the agency, please include information about your proposed book, your publishing history and any media or online platform you have developed." Accepts simultaneous submissions.

TALCOTT NOTCH LITERARY

31 Cherry St., Suite 100, Milford CT 06460. (203)876-4959. **Fax:** (203)876-9517. **E-mail:** editorial@talcottnotch.net. **Website:** www.talcottnotch.net. **Contact:** Gina Panettieri, President. Represents 150 clients.

Prior to becoming an agent, Ms. Panettieri was a freelance writer and editor. Ms. Munier was Director of Acquisitions for Adams Media Corporation and had previously worked for Disney. Ms. Sulaiman holds degrees from Wellesley and the University of Chicago and had completed an internship with Sourcebooks prior to joining Talcott Notch. Mr. Shalabi holds an MS in Neuroscience and had completed internships with Folio and Veritas agencies as well as with Talcott Notch before joining Talcott Notch as a Junior Agent in late 2016.

MEMBER AGENTS Gina Panettieri, gpanettieri@talcottnotch.net (history, business, self-help, science, gardening, cookbooks, crafts, parenting, memoir, true crime and travel, YA, MG and women's fiction, paranormal, urban fantasy, horror, science fiction, historical, mystery, thrillers and suspense); Paula Munier, pmunier@talcottnotch.net (mystery/thriller, SF/fantasy, romance, YA, memoir, humor, pop culture, health & wellness, cooking, self-help, pop psych, New Age, inspirational, technology, science, and writing); Saba Sulaiman, ssulaiman@talcottnotch.net (upmarket literary and commercial fiction, romance [all subgenres except paranormal], character-driven psychological thrillers, cozy mysteries, memoir, young adult [except paranormal and sci-fi], middle grade, and nonfiction humor).

REPRESENTS Nonfiction, fiction, novels, short story collections, novellas, juvenile books. **Considers these nonfiction areas:** biography, business, cooking, crafts, cultural interests, current affairs, diet/nutrition, ethnic, foods, gardening, gay/lesbian, government, health, history, how-to, humor, inspirational, juvenile nonfiction, literature, memoirs, military, multicultural, parenting, popular culture, politics, psychology, science, self-help, sex, sociology, spirituality, technology, travel, true crime, women's issues, women's studies, young adult. **Considers these fiction areas:** action, adventure, commercial, contemporary issues, crime, ethnic, fantasy, feminist, gay, hi-lo, historical, horror, juvenile, lesbian, literary, mainstream, middle grade, multicultural, multimedia, mystery, new adult, New Age, paranormal, police, romance, science fiction, short story collections, suspense, thriller, urban fantasy, women's, young adult.

"We are most actively seeking projects featuring diverse characters and stories which expand the reader's understanding of our society and the wider world we live in."

HOW TO CONTACT Query via e-mail (preferred) with first 10 pages of the ms pasted within the body of the e-mail, not as an attachment. Accepts simultaneous submissions. Responds in 2 weeks to queries; 6-10 weeks to mss.

TERMS Agent receives 15% commission on domestic sales; 20% commission on foreign sales. Offers written contract, binding for 1 year.

RECENT SALES Agency sold 65 titles in the last year, including *The Widower's Wife* by Cate Holahan (Crooked Lane Books); *Tier One*, by Brian Andrews and Jeffrey Wilson (Thomas & Mercer) and *Beijing Red*, written as Alex Ryan (Crooked Lane Books); *Firestorm*, by Nancy Holzner (Berkley Ace Science Fiction); *The New Jersey Mob*, by Scott Deitche (Rowman and Littlefield); *The Homeplace*, by Kevin Wolf (St. Martin's Press); *The Goblin Crown*, by Robert Hewitt Wolfe (Turner Publishing); *The Unprescription for Autism*, by Janet Lintala (Amacom); *Disintegration*, by Richard Thomas (Random House/Alibi); *Red Line*, by Brian Thiem (Crooked Lane Books); and more.

TIPS "Know your market and how to reach them. A strong platform is essential in your book proposal. Can you effectively use social media/Are you a strong networker: Are you familiar with the book bloggers in your genre? Are you involved with the interest-specific groups that can help you? What can you do to break through the 'noise' and help present your book to your readers? Check our website for more tips and information on this topic."

TESSLER LITERARY AGENCY, LLC

27 W. 20th St., Suite 1003, New York NY 10011. (212)242-0466. **Website:** www.tessleragency.com. **Contact:** Michelle Tessler. "Tessler Literary Agency represents a select number of best-selling and emerging authors. Based in the Flatiron District in Manhattan, we are dedicated to writers of high quality fiction and nonfiction. Our clients include accomplished journalists, scientists, academics, experts in their field, as well as novelists and debut authors with unique voices and stories to tell. We value fresh, original writing that has a compelling point of view." The agency handles all domestic, UK, foreign, and subsidiary rights for clients—including film and television, audio, and e-formats. Estab. 2004. Member of AAR. Women's Media Group.

Prior to forming her own agency, Ms. Tessler worked at the prestigious literary agency Carlisle & Company (now Inkwell Management) and at the William Morris Agency.

REPRESENTS Nonfiction, fiction, novels. **Considers these nonfiction areas:** animals, autobiography, biography, business, cooking, creative nonfiction, cultural interests, current affairs, diet/nutrition, economics, education, environment, ethnic, foods, gardening, health, history, how-to, humor, investigative, literature, medicine, memoirs, military, money, multicultural, parenting, philosophy, photography, popular culture, psychology, religious, science, self-help, spirituality, technology, travel, women's issues, women's studies. **Considers these fiction areas:** commercial, ethnic, family saga, historical, literary, multicultural, women's.

"Tessler Literary Agency represents a select number of best-selling and emerging authors. Based in the Flatiron District in Manhattan, we are dedicated to writers of high quality fiction and nonfiction. Our clients include accomplished journalists, scientists, academics, experts in their field, as well as novelists and debut authors with unique voices and stories to tell. We value fresh, original writing that has a compelling point of view. Our list is diverse and far-reaching. In nonfiction, it includes narrative, popular science, memoir, history, psychology, business, biography, food, and travel. In many cases, we sign authors who are especially adept at writing books that cross many of these categories at once. In fiction, we represent literary, women's, and commercial. If your project is in keeping with the kind of books we take on, we want to hear from you." Does not want genre fiction or children's books or anthologies.

HOW TO CONTACT Submit query through online query form only. Accepts simultaneous submissions. New clients by queries/submissions through the website and recommendations from others.

TERMS Receives 15% commission on domestic sales; 20% on foreign sales. Offers written contract.

THOMPSON LITERARY AGENCY

115 W. 29th St., Third Floor, New York NY 10001. (347)281-7685. **E-mail:** submissions@thompsonliterary.com. **Website:** thompsonliterary.com. **Contact:** Meg Thompson, founder. Estab. 2014. Member of AAR. Signatory of WGA.

Before her current position, Ms. Thompson was with LJK Literary and the Einstein Thompson Agency.

MEMBER AGENTS Cindy Uh, senior agent; Kiele Raymond, senior agent; John Thorn, affiliate agent; Sandy Hodgman, director of foreign rights.

REPRESENTS Nonfiction, fiction, novels, juvenile books. **Considers these nonfiction areas:** autobiography, biography, business, cooking, crafts, creative nonfiction, current affairs, diet/nutrition, design, education, foods, health, history, how-to, humor, inspirational, interior design, juvenile nonfiction, memoirs, multicultural, popular culture, politics, science, self-help, sociology, sports, travel, women's issues, women's studies, young adult. **Considers these fiction areas:** commercial, contemporary issues, experimental, fantasy, feminist, historical, juvenile, literary, middle grade, multicultural, picture books, women's, young adult.

The agency is always on the lookout for both commercial and literary fiction, as well as young adult and children's books. "Nonfiction, however, is our specialty, and our interests include biography, memoir, music, popular science, politics, blog-to-book projects, cookbooks, sports, health and wellness, fashion, art, and popular culture." "Please note that we do not accept submissions for poetry collections or screenplays, and we only consider picture books by established illustrators."

HOW TO CONTACT "For fiction: Please send a query letter, including any salient biographical information or previous publications, and attach the first 25 pages of your manuscript. For nonfiction: Please send a query letter and a full proposal, including biographical information, previous publications, credentials that qualify you to write your book, marketing information, and sample material. You should address your query to whichever agent you think is best suited for your project." Accepts simultaneous submissions. Responds in 6 weeks if interested.

THREE SEAS LITERARY AGENCY

P.O. Box 444, Sun Prairie WI 53590. (608)834-9317. **E-mail:** queries@threeseaslit.com. **Website:** threeseasagency.com. **Contact:** Michelle Grajkowski, Cori Deyoe. Estab. 2000. Member of AAR. Other memberships include RWA (Romance Writers of America), SCBWI Represents 55 clients.

Since its inception, 3 Seas has sold more than 500 titles worldwide. Ms. Grajkowski's authors have appeared on all the major lists including *The New York Times*, *USA Today* and *Publishers Weekly*. Prior to joining the agency in 2006, Ms. Deyoe was a multi-published author. She represents a wide range of authors and has sold many projects at auction.

MEMBER AGENTS Michelle Grajkowski (romance, women's fiction, young adult and middle grade fiction, select nonfiction projects); Cori Deyoe (all sub-genres of romance, women's fiction, young adult, middle grade, picture books, thrillers, mysteries and select nonfiction); Linda Scalissi (women's fiction, thrillers, young adult, mysteries and romance).

REPRESENTS Nonfiction, novels. **Considers these fiction areas:** middle grade, mystery, picture books, romance, thriller, women's, young adult.

"We represent more than 50 authors who write romance, women's fiction, science fiction/fantasy, thrillers, young adult and middle grade fiction, as well as select nonfiction titles. Currently, we are looking for fantastic authors with a voice of their own." 3 Seas does not represent poetry or screenplays.

HOW TO CONTACT E-mail queries only; no attachments, unless requested by agents. For fiction, please e-mail the first chapter and synopsis along with a cover letter. Also, be sure to include the genre and the number of words in your manuscript, as well as pertinent writing experience in your query letter. For nonfiction, e-mail a complete proposal, including a query letter and your first chapter. For picture books, query with complete text. Accepts simultaneous submissions. Obtains most new clients through recommendations from others, conferences.

TERMS Agent receives 15% commission on domestic sales; 20% commission on foreign sales. Offers written contract.

RECENT SALES Bestselling authors, including Jennifer Brown, Katie MacAlister, Kerrelyn Sparks, and C.L. Wilson.

TRANSATLANTIC LITERARY AGENCY

2 Bloor St. E., Suite 3500, Toronto ON M4W 1A8 Canada. (416)488-9214. **E-mail:** info@transatlanticagency.com. **Website:** transatlanticagency.com. The Transatlantic Agency represents adult and children's authors of all genres, including illustrators. We do not handle stage plays, musicals or screenplays. Please review the agency website and guidelines carefully before making any inquiries, as each agent has their own particular submission guidelines.

MEMBER AGENTS Trena White (upmarket, accessible non-fiction: current affairs, business, culture, politics, technology, and the environment); Amy Tompkins (adult: literary fiction, historical fiction, women's fiction including smart romance, narrative non-fiction, and quirky or original how-to books; children's: early readers, middle grade, young adult, and new adult); Stephanie Sinclair (literary fiction, upmarket women's and commercial fiction, literary thriller and suspense, YA crossover; narrative nonfiction, memoir, investigative journalism and true crime); Samantha Haywood (literary fiction and upmarket commercial fiction, specifically literary thrillers and upmarket mystery, historical fiction, smart contemporary fiction, upmarket women's fiction and cross-over novels; narrative nonfiction, including investigative journalism, politics, women's issues, memoirs, environmental issues, historical narratives, sexuality, true crime; graphic novels (fiction/nonfiction): preferably full length graphic novels, story collections considered, memoirs, biographies, travel narratives); Jesse Finkelstein (nonfiction: current affairs, business, culture, politics, technology, religion, and the environment); Marie Campbell (middle grade fiction); Shaun Bradley (referrals only; adult literary fiction and narrative nonfiction, primarily science and investigative journalism); Sandra Bishop (fiction; nonfiction: biography, memoir, and positive or humorous how-to books on advice/relationships, mind/body/spirit, religion, healthy living, finances, life-hacks, traveling, living a better life); Fiona Kenshole (children's and young adult; only accepting submissions from referrals or conferences she attends as faculty); Lynn Bennett (not accepting submissions or new clients); David Bennett (children's, young adult, adult).

REPRESENTS Nonfiction, novels, juvenile books.

"In both children's and adult literature, we market directly into the US, the United Kingdom and Canada." Represents adult and children's authors of all genres, including illustrators. Does not want to receive picture books, musicals, screenplays or stage plays.

HOW TO CONTACT Always refer to the website, as guidelines will change, and only various agents are open to new clients at any given time. Obtains most new clients through recommendations from others.

TERMS Agent receives 15% commission on domestic sales; 20% commission on foreign sales. Offers written contract; 45-day notice must be given to terminate contract. This agency charges for photocopying and postage when it exceeds $100.

RECENT SALES Sold 250 titles in the last year.

S©OTT TREIMEL NY

434 Lafayette St., New York NY 10003. (212)505-8353. **E-mail:** general@scotttreimelny.com. **Website:** scotttreimelny.blogspot.com; www.scotttreimelny.com. **Contact:** Chris Hoyt. Estab. 1995. Member of AAR. Other memberships include The Authors Guild, SCBWI, PEN America.

Mr. Treimel began his career as an assistant to Marilyn E. Marlow at Curtis Brown, a rights agent for Scholastic, a book packager and rights agent for United Feature Syndicate, a freelance editor, a rights consultant for HarperCollins Children's Books, and the founding director of Warner Bros. Worldwide Publishing.

MEMBER AGENTS Scott Treimel.

REPRESENTS Juvenile books. **Considers these nonfiction areas:** juvenile nonfiction, young adult. **Considers these fiction areas:** cartoon, hi-lo, juvenile, middle grade, new adult, picture books, young adult, All children's categories from broad books through older YA, includes picture books, easy readers, chapter books, series, etc.

This agency specializes in tightly focused segments of the trade and institutional markets, representing both authors and illustrators of books for children and teens.

HOW TO CONTACT No longer accepts unsolicited submissions. Wants—via e-mail only—queries from writers recommended by his clients and/or editor pals or that he has met at conferences. Accepts simultaneous submissions.

TERMS Agent receives 15% commission on domestic sales; 20% commission on foreign sales. Offers verbal or written contract, standard terms. Only charges fees for books needed to sell subsidiary rights—foreign, film, etc.

RECENT SALES *Misunderstood Shark*, by Ame Dyckman (Scholastic); *Crimson*, by Arthur Slade (HarperCanada); *Willa and the Bear*, by Philomena O'Neill (Sterling); *Wee Beastie Series*, by Ame Dyckman (Simon & Schuster); *A Bike Like Sergio's*, by Maribeth Boelts (Candlewick); *Lucky Jonah*, by Richard Scrimger (HarperCanada); *Other Word-ly*, by Yee-Lum Mak (Chronicle); *The Passover Cowboy*, by Barbara Diamond Golden (Apples & Honey Press); *Dandy*, by Ame Dyckman (Little Brown); *You Don't Want a Unicorn*, by Ame Dyckman (Little Brown); *Par-Tay*, by Eloise Greenfield (Alazar Press); *The Women Who Caught the Babies*, by Eloise Greenfield (Alazar Books); *Pupunzel*, by Maribeth Boelts (Random House); *The Fairy Dog Mother*, by Maribeth Boelts (Random House); *Flickers*, by Arthur Slade (HarperCanada).

WRITERS CONFERENCES Avalon Full Manuscript Writers Retreat; Pacific Coast Children's Writers Workshop; Pikes Peak Writers' Conference; Southwest Writers' Conference; SCBWI NY, NJ, PA, NC, SC, VA, Bologna; The New School.

TIPS "We look for dedicated authors and illustrators able to sustain longtime careers in our increasingly competitive field. I want fresh, not derivative story concepts with overly familiar characters. We look for gripping stories, characters, pacing, and themes. We read for an authentic (to the age) point-of-view, and look for original voices. We spend significant time hunting for the best new work, and do launch debut talent each year. It is best not to send warm-up manuscripts or those already seen all over town."

TRIADA US

P.O. Box 561, Sewickley PA 15143. (412)401-3376. **E-mail:** uwe@triadaus.com; brent@triadaus.com; laura@triadaus.com; lauren@triadaus.com; amelia@triadaus.com. **Website:** www.triadaus.com. **Contact:** Dr. Uwe Stender, President. Triada US was founded by Dr. Uwe Stender over twelve years ago. Since then, the agency has built a high-quality list of fiction and nonfiction for kids, teens, and adults. Triada US titles are consistently critically acclaimed and translated into multiple languages. Estab. 2004. Member of AAR.

MEMBER AGENTS Uwe Stender; Brent Taylor; Laura Crockett; Lauren Spieller; Amelia Appel.

REPRESENTS Nonfiction, fiction, novels, juvenile books. **Considers these nonfiction areas:** biography, business, cooking, crafts, creative nonfiction, cultural interests, current affairs, diet/nutrition, economics, education, environment, ethnic, foods, gardening, health, history, how-to, juvenile nonfiction, literature, memoirs, music, parenting, popular culture, politics, science, self-help, sports, true crime, women's issues, young adult. **Considers these fiction areas:** action, adventure, comic books, commercial, contemporary issues, crime, detective, ethnic, family saga, fantasy, gay, historical, horror, juvenile, lesbian, literary, mainstream, middle grade, multicultural, mystery, new adult, occult, picture books, police, suspense, thriller, urban fantasy, women's, young adult.

Actively seeking fiction and non-fiction across a broad range of categories of all age levels.

HOW TO CONTACT E-mail queries preferred. Please paste your query letter and the first 10 pages of your ms into the body of a message e-mailed to the agent of your choice. Please note: a rejection from 1 Triada US agent is a rejection from all. Triada US agents personally respond to all queries and requested material and pride themselves on having some of the fastest response times in the industry. Obtains most new clients through submission inbox (query letters and requested mss), client referrals, and conferences.

TERMS Triada US retains 15% commission on domestic sales and 20% commission on foreign and translation sales. Offers written contract; 30-day notice must be given prior to termination.

RECENT SALES *The Hemingway Thief*, by Shaun Harris (Seventh Street); *Finder's Fee*, by Summer Heacock (Mira); *Not Perfect*, by Elizabeth LaBan (Lake Union); *Sometime After Midnight*, by L. Philips (Viking); *The Diminished*, by Kaitlyn Sage Patterson (Harlequin Teen); *A Short History of the Girl Next Door*, by Jared Reck (Knopf); *Chaotic Good*, by Whitney Gardner (Knopf); *Project Pandora*, by Aden Polydoros (Entangled Teen); *Skulls!*, by Blair Thornburgh (Atheneum).

TRIDENT MEDIA GROUP

41 Madison Ave., 36th Floor, New York NY 10010. (212)333-1511. **Website:** www.tridentmediagroup.com. **Contact:** Ellen Levine. Member of AAR.

MEMBER AGENTS Kimberly Whalen, ws.assistant@tridentmediagroup (commercial fiction and nonfiction, including women's fiction, romance, suspense, paranormal, and pop culture); Alyssa Eisner Henkin (picture books through young adult fiction, including mysteries, period pieces, contemporary school-settings, issues of social justice, family sagas, eerie magical realism, and retellings of classics; children's/YA nonfiction: history, STEM/STEAM themes, memoir) Scott Miller, smiller@tridentmediagroup.com (commercial fiction, including thrillers, crime fiction, women's, book club fiction, middle grade, young adult; nonfiction, including military, celebrity and pop culture, narrative, sports, prescriptive, and current events); Melissa Flashman, mflashman@tridentmediagroup.com (nonfiction: pop culture, memoir, wellness, popular science, business and economics, technology; fiction: adult and YA, literary and commercial); Don Fehr, dfehr@tridentmediagroup.com (literary and commercial fiction, young adult fiction, narrative nonfiction, memoirs, travel, science, and health); John Silbersack, silbersack.assistant@tridentmediagroup.com (fiction: literary fiction, crime fiction, science fiction and fantasy, children's, thrillers/suspense; nonfiction: narrative nonfiction, science, history, biography, current events, memoirs, finance, pop culture); Erica Spellman-Silverman; Ellen Levine, levine.assistant@tridentmediagroup.com (popular commercial fiction and compelling nonfiction, including memoir, popular culture, narrative nonfiction, history, politics, biography, science, and the odd quirky book); Mark Gottlieb (fiction: science fiction, fantasy, young adult, graphic novels, historical, middle grade, mystery, romance, suspense, thrillers; nonfiction: business, finance, history, religious, health, cookbooks, sports, African-American, biography, memoir, travel, mind/body/spirit, narrative nonfiction, science, technology); Alexander Slater, aslater@tridentmdiagroup.com (children's, middle grade, and young adult fiction); Amanda O'Connor, aoconnor@tridentmediagroup.com; Tara Carberry, tcarberry@tridentmediagroup.com (women's commercial fiction, romance, new adult, young adult, and select nonfiction); Alexa Stark, astark@tridentmediagroup.com (literary fiction, upmarket commercial fiction, young adult, memoir, narrative nonfiction, popular science, cultural criticism and women's issues).

REPRESENTS **Considers these nonfiction areas:** biography, business, cooking, creative nonfiction, current affairs, economics, health, history, memoirs, military, popular culture, politics, religious, science, sports, technology, travel, women's issues, young adult, middle grade. **Considers these fiction areas:** commercial, crime, fantasy, historical, juvenile, literary, middle grade, mystery, new adult, paranormal, picture books, romance, science fiction, suspense, thriller, women's, young adult.

Actively seeking new or established authors in a variety of fiction and nonfiction genres.

HOW TO CONTACT Submit through the agency's online submission form on the agency website. Query only one agent at a time. If you e-query, include no attachments. Accepts simultaneous submissions.

TIPS "If you have any questions, please check FAQ page before e-mailing us."

UNITED TALENT AGENCY

142 W. 57th St., 6th Floor, New York NY 10019. (212)581-3100. **Website:** www.theagencygroup.com. **Contact:** Marc Gerald.

Prior to becoming an agent, Mr. Gerald owned and ran an independent publishing and entertainment agency.

MEMBER AGENTS Marc Gerald (no queries); Juliet Mushens, UK Literary division, juliet.mushens@unitedtalent.com (high-concept novels, thrillers, YA, historical fiction, literary fiction, psychological suspense, reading group fiction, SF and fantasy); Sasha Raskin, sasah.raskin@unitedtalent.com (popular science, business books, historical narrative nonfiction, narrative and/or literary nonfiction, historical fiction, and genre fiction like sci-fi but when it fits the crossover space and isn't strictly confined to its genre); Sarah Manning, sarah.manning@unitedtalent.com (enjoys crime, thrillers, historical fiction, commercial women's fiction, accessible literary fiction, fantasy and YA); Diana Beaumont, UK Literary division, diana.beaumont@unitedtalent.com (accessible literary fiction with a strong hook, historical fiction, crime, thrillers, women's commercial fiction that isn't too marshmallowy, cookery, lifestyle, celebrity books and memoir with a distinctive voice).

REPRESENTS Nonfiction, novels. **Considers these nonfiction areas:** business, cooking, history, memoirs, popular science, narrative nonfiction, literary nonfiction, lifestyle, celebrity. **Considers these fiction areas:** commercial, crime, fantasy, historical, literary, science fiction, suspense, thriller, women's, young adult.

HOW TO CONTACT To query Juliet: Please send your cover letter, first 3 chapters and synopsis by e-mail. Juliet replies to all submissions, and aims to respond within 8-12 weeks of receipt of e-mail. To query Sasha: e-query. To query Sarah: Please send you cover letter in the body of your e-mail with synopsis and first 3 chapters by e-mail. She responds to all submissions within 8-12 weeks. Accepts simultaneous submissions.

THE UNTER AGENCY

23 W. 73rd St., Suite 100, New York NY 10023. (212)401-4068. **E-mail:** jennifer@theunteragency.com. **Website:** www.theunteragency.com. **Contact:** Jennifer Unter. Estab. 2008. Member of AAR. Women Media Group

Ms. Unter began her book publishing career in the editorial department at Henry Holt & Co. She later worked at the Karpfinger Agency while she attended law school. She then became an associate at the entertainment firm of Cowan, DeBaets, Abrahams & Sheppard LLP where she practiced primarily in the areas of publishing and copyright law.

REPRESENTS Nonfiction, fiction, novels, short story collections, juvenile books. **Considers these nonfiction areas:** animals, art, autobiography, biography, cooking, creative nonfiction, current affairs, diet/nutrition, environment, foods, health, history, how-to, humor, juvenile nonfiction, law, memoirs, popular culture, politics, spirituality, sports, travel, true crime, women's issues, young adult, nature subjects. **Considers these fiction areas:** action, adventure, cartoon, commercial, family saga, inspirational, juvenile, mainstream, middle grade, mystery, paranormal, picture books, thriller, women's, young adult.

This agency specializes in children's, nonfiction, and quality fiction.

HOW TO CONTACT Send an e-query. There is also an online submission form. If you do not hear back from this agency within 3 months, consider that a no. Accepts simultaneous submissions. Responds in 3 months.

RECENT SALES A full list of recent sales/titles is available on the agency website.

UPSTART CROW LITERARY

244 Fifth Avenue, 11th Floor, New York NY 10001. **E-mail:** danielle.submission@gmail.com. **Website:** www.upstartcrowliterary.com. **Contact:** Danielle Chiotti, Alexandra Penfold. Estab. 2009. Member of AAR. Signatory of WGA.

MEMBER AGENTS Michael Stearns (not accepting submissions); Danielle Chiotti (all genres of young adult and middle grade fiction; adult upmarket commercial fiction [not considering romance, mystery/suspense/thriller, science fiction, horror, or erotica]; nonfiction in the areas of narrative/memoir, lifestyle, relationships, humor, current events, food, wine, and cooking); Ted Malawer (not accepting submissions); Alexandra Penfold (not accepting submissions); Susan Hawk (books for children and teens only).

REPRESENTS **Considers these nonfiction areas:** cooking, current affairs, foods, humor, memoirs. **Considers these fiction areas:** commercial, mainstream, middle grade, picture books, young adult.

HOW TO CONTACT Submit a query and 20 pages pasted into an e-mail. Accepts simultaneous submissions.

VERITAS LITERARY AGENCY

601 Van Ness Ave., Opera Plaza, Suite E, San Francisco CA 94102. (415)647-6964. **Fax:** (415)647-6965. **E-mail:** submissions@veritasliterary.com. **Website:** www.veritasliterary.com. **Contact:** Katherine Boyle. Member of AAR. Other memberships include Author's Guild and SCBWI.

MEMBER AGENTS Katherine Boyle, kboyle@veritasliterary.com (literary fiction, middle grade, young adult, narrative nonfiction/memoir, historical fiction, crime/suspense, history, pop culture, popular science, business/career); Michael Carr, michael@veritasliterary.com (historical fiction, women's fiction, science fiction and fantasy, nonfiction).

REPRESENTS Nonfiction, novels. **Considers these nonfiction areas:** business, history, memoirs, popular culture, women's issues. **Considers these fiction areas:** commercial, crime, fantasy, historical, literary, middle grade, new adult, science fiction, suspense, women's, young adult.

HOW TO CONTACT This agency accepts short queries or proposals via e-mail only. "Fiction: Please include a cover letter listing previously published work, a one-page summary and the first 5 pages in the body of the e-mail (not as an attachment). Nonfiction: If you are sending a proposal, please include an author biography, an overview, a chapter-by-chapter summary, and an analysis of competitive titles. We do our best to review all queries within 4-6 weeks; however, if you have not heard from us in 12 weeks, consider that a no." Accepts simultaneous submissions. If you have not heard from this agency in 12 weeks, consider that a no.

WADE & CO. LITERARY AGENCY, LTD

33 Cormorant Lodge, Thomas More St., London E1W 1AU United Kingdom. (44)(207)488-4171. **Fax:** (44) (207)488-4172. **E-mail:** rw@rwla.com. **Website:** www.rwla.com. **Contact:** Robin Wade. Estab. 2001.

Prior to opening his agency, Mr. Wade was an author.

MEMBER AGENTS Robin Wade.

"We are young and dynamic, and actively seek new writers across the literary spectrum." Does not want to receive poetry, plays, screenplays, children's books, film scripts, or short stories.

HOW TO CONTACT New proposals for full length adult and young adult books (excluding children's books or poetry) are always welcome. We much prefer to receive queries and submissions by e-mail, although we do, of course, accept proposals by post. There is no need to telephone in advance. Please provide a few details about yourself, a synopsis (i.e. a clear narrative summary of the complete story, of between say 1 and 6 pages in length) and the first 10,000 words or so (ideally as word.doc or PDF attachments) over e-mail. Accepts simultaneous submissions. Responds in 1 week to queries; 1 month to mss.

TERMS Agent receives 15% commission on domestic sales; 20% commission on foreign sales. Offers written contract; 1-month notice must be given to terminate contract.

TIPS "We seek manuscripts that are well written, with strong characters and an original narrative voice. Our absolute priority is giving the best possible service to the authors we choose to represent, as well as maintaining routine friendly contact with them as we help develop their careers."

WALES LITERARY AGENCY, INC.

1508 10th Ave. E. #401, Seattle WA 98102. (206)284-7114. **E-mail:** waleslit@waleslit.com. **Website:** www.waleslit.com. **Contact:** Elizabeth Wales; Neal Swain. Estab. 1990. Member of AAR. Other memberships include Authors Guild.

Prior to becoming an agent, Ms. Wales worked at Oxford University Press and Viking Penguin.

MEMBER AGENTS Elizabeth Wales; Neal Swain.

REPRESENTS Nonfiction, fiction, novels.

This agency specializes in quality mainstream fiction and narrative nonfiction. "We're looking for more narrative nonfiction writing about nature, science, and animals." Does not handle screenplays, children's picture books, genre fiction, or most category nonfiction (such as self-help or how-to books).

HOW TO CONTACT E-query with no attachments. Submission guidelines can be found at the agency website along with a list of current clients and titles. Accepts simultaneous submissions. Responds in 2 weeks to queries, 2 months to mss.

TERMS Agent receives 15% commission on domestic sales; 20% commission on foreign sales.

RECENT SALES *At Peace*, by Samuel Harrington, MD; *Victory Parade*, by Leela Corman (Grand Central Publishing); *Be Brave, Be Kind, Be Thankful*, by Heather Lende (Algonquin); *Three Sides Water*, by Peter Donahue.

TIPS "We are especially interested in work that espouses a progressive cultural or political view, projects a new voice, or simply shares an important, compelling story. We also encourage writers living in the Pacific Northwest, West Coast, Alaska, and Pacific Rim countries, and writers from historically underrepresented groups, such as gay and lesbian writers and writers of color, to submit work (but does not discourage writers outside these areas). Most importantly, whether in fiction or nonfiction, the agency is looking for talented storytellers."

WATERSIDE PRODUCTIONS, INC.

2055 Oxford Ave., Cardiff CA 92007. (760)632-9190. **Fax:** (760)632-9295. **E-mail:** admin@waterside.com. **Website:** www.waterside.com. Estab. 1982.

MEMBER AGENTS Bill Gladstone (big nonfiction books); Margot Maley Hutchinson (computer, health, psychology, parenting, fitness, pop culture, and business); Carole Jelen, carole@jelenpub.com (innovation and thought leaders especially in business, technology, lifestyle and self-help); David Nelson; Jill Kramer, watersideagentjk@aol.com (quality fiction with empowering themes for adults and YA (including crossovers); nonfiction, including mind-body-spirit, self-help, celebrity memoirs, relationships, sociology, finance, psychology, health and fitness, diet/nutrition, inspiration, business, family/parenting issues); Brad Schepp (e-commerce, social media and social commerce, careers, entrepreneurship, general business, health and fitness); Natasha Gladstone, (picture books, books with film tie-ins, books with established animated characters, and educational titles); Johanna Maaghul, johanna@waterside.com (nonfiction and select fiction); Kimberly Brabec, rights@waterside.com (Director of International Rights).

REPRESENTS Considers these nonfiction areas: business, computers, diet/nutrition, health, inspirational, money, parenting, popular culture, psychology, self-help, sociology, technology, fitness. **Considers these fiction areas:** mainstream, picture books, young adult.

8→ Specializes in computer and technical titles, and also represent other nonfiction genres, including self-help, cooking, travel, and more. Note that most agents here are nonfiction only, so target your query to the appropriate agent.

HOW TO CONTACT "Please read each agent bio [on the website] to determine who you think would best represent your genre of work. When you have chosen your agent, please write his or her name in the subject line of your e-mail and send it to admin@waterside.com with your query letter in the body of the e-mail, and your proposal or sample material as an attached word document." Nonfiction submission guidelines are available on the website. Accepts simultaneous submissions. Obtains most new clients through referrals from established client and publisher list.

TIPS "For new writers, a quality proposal and a strong knowledge of the market you're writing for goes a long way toward helping us turn you into a published author. We like to see a strong author platform."

⊘ WATKINS LOOMIS AGENCY, INC.

P.O. Box 20925, New York NY 10025. (212)532-0080. **Fax:** (646)383-2449. **E-mail:** assistant@watkinsloomis.com. **Website:** www.watkinsloomis.com. Estab. 1980. Represents 50+ clients.

MEMBER AGENTS Gloria Loomis, president; Julia Masnik, junior agent.

REPRESENTS Nonfiction, novels. **Considers these nonfiction areas:** ethnic.

8→ This agency specializes in literary fiction, biography, memoir, and political journalism.

HOW TO CONTACT *No unsolicited mss.* This agency does not guarantee a response to queries.

TERMS Agent receives 15% commission on domestic sales; 20% commission on foreign sales.

RECENT SALES A list of sales is available on the agency website.

WAXMAN LEAVELL LITERARY AGENCY, INC.

443 Park Ave. S, Suite 1004, New York NY 10016. (212)675-5556. **Fax:** (212)675-1381. **Website:** www.waxmanleavell.com.

MEMBER AGENTS Scott Waxman (nonfiction: history, biography, health and science, adventure, business, inspirational sports); Byrd Leavell (narrative nonfiction, sports, humor, and select commercial fiction); Holly Root (middle grade, young adult, women's fiction (commercial and upmarket), urban fantasy, romance, select nonfiction); Larry Kirschbaum (fiction and nonfiction; select self-published breakout books); Rachel Vogel (nonfiction: subject-driven narratives, memoirs and biography, journalism, popular culture and the occasional humor and gift book; selective fiction); Taylor Haggerty (young adult, historical, contemporary and historical romance, middle grade, women's, new adult); Cassie Hanjian (new adult novels, plot-driven commercial and upmarket women's fiction, historical fiction, psychological suspense, cozy mysteries and contemporary romance; for nonfiction, mind/body/spirit, self-help, health and wellness, inspirational memoir, food/wine (narrative and prescriptive), and a limited number of accessible cookbooks); Fleetwood Robbins (fantasy and speculative fiction—all subgenres); Molly O'Neill (middle grade and YA fiction and picture book author/illustrators, and—more selectively—narrative nonfiction [including children's/YA/MG, pop science/pop culture, and lifestyle/food/travel/cookbook projects by authors with well-established platforms]).

REPRESENTS Nonfiction, novels. **Considers these nonfiction areas:** biography, business, foods, health, history, humor, inspirational, memoirs, popular culture, science, sports, adventure. **Considers these fiction areas:** fantasy, historical, literary, mainstream, middle grade, mystery, paranormal, romance, science fiction, suspense, thriller, urban fantasy, women's, young adult.

HOW TO CONTACT To submit a project, please send a query letter only via e-mail to one of the addresses included on the website. Do not send attachments, though for fiction you may include 5-10 pages of your manuscript in the body of your e-mail. "Due to the high volume of submissions, agents will reach out to you directly if interested. The typical time range for consideration is 6-8 weeks." "Please do not query more than 1 agent at our agency simultaneously." (To see the types of projects each agent is looking for, refer to the Agent Biographies page on website.) Use these e-mails: scottsubmit@waxmanleavell.com; byrdsubmit@waxmanleavell.com; hollysubmit@waxmanleavell.com; rachelsubmit@waxmanleavell.com; and larrysubmit@waxmanleavell.com; taylorsubmit@waxmanleavell.com; cassiesubmit@waxmanleavell.com; mollysubmit@waxmanleavell.com. Accepts simultaneous submissions.

TERMS Agent receives 15% commission on domestic sales; 10% commission on foreign sales. Offers written contract; 2-month notice must be given to terminate contract.

⊘ CHERRY WEINER LITERARY AGENCY

925 Oak Bluff Ct., Dacula GA 30019-6660. (732)446-2096. **Fax:** (732)792-0506. **E-mail:** cherry8486@aol.com. **Contact:** Cherry Weiner. Estab. 1977. Represents 40 clients.

REPRESENTS Fiction, novels. **Considers these fiction areas:** action, adventure, commercial, contemporary issues, crime, detective, family saga, fantasy, frontier, gay, historical, horror, literary, mainstream, military, mystery, paranormal, police, psychic, romance, science fiction, supernatural, suspense, thriller, urban fantasy, westerns, women's.

This agency is currently not accepting new clients except by referral or by personal contact at writers' conferences. Specializes in fantasy, science fiction, westerns, mysteries (both contemporary and historical), historical novels, Native American works, mainstream, and all genre romances.

HOW TO CONTACT Only wishes to receive submissions from referrals and from writers she has met at conferences/events. Responds in 1 week to queries; 2 months to requested mss.

TERMS Agent receives 15% commission on domestic sales; 15% commission on foreign sales. Offers written contract. Charges clients for extra copies of mss, first-class postage for author's copies Mailing of books first class, express mail for important documents/mss.

RECENT SALES This agency prefers not to share information on specific sales.

WRITERS CONFERENCES Western Writers of America; BoucherCon; World Science Fiction Writers Conference; World Fantasy Conference; and many writer group workshops.

TIPS "Meet agents and publishers at conferences. Establish a relationship, then get in touch with them and remind them of the meeting and conference."

THE WEINGEL-FIDEL AGENCY

310 E. 46th St., 21E, New York NY 10017. (212)599-2959. **Contact:** Loretta Weingel-Fidel.

Prior to opening her agency, Ms. Weingel-Fidel was a psychoeducational diagnostician.

REPRESENTS Novels. **Considers these nonfiction areas:** art, autobiography, biography, dance, memoirs, music, psychology, science, sociology, technology, women's issues, women's studies, investigative journalism. **Considers these fiction areas:** literary, mainstream.

This agency specializes in commercial and literary fiction and nonfiction. Does not want to receive childrens books, self-help, science fiction, or fantasy.

HOW TO CONTACT Accepts writers by referral only. *No unsolicited mss.* Accepts simultaneous submissions.

TERMS Agent receives 15% commission on domestic sales; 20% commission on foreign sales. Offers written contract, binding for 1 year with automatic renewal.

TIPS "A very small, selective list enables me to work very closely with my clients to develop and nurture talent. I only take on projects and writers about which I am extremely enthusiastic."

WELLS ARMS LITERARY

New York NY **E-mail:** info@wellsarms.com. **Website:** www.wellsarms.com. Wells Arms Literary represents children's book authors and illustrators to the trade children's book market. Estab. 2013. Member of AAR. SCBWI, Society of Illustrators. Represents 25 clients.

Victoria's career began as an editor at Dial Books for Young Readers, then G. P. Putnam's Sons and then as the founding editorial director and Associate Publisher of Bloomsbury USA's Children's Division. She opened the agency in 2013.

REPRESENTS Nonfiction, fiction, novels, juvenile books. children's book illustrators. **Considers these nonfiction areas:** juvenile nonfiction, young adult. **Considers these fiction areas:** juvenile, middle grade, new adult, picture books, young adult.

"We focus on books for young readers of all ages: board books, picture books, readers, chapter books, middle grade, and young adult fiction." Actively seeking middle grade, young adult, magical realism, contemporary, romance, fantasy. "We do not represent to the textbook, magazine, adult romance or fine art markets."

HOW TO CONTACT E-query. Put "query" and your title in your e-mail subject line addressed to info@wellsarms.com. Accepts simultaneous submissions. We try to respond in a month's time. If no response, assume it's a no.

WERNICK & PRATT AGENCY

E-mail: submissions@wernickpratt.com. **Website:** www.wernickpratt.com. **Contact:** Marcia Wernick; Linda Pratt; Emily Mitchell. "Wernick & Pratt Agency provides each client with personal attention and the highest quality of advice and service that has been the hallmark of our reputations in the industry. We have the resources and accumulated knowledge to assist clients in all aspects of their creative lives including editorial input, contract negotiations, and subsidiary rights management. Our goal is to represent and manage the careers of our clients so they may achieve industry wide and international recognition, as well as the highest level of financial potential." Member of AAR. Signatory of WGA. SCBWI

Prior to co-founding Wernick & Pratt Agency, Ms. Wernick worked at the Sheldon Fogelman Agency, in subsidiary rights, advancing to director of subsidiary rights; Ms. Pratt also worked at the Sheldon Fogelman Agency. Emily Mitchell began her publishing career at Sheldon Fogelman Agency and then spent eleven years as an editor at Charlesbridge Publishing.

MEMBER AGENTS Marcia Wernick, Linda Pratt, Emily Mitchell.

REPRESENTS Juvenile books. **Considers these fiction areas:** middle grade, young adult.

"Wernick & Pratt Agency specializes in children's books of all genres, from picture books through young adult literature and everything in between. We represent both authors and illustrators. We do not represent authors of adult books." Wants people who both write and illustrate in the picture book genre; humorous young chapter books with strong voice, and which are unique and compelling; middle grade/YA novels, both literary and commercial. No picture book mss of more than 750 words, or mood pieces; work specifically targeted to the educational market; fiction about the American Revolution, Civil War, or World War II unless it is told from a very unique perspective.

HOW TO CONTACT Submit via e-mail only to submissions@wernickpratt.com. "Please indicate to which agent you are submitting." Detailed submission guidelines available on website. "Submissions will only be responded to further if we are interested in them. If you do not hear from us within 6 weeks of your submission, it should be considered declined." Accepts simultaneous submissions. Responds in 6 weeks.

WESTWOOD CREATIVE ARTISTS, LTD.

386 Huron St., Toronto ON M5S 2G6 Canada. (416)964-3302. **E-mail:** wca_office@wcaltd.com. **Website:** www.wcaltd.com. Westwood Creative Artists is Canada's largest literary agency. It's also one of the oldest and most respected. "Situated in Toronto's Annex neighbourhood, our staff of 11 includes 6 full-time book agents who are supported by an inhouse international rights agent and an outstanding network of twenty-four international co-agents. We take great pride in the enthusiastic response to our list from publishers around the world and in the wide praise our writers receive from Canadian and international critics. We are honored that many of the writers we represent have won and been shortlisted for such esteemed prizes as the Man Booker Prize, the Nobel

Prize, and the Scotiabank Giller Prize." Represents 350+ clients.

MEMBER AGENTS Carolyn Ford (literary fiction, commercial, women's/literary crossover, thrillers, serious narrative nonfiction, pop culture); Jackie Kaiser (President and COO); Michael A. Levine (Chairman); Hilary McMahon (Executive Vice President, fiction, nonfiction, children's); John Pearce (fiction and nonfiction); Bruce Westwood (Founder, Managing Director and CEO).

REPRESENTS Nonfiction, fiction, novels. **Considers these nonfiction areas:** biography, current affairs, history, parenting, science, journalism, practical nonfiction. **Considers these fiction areas:** commercial, juvenile, literary, thriller, women's, young adult.

"We take on children's and young adult writers very selectively. The agents bring their diverse interests to their client lists, but are generally looking for authors with a mastery of language, a passionate, expert or original perspective on their subject, and a gift for storytelling." "Please note that WCA does not represent screenwriters, and our agents are not currently seeking poetry or children's picture book submissions."

HOW TO CONTACT E-query only. Include credentials, synopsis, and no more than 10 pages. No attachments. Accepts simultaneous submissions.

TIPS "We will reject outright complete, unsolicited manuscripts, or projects that are presented poorly in the query letter. We prefer to receive exclusive submissions and request that you do not query more than one agent at the agency simultaneously. It's often best if you approach WCA after you have accumulated some publishing credits."

WHIMSY LITERARY AGENCY, LLC

49 N. 8th St., 6G, Brooklyn NY 11249. (212)674-7162. **E-mail:** whimsynyc@aol.com. **Contact:** Jackie Meyer. Whimsy Literary Agency LLC, specializes in nonfiction books and authors that educate, entertain, and inspire people. Represents 30 clients.

Prior to becoming an agent, Ms. Meyer was a VP at Warner Books (now Grand Central/Hachette) for 20 years.

MEMBER AGENTS Jackie Meyer.

REPRESENTS Nonfiction. **Considers these nonfiction areas:** art, autobiography, biography, business, child guidance, cooking, current affairs, diet/nutrition, design, education, foods, health, history, how-to, humor, inspirational, interior design, literature, memoirs, money, New Age, parenting, photography, popular culture, psychology, self-help, software, spirituality, technology, women's issues. **Considers these fiction areas:** commercial, inspirational, New Age, paranormal, picture books, psychic.

"Whimsy looks for non-fiction projects that are concept- and platform-driven. We seek books that educate, inspire, and entertain." Actively seeking experts in their field with integrated and established platforms.

HOW TO CONTACT Send your proposal via e-mail to whimsynyc@aol.com (include your media platform, table of contents with full description of each chapter). First-time authors: "We appreciate proposals that are professional and complete. Please consult the many fine books available on writing book proposals. We are not considering poetry, or screenplays. Please Note: Due to the volume of queries and submissions, we are unable to respond unless they are of interest to us." Accepts simultaneous submissions. Responds "quickly, but only if interested" to queries. *Does not accept unsolicited mss.* Obtains most new clients through recommendations from others, solicitations.

TERMS Agent receives 15% commission on domestic sales; 20% commission on foreign sales. Offers written contract.

WOLF LITERARY SERVICES, LLC

E-mail: queries@wolflit.com. **Website:** wolflit.com. "Wolf Literary Services, LLC is a full-service literary agency specializing in smart, quirky, ambitious books. We have a deep respect for the power of stories and we love authentic voices, compelling writing, and books that break the bounds of genre." Estab. 2008. Member of AAR. Signatory of WGA.

MEMBER AGENTS Kirsten Wolf (no queries); Kate Johnson (literary and upmarket fiction, memoir, cultural history, pop science, narrative nonfiction); Allison Devereux (literary and upmarket fiction, narrative nonfiction, cultural history and criticism, memoir, and biography); Rachel Crawford (literary fiction; high concept YA; and narrative nonfiction, particularly environmental and science journalism, ecological memoir, and queer and feminist pop culture).

REPRESENTS Nonfiction, fiction, novels. **Considers these nonfiction areas:** animals, anthropology, art, biography, creative nonfiction, economics, environment, film, foods, gay/lesbian, history, humor, investigative, literature, memoirs, parenting, science, travel, women's issues, women's studies. **Considers these fiction areas:** commercial, contemporary issues, family saga, fantasy, feminist, gay, historical, horror, lesbian, literary, science fiction, suspense, thriller, young adult, LGBTI+.

HOW TO CONTACT To submit a project, please send a query letter along with a 50-page writing sample (for fiction) or a detailed proposal (for nonfiction) to queries@wolflit.com. Samples may be submitted as an attachment or embedded in the body of the e-mail. Accepts simultaneous submissions.

RECENT SALES Dapper Dan of Harlem memoir (Random House); *Hardly Children*, by Laura Adamczyk (Farrar, Straus); *Bloodworth*, by Helen Klein Ross (Little, Brown); *Rubik*, by Elizabeth Tan (Unnamed Press).

WOLFSON LITERARY AGENCY

P.O. Box 266, New York NY 10276. **E-mail:** query@wolfsonliterary.com. **Website:** www.wolfsonliterary.com. **Contact:** Michelle Wolfson. Estab. 2007. Adheres to AAR canon of ethics.

- Prior to forming her own agency in December 2007, Ms. Wolfson spent 2 years with Artists & Artisans, Inc. and 2 years with Ralph Vicinanza, Ltd.

REPRESENTS Nonfiction, fiction. **Considers these fiction areas:** commercial, mainstream, new adult, romance, thriller, women's, young adult.

- Actively seeking commercial fiction: young adult, mainstream, women's fiction, romance. "I am not taking on new nonfiction clients at this time."

HOW TO CONTACT E-queries only. Accepts simultaneous submissions. Responds only if interested. Positive response is generally given within 2-4 weeks. Responds in 3 months to mss. Obtains most new clients through queries or recommendations from others.

TERMS Agent receives 15% commission on domestic sales; 25% commission on foreign sales. Offers written contract; 30-day notice must be given to terminate contract.

TIPS "Be persistent."

WORDSERVE LITERARY GROUP

7061 S. University Blvd., Suite 307, Centennial CO 80122. **E-mail:** admin@wordserveliterary.com. **Website:** www.wordserveliterary.com. **Contact:** Greg Johnson. WordServe Literary Group was founded in 2003 by veteran literary agent Greg Johnson. After more than a decade in serving authors, the agency has represented more than 700 books in every fiction category and nonfiction genre. "We specialize serving authors of faith in all of their creative endeavors, as well as select titles and genres in the general market." Greg Johnson represents a broad array of adult fiction, primarily in the Christian market. He works with pastors and speakers, male and female, who have important and compelling messages to author for their constituents. He has also carved a niche by representing military nonfiction/memoir for those who have served our country from WWII until today. Business books, health and humor rounds out what he is looking to acquire. Sarah Freese acquires Christian fiction, particularly in the areas of contemporary romance, historical romance, contemporary women's fiction, and suspense. She also considers memoir, narrative non-fiction, and marriage/family/parenting books from bloggers with a large platform. Nick Harrison represents character-driven historical fiction, contemporary literary fiction and some genre fiction (mystery, romance, Amish). For nonfiction, he elcomes well-written memoirs, books by high-profile speakers or entertainers, health-related books, issue-related books, and "deeper life" Christian living books. Represents 100 clients.

- Prior to becoming an agent in 1994, Mr. Johnson was a magazine editor and freelance writer of more than 20 books and 200 articles.

MEMBER AGENTS Greg Johnson, Nick Harrison, Sarah Freese.

REPRESENTS Nonfiction, fiction, novels. **Considers these nonfiction areas:** biography, business, current affairs, diet/nutrition, history, inspirational, literature, memoirs, military, parenting, religious, self-help, sports, war, women's issues. **Considers these fiction areas:** historical, inspirational, literary, mainstream, religious, spiritual, suspense, thriller, women's, young adult.

- Materials with a faith-based angle. No gift books, poetry, short stories, screenplays, graphic novels, children's picture books, science fiction or fantasy. Please do not send mss that are more than 120,000 words.

HOW TO CONTACT E-query admin@wordserveliterary.com. In the subject line, include the word "query." All queries should include the following three elements: a pitch for the book, information about you and your platform (for nonfiction) or writing background (for fiction), and the first 5 (or so) pages of the manuscript pasted into the e-mail. Please view our website for full guidelines: http://www.wordserveliterary.com/submission-guidlines/. Accepts simultaneous submissions. Response within 60 days. Obtains most new clients through recommendations from others.

TERMS Agent receives 15% commission on domestic sales; 10-15% commission on foreign sales. Offers written contract; up to 60-day notice must be given to terminate contract.

TIPS "We are looking for good proposals, great writing and authors willing to market their books. We specialize in projects with a faith element bent. See the website before submitting."

WRITERS HOUSE

21 W. 26th St., New York NY 10010. (212)685-2400. **Fax:** (212)685-1781. **Website:** www.writershouse.com. Estab. 1973. Member of AAR.

MEMBER AGENTS Amy Berkower; Stephen Barr; Susan Cohen; Dan Conaway; Lisa DiMona; Susan Ginsburg; Susan Golomb; Merrilee Heifetz; Brianne Johnson; Daniel Lazar; Simon Lipskar; Steven Malk; Jodi Reamer, Esq.; Robin Rue; Rebecca Sherman; Geri Thoma; Albert Zuckerman; Alec Shane; Stacy Testa; Victoria Doherty-Munro; Beth Miller; Andrea Morrison; Soumeya Roberts.

REPRESENTS Nonfiction, novels. **Considers these nonfiction areas:** biography, business, cooking, economics, history, how-to, juvenile nonfiction, memoirs, parenting, psychology, science, self-help. **Considers these fiction areas:** commercial, fantasy, juvenile, literary, mainstream, middle grade, picture books, science fiction, women's, young adult.

- This agency specializes in all types of popular fiction and nonfiction, for both adult and juvenile books as well as illustrators. Does not want to receive scholarly, professional, poetry, plays, or screenplays.

HOW TO CONTACT Individual agent email addresses are available on the website. "Please e-mail us a query letter, which includes your credentials, an explanation of what makes your book unique and special, and a synopsis. Some agents within our agency have different requirements. Please consult their individual Publisher's Marketplace (PM) profile for details. We respond to all queries, generally within six to eight weeks." If you prefer to submit my mail, address it to an individual agent, and please include SASE for our reply. (If submitting to Steven Malk: Writers House, 7660 Fay Ave., #338H, La Jolla, CA 92037.) Accepts simultaneous submissions. "We respond to all queries, generally within 6-8 weeks." Obtains most new clients through recommendations from authors and editors.

TERMS Agent receives 15% commission on domestic sales. Agent receives 20% commission on foreign sales. Offers written contract, binding for 1 year. Agency charges fees for copying mss/proposals and overseas airmail of books.

TIPS "Do not send mss. Write a compelling letter. If you do, we'll ask to see your work. Follow submission guidelines and please do not simultaneously submit your work to more than one Writers House agent."

WRITERS' REPRESENTATIVES, LLC

116 W. 14th St., 11th Floor, New York NY 10011-7305. (212)620-9009. **E-mail:** transom@writersreps.com. **Website:** www.writersreps.com. **Contact:** Glen Hartley. Estab. 1985. Represents 120 clients.

- Prior to becoming an agent, Ms. Chu was a lawyer; Mr. Hartley worked at Simon & Schuster, Harper & Row and Cornell University Press.

MEMBER AGENTS Lynn Chu, Glen Hartley.

REPRESENTS Nonfiction, fiction.

- Serious nonfiction and quality fiction. No motion picture or television screenplays. "We generally will not consider science fiction or children's or young adult fiction unless it aspires to serious literature."

HOW TO CONTACT Query with SASE or by e-mail. Send ms, brief biography or CV, list of previously published works, and a table of contents. Advise on submission if the projects has been sent to other agents and if it was previously submitted to publishers. Accepts simultaneous submissions.

TERMS Agents receive 15% on domestic sales; 10% for screenwriting or other consulting services. No reading fee. "We may charge clients the costs of out-of-house photocopying or for buying books or galleys for manuscript or proposal submissions, messengers, long-distance telephone and long-distance courier services such as FedEx. Any other expenses must be approved by the author. We do our best to minimize all expenses."

THE WYLIE AGENCY

250 W. 57th St., Suite 2114, New York NY 10107. (212)246-0069. **Fax:** (212)586-8953. **E-mail:** mail@wylieagency.com. **Website:** www.wylieagency.com. Overseas address: 17 Bedford Square, London WC1B 3JA, United Kingdom; mail@wylieagency.co.uk. The Wylie Agency represents high-profile and prolific authors.

REPRESENTS Novels.

This agency is not currently accepting unsolicited submissions; do not query unless you are asked.

HOW TO CONTACT This agency does not currently take unsolicited submissions. Accepts simultaneous submissions.

JASON YARN LITERARY AGENCY

3544 Broadway, No. 68, New York NY 10031. **E-mail:** jason@jasonyarnliteraryagency.com. **Website:** www.jasonyarnliteraryagency.com. Member of AAR. Signatory of WGA.

REPRESENTS Nonfiction, fiction. **Considers these nonfiction areas:** creative nonfiction, current affairs, foods, history, science. **Considers these fiction areas:** commercial, fantasy, literary, middle grade, science fiction, suspense, thriller, young adult, graphic novels, comics.

HOW TO CONTACT Please e-mail your query to jason@jasonyarnliteraryagency.com with the word "Query" in the subject line, and please paste the first 10 pages of your manuscript or proposal into the text of your e-mail. Do not send any attachments. "Visit the About page for information on what we are interested in, and please note that JYLA does not accept queries for film, TV, or stage scripts." Accepts simultaneous submissions.

YATES & YATES

1551 N. Tustin Ave., Suite 710, Santa Ana CA 92705. (714)480-4000. **Website:** www.yates2.com. "We serve as creative counsel for top-tier authors, artists, and creative organizations. Our holistic approach combines agency representation, expert legal advice, brand management, marketing guidance, career coaching, creative counseling, and business management consulting." Represents 40 clients.

REPRESENTS Considers these nonfiction areas: religious.

ZACHARY SHUSTER HARMSWORTH

19 W. 21st St., Suite 501, New York NY 10010. (212)765-6900. **Website:** www.zshliterary.com. Alternate address: 545 Boylston St., 11th Floor, Boston MA 02116. (617)262-2400. **Fax:** (617)262-2468.

"Our principals include two former publishing and entertainment lawyers, a journalist and an editor/agent. Lane Zachary was an editor at Random House before becoming an agent."

MEMBER AGENTS Lane Zachary (memoir, current events, history, biography and psychology); Todd Shuster (nonfiction: current affairs, biography, true-crime, popular science, adventure, politics and civil rights, history, memoir, business, health, parenting, and psychology; fiction: literary and "crossover" commercial novels, including mysteries and thrillers); Esmond Harmsworth (fiction: literary fiction mystery, crime, mainstream fiction, young adult, middle grade; nonfiction, including business, politics, psychology, culture, society, science); Jennifer Gates (nonfiction, including literary and inspirational memoir, narrative nonfiction, current affairs, history, pop culture, business, science, and psychology; literary and commercial fiction and children's); Janet Silver (literary fiction and narrative nonfiction, including memoir, biography, history, and cultural studies); Bridget Wagner Matzie (nonfiction and commercial fiction); Jane Von Mehren (nonfiction: business, cooking, health, history, memoir, parenting, psychology, and science; fiction: YA and Middle Grade literature, thrillers, and women's, book club, and historical fiction); Elias Altman (narrative nonfiction, memoirs, history, literary fiction, cultural criticism); Lori Galvin (cookbooks, narratives about food and drink (memoir or cultural commentary), lifestyle, self-help); Albert Lee (narrative journalism, current affairs, pop culture, music, business and technology, titles with strong book-to-film/TV potential); Michelle Brower (literary fiction, thrillers and literary mysteries, smart women's fiction, "book club" fiction, paranormal/fantasy, selective YA; nonfiction: subject-driven narratives, memoirs, and journalism); Sarah Levitt (nonfiction: biography, cultural history, memoir, science, "ideas" books, reportage, narrative; literary fiction); Jen Marshall; David Granger.

REPRESENTS Novels.

⊶ Check the website for updated info.

HOW TO CONTACT "We regret that we cannot accept unsolicited submissions under any circumstances except for short queries sent by e-mail." Use the online agency submission form to send e-mail to anyone on our staff. Accepts simultaneous submissions. Obtains most new clients through recommendations from others.

TERMS Agent receives 15% commission on domestic sales; 20% commission on foreign sales. Offers written contract, binding for 1 work only; 30-day notice must be given to terminate contract.

HELEN ZIMMERMANN LITERARY AGENCY

E-mail: submit@zimmagency.com. **Website:** www.zimmermannliterary.com. **Contact:** Helen Zimmermann. Estab. 2003.

Prior to opening her agency, Ms. Zimmermann was the director of advertising and promotion at Random House and the events coordinator at an independent bookstore.

REPRESENTS Nonfiction, fiction. **Considers these nonfiction areas:** diet/nutrition, health, interior design, memoirs, music, popular culture, sports, women's issues, relationships. **Considers these fiction areas:** family saga, literary, mainstream.

⊶ "I am currently concentrating my nonfiction efforts in health and wellness, relationships, popular culture, women's issues, lifestyle, sports, and music. I am also drawn to memoirs that speak to a larger social or historical circumstance, or introduce me to a new phenomenon. And I am always looking for a work of fiction that will keep me up at night!"

HOW TO CONTACT Accepts e-mail queries only. "For nonfiction queries, initial contact should just be a pitch letter. For fiction queries, I prefer a summary, your bio, and the first chapter as text in the email (not as an attachment). If I express interest I will need to see a full proposal for nonfiction and the remainder of the manuscript for fiction." Accepts simultaneous submissions. Responds in 2 weeks to queries, only if interested. Obtains most new clients through recommendations from others, solicitations.

TERMS Agent receives 15% commission on domestic sales. Offers written contract; 30-day notice must be given to terminate contract.

WRITERS CONFERENCES Washington Independent Review of Books Writers Conference; Yale Writers' Conference; American Society of Journalists and Authors Conference; Writer's Digest Conference; LaJolla Writer's Conference; Gulf Coast Writers Conference; Kansas Writers Association Conference; New York Writers Workshop; Self Publishing Book Expo; Burlington Writers' Conference; Southern Expressions Writers' Conference; Literary Writers' Conference, NYC.

WRITERS CONFERENCES

Attending a writers conference that includes agents gives you the opportunity to learn more about what agents do and to show an agent your work. Ideally, a conference should include a panel or two with a number of agents to give writers a sense of the variety of personalities and tastes of different agents.

Not all agents are alike: Some are more personable, and sometimes you simply click better with one agent versus another. When only one agent attends a conference, there is a tendency for every writer at that conference to think, "Ah, this is the agent I've been looking for!" When the number of agents attending is larger, you have a wider group from which to choose, and you may have less competition for the agent's time.

Besides including panels of agents discussing what representation means and how to go about securing it, many of these gatherings also include time—either scheduled or impromptu—to meet briefly with an agent to discuss your work.

If they're impressed with what they see and hear about your work, they will invite you to submit a query, a proposal, a few sample chapters, or possibly your entire manuscript. Some conferences even arrange for agents to review manuscripts in advance and schedule one-on-one sessions during which you can receive specific feedback or advice regarding your work. Such meetings often cost a small fee, but the input you receive is usually worth the price.

Ask writers who attend conferences and they'll tell you that, at the very least, you'll walk away with new knowledge about the industry. At the very best, you'll receive an invitation to send an agent your material!

Many writers try to make it to at least one conference a year, but cost and location can count as much as subject matter when determining which one to attend. There are conferences in almost every state and province that can provide answers to your questions about writing and the publishing industry. Conferences also connect you with a community of other writers. Such connections help you learn about the pros and cons of different agents, and they can also give you a renewed sense of purpose and direction in your own writing.

SUBHEADS

Each listing is divided into subheads to make locating specific information easier. In the first section, you'll find contact information for conference contacts. You'll also learn conference dates, specific focus, and the average number of attendees. Finally, names of agents who will be speaking or have spoken in the past are listed along with details about their availability during the conference. Calling or e-mailing a conference director to verify the names of agents in attendance is always a good idea.

COSTS: Looking at the price of events, plus room and board, may help writers on a tight budget narrow their choices.

ACCOMMODATIONS: Here conferences list overnight accommodations and travel information. Often conferences held in hotels will reserve rooms at a discount rate and may provide a shuttle bus to and from the local airport.

ADDITIONAL INFORMATION: This section includes information on conference-sponsored contests, individual meetings, the availability of brochures, and more.

AGENTS & EDITORS CONFERENCE

Writers' League of Texas, 611 S. Congress Ave., Suite 200 A-3, Austin TX 78704. (512)499-8914. **E-mail:** michael@writersleague.org. **Website:** www.writersleague.org/38/conference. **Contact:** Michael Noll, program director. Estab. 1982. Annual conference held in summer. 2018 dates: June 29-July 1. "This standout conference gives each attendee the opportunity to become a publishing insider. Meet more than 25 top agents, editors, and industry professionals through one-on-one consultations and receptions. Get tips and strategies for revising and improving your manuscript from keynote speakers and presenters (including award-winning and best-selling writers)."

COSTS Registration for the 2018 conference: $409 for Writers' League members and $469 for non-members through April 2, 2018. Registrations through April 2 include a one-on-one consultation with an agent or editor. After April 2: $449 for members and $409 for non-members, with consultations available for individual purchase.

ACCOMMODATIONS Discounted rates are available at the conference hotel.

ADDITIONAL INFORMATION Register before April 3 to receive a free consultation with an agent or editor.

ALASKA WRITERS CONFERENCE

Alaska Writers Guild, P.O. Box 670014, Chugiak AK 99567. **E-mail:** alaskawritersguild.awg@gmail.com. **Website:** alaskawritersguild.com. Annual event held in the fall—usually September. Duration: 2 days. There are many workshops and instructional tracks. Sometimes teams up with SCBWI and Alaska Pacific University to offer courses at the event. Literary agents are in attendance each year to hear pitches and meet writers.

ALGONKIAN FIVE DAY NOVEL CAMP

2020 Pennsylvania Ave. NW, Suite 443, Washington DC 20006. **E-mail:** info@algonkianconferences.com. **Website:** algonkianconferences.com. Conference duration: 5 days. Attendance: 12 students maximum per workshop. "During more than 45 hours of actual workshop time, students will engage in those rigorous narrative and complication/plot exercises necessary to produce a publishable manuscript. Genres we work with include general commercial fiction, literary fiction, serious and light women's fiction, mystery/cozy/thriller, science fiction/fantasy, young adult, and memoir/narrative nonfiction. The three areas of workshop emphasis will be premise, platform, and execution.

AMERICAN CHRISTIAN WRITERS CONFERENCES

P.O. Box 110390, Nashville TN 37222. (800)219-7483 or (615)331-8668. **E-mail:** acwriters@aol.com. **Website:** www.acwriters.com. **Contact:** Reg Forder, director. Estab. 1981. ACW hosts a dozen annual two-day writers conferences and mentoring retreats across America taught by editors and professional freelance writers. These events provide excellent instruction, networking opportunities, and valuable one-on-one time with editors. Open to all forms of Christian writing (fiction, nonfiction, and scriptwriting). Conferences are held between March and November during each year.

COSTS Costs vary and may depend on type of event (conference or mentoring retreat).

ACCOMMODATIONS Special rates are available at the host hotel (usually a major chain like Holiday Inn).

ADDITIONAL INFORMATION E-mail or call for conference brochures.

ANTIOCH WRITERS' WORKSHOP

Antioch Writers' Workshop, c/o Antioch University Midwest, 900 Dayton St., Yellow Springs OH 45387. (937)769-1803. **E-mail:** info@antiochwritersworkshop.com. **Website:** www.antiochwritersworkshop.com. **Contact:** Sharon Short, director. Estab. 1986. Programs are offered year-round; annual conference held in summer. Average attendance: 80. Workshop concentrations: fiction, poetry, personal essay, and memoir. Site: Antioch University Midwest in the Village of Yellow Springs. Literary agents attend. Writers of all levels (beginner to advanced) are warmly welcomed to discover their next steps on their writing paths—whether that's developing craft or preparing to submit for publication. An agent and an editor will be speaking and available for meetings with attendees.

ACCOMMODATIONS Accommodations are available at local hotels and bed-and-breakfasts.

ADDITIONAL INFORMATION The easiest way to contact this event is through the website's contact form.

ASJA ANNUAL WRITERS CONFERENCE

American Society of Journalists and Authors, 355 Lexington Ave., 15th Floor, New York NY 10017. (212)997-0947. **E-mail:** asjaoffice@asja.org. **Website:** www.asja.org. **Contact:** Holly Koenig, executive director. Estab. 1971. Annual conference held in New York each spring. Duration: 2 days. Average attendance: 600. Covers nonfiction. Site: New York. Speakers have included Kitty Kelley, Jennifer Finney Boylan, Daniel Jones, D.T. Max, and more.

COSTS Approximately $300/day, depending on when you sign up. Check website for details.

ACCOMMODATIONS Venue hotel has a block of rooms at discounted conference rate.

ADDITIONAL INFORMATION Conference program available online mid-January. Registration is online only. Sign up for e-mail updates online.

ATLANTA WRITERS CONFERENCE

Atlanta Writers Club, Westin Atlanta Airport Hotel, 4736 Best Rd., Atlanta GA 30337. **E-mail:** awconference@gmail.com. **Website:** www.atlantawritersconference.com/about. **Contact:** George Weinstein. Estab. 2008. Annual conference held in spring. 2018 dates: May 4-5. Literary agents and editors are in attendance to take pitches and critique ms samples and query letters. Conference offers a screenwriting workshop, instructional sessions with local authors, and separate question-and-answer panels with the agents and editors. Site: Westin Airport Atlanta Hotel.

COSTS Manuscript critiques are $170 each (2 spots/waitlists maximum). Pitches are $70 each (2 spots/waitlists maximum). There's no charge for waitlists unless a spot opens. Query letter critiques are $70 (1 spot maximum). Other workshops and panels may also cost extra; see website. The "all activities" option is $620 and includes 2 manuscript critiques, 2 pitches, and 1 of each remaining activity.

ACCOMMODATIONS A block of rooms is reserved at the conference hotel. Booking instructions will be sent in the registration confirmation e-mail.

ADDITIONAL INFORMATION A free shuttle runs between the airport and the hotel.

BALTIMORE WRITERS' CONFERENCE

English Department, Liberal Arts Bldg., Towson University, 8000 York Rd., Towson MD 21252. (410)704-5196. **E-mail:** prwr@towson.edu. **Website:** baltimorewritersconference.org. Estab. 1994. Annual conference held in November at Towson University. Conference duration: 1 day. Average attendance: 150-200. Covers all areas of writing and getting published. Held at Towson University. Session topics include fiction, nonfiction, poetry, magazines and journals, and agents and publishers. Sign up the day of the conference for quick critiques to improve your stories, essays, and poems.

ACCOMMODATIONS Hotels are close by, if required.

ADDITIONAL INFORMATION Writers may register through the website. Send inquiries via e-mail.

BAY TO OCEAN WRITERS CONFERENCE

P.O. Box 1773, Easton MD 21601. (410)482-6337. **E-mail:** info@baytoocean.com. **Website:** www.baytoocean.com. Estab. 1998. Annual conference held the second Saturday in March. Average attendance: 200. Approximately 30 speakers conduct workshops on publishing, agents, editing, marketing, craft, the Internet, poetry, fiction, nonfiction, and freelance writing. Site: Chesapeake College, Rt. 213 and Rt. 50, Wye Mills, on Maryland's historic Eastern Shore. Accessible to individuals with disabilities.

COSTS Adults: $100-120. Students: $55. A paid ms review is also available; details on website. Includes continental breakfast and networking lunch.

ADDITIONAL INFORMATION Registration is on website. Pre-registration is required; no registration at door. Conference usually sells out 1 month in advance. Conference is for all levels of writers.

BIG SUR WRITING WORKSHOP

Henry Miller Library, Hwy. 1, Big Sur CA 93920. (831)667-2574. **E-mail:** writing@henrymiller.org. **Website:** bigsurwriting.wordpress.com. Annual workshop focusing on children's writing (picture books, middle-grade, and young adult). Held every spring in Big Sur Lodge in Pfeiffer State Park. Cost of workshop includes meals, lodging, workshop, and Saturday evening reception. This event is helmed by the literary agents of the Andrea Brown Literary Agency. All attendees meet with at least 2 faculty members to have their work critiqued.

BLUE RIDGE MOUNTAINS CHRISTIAN WRITERS CONFERENCE

(800)588-7222. **Website:** www.blueridgeconference.com. **Contact:** Edie Melson, director. Annual retreat held in May at Ridgecrest/LifeWay Conference Center near Asheville, North Carolina. 2017 dates: May 21-25. Duration: Sunday through lunch on Thursday. Average attendance: 350. The conference is a training and networking event for both seasoned and aspiring writers that allows attendees to interact with editors, agents, professional writers, and readers. Workshops and continuing classes in a variety of creative categories are offered.

COSTS $325 for the conference; meal package is $145.00 per person (12 meals beginning with dinner Sunday and ending with lunch on Thursday). $350 conference fee for those not staying on campus. Room rates vary from $60-$70 per night.

ADDITIONAL INFORMATION For a PDF of the complete schedule (typically posted in April), visit the website.

BOOKS-IN-PROGRESS CONFERENCE

Carnegie Center for Literacy and Learning, 251 W. Second St., Lexington KY 40507. (859)254-4175. **E-mail:** ccll1@carnegiecenterlex.org. **Website:** carnegiecenterlex.org. **Contact:** Laura Whitaker, program director. Estab. 2010. This is an annual writing conference at the Carnegie Center for Literacy and Learning in Lexington, Kentucky. It typically happens in June. "Each conference will offer writing and publishing workshops and includes a keynote presentation." Literary agents are flown in to meet with writers and hear pitches. Website is updated several months prior to each annual event.

ACCOMMODATIONS See website for list of area hotels.

BREAD LOAF IN SICILY WRITERS' CONFERENCE

Middlebury College, Middlebury College, Middlebury VT 05753. (802)443-5286. **Fax:** (802)443-2087. **E-mail:** blsicily@middlebury.edu. **Website:** www.middlebury.edu/bread-loaf-conferences/blsicily. Estab. 2011. Annual conference held in September in Erice, Sicily (western coast of the island). Duration: 7 days. Offers workshops for fiction, nonfiction, and poetry. 2017 dates: September 17-23. Average attendance: 32.

COSTS $3,020. Includes the conference program, transfer to and from Palermo Airport, 6 nights of lodging, 3 meals daily (except for Wednesday), wine reception at the readings, and an excursion to the ancient ruins of Segesta. The charge for an additional person is $1,750. There is a $15 application fee an a $300 deposit.

ACCOMMODATIONS Accommodations are single rooms with private bath. Breakfast and lunch are served at the hotel, and dinner is available at select Erice restaurants. A double room is possible for those who would like to be accompanied by a spouse or significant other.

ADDITIONAL INFORMATION Application deadline for 2017 conference: April 15. Rolling admissions. Space is limited.

BREAD LOAF ORION ENVIRONMENTAL WRITERS' CONFERENCE

Middlebury College, Middlebury College, Middlebury VT 05753. (802)443-5286. **Fax:** (802)443-2087. **E-mail:** blorion@middlebury.edu. **Website:** www.middlebury.edu/bread-loaf-conferences/blorion. Estab. 2014. Annual specialized conference held in June. Duration: 7 days. Offers workshops for fiction, nonfiction, and poetry. Agents and editors will be in attendance. 2017 dates: June 3-9. Average attendance: 70.

COSTS $2205 for full participants and $1875 for auditors. Both options include room and board.

ACCOMMODATIONS Mountain campus of Middlebury College in Vermont.

ADDITIONAL INFORMATION The event is designed to hone the skills of people interested in producing literary writing about the environment and the natural world. The conference is co-sponsored by the Bread Loaf Writers' Conference, Orion magazine, and Middlebury College's Environmental Studies Program. Application deadline for 2017 conference: February 15. Rolling admissions. Space is limited.

BREAD LOAF WRITERS' CONFERENCE

Middlebury College, Middlebury College, Middlebury VT 05753. (802)443-5286. **Fax:** (802)443-2087. **E-mail:** blwc@middlebury.edu. **Website:** www.middlebury.edu/bread-loaf-conferences/bl_writers. Estab. 1926. Annual conference held in late August. 2018 dates: August 15-25. Duration: 10 days. Average attendance: 230. Offers workshops for fiction, nonfiction, and poetry. Agents and editors attend.

COSTS $3,395 for general contributors and $3,255 for auditors. Both options include room and board.

ACCOMMODATIONS Bread Loaf campus of Middlebury College in Ripton, Vermont.

ADDITIONAL INFORMATION The application deadline for the 2018 event is February 15; there is $15 application fee.

CALIFORNIA CRIME WRITERS CONFERENCE

Sisters in Crime Los Angeles and Southern California Mystery Writers of America, DoubleTree by Hilton Los Angeles—Westside, 6161 W. Centinela Avenue, Culver City CA 90230 USA. **E-mail:** ccwconference@gmail.com. **E-mail:** ccwconference@gmail.com. **Website:** www.ccwconference.org. **Contact:** Rochelle Staab and Sue Ann Jaffarian, 2017 co-chairs. Estab. 1995. Biennial conerence usually held in early June. 2017 dates: June 10-11. Average attendance: 200. Two-day conference on mystery and crime writing. Offers craft, forensic, industry news, marketing, and career-building sessions; 2 keynote speakers; author, editor, and agent panels; ms critiques (additional fee); and book signings. 2017 keynote speakers are William Kent Krueger and Hallie Ephron. Breakfast and lunch both days included.

COSTS Early bird registration through January 31: $265. Registration February 1-April 30: $300. Registration May 1-31: $335. Onsite registration: $350.

CAMPBELL CONFERENCE

University of Kansas Gunn Center for the Study of Science Fiction, Wesoce Hall, 1445 Jayhawk Blvd., Lawrence KS 66045. (785)864-2508. **E-mail:** cmckit@ku.edu; cssf@ku.edu. **Website:** www.sfcenter.ku.edu/campbell-conference.htm. Estab. 1985. Annual conference for science fiction, generally held at the University of Kansas. Established in 1985 by James Gunn and currently led by Christopher McKitterick. Writer and editor instructors have included Lou Anders, Bradley Denton, James Gunn, Kij Johnson, John Ordover, Frederik Pohl, Pamela Sargent, and George Zebrowski, and each year the winners of the Campbell and Sturgeon Memorial Awards participate as guests of honor.

ACCOMMODATIONS Housing information is available. Several airport shuttle services offer reasonable transportation from the Kansas City International Airport to Lawrence.

ADDITIONAL INFORMATION Admission to the workshop is by submission of an acceptable story. Two additional stories are submitted by the middle of June. These 3 stories are distributed to other participants for critiquing and are the basis for the first week of the workshop. One story is rewritten for the second week, when students also work with guest authors. See website for guidelines. This workshop is intended for writers who have just started to sell their work or need that extra bit of understanding or skill to become a published writer.

CAPE COD WRITERS CENTER ANNUAL CONFERENCE

P.O. Box 408, Osterville MA 02655. (508)420-0200. **E-mail:** writers@capecodwriterscenter.org. **Website:** www.capecodwriterscenter.org. **Contact:** Nancy Rubin Stuart, executive director. Announcing the 56th broad-based literary conference August 2-5, 2018 at the Resort and Conference Center at Hyannis, MA.Workshops in fiction, nonfiction, poetry, memoir, mystery, thrillers, writing for children, social media, screenwriting, promotion, pitches and queries, agent meetings and ms mentorship with agents,editors and faculty.

COSTS Costs vary, depending on the number of courses selected, beginning at $125. Several scholarships are available.

ACCOMMODATIONS Resort and Conference Center of Hyannis, Massachusetts.

CELEBRATION OF SOUTHERN LITERATURE

Southern Lit Alliance, 301 E. 11th St., Suite 301, Chattanooga TN 37403. (423)267-1218. **Fax:** (866)483-6831. **Website:** www.southernlitalliance.org. Biennial conference held in odd-numbered years. "The Celebration of Southern Literature stands out because of its unique collaboration with the Fellowship of Southern Writers, an organization founded by towering literary figures like Eudora Welty, Cleanth Brooks, Walker Percy, and Robert Penn Warren to recognize and encourage literature in the South. The Fellowship awards 11 literary prizes and inducts new members, making this event the place to discover up-and-coming voices in Southern literature. The Southern Lit Alliance's Celebration of Southern Literature attracts more than 1,000 readers and writers from all over the United States. It strives to maintain an informal atmosphere where conversations will thrive, inspired by a common passion for the written word. The Southern Lit Alliance (formerly the Arts & Education Council) started as one of 12 pilot agencies founded by a Ford Foundation grant in 1952. The Alliance is the only organization of the 12 still in existence. The Southern Lit Alliance celebrates Southern writers and readers through community education and innovative literary arts experiences."

CHICAGO WRITERS CONFERENCE

E-mail: mare@chicagowritersconference.org. **Website:** chicagowritersconference.org. **Contact:** Mare Swallow. Estab. 2011. Annual conference held in fall (typically September or October). The event brings together a variety of publishing professionals (agents, editors, authors) and brings together several Chicago literary, writing, and bookselling groups. Often sells out. Past speakers have included *New York Times* bestselling author Sara Paretsky, children's author Allan Woodrow, young adult author Erica O'Rourke, novelist Eric Charles May, and novelist Loretta Nyhan.

CHRISTOPHER NEWPORT UNIVERSITY WRITERS' CONFERENCE & WRITING CONTEST

(757)269-4368. **E-mail:** eleanor.taylor@cnu.edu. **Website:** writers.cnu.edu. Estab. 1981. Annual conference held in spring. This is a working conference. Presentations made by editors, agents, fiction writers, poets, and more. Breakout sessions in fiction, nonfiction, poetry, juvenile fiction, and publishing. Previous panels have included publishing, proposal writing, and Internet research.

ACCOMMODATIONS Provides list of area hotels.

CLARION WEST WRITERS WORKSHOP

P.O. Box 31264, Seattle WA 98103. (206)322-9083. **E-mail:** info@clarionwest.org. **Website:** www.clarionwest.org. **Contact:** Neile Graham, workshop director. Clarion West is a prestigious, intensive six-week workshop for writers preparing for professional careers in science fiction and fantasy, held annually in Seattle. Usually run from mid-June through the end of July. Average attendance: 18. Held near the University of Washington. Deadline for applications is March 1. Instructors are well-known writers and editors in the field.

COSTS $4,200 (for tuition, housing, most meals). Numerous scholarships are available. Students can apply by mail or e-mail and must submit 20-30 pages of ms with four-page biography and $60 fee ($35 if received by February 10).

ACCOMMODATIONS Students stay on-site in workshop housing near the University of Washington.

ADDITIONAL INFORMATION Conference information available in fall. For brochure/guidelines, send SASE, visit website, e-mail, or call.

CLARKSVILLE WRITERS CONFERENCE

1123 Madison St., Clarksville TN 37040. (931)551-8870. **E-mail:** artsandheritage@cdelightband.net. **Website:** www.artsandheritage.us/writers. **Contact:** Ellen Kanervo. Annual conference held in the summer at Austin Peay State University. Features a variety of presentations on fiction, nonfiction, and more. Past presenting authors include Tom Franklin, Frye Gaillard, William Gay, Susan Gregg Gilmore, Will Campbell, John Seigenthaler Sr., Alice Randall, George Singleton, Alanna Nash, and Robert Hicks. "Our presentations and workshops are valuable to writers and interesting to readers."

COSTS Costs available online; prices vary depending on how long attendees stay and if they attend the banquet dinner.

ADDITIONAL INFORMATION Multiple literary agents are flown in to the event every year to meet with writers and take pitches.

DESERT DREAMS WRITERS CONFERENCE

Desert Rose Chapter of Romance Writers of Ameica, P.O. Box 14601, Tempe AZ 85285. **E-mail:** desertdreams@desertroserwa.org. **E-mail:** desertdreams@desertroserwa.org. **Website:** desertroserwa.org/desertdreams. **Contact:** Kris Tualla. Estab. 1986. Annual conference held in summer. 2017 dates: June 1-4. Desert Dreams Writers Conference provides authors of all skill levels, from beginner to multi-published, with the tools to take their writing to the next level. Sessions will include general writing, career development, genre-specific, agent/publisher spotlights, and an agent/editor panel. The conference also offers one-on-one appointments with editors or agents (included in registration), an all-author book signing, and a keynote address.

COSTS $299 for regular registration, which includes 3 and a half days of sessions plus extra opportunities (see website), two sit-down dinners, keynote, and an awards gala announcing the winners of the event's 3 contests.

ACCOMMODATIONS Embassy Suites Phoenix-Scottsdale. "Enter the code DRE to receive the $104 per night conference rate."

ADDITIONAL INFORMATION 2017 keynote speaker: Diana Gabaldon.

DETROIT WORKING WRITERS ANNUAL WRITERS CONFERENCE

Detroit Working Writers, P.O. Box 82395, Rochester MI 48308. **E-mail:** conference@detworkingwriters.org. **Website:** dww-writers-conference.org. Estab. 1961. Annual conference held in spring. Site: Michigan State University Management Education Center in Troy, Michigan. Conference is 1 day, with breakfast, luncheon, keynote speaker, 4 breakout sessions, and 3 workshop choices. Details available online. There are 5 writing competitions with cash prizes in different categories: young adult/new adult, creative nonfiction, poetry, children's, and adult fiction. Registration and competition open in January, online.

COSTS Costs vary, depending on early bird registration and membership status within the organization.

ERMA BOMBECK WRITERS' WORKSHOP

University of Dayton, 300 College Park, Dayton OH 45469. (937)229-3255. **E-mail:** erma@udayton.edu. **Website:** humorwriters.org. **Contact:** Teri Rizvi. Estab. 2000. Biennial conference held in even numbered years. 2018 dates: April 5-7. This is a specialized writing conference for writers of humor (books, articles, essays, blogs, and film/television). "The Bombeck Workshop is the only one in the country devoted to both humor and human interest writing. Through the workshop, the University of Dayton and the Bombeck family honor one of America's most celebrated storytellers and humorists. Over the past decade, the workshop has attracted such household names as Dave Barry, Art Buchwald, Phil Donahue, Roy Blount, Jr., Nancy Cartwright, Don Novello, Garrison Keillor, Gail Collins, Connie Schultz, Adriana Trigiani, and Alan Zweibel. The workshop draws approximately 350 writers from around the country and typically sells out very quickly, so don't wait once registration opens."

ADDITIONAL INFORMATION Connect with the event on social media: facebook.com/ermabombeck and @ebww.

FLORIDA CHRISTIAN WRITERS CONFERENCE

Word Weavers International, Inc., P O Box 520224, Longwood FL 32752. (407)615-4112. **E-mail:** floridacwc@aol.com. **Website:** floridacwc.net. Jessica Everson, Taryn Souders **Contact:** Eva Marie Everson and Mark T. Hancock. Estab. 1988. Annual conference held from the last Wednesday of February to the first Sunday in March at Lake Yale Conference Center in Leesburg, Florida. Workshops/classes geared toward all levels, from beginners to published authors. Open to students. Offers 6 keynote addresses, 10 continuing classes (including teen and pastor tracks), and a number of three-hour workshops, one-hour workshops, and after-hours workshops. "FCWC brings in the finest the industry has to offer in editors, agents, freelancers, and marketing and media experts." Additionally, the conference offers a book proposal studio, a pitch and networking studio, and advanced critique services.

COSTS Ranges: $275 (daily rate—in advance, includes lunch and dinner; specify days) to $1,495 (attendee and participating spouse/family member in same room). Scholarships offered. For more information or to register, go to the conference website.

ACCOMMODATIONS Offers private rooms and double occupancy as well as accommodations for participating and non-participating family members. Meals provided, including awards dessert banquet Saturday evening. For those flying into Orlando or Sanford airports, FCWC provides a shuttle to and from the conference center.

FLORIDA ROMANCE WRIITERS FUN IN THE SUN CONFERENCE

Florida Romance Writers, P.O. Box 550562, Fort Lauderdale FL 33355. **E-mail:** frwfuninthesun@yahoo.com. **Website:** frwfuninthesunmain.blogspot.com. Estab. 1986. Annual conference held in February. 2017 dates: February 16-20. "Set sail with Florida Romance Writers and our special guests. Inspiring workshops and panels will keep your muse buzzing with plot turns. For those with a well behaved muse who continues to do her job, schedule an appointment with our guest agents and editors. Also, take advantage of the opportunities to build a website and create a marketing plan while at sea." Space is limited.

GREEN MOUNTAIN WRITERS CONFERENCE

47 Hazel St., Rutland VT 05701. (802)236-6133. **E-mail:** ydaley@sbcglobal.net. **E-mail:** yvonnedaley@me.com. **Website:** vermontwriters.com. **Contact:** Yvonne Daley, director. Estab. 1998. Annual conference held in the summer. Covers fiction, creative nonfiction, poetry, young adult fiction, journalism, nature writing, essay, memoir, personal narrative, and biography. Held at the Mountain Top Inn and Resort, a beautiful lakeside inn located in Chittenden, Ver-

Howard Frank Mosher, Chris Bohjalian, Yvonne Daley, David Huddle, David Budbill, Jeffrey Lent, Verandah Porche, Tom Smith, and Chuck Clarino.

COSTS $525 before April 15; $575 before May 15; $600 before June 1. Partial scholarships are available.

ACCOMMODATIONS Dramatically reduced rates at the Mountain Top Inn and Resort for attendees. Close to other area hotels and bed-and-breakfasts in Rutland County, Vermont.

ADDITIONAL INFORMATION Participants' mss can be read and commented on at a cost. Sponsors contests and publishes a literary magazine featuring work of participants. Brochures available on website or e-mail.

HAMPTON ROADS WRITERS CONFERENCE

Hampton Roads Writers, P.O. Box 56228, Virginia Beach VA 23456. (757)639-6146. **E-mail:** hrwriters@cox.net. **Website:** hamptonroadswriters.org. Estab. 2008. Annual conference held in September. 2018 dates: September 13-15. Workshops cover fiction, nonfiction, memoir, poetry, lyric writing, screenwriting, and the business of getting published. A bookshop, 3 free contests with cash prizes, free evening networking social, and many networking opportunities will be available. Multiple literary agents are in attendance each year to meet with writers and hear ten-minute pitches. Much more information available on the website.

COSTS Costs vary. There are discounts for members, for early bird registration, for students, and more.

HOUSTON WRITERS GUILD CONFERENCE

Writefest Houston, Houston Writers Guild, P.O. Box 42255, Houston TX 77242. (281)736-7168. **E-mail:** info@houstonwritersguild.org. **Website:** houstonwritersguild.org. Estab. 1994. This annual conference, organized by the Houston Writers Guild, happens in the spring and has concurrent sessions and tracks on the craft and business of writing. Each year, multiple agents are in attendance taking pitches from writers. Starting in 2018, the Houston Writers Guild has teamed up with Writespace Houston to enhance the conference. The festival, Writefest, is now a weeklong event with various tracks of sessions during the weekday evenings as well as during the weekend of the festival. Literary journals as well as publishing companies and agents are featured.

COSTS Costs are different for members and nonmembers. Costs depend on how many days and events you sign up for.

ADDITIONAL INFORMATION The conference dates for 2018 are April 30 through May 6; Each year the conference takes place either the last weekend of April or the first weekend of May depending on venue availability.

The Guild also hosts a conference the last weekend of September called Indiepalooza. This conference focuses on marketing and branding for all authors and specific presentations and sessions for authors who are self-publishing.

IDAHO WRITERS LEAGUE WRITERS' CONFERENCE

601 W. 75 St., Blackfoot ID 83221. (208)684-4200. **Website:** www.idahowritersleague.org. Estab. 1940. Annual floating conference, usually held in September. This conference has at least one agent in attendance every year, along with other writers and presenters.

COSTS Pricing varies. Check website for more information.

INTERNATIONAL WOMEN'S FICTION FESTIVAL

Via Cappuccini 8E, Matera Italy. (39)0835-312044. **Fax:** (39)333-5857933. **E-mail:** contact@womensfictionfestival.com. **Website:** www.womensfictionfestival.com. **Contact:** Elizabeth Jennings. Estab. 2004. Annual conference usually held in September. 2017 dates: September 28-30. Average attendance: 100. International writers conference with a strong focus on fiction and marketing to international markets. Numerous literary agents and editors are in attendance, both from the United States and from Europe.

COSTS Registration costs vary. Check website for full details.

ACCOMMODATIONS The conference is held at Le Monacelle, a restored 17th century convent. Conference travel agency will find reasonably priced accommodation. A paid shuttle is available from the Bari Airport to the hotel in Matera.

IWWG ANNUAL SUMMER CONFERENCE

(917)720-6959. **E-mail:** iwwgquestions@gmail.com. **Website:** https://iwwg.wildapricot.org/events. Marj Hahne, Interim Director of Operations **Contact:** Dixie King, executive director. Estab. 1976.

ACCOMMODATIONS Check website for updated pricing.

ADDITIONAL INFORMATION Choose from 30 workshops in poetry, fiction, memoir and personal narrative, social action/advocacy, and mind-body-spirit. Critique sessions; book fair; salons; open readings. No portfolio required.

JACKSON HOLE WRITERS CONFERENCE

P.O. Box 1974, Jackson WY 83001. (307)413-3332. **E-mail:** connie@blackhen.com. **Website:** jacksonholewritersconference.com. Estab. 1991. Annual conference held in June. 2018 dates: June 28-30. Conference duration: 3-4 days. Average attendance: 110. Covers fiction, creative nonfiction, poetry and KidsLit, and offers ms critiques from authors, agents, and editors. Agents in attendance will take pitches from writers. Paid ms critique programs are available.

COSTS $375 thru May 12, 2018; critiques additional.

ACCOMMODATIONS Accommodations not included.

ADDITIONAL INFORMATION Held at the Center for the Arts in Jackson, Wyoming, and online.

JAMES RIVER WRITERS CONFERENCE

2319 E. Broad St., Richmond VA 23223. (804)433-3790. **E-mail:** info@jamesriverwriters.org. **Website:** www.jamesriverwriters.org. **Contact:** Katharine Herndon. Estab. 2003. Nonprofit supporting writers in the Richmond, VA, area and beyond. Annual conference held in October. The event has master classes, agent pitching, critiques, panels, and more. Previous attending speakers include Ellen Oh, Margot Lee Shetterly, David Baldacci, Jeannette Walls, Adriana Trigiani, Jacqueline Woodson, and more.

COSTS Check website for updated pricing.

KACHEMAK BAY WRITERS' CONFERENCE

Kachemak Bay Campus—Kenai Peninsula College/University of Alaska Anchorage, Kenai Peninsula College—Kachemak Bay Campus, 533 E. Pioneer Ave., Homer AK 99603. (907)235-7743. **E-mail:** iyconf@uaa.alaska.edu. **Website:** writersconf.kpc.alaska.edu. Annual conference held in June. 2017 dates: June 9-13. 2017 keynote speaker is Jane Smiley. This nationally recognized writing conference features workshops, readings, and panel presentations in fiction, poetry, nonfiction, and the business of writing. There are open mic sessions for conference registrants, evening readings open to the public, agent/editor consultations, and more.

COSTS See the website. Some scholarships available.

ACCOMMODATIONS Homer is 225 miles south of Anchorage, Alaska, on the southern tip of the Kenai Peninsula and the shores of Kachemak Bay. There are multiple hotels in the area.

KENTUCKY WOMEN WRITERS CONFERENCE

University of Kentucky College of Arts & Sciences, 232 E. Maxwell St., Lexington KY 40506. (859)257-2874. **E-mail:** kentuckywomenwriters@gmail.com. **Website:** kentuckywomenwriters.org. **Contact:** Julie Wrinn, director. Estab. 1979. Conference held in second or third weekend of September. September 14-15, 2018. Duration: 2 days. Site: Carnegie Center for Literacy in Lexington, Kentucky. Average attendance: 150-200. Conference covers poetry, fiction, creative nonfiction, and playwriting. Includes writing workshops, panels, and readings featuring contemporary women writers. 2018 speakers will include Mary Gaitskill, Tarfia Faizullah, Gabrielle Calvocoressi, Angela Palm, Sherry Thomas, Jane Friedman, and many more.

COSTS $200 for general admission and a workshop and $125 for admission with no workshop.

ADDITIONAL INFORMATION Sponsors prizes in poetry ($300), fiction ($300), nonfiction ($300), playwriting ($500), and spoken word ($500). Winners are also invited to read during the conference. Pre-registration opens May 1.

KENTUCKY WRITERS CONFERENCE

Southern Kentucky Book Fest, WKU South Campus, 2355 Nashville Rd., Bowling Green KY 42101. (270)745-4502. **E-mail:** sara.volpi@wku.edu. **Website:** www.sokybookfest.org. **Contact:** Sara Volpi. This event is entirely free to the public. 2018 date: April 20-21. Duration: 2 days. Part of the 2-day Southern Kentucky Book Fest. Authors who will be participating in the Book Fest on Saturday will give attendees at the conference the benefit of their wisdom on Friday (16 sessions available). For the first time, additional workshops will be offered on Saturday! Free workshops on a variety of writing topics will be presented. Sessions run for 75 minutes, and the day begins at 9 a.m. and ends at 3:30 p.m. The conference is open to anyone who would like to attend, including high school students, college students, teachers, and the general public. Registration will open online in February.

KILLER NASHVILLE

P.O. Box 680759, Franklin TN 37068. (615)599-4032. **E-mail:** contact@killernashville.com. **Website:** www.killernashville.com. Estab. 2006. Annual conference held the late summer or fall. Duration: 3 days. Average attendance: more than 400. The event draws in literary agents seeking thrillers as well as some of the industry's top thriller authors. Conference designed for writers and fans of mysteries and thrillers, including fiction and nonfiction authors, playwrights, and screenwriters. There are many opportunities for authors to sign books. Distinct session tracks may include general writing, genre-specific writing, publishing, publicity and promotion, forensics, and ms critiques (fiction, nonfiction, short stories, screenplays, and queries). The conference also offers a realistic mock crime scene for guests to solve and an opportunity for networking with best-selling authors, agents, editors, publishers, attorneys, publicists, and representatives from law and emergency services. Other activities include mystery games, an authors' bar, a wine tasting event, 2 cocktail receptions, a guest of honor dinner and awards program, giveways, and more.

COSTS $375 for general registration. Includes network lunches on Friday and Saturday and special sessions with best-selling authors and industry professionals.

ADDITIONAL INFORMATION Additional information about registration is provided online.

LA JOLLA WRITERS CONFERENCE

P.O. Box 178122, San Diego CA 92177. **E-mail:** akuritz@san.rr.com. **Website:** www.lajollawritersconference.com. **Contact:** Jared Kuritz, director. Estab. 2001. Annual conference held in fall. 2017 dates: October 27-29. Conference duration: 3 days. Attendance: 200 maximum. The LaJolla Writers Conference covers all genres and both fiction and nonfiction as well as the business of writing. "We take particular pride in educating our attendees on the business aspect of the book industry and have agents, editors, publishers, publicists, and distributors teach classes. There is unprecedented access to faculty. Our conference offers lecture sessions that run for 50 minutes and workshops that run for 110 minutes. Each block period is dedicated to either workshop or lecture-style classes, with 6-8 classes on various topics available each block. For most workshop classes, you are encouraged to bring written work for review. Literary agents from prestigious agencies such as the Andrea Brown Literary Agency, the Dijkstra Agency, the McBride Agency, Full Circle Literary Group, the Zimmerman Literary Agency, the Van Haitsma Literary Agency, the Farris Literary Agency, and more have participated in the past, teaching workshops in which they are familiarized with attendee work. Late night and early bird sessions are also available. The conference creates a strong sense of community, and it has seen many of its attendees successfully published."

COSTS $395 for full 2017 conference registration (doesn't include lodging or breakfast).

LAS VEGAS WRITER'S CONFERENCE

Henderson Writers' Group, P.O. Box 92032, Henderson NV 89009. (702)953-5675. **E-mail:** info@lasvegaswritersconference.com. **Website:** www.lasvegaswritersconference.com. Estab. 2001. Annual event held in spring. 2018 dates: April 19-21. Conference duration: 3 days. Attendance: 175 maximum. "Join writing professionals, agents, industry experts, and your colleagues for three days in Las Vegas as they share their knowledge on all aspects of the writer's craft. While there are formal pitch sessions, panels, workshops, and seminars, the faculty is also available throughout the conference for informal discussions and advice. Workshops, seminars, and expert panels cover topics in both fiction and nonfiction, screenwriting, marketing, indie-publishing, and the craft of writing itself. There will be many question-and-answer panels for you to ask the experts all your questions." Site: Tuscany Suites and Casino (Las Vegas, Nevada). 2018 keynote speaker: Jane Friedman.

COSTS Costs vary depending on the package. See the website. There are early bird rates through January 31.

ADDITIONAL INFORMATION Agents and editors participate in conference.

MENDOCINO COAST WRITERS' CONFERENCE

P.O. Box 2087, Fort Bragg CA 95437. (707)485-4031. **E-mail:** info@mcwc.org. **Website:** www.mcwc.org. **Contact:** Shirin Bridges, Executive Director. Estab. 1989. Situated where summers are temperate and the seascape spectacular, this friendly conference emphasizes craft and community. Visiting faculty—top authors who are also outstanding teachers—will challenge you to find and express your own voice. MCWC 2018 faculty include Elizabeth McKenzie (National Book Award nominee), Indigo Moor (Sacramento

Poet Laureate), Linda Joy Myers (President of the National Association of Memoir Writers), Vanessa Hua (California Book Award finalist) and Nina Sadowsky (screenwriter, novelist, and producer of The House of Sand and Fog and The Wedding Planner), among others. You will work closely with authors, editors, literary agents, and writers of many levels of experience, interests, ages, and backgrounds. Participants meet for three mornings with their intensive workshop group. Afternoons and evenings include craft seminars, pitch sessions, open-mics, literary readings, publishing panels, and social events. Optional manuscript consultations are available with the instructor, editor, or agent of your choice, on a limited first-come, first-served basis. All registrants may enter conference contests with cash prizes and possible publication in Noyo River Review. 2018 Conference dates are August 2-4 with an optional Publishing Bootcamp taught by Jane Friedman on August 5.

COSTS $575 early bird registration includes morning intensives, afternoon panels and seminars, social events, and most meals. Scholarships available. Opt-in for consultations and Publishing Boot Camp. Early application advised.

ACCOMMODATIONS Many lodging options in the scenic coastal area.

ADDITIONAL INFORMATION "Take your writing to the next level with encouragement, expertise, and inspiration in a literary community where authors are also fantastic teachers." General registration opens March 1. Apply now for a scholarship or for the Master Class, deadline is February 15.

MIDWEST WRITERS WORKSHOP

Muncie IN 47306. (765)282-1055. **E-mail:** midwestwriters@yahoo.com. **Website:** www.midwestwriters.org. **Contact:** Jama Kehoe Bigger, director. Annual workshop held in July in east central Indiana. Writer workshops geared toward writers of all levels, including craft and business sessions. Topics include most genres. Faculty/speakers have included Joyce Carol Oates, George Plimpton, Clive Cussler, Haven Kimmel, William Kent Krueger, William Zinsser, John Gilstrap, Lee Martin, Jane Friedman, Chuck Sambuchino, and numerous best-selling mystery, literary fiction, young adult, and children's authors. Workshop also includes agent pitch sessions, ms evaluation, query letter critiques, and social media tutoring. Registration tentatively limited to 240.

COSTS $155-400. Most meals included.

ADDITIONAL INFORMATION Offers scholarships. See website for more information. Keep in touch with the MWW at facebook.com/midwestwriters and twitter.com/midwestwriters.

MISSOURI WRITERS' GUILD CONFERENCE

St. Louis MO **E-mail:** mwgconferenceinfo@gmail.com. **Website:** www.missouriwritersguild.org. **Contact:** Tricia Sanders, vice president/conference chair. Annual conference held in spring. 2017 dates: May 5-7. Writer and illustrator workshops geared to all levels. Open to students. "Gives writers the opportunity to hear outstanding speakers and to receive information on marketing, research, and writing techniques." Agents, editors, and published authors in attendance.

ADDITIONAL INFORMATION The primary contact individual changes every year, because the conference chair changes every year. See the website for contact info.

MONTROSE CHRISTIAN WRITERS' CONFERENCE

Montrose Bible Conference, 218 Locust St., Montrose PA 18801. (570)278-1001 or (800)598-5030. **Fax:** (570)278-3061. **E-mail:** mbc@montrosebible.org. **Website:** www.montrosebible.org. Estab. 1990. "Annual conference held in July. Offers workshops, editorial appointments, and professional critiques. We try to meet writing needs, for beginners and advanced, covering fiction, poetry, and writing for children. It is small enough to allow personal interaction between attendees and faculty. Speakers have included William Petersen, Mona Hodgson, Jim Watkins, and Bob Hostetler." Held in Montrose.

COSTS Tuition is $195.

ACCOMMODATIONS Will meet planes in Binghamton, New York, and Scranton, Pennsylvania. On-site accommodations: room and board $360-490/conference, including food (2018 rates). RV court available.

ADDITIONAL INFORMATION "Writers can send work ahead of time and have it critiqued for a small fee." The attendees are usually church related. The writing has a Christian emphasis. Conference information available in April. For brochure, visit website, e-mail, or call. Accepts inquiries by phone or e-mail.

MOONLIGHT AND MAGNOLIAS WRITER'S CONFERENCE

Georgia Romance Writers, 3741 Casteel Park Dr., Marietta GA 30064. **Website:** www.georgiaromancewriters.org/mm-conference. Estab. 1982. Georgia Romance Writers Annual Conference. 2017 dates: September 28-October 1. "Conference focuses on writing women's fiction with emphasis on romance. Includes agents and editors from major publishing houses. Previous workshops have included beginning writer sessions, research topics, writing basics, and professional issues for the published author, plus specialty sessions on writing young adult, multicultural, paranormal, and Regency. Speakers have included experts in law enforcement, screenwriting, and research."

MUSE AND THE MARKETPLACE

Grub Street, 162 Boylston St., 5th Floor, Boston MA 02116. (617)695-0075. **E-mail:** info@grubstreet.org. **Website:** museandthemarketplace.com. Grub Street's national conference for writers. Held held in the late spring, such as early May. 2017 dates: May 5-7. Conference duration: 3 days. Average attendance: 400. Dozens of agents are in attendance to meet writers and take pitches. The conference has workshops on all aspects of writing.

ACCOMMODATIONS Boston Park Plaza Hotel.

NAPA VALLEY WRITERS' CONFERENCE

Napa Valley College, 1088 College Ave., St. Helena CA 94574. (707)967-2900 ext. 4. **E-mail:** info@napawritersconference.og. **Website:** www.napawritersconference.org. **Contact:** Catherine Thorpe, managing director. Estab. 1981. Established 1981. Annual weeklong event. 2017 dates: July 23-July 28. Location: Upper Valley Campus in the historic town of St. Helena, 25 miles north of Napa in the heart of the valley's wine growing community. Average attendance: 48 in poetry and 48 in fiction. "Serious writers of all backgrounds and experience are welcome to apply." Offers poets and fiction writers workshops, lectures, faculty readings at Napa Valley wineries, and one-on-one faculty counseling. "Poetry session provides the opportunity to work both on generating new poems and on revising previously written ones."

COSTS $975; $25 application fee.

NATIONAL WRITERS ASSOCIATION FOUNDATION CONFERENCE

10940 S. Parker Rd., #508, Parker CO 80138. **E-mail:** natlwritersassn@hotmail.com. **Website:** www.nationalwriters.com. **Contact:** Sandy Whelchel, executive director. Estab. 1926. Annual conference held the second week of June in Denver. Conference duration: 1 day. Average attendance: 100. Focuses on general writing and marketing.

ADDITIONAL INFORMATION Awards for previous contests will be presented at the conference. Brochures/guidelines are available online or by SASE.

NETWO WRITERS CONFERENCE

Northeast Texas Writers Organization, P.O. Box 962, Mt. Pleasant TX 75456. (469)867-2624 or (903)573-6084. **E-mail:** jimcallan@winnsboro.com. **Website:** www.netwo.org. Estab. 1987. Annual conference held in April. Duration: 2 days. Presenters include agents, writers, editors, and publishers. Agents in attendance will take pitches from writers. The conference features a writing contest, pitch sessions, critiques from professionals, and dozens of workshops and presentations.

COSTS $90 for members before February 29th, and $100 after. $112.50 for non-members before February 29th, and $125 after.

ACCOMMODATIONS See website for information on area motels and hotels.The conference is held at the Titus County Civic Center in Mt. Pleasant, Texas.

ADDITIONAL INFORMATION Conference is co-sponsored by the Texas Commission on the Arts. See website for current updates.

NEW JERSEY ROMANCE WRITERS PUT YOUR HEART IN A BOOK CONFERENCE

P.O. Box 513, Plainsboro NJ 08536. **Website:** www.njromancewriters.org/conference.html. Estab. 1984. Annual conference held in October. 2017 dates: October 13-14. Average attendance: 500. Workshops are offered on various topics for all writers of romance, from beginner to multi-published. Speakers have included Nora Roberts, Kathleen Woodiwiss, Patricia Gaffney, Jill Barnett, and Kay Hooper. Appointments are offered with editors and agents.

NORTH CAROLINA WRITERS' NETWORK FALL CONFERENCE

P.O. Box 21591, Winston-Salem NC 27120. (336)293-8844. **E-mail:** mail@ncwriters.org. **Website:** www.ncwriters.org. Estab. 1985. Annual conference held in November in different North Carolina venues. Average attendance: 250. This organization hosts 2 conferences: 1 in the spring and 1 in the fall. Each conference is a weekend full of workshops, panels, book signings, keynote speaker, a variety of sessions on the craft and business of writing, and opportunities to meet with agents and editors.

COSTS Approximately $250 (includes 4 meals).

ACCOMMODATIONS Special rates are usually available at the conference hotel, but attendees must make their own reservations.

NORTHERN COLORADO WRITERS CONFERENCE

407 Cormorant Court, Fort Collins CO 80525. (970)227-5746. **E-mail:** april@northerncoloradowriters.com. **Website:** www.northerncoloradowriters.com. Estab. 2006. Annual conference held in Fort Collins. 2017 dates: May 5-6. Duration: 2-3 days. The conference features a variety of speakers, agents, and editors. There are workshops and presentations on fiction, nonfiction, screenwriting, children's books, marketing, magazine writing, staying inspired, and more. Previous agents who have attended and taken pitches from writers include Jessica Regel, Kristen Nelson, Rachelle Gardner, Andrea Brown, Ken Sherman, Jessica Faust, Gordon Warnock, and Taylor Martindale. Each conference features more than 30 workshops from which to choose from. Previous keynotes include Chuck Sambuchino, Andrew McCarthy, and Stephen J. Cannell.

COSTS Prices vary depending on a number of factors. See website for details.

ACCOMMODATIONS Conference hotel may offer rooms at a discounted rate.

NORWESCON

100 Andover Park W. Suite 150-165, Tukwila WA 98188. (425)243-4692. **E-mail:** info@norwescon.org. **Website:** www.norwescon.org. Estab. 1978. Annual conference held on Easter weekend. Average attendance: 2,800-3,000. General convention (with multiple tracks) focusing on science fiction and fantasy literature with wide coverage of other media. Tracks cover science, sociocultural, literary, publishing, editing, writing, art, and other media of a science fiction/fantasy orientation. Literary agents will be speaking and available for meetings with attendees.

ACCOMMODATIONS Conference is held at the Doubletree Hotel Seattle Airport.

ODYSSEY FANTASY WRITING WORKSHOP

P.O. Box 75, Mont Vernon NH 03057. (603)673-6234. **E-mail:** jcavelos@odysseyworkshop.org. **Website:** www.odysseyworkshop.org. **Contact:** Jeanne Cavelos. Saint Anselm College, 100 Saint Anselm Dr., Manchester NH 03102 Estab. 1996. Annual workshop held in June (through July). Conference duration: 6 weeks. Average attendance: 15. A workshop for fantasy, science fiction, and horror writers that combines an intensive learning and writing experience with in-depth feedback on students' mss. Held on the campus of Saint Anselm College in Manchester, New Hampshire. Speakers have included George R.R. Martin, Elizabeth Hand, Jane Yolen, Catherynne M. Valente, Holly Black, and Dan Simmons.

COSTS $2,025 tuition, $195 textbook, $892 housing (double room), $1,784 housing (single room), $40 application fee, $600 food (approximate), $950 optional processing fee to receive college credit.

ACCOMMODATIONS Most students stay in Saint Anselm College apartments to get the full Odyssey experience. Each apartment has 2 bedrooms and can house a total of 2 to 3 people (with each bedroom holding 1 or 2 students). The apartments are equipped with kitchens, so you may buy and prepare your own food, which is a money-saving option, or you may eat at the college's Coffee Shop or Dining Hall. Wireless internet access and use of laundry facilities are provided at no cost. Students with cars will receive a campus parking permit.

ADDITIONAL INFORMATION Students must apply and include a writing sample. Application deadline: April 8. Students' works are critiqued throughout the 6 weeks. Workshop information available in October. For brochure/guidelines, send SASE, e-mail, visit website, or call.

OKLAHOMA WRITERS' FEDERATION, INC. ANNUAL CONFERENCE

9800 South Hwy. 137, Miami OK 74354. **Website:** www.owfi.org. Annual conference held first weekend in May, just outside Oklahoma City. Writer workshops geared toward all levels. "The goal of the conference is to create good stories with strong bones. We will be exploring cultural writing and cultural sensitivity in writing." Several literary agents are in attendance each year to meet with writers and hear pitches.

COSTS Costs vary depending on when registrants sign up. Cost includes awards banquet and famous author banquet. Three extra sessions are available for an extra fee. Visit the event website for more information and a complete faculty list.

OREGON CHRISTIAN WRITERS SUMMER CONFERENCE

1075 Willow Lake Rd. N., Keizer OR 97303. **E-mail:** summerconference@oregonchristianwriters.org. **Website:** www.oregonchristianwriters.org. **Contact:** Lindy Jacobs, summer conference director. Estab. 1989. Annual conference held in August at the Red Lion Hotel on the River, a full-service hotel in Portland. Duration: 4 days. 2018 dates: August 20-23. Average attendance: 250 (200 writers, 50 faculty). Top national editors, agents, and authors in the field of Christian publishing offer 11 intensive coaching classes and 30 workshops plus critique sessions. Published authors as well as emerging writers have opportunities to improve their craft, get feedback through ms reviews, meet one-on-one with editors and agents, and have half-hour mentoring appointments with published authors. Classes include fiction, nonfiction, memoir, young adult, poetry, magazine articles, devotional writing, children's books, and marketing. Daily general sessions include worship and an inspirational keynote address. Each year contacts made during the OCW summer conference lead to publishing contracts.

COSTS $550 for OCW members, $595 for nonmembers. Registration fee includes all classes, workshops, and 2 lunches and 3 dinners. Lodging additional. Full-time registered attendees may also pre-submit 3 proposals for review by an editor (or agent) through the conference, plus sign up for a half-hour mentoring appointment with an author.

ACCOMMODATIONS Conference is held at the Red Lion on the River Hotel. Attendees wishing to stay at the hotel must make a reservation through the hotel. A block of rooms is reserved at a special rate and held until mid-July. The hotel reservation link is posted on the website in late spring. Shuttle bus transportation is provided from Portland Airport (PDX) to the hotel, which is 20 minutes away.

ADDITIONAL INFORMATION Conference details posted online beginning in January. All conferees are welcome to attend the Cascade Awards ceremony, which takes place Wednesday evening during the conference. For more information about the Cascade Writing Contest for published and unpublished writers—opens February 14. Please check the website for details.

OZARK CREATIVE WRITERS, INC. CONFERENCE

P.O. Box 9076, Fayetteville AR 72703. **E-mail:** ozarkcreativewriters1@gmail.com. **Website:** www.ozarkcreativewriters.com. The annual event is held in October at the Inn of the Ozarks, in the resort town of Eureka Springs, Arkansas. Approximately 200 writers attend each year; many also enter the creative writing competitions. Open to professional and amateur writers, workshops are geared toward all levels and all forms of the creative process and literary arts; sessions sometimes also include songwriting. Includes presentations by best-selling authors, editors, and agents. Offering writing competitions in all genres.

PENNWRITERS CONFERENCE

P.O. Box 685, Dalton PA 18414. **E-mail:** conferenceco@pennwriters.org; info@pennwriters.org. **Website:** pennwriters.org/conference. Estab. 1987. The Mission of Pennwriters, Inc., is to help writers of all levels, from the novice to the award-winning and multi-published, improve and succeed in their craft. The annual Pennwriters conference is held every year in May in Pennsylvania, switching between locations—Lancaster in even numbered years and Pittsburgh in odd numbered years. 2017 dates: May 19-21 at the Pittsburgh Airport Marriott. Literary agents are in attendance to meet with writers.

ACCOMMODATIONS Costs vary. Pennwriters members in good standing get a slightly reduced rate.

ADDITIONAL INFORMATION Sponsors contest. Published authors judge fiction in various categories. Agent/editor appointments are available on a first-come, first-served basis.

PHILADELPHIA WRITERS' CONFERENCE

P.O. Box 7171, Elkins Park PA 19027. (215)619-7422. **E-mail:** info@pwcwriters.org. **Website:** pwcwriters.org. Estab. 1949. Annual conference held in June. Duration: 3 days. Average attendance: 160-200. Conference covers many forms of writing: novel, short story, genre fiction, nonfiction book, magazine writing, blogging, juvenile, poetry.

ACCOMMODATIONS See website for details. Hotel may offer discount for early registration.

ADDITIONAL INFORMATION Accepts inquiries by e-mail. Agents and editors attend the conference. Many questions are answered online.

PIKES PEAK WRITERS CONFERENCE

Pikes Peak Writers, P.O. Box 64273, Colorado Springs CO 80962. (719)244-6220. **E-mail:** registrar@pikespeakwriters.com. **Website:** www.pikespeakwriters.com/ppwc. Estab. 1993. Annual conference held in April. 2017 dates: April 28-30. Conference duration: 3 days. Average attendance: 300. Workshops, presentations, and panels focus on writing and publishing mainstream and genre fiction (romance, science fiction/fantasy, suspense/thrillers, action/adventure, mysteries, children's, young adult). Agents and editors are available for meetings with attendees on Saturday. Speakers have included Jeff Lindsay, Rachel Caine, and Kevin J. Anderson.

COSTS $395-465 (includes all 7 meals).

ACCOMMODATIONS Marriott Colorado Springs holds a block of rooms at a special rate for attendees until late March.

ADDITIONAL INFORMATION Readings with critiques are available on Friday afternoon. Registration forms are online; brochures are available in January. Send inquiries via e-mail.

PNWA SUMMER WRITERS CONFERENCE

Writers' Cottage, 317 NW Gilman Blvd. Suite 8, Issaquah WA 98027. (425)673-2665. **E-mail:** pnwa@pnwa.org. **Website:** www.pnwa.org. Estab. 1955. Annual conference held in July. 2017 dates: July 20-23. Duration: 4 days. Average attendance: 400. Attendees have the chance to meet agents and editors, learn craft from authors, and uncover marketing secrets. Speakers have included J.A. Jance, Sheree Bykofsky, Kimberley Cameron, Jennie Dunham, Donald Maass, Jandy Nelson, Robert Dugoni, and Terry Brooks.

ROCKY MOUNTAIN FICTION WRITERS COLORADO GOLD CONFERENCE

Rocky Mountain Fiction Writers, Denver Renaissance Hotel, Denver CO **E-mail:** conference@rmfw.org. **Website:** www.rmfw.org. **Contact:** Pamela Nowak and Susan Brooks. Estab. 1982. Annual conference held in September. Duration: 3 days. Average attendance: 400+. Themes include general fiction, genre fiction, contemporary romance, mystery, science fiction/fantasy, mainstream, young adult, screenwriting, short stories, and historical fiction, as well as marketing and career management. 2018 keynote speakers are Kate Moretti, James Scott Bell, and Christopher Paolini. Past speakers have included Diana Gabaldon, Sherry Thomas, Lori Rader-Day, Ann Hood, Robert J. Sawyer, Jeffery Deaver, William Kent Krueger, Margaret George, Jodi Thomas, Bernard Cornwell, Terry Brooks, Dorothy Cannell, Patricia Gardner Evans, Diane Mott Davidson, Constance O'Day, and Connie Willis. Approximately 16 acquiring editors and agents attend annually.

COSTS Available on website.

ACCOMMODATIONS Special rates will be available at conference hotel.

ADDITIONAL INFORMATION Pitch appointments available at no charge. Add-on options include agent and editor critiques, master classes, pitch coaching, query letter coaching, special critiques, and more.

ROMANCE WRITERS OF AMERICA NATIONAL CONFERENCE

14615 Benfer Rd., Houston TX 77069. (832)717-5200. **Fax:** (832)717-5201. **E-mail:** info@rwa.org. **Website:** www.rwa.org/conference. Estab. 1981. Join Romance Writers of America for RWA2018 at the Sheraton Denver Downtown Hotel in Denver, Colorado, July 18–21. The RWA Conference is the place where career-focused romance writers gather to make lasting connections and grow their careers—and so much more. When 2,000 romance writers and industry professionals assemble in one place, the sense of community is undeniable. At the conference, career-focused romance writers can anticipate: education and information, networking with fellow writers, interaction with editors, agents, publishers, vendors, retailers, and other romance, publishing industry professionals.

COSTS $450-675 depending on your membership status as well as when you register.

ADDITIONAL INFORMATION Annual RTA awards are presented for romance authors. Annual Golden Heart awards are presented for unpublished writers.

SALT CAY WRITERS RETREAT

Salt Cay Bahamas. (732)267-6449. **E-mail:** admin@saltcaywritersretreat.com. **Website:** www.saltcaywritersretreat.com. **Contact:** Karen Dionne and Christopher Graham. Annual retreat held in the Bahamas in May. Duration: 5 days. "The Salt Cay Writers Retreat is particularly suited for novelists (especially those writing literary and upmarket commercial fiction, or genre novelists wanting to write a break-out book), memoirists, and narrative nonfiction writers. However, any author (published or not yet published) who wishes to take their writing to the next level is welcome to apply." Speakers have included editors Chuck Adams (Algonquin Books) and Amy Einhorn (Amy Einhorn Books); agents Jeff Kleinman, Michelle Brower, Erin Niumata, and Erin Harris (all of Folio Literary Management); and authors Robert Goolrick and Jacquelyn Mitchard.

COSTS $2,450 through May 1; $2,950 after.

ACCOMMODATIONS Comfort Suites, Paradise Island, Nassau, Bahamas.

SAN DIEGO STATE UNIVERSITY WRITERS' CONFERENCE

SDSU College of Extended Studies, 5250 Campanile Dr., San Diego State University, San Diego CA 92182. (619)594-2099. **Fax:** (619)594-8566. **E-mail:** sdsuwritersconference@mail.sdsu.edu. **Website:** ces.sdsu.edu/writers. Estab. 1984. Annual conference held in January. 2017 dates: January 20-22. Conference duration: 2.5 days. Average attendance: 350. Covers fiction, nonfiction, scriptwriting, and e-books. Held at the San Diego Marriott Mission Valley Hotel. Each year the conference offers a variety of workshops for the beginner and advanced writers. This conference allows writers to choose which workshops best suit their needs. In addition to the workshops, editor reading appointments and agent/editor consultation appointments are provided so attendees may meet with editors and agents one-on-one to discuss specific questions. A reception is offered Saturday immediately following the workshops, offering attendees the opportunity to socialize with the faculty in a relaxed atmosphere. In previous years, approximately 60 faculty members have attended.

COSTS $495-549. Extra costs for consultations.

ACCOMMODATIONS Attendees must make their own travel arrangements. A conference rate for attendees is available at the event hotel (Marriott Mission Valley Hotel).

SAN FRANCISCO WRITERS CONFERENCE

Hyatt Regency Embarcadero, San Francisco CA 94111. (925)420-6223. **E-mail:** barbara@sfwriters.org; www.sfwriters.org. **E-mail:** See website at www.SFWriters.org for writing contest and scholarship submissions and other details. **Website:** sfwriters.org. **Contact:** Barbara Santos, marketing director. Estab. 2003. 2019 dates: February 14-17. Annual conference held President's Day weekend in February. Average attendance: 700. "More than 100 top authors, respected literary agents, and major publishing houses are at the event so attendees can make face-to-face contact with all the right people. Writers of nonfiction, fiction, poetry, and specialty writing (children's books, lifestyle books, etc.) will all benefit from the event. There are important sessions on marketing, self-publishing, technology, and trends in the publishing industry. Plus, there's an optional session called Speed Dating with Agents where attendees can meet with literary agents. Past speakers have included Jane Smiley, Debbie Macomber, Clive Cussler, Guy Kawasaki, Jennifer Crusie, R.L. Stine, Lisa See, Steve Berry, and Jacquelyn Mitchard. Bestselling authors, agents and several editors from traditional publishing houses participate each year, and many will be available for meetings with attendees."

COSTS Full registration is $895 (as of the 2018 event) with early bird registration discounts through February 1.

ACCOMMODATIONS The Hyatt Regency Embarcadero offers a discounted SFWC rate (based on availability). Call directly: (415) 788-1234. Across from the Ferry Building in San Francisco, the hotel is located so that everyone arriving at the Oakland or San Francisco airport can take the BART to the Embarcadero exit, directly in front of the hotel.

ADDITIONAL INFORMATION "Present yourself in a professional manner, and the contacts you will make will be invaluable to your writing career. Fliers, details, and registration information are online."

SAN FRANCISCO WRITING FOR CHANGE CONFERENCE

San Francisco Writers Conference, 1029 Jones St., San Francisco CA 94109. (925)420-6223. **E-mail:** barbara@sfwriters.org. **Website:** sfwritingforchange.org. **Contact:** Barbara Santos, marketing director; Michael Larsen, codirector. Estab. 2004. Annual conference in September (September 8, 2018) held at Unitarian Universalist Center in San Francisco. Writing to Make a Difference is the theme. Presenters provide inspiration and tools to get published. Average attendance: 100 attendees and 25 presenters. Early discounts available. Includes panels, workshops, keynote address, lunch, and editor consultations.

COSTS $199. Early registration discounts available. Please visit the website for details.

ACCOMMODATIONS Check website for event details, accommodations, directions, and parking.

ADDITIONAL INFORMATION "The limited number of attendees (150 maximum) makes this a truly interactive event and a highly effective and productive conference. The presenters are major names in the publishing business, but they take personal interest in the projects discovered at this event each year." Guidelines available on website.

SEWANEE WRITERS' CONFERENCE

735 University Ave., 119 Gailor Hall, Stamler Center, Sewanee TN 37383. (931)598-1654. **E-mail:** swc@sewanee.edu. **Website:** www.sewaneewriters.org. **Contact:** Adam Latham. Estab. 1990. Annual conference. 2018 dates: July 17-29. Average attendance: 150. Accepting applications January 5-March 20. The University of the South will host the 29th session of the Sewanee Writers' Conference. Thanks to the generosity of the Walter E. Dakin Memorial Fund, supported by the estate of the late Tennessee Williams, the Conference will gather a distinguished faculty to provide instruction and criticism through workshops and craft lectures in poetry, fiction, and playwriting. During a 12-day period, participants will read and critique workshop manuscripts under the leadership of some of our country's finest fiction writers, poets, and playwrights. Faculty members and fellows give scheduled readings; senior faculty members offer craft lectures; open mic readings accommodate many others. Additional writers, along with a host of writing professionals, visit to give readings, participate in panel discussions, and answer questions from the audience. Receptions and mealtimes offer ample social opportunities. 2018 faculty includes fiction writers Jeffery Renard Allen, Richard Bausch, Tony Earley, Adrianne Harun, Randall Kenan, Michael Knight, Bobbie Ann Mason, Jill McCorkle, Christine Schutt, and Steve Yarbrough; poets B.H. Fairchild, Mark Jarman, Maurice Manning, Charles Martin, Marilyn Nelson, Mary Jo Salter, A.E. Stallings, and Sidney Wade; and playwrights Naomi Iizuka and Dan O'Brien. Allan Gurganus, Alice McDermott, Wyatt Prunty, Caki Wilkinson, and Greg Williamson will read from their work.

COSTS $1,100 for tuition, and $700 for room, board, and activity costs.

ACCOMMODATIONS Participants are housed in single rooms in university dormitories. Bathrooms are shared by small groups.

SLEUTHFEST

Mystery Writers of America Florida, **E-mail:** sleuthfestinfo@gmail.com. **Website:** sleuthfest.com. Annual conference held in February/March, at the Deerfield Beach Hilton, Florida. 2017 dates: February 23-26. Conference duration: 4 days. Hands-on workshops, 4 tracks of writing and business panels, and 2 keynote speakers for writers of mystery and crime fiction. 2017 keynote speaker: David Baldacci. Also offers agent and editor appointments and paid ms critiques. A full list of attending speakers as well as agents and editors is online. This event is put on by the local chapter of the Mystery Writers of America.

SOUTH CAROLINA WRITERS WORKSHOP

4711 Forest Dr., Suite 3, P.M.B. 189, Columbia SC 29206. **E-mail:** scwwliaison@gmail.com. **Website:** www.myscwa.org. Estab. 1991. Conference held in October at the Metropolitan Conference Center in Columbia. Held almost every year. Conference duration: 3 days. Features critique sessions, open mic readings, and presentations from agents and editors. More than 50 different workshops for writers to choose from, dealing with all subjects of writing craft, writing business, getting an agent, and more. Agents will be in attendance.

SOUTHEASTERN WRITERS ASSOCIATION—ANNUAL WRITERS WORKSHOP

E-mail: purple@southeasternwriters.org. **Website:** www.southeasternwriters.org. Estab. 1975. Annual four-day workshop, held in Epworth By The Sea, St. Simons Island, Georgia. Open to all writers. 2018 dates: June 8-12. Tuition includes 3 free evaluation conferences with instructors (minimum two-day registration). Offers contests with cash prizes. Manuscript deadlines: May 15 for both contests and evaluations.

COSTS Cost of workshop: $445 for 4 days or lower prices for daily tuition or early bird special. (See website for tuition pricing.)

ACCOMMODATIONS Lodging at Epworth and throughout St. Simons Island. Visit website for more information.

SPACE COAST WRITERS GUILD ANNUAL CONFERENCE

P.O. Box 262, Melbourne FL 32902. **E-mail:** stilley@scwg.org. **Website:** www.scwg.org. Conference held along the east coast of central Florida in the last weekend of January, though necessarily every year. Check website for up-to-date information. Conference duration: 2 days. Average attendance: 150+. This conference is hosted in Florida and features a variety of presenters on all topics. Critiques are available for a price, and agents in attendance will take pitches from writers. Previous presenters have included Debra Dixon, Davis Bunn (writer), Ellen Pepus (agent), Jennifer Crusie, Chuck Sambuchino, Madeline Smoot, Mike Resnick, Christina York, Ben Bova, and Elizabeth Sinclair.

COSTS Check website for current pricing.

ACCOMMODATIONS The conference is hosted in a beachside hotel, with special room rates available.

SQUAW VALLEY COMMUNITY OF WRITERS

Community of Writers at Squaw Valley, P.O. Box 1416, Nevada City CA 95959. (530)470-8440 or (530)583-5200 (summer). **E-mail:** info@communityofwriters.org. **Website:** www.communityofwriters.org. **Contact:** Brett Hall Jones, Executive Director. P.O. Box 2352, Olympic Valley CA 96146 (summer) Estab. 1969.

COSTS Tuition is $1,150, which includes 6 dinners. Limited financial aid is available.

ACCOMMODATIONS The Community of Writers rents houses and condominiums in the Squaw Valley for participants to live in during the week of the conference. Single room (1 participant): $700/week. Double room (twin beds, room shared by conference participant of the same gender): $465/week. Multiple room (bunk beds, room shared with 2 or more participants of the same gender): $295/week. All rooms subject to availability; early requests are recommended. Can arrange airport shuttle pickups for a fee.

SURREY INTERNATIONAL WRITERS' CONFERENCE

SiWC, 151-10090 152 St., Suite 544, Surrey BC V3R 8X8 Canada. **E-mail:** kathychung@siwc.ca. **Website:** www.siwc.ca. **Contact:** Kathy Chung, proposals contact and conference coordinator. Annual professional development writing conference outside Vancouver, Canada, held every October. Writing workshops geared toward beginner, intermediate, and advanced levels. More than 80 workshops and panels, on all topics and genres, plus pre-conference master classes. Blue Pencil and agent/editor pitch sessions included. Different conference price packages available. Check the conference website for more information. This event has many literary agents in attendance taking pitches. Annual fiction writing contest open to all with $1,000 prize for first place. Conference registration opens in early June every year. Register early to avoid disappointment as the conference is likely to sell out.

TAOS SUMMER WRITERS' CONFERENCE

Department of English Language and Literature, MSC 03 2170, 1 University of New Mexico, Albuquerque NM 87131. (505)277-5572. **E-mail:** nmwriter@unm.edu. **Website:** taosconf.unm.edu. **Contact:** Sharon Oard Warner, founding director. Estab. 1999. Annual conference held in July. Offers workshops and master classes in the novel, short story, poetry, creative nonfiction, memoir, prose style, screenwriting, humor writing, yoga and writing, literary translation, book proposal, the query letter, and revision. Participants may also schedule a consultation with a visiting agent/editor.

COSTS Week-long workshop registration: $700. Weekend workshop registration: $400. Master classes: $1,350-1,625. Publishing consultations: $175.

TEXAS WRITING RETREAT

Navasota TX **E-mail:** paultcuclis@gmail.com. **Website:** www.texaswritingretreat.com. **Contact:** Paul Cuclis, coordinator. Estab. 2013. The Texas Writing Retreat is an intimate event with a limited number of attendees. 2017 dates: January 11-16. Held on a private residence ranch an hour outside of Houston, the retreat has an agent and editor in attendance teaching. All attendees get to pitch the attending agent. Meals, excursions, and amenities are included. This is a unique event that combines craft sessions, business sessions, time for writing, relaxation, and more. The retreat is not held every year; it's best to check the website.

COSTS Costs vary per event. There are different pricing options for those staying on-site versus commuters.

THRILLERFEST

P.O. Box 311, Eureka CA 95502. **E-mail:** kimberlyhowe@thrillerwriters.org; infocentral@thrillerwriters.org. **Website:** www.thrillerfest.com. **Contact:** Kimberley Howe, executive director. Grand Hyatt New York, 109 E. 42nd St., New York, NY 10017 Estab. 2006. Annual workshop/conference/festival. 2017 dates: July 11-15 at the Grand Hyatt in New York. Conference duration: 5 days. Average attendance: 1,000. "A great place to learn the craft of writing the thriller. Classes taught by best-selling authors."

Speakers have included David Morrell, James Patterson, Sandra Brown, Ken Follett, Eric Van Lustbader, David Baldacci, Brad Meltzer, Steve Martini, R.L. Stine, Steve Berry, Kathleen Antrim, Douglas Preston, Gayle Lynds, Harlan Coben, Lee Child, Lisa Scottolini, Katherine Neville, Robin Cook, Andrew Gross, Kathy Reichs, Brad Thor, Clive Cussler, Donald Maass, M.J. Rose, and Al Zuckerman. Three days of the conference are CraftFest, where the focus is on the craft of writing, and 2 days are ThrillerFest, which showcase the author-fan relationship. Also featured: PitchFest, a unique event where authors can pitch their work face-to-face to 50 top literary agents. Lastly, there is the International Thriller Awards and Banquet.

COSTS $475-1,199, depending on which events are selected. Various package deals are available, and early bird pricing is offered beginning September of each year.

TMCC WRITERS' CONFERENCE

Truckee Meadows Community College, 7000 Dandini Blvd., Reno NV 89512. (775)673-7111. **E-mail:** wdce@tmcc.edu. **Website:** wdce.tmcc.edu. Estab. 1991. Annual conference held in April. 2017 date: April 8. Average attendance: 150. Conference focuses on strengthening mainstream/literary fiction and nonfiction works and how to market them to agents and publishers. Site: Truckee Meadows Community College in Reno. "There is always an array of speakers and presenters with impressive literary credentials, including agents and editors." Speakers have included Chuck Sambuchino, Sheree Bykofsky, Andrea Brown, Dorothy Allison, Karen Joy Fowler, James D. Houston, James N. Frey, Gary Short, Jane Hirschfield, Dorrianne Laux, and Kim Addonizio. Literary agents are on site to take pitches from writers.

ACCOMMODATIONS Contact the conference manager to learn about accommodation discounts.

ADDITIONAL INFORMATION "The conference is open to all writers, regardless of their level of experience. Brochures are available online and mailed in January. Send inquiries via e-mail."

UNICORN WRITERS CONFERENCE

17 Church Hill Rd., Redding CT 06896 USA. (203)938-7405. **E-mail:** unicornwritersconference@gmail.com. **Website:** www.unicornwritersconference.com. **Contact:** Jan L. Kardys, chair. Estab. 2010. This writers conference draws upon its close proximity to New York and pulls in over 40 literary agents and 15 major New York editors to pitch each year. There are manuscript review sessions (40 pages equals 30 minutes with an agent/editor), query/manuscript review sessions, and 6 different workshops every hour. Cost: $325, includes all workshops and 3 meals.

COSTS $325 includes all workshops (6 every hour to select on the day of the conference), gift bag, and 3 meals. Additional cost for manuscript reviews: $60 each.

ACCOMMODATIONS Held at Reid Castle, Purchase, New York. Directions available on event website.

ADDITIONAL INFORMATION The first self-published authors will be featured on the website, and the bookstore will sell their books at the event.

UNIVERSITY OF NORTH DAKOTA WRITERS CONFERENCE

Department of English, Merrifield Hall, Room 110, 276 Centennial Dr., Stop 7209, Grand Forks ND 58202. (701)777-2393. **Fax:** (701)777-2373. **E-mail:** crystal.alberts@und.edu. **Website:** und.edu/orgs/writers-conference. **Contact:** Crystal Alberts, director. Estab. 1970. Annual event. 2018 dates: March 21-23. Duration: 3 days. Offers panels, readings, and films focused around a specific theme. Almost all events take place in the University of North Dakota Memorial Union, which has a variety of small rooms and a 600-seat main hall. Past speakers have included Art Spiegelman, Truman Capote, Sir Salman Rushdie, Allen Ginsberg, Roxane Gay, Viet Thanh Nguyen, and Louise Erdrich.

COSTS All events are free and open to the public. Donations accepted.

ACCOMMODATIONS Accommodations available at area hotels. Information on overnight accommodations available on website.

ADDITIONAL INFORMATION Schedule and other information available on website.

UNIVERSITY OF WISCONSIN AT MADISON WRITERS INSTITUTE

21 N. Park St., Madison WI 53715. (608)265-3972. **E-mail:** laurie.scheer@wisc.edu. **Website:** uwwritersinstitute.wisc.edu. Estab. 1990. Annual conference. 2018 dates: April 12-15. Conference on fiction and nonfiction held at the University of Wisconsin at Madison. Guest speakers are published authors and publishing executives. Agents and publishing companies take pitches. Theme: Pathway to Publication.

COSTS $250-375, depending on discounts and if you attend one day or multiple days.

WESTERN RESERVE WRITERS & FREELANCE CONFERENCE

Cuyahoga County Public Library, South Euclid-Lyndhurst Branch, 4645 Mayfield Road, South Euclid OH 44121. (216)382-4880. **E-mail:** deanna@deannaadams.com. **Website:** www.deannaadams.com. Laurie Kincer, program coordinator, South Euclid-Lyndhurst Library **Contact:** Deanna Adams, director/conference coordinator. Estab. 1983. Annual conference now held in the spring. Duration: 1 day. Average attendance: 150. "The Western Reserve Writers Conference is designed for all writers, aspiring and professional, and offers presentations in all genres—nonfiction, fiction, poetry, essays, creative nonfiction, and the business of writing, including successful freelance writing." Site: "Formerly located at Lakeland Community College, the conference is now held at the new Writers' Center at the South Euclid-Lyndhurst Library. Included throughout the day are one-on-one editing consults, a question and answer panel, and book sale/author signings." See Deanna's website for updates: www.deannaadams.com.

COSTS The conference is now free but does not include lunch.

ADDITIONAL INFORMATION Brochures for the conferences are available by January. Also accepts inquiries by e-mail and phone. Check Deanna Adams' website for all updates. Editors always attend the conferences. Agents, occasionally. Private editing consultations are available as well.

WHIDBEY ISLAND WRITERS' CONFERENCE

P.O. Box 1289, Langley WA 98260. (360)331-0307. **E-mail:** http://writeonwhidbey.org. **Website:** http://writeonwhidbey.org. Annual conference held in early spring. Registration limited to 290. Registration includes workshops, fireside chats, book-signing reception, various activities, and daily luncheons. The conference offers consultation appointments with editors and agents. Registrants may reduce the cost of their conference by volunteering. See the website for more information. "The uniquely personal and friendly weekend is designed to be highly interactive." There are a variety of sessions on topics such as fiction, craft, poetry, platform, agents, screenwriting, and much more. Topics are varied, and there is something for all writers. Multiple agents and editors are in attendance. The schedule and faculty change every year, and those changes are reflected online

COSTS Cost: $395; early bird and member discounts available

WILLAMETTE WRITERS CONFERENCE

2108 Buck St., West Linn OR 97068. (503)305-6729. **Fax:** (503)344-6174. **Website:** willamettewriters.com/wwcon/. Estab. 1981. Annual conference held in August. 2015 dates: Aug. 7-9. Conference duration: 3 days. Average attendance: 600. "Willamette Writers is open to all writers, and we plan our conference accordingly. We offer workshops on all aspects of fiction, nonfiction, marketing, the creative process, screenwriting, etc. Also, we invite top-notch inspirational speakers for keynote addresses. We always include at least 1 agent or editor panel and offer a variety of topics of interest to both fiction and nonfiction writers and screenwriters." Agents will be speaking and available for meetings with attendees.

COSTS Pricing schedule available online.

ACCOMMODATIONS If necessary, arrangements can be made on an individual basis through the conference hotel. Special rates may be available. 2015 location is the Lloyd Center DoubleTree Hotel.

ADDITIONAL INFORMATION Brochure/guidelines are available for a catalog-sized SASE.

WISCONSIN WRITERS ASSOCIATION

Wisconsin Writers Association, Inc., WI **E-mail:** karinss1945@outlook.com. **Website:** www.wiwrite.org. Treasurer: Nancy Rafal. **Contact:** Karin Schmidt, president. Estab. 1948. The Wisconsin Writers Association is a 501(c)(3) nonprofit corporation, volunteer run, providing educational services, networking opportunities, and encouragement for writers and poets of all genres in the state. Our annual conference is held in October. Conference duration: 1-2 days. Provides workshops, speakers, and presentations for all genres in fiction, nonfiction, and poetry.

COSTS $80-100.

ACCOMMODATIONS Rooms available at the host conference center.

WOMEN WRITING THE WEST

8547 E. Araphoe Rd., Box J-541, Greenwood Village CO 80112-1436. **E-mail:** conference@womenwritingthewest.org; shanna@shannahatfield.com. **Website:** www.womenwritingthewest.org. 2018 conference dates: October 25-28; Location: Walla Walla,

Washington. "Women Writing the West is a nonprofit association of writers, editors, publishers, agents, booksellers, and other professionals writing and promoting the women's West. As such, women writing their stories in the American West in a way that illuminates them authentically. In addition, the organization provides support, encouragement, and inspiration to all women writing about any facet of the American West. Membership is open to all interested persons worldwide, including students. WWW membership also allows the choice of participation in our marketing marvel, the annual WWW Catalog of Author's Books. An annual conference is held every fall. The event covers research, writing techniques, multiple genres, marketing/promotion, and more. Agents and editors share ideas in a panel format as well as meeting one-on-one for pitch sessions with attendees. Conference location changes each year. The blog and social media outlets publish current WWW activities, features market research, and share articles of interest pertaining to American West literature and member news. WWW annually sponsors the WILLA Literary Award, which is given in several categories for outstanding literature featuring women's stories, set in the West. The winner of a WILLA literary Award receives a cash award and a trophy at the annual conference. Contest is open to non-members.

COSTS See website. Discounts available for members, and for specific days only.

ACCOMMODATIONS See website for location and accommodation details.

WORDS & MUSIC

Words & Music, A Literary Feast in New Orleans, The Pirate's Alley Faulkner Society, Inc., 624 Pirate's Alley, New Orleans LA 70116. (504) 586-1609. **E-mail:** Faulkhouse@aol.com. **E-mail:** Faulkhouse@aol.com. **Website:** www.wordsandmusic.org. **Contact:** Rosemary James. Estab. 1997. Annual conference held in November. Conference duration: 5 days. Average attendance: 300. Presenters include authors, agents, editors and publishers. Past speakers included agents Deborah Grosvenor, Judith Weber, Stuart Bernstein, Nat Sobel, Jeff Kleinman, Emma Sweeney, Liza Dawson, Brettne Bloom, Jennifer Weltz, and Michael Murphy; editors Sarah Crichton, Brenda Copeland, Andra Miller, Kristine Poupolo, Webster Younce, Ann Patty, Will Murphy, Jofie Ferrari-Adler, and Elizabeth Stein; critics Marie Arana, Jonathan Yardley, and Michael Dirda; fiction writers Adam Johnson, Julia Glass, Stewart O'Nan, Tom Franklin, Tom Piazza, Tea Obreht, Robert Goolrick, Oscar Hijuelos, Robert Olen Butler, Shirley Ann Grau, Mayra Montero, Ana Castillo, Horacio Castellenos-Moya. Agents and editors critique manuscripts in advance; meet with them one-on-one during the conference. A detailed schedule of master classes and workshops is available online.

COSTS See website for a costs and additional information on accommodations. Website will update closer to date of conference.

ACCOMMODATIONS Room blocks available at Hotel Monteleone and sister hotel, Bienville House in New Orleans.

ADDITIONAL INFORMATION Winners of 2016 William Faulkner - William Wisdom Creative Writing Competition will be presented at Words & Music.

WRITE CANADA

The Word Guild, Suite 226, 245 King George Rd., Brantford Ontario N3R 7N7 Canada. **E-mail:** writecanada@thewordguild.com. **Website:** thewordguild.com/events/write-canada. Annual conference in Ontario for Christian writers of all types and at all stages. Conference duration: 3 days. Offers solid instruction, stimulating interaction, exciting challenges, and worshipful community.

WRITE ON THE SOUND

WOTS, City of Edmonds Arts Commission, Frances Anderson Center, 700 Main St., Edmonds WA 98020. (425)771-0228. **E-mail:** wots@edmondswa.gov. **Website:** www.writeonthesound.com. **Contact:** Laurie Rose, Conference Organizer or Frances Chapin, Edmonds Arts Commission Mgr. Estab. 1985. Small, affordable annual conference focused on the craft of writing. Held the first weekend in October. 2018 dates: October 5-7. Conference duration: 3 days. Average attendance: 275. Features over 30 presenters, keynote, writing contest, ms critique appts, roundtable discussions, book signing reception, onsite bookstore, and opportunity to network with faculty and attendees. Edmonds is located just north of Seattle on the Puget Sound.

COSTS $85-285 (not including optional fees).

ACCOMMODATIONS Best Western Plus/Edmonds Harbor Inn is a conference partner.

ADDITIONAL INFORMATION Schedule posted on website late spring/early summer. Registration opens mid-July. Attendees are required to select the sessions when they register. Waiting lists for conference and manuscript appointments are available.

WRITERS@WORK WRITING RETREAT

P.O. Box 711191, Salt Lake City UT 84171. (801)996-3313. **E-mail:** jennifer@writersatwork.org. **Website:** www.writersatwork.org. Estab. 1985. Annual conference held in June. Duration: 4 days. Average attendance: 45. Morning workshops (3 hours/day) focus on novel, advanced fiction, generative fiction, nonfiction, poetry, and young adult fiction. Afternoon sessions include craft lectures, discussions, and directed interviews with authors and editors. In addition to the traditional, one-on-one ms consultations, there will be many opportunities to mingle informally with visiting writers and editors. Site: Alta Lodge in Alta Lodge, Utah. Speakers have included Steve Almond, Bret Lott, Shannon Hale, Emily Forland (Wendy Weil Agency), Julie Culver (Folio Literary Management), Chuck Adams (Algonquin Press), and Mark A. Taylor (Juniper Press).

COSTS $650-1,000, based on housing type and consultations.

ACCOMMODATIONS Onsite housing available. Additional lodging information is on the website.

WRITERS CONFERENCE AT OCEAN PARK

P.O. Box 172, Assonet ME 02702. (401)598-1424. **E-mail:** jbrosnan@jwu.edu. **Website:** www.oceanpark.org/programs/education/writers/writers.html. Estab. 1941. Annual conference held in mid-August. Conference duration: 4 days. Average attendance: 50. "We try to present a balanced and eclectic conference. In addition to time and attention given to poetry, we also have children's literature, mystery writing, travel, fiction, nonfiction, journalism, and other issues of interest to writers. Our speakers are editors, writers, and other professionals. Our concentration is, by intention, a general view of writing to publish with supportive encouragement. We are located in Ocean Park, a small seashore village 14 miles south of Portland. Ours is a summer assembly center with many buildings from the Victorian age. The conference meets in Porter Hall, one of the assembly buildings which is listed in the National Register of Historic Places." Speakers have included Michael C. White (novelist/short story writer), Betsy Shool (poet), Suzanne Strempek Shea (novelist), John Perrault (poet), Anita Shreve (novelist), Dawn Potter (poet), Bruce Pratt (fiction writer), Amy McDonald (children's author), Sandell Morse (memoirist), Kate Chadbourne (singer/songwriter), Wesley McNair (poet and Maine faculty member), and others. "We usually have about 8 guest presenters each year." Writers/editors lead workshops and are available for meetings with attendees. Workshops start at 8:30 a.m. on Tuesday and continue through Friday until early afternoon. Opening event is Monday at 4 p.m.

COSTS $200. The fee does not include housing or meals, which must be arranged separately.

ACCOMMODATIONS "An accommodations list is available. We are in a summer resort area where motels, guest houses, and restaurants abound."

ADDITIONAL INFORMATION 2017 marks the conference's 77th anniversary.

WRITER'S DIGEST ANNUAL CONFERENCE

F+W Media, Inc., 10151 Carver Rd., Suite 200, Blue Ash OH 45242. (877)436-7764 (option 2). **E-mail:** writersdigestconference@fwmedia.com. **E-mail:** phil.sexton@fwmedia.com. **Website:** www.writersdigestconference.com. **Contact:** Taylor Sferra. Estab. 1995. The Writer's Digest conferences feature an amazing lineup of speakers to help writers with the craft and business of writing. Each calendar year typically features multiple conferences around the country. In 2017, the New York conference will be August 18-20 at the New York Hilton Midtown. The most popular feature of the east coast conference is the agent pitch slam, in which potential authors are given the ability to pitch their books directly to agents. For the 2017 conference, there will be more than 50 agents in attendance. For more details, see the website.

COSTS Cost varies by location and year. There are typically different pricing options for those who wish attend the pitch slam and those who just want to attend the conference education.

ACCOMMODATIONS A block of rooms at the event hotel is reserved for guests. See the travel page on the website for more information.

WRITERS IN PARADISE

Eckerd College, 4200 54th Ave. S., St. Petersburg FL 33711. (727)386-2264. **E-mail:** wip@eckerd.edu. **Website:** writersinparadise.com. Estab. 2005. Annual conference held in January. 2017 dates: January 14-21. Conference duration: 8 days. Average attendance: 84 maximum. Workshop. Offers college credit. "Writers in Paradise offers workshop classes in fiction (novel and short story), poetry, and nonfiction. Working closely with our award-winning faculty, students will have stimulating opportunities to ask questions and learn valuable skills from fellow students and authors at the top of their form. Most importantly, the intimate size and secluded location of the Writers in Paradise experience allows you the time and opportunity to share your manuscripts, critique one another's work, and discuss the craft of writing with experts and peers who can help guide you to the next level." Faculty have included Andre Dubus III (*House of Sand and Fog*), Laura Lippman (*Wilde Lake*), Dennis Lehane (*The Given Day*), Ann Hood (*The Book That Matters Most*), Lisa Gallagher (literary agent), Daniel Halpern (editor), and more. Editors and agents attend the conference.

ADDITIONAL INFORMATION Application materials are due in November and required of all attendees.

WRITE-TO-PUBLISH CONFERENCE

WordPro Communication Services, 9118 W. Elmwood Dr., Suite 1G, Niles IL 60714. (847)296-3964. **E-mail:** lin@writetopublish.com. **Website:** www.writetopublish.com. **Contact:** Lin Johnson, director. Estab. 1971. Annual conference. 2018 dates: June 13-16. Average attendance: 175. Conference is focused on the Christian market and includes classes for writers at all levels. Open to high school students. Site: Wheaton College, Wheaton, Illinois (Chicago area). [This is not a function of Wheaton College.]

COSTS See the website for current costs.

ACCOMMODATIONS Campus residence hall rooms available. See the website for current information and costs.

ADDITIONAL INFORMATION Conference information available in late January or early February. For details, visit website, or e-mail brochure@writetopublish.com. Accepts inquiries by e-mail, phone.

WRITING AND ILLUSTRATING FOR YOUNG READERS CONFERENCE

1480 E. 9400 S., Sandy UT 84093. **E-mail:** staff@wifyr.com. **Website:** www.wifyr.com. Estab. 2000. Annual workshop held in June. 2017 dates: June 12-16. Duration: 5 days. Average attendance: more than 100. Learn how to write, illustrate, and publish in the children's and young adult markets. Beginning and advanced writers and illustrators are tutored in a small-group workshop setting by published authors and artists and receive instruction from and network with editors, major publishing house representatives, and literary agents. Afternoon attendees get to hear practical writing and publishing tips from published authors, literary agents, and editors. Site: Waterford School in Sandy, UT. Speakers have included John Cusick, Stephen Fraser, Alyson Heller, and Ruth Katcher.

ACCOMMODATIONS A block of rooms is available at the Best Western Cotton Tree Inn in Sandy, UT, at a discounted rate. This rate is good as long as there are available rooms.

ADDITIONAL INFORMATION There is an online form to contact this event.

WYOMING WRITERS CONFERENCE

Cheyenne WY **E-mail:** president@wyowriters.org. **Website:** wyowriters.org. **Contact:** Chris Williams. This is a statewide writing conference for writers of Wyoming and neighboring states. Each year, multiple published authors, editors, and literary agents are in attendance to meet with writers and take pitches.

GLOSSARY OF INDUSTRY TERMS

Your guide for every need-to-know term.

#10 ENVELOPE. A standard, business-size envelope.

ACKNOWLEDGMENTS PAGE. The page of a book on which the author credits sources of assistance—both individuals and organizations.

ACQUISITIONS EDITOR. The person responsible for originating and/or acquiring new publishing projects.

ADAPTATION. The process of rewriting a composition (novel, story, film, article, play) into a form suitable for some other medium, such as television or the stage.

ADVANCE. Money a publisher pays a writer prior to book publication, usually paid in installments, such as one-half upon signing the contract and one-half upon delivery of the complete, satisfactory manuscript. An advance is paid against the royalty money to be earned by the book. Agents take their percentage off the top of the advance as well as from the royalties earned.

ADVENTURE. A genre of fiction in which action is the key element, overshadowing characters, theme, and setting.

AUCTION. Publishers sometimes bid for the acquisition of a book manuscript with excellent sales prospects. The bids are for the amount of the author's advance, guaranteed dollar amounts, advertising and promotional expenses, royalty percentage, etc. Auctions are conducted by agents.

AUTHOR'S COPIES. An author usually receives about ten free copies of his hardcover book from the publisher; more from a paperback firm. He can obtain additional copies at a reduced price by using his author's discount (usually 50 percent of the retail price).

AUTOBIOGRAPHY. A book-length account of a person's entire life written by the subject himself.

BACKLIST. A publisher's list of books that were not published during the current season, but that are still in print.

BACKSTORY. The history of what has happened before the action in your story takes place, affecting a character's current behavior.

BIO. A sentence or brief paragraph about the writer; includes work, any publishing history, and educational experience.

BIOGRAPHY. An account of a person's life (or the lives of a family or close-knit group) written by someone other than the subject(s). The work is set within the historical framework (i.e., the unique economic, social, and political conditions) existing during the subject's life.

BLURB. The copy on paperback book covers or hardcover book dust jackets, either promoting the book and the author or featuring testimonials from book reviewers or well-known people in the book's field. Also called flap copy or jacket copy.

BOILERPLATE. A standardized publishing contract. Most authors and agents make many changes to the boilerplate before accepting the contract.

BOOK DOCTOR. A freelance editor hired by a writer, agent, or book editor who analyzes problems that exist in a book manuscript or proposal, and offers solutions to those problems.

BOOK PACKAGER. Someone who draws elements of a book together—from initial concept to writing and marketing strategies—and then sells the book package to a book publisher and/or movie producer. Also known as book producer or book developer.

BOUND GALLEYS. A prepublication, often paperbound, edition of a book, usually prepared from photocopies of the final galley proofs. Designed for promotional purposes, bound galleys serve as the first set of review copies to be mailed out. Also called bound proofs.

CATEGORY FICTION. A term used to include all types of fiction. See *genre.*

CLIMAX. The most intense point in the storyline of a fictional work.

CLIPS. Samples, usually from newspapers or magazines, of your published work. Also called tearsheets.

COMMERCIAL FICTION. Novels designed to appeal to a broad audience. These are often broken down into categories such as Western, mystery, and romance. See genre.

CONFESSION. A first-person story in which the narrator is involved in an emotional situation that encourages sympathetic reader identification, concluding with the affirmation of a morally acceptable theme.

CONFLICT. A prime ingredient of fiction that usually represents some obstacle to the main character's (i.e., the protagonist's) goals.

CONTRIBUTOR'S COPIES. Copies of the book sent to the author. The exact number of contributor's copies is often negotiated in the publishing contract.

CO-PUBLISHING. Arrangement where author and publisher share publication costs and profits of a book. Also called cooperative publishing.

COPYEDITING. Editing of a manuscript for writing style, grammar, punctuation, and factual accuracy.

COPYRIGHT. A means to protect an author's work. A copyright is a proprietary right designed to give the creator of a work the power to control that work's reproduction, distribution, and public display or performance, as well as its adaptation to other forms.

COVER LETTER. A brief letter that accompanies the manuscript being sent to an agent or publisher.

CREATIVE NONFICTION. Type of writing where true stories are told by employing the techniques usually reserved for novelists and poets, such as scenes, character arc, a three-act structure, and detailed descriptions. This category is also called "narrative nonfiction" or "literary journalism."

CRITIQUING SERVICE. An editing service offered by some agents in which writers pay a fee for comments on the salability or other qualities of their manuscript. Sometimes the critique includes suggestions on how to improve the work. Fees vary, as does the quality of the critique.

CURRICULUM VITAE (CV). Short account of one's career or qualifications.

DEADLINE. A specified date and/or time that a project or draft must be turned into the editor. A deadline factors into a preproduction schedule, which involves copyediting, typesetting, and production.

DEAL MEMO. The memorandum of agreement between a publisher and author that precedes the actual contract and includes important issues such as royalty, advance, rights, distribution, and option clauses.

DEUS EX MACHINA. A term meaning "God from the machine" that refers to any unlikely, contrived, or trick resolution of a plot in any type of fiction.

DIALOGUE. An essential element of fiction. Dialogue consists of conversations between two or more people, and can be used heavily or sparsely.

DIVISION. An unincorporated branch of a publishing house/company.

ELECTRONIC RIGHTS. Secondary or subsidiary rights dealing with electronic/multimedia formats (the Internet, CD-ROMs, electronic magazines).

EL-HI. Elementary to high school. A term used to indicate reading or interest level.

EROTICA. A form of literature or film dealing with the sexual aspects of love. Erotic content ranges from subtle sexual innuendo to explicit descriptions of sexual acts.

ETHNIC. Stories and novels whose central characters are African American, Native American, Italian American, Jewish, Appalachian, or members of some other specific cultural group. Ethnic fiction usually deals with a protagonist caught between two conflicting ways of life: mainstream American culture and his ethnic heritage.

EVALUATION FEES. Fees an agent may charge to simply evaluate or consider material without further guarantee of representation. Paying up-front evaluation fees to agents is never recommended and strictly forbidden by the Association of Authors' Representations. An agent makes money through a standard commission—taking 15 percent of what you earn through advances, sales of subsidiary rights, and, if applicable, royalties.

EXCLUSIVE. Offering a manuscript, usually for a set period of time, such as one month, to just one agent and guaranteeing that agent is the only one looking at the manuscript.

EXPERIMENTAL. Type of fiction that focuses on style, structure, narrative technique, setting, and strong characterization rather than plot. This form depends on the revelation of a character's inner being, which elicits an emotional response from the reader.

FAMILY SAGA. A story that chronicles the lives of a family or a number of related or interconnected families over a period of time.

FANTASY. Stories set in fanciful, invented worlds or in a legendary, mythic past that rely on outright invention or magic for conflict and setting.

FILM RIGHTS. May be sold or optioned by the agent/author to a person in the film industry, enabling the book to be made into a movie.

FLOOR BID. If a publisher is very interested in a manuscript, he may offer to enter a floor bid when the book goes to auction. The publisher sits out of the auction, but agrees to take the book by topping the highest bid by an agreed-upon percentage (usually 10 percent).

FOREIGN RIGHTS. Translation or reprint rights to be sold abroad.

FOREIGN RIGHTS AGENT. An agent who handles selling the rights to a country other than that of the first book agent.

GENRE. Refers to either a general classification of writing, such as a novel, poem, or short story, or to the categories within those classifications, such as problem novels or sonnets.

GENRE FICTION. A term that covers various types of commercial novels, such as mystery, romance, Western, science fiction, fantasy, thriller, and horror.

GHOSTWRITING. A writer puts into literary form the words, ideas, or knowledge of another person under that person's name. Some agents offer this service; others pair ghostwriters with celebrities or experts.

GOTHIC. Novels characterized by historical settings and featuring young, beautiful women who win the favor of handsome, brooding heroes while simultaneously dealing with some life-threatening menace—either natural or supernatural.

GRAPHIC NOVEL. Contains comic-like drawings and captions, but deals more with everyday events and issues than with superheroes.

HIGH CONCEPT. A story idea easily expressed in a quick, one-line description.

HI-LO. A type of fiction that offers a high level of interest for readers at a low reading level.

HISTORICAL. A story set in a recognizable period of history. In addition to telling the stories of ordinary people's lives, historical fiction may involve political or social events of the time.

HOOK. Aspect of the work that sets it apart from others and draws in the reader/viewer.

HORROR. A story that aims to evoke some combination of fear, fascination, and revulsion in its readers—either through supernatural or psychological circumstances.

HOW-TO. A book that offers the reader a description of how something is accomplished. It includes both information and advice.

IMPRINT. The name applied to a publisher's specific line of books.

IN MEDIAS RES. A Latin term meaning "into the midst of things" that refers to the literary device of beginning a narrative at a dramatic point in a story well along in the sequence of events to immediately convey action and capture reader interest.

IRC. International Reply Coupon. Buy at a post office to enclose with material sent outside the country to cover the cost of return postage. The recipient turns them in for stamps in their own country.

ISBN. This acronym stands for International Standard Book Number. ISBN is a tool used for both ordering and cataloging purposes.

JOINT CONTRACT. A legal agreement between a publisher and two or more authors that establishes provisions for the division of royalties their co-written book generates.

LIBEL. A form of defamation, or injury to a person's name or reputation. Written or published defamation is called "libel," whereas spoken defamation is known as "slander."

LITERARY. A book where style and technique are often as important as subject matter. In literary fiction, character is typically more important than plot, and the writer's voice and skill with words are both essential. Also called "serious fiction."

LOGLINE. A one-sentence description of a plot.

MAINSTREAM FICTION. Fiction on subjects or trends that transcend popular novel categories like mystery or romance. Using conventional methods, this kind of fiction tells stories about people and their conflicts.

MARKETING FEE. Fee charged by some agents to cover marketing expenses. It may be used to cover postage, telephone calls, faxes, photocopying or any other legitimate expense incurred in marketing a manuscript. Recouping expenses associated with submissions and marketing is the one and only time agents should ask for out-of-pocket money from writers.

MASS-MARKET PAPERBACKS. Softcover books, usually 4×7 inches, on a popular subject directed at a general audience and sold in groceries, drugstores, and bookstores.

MEMOIR. An author's commentary on the personalities and events that have significantly influenced one phase of his life.

MIDLIST. Those titles on a publisher's list expected to have limited sales. Midlist books are mainstream, not literary, scholarly or genre, and are usually written by new or relatively unknown writers.

MULTIPLE CONTRACT. Book contract that includes an agreement for a future book(s).

MYSTERY. A form of narration in which one or more elements remain unknown or unexplained until the end of the story. Subgenres include amateur sleuth, caper, cozy, heist, malice domestic, police procedural, etc.

NET RECEIPTS. One method of royalty payment based on the amount of money a book publisher receives on the sale of the book after the booksellers' discounts, special sales discounts, and returned copies.

NEW ADULT (NA). Novels with characters in their late teens or early twenties who are exploring what it means to be an adult.

NOVELIZATION. A novel created from the script of a popular movie and published in paperback. Also called a movie tie-in.

NOVELLA. A short novel or long short story, usually 20,000–50,000 words. Also called a "novelette."

OCCULT. Supernatural phenomena, including ghosts, ESP, astrology, demonic possession, paranormal elements, and witchcraft.

ONE-TIME RIGHTS. This right allows a short story or portions of a fiction or nonfiction book to be published again without violating the contract.

OPTION. The act of a producer buying film rights to a book for a limited period of time (usually six months or one year) rather than purchasing said rights in full. A book can be optioned multiple times by different production companies.

OPTION CLAUSE. A contract clause giving a publisher the right to publish an author's next book.

OUTLINE. A summary of a book's content (up to fifteen double-spaced pages); often in the form of chapter headings with a descriptive sentence or two under each one to show the scope of the book.

PICTURE BOOK. A type of book aimed at ages two to nine that tells the story partially or entirely with artwork, with up to one thousand words. Agents interested in selling to publishers of these books often handle both artists and writers.

PLATFORM. A writer's speaking experience, interview skills, website, and other abilities that help form a following of potential buyers for his book.

PROOFREADING. Close reading and correction of a manuscript's typographical errors.

PROPOSAL. An offer to an editor or publisher to write a specific work, usually consists of an outline, sample chapters, a marketing plan, and more.

PROSPECTUS. A preliminary written description of a book, usually one page in length.

PSYCHIC/SUPERNATURAL. Fiction exploiting—or requiring as plot devices or themes—some contradictions of the commonplace natural world and materialist assumptions about it (including the traditional ghost story).

QUERY. A letter written to an agent or a potential market to elicit interest in a writer's work.

READER. A person employed by an agent to go through the slush pile of manuscripts and scripts, and select those worth considering.

REGIONAL. A book faithful to a particular geographic region and its people, including behavior, customs, speech, and history.

RELEASE. A statement that your idea is original, has never been sold to anyone else, and that you are selling negotiated rights to the idea upon payment. Some agents may ask that you sign a release before they request pages and review your work.

REMAINDERS. Leftover copies of an out-of-print or slow-selling book purchased from the publisher at a reduced rate. Depending on the contract, a reduced royalty or no royalty is paid to the author on remaindered books.

REPRINT RIGHTS. The right to republish a book after its initial printing.

ROMANCE. A type of category fiction in which the love relationship between a man and a woman pervades the plot. The story is told from the viewpoint of the heroine, who meets a man (the hero), falls in love with him, encounters a conflict that hinders their relationship, and then resolves the conflict with a happy ending.

ROYALTIES. A percentage of the retail price paid to the author for each copy of the book that is sold. Agents take their percentage from the royalties earned and from the advance.

SASE. Self-addressed, stamped envelope. It should be included with all postal mail correspondence and submissions.

SCHOLARLY BOOKS. Books written for an academic or research audience. These are usually heavily researched, technical, and often contain terms used only within a specific field.

SCIENCE FICTION. Literature involving elements of science and technology as a basis for conflict or as the setting for a story.

SERIAL RIGHTS. The right for a newspaper or magazine to publish sections of a manuscript.

SIMULTANEOUS SUBMISSION. Sending the same query or manuscript to several agents or publishers at the same time.

SLICE OF LIFE. A type of short story, novel, play, or film that takes a strong thematic approach, depending less on plot than on vivid detail in describing the setting and/or environment and the environment's effect on characters involved in it.

SLUSH PILE. A stack of unsolicited submissions in the office of an editor, agent, or publisher.

STANDARD COMMISSION. The commission an agent earns on the sales of a manuscript. The commission percentage (usually 15 percent) is taken from the advance and royalties paid to the writer.

SUBAGENT. An agent handling certain subsidiary rights, usually working in conjunction with the agent who handled the book rights. The percentage paid the book agent is increased to pay the subagent.

SUBSIDIARY. An incorporated branch of a company or conglomerate (for example, Crown Publishing Group is a subsidiary of Random House, Inc.).

SUBSIDIARY RIGHTS. All rights other than book publishing rights included in a book publishing contract, such as paperback rights, book club rights, and movie rights. Part of an agent's job is to negotiate those rights and advise the writer on which to sell and which to keep.

SUSPENSE. The element of both fiction and some nonfiction that makes the reader uncertain about the outcome. Suspense can be created through almost any element of a story, including the title, characters, plot, time restrictions, and word choice.

SYNOPSIS. A brief summary of a story, novel, or play. As a part of a book proposal, it is a comprehensive summary condensed in a page or page-and-a-half, single-spaced. Unlike a query letter or logline, a synopsis is a front-to-back explanation of the work—and will give away the story's ending.

TERMS. Financial provisions agreed upon in a contract, whether between writer and agent, or writer and editor.

TEXTBOOK. Book used in school classrooms at the elementary, high school, or college level.

THEME. The point a writer wishes to make. It poses a question—a human problem.

THRILLER. A story intended to arouse feelings of excitement or suspense. Works in this genre are highly sensational, usually focusing on illegal activities, international espionage, sex, and violence.

TOC. Table of Contents. A listing at the beginning of a book indicating chapter titles and their corresponding page numbers. It can also include chapter descriptions.

TRADE BOOK. Either a hardcover or softcover book sold mainly in bookstores. The subject matter frequently concerns a special interest for a more general audience.

TRADE PAPERBACK. A softbound volume, usually 5×8 inches, published and designed for the general public; available mainly in bookstores.

TRANSLATION RIGHTS. Sold to a foreign agent or foreign publisher.

UNSOLICITED MANUSCRIPT. An unrequested manuscript sent to an editor, agent, or publisher.

VET. A term used by editors when referring to the procedure of submitting a book manuscript to an outside expert (such as a lawyer) for review before publication. Memoirs are frequently vetted to confirm factual accuracy before the book is published.

WESTERNS/FRONTIER. Stories set in the American West, almost always in the nineteenth century, generally between the antebellum period and the turn of the century.

YOUNG ADULT (YA). The general classification of books written for ages twelve to sixteen. They run forty thousand to eighty thousand words and include category novels—adventure, sports, paranormal, science fiction, fantasy, multicultural, mysteries, romance, etc.

LITERARY AGENT SPECIALTIES INDEX

FICTION

ACTION

ADVENTURE

CARTOON

COMIC BOOKS

COMMERCIAL

CONFESSION

CONTEMPORARY ISSUES

CRIME

DETECTIVE

EROTICA

ETHNIC

EXPERIMENTAL

FAMILY SAGA

FANTASY

FEMINIST

FRONTIER

GAY

GLITZ

HI-LO

HISTORICAL

HORROR

HUMOR

INSPIRATIONAL

JUVENILE

LESBIAN

LITERARY

MAINSTREAM

METAPHYSICAL

MIDDLE GRADE

MILITARY

MULTICULTURAL

MYSTERY

NEW ADULT

NEW AGE

OCCULT

PARANORMAL

PICTURE BOOKS

POLICE

PSYCHIC

REGIONAL

RELIGIOUS

ROMANCE

SATIRE

SCIENCE FICTION

SHORT STORY COLLECTIONS

SPIRITUAL

SPORTS

SUPERNATURAL

SUSPENSE

THRILLER

TRANSLATION

URBAN FANTASY

WAR

WESTERNS

WOMEN'S

YOUNG ADULT

NONFICTION

AMERICANA

ANIMALS

ANTHROPOLOGY

ARCHEOLOGY

ART/ARCHITECTURE

AUTOBIOGRAPHY

BIOGRAPHY

BUSINESS

CHILD GUIDANCE

COMPUTERS

COOKING

CRAFTS

CREATIVE NONFICTION

CULTURAL INTERESTS

CURRENT AFFAIRS

DANCE

DECORATING

DESIGN

DIET/NUTRITION

ECONOMICS

EDUCATION

ENVIRONMENT

ETHNIC

FILM

FOODS

GARDENING

GAY/LESBIAN

GOVERNMENT

HEALTH

HISTORY

HOBBIES

HOW-TO

HUMOR

INSPIRATIONAL

INTERIOR DESIGN

INVESTIGATIVE

JUVENILE NONFICTION

LANGUAGE

LAW

LITERATURE

MEDICINE

MEMOIRS

METAPHYSICS

MILITARY

MONEY

MULTICULTURAL

MUSIC

NEW AGE

PARENTING

PHILOSOPHY

PHOTOGRAPHY

POLITICS

POPULAR CULTURE

PSYCHOLOGY

RECREATION

RELIGIOUS

SATIRE

SCIENCE

SELF-HELP

SEX

SOCIOLOGY

SPIRITUALITY

SPORTS

TECHNOLOGY

THEATER

TRANSLATION

TRAVEL

TRUE CRIME

WAR

WOMEN'S ISSUES/STUDIES

YOUNG ADULT

GENERAL INDEX